THE PORTER

CONSPIRACY

A STORY *of* THE CIVIL WAR

GENE PALENO

First Printing 2016

ISBN 978-0-9894847-4-9

PAL PUBLISHING
P.O. Box 6, Upper Lake CA 95485

ORDERING INFORMATION:
Email inquiries to GenePaleno@gmail.com

Many of the portraits in *The Porter Conspiracy* are by
Mathew Brady Studio 1861 (printed 2011)
Modern albumen print from wet collodion negative

National Portrait Gallery, Smithsonian Institution;
Frederick Hill Meserve Collection

Many were found through Wikipedia with limited credits, or as public domain.
Other photographers mentioned were by C.M. Bell, c1860.

Map illustrations by Gene Paleno.

EDITING
Dolly P. Riley

GRAPHIC DESIGN
Christina Paleno Ericksen

In Gratitude

Writing science fiction…and I've written several novels of that kind…was easier by miles and miles than writing *The Porter Conspiracy*. Porter's story had to be factual. At more than twice the size of my other books, *The Porter Conspiracy*, took ten times as long. It had me sweating blood more times than I can count. I owe many people for helping me along the way.

All over America countless groups and organizations meet regularly to discuss and learn more about the American Civil War. One of those organizations, chaired by my friend, Charles T. Sweeny, is a member of the *Peninsula Civil War Roundtable* in Northern California. I am especially indebted to Charley for his encouragement and for the fine reference books and material he sent me.

In my own small town of Upper Lake, California, there is a very active similar Civil War discussion group. The organization is headed and run by Phil Smoley and his knowledgeable associate, Zane Jenson. I learned from them about the people and times of that war; memorabilia and data I would not otherwise have known. I especially appreciated their allowing me to share some of my research with them and their members.

Not to forget three excellent physicians, who helped me dodge the bullet during an illness that laid me low while I was trying to finish *The Porter Conspiracy:* Dr. Matthew Truesdale, M.D.; Dr. Herman Bagga, M.D.; and Dr. Kerry Oliver, M.D.; all good men.

There is truth in the writer's maxim that a complicated idea, to be understood, must be written in a simple way. That isn't as easy as it sounds. I doubt if I could have understood the thousand separate fights in the Battle of Second Manassas *(also known as the Second Battle of Bull Run)* well enough to understand or write *The Porter Conspiracy* if I had not read the *U.S. Forestry Historical Report on the Troop Movements for the Second Battle of Manassas, August 28 through August 30, 1862,* by John Hennessy. The report was an invaluable help and allowed me to better understand the men who fought and died during that famous battle. A hundred separate fights took place during those three terrible days and there were times when they threw rocks at each other after the bullets were gone.

Finally, I thank Christina Ericksen and Dolly Riley, without whose help in the production and editing *The Porter Conspiracy* would not be possible.

Gene Paleno
May 2016

Table of Contents

PART THREE — Second Manassas

PART FOUR — Defeat and Victory

Preface

I hated history in school. I didn't understand it. I didn't want to remember ancient dates, long-gone events, and the movers and shakers of a past era. They were dust in the wind. In school I forgot my history lessons as soon as a test was over. Probably I did not miss much. There was very little about slavery in my schoolbooks. What was taught about slavery was sugar-coated in ways that portrayed the slave as a happy-go-lucky clown, who not only enjoyed his life but cared only for merry times and serving 'Massa.'

Searching for the subtle reasons for the Civil War and, as I read more about the slave uprisings, the slave markets and the tearing apart of black families for money, something happened. I began to feel more keenly the passionate antipathy toward slavery that the nineteenth century Abolitionists, like Lincoln and others felt. I better understood the skewed and distorted ugly view some individuals held that Black men and women were *property*.

In 1939 in my high school among our nine hundred white students there were three Black students. One young man I remember, Pherris Noble, was a bright personable good-looking kid. Pherris was, to my unformed understanding, somehow *different* from all the white students I knew. I saw Pherris through the distorted glass of the bigotry with which I had been raised. If anyone had accused me of intolerance I would have denied it. Yet not once when I had an opportunity did I ever think to say hello or make small talk with Pherris as I did with other students I knew as well.

Later, after World War Two, after I got out of the Navy, I worked for a summer as a sign painter. Old man Anders, my employer, had two employees: a young Black man in his twenties, Jack Conners, and me. Jack was an experienced sign man and I was his apprentice. I knew nothing about neon tubing or painting or hanging signs and Jack went out of his way to show me how to build and set up the big painted metal signs, bend the neon tubing into letters and paint the signs we made.

He and I went through some hair-raising jobs for Mr. Anders. One windy day in June, Jack and I hoisted a forty-foot banner on the face of the Macomb Building, twelve stories high and the tallest building in Mt. Clemens, Michigan. At one point I had to tie a corner of the banner to a post, balancing my feet on a ten-inch balustrade on the top of the building high above busy State Street below. My stomach does flip-flops at the memory.

Later that summer, a week or two before I went back to college, I drove a taxicab at night. One of my fares was an older well-dressed Black man. Minutes into the ride, after we had made small talk, my Black passenger asked me, out of the blue, if I would consider becoming a silent partner in his rubbish business. He told me that Jack Conners, my one-time sign making teacher, had mentioned my name to him.

My fare's business was a going concern. It was expanding from the Black section of Detroit at Fifteen Mile Road to a part of town that was white. He asked me if I was interested in going to work for his company as a 'Front' man for him and his partner. All I had to do was to have my name and my face on a business card and show myself from time to time in the white community and in his newspaper ads.

In 1946, Blacks in business had an uphill fight. My fare needed a white man as a front for his expansion. The salary he offered me was great but I had to refuse. I was going back to college in the fall under the G.I. Bill and I had other things on my mind.

Looking back, it's hard to imagine the person that I was when I was young. I hoped Jack Conners had seen some small difference in my attitude toward Blacks from most whites.

I had to write The Porter Conspiracy. The Porter Conspiracy is the story of the man who was accused of losing the most important battle of the Civil War, Major General Fitz John Porter. He was arrested, tried, and found guilty of cowardice, disobeying orders and losing the Second Battle of Bull Run at Manassas, Virginia, August 27 thru August 30, 1862.

On September 30, 1862, after the Battle of Second Manassas and the defeat of the Union army at the hands of Robert E. Lee near Bull Run, Union Commanding General John Pope had not listened to his generals' many warnings regarding enemy positions in the updates he received. He needed a scapegoat after his mismanagement of his army. In a report written that date he derisively claimed,

"There is no doubt in the mind of any man here that the battle of Groveton would have been a decisive and complete victory on the first day (August 29) had General Porter advanced as I directed him."

Almost twenty years later the Schofield Board of Inquiry found that same Commanding General, John Pope, was the person responsible for losing that battle. Pope had blamed Fitz John Porter. John Pope and his second in command, Irvin McDowell were entirely responsible for the Union loss and the Confederate victory.

The truth was that Porter, by his actions alone, *saved* the Army of Virginia from destruction. Because of Porter, the Union army was able to fight again weeks later at Antietam and drive Lee back to Virginia.

In a broad-brush way, *The Porter Conspiracy* is a story of the American Civil War. More importantly, it is Fitz John Porter's story. Porter's story has been told against a background of the turbulent tapestry of the mid-18th century from 1820 to 1862.

Slavery was responsible for much of the tumult. However, there had been slavery in America for 300 years so it was not a new aberration. Slavery was not the only reason for the Civil War. Objections to the ugly institution *had* been growing for decades. The two-party political system, 'soft-on-slavery' Democrats and anti-slavery Republicans kept the slavery issue at white heat. Debates that often erupted into violence were common even on the floors of Congress. Double-dealing and temporary quick fixes managed to keep the beast caged for forty years... until the dam broke at last when Civil War was the only possible solution.

The decades leading to the war were a kaleidoscope of happenings. The Mexican War, the acquisition of hundreds of thousands of square miles of new land on the North American continent, a forty-year fight over States Rights between the North and the South, the skewed findings of the Supreme Court. These were all part and parcel of the same irresistible forces that made the American Civil War an unavoidable certainty. It created a world where the Porter trial and conviction was just as inevitable.

The Porter Conspiracy touches on many things. Every part of America's early history is important to Porter's story; not only as a cause of the Civil War, but also to explain and understand the reasons for the catastrophic miscarriage of justice of Major General Fitz John Porter's trial and conviction.

Since *The Porter Conspiracy* is Porter's story, the early battles of the war in 1861 leading up to the Second Battle of Manassas in 1862 are reported selectively here. More important were the beliefs and prejudices of the people, North and South, toward slavery and toward the Civil War.

A better understanding of the times allows us to peer into the reasons for the fears and prejudices of the times. These same fears and prejudices are what caused generals and politicians in high places to be corrupted. The result was that men like these packed the jury and lied through their teeth to convict Porter. Yet knowing this, one may wonder why the nine members of Porter's court martial hearing, all men of good reputation, were so biased toward General Porter as to find him guilty and subject to the death penalty regardless of the fact that he was innocent.

Porter's court martial record covers hundreds of single-spaced lines of testimony and evidence. The rehearing of that trial, twenty years later, is nearly as voluminous. I have abbreviated and condensed the record, where possible, without sacrificing any vital part. Excerpts of the testimony will show the twisted sequence of events that at first convicted Porter and then, twenty years later, proved Porter's complete innocence of the military charges.

Porter had proven his bravery and his loyalty to the Union and his good character in the Mexican War, and again during the Peninsula Campaign in *twenty separate battles*. Why should such a soldier, an acclaimed major general, well liked and known to be an honorable man of integrity, be convicted for the worst crime a soldier can commit? What had he done that had been so terrible as to merit a military crucifixion? Porter's trial was the most important military crime of the century to that time. I *had* to know *why* he had received such a *harsh* sentence if he was innocent.

To know how such a travesty of justice could happen, one need but read today's newspapers. Even in the present age innocent men have been convicted and sentenced to death. Porter's case was nothing new. On September 28, 2012, the Louisiana Times-Picayune newspaper carried a story of an inmate of prison, who, after 28 years on death row, was found to be innocent of a heinous murder after DNA test results. His case was no fluke. Of the 300 persons, which have been exonerated since 1989 by the *Innocence Project*, 16 people, condemned to death, were found innocent and set free.

The vendetta against Fitz John Porter may have had its beginning in the summer of 1862. Lincoln needed to energize the Union army against Lee and the rebels. The people of the North were discouraged. Pine box caskets crowded the New York Harbor docks like discarded lumber. Sons, brothers and husbands were dying by the thousands and the rebellion showed no signs of ending. McClellan, Porter's friend, mentor, and fellow Democrat, had failed miserably to capture Richmond despite commanding a huge army of more than 100,000 well-equipped men that outsized the rebel forces two to one.

Lincoln faced a sea of troubles. First, the *Peninsula Campaign against Richmond* failed, and the City of Washington, the Union capitol, was threatened with invasion. Second, England threatened to recognize the Confederacy. If that happened all hopes of bringing the departed Confederate States back into the Union, except by force, would vanish like snow in a hot summer's sun.

When McClellan failed to invade Richmond and end the war, President Lincoln chose John Pope. McClellan's failure was followed in weeks by the loss of the Second Battle of Manassas by Lincoln's hand-picked general. Someone had to be blamed and Major General Fitz John Porter fit the bill perfectly.

The one man most able to see that Porter was blamed for the loss at Manassas was Lincoln's powerful Secretary of War, Edwin Stanton. Secretary Stanton hated Porter. Porter was a Democrat, and Stanton would have had to carry the stain of McClellan's mistakes, ruining Stanton's reputation as a Republican. It was easy for Stanton to move the heavy shadow of suspicion for the loss from John Pope to Fitz John Porter.

Why did slavery continue to flourish? There were many reasons. The right of any state to follow its own path without interference by the Federal government was guaranteed by the Constitution. The Supreme Court had decided this in numerous earlier decisions. Even the Northern Democrats voted with the Southern Legislators to keep slavery alive and healthy in the South. The men and women of 1862 had been subjected to three centuries of teachings about the 'proper' relationships of the white race toward the Black race. It is no wonder that nearly the entire population believed in the absolute economic *need* for slavery in the agricultural South.

Major General Fitz John Porter's trial and conviction in 1862 was the result of the same forces that triggered the Civil War; the fight over states' rights and slavery. Slavery permeated every aspect of life in America in 1862. Americans were like flies on flypaper, stuck fast to the institution with no way to get free. Even Abraham Lincoln said, *'If all Black men were suddenly made free, I do not know what we would do with them.'*

Fitz John Porter, like many of his fellow Democrats in the north, was lukewarm in his views on slavery. Although Porter had proven himself to be a brave and loyal Union soldier and a highly intelligent person, he was willing to *tolerate* the institution of slavery. While he owned no slaves and did not wish to own a slave, he was prepared allow the South the liberty to continue what to all Southerners believed was an essential, even a vital part of their economy.

The Abolitionists, and the anti-slavery Republicans, were a long time gaining the political strength they needed to have their convictions spread and take root even with a leader like Abraham Lincoln pointing the way. It was unfortunate for our nation that our understanding came so late. Otherwise 650,000 men would never have died in the Civil War.

Of all the subjects I *have* chosen to write about, why would I choose to write about the Civil War? It's been done in every possible way. There are many books, good books, written by excellent writers. Yet, when I learned about Major General Fitz John Porter I *had* to tell his story.

Despite Porter's valor and monumental contribution to the winning of the Civil War, men who were his inferiors had destroyed this good man's life and reputation in a wicked way. It angered me that the nation, good men, and our greatest president stood idly by as Porter suffered his humiliation. It was unreasonable. It was wrong... especially after I found out the kind of man and true American hero that Porter was.

The proper telling of Porter's story had me pulling at my writer's bootstraps to really understand and then write about an enormously complicated subject in a clear and simple way. Even more important was my job to raise the scale of Porter's tragedy and the *meaning* of what Porter accomplished at the Second Battle of Manassas.

The prospect was daunting. Too much happened and so many people were a part of the drama of that single three-day conflict. Telling such a complicated tale in the simple straightway as it deserved was like trying to empty an ocean with a spoon. Research, especially, for such a work was something of such scope and meaning that, during my twenty years of writing stories, compiling that research was the hardest writing I had ever done.

This author came to see the Civil War in a different way than I had ever seen it before. The fighting, the dying, the heroism, the cowardly and political backbiting of the Civil War generals and politicians, the moving tide that was transforming America into a new and better nation—all of these I began to better understand. The Civil War became, for me, far more than a dry, long-dead history of an earlier America. It became a living part of my past as an American.

A story of the Civil War and the people involved was not at all like the stories I had written. Science fiction and fantasy required another kind of research, and far more of the writer's imagination. Porter's story was different. That difference and Porter's ordeal were all the more reason that troubled time had to be penned with scrupulous attention to detail and completeness. I had to understand, not only the Battle of Second Manassas, but also the history of the period that made the Civil War a certainty. I had to understand the politics; how Northerners of both political parties, Northern Democrats and Republicans, viewed the institution of slavery. I had to learn how slavery could have gained such a strong foothold in a country dedicated by its Constitution to the idea of freedom and equality for *all men*.

I became as familiar with the Second Battle of Manassas in 1862 (called the Second Battle of Bull Run by the North), by each fighting unit, every part of the fight, and each of the men, who led the infantry companies, brigades and divisions. I needed to know the complex maneuvering of every unit as it advanced and retreated, during every hour of the Battle. *I had to be there,* smell the smoke and sounds of battle during those three hellish days in August of 1862.

As much as one can relive an experience of others that occurred more than a hundred and fifty years in the past I had to know, hour by hour, exactly what happened to Porter during those three days. I learned what others did that contributed to the ruination of his career. Once I had come to grips with the challenge and studied the Porter Court Martial, I was appalled at the evil other men had heaped on a good and brave man. It was a distorted and complex jigsaw puzzle that *demanded* to be assembled so that the picture of the truth could be shown for everyone to see.

There is no possible way I, or anyone, could have resurrected the dust and the bones of the long-dead persons, who fought and died during the Civil War. Into whose eyes could I peer, whose faces could I read to know what they suffered? Today the men and women of that time are hardly more than a footnote in our history books. The soldiers, white, Black and red *(the Indians fought for both, North and South and some even took scalps)*, wives, sweethearts, brothers, mothers, fathers, are all gone away to where we all must go. What remains to fashion this tale in the way I wish are the words other men have written and the testimonies of those who lived at that time.

I asked myself why I should write such a book. I wrote it because the fate of one brave soldier, dust for a hundred and fifty years, whose honor can never be *fully* restored, deserves all the recognition and honor we can give to Fitz John Porter.

Gene Paleno

Major General Fitz John Porter
1822-1901

Confederate General Robert E. Lee:

(Porter's Defense At Malvern Hill)
"An extraordinary force of that arm of Mcclellan's Army."

Confederate General A.P. Hill:

"He *(General Porter)* had handled his defenses with an ability unsurpassed on any field during the War."

Union General John M. Schofield
1879 Court of Inquiry Chairman:

"General Porter's action during the Second Battle of Manassas saved the Union Army from disaster."

Union General-In-Chief, and President of The United States, 1864-1877, Ulyssys S. Grant:

Letter to President Rutherford B. Hayes, 1879
The President, Washington, D.C.

Dear Sir,

'I have recently reviewed the trial and testimony furnished before the Schofield Court of Inquiry, held in 1879, giving the subject three full days of careful reading and consideration, and much thought... I am convinced that for these nineteen years I have been doing a gallant and efficient soldier a great injustice. When I was President I had the power to have ordered a hearing, which he only got at a later day. In justification for my injustice to General Porter, I can only state that after the war closed I based my decision on wrong information. It is incumbent upon me to remove the stain upon his good name from him and his family and repair my own unintentional injustice to General Porter. I ask you give the subject some thought and the same study I have given to it and ask that the matter be placed before the Attorney General for his opinion.'

'Hoping you will do this for an officer who has suffered for nineteen years a punishment that should never have been inflicted upon any but the most guilty.'

I am very truly yours,

U.S. Grant

PART ONE

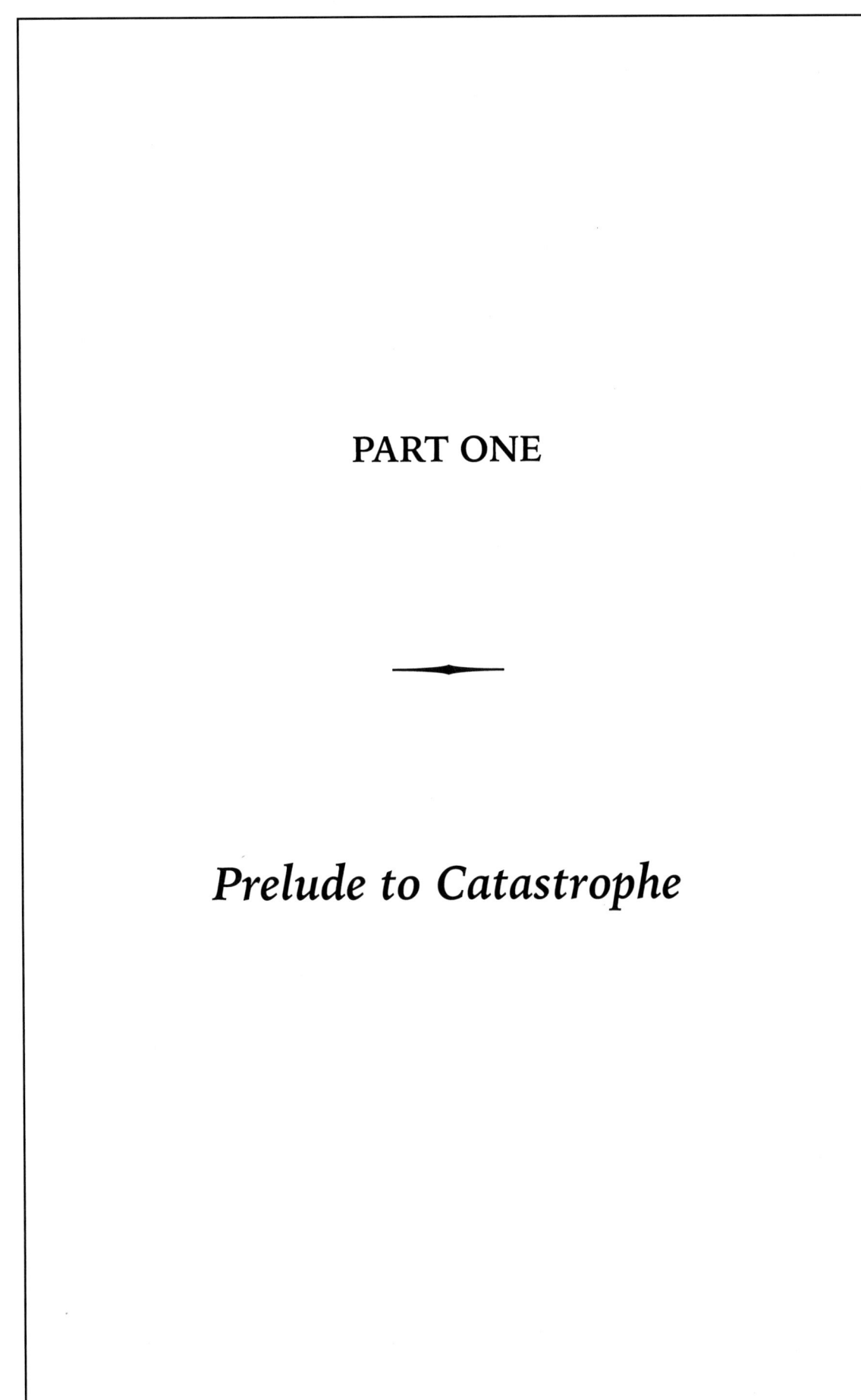

Prelude to Catastrophe

❧ 1 ❧

The Speech

On a cold February day in Washington, twenty years after General Porter had been convicted and sentenced for treason, the House of Representatives considered a Bill, Number S-1844. The Bill was for the relief of Fitz John Porter, a man who, until 1863, had been a Civil War major general, as high as a man could go in the American army. The Bill, if it passed, would be an official exoneration of the charges, which had been leveled at Porter by his superior officer, Major General John Pope, the man who commanded the troops at the Battle of Second Manassas twenty years before.

That battle was an embarrassing and a monumental defeat for the Union Army and the nation. Pope blamed one man for the defeat, Major General Fitz John Porter. A court martial was completed in February 1863 and Porter was found guilty of disobedience of orders and cowardice in the face of the enemy and drummed out of the army in abject and total disgrace.

Porter suffered the dishonor and humiliation of the court martial sentence for nearly two decades. All the while he continued to fight for his innocence and free himself of the terrible stigma of the military tribunal's decision.

In 1883, long after the Battle of Second Manassas had become one more painful memory of the bloody War Between the States, a congressman from Alabama, Joe Wheeler, gave a grand speech. He spoke in support of a House Bill to reverse the court martial conviction of 1863. The bill passed and President Chester Arthur commuted Porter's sentence. It wasn't until 1893 that President Cleveland, a Democrat, signed the order that officially cleared Porter of all charges and restored him to rank.

Joe Wheeler was quite a guy. Porter's champion in Congress, Wheeler was a plain spoken man and a good speech maker. Although he was a Southerner from Alabama, which had been one of the slave states before the war, Wheeler was an admirer of Abraham Lincoln. Furthermore, Congressman Wheeler had come to believe with all his heart and soul that Porter, a good man and a fine soldier, had been terribly wronged. Joe Wheeler decided it was time to set things right. Twenty years was a long time to make right such a terrible wrong but, in Porter's case, it was high time to correct the miscarriage of justice.

"Mr. Speaker," Wheeler began in his strong resonant voice, "As regards the conduct of man to man, the highest command given is that he do unto others even as he would that others should do unto him. When a wrong is done to *any* man it [justice] should be restored to him twofold..."

There was no apology in Wheeler's words. His message was as important as life and death. He meant every word.

"General Porter does not ask that the Scriptural precept be meted to him, that to him should be restored two-fold for the wrong that has been done to him."

"No." Wheeler's words gained strength with the conviction he felt. "The demand for justice does not come from General Porter. This demand for justice comes from the people of the United States. That he has been the victim of a great wrong has been incontrovertibly proven to the American people. General Porter has suffered and his family has shared his cup of bitterness."

Wheeler drew out each word separately to show the immenseness of the tragedy.

"Yes, Mr. Speaker, for the fifth part of our century the pangs... of... a... living... death... have... been... their... portion."

Congressman Wheeler's voice grew as somber as the grave.

"What he now endures, what he has borne for so many years, he must support for the short term God may will that he remains with us. Then the grass, perchance rose be-decked, may grow over a grave marked by a broken shaft on which will be engraved only the words, FITZ JOHN PORTER."

Wheeler launched into a review of Porter's fighting accomplishments.

"Fitz John Porter, the brave soldier, the human ideal of chivalry, was the only member of his class who won the brevet of a field officer on the plains of Mexico. He was the man selected to instill honor and chivalry into the minds of the military students of our country, the Chevalier Bayard of the Army of the Potomac. He was the man who, already covered with glory on *twenty fields of battle,* selected to command McClellan's rear guard from June 26, 1862."

Wheeler next told of one of Porter's greatest victories; the defense of Malvern Hill.

"In the darkest hours seen by the 100,000 men that the gallant and skillful McClellan had pressed to the very gates of the Confederate capitol, Fitz John Porter rallied and aligned the dispirited troops. Owing to Porter's skill and courage the sun went down on the night of July 1 upon the triumph of Malvern Hill, a victory so brilliant and so signally due to that officer as to call for the thanks of the nation. *This* is the man, who was *deliberately* selected for immolation."

"The disaster to Pope's army (at Manassas), which occurred within sixty days from Porter's victory at Malvern Hill, required a scapegoat and a blood sacrifice. When men in high places need a victim, one can always be found. John Pope... and others...needed such a victim and... he... was... found."

Wheeler paused. His speech was nearly finished. His voice became a soliloquy.

"I have never seen General Pope nor do I wish to criticize General Porter's assailants. The evidence justifies every word I have said. My object in saying these words to the lovers of right throughout our land is to add my feeble mite toward the establishment of truth, the vindication of honor, and the upholding of the sublime principles of justice."

❧ 2 ❧

Hot Day

A large housefly, which had managed to survive a hard winter in the hot courtroom and not knowing any better, buzzed desperately searching the glass in the court house window to find a way outside into the cold. It was January 1864. Major General Fitz John Porter's court martial had dragged on for 45 grueling days. Outside the courthouse workmen shoveled off the snow but they had not yet spread the rock salt and the sidewalks were as slippery as glass.

The weary fly had finally given up his buzzy battle to get out and it sat on the edge of the window ledge, disgruntled from the effort. Porter's counsel, Colonel Richard Eames, had finished his reading of the evidence in Porter's defense.

The rustle of his papers and notes in the quiet courtroom seemed unusually loud to the defendant. Judge Advocate General, Colonel Joseph Holt, completed a reading of the charges and replaced his papers on the table before him. White-haired and deliberate Reverdy Johnson, Porter's lead counsel, stood to give a final summary of Porter's defense to the five-man board of military men and to the judge advocate.

Major General Fitz John Porter, at 42, was a handsome man with a quiet demeanor that inspired respect. A full dark beard with a full head of dark hair, just beginning to thin at his temples, made him better looking if anything. Only the lines around his eyes, penetrating and dark beneath heavy eyebrows, and the firm set of his jaws betrayed his concern and his bitterness for the harsh accusations to which he had subjected.

For days he heard dozens of witnesses for his defense and those against his cause. His witnesses were his friends. They were men he knew well, the same men who had stood with him in the midst of the storm and blood of battle. They were fellow soldiers that had lived with him through the fire more than once and they had come gladly to support the truth of his testimony.

The sorry kangaroo court was a sad ending to a brilliant career. General Porter came from a family of famous naval officers. David Farragut, the first United States Admiral, was Porter's cousin. Graduating from West Point in 1845, fourteenth in a class of sixty-five, Porter planned to make the army his career. He became an instructor at West Point and, for a time, Porter was the Post Adjutant for Robert E.

Lee. At West Point Porter formed what would become a fatal friendship with George McClellan, because McClellan was unpopular with the army administration.

His rise was rapid. After the war with Mexico Porter was the only officer brevetted on the field of battle to become a captain. In August of 1861 he was made a Brigadier General. Porter commanded a division of the Army of the Potomac under his friend General George McClellan. Within only a few months, during the height of the Peninsular and Seven Days Campaigns, he was made a Major General.

Porter's brilliance as a commander became clearer during the Peninsular Campaign. He was given an entire army corps; nine thousand men. From the start Porter displayed excellent generalship in the fighting at Beaver Creek and at Gaines Mill. At Malvern Hill General Porter displayed military genius as he covered the withdrawal of McClellan's army. Had he been given free rein by the cautious McClellan to advance and counter attack, Porter might have beaten the badly mauled Robert E. Lee and moved on to take the Confederate capitol.

In August of 1862, after President Lincoln had replaced McClellan with John Pope, Porter was sent to reinforce Pope's newly-formed Army of Northern Virginia. It was an unhappy change of command for Porter.

THE IMPOSSIBLE ORDER

During the Second Battle of Manassas, Porter made a desperate attempt to carry out Pope's *impossible order*. Pope had ordered Porter to attack Stonewall Jackson, Lee's right wing. Porter did not obey the order because he was far outnumbered; and rather than offense he conducted defense. Had Porter tried to carry out the order his attack would have been fatal for the *entire* Northern army. Longstreet's Southern army had come to the field, and this factor was not included in Pope's decision-making. Perhaps negotiating the chess pieces of war was beyond Pope's ability.

With a three-to-one advantage in numbers and position, Longstreet would have easily crushed Porter's troops and gone on to destroy the unsuspecting Federal army. Instead, Porter held Longstreet and the larger part of the Confederate army for a full day. By this action Porter saved the Union army from annihilation and allowed Pope the time to retire in an orderly retreat and to fight another day. Regardless of these facts, Pope acted as if he was ignorant of the truth. Pope placed blame for the loss of the Battle of Second Manassas on Porter.

THE CHARGES

General Porter's court martial hearing began the fall of 1862. There were five specifications to the first charge and three specifications to the second charge. The charges amounted to disobeying orders during a battle and cowardice under fire; violations of the Ninth and the Fifty-Second Articles of War. The specifications to the charges against Fitz John Porter, cut to the bare essentials, were three accusations of disobedience to General Pope's orders.

First: Disobedience to the August 27, 1862 order, the 1:00 AM Order. That order from Pope required Porter to march his 10,000 troops from Warrenton Junction at 1 AM and be at Bristoe Station, nine miles away, by daylight, by marching over twisted railroads in the dark all night.

Second: Disobedience to a Joint Order Pope sent to McDowell's and Porter's corps on August 29, while Porter was in front of the enemy. The Joint Order directed Porter to march toward Gainesville and establish a connection with the corps of Generals Heintzelman, Reno and Siegel.

Third: Disobedience to an August 29 order while Porter was facing an enemy. That order became known as the *4:30 Order* and it ordered Porter to attack the enemy's flank and rear.

The Court alleged Porter had been insubordinate, disobeyed orders and displayed cowardice in the face of the enemy. Secretary of War Edwin Stanton, the man behind the scenes and speaking for General Pope, brought charges against Porter and Porter was found guilty. Porter was cashiered (dismissed) from the army and forever disqualified from holding any office of trust or profit under the government of the United States. Porter's witnesses, their testimony, and the facts of what *truly* happened, all came to nothing.

THE COURT MARTIAL

The nine members of the court martial against General Fitz John Porter were picked carefully for a specific task, all 'reliable' officers, carefully chosen by Edwin Stanton, to carry out the administration's will and to place blame for the Union defeat at Second Manassas anywhere except on the two men truly responsible for the disaster: General John Pope and his second in command, Irvin McDowell.

Major David Hunter, president of the court, was Lincoln's close political ally. Major General E.A. Hitchcock, one of the judges, had advised Lincoln during the time when McClellan had repeatedly failed to go on the offensive against Lee. McClellan had shown himself to procrastinate in attacking, and generally losing the advantage, despite commanding large numbers of soldiers. Finally, a last nail in Porter's coffin, Fitz John Porter was well known as George McClellan's protégé and fair haired boy, not a beneficial association for Porter.

General Napoleon Bonaparte Buford, another member of the nine-man court, was the half- brother to the cavalry officer, John Buford, the cavalry officer who had first reported Longstreet's arrival at Manassas as Lee and Longstreet poured out of Thoroughfare Gap. Buford had given the report of the enemy's arrival to General Irvin McDowell, who had a tendency not to share information. Irvin McDowell had failed to forward the news to John Pope.

The others members of the court martial were Generals King, Prentiss, and Ricketts; all officers in McDowell's corps. Two of the members, against all the rules of fair play and justice, *testified against accused*, then returned to their chairs to sit in judgment.

As the court martial marched its slow and deliberate way to a finish, General Porter sat and watched the parade of witnesses. He must have grown weary of the prosecution's half-truths and rhetoric. Like the handpicked Republican members of the court, these men and the judge advocate had found him guilty from the beginning. They were, one and all, a reflection of General Pope's effort to place the blame for the loss of Second Manassas on Porter.

Glancing about the courtroom Porter might have been comforted. His supporting witnesses had been a part of the battle during most of the fighting. Testimony was winding down at last to the end of the trial. Porter's witnesses, Generals Sykes, Morell and Griffin, and other officers, had served with him during the Peninsula Campaign and these same officers had been with him during the bloody fight on Malvern Hill when Porter might have defeated Robert E. Lee if he had been allowed to attack his fleeing enemy. The fleeting thought must have come to Porter, *'I would have beaten Lee, too, if I had been not ordered to withdraw after I had nearly destroyed their forces.'*

By the forty-fifth day of the trial Porter must have numbed himself to the litany of accusations, misstatements and the outright lies by Pope, McDowell and their sycophants. The muted sounds of the workmen working on the street, the clopping hoofs of horse drawn carriages passing, might have been a dirge to the melancholy he must have felt.

As he listened inattentively to the last of the witnesses, General Porter might have recalled what he had been told by friends when he learned that John Pope refused to appear against him at the court martial. Porter might have grimaced at the recollection. Someone watching him closely would have thought the slight tightening of his mouth was a wry half smile instead of sudden anger. He had been told that John Pope did not *wish* to appear to testify. Instead, Pope had directed Ruggles, his aid-de-camp and his chief of staff during the Battle of Second Manassas, to repeat his words to the court like a puppet.

Pope made no bones about his express wish when he directed Ruggles to testify on his behalf.

"General Ruggles, when you are cross-examined tell the court what I said on the County courthouse steps."

Pope was referring to the infamous *4:30 Order* he had given Porter during the third day of the Battle of Second Manassas. When Ruggles hesitated, saying that he was not acquainted with the circumstances of the case, Pope 'refreshed' his memory.

"You know what orders I gave to Porter."

Ruggles' answer was reluctant agreement. He knew what his commanding officer wanted him to say.

"Yes Sir."

"You know that they were not carried out?"

Ruggles' answer was non-committal.

"That is what I have been told, Sir."

"That is sufficient for you to know. You will be summoned as a principle witness..."

SENTENCING

The trial dragged along for more than six weeks as the Court carefully built its case. The accused presented his defense summation, a written address, which was read by his attorney. When he was finished, Judge Holt said his piece.

It is difficult to accept that Judge Advocate Holt truly *believed* his final pronouncement of the court's findings. His remarks were pure gobbledygook as he defended his reasons for refusing Porter's request for written findings:

"Whatever, therefore, of inaccuracies of interpretation of testimony, and whatever of illogical deduction from it, may be found a place in the very elaborate defense of the accused, which has been read, may be safely left for their correction to the recollection and judgment of the court."

Judge Holt finished this obscure pronouncement with an excuse that there was *no time* to answer Porter's defense.

"To prepare a written reply, in keeping with the gravity of this proceeding, to the argument of the accused, would require several days. It is felt that the *'public interests'* will be best served by asking, as I do, that you will proceed at once to deliberate upon and determine the issues which are before you thus involving a delay *which it is most important to avoid.*"

The Court had doomed a man to the most severe possible sentence; short of death. Holt sealed the fate for life of an innocent man. Why did Holt feel compelled to deny Porter a written reply, which would help Porter in an appeal? Judge Advocate's Holt reasons were curious. He claimed, "Finding generals as a part of a panel to listen to Porter's defense was difficult as they were needed to fight in the existing war." However, there were *900 generals* in Washington, *who were not needed in the fighting and who could have been selected to serve.* Holt's written reply to deny Porter's defense argument.

Secretary of War Edwin Stanton had chosen to 'pack' the court and rush a conviction as quickly as possible. The so-called *'public interests'* to which the judge advocate referred were nothing more than a reflection of Secretary Stanton's personal desire to find Porter guilty quickly,

possibly to diminish his own obvious error in the appointment of Irwin McDowell and John Pope after their egregious errors in war.

When the trial was finished, Colonel Judge Advocate Holt submitted the case to the court.

He said, "This case has been thoroughly and most patiently investigated. A continuous session of forty-five days sufficiently attests to this. Indeed, the greater part of the evidence, touching the more important and more severely contested points, has, by examination and cross-examination, been again and again impressed upon your *(the judges and members of the court)* minds. I feel entirely satisfied that the facts are completely comprehended and appreciated by you in all its bearings."

Porter was convicted. General of the Army, H.W. Halleck laid the proceedings and the court martial sentence before the president of the United States and Abraham Lincoln signed them. It was over.

The fact that Lincoln approved the court martial proceedings against Porter led me to revise my opinion in the beginning of my research for Porter's story; I believed that Lincoln had sacrificed his moral beliefs in this case for what he may have considered the greater need to save the Union.

That was not true.

Lincoln *did not* betray his beliefs. The judge advocate had *lied to Lincoln* with the sin of omission; he gave Lincoln only the evidence *against* Porter. When Judge Holt appeared before Lincoln to explain the proceedings and the evidence, he withheld the evidence *which would have given the lie to Pope's charges*.

∞ 3 ∞

Early Troubles

Major General Fitz John Porter's unhappy future, because of his liberal politics, was predestined. Never a slave owner, like many men of his time, he believed slavery would die of its own weight. Yet, as early as 1803 events had begun their march, like gloomy road markers, to line the way toward the nation's inevitable bloody future. It led to the destruction of men like Porter, whose politics did not fit the slaveholder's mold.

The first of the measures that pointed the way to America's greater future had dark repercussions. It was the bold purchase of an enormous chunk of land in 1803 by Thomas Jefferson... and that far-sighted American did it with an empty purse; money he did not have in the treasury.

The Louisiana Purchase was a vast area of wild, unexplored plains, rivers and mountains inhabited only by Indians, trappers, hunters and wild animals. The land stretched across the continent from the wide Mississippi to the Pacific Ocean and from Canada to Mexico. Foreigners owned it. Napoleon Bonaparte, Emperor of France, claimed most of the land in North America beyond the United States.

Clever as Jefferson had been, luck played a part. The French had no choice but to sell. France was at war with England and Napoleon needed money to fight the war. The war was not the worst of Bonaparte's troubles; if the real estate wasn't sold, and quickly, England would take it from him by force.

When President Thomas Jefferson came to France he headed straight to the Emperor's Palace in Paris. He knew all about Napoleon's dilemma.

"Sell us your North American holdings," the wily Jefferson suggested

Napoleon Bonaparte was the leader of the most powerful military power in Europe but he was between a rock and a hard place. His enemy, England, possessed the greatest naval power in the world. Bonaparte could not compete with England's navy and he could not prevent the British takeover of his New World holdings. With nothing to lose Napoleon agreed to sell that great chunk of real estate to the United States. This would affect the future of slavery in the United States.

Two weeks earlier, before Jefferson arrived, Napoleon met with his advisers. In that meeting of the First Counsel of France, grim with certain knowledge, he laid out the facts.

"Messieurs," he began, "I *know* the full value of Louisiana. I had it, and now I must lose it to the English. They will take it from France. They will start a war, and then we *must* fight. With twenty ships in the Gulf of Mexico, their conquest of Louisiana will be easy."

Napoleon laid out the cold truth. He gave his advisers the only answer to the problem that was possible.

"That possession (the Louisiana Colony) must be taken out of their reach and there is not a moment to lose. *The English shall not have that land.*"

More was discussed and the weary conference dragged on far into the night. At daybreak the First Counsel made its decision.

"No more deliberation. I shall cede New Orleans and the *entire Louisiana Colony* to the United States without reservation. I *know* the value of what I abandon. I give it up with the greatest regret but to try to hold it would be folly."

He instructed his Charge d'Affairs, "Negotiate the affair with the United States."

Timing is everything. The heating war with England couldn't have come at a more opportune time for the young republic. Had France not sold and the English claimed the land, with a foothold on the continent, their next step might have been a new conquest to regain their American colonies.

Bonaparte agreed to sell a third of North America to Jefferson for *fifteen million dollars, at pennies an acre…* and he was happy to be rid of the burden. President Jefferson returned to the United States with a Bill of Sale and a Deed in his pocket, the ink not yet dry on the document. With one stroke of a goose quill pen, Jefferson had purchased the center part of a continent along with a very, very, very large I.O.U.

When Jefferson announced his '*Good News,*' instead of the praise, the acclaim, and the grand celebrations he expected from his fellow citizens, they called him every bad name in the book. His public stated,

"Jefferson is a madman. He has ruined us before we are barely established. He has committed the greatest folly possible."

No abuse was too malignant, no epitaph was too coarse, and no imprecation was too savage to be employed. Here was President Jefferson, head of a feeble republic, buying a colossal part of a continent that would take every penny the young republic could beg borrow or steal for a generation or more to repay. Most of Jefferson's fellow citizens thought he was crazy. The Halls of Congress reverberated with the cries of the legislators.

"We cannot afford such a wild expenditure so early in our history. The purchase is insane. Jefferson has saddled us with a mortgage we can *never* repay."

The deal was no trifling acquisition. America's new Louisiana Territory included what would later become the states of Louisiana, Arkansas, Missouri, Iowa, Kansas, Nebraska, Minnesota, Colorado, North and South Dakota, Wyoming, and Montana. Also, because of Jefferson's bargain basement steal, the purchase opened the way, soon after, to acquire Washington State and Oregon from Spain.

The American purchase had a direct effect on the irritating and troublesome matter of American slavery. The Louisiana Territory, from the beginning, had been accepted as a territory where slavery was permitted. The territory had no legislators so it had no players in a game that might otherwise have joined in the pro-slavery and anti-slavery tug of war.

Early on the question came, *'What if the territory is divided into more states?'* When that happened, and it was a certainty, then each state would have its share of senators and representatives. Who would they speak for, supporters of slavery or the Abolitionists? That huge land acquisition had, overnight, created new problems for the young republic.

Sure enough, before the century was twenty years older, by 1819, the specter of slavery reared its head higher than ever. The all-important balance between those states that allowed slavery and those states that did not allow slavery had been carefully kept equal. There were twelve slave states and twelve free states. Peace over the question had reigned... until then. At least, the slave question had not so far caused any serious disputes, violence or killing. Now the new territory threatened to upset the precarious balance.

There were three main triggers that caused the civil war. First, there was the Abolitionist movement that raised tempers to a fever pitch. The second was the fact of slavery, a human condition no one liked, but one for which there appeared to be no easy answer. The third cause was the continuing dispute between the states and the central government. One writer on the Internet, known only as the *'History Guru,'* drew a curious but interesting analogy to Abolition as one of the causes of the Civil War.

In a Wikipedia article he wrote, *'The suggestion that the abolition movement was a cause of the Civil War is like saying that Poland caused WW II. If only Poland had kept their mouths shut as the Nazi's invaded, we could all have been spared.'* I liked the History Guru's acerbic analogy.

Anti-slavery sentiment had been strong and healthy since the American Revolution. Yet, it wasn't until 1820 that the Abolitionists turned it into a crusade. As a seventeen-year-old growing up in America, young Fitz John Porter probably considered the Abolitionists to be one more crackpot organization.

Porter came from generations of conservatives who had accepted slavery as a natural way of life. His ancestors were military men of great renown. It was natural for Porter to drift toward the Democratic Party, an organization that was very much socialist in its ideas. Democrats in 1820 were laissez faire capitalists, and property owners said slaves were considered property. That three-hundred-year-old practice was accepted as part of *'the way things were'* in America. Democrats believed without a twinge of conscience that owning slaves was right and proper.

For the growing numbers of Abolitionists, the buying and selling of men was an indigestible fact. There were slaves in nearly all the states. As hard a row to hoe as it was, the anti-slavers were forced to accept the uneasy balance between the pro and the con states, twelve slave and twelve free, as the best bargain they could get from the powerful pro-slave block of legislators, which dominated Congress.

Four landmark events affecting slavery followed. Each came fast on the heels of the other. They were; the Missouri Compromise of 1820, the 1850 Missouri Compromise, the Kansas-Nebraska Act, and the Fugitive Slave Laws. Each led like pointers on a map toward a day of reckoning and the opening guns of the Civil War.

The ordinary farmer and city dweller didn't think much about the *'slave question'* in 1820. Business in America was like a healthy child on growth hormones. The Northern states of New York, Illinois, Ohio and Indiana were fast becoming a powerful industrial force with a strong influence on legislators in Congress. Meanwhile, the South was building a strong agricultural economy based on cotton, tobacco and sugar… and slaves.

The Missouri Territory had enough people and they were ready for statehood. Maine wanted to become a state. Missouri wanted to be a slave state but Maine wanted to be a free state. No problem. The balance between slave states and free states would be maintained.

Before Congress could approve statehood, the new want-to-be-state territories had to have a constitution. From Missouri, Congressional Representative James Talmadge was one of the growing numbers of Abolitionists. He proposed an amendment to the new Missouri constitution and his amendment was aimed at eventually ending slavery in Missouri. It stated, *'All slaves, upon reaching the age of twenty-five shall be given their freedom.'*

That short sentence was a dagger at the heart of slavery. It woke up the Missouri slave owning legislators like a jab in the eye. With a hue and cry of outright fury at changing the rules *and the balance of power* they opposed Congressman Talmadge's amendment.

White-haired Henry Clay, with a voice like a trumpet, and a leading Senator, watching the hubbub over the proposed amendment, saw the handwriting on the wall. He gave bleak notice in his speeches in Congress to all who would listen. The prophet warned of Armageddon.

"These continuing disputes and arguments between the two parts of the United States, will surely, someday, and soon, *lead to war.*"

Clay was only saying what most men and women already knew in their hearts. As it is for most humans, war was only a possible future event on the far horizon. People were perfectly willing to wait and see, to bury their heads in the sand, hoping it would all go away.

Henry Clay was a realist. He suggested a compromise, knowing the people could not afford to *'wait and see.'* Clay had only a year or two of formal schooling, and like Abraham Lincoln, he was a lawyer. Like Lincoln, Henry Clay fought all his life to preserve the Union. Clay offered a different and unique arrangement. Clay's compromise would get rid of the vagueness of Missouri's status. He proposed the *Missouri Compromise of 1820.*

Both the North and South were as anxious to avoid strife and unpleasantness as they would have been to avoid the plague. They accepted the Act and it passed into law. Missouri was admitted to the Union as a slave state and, to balance the books, Maine was made a free state. A second clause in the Act specified that free *negroes and mulattos were excluded from the state of Missouri.*

That small clause in the Compromise caused an explosion of anger. Anti-slavery people were a majority of the Missouri population and those few words caused wide-spread outrage.

"What," they cried, "There are already hundreds of *freed* negroes, who are *already* free citizens in Missouri. Why should they be excluded from living in Missouri?"

It was a standoff. The Missouri Compromise of 1820 stated quite clearly that freed negroes *could not live in Missouri*. What to do? The law was an insult to the Abolitionist citizens of the State. The law was an insult to every state where there were free Black American citizens. It was a calamity. The clause was a *flat contradiction* to the Federal Constitution. Article IV, Section 3, of the Constitution, which stated: '*The citizens of each State shall be entitled to all the privileges and immunities of citizens in the several States.*'

Clay offered *another* compromise. In place of the *Amendment excluding free Black citizens from Missouri,* he proposed to set an arbitrary line separating the mostly pro-slave states from the anti-slave North. The line, later called the Mason-Dixon Line, was set at 36 degrees, 30 minutes latitude. Above that line all new states in the Louisiana Territory would be forever free. Below that line all new states would become slave states. Furthermore, the troublesome Amendment in the Missouri Constitution was done away with; there would be no special restrictions on slavery in Missouri. Everything seemed to be settled for Missouri's statehood.

The Northern anti-slavers balked.

"What about *free* Black men and women citizens that come to Missouri? The Compromise keeps free Blacks out of Missouri."

It was a quandary. The knotty problem kept the legislators up drinking gallons of black coffee far into the night. Finally, after hours of debate, Senator Henry Clay and his friends hit on still one more smart solution. They drafted a *new* Compromise. This one, they promised, would solve the problem.

They labeled this brilliant idea, the *Second Missouri Compromise*. Henry Clay saw to it that Missouri's statehood was delayed... until Missouri's legislature agreed that *nothing* in its constitution would '*abridge the immunities and privileges of its citizens.*'

This *final Missouri Compromise of 1820,* with all its clauses and clever promises, only prolonged the inevitable dispute. The streamlined agreement was an easy answer but those clever tacked-on promises for parity would come back to haunt America. Thomas Jefferson knew it. He was an old man by then and he saw the storm coming; not right away, not in a decade, but it *was* coming.

Jefferson said, "The Missouri question is the most portentous one that has ever threatened the Union. In the gloomiest hour of the Revolutionary War I never had any apprehensions equal to *those, which I feel from this source.*"

The Slavery Question was growing hotter. Abolitionists had rocked the 'ship of state' to the point where, for the first time, Northerners saw what Jefferson saw. It scared them. Pro-slavery mobs attacked the anti-slaver's homes and businesses. Southerners burned their pamphlets, wrecked their presses and, in some towns and places, the pro-slavery officials did not allow Abolitionists to use the U.S. Mail.

It came to a head in 1837. Elijah Lovejoy, a newspaper editor, was murdered by a pro-slavery mob. Twenty years before the Civil War, Lovejoy set up shop as the editor of a St. Louis Abolitionist newspaper, the *Alton Observer*. After anti-abolitionists destroyed his printing press for the third time he hid his remaining press in a warehouse. When he rushed out to stop the mob from burning down the warehouse and his precious printing press, he was shot and killed on the spot.

Lovejoy has been called 'the *first casualty of the Civil War.*' His death and the furor that came from that tragedy so frightened the pro-slavery Democratic Congress that they passed the *Atherton Gag Rule. That infamous rule* prevented *any* discussion of slavery by any person. That Congressional piece of inane legislation made the Abolitionists more fearful than ever that their constitutional rights were threatened. The country slid inexorably to the precipice.

❧ 4 ❧

Mexico

Porter's part in the Mexican American War established a milestone in his brilliant career. The Mexican War brought Fitz John Porter one step closer to raising him to the heights as a hero and a great leader, and after that, the abject destruction of his promising career.

That story began in 1821. Texas was an open lawless territory. Longhorn cattle, with horns six feet across, grazed the chaparral and grassy plains. Wild mustangs, descendants of the Spanish horses from the time Spain conquered Mexico, roamed the plains. Pioneers, who survived the hard country, were tough hard-fighting, hard-living men and women with a strong sense of independence from any autocratic government.

The vast new area of Texas was home to 35,000 persons: 5000 Mexicans, 10,000 Americans, and 20,000 Comanche Indians, although few paid much attention to Comanche ownership rights. Texas was a rich land. Every kind of tropical crop could be grown, including cotton, and it was good land for the herds of cattle and sheep needed by a growing America.

Texas belonged to Mexico. Mexico, with its new-found independence from Spain, was suspicious of strangers. The growing numbers of settlers in Texas frightened the Mexicans and Mexico tightened its hold on its new inhabitants. Twelve military garrisons of Mexican soldiers administered the area and military law was harsh with few individual civil rights.

When the settlers showed signs of wanting independence the Mexican government made an attempt to compromise. The Mexican Constitution of 1824 gave the Americans the right to live on Mexican land if they swore an oath of allegiance to the Republic of Mexico and became Catholic. To sweeten the pot any American who married a Mexican woman was given 4605 acres of land. Steven Austin was delegated by the Mexican government to enforce the decree.

Most Americans believed in manifest destiny; which held that America was *fated* to control a greater part of North America, and Texas was the doorway to that hope. Americans living in Texas were tired of Mexican rule. They wanted their independence from Mexico and it mattered little to these settlers whether they would become an independent country or a part of the United States.

The war with Mexico was like a trial first-night opening for the greater show to come. It was an elaborate confidence game purposely started by politicians in Congress to add new territory to the United States. Popular in the South, the average southern slave-owner believed *if the United States could acquire a vast new territory on its borders from a weak and disorganized Mexico then that territory should become slave territory.*

American leaders told Steven Austin that it was time for Texans to revolt from Mexican control. They whispered in his ear that Texans *must declare their independence; Texas must become a separate country. Sam Houston delivered that same message to Austin right from President Andrew Jackson* and, in 1834, Sam Houston fought and defeated the Mexican army at San Jacinto. Texans declared their independence.

An unpleasant new problem reared its head. It was a dilemma for the pro-slavers and for Abolitionists as well. If Texas became a *separate country* the new Republic of Texas would form alliances with other countries. Those alliances might be *against* the United States interests and one of those 'interests' was slavery.

England and France had abolished slavery by that time, and both countries wanted an end to slavery in the United States. France and England might give the new country of Texas their support. That could mean a second war with English troops at the United States' back door. The choice was clear to Congress and to President James K. Polk. The United States *must* annex Texas and make it a State, with or without slavery.

In spite of Texas' new independence, Mexico had never given up on Texas. She continued to claim Texas territory south of the Nueces River as a part of Mexico. Mexico's constant attacks on the Americans in Texas were repeatedly resisted and Slidell, the U.S. Minister to Mexico, was unable to negotiate a treaty with Mexico or even secure official recognition from Mexico for the Texans.

The idea of a war with Mexico was appealing to most Americans; Texas settlers would be rid of Mexican domination once and for all. More importantly, this was the chance for those in Congress who wanted to expand U.S. territory on the North American continent. The decision was made.

In 1845, on 11 May, President Polk sent a war message to Congress. He enumerated the wrongs committed by Mexico against the United States *(while conveniently ignoring Mexico's reasonable claim to the country between the Nueces River and the Rio Grande).*

The President asserted before a packed house in Congress, "Mexico has passed the boundary of the United States, has invaded our territory, and she has shed American blood on American soil."

Congress naturally declared war.

Fifty thousand men were called up to fight. The Regular army was increased to thirty thousand. A week later, Mexican General Arista evacuated Matamoros and prepared for the American attack. Four days later at the Port of Vera Cruz, America invaded Mexican territory by sea and the Mexican Ulna Fortress began bombarding General Scott's ships.

They missed the American reconnaissance vessel. Had their aim been a little better, three of the leading Confederate generals of the Civil War, Robert E. Lee, Joseph Johnson, and Richard Meade, would have gone to the bottom of the ocean with the ship.

Soon after the Mexican bombardment President Polk ordered General Zachary Taylor to march to the Nueces River, which was the dividing line between Mexico and the disputed Texas Territory. Young Lieutenant Ulysses S. Grant and other men read the order with wry amusement. As Grant later penned to his wife, *'The government sent a small force on purpose to bring on a war and have a pretext for taking California and as much of Mexico as it chose.'*

The small but well-disciplined Regular army, men of the South and the North *(who would be killing each other in a few more years)* assembled at Corpus Christi. Two weeks later, the American army, less than eight thousand men, crossed the Nueces River and neared the Rio Grande. They reached the Rio Grande River at a point opposite the Mexican City of Matamoros. Then, at Matamoros, the Americans waited. They were about to make war against an enemy three times their size.

Despite their small number, they were well disciplined and efficient. Most were graduates of West Point. Adding to that, their fighting quality was excellent and many had fought in the Indian Wars. To top off the American strength they had a navy much superior to the Mexican navy.

Junior First Lieutenant Fitz John Porter served in Mexico as a young man from the beginning of the war. When the Americans invaded Mexico in 1847, Porter was posted to artillery and joined the forces of Zachary Taylor. On September 12, 1847, the Americans assaulted Chapultepec where Mexican General Nicolas Bravo commanded a garrison of 800.

Five thousand Mexican troops held the approaches to the city and Lieutenant Porter led his regiment under plunging fire. He attacked the walls with ladders, picks, axes and crowbars. Wounded in the fight, Porter was cited for gallantry in the storming of Chapultepec, and because of his heroism he earned the rank of second lieutenant. Later Porter earned captain's bars and then Porter was the only officer brevetted in the field as a major at El Molino.

As the Americans stood on the shores of the Rio Grande, Taylor, his position fortified, had help. The United States Navy had blockaded the Rio Grande at the mouth and no supplies could reach the Mexicans at Matamoros.

The Mexican army numbered 30,000 men at arms, a mixed bag of quality. The cavalry lancers were excellent horsemen. Unfortunately for the Mexicans, they were poorly mounted and poorly armed. On the other hand, the artillery officers were good but the guns were heavy and difficult to move around the battlefield quickly. The infantry was well drilled but its muskets were ancient. Adding to their burden, the officers were politically elected and not chosen on the better basis of their leadership ability and experience. Nevertheless, that deficit was balanced by the fact the Mexican soldiers always fought with their friends beside them, many brigades from the same village, and they fought from behind strong fortifications.

In early April of 1846, General Mariano Arista replaced General Pedro de Ampudia in the Mexican forces at Matamoros. Bold General Arista immediately crossed the Rio Grande to confront the Americans. General Taylor, when he learned of the move, sought to obtain intelligence on Arista's movements. He sent a squadron of fifty-seven men to spy out Arista's intentions. Before he could act on the information, Arista attacked. Eleven Americans were killed and wounded and the rest were captured.

Taylor called the governors of Texas and Louisiana for reinforcements asking for 5000 men. Five days later, Taylor went to Point Isabel to spread the word of the Mexican attacks. Taylor left a regiment and two artillery companies behind to protect the fort, now known at Fort Brown (Brownville, Texas) in front of Matamoros. The Mexicans attacked the fort but the Americans held. Taylor returned in a week with more men. He encountered Arista, who had 6000 men and ten guns barring Taylor's road, nine miles from Matamoros. Taylor's men numbered 2300 by this time with ten guns. In the furious fight that followed Arista fell back with a loss of 252 men while the Americans lost only 54.

Taylor continued his march toward Fort Brown and set up a defense on a ridge overlooking the road to Matamoros. The chaparral brush was exceedingly dense and mass movement was impractical so Taylor sent skirmishers with artillery supported by dragoons upon the road to wait for Arista.

Reinforced by the Mexican government with 2000 more men, Arista arrived and an artillery duel began. Taylor sent a squadron of dragoons to capture the Mexican cannon. They not only succeeded but captured the guns, a Mexican general, fourteen officers, and sent the Mexican army fleeing from the field in confusion. During the melee many more of the Mexican soldiers were drowned in the river crossing. Arista lost more than a thousand of his troops.

In August, Taylor crossed the Rio Grande and took possession of Matamoros. Three days later, he marched on Monterey with 6700 men against General Ampudia's 10,000 men. Meanwhile, Santa Ana had taken power in Mexico.

Ampudia surrendered Monterey after three days of intense fighting, losing a thousand men. General Scott took most of Taylor's army and Taylor established his headquarters at Monterey. The Mexican general was allowed to march away in honor and an armistice was signed eight weeks later.

Santa Ana learned that Taylor's force had been depleted so he advanced quietly to Saltillo with 20,000 men. Taylor discovered Santa Ana's surprise and waited to ambush Santa Ana with 4600 men near Saltillo at the City of Angostura. Lieutenant Ulysses S. Grant was in charge of the mules during the move.

Ulysses Grant was a young lieutenant then. No one could know he would become the man who, a few years later, led the Union to victory in the Civil War, became president and then, twenty years later, testified for Porter in the rehearing that would declare Porter innocent. Grant was the man who saved the Union army from annihilation at the Second Battle of Bull Run.

Grant became restless as he waited for the battle to begin in Angostura. He left the mules, borrowed a horse and rode to the front as the fourth infantry regiment was about to attack. When Grant arrived at the front he discovered that he was the only officer in the assault.

He later wrote, *'I lacked moral courage to return to camp where I had been ordered to stay so I charged against Fort Teneria defenses with the regiment.'*

The Americans killed a third of the defenders then pulled back to regroup. Grant gave his horse to another officer and went back to his mules.

The fourth temporary regiment was nearly down to their last bullets and powder. As West Point's best horseman in 1843, Grant volunteered to go for the ammunition. He galloped off, sliding down behind the side of his horse to keep the horse between him and the enemy's bullets while exposing one foot for holding the cantle of the saddle and an arm over the horse's neck. At nearly every street crossing the Mexicans fired at him but he got his ammunition and made it back to his friends without a scratch.

Young Lieutenant Grant saw plenty of blood; he would see more. With the 4th regiment in Mexico, he wrote, *'I saw a ball crash into ranks nearby where my regiment stood. A single ball tore the musket from one soldier's grasp, rip off another man's head, then dissect the face of a captain I knew.'*

Grant was a stubborn man. After the war was over Grant tried to climb the 15,000-foot high Mt. Popocatepetl that overlooked Mexico City but failed to make it to the top; the snow blinded him. He tried once more, donning green spectacles, and overcame his altitude sickness. This time he succeeded in scaling the volcano.

During the battle for Vera Cruz, Robert E. Lee had his first taste of the fighting. The young captain attacked a six-gun battery that had been pummeling the stronghold and forced the battery's gun crew to surrender. At Cerro Gordo, Lee guided a Brigade of troops behind the Mexican lines, passing over a lava field that was thought by to be impassable. Once reaching the objective he and his men forced the enemy to retreat.

General Winfield Scott said of Lee, "He is the very best soldier that I ever saw in the field."

In February the Americans fought Santa Ana. Colonel Jefferson Davis, the man who would later become the President of the Southern Confederation, headed the Mississippi volunteers and for two days, as the battle see-sawed in doubt, Santa Ana was finally forced to withdraw.

For the next three months, until March of 1847, the United States sent more expeditions into California and New Mexico. The flag was hoisted at San Francisco and Santa Fe and the Mexican Pacific seaports were blockaded. General Winfield Scott landed at Vera Cruz with 12,000 men and took occupation. When Scott demanded surrender the Mexicans refused. Scott bombed the port city for four days at the Castle of San Juan de Ulúa. Ultimately, Scott suspended the hostilities to allow the resistance to bury their dead. By the end of March, Vera Cruz had wearied and surrendered the city. Thereupon, Scott marched on Mexico City where Santa Ana waited with his own 12,000 soldiers.

What small accidents may sometimes decide our fate? It was at the beginning of this final battle for Mexico City, that the Confederacy nearly lost their greatest General. It happened at a checkpoint; an antagonistic sentry stopped Lt. Robert E. Lee, forbidding him to proceed.

Lee replied to the sentry's challenge, "Friends."

At the same moment another officer with Lee said, "Officers."

The confused sentry fired his pistol at Lee, the ball passing between his left arm and his body, the flames singing his coat. Lee was shaken but unharmed and able to continue in his destiny.

Winfield Scott attacked Mexico City on March 18, 1847, as Santa Ana waited with a force grown to 36,000 men and 100 pieces of artillery. More Americans kept arriving until the U.S. force had grown. Leaving a small detachment of five hundred soldiers at Puebla, Scott advanced on Mexico City entering by three roads, each guarded by rocky hills and each well-fortified.

On one of those roads, El Pinon, 51 guns flanked by lava fields stood on the high side and marshes bordered the other side. Large lakes southeast of the city helped to protect the city's inner fortifications stopping the American advance cold.

General Scott's engineers cut a new road around Lake Chalco in a twenty-seven-mile circuitous route leading to the most vulnerable part of town. In a macabre quirk of fate, the man who would lead the South to a near victory in the Civil War, and the man who for most of the Civil War would be his opponent, were now *in the same U.S. Battalion.* The expedition was under the command of Captain Robert E. Lee and Captain George McClellan.

After a reconnaissance of the land around the massive fortifications, Lee completed a rough road near Mexico City at El Penon, which allowed the American troops to position between Contreras and the capitol. Five times Lee walked the lava fields to reconnaissance the enemy and then, when he was satisfied with the route, he guided General Pierce on a diversionary attack on Contreras. Although he had been on foot or on horseback for 24 unbroken hours, Lee finished the reconnaissance. In the fight that followed Lee received a flesh wound and collapsed. His commander made an observation that would prove to be apocryphal ten years later in the War Between the States.

Lee's talent for topography was *peculiar.* He seemed to receive impressions intuitively, which cost other men much labor to acquire.

By noon the Americans swept over Cerro Gordo, an outlying village, and had driven the Mexicans ten miles down the road, capturing 3000 prisoners. They also bagged a general and forty bronze cannons. The Mexicans lost 1000 men, while the victorious Americans lost 431. The Hill of Contreras was taken along with the capture of four generals, 800 prisoners and 22 cannons. The Americans numbered 4500 against a Mexican defense of 7000.

Losses were lopsided in the other direction; Mexico lost 700 and the Americans lost less than seventy. On the same day Churubusco and San Antonio positions were taken with the further captures of four Mexican general officers and nearly two thousand prisoners. Once more Mexican battle casualties of three thousand were balanced by only a third of the Americans lost.

With the outer walls of the city taken the American advance halted. An armistice was declared. At Chapultepec, Lee's ability to understand the lay of the land helped him direct the positioning of American guns in range of Chapultepec and the final American attack began on the morning of September 7. After fierce hand to-hand fighting the Americans carried the day at Molino Del Rey, and Fitz John Porter was promoted to captain in the field because of his leadership and bravery.

A week later Chapultepec was stormed. Chapultepec is on a small hill three miles southwest of Mexico City and the city was once the summer home of the Aztecs. The land rises 150 feet above the plain. The Americans fortified Chapultepec after they took it. Within hours Sam Grant and the other marines in his brigade advanced down the streets of Mexico City against barricades of hundreds of Mexicans.

Moving forward, 'an arch at a time' toward the City Gate, they reached and held the Gate at last. Grant, spotting the belfry in a church that overlooked the San Cosme Gate, devised an audacious plan. He and other marines dismantled a mountain howitzer and carried the pieces, under fire, to the church.

Grant explained to the unwilling priest, "The only way you will save this church is by opening the door for us."

The troops trundled the gun up a narrow staircase one step at a time to the belfry and assembled the gun. Three hundred yards from the Cosme Gate, directed at their objective, the cannon was fired. The enemy scattered allowing the Americans to advance and Grant was praised for his resourcefulness.

Robert E. Lee, another young Union officer, also could not know that in a few more years he would lead the Confederate Army against Pope at the Second Battle of Bull Run. The only Union Officer that stopped him long enough in that Civil War battle was a fellow officer, Fitz John Porter, fighting with him at the Cerro Gordo battle.

Lee's dangerous reconnaissance and near-capture and death at the hands of the Mexican soldiers resulted in finding a new way to the top of Ayala, a hill opposite Cerro Gordo, for General Twiggs' guns. The Mexican army evacuated the capitol and General Scott entered Mexico City.

American total losses had been light compared to the Mexican loss of 14,000 troops. General Scott captured more than a hundred cannons and when the city had been captured, he levied a tax of a hundred and fifty thousand dollars on the city to pay for the care of the American dead and wounded. Thousands of troops soon arrived to reinforce Scott and Captain Porter. Porter was promoted to brevet major for his part in the battle.

Many of the men who fought in the Mexican-American battles, like Robert E. Lee and Ulysses S. Grant, later realized the horror of the trumped up reasons for that war. Grant wrote later, "*Nations, like individuals, are punished for their transgressions; we got our punishment in the most sanguinary and expensive war (the Civil War) of modern times. I should have resigned… but I had not the moral courage.*"

On 28 February 1848, the Treaty of Hidalgo was signed. Mexico had lost half her territory in the war that included New Mexico, Upper California, Arizona, and parts of other states and Texas. That same year in December, the Thirtieth Congress supported the principle of the Wilmot Proviso by voting to *prohibit* slavery in the new territory acquired from Mexico.

In the following year slavery was excluded from *all* Federal territories and it was abolished in the District of Columbia. Lee, Grant, Porter, McClellan, Sherman and others were the same men who would soon be fighting and killing each other fifteen years later over the same question of slavery and state's rights.

When the peace was signed with Mexico, Captain Robert E. Lee, one of the greatest tacticians of all time, was a thirty-nine-year-old army engineer, commanding a company of Pioneers. All during the fighting Lee had led reconnaissance missions, and as a result of his accomplishments his senior officers recognized that he was one of the best soldiers in the American force.

Lee was General Scott's 'favorite' officer and, later, when the Civil War drew closer, the North tried their best to persuade Lee to lead the Union against the rebellious south. He refused; Lee could not fight against his own people in the State of Virginia. Like Grant, Lee believed that America had 'bullied' Mexico into that war. He said he was ashamed of his part in the conflict. Yet, always a pragmatic soldier, Lee believed that to give the land back to Mexico would be suicide.

He was not alone. Colonel Ethan Allen Hitchcock, commander of the 3rd infantry regiment, wrote in his diary about the war with Mexico, *'I have said from the first that the United States is the aggressors. We have not one particle of right to be here. It looks as if the government sent a small force on purpose to bring on a war, so to have a pretext for taking California and as much of this country as it chooses, for, whatever becomes of this army, there is no doubt of a war between the United states and Mexico. My heart is not in this business… but, as a military man, I am bound to execute orders.'*

There were lessons to be learned by the officers who fought in the earlier conflict. For one, the Mexican-American War taught Grant that the man he would one day face in a final battle for the Union, Robert E Lee, was mortal. When Grant became general of the armies for the North in 1863, he applied the same aggressive tactics that General Winfield Scott applied in that earlier war. General William Tecumseh Sherman, Grant's right-hand man, did the same in his scorched earth policy as he marched with a hundred thousand men from Atlanta to the sea. Fitz John Porter learned what a determined defense could do in his delaying action and counterblow toward Lee at Malvern Hill during the early years of the Civil War.

With victory over Mexico, a huge new territory had been added to the United States boundaries. With the acquisition, the question of slavery became paramount once more. What part of these new territories would be slave and what part would remain free? That was the question that haunted the nation and it was a question without an answer that anyone wanted to hear.

Leaders in the South were deeply discontented. Henry Clay's 1821 Missouri Compromise could no longer survive with the acquisition of so much new territory from the Mexican-American War. The war had given the Union a huge, rich free state on the Pacific. California was large enough and with the potential wealth of a country all by itself

The two senators from California voted for a free state in the U.S. Congress. This sounded the death knell to slavery. The balance between North and South was broken. The new territory, which would be parceled out as free states or slave states, according to the rules of the 1821 Missouri Compromise, would prove to be the death of slavery.

Although that same Compromise assured the South that New Mexico, Utah, and Arizona would be slave states, what good would that be? These territories were open wastelands.

The *Treaty of Hidalgo* gave the American republic the land that would become California, New Mexico, Arizona, Utah, and Texas. With the pending acquisition of seventeen future states, the slave question became all-important. From what part of the Union could this anti-slavery aggression be checked? What could be done? What about Texas? If Texas became a slave state it might be partitioned into four smaller states. That *might* repair the imbalance.

That idea fell like a lead balloon on the inhabitants of Texas. There was not a cotton planter or a cattle herder who was not inflamed by the suggestion that majestic Texas, as large as the country of France, should be split into smaller states. They would not part with a shovel-full of the earth of their magnificent domain.

Thus was born the legislation for the Kansas-Nebraska Act. From the beginning, as more states were added to the Union, they were made states two by two. Always one free state was added and one slave state to keep the balance. Now Texas was added to the Union as a slave state. The balance was upset.

What of Captain Porter? After the peace was signed with Mexico in 1850, Porter was transferred to the Adjutant Generals Department. He'd had a meteoric rise and he became assistant to a general. He continued his rise to be made a colonel of the Pennsylvania 15th Infantry Brigade, followed by the appointment as Chief of Staff for the Military Department of Pennsylvania. In 1860, as war loomed closer, Porter was sent to Charleston, South Carolina to prepare for the inevitable.

Across the narrow isthmus Fort Sumter looked over the waters of the Mississippi and the City of Charleston. Colonel Porter advised his superiors that Major Robert Anderson should be placed in charge of the defenses of South Carolina and those Federal defenses should be consolidated at Fort Sumter. He was prophetic.

❧ 5 ❧

States Rights

It was the end of innocence.

For decades, there had been a growing certainty in the South that the U.S. Government would one day acquire the power to regulate and control some interstate matters. When that happened the South knew it meant the death of slavery.

Events beyond the control of any man were changing the balance of power away from slavery in America. The industrial revolution, the rising strength of the Abolitionists, a worldwide antipathy against slavery; these were like locomotives rushing through a dark night toward a bloody collision.

Fitz John Porter was like most men and women of his times. Like Alexander Hamilton, Horace Greely, Daniel Webster, and Samuel Adams, Porter believed the states had the constitutional right to secede. Like many Americans he believed that the Constitution allowed the states to run their own affairs. Yet, Porter was a patriot and a loyal Union soldier, who believed in the need for a strong central government.

Porter was a man of strong opinions. Other than the private thoughts he may have expressed to close friends, and in the several letters he wrote during the Second Battle of Manassas to his friend General Ambrose Burnside, Porter kept his views to himself. He never allowed them to interfere with his duty.

In the new and different Republican atmosphere of an anti-slavery administration, the greater power of the central government over the power of the individual states was, for the first time, about to be established by force of arms. Fitz John Porter, a silent Democrat, yet still a Democrat, and worse, a friend of George McClellan, was fed into the grinder of change as an example of those who did not agree openly with the new ideas.

Here was another puzzle. How did it happen that the Union went to war with the Southern Confederation if the Southern states had a *legal right to secede*? The answer depended on how the Constitution was interpreted. Abraham Lincoln, like Alexander Hamilton, believed *absolutely* in a strong central government.

The element that changed this simple premise to something brand new and utterly dangerous was the addition of the element of slavery. That dark institution, with all its evils, was the explosive catalyst in the mix.

President Lincoln, without doubt, was sure that the only way to preserve the Union and at the same time rid the country of the anathema of slavery, was to consider the seceding states as being in rebellion. Lincoln would do anything necessary to preserve the Union. Like adding sulfur to nitrates to make explosive gunpowder, Lincoln intended to create by force a new idea of democratic government.

How did Porter and other neutral or anti-slavery people feel about the South's die-hard attitude? First, it must be made clear that slavery was never the only reason for the Civil War. The industry and machinations of the North and the agrarian economy of the South put the South at a disadvantage as far as the need for mass labor was concerned. Slaves provided free labor. Some say the root cause of the Civil War was linked to the struggle for the states' right to secede as opposed to the nation's right to halt treasonous acts such as secession. Either way, the stalemate between the two views caused a sharpening discord, and looming war hastened on its way like street fighters egged on by pro-slavers and Abolitionists.

Where did a man's *first* loyalty lie in 1861? Was it to his State or was it to the Nation and the Federal government? Every citizen and every soldier had to decide. Like Robert E. Lee, the Southerner had no difficulty deciding; their loyalty was to the State of their birth. The Confederate soldier had simple loyalties but they were strong. It helped him through his travails on the march and in battle.

Southerners give us their reasons behind the ideals for which they fought. Knowing these things may help us to understand better, not only the Civil War but also Fitz John Porter. One Confederate officer, who shared the same experiences of his men, was a Captain of the Richmond Howitzers. Captain Carlton McCarthy served in the second company heading an artillery battery, Colonel Cutshaw's battalion of the second corps. Captain McCarthy fought in many battles during the four years of the war and his brother was killed at Cold Harbor. McCarthy, in his writings, tells his reasons for fighting and the obstacles he faced. He claimed to speak for all of his comrades in arms.

"It is not fair to demand a reason for actions above reason. The heart is greater than the mind. No man can successfully define the cause for which the Confederate soldier fought. He was above human reason and above human law, secure in his own rectitude of purpose, accountable to God only, having assumed a 'Nationality,' which he vowed to defend with his life and his property, and therefore pledged to his sacred honor."

"He would not obey the dictates of tyranny. To disobey was death. He obeyed and fought for his life. He dared not refuse the call to arms, so plain was his duty and so urgent the call. His brethren and friends were answering the bugle call and the roll of the drum. To stay at home was dishonor and shame. The Confederate soldier was a monomaniac for four years. His mania was the independence of the Confederate States of America, secured by force of arms."

Perhaps more to the point of McCarthy's statement is the story of a rebel prisoner. When he was asked why he fought, his answer was direct, *"For my rights."*

His interrogator, puzzled, asked, *"What rights have I tried to take from you?"*

The rebel thought and then answered, "Well, I don't rightly know but whatever they are that's what I'm fighting for."

You and I may see his words as a confession of a purpose that he was unable to define. Yet, to McCarthy and the hundreds of thousands like him, his purpose was real enough to die for. The earth on which we were born becomes a part of us perhaps, our identity worth defending. And perhaps in the clearer light of time, the imperative of the North to limit and abolish slavery was to the rebel soldier an assault on a greater principle; the action of a heavy-handed, authoritarian central government to *supersede* the power of the State and thereby, take away the rights guaranteed to the individual under the Constitution.

Very few rebel soldiers owned a slave. They fought for the idea that they *should have the right* to own slaves as the law provided. The Constitution provided for that right according to the interpretation of the Supreme Court of that time. Fitz John Porter believed it. To deny a man the right to hold a slave as property, a right sanctioned under the laws of a state, was to deny all men the right to hold any property. Perhaps, in his convoluted way that might have been what the rebel prisoner was trying to say.

The Confederacy fought with one hand tied because it lacked the industrial might of the North. In his writings, Captain McCarthy boasted of Southern victories. Despite the disparity of numbers between the forces of the Confederacy and those of the United States in the Civil War, he had a right to brag:

"The Confederate soldier faced immense odds. In the Seven Day's Battle of July of 1862, 80,000 men drove the Federal force of McClellan's 115,000 to the James River and away from Richmond. At Fredericksburg, 78,000 Confederate troops routed 110,000 Federal troops. At Chancellorsville in 1863, 67,000 under Jackson and Lee for the South whipped and, except for the death of Jackson, would have annihilated 132,000 men; more than double their own number. At Gettysburg, 62,000 Confederates assailed the heights manned by 112,000. In 1864, in the wilderness, 63,000 Confederates met and successfully resisted 141,000 of their enemy."

"Well supplied Union arms depots were an ever handy source of supply for the Confederate soldiers. The Federal soldier boasted arms and ammunition that was abundant and good; so abundant and so good they supplied both armies. The facilities for manufacture were simply unlimited. The nation thought no expenditure of treasure too great, if only the country, the Union, could be saved. The factories and the foundry chimneys made a pillar of smoke by day and by night. The latest improvements were hurried to the front, and adopted by both armies almost simultaneously; the Union stores were hardly bought, when the Confederates captured and used the very latest. Commissary stores were piled up all over Virginia for the use of the invading armies but, to the Confederate's good fortune, the Union forces had more than they could protect. Their loss was gain to the hungry defenders of the soil."

McCarthy's numbers were not always accurate but his basic truth was there. One indication of the Northern army's will to fight (compared to those of the South) might be measured by the number of the men 'missing' after the Second Battle of Manassas. A 'missing' man was often a man who had decided that he had enough of war and had gone home. Of course, sometimes a dead man was buried and never identified. Nevertheless, the wide disparity in the number of the missing pointed out a difference in the fighting attitudes of each side.

The figures paint a macabre picture. After the Battle of Second Manassas (called Bull Run by the South) the North had 13,000 casualties: 1716 killed, 8215 wounded, and 3893 'missing.' Because of Porter's strong defense, a great number of these included many of Porter's men. The South's casualties were about 8,000: 1305 killed, 7048 wounded. The numbers of Lee's 'missing' men were conspicuous by their absence.

The Confederate soldier fought greater obstacles than battle. If asked what the Confederate soldier most resented as he marched to battle, he might have said:

"I fight against the regular monthly pay which all Federal soldiers receive, pay which no rebel receives. I fight against the embargo by the Northern blockade that denies the wounded soldier of morphine and chloroform. I fight against the well-equipped ambulances that bring the wounded Federals to good surgeons, nurses and hospital stewards and are given the best surgical applications known to the medical world while the Southern soldier suffers amputation without any anesthetics. I fight the good wagons, the fat horses, the tons of quartermaster's stores, none of which the Southern soldier has except by capture."

North and South fought for reasons that were as different as day and night. The Union army fought to put down the rebellion, to hold the Union together and to end slavery. The rebel took up arms because, in the words of a Confederate soldier, 'I refused to obey the dictates of tyranny.' One man fought to keep the status quo; the other fought for his home and family.

In 1860, most citizens sincerely believed that any state in the Union had a legal right to secede from the Union and go its own way. Porter felt that way. At the Alabama Convention that year, the majority Democratic Party's platform stated, *'We hold it to be our duty, first, to use all honorable exertions to secure our rights in the Union. If we should fail in this, we shall maintain our rights out of the Union, for as citizens of Alabama, we owe our first allegiance to the State.'* With rare exceptions, Alabama's convention platform was accepted and recognized as the supreme law of the land.

New England had been the first of the states to advocate the Doctrine of the *Right of Secession* by any state. The right of individual freedom, the freedom of the states to be sovereign over the government was sacred. The people of Massachusetts always sanctioned the *Right of Secession*.

Why citizens all over America felt this way, why Fitz John Porter felt that way, was no mystery. One had only to look at their heritage. New England was pioneered and populated with Puritans; Cavaliers settled in Virginia, Quakers came to Pennsylvania. South Carolina was peopled with Huguenots and early Georgia was filled with the followers of Oglethorpe. They were all, without exception, refugees from governments that insisted on restricting their freedoms.

With Quakers and Puritans, it was religion. The followers of James Oglethorpe had fought with Oglethorpe against English despots. The Cavaliers, who followed the trappings and knightly behavior of olden times, had been knights that fought repression. The Huguenots fought their way against the domination of the Catholic Church. The binding force that welded all of these very disparate citizens was a determination to remain free and independent as individuals and as States.

The Supreme Court, in 1861, in all their decisions, maintained the principle of the absolute sovereignty of the states. The Tenth Amendment of the Constitution stated, *'The powers not delegated to the United States by the Constitution, nor prohibited by it to the States, are reserved to the States…'*

The Constitution further stated that the central government could not use force to bend the states to the government's will. When the states ratified the Constitution they expressed in no uncertain terms that the states could not be coerced and could, at any time, withdraw from the federation and retake the powers granted to the central government.

Alexander Hamilton, one of the most extreme advocates for a strong central government, emphatically stated, "Any attempt by the central government to enact a law, which was not granted by the Constitution, *would be an invasion of the powers reserved to the states.*"

John Quincy Adams said, "The indissoluble Union between the states and the central government was not a right; it was *in the heart.*"

Daniel Webster denounced the anti-slavery agitators who opposed the Fugitive Slave Law demanding, "They should observe the laws and the Constitution."

Horace Greely, a powerful Abolitionist, strongly insisted in 1860 upon the rights of the Southern states to secede.

The New York Tribune, 8 October, 1860, quoting Greely, reported, "If the cotton states shall become satisfied that they can do better out of the Union than in it, we insist on letting them go in peace. The right to secede may be a revolutionary one, but it exists nevertheless."

No, the issue of slavery was not the sole reason for secession and the Civil War, but slavery became the reason and changed our nation forever.

Slavery

From the beginning, slavery was the *'skunk in the parlor.'* Nobody *liked* slavery. As a slave state, in 1760 Virginia tried to monitor the slave trade. South Carolina, another slave-holding state, prohibited the importation of slaves while that state was yet a colony, but she was overruled by her British masters.

A large, heavy, and very old encyclopedia, published in 1880, dealt specifically with the causes and the subject of secession. It was told in a way this writer had never understood before. It was a collection of quotations, speeches and news articles by leaders in the northern *frees states*. More to the point of Fitz John Porter's story, these facts helped explain why Porter thought as he did, and why that good man was pilloried and dishonored for his popular beliefs.

Porter, George McClellan, Stephen Douglas, and most of the leading Democrat politicians, citizens, and leaders of the day in the North believed secession was entirely legal. They believed the Constitution allowed for the right of some states to conduct the business of slavery.

Slavery was always the *'elephant in the room.'* As a practice that made human beings nothing more than property, to most it was a hideous concept. Some attitudes toward slavery were hard to explain and harder to understand. Many people believed slavery was not the horror that it was. Slaves were valuable property for the Southern planter and Southern businessman and good property, like a valuable machine, was well cared for.

Yet, there were some men, even in those early days of 1831, that knew slavery for what it was. These first Abolitionists were a persecuted and proscribed class. They were denounced with unsparing severity by both political parties. They were condemned by many of the leading churches. They were libeled in the press and they were maltreated by furious mobs. No more than a handful of the population, the Abolitionists continued to work against the institution of slavery.

Many of the Abolitionists were recruited from the Society of the Friends, the Quakers, whose religion relied on non-violence and an appeal to the reason and the conscience of men and women. Congress was besieged with petitions from the Abolitionists that might free the Black man and they were met with powerful resistance. They were denied a hearing and warned the mere presentation of their petitions might precipitate dissolution of the Union.

THE GAG RULE

John Quincy Adams, while he was not an Abolitionist, waged constant war against Congress's refusal to discuss the question. He maintained that the Abolitionists had a *right* to be heard. The pro-slavery congressmen in the House of Representatives finally got so sick and tired of hearing the Abolitionists' protests that one of their number, Congressman James Atherton, threw up a barrier to free speech. He concocted an odious rule, which was called the *Atherton Gag Rule*. It was the Twenty-First of General House Rules in common use to stifle unnecessary speeches and debate. The Gag Rule was thorough. The House voted that '*every petition, memorial, resolution, proposition, or paper, touching on or relating in any way whatever to slavery or the abolition thereof, shall on presentation, without any further action thereon, be laid on the table without being debated, printed, or referred.*'

The Abolitionists were not to be so easily discouraged. The sheer injustice and stamping of heels on the Constitution by the pro-slavers only inspired more and more citizens to become Abolitionists. By 1860 Abolition was added to the Republican platform.

The Abolitionists struck out many times but could not give up.

The slave overseers were the worst offenders. They did their best, at any cost, to squeeze the most work possible from the slaves under their control. The main job of the overseer was to sweat his workers to the limit. But beware retribution from the owner of the slaves if the overseer did not keep the owner's property in good repair, like any good, expensive machine, reasonably happy with their lot, and unlikely to run off or rebel.

We know and accept without thought that no matter whether the Black man was cared for well by some slave masters or treated with the gravest cruelty, the fact then and the fact now is that to take freedom from any person diminishes all persons. Certainly there *were* abuses but the greatest abuse was the *existence* of slavery. For one man to lay claim to the body, the spirit, and the mind of another was the worst kind of abuse. America was not like that… for many reasons.

PART OF THE FAMILY

One Southern writer, Colonel John Scott of the Confederate Army, wrote about the South before the Civil War. He described what he believed was the common feeling by most of the Southern slave owners towards slavery.

'… *The real old settlers regarded the slaves as a part of their families. It was a cause of considerable grief to a family if any of their Negroes became such bad subjects as to require to be severely punished or sold. The planters and their Negroes were born together on the plantation; they had played together in childhood. Sons of the planter might branch off to follow some profession. Others, as they grew up, fell into their respective positions as master and slave. Both were contented and, like many others, they saw themselves and their position in the light of their own eyes and not as others saw them. They did not understand why any outsiders should interfere with them.*'

One might wonder what the slave might have said in his own behalf once forever out of range of the whip and the leg irons or the auction block.

More and more often, as the nation hurtled toward Civil War the Northern newspapers in dozens of articles by Abolitionists, defamed the slave owners. They presented the Southern slave owners' treatment of slaves as cruel and immoral. The slave owners fought to defend the practice in the Southern press and in the halls of Congress. They were certain the barrage of Abolitionist charges would surely lead to an attempt by the national government to interfere with the states' right of self-government.

When Abraham Lincoln was elected to the presidency he presented a thoughtful point of view on the subject of slavery so that not all Southerners were terrified of his election in 1860. Most believed he was a moderate, always willing to compromise on any question. Yet, by the vote that elected Lincoln to the presidency and the growing power of the Republican anti-slavery party, the South soon became fearful that the Constitution would be disregarded and slavery would be destroyed. They believed that the end of slavery would bring financial ruin and utter annihilation upon the South.

THE PECULIAR INSTITUTION

Most people in the North, men like Fitz John Porter and General McClellan, believed that the *'peculiar institution'* of slavery was a phenomenon that they could live with, as repugnant as it was. They believed slavery would die by itself. The problem was, until it did, no one, not even Abe Lincoln knew what to do with a million Black men and women if and when they were freed.

Here is a mystery. Why did slavery gain such a strong foothold in the Southern states, while, much earlier, the North turned its back on the institution? The reasons were hard to define, but the Southern agrarian economy required little education and many souls to do back-breaking labor. Meanwhile, Americans were gradually being transformed into a nation of curious, inventive self-sufficient innovators. Men and women thought of ideas on every conceivable subject to make life better. The ideas came; one after another in an avalanche of new inventions: Morse telegraph in 1840, the McCormick reaper in 1847, the Singer sewing machine in 1855. The early settlers were driven to anything that would make life more agreeable and make 'Yankee' traders rich.

Maybe it was something in the air or in the water of this new land. How was it a backward dozy America managed to change Robert Fulton's steam ship which had a low pressure steam engine into, by 1830, the high pressure engine of original American invention that drove the massive steamships plying the Mississippi?

Archeologists sifted the sand around the original site of Jamestown and they found an earthen ware oven, a swept hilt rapier, pieces of ivory chessmen, a small caltrop with wicked spikes to throw in the path of the Spanish cavalry, scissors, needles and thimbles, a branding iron, candle snuffers and an ice pit for storing food; all innovations and new creations of the settlers. Even the soldier's armor was cut up into cooking pans. Europe had loosed a pack of wild eyed but thoroughly practical innovators on the world.

People in Pennsylvania, Illinois, New York, and the cities, mostly in the north, invented everything from Colt repeating revolvers to Singer sewing machines to the hitherto unheard of idea of selling on credit.

Lewis Tappan hired no less such persons to search out credit worthy customers on whom to sell their goods as certain young men who would find higher employment later in life. Some of the young men who worked for Tappan included Abe Lincoln, Ulysses Grant, and Salmon Chase, later secretary of the Union treasury during the Civil War.

The South took an entirely different road from the North. While the North built their factories and railroads, the South became an agrarian society. Labor was cheap and the Southern planters grew cotton, tobacco, and crops on the rich semi-tropical lands of the Southern states. And they came to depend entirely on slave labor.

One explanation for the flourishing of slavery in the South, but which died on the vine in the Northern states, was suggested by Charles Mann in his book, '1493.' Mann linked the cause of slavery to a *mosquito*.

Before you laugh or doubt Mann's reasoning, hear what he says. It makes sense. The answer to the mystery of why slavery flourished in the South and not in the North might have been because of *malaria*. At the time malaria was called *turkey fever*. Malaria flourished where the disease carrier, the Anopheles mosquito lived and where wild turkeys thrived. The mosquito eggs need but a couple of weeks of warm humid weather and that kind of weather had to be consistent during both night and day. One place fit the bill; the Southern states.

This kind of moist hot weather with mild winters exists in a broad band, between Southern Brazil and below a line that separates the Southern states from the Northern states. Roughly, that line may be defined as the *Mason-Dixon Line*. It was no coincidence that the Mason-Dixon Line became the dividing line for slavery between the Southern rebels and the Northern states.

The changes in America that allowed slavery to flourish came in two steps. When the first Europeans arrived, along with their worldly possessions they also brought the unwelcome baggage of the measles, smallpox, and other diseases. The Native Americans had no defense against these newly-introduced diseases and they died like flies. European diseases killed ninety percent of the Indians. Once the natives were no longer a threat to prevent settlement and growing crops, it was easy for the new Americans to set up shop.

For centuries wealthy European settlers used the practice of *indentured servitude*. First cousin to slavery or serfdom, indentured servitude was a good, inexpensive way to acquire cheap labor to work the farms. A wealthy European paid a sum of money to a poor man and, in return, the laborer agreed to serve his master for several years until the money given to him was repaid in labor. The practice seemed perfect for the settlers of the new world who wished to build large plantations on the rich southern lands and enjoy year 'round good weather. Men were brought to the new world and they promised to work for their masters as indentured servants for seven years. The indentured servant planted the master's corn, cotton, tobacco, or whatever crop was grown. Generally, the servant also waited on the master and worked his farm or plantation. At the end of seven years if he had paid off the passage money he was free to start his own farm.

According to author Charles Mann, because of the Anopheles mosquito and the fact the Anopheles mosquito thrived below the Mason-Dixon Line, that pesky insect killed their indentured servants in droves.

Some observant planter made the convenient discovery that the Black Africans of Central Africa *(where the mosquito and malaria also thrived)* had developed an immunity to the disease. Only one in a hundred Blacks died as compared with the white population in Africa. Why not use Black Africans in place of the fragile white indentured servants to farm the cotton and tobacco in America?

The planters of early America and in those places between Southern Brazil and below Washington D.C. *(exactly the division between North and South where the Mason-Dixon line runs)* must have asked themselves that question. Was it better to have a willing servant for a few years, whom often died before his indenture was finished, or a Black African who did not die and stayed around to work the plantations for life? Never mind that the Africans might want to kill you for taking their liberty. By exercising strict controls, Black Africans were more cost effective by far. Hence, the practice grew in the South until the Southerners became so dependent on the need for slave labor they were willing to die to keep it.

The Southern attitude toward slavery was an even a greater puzzle. Other than the Constitutional defense and opposition to anything 'Yankee,' Southerners that shifted uncomfortably in their seats when confronted with the idea of enslaving other men, could only reply with bland philosophy.

'Leave the institution alone. It shall fade away of its own accord.'

Nevertheless, slavery was at the core of secession. I quote from the observation by Fergus Bordewich, who reviewed the book by Eugene D. Genovese and Elisabeth Fox-Genovese, *'Fatal Self Deception:'*

'If you were from the South, and you were white, slavery was the embodiment of the American Dream.'

A South Carolinian and Buchanan's Secretary of State wrote in 1860, *'In a word, for all that we are, we believe in ourselves, under God, indebted to the institution of slavery… for a national existence, a well-ordered liberty, a prosperous agriculture, an exulting commerce, a free people and a firm government.'*

Slave owners insisted slavery was a blessing for all, their slaves as well as for them. Opinions of most Southerners about the condition of slave servitude varied from *'the happiest of earthly conditions'* to an attitude by the enslaved of being *'loyal and loving to their masters.'* Blacks were creatures of a *'mental incapacity.'* All the while the slave owner complained bitterly of the heavy cross of responsibility he must bear and the household and field problems he had with his slaves.

John C. Calhoun, the father of secession exclaimed to a British Abolitionist, "Liberate a slave? God forbid I should ever be guilty of such a crime."

It is little wonder that men in the North, like McClellan and Porter, both of whom had friends in the South and traveled often, would feel some of the illusionist and grand beliefs that festered among Southerners. Blacks were incompetent. Everyone believed it. Even Abraham Lincoln could not fathom the possibility or the likelihood that a Black man might ever aspire to any higher position, much less the presidency of a world power of three billion citizens because of a *'lack of capacity and intellect.'*

Indeed.

THROUGH A GLASS DARKLY

Slavery was essential to the economic life of half of the United States in 1860. Fitz John Porter, like most Americans, saw slavery *'through a glass darkly.'* It was an essential part of the operation of half of the country. In the short run slavery was unpleasant but a necessary evil. Porter's own government, the United States, and the revered Constitution seemed to support an institution that had tremendous practicality.

Just before the Civil War, a million tons of cotton was being produced every year in the South. The underpinnings of that accomplishment was the sweat and labor of four million slaves, who worked the fields and reaped the cotton harvests for their masters. Everything the national government did was a constant barrage of propaganda, which supported the *'rightness'* and the *'need'* for slavery in America.

It is no wonder that there were men of intellect and good judgment, while not favoring slavery, were willing to let it lay unmolested. Until Abraham Lincoln forced the issue with a Civil War and the Emancipation Proclamation, that was the way it was.

What happened to the Black men who managed to tear off their chains and fight for their freedom? Their fate was a well-kept secret. Three major rebellions, the destruction of millions of Black families, the cruelty of slave masters; these tales never reached the North. Most likely, Fitz John Porter never heard of these slave uprisings.

Lewis Clark, an escaped slave, may have given us a kernel of the true state of affairs. In his memoirs as a slave, Lewis Clark wrote, *'There is nobody deceived quite so bad as the masters down South; for the slaves deceive them and they deceive themselves.'*

Where did it begin? It began when the first slave was brought to Jamestown 250 years before the Civil War. By 1631 the colonies were regularly importing African slaves to do their work. During the Colonial period slaves were in all the colonies, north and south. Only *after the Revolutionary War* did the Northern states abolished slavery by gradual emancipation. The Southern plantation owners kept their source of cheap labor and all was peaceful in all parts of the country.

It was not until 1787, at the Constitutional Convention, that there was a North-South disagreement on the slave issue. Slavery was prohibited that year in the Northwest Territory and confined to a region south of the Ohio River and the Mason-Dixon line. However, the territory of the Louisiana Purchase was tactfully ignored. No slave policy marred the peace in that large new territory.

King Cotton tightened the manacles on the slaves ever more and more securely. By1793 the first *Fugitive Slave Law* guaranteed the return of runaway slaves to their owners. Along with that, Eli Whitney and his miraculous cotton gin made the cotton industry grow overnight to become one of the great American exports to the Old World of Europe and England. Sugar plantations became another gold mine for Southern agriculture. The demand for slaves shot up like a rocket. Slavery became a gang system of enforced labor that *eliminated the need for any white labor* or taxes for the Southerner.

At the start of the Civil War there were six million slaves in America. From the beginning the existence of slavery in America molded the minds and the prejudices of its citizens. The Fathers of our Country were plagued by the fact of slavery. Judging from this sentiment, you would have thought that the first act of the new government *should have been* to *prohibit* the slave trade.

Some tried. The Supreme Court decision of 36 U.S. 136, the majority opinion expressly declared, *'Persons are not subjects of commerce.'* Because of the growing power of the slave states of the South, and the slaveholder's consideration of the slave as property, the difference between a slave as property and a slave as a person was purposely blurred.

A later Supreme Court decision, 40 U.S. 558A, *expressly protected property rights.* The alert Southern politicians and leaders latched on to *that* pretty definition as quick as scat. However, the Court's decisions and the laws that followed were *supposed* to apply to *inanimate* things or to animals. They were never supposed to apply to human beings. Nevertheless, because of the *vagueness* in the slave laws, the Southern states took full advantage of the generous misinterpretation.

To form a *More Perfect Union* the Founders of our Nation were forced to compromise their ideals of freedom. If they had not compromised, there would have been *no* republic and the *Ordinance of 1787 (which included the Fugitive Slave Law)* was a reflection of those compromises. With gritted teeth, the founders of our country passed the first of the slave laws, hoping that slavery would fade away of its own accord.

The Ordinance of 1787 declared the slave trade must continue for twenty years… and then cease. Second, the Ordinance declared that Congress would determine the Congressional voting power of the total population of a state. Third, the Ordinance declared that all territory *south* of the Ohio River belonged to the land that would later become the states of Virginia, South Carolina, Georgia and North Carolina.

That land was already occupied with Southern landowners, whose crops and homes were worked by slaves. The 1787 Ordinance had to make allowance for this and to satisfy the Southern slaveholders so the Ordinance of 1787 decreed that all runaway fugitive slaves would be returned to their masters.

The Founders agreed to the compromise. They were forced to recognize the fact of slavery. Yet, the Founding Fathers were careful to exclude from the Constitution *every expression that might be taken to mean that men were property.* You may search the Constitution in vain for *any* expression recognizing human beings as merchandise or legitimate subjects for commerce.

Moving like a mindless juggernaut toward the apocryphal conclusion, other events followed. Southern slave owners found it was *easier* to have other men do their work. Later, dependence on servile labor became a part of the basic survival of the

South. They no longer wished to change the practice. After all, if their slaves had been magically taken from them who would work their farms? Who would carry on the labor of their households?

It was *never* the cry of the fighting men in the South to protect the institution of slavery. The rallying cry was always *states' rights* over the power of an oppressive federal government. Few Southern small farmers owned slaves. It was only the upper class, one-third of the wealthier planters, who had all the slaves. The poor man could not afford a single slave, let alone the hundreds, which the large cotton plantations needed.

God was given the credit. The Southern slave owners rationalized the 'rightness' of slavery and took the words of their Old Testament Bible to justify the practice of enslaving the black man. Yet, in the years after, the South's utter dependence on slaves to do their work came to be a double edged sword. When war came the South had no industry, few railroads and limited steel-making works. They had a much smaller capacity than the North to make guns and ammunition and only a tiny fraction of the war-making armament potential of the industrial-rich North. Nevertheless, they marched to war with supreme confidence in the rightness of their cause and the certainty that it was God's Will they would prevail.

THE SLAVE REBELLIONS

There were plenty of slave rebellions, seldom reported and largely kept secret. Not all Black men loved Massa and accepted their bondage… far from it. In 1811, four hundred slaves gathered after an uprising on the Major Andry plantation. Armed with primitive homemade weapons, the rebellion spread from plantation to plantation. Like the march of the Roman slave, Spartacus, they gathered more slaves as they passed.

The U.S. Government Forces sent soldiers to end the rebellion. They attacked and killed sixty-six men and the rest were tried for their crimes. Sixteen more Black men were executed as criminals before it was over.

In 1827 a freed Negro, Denmark Vesey, planned to burn Charleston, South Carolina. It was Vesey's plan to initiate a general revolt of the slaves. Before it was over, Southerners were convinced that thousands of slaves, instead of dozens, were involved. Vesey's plan was betrayed and Vesey and thirty-five blacks were hanged. The trial record, published in Charleston, was ordered destroyed because it was too dangerous for slaves to see (*and for the slave sympathizers in the North to know about*).

The 1831 Nat Turner rebellion threw the entire South into a frantic state of emergency. For ten days, Nat Turner and twenty other Black men, unable to take any more of the terrible conditions on their plantation, rebelled. They killed their masters, and 57 white men, women, and children died in the blood bath. The entire region around South Hampton, Virginia, reeled in fear.

A hundred Blacks were killed in revenge although most of the murdered Blacks were innocent and not a part of the rebellion. When, two days after the rebellion began, they captured Turner, one of his captors, in describing his physical characteristics, noted he had several scars and a large knot on one of the bones of his right arm, probably from repeated beatings and blows from his master, plantation owner, Samuel Turner.

Turner and his twenty young co-conspirators were hung. The rebellion was over but the nightmare of future uprisings and runaway slaves left a vivid impression on the Southern slave owners. It sent an unforgettable message. From that time on the slave laws were more strictly enforced.

The Nat Turner slave rebellion galvanized the South to action. Even before the rebellion, and from the beginning of slavery, there had always been codes and rules for conducting the slave business. Slaves were slaves for life. The child of a slave was also a slave and all slaves were chattel.

The threat from Black rebels grew so great that in the South, when Black parishioners were seated in the church and the minister began the service, a white minister-observer was always seated near the back in the audience to monitor the sermon and watch for Black demonstrations or expressions of individual thought which might become rebellion.

Across Virginia and other Southern states, state legislators passed new laws to protect them against another such Black uprising as the Turner rebellion. The rules stated that slaves and freed Blacks *could not be educated*. They could not assemble in groups greater than three persons. A white minister had to be present at all Black religious services to ensure the church assembly had not been called to foment a new slave uprising. Each slave owner set his own rules of behavior for his slaves, different for field laborers than for domestic workers.

The *Amistad Affair of 1839* brought the fugitive slave laws, once more, to the front row of attention. The laws enforcing, controlling, and opposing slavery had become a twisted maze of wrong turns and hazy definitions. They varied from state to state. There were differences from one state to another even in the Northern free states.

All of the laws boiled down to a single question: is the slave a person or is he property? Opponents and adherents alike faced this hard question. Before a man is enslaved, what is he then? If he is *not* a possession of any person, how can he be property? Therefore, he *must* be a person.

According to this logic, then a miracle occurs. Once the slave merchant visits a village, catches and shackles a man so he cannot flee to his wife and children, the captured man is no longer a man; he becomes property.

How did this miraculous transformation occur? How do a set of manacles and an auctioneer with a bill of sale take away a person's humanity? What transformation has made the human being into a something no different from a beast to be used, sold and traded like any other parcel of property? That *was* a difficult question, anathema to Abolitionists and downright embarrassing to any fair-minded Southerner.

The Question was put to the test on July 27, 1839. Forty-nine black men were kidnapped from their village on the coast of Sierra Leone, West Africa. The men were put aboard the *Tecora,* a Spanish ship. The Tecora and its human cargo sailed to Cuba, then a Spanish colony. From Havana, the prisoners were taken to barracoons, or slave markets, a common holding station for slaves about to be sold or moved to the United States, where there were willing buyers in the South.

There were five slave markets within a mile of the Havana City walls, all near the governors' house. From the barracoons they were to be taken to different parts of the island and sold. The 49 captured Africans were shipped aboard the *Amistad* for delivery to America where the slave captors intended to sell them into slavery after their stay at Puerto Principe, Cuba, a major way station for the slave trade.

One of the Africans, Cinque, knew something of metalworking. Cinque managed to free himself from his chains and then he freed the other captives. He used an iron file that one of the women, who had not been chained, had found on the ship.

Cinque and his comrades attacked and killed the ship's cook but they spared the lives of two of the slaver's crew. The crew members promised they would sail the Amistad to Africa and return the forty-nine persons to Africa.

The navigator deceived the Africans. Instead of setting sail for Africa, he steered a course along the United States coast. The ship dropped anchor a half a mile off Long Island, New York under the pretext of needing water and food. Some of the Africans went on shore for the needed supplies when the U.S. Naval brig, under the command of Lt. Thomas R. Gedney of the USS warship, Washington, took custody of the Amistad and the Africans.

Gedney wished to claim the salvage rights. Under Admiralty Law, the ship, its cargo and the Africans could be claimed and sold. Thereupon Gedney sailed to Connecticut because, unlike New York, slavery was still legal in Connecticut in 1839.

A Federal Court found the transport of the Africans across the Atlantic had been illegal. The forty-six men, the two women and one child were not legally slaves; they were free persons, which the Supreme Court affirmed on March 9, 1841. The findings of the U.S. Supreme Court were a summary of the status of the current slave laws of that time.

Slaves were legally recognized as property *in Connecticut and some other states* until 1848. It was, and had been, illegal to import slaves since 1808.

The United States had a treaty with S*pain (Pinckney's Treaty of 1795)*. The Treaty stated if a vessel of either Spain or the United States was forced to enter the others ports that ship would be immediately released.

Slavery was outlawed in Spain. Spanish law made it legal to *keep* slaves *if* they were born *before* 1820. This was the neat and often used loophole in Spanish law. The excuse allowed greedy slavers to change birth documents of nearly all the imported Africans into Cuba. Ships and property *(this mostly applied to slaves as property)* found helpless at sea were subject to salvage rights and might be claimed by those who had rescued them.

Now began a tug of war. The Spanish government asked that the *Amistad*, the cargo, and the slaves be restored to Spain under the Pinckney Treaty of 1795. Meanwhile, Abolitionists collected money and mounted a defense for the Africans. Their biggest obstacle was the lack of understanding of the African citizens' foreign speech. Unless their testimony could be translated from the *Mende* tongue to English there was no way the court could evaluate their claims. They were hard put to find someone who could speak the native Mende language of the Africans.

One of the Abolitionists, a professor of languages, had learned to count to ten in the Mende language. He searched the docks among the workmen, many of whom were Black. By walking along the docks and shouting out the numbers aloud repeatedly, he found at last a twenty-year-old sailor from a British man-of-war ship who understood. The seaman's name was James Covey and Covey was a former slave. Most important to the Africans and the Abolitionists defending them, Covey spoke the Mende language.

In court Covey testified, "All these Africans were from Africa. I could talk with them. They say they came from Lumboko. They all have Mende names."

The Abolitionists' further claimed the Spanish government had *outlawed* the slave trade. The Africans had been captured from their village. Therefore, the Africans were *not* slaves but victims of an illegal kidnapping. Their papers claimed the Africans had been in Cuba *before 1820,* which by Spanish law would have made them slaves. However, it was discovered that the papers that certified the Africans as slaves were *forged and false,* a common practice by Spanish officials. The Circuit Court in Hanford ruled it lacked jurisdiction. The alleged acts took place in Spanish waters on a Spanish ship.

Then a President intervened and illegally bent and flouted the law. President Martin Van Buren made a decision that defined his character as a man. He *knew* the Africans had been kidnapped. Nevertheless, he ordered the Africans to be taken back to Cuba as slaves.

Van Buren's political motivation was clear. The President did not want to make Spain unhappy in this widely-publicized case. Also, he needed the Southern vote in the upcoming presidential re-election. Not wishing to run the risk of having the jurisdictional judgment overturned with an appeal, Van Buren issued his order quickly before any new appeals could be made.

In the nick of time the District Court *agreed with the Abolitionists*. They were willing to hear the case. In a new appeal, the District Court decreed the Africans were, indeed, free persons and not slaves.

Now Van Buren was nervous. He knew he would be found out and be placed on the hot seat. Van Buren ordered the U.S. Attorney for the District of Connecticut to appeal for a reversal. The U.S. Supreme Court agreed to hear the case for a reversal of the District Court's decision. John Quincy Adams was ready to argue for the Africans and the case was heard and the Supreme Court affirmed; *the Africans were persons and they were free men.*

Van Buren and the pro-slavers were not finished. The seven Africans were then accused of murder and piracy on the high seas. Under the Pinckney Treaty with Spain the U.S. had a duty to return such renegade Africans to Spain for trial. However, thanks to a blow for right and justice, the courts ruled that if Cinque and his brother Africans had killed the captain and the cook during the course of their escape from captivity, how was their act any different from the actions of American sailors imprisoned by a foreign power and fighting by any means at hand to gain their freedom?

According to Chief Justice Marshall in *40 U.S. 559A,* "Killing during an effort to escape a criminal kidnapping is not murder."

The Court's ruling had set a precedent and defined the Africans as persons and not property. The echoes of that decision reverberated down the years like the echoes of the Liberty Bell. Ten years later when American warships captured an English vessel with slaves aboard, because of the earlier decision, the Negros aboard were considered to be prisoners of war and never property to be sold or distributed as merchandise.

Southern pro-slavery men continued to ignore the Amistad decision. Slaves had been, were, and would continue to be property, as far as they were concerned.

The North, following Clay's attitude, agreed that slavery was bad. Nevertheless, they were determined never to force their will on the slave owners. The return of runaway slaves to free territory was always difficult and a source of friction between the North and the South. It was ever a subject of heated discussion in the North and especially in Congress. Those heated debates were the last angry voices of men who would shortly become mortal enemies during the cataclysm that was nearly upon them.

❧ 7 ❧

Politics

Twenty years before the Civil War, William Lloyd Garrison spoke about compromise at a Massachusetts Anti-Slavery Society meeting. He talked about the slavery issue and the laws that made slavery legal.

In a statement hot with passion he told his audience, *"The compact, which exists between the North and the South, is a covenant with death and an agreement with hell."*

Not everyone in the North understood that in 1862, but in the next three years they would become educated.

America was evolving. It had become like a family. The central government in Washington made the big decisions, regulated the mail, mediated disputes and saw to the defense. The states, like wives careful of their wards, decided the 'small' matters: how their money was spent, having all rights not prohibited by federal law, and how they ran their state. Political parties evolved along with the growing republic. Federalists became Democrats, and Republicans championed states' rights.

The evolution had started years earlier. Before the ink of the signatures on the Constitution was dry, slavery became an issue. Legislators in both parties and in all the states, did not always see clearly that far horizon when the slave issue must be fully confronted. As Shakespeare's King Lear said of political blindness and short-sighted views,

> '...*Get thee glass eyes;*
> *And, like a scurvy politician seem*
> *To see the things thou dost not...'*

Moral men were quite willing to acknowledge the evil of slavery but for the sake of compromise and to avoid war, they continued to make *"covenants with death and an agreement with hell."*

When Thomas Jefferson became president the power of the Federalists declined. In 1824, with Monroe, another Republican, the Federalists died as a national party. In 1829 Andrew Jackson was elected. The 'people's president' was a strong supporter of laissez faire, a relaxing of governmental oversight. Jackson believed

The Porter Conspiracy | Gene Paleno

the states should be allowed to run their own houses with minimal interference from the Federal Government.

Conflict and disagreements in the Republican Party created questions without answers. When matters of national importance came up who should call the tune? Should it be the states or should the Federal government decide? Because of these differences, some Republicans who were less rabid supporters of the preeminence of states' rights, split away and became *National* Republicans.

The National Republicans, like the old Federalist Party, favored a strong central government whereas the Jacksonian Republicans favored states' rights. Jackson's camp changed their name to Democrats. President Jackson, their leader, was a strong believer in giving the states free rein to do as they wished and the new Democrats believed in state's rights and the equality of mankind... provided they were white.

In the mid-eighteen-thirties there was another shift in politics. A major political party rose in opposition to the Jacksonian Democrats, the Whig party. They were similar in their philosophy to the old Federalists in wanting a strong central government. Just before the Civil War the Whigs fragmented into 'Cotton Whigs' and 'Conscience Whigs' over slavery. Abraham Lincoln joined the Conscience Whigs.

The Whigs didn't last. In 1856, Lincoln and others went over from the Whigs to the 'Know-Nothing' party. The Know-Nothings were a movement created by native-born Americans, white Protestant males of British-American lineage.

Beginning as a secret order, members, when asked about the party's activities, always answered, "I know nothing."

In a few years more, many, like Lincoln, joined the New Republican Party, which became just plain Republican. Now the pro-slave Democrats opposed the anti-slavery Republicans.

Prejudice was rampant. Native-born Americans hated Irish immigrants, Southerners looked down on all things 'Yankee,' Protestants hated Catholics. Northerners had little use for the slave holding Southerners, and Major General Franz Siegel's Union army corps of German troops were looked down upon with suspicion by some of Siegel's fellow officers and men. Yet, when the fighting started, native-born Americans, Irish, Germans, Catholics, Protestants, Southerners and Northerners all fought and died in the same way.

In 2002, Martin Scorsese directed an award-winning motion picture, 'The Gangs of New York.' The gang fights, portrayed in the poorest *Five Points* section of New York, were fought to the death with clubs, knives and guns. Often dozens were left dead and wounded. That excellent motion picture was a dramatic example of the bitter antipathy between the Irish immigrants and the native-born Americans in early New York.

Many political parties arose at the same time that invention and innovation exploded in the North, around the 1850s. Thick and fast, Americans invented every new thing imaginable, previously mentioned as the cotton gin to scoop up and process cotton in the fields faster than any mass of men might do, sewing machines and power looms to make cloth and clothing cheaper and better, and the Bessemer process for making iron for the mass of machinery a new country needed. The idea of interchangeable parts and mass production was another such innovation. Coal and water power became more in use instead of burning wood. Fulton built his steamboat. The miracle of the telegraph and of steam locomotives became reality. Taxes supported public schools. Women began to fight for their rights... and, for the first time, there was a strong unified, well-financed anti-slavery movement.

One striking example of the growing differences between Southern and Northern states, triggered by a federal tax on industrial goods, was the Tariff Act of 1832. The tariff jacked the tax rates higher on all goods brought into the Southern states and the Southern planters howled with rage. The South hated the tax. They were forced to buy the industrial goods the South could not produce and they called the tax, the *'Tariff of Abominations.'*

The South had no choice but to pay the tax. After all, everything from wagons, tools, arms and all kinds of machinery were imported by a South that depended on agriculture. The South had no industrial work force, except for their slaves. The slaves were better suited to plant and pick cotton and tobacco where they could be controlled and watched. Who knows what would happen if they were sent off to the cities to work in the factories?

When the Southerners objected to the tariff, the U.S. Government used force to make the Southern tobacco and cotton growers pay the added tax. It got to the point where South Carolina threatened to secede from the Union over the hated tax but, in the eighteen-fifties, such a warning was still no more than an idle threat. South Carolina stood alone. Still, South Carolina had sounded a clarion call that woke many men to dire possibilities. A compromise was found and the tariff was lowered over a ten-year period and the crisis ended for a time.

THE WILMOT PROPOSAL

In 1852 David Wilmot lit a new firestorm over slavery. He excited the nation as much with his creative proposal as the original Compromise of 1820. Knowing that very soon the United States would add millions of acres of new territory to its holdings in North America with the conquest of the southwest and Mexico, David Wilmot made a proposal.

Wilmot was a giant of a man, powerful in physique, and a man with strong common sense. He was a young Congressman from Pennsylvania, from a district which had strong Democratic majorities. Phlegmatic, with no pretense to eloquence or oratory and no claim to genius, Wilmot decided the time had come to stop the spread of slavery. He stood in Congress and stated what the Bill should do.

"The President's two-million-dollar Bill is intended to pay off Mexico for what the United States took from that country in the Mexican-American war. My proviso, added to the President's Bill, declares that in any territory taken from Mexico, *neither slavery nor involuntary servitude shall ever exist in those lands.*"

The Wilmot Proviso, as it came to be called, was a revolutionary idea. It was a bomb about to explode. It was David Wilmot's first session in Congress. He was thirty-three years old and, until then, David Wilmot had been unknown outside of his small district in Pennsylvania. At once Wilmot's Amendment made his name familiar throughout the length and breadth of the republic. Nothing like the Wilmot Proviso was so hotly debated since the 1820 Compromise. It split the Democratic Party in the North and raised the courage of all anti-slavery adherents.

Daniel Webster, the great orator, voted for the Proviso. In doing so he warned the nation of dire consequences from the South when and if the Proviso became law.

"I see little in the future and the little I do see gives me no satisfaction. All I can see is contention, strife and agitation. The future is full of difficulties and full of dangers. We appear to be rushing into peril headlong and with our eyes open."

When Daniel Webster uttered these gloomy words the Civil War was barely little more than a decade in the future. The pro-slavery legislators delayed the bill until the original Act was passed without the Proviso. Yet, the Wilmot Proviso left its mark and Wilmot's idea was one more powerful piece of evidence of the rising fever in the land over the slavery question. David Wilmot lived to see his Proviso become national law in 1863.

As the Democrats and the Republicans faced the problem of slavery head-on for the first time, the country moved toward a final reckoning. The stage was set for war. Men raced to fight for their individual countries, North for the Union and South for the new Confederacy.

❧ 8 ❧

Runaway Slaves

By 1860 it was beginning to be tough to keep slaves. Without slave labor the South was doomed. Yet, to stand still was to allow the slow and certain death of slavery. On top of that dark menace to the South, in 1848 the people of the Nebraska Territory changed the rules again; they wanted to be a part of the United States.

Their request was sent to the Congress and it passed the House of Representatives. Not everybody noticed the Southern legislators grinding their teeth in frustration and rage. When the Bill was sent to the Senate for final passage every Southern senator voted a resounding NO.

Here was a new impasse. Nebraska had been a part of the promises of the 1820 *Missouri Compromise*. It was in the 'Free Zone,' above Latitude 30 degrees 30 minutes, the Mason-Dixon Line. There was no question about it. The majority of Nebraskans had voted to be free. It *had* to become a free state. It was there in the plain words of the *Compromise of 1820* in black and white. There were no 'ifs' or 'buts' to the matter; the 1820 Compromise said Nebraska would be a free state because Nebraska was in free territory.

The slaveholders panicked. Furthermore, the balance of congressional power had shifted against the Southern states. Senator Archibald Dixon of Kentucky, the man who replaced Senator Henry Clay in the Senate, stood in the Senate chamber and made Southern intentions clear as crystal. To the whoops and hollers of joyful agreement of all the Southern senators… and some Democratic Northern senators, in 1848, Dixon proclaimed a new message of tolerance to the slave holders.

"Let the *Missouri Compromise* be repealed. Let us make a *New Compromise*. Let us allow the citizens of all the states named in the Missouri Compromise to be at liberty, if they wish, to take and hold slaves in that territory."

His statement rocked the Senate. What did Dixon mean? Was Dixon's proposal so bad? People could make up their own minds and not be forced to accept something they didn't want. What could be more fair? The *majority* of the citizens in a state could decide to be free or slave as they chose.

The other shoe hadn't dropped. There was a darker purpose to Dixon's proposal that had not yet seen the light of day for the Abolitionists. That 1848 speech was no spur-of-the-moment change in the Missouri Compromise. Dixon's proposal was part of a well-thought-out plan that had been discussed with fellow Southern slaveholders in smoke-filled rooms for years since 1820. Since the day that Clay's original Compromise Act had passed, the South had secretly plotted, schemed and waited for this moment.

Behind Senator Dixon there was a settled Southern determination to *break down the ancient barriers* of the 1820 Missouri Compromise, which might prevent some states from keeping slaves. Nobody knew it then but Archibald Dixon's speech was the *opening salvo of the Civil War*.

Southern reasoning for Dixon's *'outwardly'* liberal idea was based on these facts: The Senate at that time was mostly Democrat. The Democratic Party in the North was soft on slavery. They nearly always voted with the Southern Democrats. Democrats were for states' rights and for government protection for the ownership of property. That included *all* property, including slave ownership and the U.S. Constitution *protected* property.

The passage of Dixon's Act was a turnabout of monumental proportions. Calhoun, Webster, and Henry Clay debated the newly revised Compromise all summer. They discussed and talked about the idea of replacing the 1820 Compromise with something new and better. Clay continued to offer several alternative compromises when he rejoined the Senate in 1849, but each time they were set forth for a vote they did not receive the majority a new Act required. It was another impossible logjam.

At that moment Stephen Douglas jumped into the fight.

He offered the South an extra plum: *'Take the wastelands of New Mexico and Utah.'* His offer was hollow and of little help. It did not help to ease the pain for the pro-slavers, who had seen California become a free state.

There was an accident in the White House. President Zachary Taylor, cool to the idea of any change in the old 1820 Compromise, suddenly died of food poisoning. Before the crisis got any worse, Taylor's successor, Millard Fillmore, assumed power. The new president was much more receptive to compromise and a deal was made changing the terms and restrictions of the 1820 law. The newest compromise in 1850 became law.

The 1850 Compromise was a massive betrayal of all that the Abolitionists held dear. It was a sea change. After vowing not to change the terms and restrictions on slavery of the 1820 Compromise, the freedom that had been guaranteed for Blacks in states above the Mason-Dixon Line was demolished.

Every leading politician, from the President on down had turned about like changing a suit of clothes. They had broken their promise to support the original 1820 Compromise. They had opened the doors to slavery in *every state in the Union*.

The Act, as onerous as it was to Abolitionists, was a true compromise that kept a Civil War at bay for ten more years. California, by state constitution had declared itself to be a free state and the South let go their demands to make California a slave state. Almost as an afterthought, the District of Columbia was made free. Most important for the Abolitionists, a free state could be admitted into the Union *without requiring the Federal Government to pair the new free state with a new slave state.*

For its part in the compromise, the North gave the slave holders a revised much stronger *Fugitive Slave Law*. Almost as an innocent afterthought, the newer Fugitive Slave Law also included another not-much-noticed agreement. The law allowed *interstate slave trade*.

The *Samuel Prigg Incident and that not-much-noticed agreement in the Fugitive Slave Law was the* spark that lit the fuse for the final explosion over runaway slaves. On a warm moonless night in 1848, a mother bundled up her four children in blankets, carrying all the cornbread she had saved, and ran with her family through the fields and across back country roads to a horse drawn wagon that waited a mile away. Abolitionist friends carried her and her children on the first step along the Underground Railroad toward the free State of Pennsylvania.

A few weeks after she had found freedom in the North, Samuel Prigg, the Southern attorney who had been hired by Mary's slave owner, took Mary and her children into custody. He carried Mary and her children back to Virginia in chains.

Shortly after, federal officers arrested Prigg for the crime of kidnapping. Prigg appealed his sentence to the courts. By the following year his appeal reached the Supreme Court of the United States and the Court affirmed the decision that Mary and her children had been kidnapped.

It was a close vote; five to four. The Court's legal opinion established a new *federal* interpretation of the *older*, hardly noticed *Fugitive Slave Law of 1824*. The Court's judgment weakened the old Fugitive Slave Act and the South rocked with fear they might lose their slaves.

There was a wail of indignation from the twelve Southern states. They demanded their *right* to enforce the Fugitive Slave Laws, to bring back runaway slaves *by any means necessary* without risking a kidnapping arrest and jail. Two years later, their loud and repeated demands led to another new law; Senator Archibald Dixon's *Compromise Measure* of 1850.

The infamous sleek new *Fugitive Slave Act* decreed:

1. The *Fugitive Slave Act* protected the right of a slave owner to recover his runaway slave *wherever the fugitive should go*. No matter where his slave had fled, to another slave state or to a free state, the slaver had the *legal right* to recover his property. A runaway slave could never be free of his chains, even in a free state.

2. The *same Commissioners* who decided a particular case of a runaway slave were paid an *extra ten dollars* if they decided *for* the slave owner rather than in favor of the slave. That ten-dollar bonus was a prize in 1850.

3. Adding insult to injury, the *slaveholder's testimony alone* was enough to identify the runaway slave. The law did not allow the runaway slave to speak in his own behalf and the slave was denied a jury trial. After all, he was not a person but merely a thing of property.

In its effect, the Fugitive Slave Act of 1850 gave the thief the right to decide to whom the stolen property belonged. A knockdown, drag-out constitutional fight began. The South claimed their right to the revised Fugitive Slave Act as guaranteed by the United States Constitution.

"Not so" cried the Abolitionists.

The Abolitionists followed their objections with violence. In 1854 a slave, Anthony Burns, was captured and returned under the Fugitive Slave Act. But not before the Boston courthouse door was beaten down with a battering ram, a deputy was stabbed and President Pierce ordered Marines and artillery to guard the prisoner. Burns was returned to Virginia after the trial, and his freedom was later purchased by Boston sympathizers. Burns attended Oberlin College and became a minister, despite the hue and cries from both sides.

After Burns' trial, a temporary peace was accepted.

❧ 9 ❧

Kansas-Nebraska Act & Popular Sovereignty

In 1863 an anti-slavery military court persecuted General Fitz John Porter for his Democratic leanings. If people of our present time were to travel back to 1850 and live as typical Northern Democrats, they would find there existed a tolerance for slavery. Porter might have abhorred slavery, but he was tolerant of that dark institution.

Part of the reason for that forbearance was because slave abuse was carefully kept in the dark. Southern newspapers did not print such tales and Northern newspaper reporting criminal slave abuse was discouraged. Only if one had been a witness to the cruelty of the slave markets and the slave auctions would one have known the reality.

The practice of beating, torture and death, mainly to keep another person in servitude, was horrendous and evil. Yet, having been the law of the land for three hundred years, it was accepted.

Fitz John Porter had never owned a slave. It is probable that he had only seen the whitewashed part of slavery practiced by the less cruel slave owners. It is reasonable to think that moral Americans, like Porter, might have closed their eyes to the terrible wrongness of slavery.

White men weren't the only persons who had a sugarcoated view of slavery. Even some freed Black men took the part of the slave owners. Booker T. Washington, a Black writer, claimed to be an eyewitness to the 'truth' that most slaves were devoted to their masters.

Writer Washington, in his book, 'Up from Slavery,' wrote about black attitudes.

'One may get the idea that there was bitter feeling toward the white people on the part of the people of my race, because most of the white population was away fighting a war (the Civil War) which would result in keeping the Negro in slavery. In the case of the slaves in our place, this was not true. And it was not true of any large portion of the slave population in the South where the Negros were treated with anything like decency.'

'During the Civil War one of my young masters was killed and two were severely wounded. I recall the feeling of sorrow that existed among the slaves when they heard of the death of 'Marse Billy.' It was no sham sorrow but real. Some of the slaves had nursed and other slaves

had played with him as a child. Marse Billy had begged for the slaves' mercy when the overseer or master was thrashing them. The sorrow in the slave quarter was only second to that in the Big House.'

The 1850 Final Compromise declared that its people should decide slavery in the new territory of Nebraska, Kansas and Missouri. The majority of the free-state men of Missouri were allowed to vote to *abolish slavery.*

Stephen Douglas, an important voice in 1850, supported Clay's compromise solution. Southerners hated the solution but Jefferson Davis and most Southern congressmen were able to swallow the Compromise because of the Fugitive Slave part of the Compromise. Immediately, that is what they did.

Political power in the Senate tilted toward the North. Southern planters, factories, homes and farms depended mightily on slaves for their manpower. They saw that the *Act of 1850* had turned out to be a deadly threat to slavery. No issue was more burning or engendered more strong feeling and violent action. New territory, originally meant to be free of slavery, now might become slave if the inhabitants decided that it should be so... or the reverse might occur. In Kansas, the question became overnight the most important and divisive question in politics. People were killed, presses were burned and blood flowed in the streets.

The vague interpretation by Southerners of Article IV, Section 2 of the Constitution, suddenly became the preamble to a larger fight. Free State Abolitionists balked at the legal farce of the wording. They refused to accept the finality of the *1850* Compromise and the wide-open liberal Fugitive Slave Law that was a part of the Compromise.

Like unwanted poisonous new weeds popping up unexpectedly in the American political garden, one more new problem arose. Nebraska Territory wanted statehood. Since Nebraska was part of the Louisiana Territory, it could become a state. A bill was introduced in Congress to make that happen. Every Southern legislator voted against it because Nebraska would most likely vote to be a free state. By the old 1850 law, Nebraska would be free soil and also tip the balance of Congressional voting power further against the South.

Senator Stephen Douglas was an inventive man with imagination. He proposed the *Kansas-Nebraska Act of 1854*. Senator Douglas was a consummate politician. Called affectionately by his supporters, *The Little Giant* because of his short stature but mighty voice, Douglas had his sights set on the presidency. In Douglas' effort to curry favor in the South for his climb to the presidency, Douglas coined the term, *Popular Sovereignty*. His new Act, the *Kansas-Nebraska Act of 1854* would *include* Kansas in the Bill *with* Nebraska. His bill included the brand-new idea of '*Popular Sovereignty,' which allowed states' citizens to decide their laws.*

Stephen Douglas stated in Congress, "*Popular Sovereignty will* give the people, in any state, leave to regulate their domestic institutions in their own way."

"The policy of the United States should be non-intervention in the will of the majority of the people."

Douglas believed the majority opinion should rule. Those who opposed Stephen Douglas' premise of majority rule cried out in horror, '*If a majority of the people believe we may burn witches at the stake, then should that also become law?'*

Douglas claimed his proposal to bring statehood to Kansas and Nebraska, or to *any* state, would not interfere with the will of the majority of the citizens of that state regardless of past laws or Acts, which may have banned slavery. His policy of *Popular Sovereignty* made the *1850 Compromise* yesterday's news.

The Abolitionists were stunned. It might mean a colossal *spread* of slavery. The Northern Abolitionists, who hoped for the end of slavery, were rocked to their foundations. The revered *Missouri Compromise* had kept a free state from becoming a slave state. The people of the United States, particularly in the North, had come to regard the Missouri Compromise with as much profound respect and veneration as they did the U.S. Constitution. Now, out of the blue, Senator Douglas proposed the *Kansas-Nebraska Act* and absolutely *destroyed* their precious *Missouri Compromise*. If the proponents of slavery could finagle a majority vote for slavery in *any* state, *even in a free state,* that state would become a slave state. *All* states were open to slavery.

In 1850, Senator Douglas believed in 'live and let live.' His watchword and beliefs were, *'Let the South have their slaves. Allow the institution to continue. It will eventually die of its own accord.'*

To men Like Clay, who hated slavery with a passion, such lukewarm anti-slavery men were anathema. In 1850, rising from the ashes of the Whig Party and anti-slavery men, there arose a new party, the Republican Party. One of its new members and one of the first of the Whigs to join the Republican Party was a young Senator. His name was Abraham Lincoln.

It was time for the South to put their *Grand Plan* into action. The Southern businessmen, politicos, and planters began by gathering as many states as possible, whose populations would vote for slavery. If they lost the fight to the Abolitionists, the South hoped, by that time, they would have enough slave states south of the Mason-Dixon Line *to form a new country*.

What should have been crystal clear but befogged their thinking, because of their total dependence on slave labor, caused them to refuse to accept a sorry truth. Servile labor was their strength *and* their greatest weakness. If they hoped to build a continental empire outside of the Northern states, the South would have built their hopes on a foundation of sand.

Not all Southern congressmen were ready to abandon the Union and form a new confederacy. Three or four Southern senators believed the preservation of the Union was more important than saving slavery. Still, the Northern Democrats, who one might have thought should support the central government, had broken their pledges to support the Missouri Compromise.

When the Kansas-Nebraska Act came to a vote, in an act of national betrayal, the Northern Republicans, along with President Pierce, supported the Kansas-Nebraska Act. They voted with every Southern senator for Stephen Douglas' Act and on that day, May 30, 1854, the Missouri Compromise died. *Popular Sovereignty* opened the way for slavery in any state.

Nothing incited the wrath of the Northern peoples as much as the despicable *Kansas-Nebraska Act* and *Popular Sovereignty*. There were riots in the streets. Pro-slavery *Border Ruffians* fought the Abolitionist *Jay Hawkers*. Weapons were brandished on the floor of Congress and congressmen were arrested. There were filibusters consisting of five-hour speeches. There was grief and sorrow over the death of the last bulwark against slavery, the *1850 Compromise Act*. The *Kansas-Nebraska Act* with its idea of *Popular Sovereignty* produced a frenzy of wrath from people that had never taken part before that day in anti-slavery demonstrations. It was a fight that became more violent and more intense day by day. The people of the North realized it was now going to be a struggle to the death.

The *Kansas-Nebraska Act* weighted the laws, once more, heavily in favor of preserving the institution of slavery. One of the most horrendous parts of the Fugitive Slave Act, most repugnant to the free-staters, provided *more pay* for a Commissioner who decided in favor of the slave owner. For those who hated slavery, a part of the Compromise was found to be even more onerous, that part which allowed the owner's testimony to be sufficient to determine ownership and provide the last word on the identity of the runaway slave.

The gathering storm on the horizon was not all dark and ominous. The new state of California, peopled with a majority of anti-slavery citizens, was added to the Union as a free state. The principle of *Popular Sovereignty* was also to prevail in the New Mexico and in the Utah territories. The local inhabitants would decide whether or not slavery would be permitted. Thereupon, when that happened, California and those western states might spell the death of slavery in Congress if a new majority vote favored the Abolitionists.

Everything was in turmoil. In that turbulent year a further revision was made to the Fugitive Slave Laws. The *federal government*, and not the states, was given *exclusive jurisdiction* over fugitive slaves. This made it much easier for Southern planters to recover their escaped slaves. However, the change in the law also *prevented* state officials in free-soil states from *assisting* runaway slaves.

The part of the law ordering non-intervention from the states for helping runaway slaves, created more resentment among the Northern Abolitionists. At the very least, the Abolitionists demanded that the runaway fugitive slave should be entitled to a *Writ of Habeas Corpus (bring the person before the court)*. And here was another colossal dilemma for Southerners. *Habeas Corpus Writs,* and the power such legal writs carried, made a slave a *person* and *not property*. If the law passed Congress, the entire character of the *Fugitive Slave Laws* would become what they were *before* the Compromise Act of 1850… looser and more difficult for the slave owner to catch his escaped slave.

LINCOLN

On an August afternoon in 1842, Congress was in the midst of a hot debate to talk about stricter enforcement of the *Fugitive Slave Laws*. The speaker arguing the cause for the Southern slave states at the moment was a prominent slave owner. This plantation owner had two hundred slaves to work his cotton plantation in Mississippi. His opening statement was a clear definition of the quandary that set limits on the *Fugitive Slave Laws* in the South. The Congressman, a well-respected church-going person, believed implicitly in what he was saying.

"Slavery is the natural order of things," he declared. "That a superior man should be able to hold a lesser human as property is right and proper. The Holy Bible supports slavery. Without our slave labor the South would fall into chaos. God has given the white man the heavy *responsibility* to care for and protect the black man. Shortsighted Northerners, whose economy does depend on black labor, might criticize and condemn the South all they wish; they have no right to interfere with the institution of slavery. Slaves are property. Since that is so, as defined by the existing Fugitive Slave Laws, and the United States Constitution, it is the duty of our government to protect its property on land or on the seas."

The Speaker's face, a mask of piety, examined the faces of the men around him for support. Many, both among the Southern legislators and among the Northern Democrats, nodded agreement.

"A runaway slave, who escapes to a free state, *must* be held imprisoned and returned to his Southern master. The voices of disagreement I have heard from my friends among those who favor abolition is unreasonable. Their objections run counter to our laws *and to God's law*. Their opposition threatens to destroy the very fabric of our Union."

Now it was in the open. The destruction of the Union meant only one thing: rebellion and disunion. His voice broke. His patrician features strained in passion.

"The law *must* stand *without* changes. Only that will settle the difficulty."

Hardly before he had regained his seat, still mopping his brow in the unaccustomed warmth of the afternoon, a second slaveholder and a fellow Congressman stood to speak. The Chairman acknowledged his wish to address his fellows with a nod and a word. Jefferson Davis, hero of the Mexican-American War and future President of the Confederacy, began his affirmation for the existing law without change.

"Gentlemen, I remind you all of a fact that may not be denied. Slave property is the only private property specifically recognized in the Constitution. It is protected by the Constitution. The *New* Fugitive Slave Law, if it is passed, will be unconstitutional. If you would settle this matter, then declare that slaves *are* property. Like all property, the owners have the right to be protected against loss of their property. Furthermore, in the spirit of justice and right, missing property should be returned to the rightful owners."

A third Southern sympathizer rose to add his objections to passage of the law. The Georgia speaker began in a conciliatory way. He spoke as if his logic was irrefutable.

"In the South the slaves are at peace and live lives of comparative comfort and happiness. Slaves are not driven to crime by hunger or want as the poor white man in the North is forced to do. In the North, hunger drives thousands of men and women daily into the abyss of crime."

He warmed to his task. With a flash of fire in his eye, his voice rose to enforce his certainty.

"Look you to the poor Irish and the immigrants from the Old World. See the results of their misery and squalor. I say to you, gentlemen, fewer children are born out of wedlock among slaves than in the capitols of any Northern American City like New York or Philadelphia."

In his seat near the very back of the hall the new representative from Illinois listened intently. To anyone watching the tall rawboned young Congressman it would have been clear that he followed every word closely. When a strong point was made he would run his callused hand through his shock of coarse black hair. At times he would sit up abruptly at a score. Several times he uttered a short laugh and a grunt of disbelief at something said.

The Georgia man's claims at one point in his speech caused Lincoln to make so loud an outburst of disagreement the men closest to him looked away from the speaker to see who had made the interruption. Lincoln's sarcastic laugh was loud enough to cause the speaker to look around to seek out the man who was voicing his disdain so loudly. The young politician from Illinois knew from personal knowledge that millions of mulattos in the South were the result of rape and abuse by their slave masters.

The Georgia man was an expert duelist. He was a man to be feared. He had also heard Lincoln's blatant challenge. Pausing for the briefest of moments in his speech, he swallowed his anger and finished his say, striving to keep the debate on a civilized and reasonable level. Turning to include the representatives in the rear of the gallery, his next words were uttered with a barely disguised sneer.

"If Northern common laborers who work at barely subsistence wages were sent to the South to work we would not need slaves." To enforce his statement and emphasize the difficult lot of the slave owner, he added, "The slave owner spends all his money to support his slaves."

Instead of the hums and nods of support he expected, there was in its place, a ripple of laughter. Even the men who were slave owners and believed in the need for slavery found his words ludicrous. The congressman's claim was implausible. To a man, for or against the Fugitive Slave Laws, they knew to a certainty that no man would work in the South in hard labor to the degree that the Black man was forced to labor in.

When the third speaker finished, another congressman stood to speak for slavery and the further stiffening of the Fugitive Slave Laws. This man was a Virginia Senator. He spoke on a question that was part and parcel of the subject under discussion; the outlawed slave trade.

"The slave population is not increasing as much as we in South wish and need. We must have a greater source of slave labor. The outlawing of the slave trade in 1841 has had a serious damaging effect on the South's ability to be economically self-sufficient."

The speaker's next words held a strong note of wry censure.

"In its wisdom some members of this august body saw fit to outlaw the trading of slaves eight years ago. That was truly unfortunate for there is a great need for more slaves in the South."

He chose a fact that was well known to all; slave traders continued to bring slaves to America in secret.

"Yes, the punishment for bringing in slaves is hanging. Still the need remains. Slaves bring a fortune to the daring. That indisputable fact is a demonstration of an unjust law that drives honest men to subverting the law."

He lowered his voice to sweet reason and persuasiveness.

"Let the slave trade be made lawful again," he said. "With a heavy importation of new slaves the prices will drop. Negroes fresh from the African jungles will be sold in Southern seaports for cheaper prices. All men will benefit and our country will be the stronger for such a reasonable change."

He appealed to their pocketbooks and the state of the nation's economy.

"At the present time only a mere fifteen percent of the wealthiest Southerners have slaves. With more slaves on the market the prices will drop. The poor man might hope to own a Negro or two. The price of labor will be within his reach. He will become a man of property and the small farmers will be raised one step higher to respectability and greater wealth. The South will prosper and so the nation will prosper."

He was nearly finished.

"The difference between us in the South and you Northerners," he said, "Is that *our* slaves are hired for life. They are well compensated. There is no starvation. There is no begging, and there is no want of employment."

Now he turned to address his final argument to the Republican Abolitionists in the chamber. The Abolitionists championed freedom for the slaves. They wanted no increase in the number of slave states.

"Your laborers in the North are hired by the day. They are not cared for and they are scantily compensated. Why, you meet more beggars in one day in any single street in New York than you meet in a lifetime in the whole South, gentlemen."

He thought that he had struck a chord that would reach the staunchest of his opponents.

"We Southerners do not think that the poor whites should be slaves either by law or necessity. Can you say that the beggar is any more than a slave to his misery? I say to you, nevertheless, they *are* slaves nonetheless. We in the South have slaves. Our slaves are Black but, unlike the white beggars, the Black man is of an *inferior* race."

Sure of his ground, he smiled beneficently.

"Yet, I say that none of the Negro race on the whole face of the globe can be compared with the slaves of the South," the man insisted. "They are happy, content, and cheerful. They are utterly incapable, from their inborn natural intellectual weakness, ever to give any trouble by their aspirations."

His fellow Southern sympathizers nodded and hummed in agreement. Most had no recollection *(by choice or a convenient lapse of memory)* of the several major slave insurrections or the great numbers of slaves for whom the fugitive slave laws were intended.

"I say to you, Gentlemen, the fresh stream of white labor arriving in the North from Europe must be met by fresh importation of slave labor from Africa if the South is to grow and hold its own."

The Missouri Compromise and slavery was a white-hot subject in 1854. At that moment the Copperheads, Northern *adherents of slavery*, were a majority in the states of Nebraska, Kansas and Missouri. They were trying with all their might to bring slavery into Nebraska. The basis for their efforts was that the existing laws *permitted* a slave owner to bring his slaves into any 'free' state. Yet, Nebraska did not allow slavery within its borders. Therein was the conundrum.

At the very back of the hall in the shadows, two clerks followed the debate with consuming interest. At the moment, they were free of their duties and listened, as much a part of the audience as any person in the hall.

The older man wore the fashion of the day, stovepipe trousers and a high collar. He had recently grown a beard. His friend was younger, red-haired and clean shaven. They held a whispered discussion. They spoke of the tall man in the back of the Congress Hall, who was waiting his turn to speak.

The red-haired clerk whispered first, "Abe is going to speak. He always does when the subject has anything to do with slavery. Look at him. He is champing at the bit for his turn."

He added an observation that betrayed a small anxiety.

"I worry that Abe, with his raw unpolished speech and lack of sophistication might not be able to match Stephen Douglas when his turn comes."

The bearded clerk from Kentucky knew Abe from earlier times and he smiled tolerantly at his worried friend.

"One time I heard Abe say, *'Have you seen two men about to fight?'*"

With no other response from the other, the older man explained, "Abe said 'One of the men will brag about what he means to do. He will jump high, crack his heels together, smite his fists and waste his breath trying to scare somebody.' "Then Abe said, 'I am like the other man. He says not a word. His arms are at his side, his fists doubled up, his head is drawn into his shoulder, and his teeth are set firm together. He is saving his wind for the fight and as sure as it comes off he will win it or die a-trying.'"

The redheaded clerk chuckled.

"Sounds just like Abe, plain and direct."

The turn came for the next speaker. Stephen Douglas was a pro-slavery Democrat from Virginia. Douglas was one of the most powerful orators in the Congress. Despite the shortness of his stature, he was a powerhouse and a rabble-rouser, one of the best orators of his time. His blue-eyed gimlet stare, his shock of black hair swept back in curly waves and his lion-like head drew men to his magnetic personality like a magnet. Of all Democrats, Stephen Douglas' voice had been the loudest for the primacy of *States Rights* over *Federal Rights*. He was committed to his idea of democracy, which he defined as the *Rule of the Majority*.

Not all people agreed with Stephen Douglas. In Ohio, angry women threw thirty pieces of silver at Douglas as he went by. He was called a Judas. Men said that his middle name, Arnold, was proof of his relationship to Benedict Arnold, the betrayer of the Union.

With a touch of his usual arrogance, the short powerful man began with a patient explanation of the phrase, *Popular Sovereignty.*

"You have heard me say that *Popular Sovereignty* is a compromise in that it gives each state the right to decide for itself whether slavery should enter their state."

The term of *Popular Sovereignty* was hated by the Abolitionists. They cried out at every opportunity that the majority was *not always in the right*. There were greater and better measures of what was moral and correct than the will of the mob. Abolitionist sentiment demanded all men should be free. At the very least any new states like Missouri, Kansas and Nebraska should *not* be added to the existing twelve slave states in the South.

As Douglas spoke for the Compromise, Lincoln listened with a serious woebegone expression on his lean dark face. Stephen Douglas known by many as the 'Little Giant' made his powerful voice almost a roar.

"The real question is whether the people should rule and control their own affairs. If the people of a state are able to govern themselves, they should be able to govern a few miserable Negroes in Missouri and all other free states."

The redheaded clerk was upset. He whispered to his friend, "I don't like Douglas' speech much."

His Bearded friend's easy reply was, "Don't bother about it, Abe will hang the judge's hide on a fence when he gets up to speak."

The tall lanky man with the crooked tie and tousled hair lounged carelessly in his chair at the rear of the hall. His collar was askew and he glanced idly at his notes before asking to speak.

The day had become warmer still as each of the representatives spoke through the afternoon session in the Maryland Capitol House. From time to time, as Douglas and the others had their say, the Illinois politician looked up at some telling comment. Other times, all six feet four inches of his long body slumped in his chair further wrinkling his newly pressed rumpled black frock suit.

As the pro-slave men continued their harangues, Lincoln's long melancholy features grew sad in repose. From time to time Lincoln appeared amused. He chuckled while Douglas made his argument for the Compromise Bill. Lincoln seemed to genuinely appreciate Douglas' oratory. He laughed along with the other congressmen when Douglas said something humorous. The bearded clerk listened and watched the congressmen speak. He whispered his criticism to his friend. Abe's chuckle over Douglas' humorous remark seemed be a small betrayal to the bearded clerk.

"Abe should feel guilty at laughing at *anything* Douglas says," the bearded clerk said.

His friend grinned. "Judge Douglas feels like most slave owners. Abe says Judge Douglas and the Copperheads are like the boy skinning eels, who explain that it don't hurt the eels much. It's always been done. They're used to it."

When Stephen Douglas sat down, men in the audience filled the air with their applause. There were shouts of *'Go for it Judge'* and *'That's what we want.'* Lincoln rose from his seat to speak his turn. There was a loud booing from the chambers. Abraham Lincoln was a Republican. They expected Lincoln to speak in support of the *Missouri Compromise* that limited slavery in the new states.

Lincoln unraveled his six feet four inches of lanky homespun height and stood up. As different from Douglas as a cat is from a canary, he stooped yet he looked even taller than he was because he was thin. There was strength in his sinewy arms and shoulders. The collar of his black broadcloth suit coat was partly turned up in back. His long black coarse hair needed a haircut. From time to time, when he turned his head his dark leathery features and his long angular face and large nose appeared to be fashioned from a woodsman's axe.

This was the man who had lifted a three-hundred-pound barrel of liquor to his chest as a trick to amuse the folks of Sangamon County. This was the man who had out-wrestled the best men in his regiment during the Black Hawk War. This was the gentlest of men who refused to shoot a wild turkey. Yet, when it was necessary he threw the toughest bully in the Grover's Corners Gang ten feet into the dust.

As he waited for quiet his eyes were deep-set and brooding. His shock of black hair was disheveled. He appeared to be some gaunt harbinger of doom warmed over. Lincoln began with a short history of slavery in America. Yet, he did not directly answer Judge Douglas' arguments. Abe neither shouted nor did he rant. In the easiest and gentlest of manner he gave his reasons for his hatred of slavery.

"I do not propose to question the patriotism or assail the motives of any man. Let me say I think I have no prejudice against the Southern people. They are just what I would be in their situation. If slavery did not exist among them they would not introduce it. If it existed among us, we should not instantly give it up. In both North and South there are some that would free their slaves and there are others who would become slave owners. Slavery is difficult to get rid of in any satisfactory way. Surely I do not blame the Southerners for not doing what I should not know how to do myself."

Some time before as he was growing to his maturity, Lincoln had written in a notebook quoting Socrates, the Greek philosopher. The homily that Socrates had written two thousand years ago was *'Deliberate slowly, and execute promptly.'* Abe gave that impression now as he spoke. The two clerks, watching him, waited expectantly for the moment when the tall dark scarecrow of a man would begin his blast away at slavery. Instead, he proceeded to speak with deceptive moderation.

"What shall we do next?" Lincoln asked his peers quietly, searching their faces with studied seriousness and concern.

"Shall we free the slaves and make them socially and politically our equals?"

Here, Lincoln paused, shaking his head ever so slightly, as if searching for his own feelings on the enigma.

"My own feelings will not admit of this. If mine would, we know the great mass of whites will have no better reply to this question."

Now he smiled. Abraham Lincoln was, once more, the storyteller and cracker barrel philosopher. It was a quality that had endeared the young Abe Lincoln to the hearts of his fellow villagers in Salem.

"Inasmuch as you do not object to my taking my hog to Nebraska to sell, therefore I must not object to taking your slave."

He waited until his analogy had soaked in, watching faces.

"Now, I admit, that is perfectly logical... "

Here, Lincoln paused a full three seconds, and then finished his point.

"... If there is no difference between a hog and a Negro."

The audience woke as suddenly as though he had thrown a firecracker into church. He had struck home.

"There are laws that provide for hanging slave traders as pirates. Is this not true? If you feel slavery is *not* wrong..." here again, a long pause to let the idea percolate in their heads, "why did you join in providing that men should be hung for being a pirate in the slave trade?"

The question was rhetorical, one not intended for response. Lincoln intended to probe their deeper feelings on the troubled subject.

"You never thought of hanging a man for catching and selling wild horses?"

It was stated as a question and it hit home. Even the die-hard slave sympathizers were forced to struggle with the raw logic of his question.

"You despise a man whose business it is to operate a sort of Negro livery stable buying and selling slaves. But, if financial necessity requires it you will sell him your slave."

Lincoln looked fixedly at the Georgia man and the man from Virginia, both of whom had spoken earlier.

"If you can help it and you do not need to sell your slave, why then, will you not drive the slave trader from your door? You despise the slave trader utterly. You do not recognize him as a friend or even an honest man. Your children do not play with him. They may rollick with little Negroes... but *they do not play with the slave dealer's children*. You ban intercourse with the slave trader and his family. You do not treat him as a man who deals in corn, cotton or tobacco. Why is this?"

The two clerks watched the faces in the chamber. Everyone had turned to listen better to Lincoln's words. It took no special skill or a skilled understanding of human emotions to know the feeling that was reflected on the faces of Lincoln's listeners. They pondered his simple question. Many nodded in agreement. There was a nervous shuffling of feet. Even the most dedicated of the pro-slave men were forced at the moment to face an unpleasant truth.

Sometimes Abe devoted as much time to a word or two as he would to a half dozen less important words that followed. He spoke slowly at times, making a distinct pause at the end of each word, but giving that simple word or phrase as much force and accent as possible. Other times, in the heat of his passion, he spoke so fast that the half dozen newspaper writers nearest to the stage had difficulty taking shorthand quickly enough to keep up with his words.

"There are... 433,643... *free*... Black.... men... in this country. At five hundred dollars a head... they... are... worth... two hundred million dollars. How does it come to be that these *vast* amounts of valuable property are to be running about without owners?"

Another pause, he waited, he waited.

"We do not free *horses*. We do not free *cattle* to allow them to run at large. How is this?"

Now, again, he waited for his thought to mature in the minds of his listeners. His voice dropped to a near whisper. Those farthest from his place strained to hear.

"*Something* has operated on their white owners to give them freedom. *What is this something?*"

He paused again.

"In all cases does not your sense of right and justice tell you that the poor Black man has a natural right to himself? Why do you deny the humanity of a slave and make him only the equal of a dog? Why do you ask us to do nothing of what two hundred millions of dollars could not induce you to do?"

His voice grew stronger. His words and phrases rolled over the hall and over his listeners like a rising tide.

"If the Negro is a man, then my ancient faith teaches me that '*all men are created equal.*' There can be no moral right in making one man the slave of another."

He spoke several words swiftly, then arriving to the word or phrase that he wanted to stress, he let his voice linger and bear hard on the idea. Then he might rush to the end of the sentence like lightning. His words were true and what he was doing to Douglas could hardly be considered a debate. He was electrifying.

At the end of his speech he reached his conclusion. Now his voice rose to power and he spoke quickly, enunciating each word like driving a nail into a plank.

"All of your senses of justice and human sympathy tell you that the Negro has some natural right to himself. Should not the hands that plant, till the soil, and harvest also have the right to the bread he eats? The question all depends on whether the Negro is a man. The white man does as he pleases with the Negro. But if he is a man then the white man, who not only governs himself also governs another. That is *more* than self-government; that is despotism."

"Nearly eighty years ago we declared that all men are created equal. From that beginning we have run down to the *other declaration,* the declaration that it is a sacred right of self-government for some men to enslave others. These two principals *cannot* stand together. They are as opposite as God and Mammon. Whoever holds to one must despise the other. Judge Douglas believes that democracy means that the majority rights must always prevail. I tell you with all the force and conviction I possess that I believe that our democratic government is only… a… means… of… doing… what… is… RIGHT."

Lincoln was drained. His dark face was shining with sweat and from the emotion he had poured into his speech. The house was as still as death, silent, the perfect logic of the speaker's words resting on their minds and conscience. A voice uttered a sound and they began to cheer and shout. There was an ever-rising storm of acclimation. Abraham Lincoln stood for a long pregnant moment in silent acceptance of their applause.

Lincoln's star was rising but slavery would not go away with a single magnificent speech. The problem would erupt with greater force in three more years.

I have said earlier that Fitz John Porter was a creature of his times. Yes, he criticized Lincoln for Lincoln's Emancipation Proclamation. Yes, he was angry with Abolitionists for their stand on slavery and their burning desire to force the South to abruptly lose the power base of their economy. Like most people, Porter believed the ugly practice would die of its own weight and fade away without employing the terrible necessity of war. What else could anyone do about slavery?

Listen to Lincoln's *own* words. They show that even that great and wise man, our greatest American hero to my mind, was as much a product of his time as was Porter. In Lincoln's second debate of his seven debates with Steven Douglas, August of 1858, Lincoln revealed that he, like Fitz John Porter, was a product of his time.

"I have no purpose to introduce political and social equality between the white and the Black races. There is a physical difference between the two, which in my judgment will probably forever forbid their living together upon the footing of perfect equality. Inasmuch as it becomes a necessity, there must be a difference. I, as well as Judge Douglas, am in favor of the race to which I belong, having the superior position. Notwithstanding all this, there is no reason in the world why a Negro is not entitled to all the natural rights enumerated in the Declaration of Independence; the right to life, liberty and the pursuit of happiness."

❧ **10** ❧

John Brown & The 1856 Pottawatomie Massacre

There was one incident in 1854 that did more to trigger the war than the congressional hop-scotch. That incident was the work of a single, highly motivated Abolitionist. His name was John Brown. In his rugged appearance John Brown was the very picture of an Abolitionist revolutionary. A shock of thick unruly hair, a craggy face and with a stubborn iron jaw that brooked no opposition, he looked the part to a tee.

Brown read the newspapers. The *Squatter Sovereign* and Northern papers carried a clear message for John Brown; Kansas was about to become a slave state.

Brown and his three sons had more bad news that year. Brown's father had just died. John Brown was in dark despair. His utter hatred of slavery was further inflamed by other news. Preston Brooks, a Southern senator, had recently caned and smashed a fellow senator, Charles Sumner, about the head many times until the anti-slavery legislator lay senseless on the floor of the Senate and was left with a permanent disability.

The *Border Ruffians*, hoodlums from Missouri, invaded Kansas. John Brown's own family in Kansas was threatened with violence. These hoodlums were intent on making Kansas a slave state. They used terror, fraud and deadly attacks to promote fear in Kansas and they worked to seize Kansas by force of arms.

In May of 1856, the town of Lawrence, Kansas was sacked and burned. The Border Ruffians, shouting curses and brandishing weapons, were personally led through the streets by the Sheriff of Lawrence. They demolished a bank, destroyed newspaper presses and generally added to the death and destruction of people and property in Kansas.

Before the Civil War began and long before Brown's last ditch fight at Harper's Ferry Arsenal, one of the most vocal Northern voices against slavery had been Elijah P. Lovejoy—in outrage for the murder of John Brown.-

When John Brown had heard Lovejoy speak and read his writings, Brown declared in public, "Here, before God, in the presence of these witnesses, from this time I consecrate my life to the destruction of slavery."

The Bible described for John Brown the Mountain of Gilead, where only the bravest of the Israelites would gather to face the enemies of Israel. After Congress passed the notorious 1850 Fugitive Slave Act, Brown, a deeply religious man, founded the *League of the Gileadites*. The simple policy to his followers was direct: *'Go quickly, quietly, and efficiently to protect slaves that escape to Springfield.'*

The League was effective. Springfield was one of the last stops for runaway slaves on the Underground Slave Railroad to freedom in the North. No slave that reached Brown and his Gileadites was ever returned to slavery. John Brown could stomach no more from the forces of slavery. He established an armed camp made up of fugitive slaves hoping to start a slave insurrection in Virginia and other Southern states. In the Spring of 1856, he staged retaliatory raids against those that wanted the territory to be slave. John Brown with his two sons rode into the tiny settlement of Pottawatomie, Kansas and hacked five pro-slavery men to death *(none of whom happened to own any slaves)*. The son of one of the murdered victims, Pleasant Doyle, described the bloody scene of that night to others.

"John Brown, with about twenty-five men came to our house and demanded admittance. When refused, they set fire to the house with torches made of prairie hay. To keep us all from being burned to death my father opened the door. They came in and handcuffed my father and my two older brothers and started to take me but my mother begged them to leave me, as I would be all the protection she would have. They took them about three hundred yards from the house and murdered them. My father was shot in the head, my brothers all cut to pieces. They left them all dead in a heap."

Finally, Brown raided a federal arsenal at Harper's Ferry. The U.S. Government sent a military force to Harper's Ferry to put down Brown and his associates. It was rebellion and terrorism by their lights. The soldier in charge of the government force, Robert E. Lee, completed the job with dispatch. John Brown's sons were killed and Brown was hung.

The fires had been set. Each act generated more acts of reprisal and revenge. The Pottawatomie massacre, May 24, 1856, set off a guerrilla war that caused the massacre of 200 lives and Kansas became known as *Bleeding Kansas*. The term aptly described the situation in Kansas after the passage of the Kansas-Nebraska Act. Both Northern and Southern settlers moved into the territory. The Northern anti-slavery men were intent on making Kansas a free state and the Southern settlers were intent on making it slave. The result was a Civil War in microcosm, a smaller version of the greater Civil War that was to follow.

There were plenty of other die-hard people for slavery as well as many men and women who were against that institution. Three years before the Civil War, Benjamin Stringfellow, a newspaper writer for the *Squatter Sovereign*, a newspaper that was typical of Southern attitudes toward the institution of slavery wrote, *'Pro-slavery forces are determined to repel this Northern invasion, and make Kansas a slave state. Though the rivers shall be covered with the blood of their victims, if the carcasses of the Abolitionists should be so numerous in the territory as to breed disease and sickness, we will not be deterred from our purpose.'*

Stringfellow's hope and determination was no mystery. Stringfellow and his supporters wished to spread slavery into all parts of the United States and its territories. With the able help of the chief justice of the Supreme Court, two presidents, a Senator and the *Dred Scott* Supreme Court decision, that was about to happen.

In the early fall of 1853, the Democratic Party was the leading pro-slavery party in the North and now believed they were all-powerful. They helped to made their man, Franklin Pierce, President of the United States. They believed they were unstoppable. They were sure that the legislation they wanted to pass through Congress was certain for passage.

The Northern Democrats had overlooked one detail. Although Pierce was a Democratic pro-slavery man, President Pierce had won his election with an *electoral* vote; *not* with a popular vote. Had the bean counting winners stopped to see, they would have known that the majority of the population in the North was *against* slavery. They *did not support* the Democratic view on slavery. Pierce *had* won the electoral votes, it was true… but by a *mere fifty thousand of the popular votes.* That was hardly the swamping majority about which Southerners and the right-leaning Democrats bragged.

In the South, men planned and plotted to split the country into half slave and half free. The original Compromises of 1820 and 1850 had prevented that from happening… until the year 1858. Southern leaders waited for the right moment and in the Spring of 1858, it came at last.

The trigger was a presidential race. James Buchanan, a Democratic 'soft' pro-slavery candidate and John Fremont, the anti-slavery candidate, fought for the presidency. Buchanan was elected with the support of the Southern Democrats. With his election the cards were stacked for the pro-slavery cause.

❧ 11 ❧

Buchanan & The Dred Scott Decision

"... I will make sure the peace guaranteed by the *Compromise of 1850 (which guaranteed that some states would remain forever free of slavery)* is left undisturbed. The year 1850 shall be remembered as the year of anxious appreciation. I shall resist all attempts at renewing the agitation of the slavery question in or out of Congress. I give you my emphatic assurance that this repose shall suffer no shock during my term if I have the power to avert it."

President Buchanan's 1850 Inaugural Address to Congress

Most Americans were yet willing to let that particular sleeping dog lie unmolested. Yet, any Northern pro-slavery Democrat with his head on straight would have been less certain the slavery issue had been settled. It appeared that newly elected President James Buchanan, who succeeded Pierce, was cut of the same cloth. No man could have been more wrong.

President Buchanan's bombastic promises were short-lived. As if the people had not suffered enough of smoke-filled back room treachery and backstabbing politics to save slavery, a new case came before the Supreme Court. That case was the *Dred Scott Decision* of 1858.

Dred Scott's luck had not been good. His master, Dr. John Emerson was a doctor in the U.S. Army. Dr. Emerson went where the army ordered and the doctor was on duty for the army in Illinois, a free state. Emerson was transferred to Wisconsin Territory and took Dred Scott with him.

Slavery was prohibited in Illinois and Wisconsin Territory. Scott could have applied for his freedom, but for some reason, he did not. Maybe because he didn't know he could or maybe he was afraid of the upshot of his bid for freedom from Dr. Emerson.

Dred Scott fell in love. He met Harriet Robinson, whose master was also an army officer. Major Taliaferro approved the marriage, transferred Harriet's ownership to Dr. Emerson. Dred and Harriet were married. After two years the army transferred Dr. Emerson again. This time Emerson went to slave territory in Missouri. Dr.

Emerson got married and summoned his slave couple to come to Missouri to join him.

Soon after they came to Missouri, Dred and Harriet had two daughters. Dr. Emerson died and Dred Scott asked Emerson's widow to allow him to buy his freedom for $300, which was today's equivalent of $7000.

She refused. Dred Scott sued for his freedom in St. Louis. He lost in the local court but his case was taken by Abolitionists to the higher courts and ended up in the Supreme Court. Then occurred one of the most heinous parodies of justice ever recorded in American jurisprudence; the *Dred Scott Decision.*

Three questions had to be decided by the Supreme Court in a decision of Dred Scott v Sanford in 1857:

1. Was Scott an American citizen that had a right to sue in the American Courts?

2. Did the fact that Dred Scott had resided on free soil for a time before returning to the slave state of Missouri mean that he had become free during his residence on free soil?

3. Was the Missouri Compromise constitutional, which made Wisconsin a free state?

Chief Justice Taney ruled that, *"Any person descended from Africans, whether slave or free, is not a citizen of the United States, according to the Constitution."* (a loose and incorrect interpretation of the Constitution). The Court found that Scott and all Negro slaves *could not be U.S. citizens*; they were property. Therefore, no slave could sue in federal courts.

The court ruled the *'Once free, always free'* rule was no longer the case, overturning twenty-eight years of legal precedence.

The court found that Scott's residence in free territory did not affect his status as a slave. The Compromise of 1820 violated the Fifth Amendment's protection against depriving anyone of property without due process of law. Therefore, the Court found the Missouri Compromise of 1820 was unconstitutional.

The decision pushed the country ever closer to the brink of civil war.

Abolitionists asked, "How could a man be declared a slave and thus have no recourse to the courts... *before* the court decided that he was a slave?"

The question was embarrassing. The Southern-leaning pro-slave members of the stacked court had placed the cart before the horse. It was a blatant misuse of judicial reasoning. The Supreme Court affirmed, once again, that a slave was not a man; he was property. This was declared in spite of what the original framers of the Declaration of Independence and the Constitution had written or had intended. This was said, despite the obvious fact that nowhere in the Constitution was a Black person declared to be property. Rather, Article IV, Section 2 of the Constitution provided an extradition rule for when an alleged criminal flees from justice to another state, for the person to be delivered back to the jurisdiction of the crime, and a rule regarding a person fleeing from labor.

Specifically, Article IV, Section 2 of the Constitution stated with crystal clarity, *'The citizens of each State shall be entitled to all privileges and immunities of citizens in the several States. A person charged in any State with treason, felony, or other crime, who shall flee from justice and be found in another State, shall on demand of the executive authority of the State from which he fled be delivered up, to be removed to the State having jurisdiction of the crime. No person held to service or labor in one State, under the laws thereof, escaping into another, shall, in consequence of any law or regulation therein, be discharged from such service or labor, but shall be delivered up on claim of one party to whom such service or labor may be due.'*

The stacked Supreme Court went far beyond the real question at issue. By making the *Compromise of 1820* unconstitutional, the Court declared that the territories north of Latitude 36 degrees, 30 minutes (the Mason-Dixon line) were no longer immune from becoming slave states. After 34 years the Supreme Court declared that slave owners were as much entitled to protection of their slave property as any other property. It was unlawful for Congress to decree freedom for any territory of the United States. Slavery, by popular vote of a state's citizens, could now be introduced to any state in the Union.

How could this be?

The answer lay in thirty-four years of careful planning by the South. Five of the Supreme Court judges, an absolute majority, were Southern men, all partisans Democrats of the States-Rights school. The Southern leadership for thirty years had rigidly and cleverly excluded from the bench any class of lawyer that was not of that same class.

Southern leaders like John Crittenden and George Badger of North Carolina, who believed the Union's integrity was more important than the question of slavery... such men were rejected by a Democratic pro-slavery Senate. They followed Henry Clay's principles and the South distrusted them. Southerners rejoiced. The slavery question had been settled once and for all time in their favor.

Regardless of the hailstorm over the new pro-slavery decision, Dred became a free man after all. Irene Sanford, Dr. Emerson's widow, married Calvin Chaffee, an Abolitionist. By the time Chaffee discovered that his new wife owned the most famous slave in America it was too late to do anything about that disturbing fact. Chaffee finally persuaded his wife to return Scott to his original owners, the Blow family. Three months after the Supreme Court decision Henry Blow granted Dred Scott his freedom.

In 1856, just prior to the Civil War, Congressman Abraham Lincoln was beginning to be appreciated. In a public speech in Illinois he attacked the Supreme Court's doctrine for the Dred Scott case... not just for bad policy but also for the clumsy and irrational way the decision had been made. To most Northern citizens the political intent of the Southern judge, when he made the decision, was obvious. Lincoln's speech lampooned the Dred Scott decision.

Lincoln said, "The Kansas-Nebraska Act left the people of the territories perfectly free to settle the slavery question for themselves, subject only to the Constitution of the United States... The right of the people to exclude slavery was voted against (by the Supreme Court) because the adoption of it would have spoiled the niche for the Dred Scott decision which declared the perfect freedom of the people to be just no freedom at all." Listeners, who were there when he gave that opinion, later reported that Lincoln stated his opinion with a powerful ring of sarcasm in his voice and in a tone of utter disdain and bitterness.

Abraham Lincoln was a master at framing his arguments in humorous analogy. On the outcome of the Dred Scott case he made such an analogy. That analogy was so powerful and on point that it left its mark all through the country.

"If we saw a lot of cut, notched and ready framed timbers that had been gotten out at different times in different places and by different workmen," Lincoln began with a serious but simple question, "... and Stephen and Franklin and Roger and James were the four workmen who did the work..." The names he had given his audience just *happened* to be the same first names as Roger Taney, the Chief Justice of the Supreme Court, Senator Stephen Douglas and the two presidents, James Buchanan and Franklin Pierce. Each of these four men had played their part in the conspiracy. "...If we saw those timbers joined together and exactly made the frame of a house, with tenons and mortises all fitting, what is the conclusion?" He asked his listeners.

Then he lowered the boom drawing to an irrefutable finish.

"We find it is impossible *not to believe* that Stephen and Franklyn and Roger and James all understood one another from the beginning, and *all worked upon a common plan before the first blow was struck.*"

Lincoln's homely humor and his quaint way of arraigning the two presidents before the public bar of justice, Chief Justice Taney, and Senator Douglas, was extraordinarily effective with the mass of Americans. In a single paragraph of plain humor Abraham Lincoln had framed an indictment against four powerful men and he lived to secure the conviction of these four men before the jury of the American people.

Historical Note: Ten years after the Supreme Court decided the Dred Scott decision a friend of Scott's went to the Calvary cemetery in St. Louis, where Dred Scott was buried. He placed three Lincoln head pennies on Scott's gravestone for good luck.

A PRESIDENTIAL CONSPIRACY

Men like McClellan and Porter, while not for slavery, did not want slavery in the free states of the North. Such Democrats left the party and a determined anti-slavery feeling swept the North like a typhoon. Reaction to the Dred Scott Decision was immediate and powerful. What happened was something the South and the Southern Democrats had not counted on. Northern Democrats realized at last what had happened.

The dissenting Judge, Benjamin Curtis, was a man of high legal learning and a man of sterling character. He declared, like most learned jurists of that time, that despite the Court's decision, *'Congress has an absolute right to prohibit slavery in all the states of the Union.'*

When Judge Curtis spoke people listened. In the history of jurisprudence, no two judges and no two different opinions had ever been so widely read by the masses of American citizens. Most folks believed the whole Dred Scott case had been ruled the way it was for the single purpose of destroying the *Compromise of 1820, which had allowed some states to be free of slavery.*

To make a bad situation worse, it was learned that both presidents, Buchanan and Pierce had privately (and illegally) informed the Court of their intentions to support the pro-slavery measure. This was done *before* the Court had rendered its decision and that was illegal by any measure. The Dred Scott decision, the actions of a president and of the highest Court in the land, were hammer blows against the Constitution.

More damning evidence for this belief was Buchanan's inaugural address.

He said, "The point in time when people of a territory can decide the question of slavery for their state or territory… will be speedily and finally settled by the Supreme Court, before whom it is now pending."

People wondered how Buchanan could have known the Court's decision *beforehand?* More seriously, how was he *entitled* to know the Court's decision before the case of Dred Scott had been decided?

Senator William Pitt Fessenden, a Congressman who always spoke with precision and never with passion, added fuel to the fire. He asserted in the Senate that the Court had *purposely* reserved its judgment until after Buchanan's election.

Senator Pitt said, "I believe firmly that Mr. Buchanan would have been defeated if the Court had not withheld their decision to the public until after his election. If John Fremont had been elected *(he most probably would have)* we should never have heard of a doctrine so utterly destitute of all truth, so founded on error, and so unsupported by anything resembling argument."

The Court's decision gave the lie to Buchanan's promises but it was good timing for the president. Had the *Dred Scott* case been decided *before* Buchanan's election he would have lost. The Courts' decision blew the lid off the boiling pot of revolution.

Fitz John Porter, a colonel in the United States Army by this time, had not yet been sent to Fort Sumter to help the North prepare for civil war. He was well read, fully aware of the tumultuous politics in 1858. The Dred Scott decision and the pro-slavery Democratic administration had just been elected. The struggle to make Kansas a slave state, regardless of the will of the majority, was in ferment.

Surely, in August of that year, Porter was interested in the presidential election that would come in 1860. He had read about the seven debates on slavery between Senators Abraham Lincoln and Stephen Douglas, a debate that had been heard or read by tens of thousands of citizens in the Northern states. Porter must have known the Dred Scott decision would affect all states and territories. Slavery could be legal anywhere.

Did Fitz John Porter hear or read the question Lincoln asked Douglas during that most important second debate? He must have. Despite growing up a Democrat, with a live and let live attitude toward slavery, he must have wondered at Lincoln's words and Douglas' reply. Lincoln asked Douglas, a pro-slavery Democrat, the question during the August debate:

"If the people of a territory, before they became a state, decide they will not allow slavery on their soil, can the government force that new state to accept slavery no matter the will of the majority?"

The Supreme Court had decided, in the Dred Scott decision, that *'a slave is property and therefore, since the U.S. Constitution protects property no matter in what state or territory that property might be, no state may exclude slavery.'*

The question posed an enigma for Douglas. If Senator Douglas *agreed* with the Court's decision that no state could exclude slavery, according to the Dred Scott decision, Douglas would be supported in his bid for the presidency by the Southern Democrats *(which was Douglas' great wish)*. If he *disagreed* with the Court's decision, as Lincoln did, he might keep his senatorial seat in Illinois, but the Southern Democrats would never allow Douglas to become president. He might as well have conceded the coming presidential election to Lincoln then and there. What was Douglas to say?

Douglas answered with a lame, illogical, evasive reply. Lincoln's analysis of Douglas' position was thorough and Lincoln's ridicule for Douglas' lame reasoning was effective. Douglas answered:

"The people of a territory have the lawful means to introduce or exclude slavery as they choose. Slavery cannot exist unless supported by local police regulations. Those police regulations can only be established by the local legislature. If the people are opposed to slavery they will change the legislation and prevent its introduction."

Senator Douglas' inventive but illogical answer to the nation settled nothing, and did not reflect the Supreme Court decision Douglas had supported. The public saw through the foggy rhetoric. Douglas' glib solution was to use a local police force. Douglas' reply, the debates, and Lincoln's stunning speeches made Abraham Lincoln President in 1860.

An American victory in the Mexican War added new states to the Union. Like weights added to the delicate balance, people wondered, Would these states become slave or free? Independence for Texans put Texas in the slave column. 'Bloody' Kansas was up for grabs in either column. Men were dying in Kansas. John Brown's death sparked a martyr's song and raised new cries of outrage from the Abolitionists. The halls of Congress were places filled with brutality; Senator Charles Sumner of Massachusetts had given a vitriolic speech on the crime in Kansas, the and the bloody battles to decide whether or not Kansas would be free or slave. That was when Preston 'Bully' Brooks, a nephew of Senator Andrew Butler, whom Sumner had vilified in a speech, walked into the Senate and broke a rock-hard gutta-percha cane over Sumner's head, crippling Sumner for life.

The Supreme Court's skewed decision on the Dred Scott matter, destroying the right of a freed slave to remain free, no matter where he chose to travel, was a brazen reflection of the desire by the pro-slavers to ignore legal means. The Country, both North and South, was faced with a problem without an answer... at least an answer than most people were willing to face or accept.

PART TWO

War

〜 12 〜

Fort Sumter

A year before the firing on Fort Sumter, in 1860, Major Fitz John Porter was given the job of inspecting Charleston Harbor and reorganizing Union defenses. When war became imminent, Porter was ordered to Texas to help evacuate military personnel loyal to the United States. Abraham Lincoln became President. The Southern states began, one after another, to secede from the Union. With a federal army of a mere 16,000 troops, all busy fighting Indians, there was not much Lincoln could do to stop the seceding states from grabbing up every arsenal and fort in their state's territories.

The showdown came in April of 1861. The City of Charleston made ready to storm and take possession of Fort Sumter. Charleston's 43 cannons blasted away at Sumter for 34 hours until the men inside were in danger of bursting eardrums. Only when shells came close to the powder magazine was Major Robert Anderson forced to surrender. The single fatality was a mule.

The day after the surrender, Major Anderson was assigned to recruit volunteers for the Union in Kentucky. The breech between North and South had become an unbridgeable chasm, deep, but not as deep as it would soon become. The streets of Washington and the other Northern cities were ablaze with torchlight parades; the people were wild with mass hysteria and thousands of boys and men signed up to fight the rebels. Yet even while Sumter was still burning there were men who continued to try to save the Union. President Lincoln's first Inaugural Address in 1860, on the eve of secession and the Civil War, made one last effort to stop the cataclysm. He spoke to the seceding Southerners:

"I have no purpose directly or indirectly, to interfere with the institution of slavery in the states where it exists. It follows that no state, upon its own mere motion, can lawfully get out of the Union... that acts of violence, within any state or states, which are against the authority of the United States, are insurrectionist or revolutionary. Why should not there be a patient confidence in the ultimate justice of the American people? If the Almighty ruler of nations, with His eternal truth and justice, be on the side of the North or on yours of the South, that truth, and that justice, will surely prevail, by the judgment of this great tribunal, the American people."

"I am loath to close. We are not enemies, but friends. We must not be enemies. Though passion may have strained, it must not break the bonds of our affection. The mystic chords of memory, stretching from every battlefield, and patriot grave, to every living heart and hearthstone, all over this broad land, will yet swell the chorus of the Union, when again touched, as surely they will be, by the better angels of our nature."

The American Union continued to crumble. In the North, as much as possible with the house falling around the Country's ears, business continued as usual. In the South, South Carolina's secession was followed by Mississippi, Florida, Alabama, Georgia, Louisiana, Texas and Virginia. On the sixth of May, in Little Rock, the Arkansas legislature voted 69 to 1 in favor of secession *(the single hold out must have been pilloried for being the odd man out)* and Arkansas was followed by North Carolina.

The State of Virginia, where the Northern capitol stood, was divided in her loyalties. On May 23, Virginia voted three to one for secession but the upper third of the state was of a different mind altogether. That part of Virginia was strong for the North. They asked to break away and become the separate state of West Virginia. That troubled place was also where both capitols stood only a hundred miles apart: Richmond for the Confederacy, and Washington D.C. the Northern capitol. Ironically, the first two major battles of the Civil War, First and Second Battles of Bull Run (Manassas), would be fought on Virginia's soil.

Next day, after the fall of Sumter, Union troops quietly moved into Alexandria just across the Potomac River, to better defend Washington. Feelings ran hot. When Elmer Ellsworth, a 24-year-old Union soldier, removed a Confederate flag from the roof of a Washington hotel he was shot by the hotel owner, Isaiah Jackson. Jackson was immediately shot and killed by Federal soldiers and both the North and the South immediately made the two men martyrs. Southern newspapers blasted the killing of Isaiah Jackson with black headlines:

JACKSON PERISHES AMID A PACK OF WOLVES

Twenty-nine people were killed when a Northern army took possession by force of the armory in St. Louis. By early May, the riots had killed thirty-five persons. Two days after the killing, Newport, Rhode Island became the new Union's Naval Academy, since Annapolis was deep in rebel territory.

An opportunistic Northern businessman, James Bullock, purchased guns and ships for the Confederacy. The Union authorities charged Bullock with a crime.

The next day the new president of the Confederacy, Jefferson Davis, ordered arms from England. Wisely, the new Confederate naval secretary, Mallory, suggested to President Davis that they should build an ironclad ship or two to match the overwhelming naval power of the North. While the Confederate leaders struggled to prepare for war, the British watched but made no commitments and Queen Victoria announced a hands-off policy.

In the North, a host of smaller changes followed the hostilities. Lincoln ordered U.S. Marshals to appropriate all telegraph dispatches for the previous year. The administration was searching for any pro-secessionist dispatches and they acted quickly to weed out any persons, who might try to undermine Lincoln's war preparations.

That same day, newspaper editors in the North asked a disturbing question: *'Will slaves, which are taken out of bondage in the hostilities, become contraband… or are they free men?'* By the end of May that year, the U.S. Postmaster cut all postal service to the Confederacy and the split became a little more official and more permanent.

In the beginning there were a series of clumsy fights between Northern soldiers and the Southern rebels. The bloodletting had not started in earnest. Young men were learning war, but the line had been drawn in the sand. Still, Lincoln looked for ways to save the Union without war. Northern politicians and men who gladly carried the banners for war with the South, like Senator Douglas, watched from the sidelines at a president who seemed hesitant to fight. Douglas, an important Senator, thought Abraham Lincoln had forsaken his antislavery views in the face of an all-out civil rebellion.

He was mistaken.

Even as the fighting heated up, Lincoln took steps to end the uncertainty by signing the Confiscation *Act*. The Act authorized the seizure of slaves and other property of any person that was found to be supporting the rebellion. Southern screams over Lincoln's signing of the Act gave rise to more acts of violence against the federal government. That growing Southern violence against the *Confiscation* Law gave the government the excuse they needed to seize the slaveholder's slaves. The South saw this as the death of slavery.

After both the First and Second Battles of Bull Run, the latter in which Fitz John Porter saved the Union Army from annihilation, there was a tenuous victory at Antietam in September of 1862. In 1863 Lincoln signed the *Emancipation Proclamation*.

A measure of the man was the firmness and resolve with which he gave to what he believed. Lincoln had been shaking hands all that morning. When Seward and his son, Frederick, brought the roll to him, he unrolled the document, took up a pen, dipped it into the ink… then paused before writing his name.

"I have been shaking hands since nine o'clock this morning, and my right arm is nearly paralyzed. If my name ever goes into history it will be for this act, and my whole soul is in it. If my hand trembles when I sign the Proclamation all who examine the document will say that I hesitated."

He turned to the table, took up the pen a second time and firmly signed his name.

With a smile he looked up and said, "That will do."

The Emancipation Proclamation, a most severe attack on slavery, was to take effect January 1, 1863. It provided that all territory in rebellion would be affected by the proclamation. There was no going back. The die was cast.

Commander-in-Chief,
President Abraham Lincoln

❧ 13 ❧

Lincoln

From his earliest beginnings, Lincoln was always rock hard against the institution of slavery, although he recognized the quandary of what to do with newly-freed slaves, if that came to pass. One anecdote is told of a visit by two Confederate ladies who came to the White House in the midst of the Civil War. A measure of Lincoln's powerful support against slavery was recorded by others who were present when the two ladies from Tennessee asked for the release of their husbands, Confederate prisoners of war.

"My husband is a religious man, please release my husband," one of the wives asked Lincoln.

Lincoln obliged. Three days later the president ordered the release of the prisoners. The day after the prisoners' release, Lincoln made clear his feelings in the matter.

To the woman he said, "You have said your husband is a religious man. Tell him when you meet him that I say I am not much of a judge of religion, but in my opinion, the religion that sets men to rebel and fight against their government, because, as they think, that government does not sufficiently help some men to eat their bread on the sweat of other men's faces, is not the sort of religion upon which people can get to heaven."

Another time, in an address to the people, Lincoln summed up the terrible dichotomy of the slave question.

"Neither side, North or South, has expected a war of such magnitude or duration. Each side may have looked for an easier triumph and a result less horrifying and destructive. Both read the same bible, and both pray to the same God. Each invokes His aid against the other. It is strange that any man should dare to ask a just God's assistance in wringing the bread from the sweat of other men's faces. But let us not judge that we be not judged."

"With malice toward none; with charity for all; with firmness in the right, as God gives us the ability to see the right, let us strive on to finish the work we are in; to bind up the nation's wounds; to care for him who shall have borne the battle, and for his widow, and his orphan to do all which may achieve and cherish a just and a lasting peace, among ourselves, and with all nations."

What most inflamed the populace in the North was the *ownership* of men. The Southern slave owners insisted slaves were property. Slave ownership was as much entitled to protection under the Constitution in the territories as any other kind of property. Congress had no power over the subject except to aid slavery.

What most persons in the South *(and some in the North)* did not... or were not able to understand, because of their mindset toward three hundred years of slavery, was a simple truth.

Although our Constitution does and should support right to property, just as the Dred Scott decision ordained, the slave was *not* property. Therefore, slaves were not subject to the rules of the Constitution as it dealt with property rights. Since the slave was a *person and a human being* in every possible sense that any man is defined by those words, he was protected by the Constitution like any other American.

A while later, after Lincoln became president and the nation was in the second year of the Civil War, an incident is told by Mr. Albert H. Griffith, a person who claimed to have witnessed the incident told here. It revealed Lincoln's compassion for people, whether they were members of the Confederacy or part of the Union; anyone, who had suffered from the fighting was his concern.

After the Second Battle of Manassas, Lincoln visited every hospital in Washington. More than forty were filled with the sick and wounded. Weary from his all day tour, late in the afternoon he knelt beside the cot of a young Confederate soldier. He prayed for the boy and then he returned to his carriage.

A nurse called to say, "The Confederate boy is asking for you, Mr. President."

Lincoln left the carriage, as weary as he must have been, and went to the dying boy's bedside.

"What can I do for you?" the President asked.

The boy replied, "I am so lonely and friendless, Mr. Lincoln. I am hoping you can tell me what my mother would want me to say and do now."

"Yes, my boy," Lincoln said. "I know exactly what your mother would want you to say and do. Now, as I kneel here, please repeat the words after me."

The lad, facing eternity, with recollections of his good mother, rested his head on Abraham Lincoln's arm and repeated the words his mother had taught him to say at bedtime.

> 'Now I lay me down to sleep;
> I pray the Lord my soul to keep,
> If I should die before I wake
> I pray the Lord my soul to take,
> And this I ask for Jesus' sake.'

FISH OR CUT BAIT

In the early Summer of 1862, after fits and starts, the argument over slavery was about to become something new and different. Abraham Lincoln was faced with a tidal wave of weak-willed Northern men, who hardly believed in either emancipation for the Negro or that a war to the finish was necessary. Few men understood the depth of conviction in the beliefs held by the other side.

Paraphrasing his words that might have applied to the North and the South, Benjamin Disraeli said, *"They were two nations, between which there was no intercourse and no sympathy, who were ignorant of each other's habits, thoughts, and feelings, as if they were dwellers in different zones, or inhabitants of different planets."*

When the final break came in 1861, most persons didn't know what to do. Joseph Johnson and Robert E. Lee, West Point graduates, who later went on to lead the Confederate army in battle against the North, continued their army duties for the United States for two months after Lincoln was inaugurated. Some states had already seceded. Men had hard decisions to make. Dozens of officers who came from the South resigned their commissions to serve where duty dictated was their first commitment.

As war loomed on the horizon, Robert E. Lee was offered an appointment as General of the United States armies. Once Virginia had made her choice, Lee, a Virginian, chose to remain with his first allegiance.

Abraham Lincoln, the peace maker, even when these embarrassing defections occurred, *never* used the word 'treason' for those defections from the Union. Ultimately, Lincoln was forced to fight; fish or cut bait, a country phrase he would have understood. He made his decision and the ax fell at last.

As a last-ditch method of ferreting out Southern sympathizers, President Lincoln suspended the *Writ of Habeas Corpus. Habeas Corpus was* a Constitutional guarantee of fair hearing for those accused of a crime. It meant that anyone merely *suspected* of a crime could not be arrested and slapped into prison without a hearing or a trial. Even yet, after a hundred and fifty years, Lincoln is still criticized for suspending a vital Constitutional guarantee.

He was judged harshly by some, but Lincoln *(and many Northerners)* saw the absolute necessity for such a strong measure as the *only way* to weed out Southern sympathizers in the North. He was prepared to use every last tool at his disposal to win the war and preserve the Union. The Constitution, Lincoln's supporters claimed, justified Lincoln's action. Under Section Nine of the Constitution it is stated: *'The privilege of Writ of Habeas Corpus shall not be suspended, unless when in cases of rebellion or invasion of the public safety may require it.'*

Lincoln, statesman that he was, saw beyond the fog of violent rhetoric and the growing conflict. While many considered the secessionist movement to be only a temporary act by a fast growing new nation, Abraham Lincoln understood it was more. The war was the culmination of a century of a very old and ugly problem that had been festering and bubbling into an explosion. The rebellion required the strongest action. It was a desperate time and President Lincoln was not afraid to take such a serious step as proclaiming the suspension of Habeas Corpus.

The part of the law, *Ex Post Facto (from after the action)*, which Lincoln used to support what he did, is hard to justify. Lincoln's application of the *Ex Post Facto* law made consequences retroactive for individuals that had expressed anti-government and pro-South opinions *before* the Writ of Habeas Corpus was suspended. That is to say, if a person expressed pro-slavery or pro-Southern views or violent acts at a time *before* the act had been made a crime, that person could be arrested and suffer the same punishment as if he had committed that crime *after* the act had become a crime. For example, the burning of the flag, if such an act was not a crime at the time the person committed that act, and later the burning of the flag was made a criminal act, then the person would be charged and sentenced for that crime as if he had committed the act while it was a crime. Such persons were jailed in wholesale lots. Lincoln completely ignored the dictates of the Constitution in his determination to squelch and stamp out all pro-slavery speech, actions and violence.

His action was challenged. In a famous Supreme Court case that year, the *Ex Post Facto* application *(punishing a person for breaking a law before that law was enacted)* of the Writ of Habeas Corpus was claimed to be *counter* to the rights stated in the Constitution. But without ex post facto law, it would be logically impossible for there to be justifiable reparations for slavery because slavery had been entirely legal prior to the Civil War.

Article 1, Section 9, of the Federal Constitution very plainly stated, *'No Ex Post Facto Law shall be passed.'* Nevertheless, the law was placed in effect and people were arrested. In its detailed application the Ex Post Facto Law allowed for:

1. Infliction of punishment upon a person for an act done which, when it was committed, was not yet a crime.

2. Change to a more severe punishment than the lawful punishment when the crime was committed.

3. Change to the rules of evidence; the acceptance of less or different evidence than was required than when the offense was committed to ensure that the offender would be found guilty.

4. Imposing a penalty on a citizen for an act, which when done *before* the law was passed was still a lawful act.

5. Depriving citizens of the protections to which they were entitled at the time of the crime, such as amnesty or acquittal.

President Lincoln, a brilliant politician, used several means of gaining support for the war. Many working men believed emancipation of the Black man would reduce the working white man's wages. Had Lincoln tried early in the war to persuade the laboring men of the North to aid him in abolishing slavery, such a stance would have hurt him politically. Yet this is what he wanted.

The passing of the Ex Post Facto law was only one of the steps Lincoln took. Lincoln erased the working man's fears by raising his argument to a higher plain. He appealed to the worker's humanity, their sense of manly independence and their instinct for self-preservation against the mastery and oppression of mere wages. A master of human psychology, he worked to find a way to bring the white working man to realize that the Black man, once free, would *not* be a challenge to his livelihood. Besides, Lincoln was convinced that keeping the Union intact was the right thing to do.

He argued to the nation, "The spirit of the Southern insurrection is hostile to all free labor. A triumph of slavery will not only take away your self-defense and your protection against the abuses of capital and of your employers, but it shall take away your independence."

"Let freemen beware. Surrendering to a political power that does not recognize that some men shall have no liberty will surely to close the door on *all* liberties."

The administration knew they could not take half measures to keep the Union intact. Any person, who winked at secession or who was not rigorously opposed to slavery was an abomination to the administration. The time had come when most 'soft on slavery' Democrats could not be counted among the supporters of the Union. This fact, more than any other, was responsible for the carnage wrought upon Major General Fitz John Porter when General Pope accused Porter of disobeying orders for cowardice, and for the loss of the Second Battle of Bull Run. This truth is especially egregious because that battle was lost not by Porter, but by Porter's accuser General Pope.

One of the first steps of the new Confederacy toward war was to defend Charleston. Fort Sumter's guns overlooked Charleston. After its commander, Captain Anderson refused to abandon Fort Sumter on the city's demand, General Beauregard's batteries on the coast of Charleston opened fire on Sumter. The Fort ran out of food and supplies quickly. They were not equipped to fight the city and they surrendered. That act by the Confederacy cut the last remaining tie of the slave states to the Union. The North and the South were committed. Upon the fall of Fort Sumter, war was unavoidable.

Lincoln said, "In this act, discarding all else, they have forced upon the country the issue of dissolution or blood."

As soon as the Confederacy was established, Jefferson Davis was made its president. Davis used the very words of the U.S. Constitution to raise a rebel army, *'Congress has the power to raise and support armies and provide for the common defense.'* In March, 1861, the South created a national act to force all able-bodied Confederate men into military service for three years.

Slave overseers and militia officers were exempt from the act and the clever governors of Georgia and North Carolina made hundreds of men *'Militia Officers.'* Men could buy their way out of serving by paying the price of having another man go to war in his place. Wealthy men were given officer's commissions in the hope they were less likely to face combat directly.

The top-heavy preference in the South for the wealthy and the favored few was obvious to the poor man. Yet, in both armies, North and South, hiring exemptions were so common there was a saying, *'It was a rich man's war and a poor man's fight.'*

A Richmond citizen sold himself thirty times over, once for $6000. One poor recruit complained, "A militia regiment in those states contained fifty officers and one private with misery in his bowels."

President Jefferson Davis was forced to declare martial law in Richmond because of the outrage over the deceptions. He threatened to jail 'disloyal' citizens without trial and close offensive printing presses.

He said, "We need a large army. No man has any individual rights, which come into conflict with the welfare of the country."

It is curious to note that the *Richmond Whig Newspaper* branded Davis' actions similar to Lincoln's suppression of civil liberties. However, two-thirds of Southern congressmen agreed such a step was necessary.

A glaring example of hypocrisy in using states' rights as their excuse for secession was their anger and opposition to Davis' necessity to conscript soldiers by order of a central government. Yet the Southern states' *unwillingness to accept a central government's power* to do anything over the opposition of the states *was the very reason the South had separated from the Union.*

The South needed taxes to pay for the war. Slaves eliminated the need for most public services and the taxes were light. Bonds sold to the Southern people promised eight percent return, but by 1862 inflation was already at twelve percent and rising fast. By 1863, it took the equivalent of twenty dollars in today's money to buy a loaf of bread.

Southerners blamed the Jews. Many Jewish merchants were just good businessmen, yet they were labeled as extortionists. As an ethnically warped Charleston newspaper complained in an editorial, *'Jews eat up the substance of the country and are more numerous in Charleston than in Jerusalem.'*

Right to the end no one believed there would *really* be a war. Abolitionists argued the South was *'too cowardly to fight for slavery.'* The 'fire-eaters' in the South and their Northern pro-slavery friends had been lulled into believing that the *'North anti-slavers could not be kicked into fighting.'*

With the coming of war, the North had her hands full just keeping her enemies at home in check. Neither side, North or South, understood the other. It was much like the hoary tale of the two Irishmen told by John Billings in his 1882 writings of being a Massachusetts Union soldier.

Meeting one day in the army, one says, "How are you, Mike?"

"How are you, Pat," says the other.

"But my name is not Pat, the first man says.

"Neither is my name Mike," replies the other man.

"Faith and begorra, then," says the first man. "It must be nayther of us."

Nothing could be more perfect than this anecdote to illustrate this mutual misunderstanding each displayed and the temper of the other as events soon showed. The people of the North held the common belief that the troublesome insurrection would collapse when the blue uniformed Union soldiers marched in earnest. The Union had considered the secessionist South to be a temporary aberration. The Southern opposition and cries of outrage over the growing support against slavery in the North was something not quite *'normal.'*

Secretary of War Edwin Stanton under Lincoln, was so certain of the temporary nature of Southern opposition that in April of that year, he ordered all recruiting offices to be closed. The government thought they could handle the irritating rebellion with a few volunteers.

Secretary Stanton filled the new Union army with the recruitment of 'Three-Months-Men.' That first passel of fighting men were all that Stanton thought were needed to put down the small rebellion. Bills were passed in the states to pay for the troops and provide the money for the volunteers: uniforms, overcoats, blankets, knapsacks, muskets and ball cartridges; for only *three months* of service.

Before many months had passed, the reality of going to war became more than the new militiaman had bargained for when he agreed to attend his easy monthly drills and comradely excursions. More men were needed. Many men found all sorts of reasons *not* to enlist and avoid the draft. Recruitment grew so thin and the situation so precarious that Oliver Wendell Holmes, the poet, aimed a spotlight of ridicule on the *'Stay-at-Home Rangers'* in a satiric and damning poem:

> 'THE SWEET LITTLE MAN
>
> (Dedicated to the Stay-at-Home Rangers)
> *Now while our soldiers are fighting our battles,*
> *Each at his post to do all he can,*
> *Down among rebels and contraband chattels,*
> *What are you doing, my sweet little man?'*
> (Fourteen stanzas followed, ending with:)
> *'Now, then, nine cheers for the Stay-at-Home Ranger!*
> *Blow the great fish-horn and beat the big pan!*
> *First in the field, that is farthest from danger,*
> *Take your white feather plume, sweet little man!'*

Hardly had the *'three-month'* men reached the field and faced a determined enemy when they discovered that they had made a huge and terrible mistake. It took a very long time for everyone to realize what a gigantic rebellion the Union had on its hands. On May 3, 1861, President Lincoln issued a call for volunteers to serve *three years*. By now the emergency had become something closer to home that endangered all men's families and all men's rights. War fever erupted. Thousands sprang to arms, so many at first the regiments had to turn some away. Money was offered. Massachusetts, working hard to fill their quota, promised to pay volunteers for 21 months' service at $578.50. The volunteer's family *(four or more)* would receive $252.00 and he was given another cash-in-hand amount of $125.00, a munificent sum.

The dreadful calamity became a more sober and grim reality in 1862, when the pine coffins began to fill the docks of New York Harbor, lying side by side by the hundreds in long lines. The common reaction to the growing war by the men and women on the streets of the cities of the North, was as one woman wrote, *'Could it really be so? We would not believe it. Yet, the daily happenings forced the conclusion upon us. It seemed so strange. We had nothing in our experience to compare it with. True, some of us had dim remembrances of a Mexican war in early childhood, we could only run back in memory to the stories and traditions of wars of the Revolution and 1812. These were utterly inadequate pictures to do the subject justice.'*

By May 1861, the spirit of patriotism was at a fever pitch and flag raisings were the order of the day. The War Between the States had reached a new level of violence in the rolling countryside of Virginia. The *'elephant in the room'* had taken a long time for his trumpeting to be heard but the trumpeting was loud beyond imagining and terrifying in its portent.

Following the fall of Fort Sumter there was a flood of patriotic enthusiasm in the loyal states. Lincoln purposely delayed his presidential Declaration of War until July 4, the day of celebrating America's independence. The people approved and the temper of the population to repair the break between North and South could not have been better. Many in the North believed the very shock of arms might make sober men reflect and come to a solution.

The war of nerves took on substance. Lincoln called up 75,000 men to the Army and Jefferson Davis, not to be outdone, announced a call for 100,000. There were a few other minor scuffles between General George McClellan and the Confederates but all these small encounters merely foreshadowed the desperate character of the contest to come.

President Lincoln, in his statement to the 37th Congress, hit hard on two matters only: the raising of an army and finding the four hundred million dollars needed to pay for the troops required. Lincoln minced no words in sounding his alarm.

"Our forts, our arsenals, dock yards and custom houses have been seized by the rebels. Seven states had seceded and their new separate government is already calling on European governments for recognition and help."

This matter of a minor rebellion was proving to be no small temporary insurrection. The signs were everywhere that it was going to be a long war. In spite of the increasing dark signs of a desperate revolution, Lincoln continued to work to preserve the facade of a unified country. He went so far as to promise to continue to deliver the mail to the very people who were rebelling, pledging, *"Everything should be forborne without which it was possible to keep the government afoot. There should be no disturbances to any of the people's rights."*

Many Northerners still believed that secession was legal. Lincoln made clear that that belief was wrong. For the first time Abraham Lincoln stated his determination to correct that skewed reasoning. In a few words Lincoln established the bedrock reason and the purpose of the war.

"The Union *must be preserved.* The question must be decided whether a Constitutional Republic can maintain its territorial integrity against its own domestic foes and thus put an end to free government anywhere on earth."

Lincoln's words made matters easier to accept and embrace. His words restored enthusiasm. There was a new, growing determination to restore the Union and Congress responded. They enacted new laws, laws that would allow the Union to more actively pursue action against the seceding states and end the rebellion.

The first direct hammer blow to slavery was Lincoln's *Confiscation Act, which authorized the federal government to seize property, including slave property, of those participating in rebellion.* The Southern states used thousands of their slaves to build earthworks, for driving teams, for cooking, for doing the work of the quartermaster and commissary departments, and all the camp drudgery. Lincoln struck at that critical Confederate lynch pin. Stopping the South from using their slave labor would cripple the Southern armies; working slaves freed Southern men for service in the Confederate army to fight the Union. The Confiscation Act offered a 'carrot on a stick' advantage to the Black men who participated in such work; it promised freedom to any Negro when it was shown he had been employed for war by the rebels.

Such a move as a Congressional Act to take away the Confederate's slaves from them and give the Black man freedom was easier said than done. Lincoln didn't entirely approve of the Act; still he signed the law, believing such a move might frighten the slave states that were still on the fence to keep them from joining the rebellion.

PEA RIDGE

The Battle of Pea Ridge was one of the earliest confrontations between the rebels and the Federals and the first where the Confederates outnumbered the Federals, 16,500 to 10,500. Following a dozen confused minor actions along borders and coastal areas, the Confederate troops were driven out of Missouri into Indian Territory. Union Brigadier General Samuel Curtis had received word from his scouts that a force of rebels was marching against him toward Fayetteville, Arkansas. Curtis strengthened his position at the Union base by moving back to Sugar Creek, which is a small stream that encircles a high plateau cut by ravines and known as Pea Ridge.

The rebel general, Earl Van Dorn, was bent on defeating Curtis. It was freezing cold as Dorn swung his army around to Curtis' rear. On the morning of March 7, in a fierce two-day battle, which involved a mix of 800 Cherokee, Choctaw, Chickasaw, Creek, and Seminole Indian cavalry on the Confederate side, the rebels decimated Curtis' army. In seven hours the Union lost a quarter of their troops and eight men were scalped.

Just in time Brigadier General Franz Siegel arrived with a brigade to reinforce Curtis and after another hard fought struggle, the Confederates retreated with a loss of 2000 men, compared to the victorious Federals, who lost 384.

FIRST BULL RUN

The first truly large, full-blown battle of the Civil War was July 1861 near Bull Run, Virginia, forty miles from Washington D.C. It began like a holiday for the Northern citizens, an outing or a festive occasion like a Fourth of July celebration. At least that was the way it seemed to the citizens of Washington. Hundreds of the men and women of Washington society watched and cheered as General Irvin McDowell's troops passed in review on the streets of the Capitol before marching to Richmond to destroy the Confederate army and end the rebellion.

Most of the soldiers of both armies carried the new model M-1855 percussion rifle-musket. The South had purchased several thousand of the military firearms before the war and when they raided the Baton Rouge Arsenal in early January, they picked up another thousand muskets.

This new weapon fired a large .58 caliber bullet, the size of a small crab apple that left an ugly hole when it struck a man. Usually an injury in an arm or a leg meant amputation.

To make firing easier and quicker, a Baltimore dentist, Dr. Edward Maynard, had recently invented a feature for the weapon, just beginning production, that he called a Maynard Tape Primer System. What the tape primer did for the soldier was eliminate the old need to place the percussion cap on the nipple of the weapon's firing chamber by hand every time he fired the gun. Much like the cap pistol the author and his friends played with as boys, a paper roll, carrying the priming compound filled with a fulminate, started burning furiously as soon as the nipple moved and the cocked hammer was released. When the soldier pulled the trigger of his rifle, the hammer struck the fulminate on the paper strip, and the fulminate was detonated sending a flame through the nipple to ignite the powder charge inside the barrel and send the bullet flying at the enemy.

The 40-inch-long, bright-finish barrel *(the whole weapon was just under five feet in length)* had a socket for a bayonet. The men on both sides never got used to using bayonets for infighting. Less than one percent of all deaths and injuries in the Civil War were caused from bayonet charges. It is worth noting that even in close fighting the soldiers were more liable to use their fists or a gun stock as a club. Rocks served sometimes, as it happened during the Second Battle of Bull Run when the feisty rebels ran out of ammunition.

The M-1855 Springfield musket was a reasonably accurate weapon. A good sharpshooter could hit a bird's eye half a mile away nine times in ten. However, at the First Battle of Bull Run, these boys, especially from the North, had some soldiering to do before they could claim that kind of expertise.

The grand hope and expectation *before* the battle in the North was a smashing victory and an end to the rebellion. Neither McDowell nor most Washingtonians expected there would be much trouble subduing the rebels. However, General McDowell proved not to be as able an organizer as he might have been for this affair. His eager, mostly green recruits, their muskets brand shiny new and still unused, except for a few practice shots and minimal training, began their forty-mile march to meet the rebels on a battlefield near the Bull Run Creek not far from the village of Manassas.

Nearly the entire population of Washington followed in the van. It was a gala occasion. They came by the hundreds, dressed in their finery, riding in their polished carriages and on horseback to have a ringside seat at the glorious victory and watch a wonderful outdoor spectacle.

'Why not go see the show,' would have been the ready reply by most of the spectators should anyone have asked. '*This will end the rebellion and return the country to its senses.*' McDowell's army was, in the words of many who saw the parade through the streets of the capitol, and in the words of several Washington newspapers, '*The Greatest Army in the World.*'

A pretty sixteen-year-old Northerner, dark-eyed Betty Duval, a spy and a rebel sympathizer, slipped into General Beauregard's lines two weeks before the battle to let the rebels know General Irvin McDowell was about to march on Richmond. Within hours, her message had been confirmed and passed along the line.

Union spies, new at their business, failed to notice that while McDowell paraded on his way to Bull Run, *another* army of rebels had marched from Richmond to follow Beauregard's first army. This force was led by a tall, intense, no-nonsense determined soldier, who would, very shortly, learn to practice war in ways the Northerner never expected.

86

Thomas Jackson moved fast to join Beauregard and it was in that battle, the First Battle of Manassas, called Bull Run by the North, that Jackson earned the nickname of 'Stonewall.' Jackson was a man who wouldn't quit. His affectionate handle was one he would keep from then on.

General Pierre Gustave Toutant de Beauregard and his rebel army had fortified the Bull Run Bridge on the Warrenton Turnpike. The Turnpike was a wide graveled road which ran roughly north and south, from northeast Virginia, south through the town of Centreville, through the village of Groveton and beyond to Gainesville. Then the highway goes farther south to Warrenton. All told the Pike was part of a hundred-mile roadway that connected Washington and Richmond.

The Southerners were ready and they meant business. They were not about to lie down and be trampled under the boots of the Union army. None of them had seen McDowell's big parade in Washington and even if they had, these country boys, handy with a rifle, would not have been much impressed.

By afternoon of the first day of the fighting, the Union appeared to be on the verge of a victory but then the tide turned against the Union. Jackson launched a counter attack.

It wasn't supposed to happen that way. General Irvin McDowell had numerical superiority. His army outsized the rebels by two to one. McDowell (and Washington) had no doubt of victory. The Federal forces had expected an easy win with an army that was much larger than the Confederate force, but now they were compelled to retreat.

With the second rebel force on the scene, McDowell no longer had the advantage of numbers. McDowell's 28,000 Union troops now faced 31,000 determined rebels. More than mere superior numbers, many of the Confederate soldiers, unlike most of the city-soft Northern troops, had used weapons all their life. They were brought up from birth to hunt and learn the practiced use of firearms. Besides, these Southern men believed their very freedom was threatened. General Joe Johnston and Thomas Jackson, and 22,000 Confederates waited for McDowell just beyond a seedy creek named with the odd name of Bull Run. So fierce was the fighting, the gunfire and cannon were heard 25 miles away in the Union capitol.

After a short fierce fight, and against all odds, the Confederates turned the tide of battle and sent the Northern troops running in defeat. The ignominious foot race to the defenses of Washington became a grand parade of disorganized troops and fleeing civilians in fancy buggies and riding horses that had come to watch and applaud the Northern triumph.

After the Union defeat Jefferson Davis boasted to his fellow Southerners, "Our Confederate force was 15,000 and the Union army had more than twice as many men opposing us, yet the enemy fled the field."

The Southerners loved the comparison. They came to believe that a rebel could outfight any two Federals. The truth was that in the First Battle of Manassas General McDowell's army was *smaller* than the Confederate army. Yet the praise must still go to the rebels because Johnson and Beauregard simply out-generaled Irvin McDowell.

That was bitter consolation for Washington. There was deep gloom over the destruction at Bull Run. The surprise Confederate victory was an eye opener for the Northerners as well. For the first time they saw the Southern rebels no longer as just an irritating rebellion. The United States had been plunged into a full-scale war of survival.

The loss haunted the Union leaders. If the South won their independence, the North American continent would become two countries. Waiting in the wings, should that happen, England and France, both of who had fat claims in the new world, would come calling. They would recognize the Confederate States of America and they would exchange ambassadors. The time might arrive, when the British had enough troops on their land holdings, they might try to regain their lost colonies by force.

Union General Irvin McDowell

It was only the beginning. Other misfortune followed. At Balls Bluff, soon after the Bull Run defeat, an eloquent Union senator from Oregon, leading the Union troops, lost his life. To make makers worse, the administration was abysmally ignorant of the necessities of war. They had no idea of how great the effort would have to be to end the rebellion. With troubles at home and on the battlefield, Lincoln looked to his fighting men and his generals for a quick end to the rebellion. He started by working to change the course of the war in the peninsula between Richmond and Washington. After Irvin McDowell was defeated at the First Battle of Bull Run, Lincoln appointed Major General George McClellan as commander of the Army of the Potomac in 1862. But Lincoln had a stormy relationship with McClellan, who seemed unable to muster the courage to engage an attack with Robert E. Lee's Army of Northern Virginia.

Lincoln was not the only president that was having problems with generals. Jefferson Davis, the Confederate president, had his own troubles. Joseph Johnston, the first general of the Southern army, had a stormy relationship with Davis; they did not get along. Like the relationship between Lincoln and McClellan; Davis was unhappy with Johnston because he was too cautious.

Johnston's advantage over McClellan was that Johnston spoke directly with Davis, while McClellan had to speak through Stanton and the Union chain of command. Furthermore, Stanton, an ardent anti-slavery Republican, disliked George McClellan intensely because of General McClellan's tolerant attitude toward slavery. Stanton's dislike towards McClellan and everyone who shared McClellan's convictions later became for General Fitz John Porter like a Damocles' Sword waiting to fall upon his head with terrible consequences.

Robert E. Lee, up to then an adviser to President Davis, was added to the chessboard of battle. When Johnston was critically wounded (but survived) during one of the early battles, Lee was named to take his place. As a master tactician, a general willing to face long odds for the sake of a victory, and a man with a killer's instinct, Lee hopelessly outclassed most his more timid Northern opponents. During the summer of 1862 and the *Peninsula Campaign*, McClellan was repeatedly out-maneuvered by a general that knew how to fight and was willing to risk all on a slim hope of victory.

In the spring of 1862 the war was at low ebb for the Union. In spite of larger armies, a greater industrial base, and a president that was determined to hold the Union together at any cost, Lee's army continually stopped, outfought and defeated the Northern armies sent against him. People in the North were discouraged. The two capitols and the fighting ranged in close proximity to both cities' front yards; they were only a two days' march apart.

After First Manassas *(called Bull Run by the North)*, Confederate troops remained at the gates of the Capitol. If Washington was lost it would be proof of the Union's failure and England would recognize the Confederacy. Lincoln wanted, and he *had* to have, quick and decisive action.

The North had been dreadfully naive; they had been sure their raw militia, with the simplest of training, could easily crush the Southern opponents with a single blow. Besides a lack of experienced professional soldiers and officers, their weapons were outdated and antiquated.

Most of the weapons were muskets, holdovers from the earlier War of 1812 with England and from the Indian Wars. So, during the rest of 1861, after the Bull Run fiasco for the North, there was little heavy fighting as they geared up for a greater war. Both sides had to learn how to fight a war. The North had the good sense to immediately devote the country to training, enlarging their armies, equipping their forces and establishing battle lines.

WILSON'S CREEK

During the hiatus, the only large military engagement was in the west in August of 1861. At a village called Wilson's Creek, ten miles from Springfield, Missouri, General Lyon, with 5400 Federal troops met a Confederate army twice his size. His ambitious attack failed and the rebels forced Lyon to retreat, killing Lyon in the melee.

BALL'S BLUFF

There was another small battle in October. There, again, the Union lost at Ball's Bluff, Virginia. Ball's Bluff rises 130 feet above the Mississippi, a strange place for a fight but a place of tactical importance because the guns of the town, placed on the bluff above the Mississippi, controlled that part of the river very effectively. Ships trying to run the gauntlet had a pretty good chance of being sunk before they managed to reach the bend in the river.

The Union defeat at Ball's Bluff was of little importance, but the Union defeats one after another dismayed Northerners. 1862 arrived, and with the new year, the list of deaths and injuries was growing. Both sides were desperate for a quick end to the dispute and both North and South began to understand the quicksand they had fallen into.

Battle lines were being set. The Confederate defense line extended all the way from Columbus, Kentucky, on the Mississippi, through Fort Henry on the Tennessee River, and Fort Donelson on the Cumberland River, to Mill Springs.

MILL SPRINGS

Mill Springs was the Headquarters of the Confederate general, Felix Zollicoffer. Here, in January of 1862, at Mill Springs, was the scene of the first important Union land victory of the Civil War. General Albert Sidney Johnston commanded the rebels. A Union army approached the rebel lines but before the Northerners could concentrate their forces, the rebels attacked.

Six Union infantry regiments, one battery and part of a cavalry regiment were brought into action. A bayonet charge by the Union forces broke the Confederate lines and the rebels retired in confusion. The Federal force continued chasing the Confederate soldiers all the way to their rebel entrenchments. The Confederates left everything behind in the rush: artillery, cavalry, horses, mules, private baggage, camp equipage, wagons and everything else they could not carry. The entire right wing of the Confederate army was broken and dispersed.

Despite that small victory, it was clear to Lincoln and the army heads that the Federal army badly needed to be reorganized. Weary arthritic 75-year-old Winfield Scott could hardly move from his easy chair. He was more than ready for retirement. George B. McClellan was picked for the job and he was a good choice. McClellan, whatever his other faults as a general, was an excellent organizer. He took command of the army and began to turn the raw recruits into a fighting machine.

FORT HENRY

In February, Commodore Andrew Foote's fleet of four ironclads and three wooden gunboats attacked Fort Henry for the Union. At the same time, to assist in a joint effort, General Ulysses S. Grant's army of 17,000 men advanced overland to seize the road between that Fort Henry and Fort Donelson. Grant's intention was to isolate the Fort Henry garrison of 2500 men. By isolating the Fort, he reasoned it could be subdued more easily.

Grant had an easy victory for the Union. In the dead of night, the Fort's commander quietly *left* Fort Henry and went to Fort Donelson. He left behind only ninety men to man the Fort's guns and slow the Union attack. Fort Henry surrendered to Grant, Commodore Foote returned to Cairo to make fleet repairs, and Grant made ready to march on Fort Donelson.

FORT DONELSON

The South, knowing the loss of Fort Donelson meant severing the line of communications for their army, sent 12,000 fresh troops to reinforce Fort Donelson's defenses. To lose Fort Donelson would be a disaster. Its loss would sever the lines of communication to the major parts of the rebel army.

Grant advanced. Fort Donelson was on a ridge about 120 feet above the river and strong entrenchments protected the Fort on the land side. Two powerful batteries of ten-pounder Parrott cannons covered the water approaches. Foote's fleet, now repaired, attacked. They were repulsed when the Fort's artillery badly damaged several ships of the Union fleet. Two of the ironclads and two wooden ships floated helplessly downstream, their motive power gone. Commodore Foote was wounded but, in the exchange, not a single Confederate soldier suffered a scratch.

Grant was nonplussed. He had depended on the fleet to support his land attack. What was he to do? A siege would be difficult. Grant's men were not prepared for a long winter's wait, for the Fort to surrender to him eventually for want of food and supplies.

On the following day the Confederates made the decision for Grant. They broke out of the Fort in a surprise attack and overran a Union position. Grant immediately counter attacked and the rebels ran back to their trenches. Knowing the Fort must surrender, during the night, 1500 of the rebels escaped in two small steamers. A similar force of rebel infantry and the Confederate cavalry escaped on a muddy river trail. Next morning, the Confederate commander, still manning the Fort's defenses, expected a gentlemanly agreement to allow the rebels to save face. Under a flag of truce, General Buckner asked for an armistice 'to settle the terms of capitulation.'

Grant's reply made him a household word overnight. Buckner must have been quite perturbed when General Grant gave him his answer. Grant, a very loyal Union man, was already quite unhappy with Buckner, a one-time Union officer, who had joined the rebellion. Buckner had gained much ill will in the United States so Grant spoke for many Northerners when he answered Buckner's request, 'No terms, except unconditional surrender.' Grant followed his short reply with the hammer blow: 'I propose to move on your works immediately.'

Buckner knew what that would mean.

As he wrote later to sympathetic ears, "I was compelled to accept the unchivalrous and ungenerous terms."

Grant became known by his admirers, who took a cue from Grant's initials, as *'Unconditional Surrender Grant.'* The remaining 11,500 troops in the Fort surrendered. That caused a split of the Confederate defensive plan for a large part of Confederate soil, and as a result of Grant's win the rebels were forced to withdraw their Confederate forces from Kentucky and most of Tennessee.

Things were looking up in early 1862, at last. Ulysses Grant had captured two forts; Donelson and Henry. Here was Grant, for the first time revealed to the public for the sort of leader he was.

Grant, despite his quiet demeanor, had a flare for the dramatic.

"Your victory," Grant told his men, "is not only great in the effect it will have in breaking down the rebellion, but has secured the greatest number of prisoners of war ever taken in a single battle on this continent."

He had a right to blow his horn a little; after a hard-fought battle, Grant's men took 10,000 rebels, forty cannons, and piles of military ordinance, which had been the property of the Union in the first place. Poor General Buckner was twice unhappy; the other two Southern generals, both of whom outranked Buckner, had skedaddled in the night with 5000 men leaving General Buckner to his mortification.

The effect on the Country was like a fireworks celebration in the middle of a string of depressing setbacks. Ulysses S. Grant's name was on every tongue. Grant became overnight the hero of the war. He was 'Uncle Sam' Grant, 'United States' Grant and all thirty regiments of his command were, like Grant, from Illinois (which pleased Abe Lincoln no end). Besides, most of Grant's officers were, like Grant, Democrats and Abolitionists.

Jefferson Davis was another Southerner that Grant had humbled. When President Davis reported the defeat to his congress, Davis did his best to color the official reports of the fight as 'incomplete' and 'unsatisfactory.'

MONITOR AND MERRIMAC

Most great scientific advances have come from war; armor-plated vessels were one of these new inventions of the seventeenth century. When the *Merrimac* arrived in the Northern port of Hampton Roads in March of 1862, the Southern ironclad sent the United States' sloop-of-war, the Cumberland, to the bottom of the bay in minutes.

Watchers were amazed and appalled. They were forced to accept a frightening fact: this new Confederate armor-plated ship could just as easily destroy the *entire* American navy. Next day the *Merrimac* was surprised by the sudden appearance a small cheese-box-on-a-raft. It was the Union's own surprise, the *Monitor*. After a ferocious contest that lasted many hours, with cannon balls bouncing harmlessly against each other's' armor plates like so much confetti, the rebel craft was forced to run for the shelter of the Confederate battery at Sewell's Point. It never reappeared.

NEW ORLEANS

Captain Farragut and General Butler captured New Orleans for the Union in April. That feat opened up the Mississippi along its entire length for hundreds of miles. The American Navy had come of age and was reorganized. Naval leaders, men like Farragut and Worden, were given the rank and responsibility they needed and deserved. The Union was riding high.

SHILOH

Then the house fell in. At Pittsburg Landing, Grant and the Union Army narrowly escaped a crushing defeat. The loss of life for both sides was catastrophic and Grant became a villain overnight. Only a spirited defense in Congress for Grant's actions for finally winning the battle saved him from more serious censor. Grant was demoted to command a wing of the army he once led and Halleck replaced him with McClellan in the top job as Commander of the Army. McClellan was directed to take Richmond and end the war. Now it was McClellan's time to show his colors.

The two worse days of the war for the North so far in 1862, had been the *Battle of Shiloh* in early April. The defeats convinced Grant, for the first time, the South *would not be beaten until they simply could not fight any longer.* The battle began with Generals Grant and General Buell fighting Johnson and Beauregard. Before the battle Grant had intended to march on Corinth next. He was waiting for all of the Union forces to be assembled. With no expectation of attack by the rebels and planning to begin the grand assault soon, Grant had not bothered to build trenches or fortifications.

In his memoirs, Grant said, *'We did not fortify our camp against an attack because we had no idea the enemy would leave strong entrenchments, to take the initiative when he knew he would be attacked where he was if he remained.'*

The night before the hostilities, General Sherman, Grant's second-in-command, sent a dispatch to Grant, *'All is quiet along my lines.'* Later he wrote, *'I have no expectation anything will happen along my lines except some picket firing.'*

The Confederates hadn't read those dispatches, nor would it have made any difference if they had. They had to act boldly and they did. The Confederates advanced and by 8 AM, Sherman was convinced it was an attack in force. By 10 AM it was all over. The rebels captured the Union camp and caused the Union forces to retreat to a bend in the river.

It didn't go all one way for the rebels. General Albert Sidney Johnston was wounded and died during the assault. His injury caused a delay in the fighting and in the meantime fresh Union soldiers were coming fast upon the scene. The fighting was renewed fiercely and on the second day the tide turned. The Union army was satisfied to end the fighting and the rebels were happy to get away. Six thousand Union dead was one more tragic convincer for the North that the war was a battle to the finish.

Union General George McClellan

❧ 14 ❧

Musical Chairs

When George McClellan took his hundred thousand well-armed and well trained Federal troops down the Virginia Peninsula, the North was jubilant. Since the rebels had whipped Irvin McDowell's army at the First Battle of Bull Run, now, at last, everyone was sure that dapper *'Little Mac'* would give the Confederates what for. Shortly, McClellan would invade Richmond and end the rebellion.

It shouldn't have been hard. Richmond was only a hundred miles from the Northern capitol. The troops could reach the outskirts of the Confederate capitol by ships on the Potomac in a couple of days. The roads were good and there were no obstacles to speak of. McClellan had plenty of men, the industrial North had turned out guns and artillery by the ton and the U.S. Navy was entirely in the hands of the North.

But something went wrong. It wasn't to be. There were some elaborate maneuvers inspiring boastful telegrams from McClellan talking much of an impending victory. Instead, a much smaller rebel force with a general who had an understanding of clever battle strategy (and a killer's heart) outclassed McClellan at every turn.

Finally, after the month-long Peninsula Campaign ended with seven days of hard infighting, Robert E. Lee forced the Army of the Potomac to *'change position.'* That phrase, used by McClellan, was a euphemism for running with one's tail between their legs in retreat back to Washington's defenses.

Seen through the kinder lens of hindsight past the deadly fog of war, March thru July of 1862 in Virginia west of Chesapeake Bay and around the southern capitol of Richmond, was a campaign of military musical chairs. The North could have ended the rebellion then and there. All George McClellan had to do was to move fast and hit hard.

Most of the rebel's potential for making war was in Richmond because the South hadn't moved their war-making industry into high gear. Although there was no way they could match the industrial might of the Northern states, the rebels were ready to do their best, and their best might be good enough.

Chesapeake Bay sliced northwest into Virginia, starting twenty miles from Richmond. The twenty-mile wide-mouthed bay is more like a fat river a hundred and fifteen miles long. The water way is like the trunk of a tree beginning from the Atlantic Ocean and curving slightly to the west as it narrows to less than a mile or two above Washington, across from Alexandria, eighty miles north of Richmond.

From the left side of Chesapeake Bay near Richmond, four rivers spring out like branches of a tree. From its base there is the James, then the York, where a battery of 32 pounder heavy guns commanded the York channel, then the Rappahannock River and finally the mighty Potomac.

An offshoot of the James River, twenty miles from the ocean, is the narrower, marshy, sluggish Chickahominy River. That mosquito infested stream meanders like a protective snake guarding Richmond and then peters out to a swamp a few miles past the Southern capitol.

Tucked into the land between the York and the James Rivers, there are a dozen villages, creeks, dams, bridges and small farms clustered about the outskirts of the Virginia capitol. Those landmarks are unfamiliar to most Americans but in that time and place, Drewry's Bluff, Fair Oaks, Seven Pines, Hanover Court House, Beaver Dam Creek, Mechanicsville, Cold Harbor, Gaines Mill, Savage Station, Golding's Farm, Garnett's Farm, White Oak Swamp and Malvern Hill were names forever marked by three of the bloodiest months of conflict of the war to that day.

General George McClellan's campaign began along the Virginia Peninsula with a dozen struggles in and around the hamlets, rivers, creeks and countryside near the Confederate capitol. It ended in seven days of blood and terror for the thousands of men who were wounded, maimed, taken prisoner and who gasped their last breath on the marshy, humid lands of Southern Virginia. When it was over, little was proved... except to guarantee that the Civil War would continue with even greater force.

In 1862 the North wanted victories. They needed victories desperately. Northern men were dying in wholesale lots to no purpose. President Lincoln watched his beloved Union threatened with dissolution on every side. There were riots over slavery and against forced enlistments in nearly every city. General Ulysses S. Grant was doing well in the West and that was all to the good. But, after the recent humiliating loss at the first Battle of Bull Run eight months earlier, the nation was no nearer to ending the rebellion than it was at the start. The rallying cries and Northern hopes were in those cries of "On to Richmond!" Everybody wanted to capture the Southern stronghold, hoping that victory would bring the hostilities to a close.

Richmond was close, by anyone's reckoning. The rebels' stronghold was a mere two days' march from Washington. However, that fact brought another disquieting truth to mind in the North. Washington was just as close to Richmond and just as close to a very determined enemy. More than that, in May of 1862 the people in the North and in the Union capitol faced the unpleasant fact that they also were threatened by a Confederate army at their very gates.

The Administration searched about for a general who could end the stalemate. Listening to advice about the kind of man the nation needed, Lincoln picked General George B. McClellan. The thirty-four-year-old McClellan was to take command of the Army of the Potomac and he was told to start things moving in the right direction quickly.

George Brinton McClellan looked good by any measure. Handsome, energetic, with a proud military bearing, McClellan seemed to have all the qualities of a great general. He was a distinguished graduate of West Point with exceptional military skill (this was according to older officers who carried weight with Lincoln). Not only did McClellan come with these fine credentials, he had a wonderful ability to organize the thousands of grass-green recruits, most of whom were fresh from the country or the city life, into a well-disciplined, well equipped, and well supplied army ready to fight. McClellan was meticulous in planning, but slow to aggressively challenge his opponents in battle.

Whatever the cause, McClellan's procrastination served no one. It might have been McClellan's innate caution, or perhaps hesitancy which sprung from a lack of self-confidence. And from the very start the relationship between the president and McClellan was rocky. There were other differences between them. Lincoln, a Republican, was a staunch anti-slavery man. McClellan, like most northern Democrats, was quite willing to let the South keep their slaves. Before the war Northern Democrats like McClellan usually voted with the Southern Democrats on matters of slavery. Nevertheless, McClellan was their man.

After the torchlight parades in the Nation's capitol and the colorful balloon ascensions on the Potomac to celebrate the appointment of the brilliant new General-in-Chief of the United States Army, Lincoln went to McClellan's home. He wished to discuss plans for the war. The president had been waiting until after the festivities to speak to the new commander of the Union army. When he arrived he was told by an attendant that the new Commander of the Union army had retired for the night and was unable to speak with the president. That was *not* a good beginning.

Lincoln let it pass. He needed a good general more than he needed his pride repaired. General McClellan continued to stall when the subject of planning for war came up. After six months, for reasons no one could figure out, nothing much had happened to the Army of the Potomac. There was plenty of marching and fanfare around Washington as McClellan whipped the soldiers into shape.

They were good marchers. Beyond that there was not even a hint of an announcement that McClellan was about to obliterate the rebels and take Richmond with all the power, the style and the dispatch the Northerners expected of such a grand army.

The truth was less visible. McClellan had plenty of show and ability, but when push came to shove, he had very little of the 'go' that President Lincoln needed. Autumn came. The leaves fell on the streets of Washington and the winds blew strong, heralding the coming of a colder time. Winter arrived and wore away with yet nothing much from McClellan.

At long last Spring came around again. McClellan was still not ready to send his 105,000 men into battle against the much weaker rebel force. All that Lincoln heard from McClellan were complaints and whining over his lack of support by the Administration and that he 'must have more men before he could take Richmond.'

Of all the persons in the capitol and in the streets of every city of the North, the one man that had grown most unhappy over the army's long pleasant vacation was the president. Lincoln had grown desperate.

After months of no action with the Republic's house falling away by bits and pieces, I can imagine, had I been a fly on the wall in Lincoln's presence, the tall rail splitter of his youth might have raised his long arms, fists clenched and growled his frustration: "Why won't McClellan fight?"

Abe Lincoln was no ordinary president. He had never seen action in the Indian Wars but he had never turned from a fight. He had studied battle tactics of every great campaign in history. A quick learner, Lincoln saw clearly what had to be done. He bit his tongue and waited some more. As time went by, Lincoln coppered his bets. Without depending on McClellan to keep the rebels at bay, he kept McDowell and his home guard near to protect Washington. The threat to Washington from the South remained very real.

In early April, Lincoln wrote another note to General McClellan. The concern and impatience in his writing dripped with his distress and his impatience over the long delays and lack of support: 'Your dispatches complaining you are not properly sustained, while they do not offend me, do pain me very much.'

What was George McClellan's response? He continued to complain and ask for more troops. Before he could defeat the Confederate army and take Richmond he must have a larger army. McClellan's grumbling might have had some basis had he truly lacked for the men he needed, except McClellan's army, now trained and ready, was several times larger than anything Jefferson Davis might have sent to oppose him.

'I have but 85,000 men,' he wrote to the President. Lincoln responded, 'General by my count and that of the War Department you have 108,000 men ready to fight. It is indispensable to me that you strike a blow.'

Lincoln knew something else about proper strategy. It was a fact of war that George McClellan would not admit or chose not to see because of his innate reluctance to fight. It was that to win a war, an army must destroy the enemy army. Occupying a city, even the Southern capital, counted for little. Until the enemy had lost the power of defense, ground and cities meant nothing.

He wrote to McClellan, *'Search for a field of battle, I have never written you or spoken to you in greater kindness.'* Later on another occasion, he was overheard to quip to others, "If General McClellan does not intend to use his army, I would like to borrow it!"

The President's urging came to nothing. It was all useless. Before the summer of 1862 had hardly begun, the fatal weakness in George McClellan came to light. That weakness, had anyone paid attention, revealed itself before the war, at West Point.

When Robert E. Lee, McClellan, and the other officers gathered about the poker table, and when the chips were down and the bet was a risky one for high stakes, McClellan generally folded. McClellan would not move his army. In the end, when he did move, the entire Peninsula Campaign became a succession of disappointments, of hopes deferred that made the heart sick, of a sacrifice of life and treasure, and, in the end, a disaster and humiliating retreat.

❧ 15 ❧

McClellan Prepares... and Prepares

In the spring of 1862 Lee's army of Northern Virginia, and the Confederate capital of Richmond, lay between two powerful Union forces: the armies of George McClellan and the smaller but powerful army of John Pope. By bluff and sheer aggressive élan, Lee stopped McClellan's invasion of Richmond. He fooled McClellan into believing Lee's army was far larger than it was. McClellan retired to Harrison's Landing and waited for better days. Abraham Lincoln had discovered that McClellan, a good organizer, had no will to win the war.

The Peninsular Campaign revealed the character of men, in both their strengths and their weaknesses. A special strength and ability came to light in one Southern leader. After Robert E. Lee replaced Joe Johnston early in the campaign, Lee's reputation became firmly established as a superlative tactician and a fighter. He was a general that was willing to risk all for the chance of victory. When war was declared, the men of West Point had to choose sides. For some of them the choice was a hard trial of conscience. Men like Robert E. Lee and the other Southern generals, who had been trained at West Point, were deeply troubled by the decisions they made.

One Union officer, Major General Fitz John Porter, who from his military record during the Mexican War and now in this war, was proving to be one of the best the North had to offer. McClellan was a good judge of a soldier and he made Porter his protégé, and soon, a Brigadier General. Before the Peninsula fight was over, Porter was promoted once more to the highest military rank of Major General. The promotions and McClellan's judgments proved to be the right choice. At Malvern Hill, Porter was so admired by his foe that Robert E. Lee said afterward, "Porter's defense was an extraordinary force of that arm of McClellan's army."

Longstreet's Second Division head, General A.P. Hill, paid Porter another accolade when he wrote, after the battle, *'He handled his defenses with an ability unsurpassed on any field during the war.'*

Porter was a good soldier. All of which made his dishonor by the Lincoln Administration more difficult for him to bear. I do not include President Lincoln, personally, in the miscarriage of justice at Porter's trial and sentence. When the trial facts were presented to Lincoln by Judge Advocate Colonel J. Holt, Holt purposely did not tell the President the truth; he purposely withheld evidence, on Secretary of War, Edwin Stanton's order. It was the evidence that would have supported Porter's complete innocence of the charges. Had he seen the evidence, Lincoln would never have signed the order of conviction.

It was another President, Ulysses S. Grant, who saw that missing evidence long after he had the power to pardon Porter, and who wrote, 'I am convinced that for these nineteen years I have been doing a gallant and efficient soldier a great injustice.'

Fitz John Porter, a Democrat, as wrong as he was and as badly educated to the true evils of slavery, was like tens of thousands of Northern, states-rights, Democrats in 1862. These citizens of free states of the North did not want to own a slave and they did not like slavery. In their ignorance and in the mantle of false beliefs of the period, which misled the minds of many, they honestly believed the Black man was inferior. They believed it was better to allow the South to keep its slaves in peace, rather than tear the country apart in a terrible war since most surely slavery would die of its own accord.

Porter was an outspoken man, who expressed his opinions openly. In such a time when men killed each other for a difference of opinion, it is small wonder that Porter did not feel Stanton's wrath earlier than he did.

Porter and Lincoln got along together well. Porter was as well respected as anyone in the country. Secretary Stanton, no matter how much he wished, could find no fault in Porter great enough to bring him to his knees. Unfortunately, Porter's opinions, some of which were published by the newspapers, inflamed Secretary Stanton to the point that Stanton was determined to punish the anti-abolitionist if ever he had the opportunity. That opportunity would come soon enough.

A series of '*Letters to the Editor*' from Porter gives us insight into his feelings and attitude toward slavery. He was as typical of any intelligent person in the North who was a Democrat. Democrats were dead certain that the Abolitionist anti-slavery rhetoric did no good and most surely was the cause for the war.

If asked how they felt about Abolition, any Democrat of that day might have replied with the typical Democratic outlook on slavery:

"Abolitionists should be tarred and feathered. They are rabble-rousers. They create dissension over something they cannot change and should not be changed by force. Slavery will die in time. The Constitution protects the right of the Southerner to own slaves. The Black man, if he was free, could not support himself in our society. Slaves need to be protected and cared for. They know no other life than to work for their masters and be cared by him. The Country was doing fine before Lincoln considered secession as a rebellion. Let the states secede. The Constitution gives them that right. The states should govern themselves and an autocratic central government should not force its will upon the states. That being said, I am a loyal American and I support the Constitution."

In April 1862, Porter made a mistake. Bitter about the continuing war with friends dying around him, he wrote a series of letters to the Editor, Manton Marble, of the strongly Democratic *New York World* Newspaper. The World shared the tolerant attitude of many Northerners toward the institution of slavery, '*This army will cause a revulsion of opinion on its return home. I hear that the most conservative opinions are expressed everywhere. Few Abolitionists in the armies of the U.S. are looked upon as friends to the Union. The conservative element throughout the army will make itself felt at the next election.'*

A few weeks later Porter assured Editor Marble, *'Our men wish to go home, and wish the war to cease, but they say they will whip the Abolitionists when they get home, especially for trying to prolong this unnatural war. Our men will speak, and goodbye to the Abolitionist traitors, who try now to defend themselves by publishing falsehoods.'*

In late June, Porter wrote to Marble again. *'I wish you would put the question. Does the President, controlled by an incompetent secretary, design to cause defeat here for the purpose of prolonging the war?'*

This letter to the Editor might have been the straw that broke the camel's back. In the letter Porter's words indicated that he suspected the Peninsula Campaign might have been purposely prolonged by withholding the troops and the help from the president that his friend, George McClellan had requested. Porter blatantly insulted Secretary Stanton and President Lincoln, while Porter's allegiance to George McClellan (a man hesitant to fight) did no favors for Porter.

When Secretary of War Edwin Stanton read the line of the article that referred to Stanton, *'a President controlled by an incompetent Secretary...'* he must have raged. It may have been at that same moment that Stanton vowed to destroy his nemesis. Porter embodied in Stanton's mind all that the Abolitionists most hated. Fitz John Porter, an important general, was like most Democrats in the North, ignorant of the immorality of slavery and tolerant of the institution.

On Lincoln's Emancipation Proclamation, Porter wrote to Marble, *'The proclamation was resented in the army, and led to expressions of discontent amounting, I have heard, to insubordination.'*

Porter carried with him a history that was as proud as any general in the Civil War. He was a cousin of David Farragut, the navy hero. Porter was wounded and cited for heroism in the Mexican War and brevetted to a captaincy in the field. He was an instructor of cavalry and artillery at West Point and he assisted in the evacuation of Texas after Texas seceded from the Union. Later he inspected defenses at Charleston Harbor and at Fort Sumter. Given provisional, and then permanent, command of the Fifth Corps of the Army of the Potomac in July of 1862, Fitz John Porter proved himself to be a loyal, heroic soldier with ability, a fighting spirit and strength of character. But he misunderstood the Abolitionists' message of humanity, seeing it as rabble-rousing.

I would like to think that a man of his compassion and intelligence would, in time, come to see the truth and shed his ignorance. There was little in my research to tell me this but I think it might have come to pass at a later time.

Union General
Samuel P. Heintzelman

❧ 16 ❧

Peninsula Campaign

In the Spring of 1862 McClellan was handed the Union armies on a platter. His only orders from President Lincoln and Edwin Stanton, the Secretary of War, was to win the war and end the rebellion. The citizens in the North were jubilant. With 'Little Mac' in charge hopes were high for an early end to the troubles. After Irvin McDowell's humiliating defeat eight months before at Manassas the North needed a victory. It was embarrassing that Joe Johnston and his Confederate Army was an easy day's march from the Union Capitol. Given any chance, Johnston's rebels would try again to force the North to recognize the Confederacy as a new and separate country. There the rebels sat, on the Plain of Manassas, thumbing their noses at Washington forty miles away and watching the Capitol like a cat watching a canary.

George McClellan had all the tools he needed to turn the tables on the rebels. He had plenty of men; a huge army he had trained well. Training and organizing an army was his talent. Besides the men, he had all the resources of the powerful industrial North at his disposal: guns, artillery, ammunition and supplies.

McClellan began with a plan. His plan was first to catch and destroy the Confederate army at Manassas by marching north from the Union Base at Fort Monroe near Richmond and up the Virginia Peninsula toward Johnston's army. At the same time, his plan called for General Irvin McDowell to leave Washington with another army and march south. The two Federal armies would catch the rebels neatly in a vice and crush them once and for all.

That accomplished, McClellan would march, unopposed, to the Confederate capitol at Richmond. He would capture it and the Confederacy would be no more; at least, on paper. That was McClellan's plan.

When General Joe Johnston heard the news McClellan had landed troops at the mouth of the James River thirty miles from the Confederate capital, Johnston packed up post-haste to go home and defend Richmond. He was not about to let McClellan catch him in a vice. After their victory at the First Battle of Bull Run (Manassas) and before leaving the main Union supply depot at Manassas Junction, Johnston's rebels took everything that wasn't nailed down. Anything that could be eaten, worn or used was taken. Nothing was left. One rebel company hauled a ten-gallon keg of whiskey all the way to the Rappahannock River.

When McDowell (on his way south to reinforce McClellan) arrived at the ruins of the burnt out Union supply base all he found were a few scattered bread pans, unusable water buckets and some battered frying skillets. By the time McClellan had gotten around to starting his march up the Peninsula from Fort Monroe, all set to bag the Confederate army, Joe Johnston was long gone. By then the rebel army was safely lodged behind the defenses of Richmond.

McClellan may have tried to keep his attack plan a secret but, like most of McClellan's grand endeavors, he either moved like 'molasses in January' or, he made such a fuss and fanfare about what he was planning to accomplish, the enemy heard about it much sooner than they should have.

There was another unpleasant rumor going around Washington: McClellan's attitude toward the war. Some even thought he wanted the Confederacy to be allowed to keep their slaves and be left alone in peace. True or not, McClellan was the popular choice and the man picked for the job of ending the war.

After a hard winter the 35th Georgia Infantry Regiment was especially grateful to be back in Richmond. The cold wet climate of Virginia in the winter of 1861, following the First Battle of Manassas (Bull Run) had been deadly for the Confederate forces… not because of battle casualties but because of disease. These Southern boys were used to the warmer, milder climates of Georgia and the other Southern states.

Measles was an especially merciless killer. The germ had spread quickly leaving many dead in its wake. These men had grown up on farms. All their lives they had lived isolated lives and their immune systems were very susceptible to many diseases more commonly found in the cities and the more northern, wetter climates.

As the high number of sick and dying grew, the commander of the Georgia 35th asked Secretary of War J.P. Benjamin to withdraw his men from battle. As much as Benjamin wished to oblige the commander he could not. The commander of the 35th was advised that he could not withdraw his regiment despite the high mortality because of the pressures of war and the imminent threat of invasion by the North.

"Humanity requires that I should try some way to prevent suffering and mortality among these troops just called from a southern clime and weakened by disease," J.P. Benjamin wrote to General Holmes. "I can only suggest that you lighten their duty as much as possible to give them a chance to recover."

Sick or not, these Southerners were ready to fight McClellan or anyone else bent on taking, what every solder believed were *'their rights.'*

Defending Confederate General, Joseph Johnston had his troubles as well. If having more than 100,000 federal troops on his doorstep about to invade wasn't enough to give him a headache, Joe Johnston had problems with his president. President Davis didn't like him. A Southern lady, close to the political heartbeat of Richmond, wrote in her diary about Joe Johnston's abrasive relationship with the Confederate president.

'The President detests Joe Johnston for all the trouble he has given him and General Joe returns the compliment with compound interest. His hatred of Jeff Davis amounts to a religion. With him it colors all things.'

Maybe Johnston's pique was because President Jefferson Davis had passed him over for the top general's position in Virginia. And maybe it was because Johnston was a Quaker. Davis believed that Johnston never seemed to want to fight. Whatever the reason for the bad blood, it was clear there was no love lost between the two men.

Joe Johnston had a job to do right then and he already had worries enough. Defending Richmond was quite a job for any man. If the Federals broke through his defenses the war would be over and capitulation would be the death of the short-lived Confederacy.

McClellan planned to take Richmond with a massive invasion starting from Fort Monroe. Fort Monroe was a major Union naval base with a difference; it had a moat like the castles of old. McClellan had brought his army down the Atlantic coast to Chesapeake Bay with the help of dozens of well-armed navy gunboats. Additional artillery was at his disposal and sure of success he reported to Lincoln his conviction of certain victory. His report to the President was also a bit peevish. McClellan was still upset because Lincoln had stopped him from a march down the Peninsula to invade Richmond, instead of a sea invasion which Lincoln preferred.

McClellan wrote: *'The Army will march against Richmond with complete security... although with less brilliance of results than down the Peninsula.'*

Now ready for his big move, out of the blue McClellan got a surprise that was totally unexpected and certainly not welcome. As he was all set to march, along came the rebel ironclad, the *CSS Virginia*. The monster rebel iron-cabin-on-a-tin-can put a crimp in McClellan's plans. It attacked the Union's wooden sailing ships in Chesapeake Bay like a sudden tornado.

The *CSS Virginia* had been built on the hull of the old *USS Merrimac*, which was now scuttled and burned when the rebels grabbed the nearby U.S. Navy Yard the year before. With its iron prow and cannon-proof armored deck, the *Virginia* began methodically, and without much effort, to send the entire Federal Navy to the bottom of the Bay. She started with the 24-gun *USS Cumberland*, ramming the pride of the U.S. Navy and sending her to the fishes forthwith. The Navy watched with growing panic; they were losing their Navy to the ironclad. The behemoth *Virginia* looked like no other ship ever seen. Federal cannon balls bounced off the *Virginia's* deck like pebbles.

Next, the *Virginia*, flushed with victory, headed for the 50-gun frigate the *USS Congress*. With all guns spitting twenty-pound iron cannon balls, the awestruck sailors watched the shots from the *Congress* bouncing off the iron-plated sloping sides of the *Virginia* with loud clangs and as effective as water bouncing off a duck's back. As if the cannon balls that struck the iron clad were nothing more than snowflakes, the *CSS Virginia* proceeded to demolish the *Congress* and then drove aground every other ship she could find.

When news of the destruction reached the White House it drove Stanton to a frenzy. The rebel navy turnabout in Chesapeake Bay shocked the president more than the loss of the First Battle of Bull Run eight months earlier. Drastic steps were called for.

Panicked, the Union naval officers called for the *USS Monitor*, the Union's own iron clad moored not far away. The next day the *Monitor* arrived on the scene just in time to challenge the *Virginia*. At the end of several hours the battle of the ironclads was a draw. Like two Goliaths, equal in strength and pitted against each other in battle, neither ship did much damage to the other.

A Lieutenant on board the Monitor said later, "Our turrets and other parts were repeatedly struck but the tower was intact and continued to revolve. We were confident the *Virginia* would not repeat the work of the day before."

The *Virginia* limped off at last, her motor not working well and threatening to quit. But a new age had come to naval warfare.

McClellan's elaborate invasion timetable moved at a snail's pace. It was weeks late. His delay was perfectly acceptable to the Southerners in Richmond. The extra time gave Joe Johnston the time he badly needed to be ready for the attack that everyone knew was inevitable. The thousands of Union infantrymen, outfitted to the nines and loaded down with gear, had been shipped aboard navy transports and carried on navy steamships down the Potomac River. Once ready to march, McClellan would move them up the York River toward Yorktown twenty miles away.

At last, with the sea battles over, the Federal army poured ashore. Whooping and shouting, confident the rebels would be brought to ground and defeated in short order, they prepared to leave Fort Monroe. The blue-uniformed regiments and companies were ready to march. However, McClellan was *still* not quite ready. He had to wait for Banks and McDowell to show up to add the strength he thought he needed for the final blow.

Pressure to do… something… mounted from Washington. Finally, McClellan had no choice; he had to move. Washington was on his back for action but it wasn't until April 5 that his troops began their advance toward their first objective, Yorktown.

The move had taken such a long time already that President Lincoln, watching McClellan's army doing nothing much, was frustrated nearly beyond endurance. He decided to see for himself what was holding up the invasion of Richmond. Thereupon, Lincoln, along with Treasury Secretary Salmon Chase, holder of the purse strings, and Edwin Stanton, Secretary of War, came sailing down the Potomac with staff members to see firsthand what was delaying McClellan.

The first thing the President noticed when he arrived was that the nearby city of Norfolk was in rebel hands. That wouldn't do. As Commander-in-Chief, Lincoln ordered the bombardment of the navy stronghold and, shortly after, Norfolk surrendered.

That night the regimental band serenaded the president with *The Bonnie Blue Flag* and *Home Sweet Home*. The 76th New York Regiment was especially proud of their 24-member brass band. These were the men with the best horses and special uniforms. Music was an important part of the war and every regiment, North and South, had a regimental brass band. Robert E. Lee said, *"I don't think we could have an army without music."*

Now Robert E. Lee entered the stage. Shortly, he would play a much larger part in the war. Lee was Jefferson Davis' military adviser. As a strategist he saw, and fully understood McClellan's delay. He knew McClellan's mind. From his days at West Point, when McClellan, Lee and the other plebes played cards, he knew something of McClellan's character. When push came to shove McClellan always folded. Despite the looming catastrophe Lee saw possibilities in the Union operations.

Confederate spies watching the byroads and the Washington troop reports, reported to their superiors in Richmond that Generals Banks and McDowell were on their way to reinforce McClellan. Although that was bad news, Lee, always an optimist, saw an opportunity if he could manage it. If Banks and McDowell had left Washington to join McClellan, who was left to defend Washington? Washington was unprotected.

Now it was that Lee's flare for strategy marked an example of his military genius. The plan he suggested to President Davis could change, what was, otherwise almost certainly the end of the Confederacy, into a victory. Lee intended to use some good old-fashioned psychology. He planned to kill several birds with one stone: First, he would confuse McClellan and delay Banks' and McDowell's arrival. Second, he might scare the hell out of Washington.

Lee intended to send his fast-moving General, Stonewall Jackson, up the Shenandoah Valley north toward the Union capitol. Once Washington knew Jackson was coming toward the Northern capitol, its citizens would demand protection against what might be an invasion. Their fear of Jackson might be great enough to force the administration to recall and keep General McDowell's army near the capitol's defenses.

Lee expected that Jackson might also run into and engage General Banks' smaller force. Lee hoped Jackson would hurt the Federals badly enough to disrupt McClellan's plan entirely for a while.

There were a lot of 'ifs' and 'hoped-for results' in Lee's strategy, but that marked the man. Robert E. Lee was willing to take a chance if there was the reasonable possibility of a large reward. Besides, his options were limited. It was a good plan and that is what happened. With Lee at the controls, the free-wheeling Confederate general, Thomas Jackson, was sent up the Shenandoah Valley with his small force to do what damage he could. Lee's order to Jackson was short and direct.

"Find Banks and McDowell. Delay them any way you can."

Within the hour Jackson's 'foot cavalry' (so named because they moved fast when necessary) were on the move up the Shenandoah Valley toward the Northern heartland. To the Union's detriment, Washington had not yet learned the good sense of coordinating their considerable military forces. Banks and McDowell were two fairly good-sized Union armies wandering uselessly around the Shenandoah Valley with little or no coordination with McClellan or with Washington.

Twenty years after Jackson's ride, published in 1884, still fresh in the minds of the citizens, James G. Blaine, twice Secretary of State under two presidents and once a Senator and Speaker of the House, compiled a five-inch-thick leather-bound volume. The title was, *Twenty Years of the American Congress*. The four-inch-thick volume was a detailed compendium of the affairs of Congress from 1860 to 1880.

The dusty compendium told what the Congressmen talked about, what speeches they gave, and what their comments were on Jackson's ride in early August of 1862. Blaine described the wild-eyed reaction by the Northern citizens and the government when they learned about Jackson's Shenandoah Valley Campaign. Blaine's words in the lawyer-like tome, offered his graphic description of the panic, the horror and the fear that swept over the population. Jackson and his few 4200 rebels scared the liver out of Washington in 1862.

Blaine wrote, '*Stonewall Jackson came thundering down the Shenandoah Valley with a force, which the exaggeration of the day placed beyond his real numbers. He brushed aside the army of General Banks at Winchester by what might well be termed a military cyclone, and created such consternation that our troops in the Potomac Valley were at once thrown upon the defensive.*'

McDowell, with his corps, was at Fredericksburg hurrying toward Hanover Court House for the purpose of aiding McClellan. With U.S. forces thus remote from Washington and the fortifications around the city imperfectly manned, something akin to panic seized upon the government.

Governor Anderson, with evident apprehension of the worst, informed the people of Massachusetts, "A wily and barbarous horde of traitors to the people menaces the National Capitol. They are marching on Washington. The National Capitol might soon be in the possession of the Confederate army, and the senators and representatives in Congress will be seized as prisoners of war."

Confederate General
Thomas J. "Stonewall" Jackson

Blaine, in that dusty leather-bound volume, offered his opinion of the aggressive Secretary of War. It was probably sound. He wrote, *'Secretary of War Stanton, undertook to perform the duties of General-in-Chief and, by his order, McDowell was diverted from his plan to aid McClellan and invade Richmond.'*

'Stanton was unfitted for the job. Had anyone of McDowell, Banks, or Fremont's military experience been in chief command of Washington at that moment, Jackson would not have been successful and Richmond would have been taken.'

Eating up the miles, by the second day Stonewall Jackson's rebels had reached the outlying small farms around Kernstown and Winchester. General Fremont was near and Jackson's troops knocked Fremont back on his heels. Next, Jackson destroyed Banks' supply lines. General Banks had been given the job of stopping Jackson and keeping the rebel intruders from getting back to Richmond to reinforce Lee but Jackson struck first.

On May 23, at Front Royal, Jackson and Ewell's division attacked and overwhelmed the Union outpost. The fast-moving Jackson reached Bank's left flank with twice the number of troops Banks had. Banks was forced to fall back from Strasbourg to his base at Winchester. With no idea where Jackson's main force was and without a steady flow of supplies Banks had no choice; he had to retreat to resupply his army.

The following day, Jackson sliced into Banks' wagon train of supplies. Banks' troops were hit hard and the attack turned into a rout. Stonewall next attacked Fremont's smaller army.

Jackson had accomplished exactly what Lee wanted him to do, and more by forcing Fremont and Banks into retreat. Washington had been frightened half to death over a possible invasion, and Jackson had succeeded in delaying McDowell from joining McClellan. That added delay gave Jefferson Davis the time he needed to gather and arm more Confederate troops for the defense of Richmond.

One of Stonewall's soldiers described their general's no-frills fighting rule in a letter he sent home. *'All old Jackson gave us was a musket, a hundred rounds, and a gum blanket and he druv us like hell.'*

Not knowing Jackson's true intentions, Lincoln canceled Bank's transfer to McClellan and he ordered McDowell's 35,000 men to stay close to Washington to protect the capitol. What Jackson had accomplished in his march northward up the Shenandoah Valley was a powerful and decisive psychological strategic victory for the Confederates. Although the Confederates lost the Kernstown battle to Banks, Jackson had convinced the Federal authorities in Washington to keep McDowell in front of the capitol despite McClellan's loud protests.

There was another psychological plus for Lee. Jackson had, by his bold aggressiveness, impressed the Union administration in that he made them believe the Southern armies were *much larger* than they were. Furthermore, Stonewall Jackson had given General Shields, Banks' division commander, such a hard fight that Jackson's ability to lead such hard-fighting troops made an even greater impression on the administration.

Jackson's speed and the fierceness of his raw-boned rebels were a foretaste of things to come. Lee was also impressed. During the next few days, he sent Jackson more men until Jackson's army swelled to 80,000 troops.

General Nathaniel Banks would not forget his ignominious retreat from Jackson's men at Kernstown. They would meet again. In August, a month later, at Cedar Mountain, still smarting from the defeat, Bank's men would give Stonewall as good as he had been given at Winchester.

General Banks had been a politician before the war. He was a pretty good soldier, despite losing the fight at Cedar Mountain. Before the war, he had been Speaker of the House of Representatives and, like Lincoln, he belonged to the anti-slavery *Know-Nothing* Party *(later, the Republican Party)*. It made Banks feel no better when he heard later that Jackson had also sent Fremont running.

While Jackson was working hard for the Confederacy, General James Longstreet, Lee's other wing commander, was equally busy. Longstreet guarded the roads around Richmond. News of Jackson's resounding success got home. The newspapers and the citizens shouted the news on the streets of Richmond. Longstreet also heard the good news, as he trudged with his troops through the mud and rain around the capitol establishing a defense line. He sent a cheery letter to President Davis that reflected the new optimism of the Confederacy.

'If you see General Johnston, say to him that we are happy as larks over here. If your roads can beat this for mud, I don't want to see it. We have 126 wagons up to the hub at one time but I don't fear McClellan or anyone in Yankeedom.'

MCCLELLAN ATTACKS

McClellan's Peninsula Campaign began with an attack on Yorktown, fifteen miles away. Brigadier General Porter *(he wouldn't remain a Brigadier for long)*, McClellan's favorite general, commanded a full division of 2000 men. Fitz John Porter had been on a fast track for promotion after West Point, from the beginning of his career. His division upped to a full corps of 6000 troops. Most were regular army men.

By any measure, Porter was a pretty good soldier. It is not a usual matter to have a general commend his *enemy's* fighting ability. After the Civil War two of the Confederacy's best generals praised Porter: General A.P. Hill, one of the Confederacy's finest division heads, and their best, Robert E. Lee.

Along with Porter, McClellan's forces included Sumner's Fifth Corps, Heintzelman's Third Corps, and Keyes' Fourth Corps. Beside that impressive array of fighting men, McClellan expected, shortly, he would be joined by Banks' and McDowell's Corps.

After taking Yorktown, five more brief and bloody battles followed with both sides suffering casualties: The Battle of Williamsburg, Eltham's Landing, Drewry's Bluff, Hanover Court House, and Seven Pines *(also called Fair Oaks)*.

On 5 May, Williamsburg was followed by an unsuccessful try with an amphibious landing to cut off fleeing rebels at Eltham's Landing. U.S. Naval gunboats sailed up the James River on 15 May, and attempted to blast away at the artillery on top of Drewry's Bluff, three miles from Richmond. They were repulsed.

A minor battle occurred at the outskirts of Richmond near Hanover Court House and finally an attack by Confederates General Johnston caught McClellan by surprise at Fair Oaks. The Fair Oaks fight *(also known as Seven Pines)* was a hard fight and both sides had heavy casualties.

One of those casualties changed the course of the war. General Johnston was mortally wounded and Robert E. Lee took his place.

YORKTOWN

McClellan's first objective had to be Fort Yorktown, the first town in his way. A town of considerable size, Yorktown was a mere twenty miles from the capitol. It had respectable defenses, but McClellan *hardly expected* those defenses to slow *his* huge army.

Lee was fighting for more time to prepare for the giant assault and a way to further delay McClellan. He sent word by way of Johnston to General Magruder who was near Yorktown: '*Delay McClellan. Johnston is sending more troops.*'

The next day the Union troops marched. The day was sunny and warm and the marching was pleasant. Ten miles from Ft. Monroe, on April 5, McClellan had another surprise: rebels were not supposed to be at Yorktown in any force. Until then there had been no sign of rebel troops. The rebels had not only failed to attack the Union troops on the beaches but they appeared to have all high-tailed it to Richmond.

Despite appearances, Confederate General John B. Magruder, sometimes called, 'Prince John' because of his gaudy dress uniform and his well-known history of stage acting, was a pretty smart general. He arrived in Yorktown ahead of the Federals and made his preparations to meet them. The ex-actor-come-general had found a way to delay McClellan at Yorktown. At that point in the invasion of Richmond, Fitz John Porter had been assigned to lead McClellan's army.

By the second day of marching, war became a little more real for the Federal infantrymen. It began to rain. The rain came down hard and, before long the road to Yorktown was a river of mud worse than a pig sty. With each step the soldiers were ankle-deep in the mire. The roads turned to mud pits, and just when the foot-slogging Federals thought things could get no worse, General John G. Magruder and 13,000 desperate rebels reared up in their path. A fight began and Magruder's smaller force stopped Porter's juggernaut in its tracks.

Keeping in close charge of Porter's army, McClellan was fooled again. Instead of bothering to ferret out the enemy's true weakness, he had assumed Magruder's make-believe strength was real. McClellan ordered Porter to lay siege to Yorktown. George McClellan, with his past as an engineer and an engineer's careful detailed point of view, made a siege the easy thing to do. His army remained conveniently close their base at Harrison's Landing on the James River. He gave Lee the precious time he needed for new devilment.

McClellan chose General Fitz John Porter to conduct the siege. Porter was ready to carry out the order but he wanted to know what size of force opposed him. A story about Porter gives us insight into the kind of person he was.

At the outbreak of the war, Thaddeus Lowe was authorized to create an Aeronautic Service. He built five balloons, which were used during the Peninsula Campaign and later on in other battles. On April 11, at five o'clock in the afternoon when the air was clear and it had stopped raining, an observation balloon was sent up to spy on the Yorktown forces. General Porter decided he would be the observer and he would ascend and personally reconnoiter the enemy. As a first-hand observer that day, the teller of this tale, a civilian, who knew Porter as a friend, described the ascension and what happened afterward.

"Porter was a polite soldierly gentleman who had been in the regular army since early manhood. He had fought in the Mexican War, been wounded and was now forty years of age. He was handsome, enthusiastic, ambitious and popular with his men and fellow officers. He had ascended thrice before and seemed as cozily at home in the firmament as upon solid earth."

"On this day he leaped into the car and called out, *'Let the cables out with all speed.'* I saw the flurried assistants send up the great straining canvas with but a single rope attached. The enormous bag had only partly inflated. The loose folds opened and shut with a crack like that of a musket. Noisily, fitfully, the yellow mass rose into the sky, the basket rocking like a feather in the zephyr."

"Just as I turned aside to speak to a comrade, a sound came from overhead like the explosion of a shell and something struck me across the face, laying me on the ground. Half blind and stunned, I staggered to my feet but the air seemed full of cries and curses. Opening my eyes carefully, I saw all faces turned upwards. When I looked up the balloon was adrift and rising swiftly."

"The treacherous cable, rotted with vitriol, had snapped in twain. One whipping fragment had been the cause of my downfall. The other hung from the receding car beneath the balloon like a great entrail. General Porter's balloon was bounding like a Pegasus that he could neither check nor direct."

"Presently, the General appeared directly over the edge of the car. He shouted something we could not comprehend. Below, on the ground, among the crowd of fearful onlookers, the maker of the balloons, Lowe, called out to General Porter, now a speck in the sky."

"*Open the valve!*" Lowe called, "Climb to the netting and reach the valve rope!'"

"'The valve, the valve!" a multitude of voices echoed in chorus."

The unnamed soldier continued, "We saw him, no bigger than a child's toy. Clambering up to the netting and reaching for the cord. Then we saw him descend and peer toward the enemy with a long black spyglass. He was reconnoitering the enemy. Had he been reconnoitering the moon he could not have been more vigilant."

"A few enemy muskets fired at the balloon but to no effect. A grand Hallelujah that shook the spheres went up from our camp. A huzzah was on every lip. The balloon descended at last, struck a canvas tent and the General was seen clambering out of the basket. A band marched up and they played as the men bawled their satisfaction in hurrahs while a throng of horsemen gave General Porter a vociferous escort back to his quarters."

When General Porter had finished his cloud-high first-hand reconnoiter of the enemy, looking toward the city he realized that Magruder had practiced nothing more than the con of legerdemain. Magruder, an old-style stage actor and showman, had created the illusion of a mighty army at Yorktown. He had his men moving back and forth, well out of artillery and musket range, giving the impression to the watching Federals of a very large army, instead of the small force Magruder really had.

There was more to the charade. There were plenty of cannons in Yorktown. Fifteen huge mounted mortars stood before the city with five-foot-long barrels and thirteen-inch openings in the barrels that were large enough to swallow a horse but these monsters were useless. They were aimed at the Yorktown River and not toward the Union army. The rebels had also chopped down trees, shaved the bark and threw up dozens of very real-looking (from a distance) dangerous cannons. The clever and artful 'Prince John' used every trick in his bag of tricks to fool McClellan… and it had worked like a charm.

The sorry fact was that any Union general could have easily smashed through the rebels. Porter had three times that of the rebel forces that faced him. Had McClellan not been fooled and not given Porter the order to halt, Porter might have moved against Richmond much more quickly with a pretty good chance of success.

George McClellan's weeks-long siege preparations had been completed. A complicated matter of digging miles of trenches, installing dozens of cannon mounts, and moving heavy firepower into position, all came to nothing. It was an exercise in futility. The canny rebels, guided by the mastermind of Jefferson Davis' military adviser in Richmond, waited until all of McClellan's careful engineer's preparations were in readiness.

Lee then told Magruder, "Take your men back to Richmond and join the rest of the Confederate army."

President Lincoln had not been as easily fooled. He suspected from the start, and he was dead right, the Confederates had been putting on a show worthy of a New York Opera House extravaganza. By the time 'Prince John' had finished his sleight of hand, the cautious McClellan was sure the Confederate line was too hard to break. His timidity had cost the Union army five weeks in valuable time.

The trenches at Yorktown were evacuated and Magruder retreated up the Peninsula. McClellan had to leave his fine arrangements, worthy of holding any city siege for years, let alone a small seaport town. McClellan sent General Heintzelman forward to find 'Prince John' and destroy his small army while Porter remained with him for the final push on Richmond.

Then commenced a comedy of errors. General Johnston planned to attack the Federals with Longstreet's division *before* the Federals reached Richmond. He started 55,000 Confederates against Sam Heintzelman's 33,000 men of the Third Corps and Erasmus Keyes' Fourth Corps, but Longstreet was late getting started.

It was not until ten o'clock that Longstreet's division began to march. His divisions got tangled up and the advance was slowed even more. Union observation balloons were not in the air so there was no aerial reconnaissance to let the Federals know what was happening. When Longstreet's skirmishers finally contacted Heintzelman's men it was near the small town of Williamsburg.

WILLIAMSBURG

By May 5, Stoneman's Union cavalry was skirmishing with Jeb Stuart's Confederate cavalry, which were posted as Johnston's rearguard. The Federals, led by Sam Heintzelman's Third Corps, were hard on Magruder's heels so Magruder decided it was time to make a stand. Part of his force got behind a large earthen fortification, which had been constructed beforehand for just such an occasion. The defense straddled the Williamsburg Road and the battle that followed was fair-sized with 41,000 Federals fighting 32,000 Confederates.

Heintzelman tried to cut off Magruder's retreat but that turned out to be more of a job than he or McClellan had anticipated. By then Johnston had sent General Magruder more troops and General James Longstreet had arrived.

Hooker's Second Division was in the lead of Heintzelman's forces. He launched an assault on the rebels behind the earth mound, what had come to be called 'Fort Magruder' in honor of the Fort's far-sighted general. The butternut uniforms of the Confederate counter attacked, and there the fighting got hot. A battery of three-inch guns from the Union artillery turned to meet the enemy. Bullets were flying so fast a North Carolina man said afterward, *"I came out safe with a bullet hole in my cap. This is what I call pretty close work."*

All morning they fought. With more Confederate on the field, Longstreet's rebels threatened to overwhelm the Federals. The rebels now numbered 32,000 men and they were more than equal to the task of holding and delaying Heintzelman's 9000 troops.

In the fighting that followed, the Federal troops were pressed back. General William *'Baldy'* Smith, ex-math professor and civil engineer, proved to be quite a soldier. He heard the uproar of the guns and brought his brigade on the run to support Hooker. It was still nip and tuck. At one crucial point in the melee, the fierce one-armed General Phil Kearney joined the fight. His saber raised high with a string of curses and a shout, he galloped forward to lead Union infantrymen into the fray.

General Winfield Hancock attacked. He bombarded the rebels with more artillery and the fight continued back and forth until late afternoon. That night, after both sides had stopped shooting and nursed their wounds for the next day's battle, General Heintzelman saw many of his musicians standing at the back of the lines. Knowing his troops were discouraged by the unexpected heavy resistance, he ordered the band to play *anything*. Their music rallied the Union forces and the following day they forced the Confederates to withdraw toward their defenses in Richmond.

DREWRY'S BLUFF

Next, fifteen naval gunboats steamed up the York River to Drewry's Bluff to blast Richmond. On the south bank of the James River, Drewry's Bluff rears up 110 feet and overlooks a bend in the river. The outpost is a mere seven miles from Richmond. The U.S. Navy sent gunboats steaming up the James to knock out the rebel guns, and if they were successful it would help McClellan immensely; those guns were Richmond's last line of artillery defense. The Union sailors were confident the Union Ironclad, the Monitor, would make short work of the battlements protecting Drewry's Bluff so up the river they steamed.

That trip up the James River would have been much more difficult except for the new temporary field commander; Abraham Lincoln. On 6 May, when the President and his cabinet officers came down to Fort Monroe to see how McClellan was doing, Lincoln saw that the City of Norfolk was still in Confederate hands. As Commander-in-Chief *(McClellan was too busy planning the push toward Richmond to discuss the matter with the President)* Lincoln ordered the naval bombardment of Norfolk.

The City caved in quickly. Federal forces took their surrender, and that was that. It also meant that the Confederate floating tin can, the CSS Virginia, no longer had a home port. Not able to get through the shallow waters of the James River to escape to Richmond, her captain scuttled her. The flat top iron ship was no longer a threat to the wooden Union gunboats and because of Lincoln, the Union ships were able to navigate toward Drewry's Bluff, seven miles from Richmond, to attack those defenses without worrying about the CSS Virginia sinking the gunboats.

More unexpected problems popped up for the attackers. When the navy gunboats fired at Drewry's Bluff, they found, to their consternation and frustration, the guns aboard the Union ships could not elevate high enough to 110 feet above the river and therefore could not do much damage.

Reluctantly, they had to turn around and steam back down the James with the taunts of the rebel defenders in their ears yelling their derision with cries of *"That is not the way to Richmond,"* and *"Come back and see us again, Yankee, when your guns can shoot."* As a final insult to the gunboats, the rebel guns continued to fire, peppering away and succeeded in blowing a few more holes in the Union ships until they were out of range.

Moving in snail-slow-motion, George McClellan set up his base of operations at Eltham's Landing near Rooney Lee's plantation, Robert E. Lee's son. Johnston pulled his army back to the defenses of Richmond and 60,000 Confederates faced McClellan's 105,000 troops.

Pinkerton had done his usual job of incorrectly gauging enemy strength. He informed McClellan that he was outnumbered two-to-one so McClellan settled down to wait for General McDowell's army before going forward, taking the time to arrange his siege guns for the big show, which he expected to come soon.

HANOVER COURT HOUSE

While the skirmishing was going on around Richmond, McClellan heard a rumor that *'Seventeen thousand rebels were moving toward Hanover Court House, north of Mechanicsville.'* George McClellan was ready to believe any rumor that supported his persistent conviction of a vastly superior enemy force. That imagined monster was always waiting in the wings. If it was true, that meant that his left flank was threatened.

He sent General Porter and his well-disciplined regular army infantrymen to Hanover Court House to protect the army's flank. Porter was told to drive any

Confederate soldiers away from that part of the country so that McClellan would be free to attack Richmond without having to worry about having an enemy at his back. By this time Porter had been upgraded to Major General with his own corps. General Pope, who had come from Washington, for his part in clearing away any threat to McClellan's rear, tore up the railroads and bridges over the Pamunkey River.

Hanover Court House was 14 miles north of Richmond. Before the sun was up Porter sent Morell's First Brigade and Sykes's Third Brigade; 2,000 infantrymen, to search and reconnoiter the area. They were ready to fight whoever they found. The day turned gray and it started to rain about noon. It was a gully washer. Most of the way the road was shoe-deep in mud because it had been raining for a week. As one wet soldier described the road to Hanover Court House, *"It was twenty miles long and one foot deep."*

Maps of the area were about as poor as they could be and Porter and the rest of his men did not arrive to the place where they were supposed to march. Instead of Hanover, his men had come to another wide spot in the road named New Bridge. Held up by the swampy roads, Porter sent his cavalry and artillery along Ashland Road to destroy the Railroad and the telegraph lines at the crossing.

General Porter often also used lookout balloons when the weather allowed, gaining more intelligence about the enemy. His balloon lookout that day, lifting to 300 feet and at times, rising to 1000 feet, reported the Confederates were about to attack his rear guard. Porter's rear guard, men of the 44th New York and the 25th Main infantry companies, along with two pieces of artillery, had started their journey with sixty rounds of ammunition. The tenacious rebels, always searching for an opening or a weakness, hit hard. The Federals had one fight already, and the rebel commander attacked with his full force. It became a hot fight and Porter's men were running out of ammunition. Their muskets got so hot they had to cool the barrels with water from their canteens. The blue lines were breaking. Porter's main army, hearing the racket, knowing the rear guard was in the soup, faced about and double-quick marched to the aid of the beleaguered rear guard. Expecting to find the whole Confederate army at Hanover Court House, instead, Porter found a far smaller force. Once on the scene Porter's assault force made short work of the Confederates. It was a hot fight while it lasted and a Lt. Colonel of the 9th Massachusetts wrote to his wife about the busy afternoon,

'The woods all around were swarming with rebels. We met the rebels on the verge of the wood and whipped them out of it in no time... such quick work I never saw... the rebels made a stand in the open... again we pressed upon the enemy... captured one of their flags and drove them from the field in the most indescribable disorder.'

The rebels were routed. Porter's men took 730 prisoners and moved toward Hanover Court House only to find the Confederates had abandoned their camp. Measured by the number of prisoners taken, the count was ten to one in Porter's favor.

Although it was a minor fracas, McClellan, always bombastic in touting any victory, claimed the affair at Hanover Court House was a *'Glorious victory over superior numbers'* (untrue) and *'One of the handsomest things of the war'* (it was a good performance but hardly that).

As small as the skirmish that afternoon turned out to be, Union and Confederate casualties totaled to more than *two thousand men*. Small as it was, it led McClellan to trumpet, *'A glorious victory over superior numbers.'* The fight was an example of the training and fighting spirit that General Porter had instilled in his men. His organization, his methods of discipline, his excellent communications and his quick response to trouble were all responsible for the rapid resolution of an unexpected problem. It was another measure of a commander, who was fast becoming one of the Union's best.

McClellan was depending too much on Porter. Because Porter had been busy at Hanover Court House, McClellan delayed, reluctant to move more troops south of the Chickahominy River to join his main force. That exposed his left flank to Johnston. Part of the reason for McClellan's lack of sharpness was because he was in bed with a flair-up of his chronic malaria.

FAIR OAKS *(SEVEN PINES)*

Johnston knew he could not survive a massive siege of Richmond so he decided to attack. What followed next was a two-day battle with heavy casualties on the last day of May. Everything went wrong for the Confederacy.

It was the first time the 35th Georgia would see action and before the sun had set they had paid a heavy price. Longstreet's force, most of it, was stuck too far from the fight to join in. To keep the Union forces from overrunning Longstreet's right flank, the rebels advanced against a murderous artillery fire from a Federal 6-gun battery of Napoleon cannons. Eventually, the Confederates realized they faced overwhelming odds and they fell back, leaving scores of wounded and dying. Of the more than 500 men of one Southern regiment, the 35th Georgia, 53 were battle casualties, along with two Confederate generals. The battle was fought amid thick woods in small clusters of men and the wounded were propped against trees so they would not drown in the muck.

Joe Johnston stood watching the battle six hundred feet from Fair Oaks Station. The fighting was in range of the Yankee guns and his men were dodging as the metal sang by. His staff worried for his safety, prodded him to move to less dangerous place but Johnston refused.

He wished to be near his troops, saying, "I have been hit five times, sir. It is no use dodging when you hear the bullets pass it is already too late to dodge."

At that moment a bullet struck him in his right shoulder and a shell exploded slamming a large fragment of metal into his chest with force enough to knock him from his horse. The blow broke several ribs and left him painfully wounded. The more far-reaching result of his injury would not be made manifest for a while… but when it was clear how badly he had been hurt it changed the course of the war for the South. Ultimately, Jefferson Davis gave the command of the Confederate army to Robert E. Lee and his leadership would make all the difference.

At first, after the battle, President Davis replaced Johnston with Major General Gustavus W. Smith, a man in whom Davis had little confidence. Davis felt he had little choice; the enemy was at the gates of Richmond. It was only later, in a bright moment of decision, that President Davis asked Robert E. Lee to take Smith's place on a temporary basis. Lee accepted and he changed the course of the war.

McClellan claimed a victory at Seven Pines but he was shaken by the near defeat. The shock of a near catastrophic loss (plus he was still suffering from a miserable ear infection at the time) made him send his entire army south of the river, except for the Fifth Corps, General Fitz John Porter's men. He still planned for a siege of Richmond when the time was right, but something had snapped in him. He had lost the initiative and he never got it back after Seven Pines.

He made his main supply base at White House on the Pamunkey River and more troops were coming from Fredericksburg every hour to swell his ranks. McClellan's 100,000 men were close enough to hear the Richmond church bells. McClellan arranged his five divisions on the banks of the Chickahominy in a vast horseshoe-shaped semi-circle before Richmond; three divisions were posted north of the river and two divisions were placed south of the Chickahominy.

General Fitz John Porter was sent north to pursue the enemy and destroy bridges, camps, trains, tracks and boats on and along the Pamunkey River. Lee had half that many Confederate soldiers to meet the threat. Despite the optimism that persisted among the rebels, prospects were still bleak for the Confederacy.

LEE TAKES CHARGE

Lee got busy. He spent almost a month stretching his lines and immediately reorganizing his army into a new and better arrangement of forces. Jackson, just back from his coup in the Shenandoah Valley, was given his own division. Lee's half dozen separate parts included A.P. Hill's Light Division and General Hill's men were a force that traveled with a minimum of encumbrances. Like a rattler, on short notice they could strike the enemy quickly.

When A.P. Hill went into battle General Longstreet was given operational command of Hill's force. General Magruder, the old-time showman of the Yorktown siege, kept his division. Aging General Benjamin Huger's division was given a brigade headed by one of the heroes-to-be of the tragic rebel charge at Gettysburg, General Lewis Armistead. General Theophilus Holmes rounded out the Sixth Division of Lee's nearly 80,000 Confederate troops defending Richmond.

Meanwhile, like a bump on a log, McClellan sat by waiting for dry weather, better roads, more men... or whatever seemed to be what kept him from attacking. Perhaps untold numbers of men and the most perfect roads and weather might have been enough. While he waited for McDowell he made good use of his engineering skills. Engineering was what he knew best and his men built beautiful bridges complete with strong log piers, and corduroy paving.

McClellan got a report that Lee was on the move. Robert E. Lee sent 17,000 rebels to roll up McClellan's exposed right flank. The bridge nearest to the expected attack was finished and his men had christened the overcrossing, Grapevine Bridge. To counter Lee's threat McClellan marched his men across the Chickahominy. Lee drew back to Richmond.

Things were about to change in the Confederate's favor. The Seven Days Battle was about to happen with Lee, not McClellan, on the offensive.

⪦ 17 ⪧

Robert E. Lee

Like many officers, Union and rebel, Robert E. Lee came of great military forebears. One of Lee's ancestors fought with William the Conqueror, another had been knighted by Queen Elizabeth and still another had marched in the crusades to the Holy Land. A man of iron self-control, many considered Lee to be cold and aloof. In truth, he was not. Lee was compassionate, moved to tears upon learning of the death of a fellow soldier. In the few times when Lee became angry, those who saw his rage quickly left his presence. His experiences, added to his natural genius for judging his enemy's strengths and weaknesses, and most of all, his audacity and willingness to risk all for a great advantage were qualities that made Robert E. Lee one of the most skillful generals of the War.

When President Davis appointed Robert E. Lee to lead the Confederate armies, it was the best decision Davis ever made. In the months that followed, Lee bluffed and out-generaled nearly all of Lincoln's generals. Lee had the added advantage over the Union by having two superb corps commanders, Jackson and Longstreet, both superior leaders. These two men were excellent tacticians and they were unmatched in their raw desire to win.

In the Fall of 1861 it was taken on faith by the Union that the Confederate army vastly outnumbered the Union forces.

Allan Pinkerton, of the Pinkerton Detective Service, told McClellan as he stood before Richmond, "General Robert E. Lee has 200,000 troops before Richmond, maybe more."

Pinkerton had gained importance in the North since the days when he had been a barrel maker and it was his barrels that brought him to fame. After he found the thieves that had stolen his barrels, and brought them to justice, he was made a Chicago Deputy Sheriff. Soon after, he founded a detective agency. Pinkerton, an ardent Abolitionist, made his staff follow strict rules (*one of them was a woman, America's first woman detective*). His 'Pinkertons' could not smoke, drink, play cards, hang about low places with the riff-raff or use slang. The sign on the front of his Chicago headquarters bore the picture of a huge eye, two-feet in diameter. The motto below the eye read 'We never sleep.'

In 1861, when the president elect, Abraham Lincoln, boarded the train for his inauguration in Washington, there were rumors of a possible assassination attempt. Most of the army was off fighting Indians. A local paramilitary group, 300 men of the *National Rifles*, offered to guard the president. Not known to the president's people, the generous offer was like the fox offering to guard the chickens. Some of the leaders and the group's captain were Southern sympathizers. They were planning to storm the Treasury building and take over Washington.

Pinkerton uncovered the plot. The 'Rifles' captain fled the capitol and became a Confederate intelligence officer. The rest, with the secessionists cleaned out, were converted into companies of men loyal to the Union and ready to defend the capitol and the president. When McClellan asked Pinkerton to establish a Union intelligence operation Pinkerton agreed. Thereafter, Pinkerton's stock was so high that whatever he said was taken as true.

When Allan Pinkerton reported huge Confederate numbers of enemy troops to McClellan, his estimates were accepted as probably correct. What McClellan believed, the entire officer corps accepted as gospel truth. The intelligence reports were detailed and explicit... but they were *dead wrong*.

Not everyone believed Pinkerton's high numbers. General Montgomery Meigs, the Washington quartermaster, had his doubts that the number Pinkerton quoted was right. He combed the Richmond newspapers, noted the numbers and size of brigades and regiments, and he came up with a pretty good estimate. Meigs guessed the rebels had less than *half* the figure McClellan or Pinkerton claimed. Nevertheless, despite the army quartermaster's better estimate, General McClellan continued to believe he was vastly outnumbered.

That false perception and Pinkerton's inflated reports gave George McClellan the perfect excuse to wait and wait and wait some more... to believe he was always outnumbered. It was a mistake that was to haunt McClellan and all of the generals that followed him until Ulysses S. Grant took charge two years later.

The added delay Magruder had caused along with Longstreet's spirited fight at Williamsburg persuaded McClellan all the more that Pinkerton was right. He called Washington for more troops. The President's reply to McClellan was discouraging. Lincoln had decided not to send him more men and the unhappy McClellan's disappointment was compounded with Lincoln's correspondence, which for McClellan was the coupe de gras. Lincoln wrote, *'I shall not send you McDowell's army. His troops are needed to defend Washington.'*

McClellan should have been happy with what he had; the Federals outnumbered the rebels two to one. Beside his own powerful forces, he would soon have another 50,000 soldiers to use from John Pope's command. To top off his superiority over the rag-tag rebels, the industrial might of the North guaranteed an unlimited supply of guns, food and artillery. McClellan had the best-trained, mightiest military force ever assembled. The hard cold truth was that McClellan had no belly for war.

McClellan had trained an army to fight but he had a defect that was fatal for a general that was expected to win a war and save the country. Abraham Lincoln saw it. Lincoln once remarked in a moment of irritation over McClellan's repeated delays, *'McClellan has a case of the slows.'*

The reason for McClellan's excessive military caution had a simple explanation: George McClellan lacked the killer instinct. Any champion must have it. Robert E. Lee had it. It was a trait Lee had in spades. Moreover, Lee *knew* McClellan's weakness from their days at West Point. Lee recalled the young officer candidates around the poker table, and when the betting got steep, George McClellan always folded. Lee used McClellan's weakness against him at every opportunity.

After his newest setback in an attempt to take Richmond, McClellan waited for more men at Harrison's Landing. He had 100,000 troops in position, twice what Lee had; Richmond was about as close as it could be. Still, time and again, McClellan called Washington for more troops. Only *then* could he invade Richmond.

Lee's options were limited. He could not remain where he was; reinforcements were coming to join McClellan.

It began to rain again around Richmond, as it usually did in midsummer. Lee watched the Union army positioning itself on the Chickahominy River and saw they were settling into position to prepare for an attack against the city. Word also came to Lee that General McDowell had left Fredericksburg and was on his way. Lee had to act swiftly. He had to take the offensive. All that remained was to decide where and how to begin.

James Longstreet had operational command of half of Lee's army. He commanded 92,000 men, the largest force assembled during the war. Moxley Sorrel, his aid, wrote of Longstreet's calmness in battle.

"He was a like a rock in steadiness when sometimes in battle the world seemed to be flying in pieces."

Robert E. Lee said of him, "Longstreet is the staff in my right hand."

That 'staff' to whom Lee referred was highly supported by the Confederate soldiers. In Lee, Longstreet and Jackson, one could see three of the best generals of the Civil War. And the rebel infantrymen were fighters to be reckoned with no matter the odds.

On June 23, McClellan had drawn up his forces on the Chickahominy River, a slow-moving marshy river, six miles from Richmond. When McDowell learned Jackson was nowhere to be found near Washington, he went north to help McClellan capture Richmond. Everyone had been completely fooled by Lee's clever battle strategy. Jackson, his job of fakery finished, also marched back to Richmond to join the rest of Richmond's defenders.

The Chickahominy River flows from the James River in a roughly southeast direction. It winds above and around Richmond like an encircling snake, and protected the Confederate capitol. The river (if one can call a sluggish swampland tangled with rank thick water, reeds and plants a true river) was as much as a mile across in some places. The width and depth of the river changed all the time. How much it changed depended on the weather and the rain. As the river rose and fell in the rainy season, the stagnant waters were a breeding ground for mosquitoes and biting flies. Malaria was common. Next to the river was a bad place to camp.

The Army of the Potomac had been split in two parts straddling the rain-swollen Chickahominy River. Most of the Union army, four of McClellan's corps, was in a great semi-circular line along the south side of the river four miles from the city. However, General Fitz John Porter's Fifth Corps was on the other side, north of the river near Mechanicsville and behind Beaver Creek. McClellan had sent Porter to guard the Union supply line north of the Chickahominy and Lee's plan was to cross the river and attack Porter's right flank.

Early in the morning of June 26, Lee left enough troops on the south side to distract McClellan. He advanced on Porter's trenches with the hope Porter's men might leave their trenches and retreat. Then Longstreet and A.P. Hill would join the battle and Porter would be overwhelmed by the two-point attack. Lee planned

**Confederate General
Robert E. Lee**

then to move on Cold Harbor and cut McClellan's communications with White House Landing.

Lee guessed that Porter might not be prepared for an attack against his rear guard but first he had to make sure. To confirm Porter's position Lee ordered J.E.B. Stuart, his eyes and ears, to ride out and see.

August 20, 1861, was the day J.E.B. Stuart lost his hat. Stuart's 1200 cavalry, horsemen lugging a pair of cannons, went to find out what McClellan's defensive strength was on the Union right and north side of the river. On the way, at an hour when Stuart and his aid, Major Heros von Borcke, were far ahead of his brigade, they ran into a squadron of Union soldiers who were a part of Pope's army. The rebel officers escaped but just barely. In his haste to keep from being killed or captured by the Federal troops, General Stuart lost his hat.

General Stuart was highly indignant over the loss of his hat, which the enemy had recovered and triumphantly carried off, along with Stuart's haversack. Stuart covered his head with a handkerchief and tied it around his head against the scorching sun. The hat was a beautiful plumed affair and Stuart's pride and joy. Major von Borcke told about the embarrassing encounter, which caused some hilarity.

"We could not look at each other despite our inner rage. When we fell in with our regiment the driver of the sutler's wagon presented the general with another hat. News of the loss of General Stuart's hat spread through the army and created quite a sensation. Venting his rage over the loss, Stuart's cavalry took off and entered Culpepper. In no mood to be gentle, Stuart's men charged down the Culpepper Main Street, scattering pistol balls right and left to the laughter and jeers of his fellow Confederates. Supper tables were upturned, tents were broken, and everything that was not tied down was thrown galley west in the mad rush of the Union soldiers to escape and get out of the rebels' swath of destruction."

Later, a soldier remarked, "A few of us were gathered at a table with some toddy someone had made. I heard one of the diners say, '*Now this is something like comfort. I hope Jeb Stuart won't disturb us tonight.*'"

"Just then a yell broke upon our ears." The speaker, striking his fist on the table, said, "None of us at that table that night ever finished our drink."

Stuart's several hundred mounted troops next set fire to the bridge at Cedar Run near the Culpepper Court House, cut Pope's supply lines by tearing up the railroad, and burned every Yankee supply train car his men could find. What the rebels could not carry they burned. After riding all the way around the Union army Stuart made his report to General Lee; '*Porter is vulnerable.*' Lee made ready to attack.

Historical Note: The saga of Confederate General J.E.B. Stuart's many amazing exploits made him the most famous Cavalry General of the Civil War. Standing at six-foot-four and weighing 240 pounds, he had an ego to match his imposing appearance. His bold exploits had already stunned the Federals.

Until 1864, after two more years of running rings around the Union army and cavalry, J.E.B. Stuart was to suffer the fate of many brave men during the Civil War. During the battle of Todd's Tavern, Grant held the line waiting for Lee to come out of the wilderness. Sheridan, commanding the troops on Grant's left flank, had been trying to catch Stuart, until his orders were countermanded by General Meade.

Sheridan responded to Meade, *"As my plans were interfered with, and my orders countermanded, I will decline to give further orders. You may run my troops yourself, as you seem to wish to do."* To lighten the appearance of insubordination, Sheridan added, *"However, I would like the opportunity to take my corps and go after Stuart. I believe I can whip him in a fair fight."*

Grant was given Sheridan's request and gave his permission. The battle continued to rage while Grant had Lee bottled up. At an early hour in the darkness, Sheridan's cavalry headed by Custer, found the rebel horsemen. Stuart's men were waiting for Custer... but did not attack. When Custer came near, Stuart dismounted his cavalry and the battle was on. Custer gave the command to charge and Stuart tried to stem the tide with a few mounted men. One Federal cavalryman who had been unhorsed, shot and mortally wounded Stuart. General Stuart was taken to Richmond, where he died. He left behind a record of which those who wore blue and those who wore gray took equal pride, and both paid tribute.

General Sumner was a part of Porter's force and Lee decided to strike Sumner first. Jackson was summoned from the Shenandoah Valley and given some of Magruder's troops swelling Jackson's forces to 47,000.

McClellan, whatever his shortcomings, was not asleep at the switch. He also had a plan. When he found out that Lee was on the move, with Jackson back from the Shenandoah Valley, he decided to upstage Lee. He decided to take the offensive before Lee could carry out his plan. Even with the foreknowledge of Lee's plan and *knowing* Lee was coming to strike Porter, McClellan may have acted on his own behalf, but did nothing to support Porter.

It began to rain again around Richmond... as it usually did in midsummer. Lee watched the Union army positioning itself on the Chickahominy River, seeing they were settling into place to prepare for an attack against the city. Word came to Lee that General McDowell had left Fredericksburg, which increased the threat to the Confederate capitol. McDowell was on his way to add his considerable numbers to the Union Army. It was time for Lee to make his counter move.

Longstreet and Jackson, temporarily, with the larger force, began by pushing McClellan's men back. The Confederates moved the Union troops slowly up the Virginia Peninsula. The fighting never let up. The men in blue and gray fought each other in marshes, near creeks and rivers, on hillsides, in hamlets and in small towns, all within thirty miles of Richmond. It spread through small towns and villages, finally spilling over into the Battle of Cedar Creek and then... into the much greater Second Battle of Bull Run.

❧ 18 ❧

The Soldier

The single most obvious outward difference between the rebel and the Federal soldier was in the way each was outfitted for marching and for battle. The difference in their beliefs and personal prejudices was just as different. A Confederate soldier described the evolution of appropriate Confederate outfit.

"At the beginning of the war, the Confederate volunteer made extensive preparations for the field. Boots, he thought, were an absolute necessity; the heavier the soles and the longer the tops, the better. His pants were stuffed inside the tops of the boots. A double-breasted coat, heavily wadded, with two rows of brass buttons and a skirt was considered comfortable wear. The long overcoat was heavy with a cape reaching nearly to the waist. A small stiff cap with a narrow brim finished the ensemble."

"On his back he strapped a knapsack, which held a full stock of underwear, soap, towels, comb, brush, looking glass, tooth-brush, paper and envelopes, pens, ink, pencils, blacking, photographs, smoking and chewing tobacco, pipes, twine, needles and thread, buttons, knife, fork, spoon, cotton strips for wounds and other emergencies, and many other things, according to each man's idea of necessities."

"On the outside of the knapsack were two great blankets and a rubber oilcloth. The knapsack weighed in at twenty-five pounds and sometimes more. In addition, each man had a haversack stored with provisions enough to carry him in comfort across the greatest desert. To be prudent a canteen was kept filled with water. For hand-to-hand encounters, many carried revolvers and Bowie knives. Gloves were considered to be a good thing, especially in winter."

"Beside his private luggage, each mess, generally composed of five to ten men, carried a skillet, frying pan, coffee boiler, a bucket for lard, coffee box, salt box, sugar box, flour box, knives, forks, spoons, plates, and cups. It took a large army wagon to carry these supplies. It was all that two strong men could do to lift and get the chest into the wagon. Each mess owned an ax, water bucket and a bread tray. Then the tents in each company had little sheet-iron stoves and a stove pipe."

The Southern soldier's attitude toward the idea of slavery was markedly in opposition to most Northern soldiers. Whether he was even *acquainted* with a landowner or an individual who owned slaves, the Southerner and his Northern counterpart thought of the Black man in much the same way. To own another man or woman, to work them as they would any machine, was accepted with no thought that the Black man just *might be their equal*. Most certainly, if any rebel or Federal had been told that one day a Black president would lead our nation, they might have been unanimous in their views. They would have scoffed at the very possibility of such an idea.

The Confederate soldier, more used to a Black person as a servant, told of the hope that he might *'have a "boy" along on the march and in camp to do his washing and his cooking, a body servant all his own to bring him a drink, black his boots, dust his clothes, cook his corn bread and bacon, and put wood on his fire.'*

The Southerner's point of view was not unique; Abraham Lincoln freely confessed that *'If the Black man is free, I would not know what to do with him.'*

The rebel lived under the illusion that the Black man was docile and accepted his lot. In the words of a rebel soldier, "Never was there a fonder admiration than these darkies had for their masters. Their chief delight was to praise the courage and good looks of *'Marse Tom'* and prophesize great things for him in the future." This misconception of the slave endured until long after the Civil War.

As the war went on its weary way the Southern soldier's uniform and the necessities he carried into battle grew more streamlined and down to the bare necessities of marching and fighting. The heels of his boots wore down on the long march causing the ankle to twist nearly out of joint. The boots got wet. By the time the volunteer managed to pull on his soggy boots, morning roll call was missed. A simple gray jacket replaced the overcoat. A good felt hat was worn instead of the brimmed and utterly useless top hat. The few overcoats worn in winter were those captured from the 'bluecoats.' Rebel soldiers wore the same underclothes until worn out or replaced by wear sent from home. The luxury of washing clothes went by the wayside; cold water would not destroy the vermin and hot water was scarce. A single blanket was all any man wished to carry and with an oilcloth outside the blanket. That was enough for the most severe weather. This bundle was carried by rolling the blanket and the oilcloth sheet lengthwise with the protection on the outside, then tying the ends of the roll together, and throwing the loop that had been made over the left shoulder with the ends fastened together under the right arm.

The last of the rebel soldier's *'necessities'* to go was the haversack. That food container seldom carried rations of any sort. Anything absolutely necessary, a piece of hard tack, an apple, an ear of green corn, minie balls (bullets), were carried in their pockets. A good tin cup served to carry water from the nearest stream or well to boil coffee. Gloves were useless. They made it impossible to load a musket or handle a rammer at the piece. For the mess, when there was something to fry, one skillet passed from mess to mess. A couple of frying pans, a bag for flour or meal, another bag for sugar, salt and coffee served them well. The conglomeration of bags was divided by a knot between each item.

Tent use passed away for the rebel soldier in bivouac or on the march at night. Two men slept on the ground together, each having a blanket and an oil cloth next to the ground and with the second blanket and oil cloth on top to protect them from the rain, snow or hail.

The Southern soldier had no pay because there was nothing to buy. When rations got short, the few Black servants remaining from the start of the war were sent home. Reduced to a minimum, the private soldier's wardrobe consisted of one hat, one jacket, one shirt, a pair of pants, one pair of drawers, one pair of shoes, and one pair of socks.

His baggage was one blanket, one oilcloth sheet and perhaps a haversack that carried his smokes, a piece of soap, apples, berries and whatever he found on the march from some farmer's orchard. The handle of the fry pan was stuck in the barrel of the musket to carry it in place of a heavy bayonet and scabbard.

A Confederate writer said, *'In spite of hardships they laughed at their own bare feet, ragged clothes and pinched faces. Weak, hungry and cold, they marched with no hope of reward or rest, cheerfully to meet the well-fed and warmly clad host of the enemy.*

Field illustration by Edwin E Forbes
Confederate prisoners captured at Woodstock, Virginia, ca. 1862, Library of Congress

**Confederate General
James Longstreet**

❧ 19 ❧

Seven Days

In 1862, at the end of June during a period of seven days, six battles took place on the Virginia Peninsula, all within five miles of Richmond. Blue and Gray fought each other at Oak Grove, Mechanicsville, Gaines' Mill, Garnett's and Golding's Farm, Savage Station, Glendale, and Malvern Hill. The fighting ended with 36,000 casualties, who were wounded or captured or missing, and included more than five thousand men killed.

What did fighting accomplish? Quite a bit. Northern morale was crushed. The casualties, one out of every five of Lee's men, stunned Southerners. Yet for Robert E. Lee and his officers the blood was worth the price. Morale in the Confederacy skyrocketed.

When the fighting ended McClellan retreated to the safety of the James River defenses. Lee, convinced that the offensive against Richmond was over, was emboldened. Shortly he would begin his Northern Virginia Campaign, which would culminate with two terrible battles; the Battle of Second Manassas (Bull Run), and two weeks later, the Battle of Antietam.

In May, the 10,000 men of McClellan's Fifth Corps had been given to Major General Fitz John Porter. Porter was made a Corps Commander. Up to that point Porter had commanded the Third Division only. From then on his Fifth Corps fought in most of the battles of the Peninsula Campaign and during the Seven Days of fighting that followed. His leadership in all of the separate smaller fights was characterized by good generalship, especially at Gaines' Mill and Malvern Hill where Porter demonstrated outstanding skill.

A powerful testimony to Porter's will-to-fight was the terrible numbers of his men that were wounded and killed. Yet, General Porter's losses were always less than those of the rebels he fought. In the end, Porter's battle losses totaled 7,601 men; nearly half the entire losses of the Union army.

Porter and Longstreet were fated to meet several times more during the Seven Days and again, for the last time, at the Second Battle of Manassas near Bull Run, Virginia. There, on the plain of Manassas, Porter would lose a third of his troops defending John Pope's army against Longstreet's hammer assault as Lee swept over the Federals. Since this is, mostly, Major General Fitz John Porter's story, it must be said that only Porter's stubborn resistance to that assault on August 29 and 30, of 1862 saved the Union Army from complete destruction.

OAK GROVE AND WHITE OAK SWAMP

McClellan made one last try to overpower the Richmond defenders. Just after daylight two brigades of Hooker's division stepped off to attack. Advancing west, along the Williamsburg Road toward the capitol, they came upon a small, half-mile wide, dense forest: White Oak Swamp, the headwaters of a narrow river. A miasmic, humid, pest-ridden boggy field cut through the center of the woods.

The rebels had set an abatis defense (felled trees with sharpened tops as a barrier) in the muddy swampy waters to slow the Federal advance. The sharpened stakes made passage through the swamp difficult and downright dangerous. Long after the battles that took place that day, photographer Alexander Gardner wrote of the swamp, *'The air seemed to be suffocating with stagnation... beneath the pall of mist.'*

Slugging their way through the muddy swamp and climbing over the stakes was hard going for the marchers. The pace was slowed to a crawl and the beautifully formed lines of the advancing infantry became ragged and out of alignment. The aging Confederate General, Benjamin Huger, was waiting on the other side with plenty of rebels. Huger took full advantage of the confusion in Hooker's lines. He sent his expert riflemen to greet the attackers, and Hooker's men ran straight into the hellish musket fire of a perfectly synchronized volley blast from dozens of rebel guns.

The rain of bullets turned Hooker's charge into a panicked retreat. General Sickles, leading a brigade, described the morning debacle, *'the men fled in disgraceful confusion.'*

The fight might have gone badly for the Federals. At a critical point in the battle on Williamsburg Road, the one-armed Union Brigadier Commander, General Phil Kearney, led a Federal counter attack. As he came riding before the ranks of his troops he cried out to all that were in range of his shout, "I am a one-armed New Jersey son-of-a-bitch. Follow me."

The counter attack and his fearless challenge were successful. With three cheers from Kearney's brigade, the Confederates were forced to give ground to the fired-up Federals. Each side had lost a couple thousand men, but that was small change for any battle in the Civil War and no big thing in the larger scope of the more desperate fighting to come.

While the fighting was going on, George McClellan was three miles away. He was busy supervising the unloading of more supplies and arms at the Monroe base. When he got word of the fight he immediately sent a messenger to order Hooker to retreat. It was an odd order. Heintzelman had already sent plenty of reinforcements and they would have beaten back the rebels handily.

Luckily, McClellan heard of Heintzelman's action before his order had been carried out and a new attack was ordered. The Union men charged ahead a second time and retook the same 1000 yards they had given up after being ordered to retreat... all of which mystified Hooker and his men.

The Battle of Oak Grove was a minor affair as Civil War battles went. It is worth noting that that Battle was the *only offensive action* that McClellan undertook against Richmond. Still, it cost a thousand dead and wounded.

MECHANICSVILLE AND BEAVER CREEK DAM

The last battle of the military minuet, before McClellan finally gave up his attempt to invade Richmond, was June 26, 1862. It was at Mechanicsville near Beaver creek. A Union spy, pretending to be a new recruit for the rebel army, discovered that Lee was planning to take the offensive by sending Jackson to attack Porter's rear guard. The spy found McClellan and informed him what was about to happen. Upon receiving this news, General Porter had already expected Jackson's attack on the morrow.

"General," Porter told McClellan that morning, "I am quite willing to fight. Yesterday, at Beaver Creek, when A.P. Hill attacked my men, we took all that Lee sent against us."

"Jackson may attack your right flank," McClellan warned.

With that warning in his ears, Porter ordered his men to Mechanicsville to meet Confederate Commander A.P Hill and Stonewall Jackson.

The Confederates had been busy near Mechanicsville. For the first three weeks in June, A.P. Hill, now a Commander of the new Confederate Light Division, had been at work building earthwork defenses on the south side of the Chickahominy, east and west of the Mechanicsville bridges. By June 25, his Light Division was amassed in the woods southeast of Mechanicsville as part of Lee's plan to strike Porter's corps.

The Confederacy always identified General Ambrose Hill as A.P. Hill, to tell the difference from another Confederate general with the same last name, D.H. Hill. Ambrose Hill was an excellent general and a part of Stonewall Jackson's Left Wing. He was Jackson's opposite in many ways. Jackson was deeply religious and A.P. Hill was not. From their time together at West Point, Hill did not get along with Jackson. Hill, unlike Jackson, missed his classes and was an all-around Good-Time-Charley. Jackson was more reserved. He scorned levity and practiced his religion fervently. Nevertheless, Robert E. Lee called A.P. Hill his *'fightingest general.'*

Hill was known to be short-tempered. At one time, Hill and Longstreet were at such loggerheads with one another that Longstreet challenged Hill to a duel.

Hill had written a newspaper article in the *Richmond Examiner* that Jackson considered an insult. Lee resolved the argument by assigning Hill to Jackson's command. It was a good answer to the trying personnel problem. After Jackson was killed in 1863, Hill took Jackson's place as Commander of Lee's Left Wing.

Lee's original plan of attack at Mechanicsville was for A.P. Hill to advance into Mechanicsville against Porter but to wait for Jackson before his men left the woods. Magruder and Huger were to make a show on Porter's front of their intention to make an advance. Their 'demonstration' was meant to deceive Porter about what Jackson and A.P. Hill were doing secretly in Porter's rear. Then Jackson would attack.

As a part of Jackson's assault, A.P. Hill was supposed to move his division to Beaver

Dam Creek, Near Mechanicsville, and hit Porter's front lines with everything he had... but not until he heard Jackson's guns.

Each of the Confederate units did their part right on schedule as expected. Then, just when all was in readiness for the attack on Porter, Lee's plan fell apart; Jackson was late. Porter was kept busy and was making his position stronger. By 3 PM, still without having heard any sound of Jackson's guns, A.P. Hill began his attack anyway. With his 11,000 men and without orders from Lee, his men pressed forward emerging from the trees, and pushed into Mechanicsville to attack Porter.

Instead of resisting A.P. Hill's advance, Porter had his men pull back to the fortified heights above the town. The heights were tough to reach because of a natural barrier that faced the base of the slope. A creek surrounded by a fifteen-foot-wide swamp made a rapid assault on Porter's high position all but impossible.

Hill decided to assault the heights anyway. At 6 PM he gave the order to advance and his 11,000 Confederate troops attacked Porter's 14,000 well-entrenched Union soldiers. Porter was ready. His men were supported with six batteries of 32-pound rifles, howitzers and other artillery. The rebel division began climbing the hill. At the top were Porter's Pennsylvania men which included Berdan's Sharpshooters and John Reynolds' First Brigade, and there were none better.

The Confederates were instantly under fire from the Federals. The Federal guns ripped away at the Confederate attack and Hill's rebels suffered heavy casualties. By dusk the only rebels that had been successful in crossing the chest-high waters of the 15-foot wide swamp surrounding the creek was a Georgia regiment. They established a beachhead on the other side and made ready to storm the heights. But they could not remain there for long. Under heavy infantry fire from the Pennsylvanians, with Captain Mark Kern's Napoleons firing double canister into the rebels, the Confederate attack was doomed from the start.

Historical Note: Captain Kern was to fight again at the Battle of Second Manassas... and die there. Captain Kern was an exceptionally brave soldier. During that fight all his gun crews had been killed or were running. Kern tried to load and fire all six artillery pieces at the rebels without help. Confederates soldiers, seeing his bravery, called, "Don't fire at him." Captain Kern succeeded in aiming and firing one of his guns before he was finally shot and killed.

Without Jackson's support, the rebels began to crumble. Before they could be captured wholesale, A.P. Hill's men retreated back across the swamp and the creek. As night fell, the Confederates gathered up their wounded and their dead; a total of seventy-nine men. When it was over, Hill's troops were thrown back on their heels in confusion with *five times* the casualties that Porter had.

The Confederates intended to renew the attack the next morning but now one of those odd incidents happened, a situation which belied Jackson's reputation as an aggressive fighter. Jackson and his men were weary from their long march. After he arrived on the scene, instead of joining the fight, he made bivouac and he went to sleep. The fight that night raged within earshot of Jackson and his men, but they slept on.

The next day, General George McClellan, knowing Jackson's army was still close to his flank, became worried all over again that Jackson might try to break the Union's supply line on the Richmond and York railroad. Without a supply line McClellan would be forced to abandon his siege of Richmond. Continuing his usual cautious approach to all such dilemmas, McClellan ordered Porter to withdraw his force.

Part of the reason McClellan gave that order to Porter, even though Porter had gotten the best of the fight, was that Lee had fooled McClellan again. McClellan thought Huger and Magruder had a *much larger force* than it had. McClellan had another attack of the 'cautions' and Porter had to abandon his well-fortified position.

The Battle of Mechanicsville was a major Union tactical victory. The fight cost the Confederates heavy casualties and Robert E. Lee had failed to achieve any of his objectives. The fault lay with Lee. Instead of 60,000 men crushing Porter's flank, only a quarter, 15,000 troops, had seen action and they had been sent into the assault in parts and pieces. Overall, the rebels lost four times the men as Porter, 1400 to Porter's 350.

McClellan's generals urged McClellan to attack Magruder, who remained in the front position of most of the Army of the Potomac. McClellan, had he not been fooled by Magruder, had an overwhelming superiority. Magruder had been up to his old show business tricks. He had ordered small groups of men to parade back and forth and using groups of slaves beating drums to simulate a larger force. Also, to cap his magic with a showstopper, Magruder sent up a balloon tethered to a railroad car floating on a barge down the York River.

That was the last straw for the confused George McClellan; he was more certain than ever that Lee's forces far outnumbered his own. Although it was a tactical victory for the North, McClellan, from that time on, never regained the initiative.

GAINES' MILL

By the end of June, Porter had retired from Mechanicsville in good order. McClellan gave hurried instructions to *'head toward the James River Base in all haste,'* so Porter followed the orders to make haste, but his rear guard had not been sufficiently strengthened. As a result, McClellan's perennial fears and need to rush caused the loss by capture of some of Porter's men. Porter's Union reinforcements had arrived too late on the field.

Porter withdrew to another slow-moving stream called Boatswain's Creek. This place was an even better place to defend than the plateau above Beaver creek where he had been. Once there, his men set themselves in a new strong line around a crescent-shaped plateau 15 feet above the stream. Before him, where Lee was expected, the high ground faced the marsh and a fringe of pine trees stretching to the water. With General George Morell's First Division on the right and General George Sykes' Second Division on the left, McClellan's division was held in reserve. To complete his defenses, Porter deployed 80 pieces of artillery along the ridge behind him. To make his line stronger yet, crude breastworks were constructed from felled trees and pillaged fence rails. Rifle pits were dug then the boys in blue settled back to wait.

Porter was not yet out of danger. The Confederate forces of General Huger and General Magruder were coming. The 85,000 Confederates approaching his lines were several times larger than his own. Lee intended to use the strategy he had used the day before: A.P. Hill and Longstreet would pressure Porter, while D.H. Hill and Stonewall Jackson were supposed to hit Porter's right flank and rear.

General Daniel Harvey Hill, (called D.H. Hill to tell the difference between himself and A.P. Hill), had a powerful dislike of all things 'Yankee.' D.H. Hill began life as an iron worker. He worked and educated himself with great tenacity, and went on to become a professor of mathematics at a college in Virginia. While he was teaching at Washington University, he wrote a college textbook, written purely for the Southern market, The Elements of Algebra. The book, with sardonic scorn, pointed the finger of ridicule at all things 'Northern.' Even his word problem illustrations pictured Yankees as cowardly, fraudulent, and heartless individuals. The Southern characters that he used in the algebra problems were typified as kind, generous and brave. One example was this:

Problem: *A gentleman in Richmond expressed a willingness to liberate his slave, valued at $1000, upon the receipt of that sum from charitable persons. He received contributions from 24 persons. Of these contributions there were 14/19ths fewer from the North than from the South. The average donation from the Northerners was 4/5ths smaller than from the Southerners. What was the entire amount given by each?*

Answer: *The Northerners contributed $50 and the Southerners contributed $950.*

Unfortunately for D.H. Hill, in spite of his mathematical ability, he had misread his map and mistook Porter's true position and struck what he thought was Porter's *rear guard.* At one o'clock, near an old five-story gristmill, known as Gaines' Mill, D.H. Hill attacked a part of General Porter's *powerful front line.*

Porter had plenty of artillery waiting, along with Berdan's ace sharpshooters and well-fortified seasoned Union troops. After his attack was easily repulsed, General D.H. Hill, much chastened, decided to wait for Jackson, who was supposed to join in the attack as soon as he arrived. That was when Lee's main force of 12,000 Confederates, headed by General A.P. Hill, would also join in a massive attack.

The Confederate attack, when it finally came, was the largest of the war; 57,000 Confederates, six divisions, smashed against Porter's 34,000 Federals. A mile and a half past a country road and across an open field, the rebels came in a gray mass. The rebels started down a long grassy slope toward Boatswain's Creek… and hit smack up against Porter's defense line.

Porter's men had been battered all day, and now they were heavily outnumbered. Still they fought on and put up a strong resistance. Gradually the Federals were pushed back but they gave ground at an enormous cost to Lee's troops. Porter's colorful Zouaves, whose motto was, *'Death before Retreat,'* cut down an astounding sixty percent of the South Carolina regiment that tried to capture the Federal cannons. A.P. Hill's division, all told and counting the day before at Mechanicsville, *lost a quarter of his men* in the two fights with Porter's men.

Historical Note: The Zouaves were tough cookies. In spite of what by today's standards might have appeared somewhat feminine dress for a soldier, they patterned themselves after the most vicious and tenacious solders of the French-African and Turkish fighters from wars stretching past to the sixteenth century and a dozen wars.

Their uniform could be described as: a bright red chasseur cap with gold braid; a light blue shirt with moiré antique facings, a dark blue jacket with orange and red trimmings, brass bell buttons, placed as close together as possible, a red sash and loose red trousers reaching below the knee, and white waist belt. They won all drill competitions and McClellan described them as the best ideal of a soldier. During the Seven Days battles, they were in every battle. Porter's

Zouave troops lost more men (and inflicted more casualties on the enemy) than any other regiment.

D.H. Hill's attack on Porter's rear and right flank quickly turned out to be more than he had bargained for. He had expected a lightly defended rear guard but the result was a catastrophe. When McClellan heard how well the fight was going, he was elated. He told Porter to *'Pitch in. Reinforcements are coming over the river.'*

Porter never got the help he had been promised. On the south side of the river, where most of the Union army was, General Franklin had destroyed the bridges near his corps. At the same time, Lee's skeleton forces, Magruder especially, on that same south side of the river, flimflammed McClellan into believing Lee still had a massive force in front of his army so *he withheld the help he had promised Porter.*

Lee's assault came after the sun had set. Jackson had not come up yet so the two forces were about even in size; 34,000 to 32,000. However, Porter's defense position was good, and he had better artillery than the Confederates who were advancing over a quarter mile of open wheat field. Stonewall Jackson finally joined the fight and the massive rebel advance broke through Porter's line. Porter's reinforcements had arrived too late to fight but the new men filled the broken gaps quickly and made an orderly retreat possible. Porter withdrew across the Chickahominy River that night, burning the bridges behind him with his army still intact and well able to fight.

GARNETT'S AND GOLDING'S FARM

By now General Lee was convinced McClellan was heading for the James River. There were large clouds of dust south of the Chickahominy River and the Confederate troops were heartened at the sight. It was true. The Yankee's were pulling out. There was a half-hearted attack on "Baldy" Smith's Sixth Division but General Hancock repulsed the Georgians easily and inflicted 271 casualties.

Next day Toombs conducted a reconnaissance going over the pasture and skirting the woods on Golding's farm but the rebels charged his regiment and it turned into a larger fight. Two rebel regiments joined in the attack but Pennsylvanians and some New York infantry countered with another loss of 151 men.

CONFEDERATE PURSUIT

No matter that Porter's men had won their fights and were ready to counter attack but McClellan had already made up his mind. He believed that 200,000 Confederates were about to destroy his army. He had to reach his base at Harrison's Landing in safety before they attacked in force. McClellan saw he had two choices. He could assault the Confederate army south of the Chickahominy. If he did his army was larger with a good chance of going all the way to Richmond. Or he could retreat into the Peninsula. That move would give Lee the advantage and time to put his scattered rebel army together.

Despite the courage and determination to fight possessed by McClellan's men, Lee was certain McClellan would fold. An excellent demonstration of the mettle of the army's rank and file was General Fitz John Porter's stand at Gaines' Mill and Beaver Dam. General McClellan had called a war council. On the night of June 27, near midnight, Fitz John Porter listened with the other four corps commanders as

General McClellan gave his reasons for the retreat. Porter had his doubts.

Porter's later memoirs spoke for the opinions of most of the other generals at McClellan's staff meeting that day.

'That wasn't at all like General McClellan. He always made his own decisions. When he gave us his decision we were all set back on our heels. He was going to abandon our entrenchments before Richmond. The entire Army of the Potomac was moving to a new position on the James River. He called it a "change of base."'

'Some of the order made sense. Our food and supplies had been moved to Harrison's Landing on the James. What did not make sense was that the army would move also, under the protection of the navy's gunboats and wait for reinforcements from Washington. The rebels would cut the railroad supply from White House Landing. We weren't ready to quit.'

'Later, when the division commanders, Kearney and Hooker heard about the decision I was there when they rushed into McClellan's headquarters. Most of us heard some of what they were shouting and I was sure that George was going to fire both of them. I must say I agreed. But General McClellan gave me command of Fifth Corps just a week ago and I have always respected the man. Nobody could have put together this army so quickly. The men are ready and willing to fight.'

Phil Kearney, always willing to fight no matter the odds, was angry.

He was heard to say, *"Dammit, General. We can't quit. We can beat them and we can take Richmond. I know. I watched them attack my division and I saw them run like sheep when we drove them off at Gaines' Mill."*

Hooker spoke less but he swore once or twice. One time he said, *"It would be a damn shame to turn and run now."*

The fact was George McClellan believed his own lies. He believed the Confederates were fighting on their home ground and they outnumbered him. He had to have reinforcements before he did anything. McClellan could not bear the faintest possibility that the magnificent army he had made single-handedly might be destroyed. If that happened, and he lost his army, he would have to return to Washington in shame and disgrace. He *had* to save his army.

As McClellan later wrote to his wife, *'Certainly, some would call it a retreat, but when reinforcements arrive there is always the possibility of a new offensive against Richmond.'*

McClellan's newest plan for the retreat was this. He would send two corps to establish a foothold at Malvern Hill. While this defensive position was being held, the other three corps would stay behind to slow the Confederate pursuit so he could assemble his troops and wait for more men for a new advance on Richmond.

The Union Army move began late that night. On the morning of June 28, Robert E. Lee awoke in surprise *(and some relief, most likely)* to find the Yankees gone from the Chickahominy River's north bank. It had been done quietly; not a single rebel commander had any inkling what the Federals had been doing all night, so quietly and well executed was the move. Reports from his scouts came in a hurried gallop racing to bring the news. All the signs of a monumental retreat were there. Locomotives and cars at the White House Union Supply Depot had been set afire. Explosions signaled the destruction of Federal ammunition dumps. McClellan was pulling out.

SAVAGE STATION

Lee was a man with focus. With single-minded intensity, Lee sent his whole army to pursue and destroy the Army of the Potomac before McClellan could assemble the scattered forces or regain his courage. Longstreet, Jackson and the rest of Lee's men were sent to cut off and trap the fleeing Union troops. Lee felt a deep satisfaction; Richmond was saved. Now he had been given a new opportunity to force the Union to concessions and allow the Confederacy to exist in freedom from Federal domination.

Three miles east of Savage Station, General Magruder was fresh from his outstanding performance before the Union Army. He left his place before Richmond and joined in the pursuit of the fleeing Yankees. He found part of them at Savage Station, Sumner's Second Corps, who were acting as the Union rearguard. Most of McClellan's army was clustered around Savage Station waiting to get through the difficult crossing through White Oak Swamp. Nobody was in charge; the mob was leaderless. McClellan had moved on without leaving directions or a second-in-command.

The retreating Yankee corps did the best they could to keep some semblance of a coordinated command. Heintzelman's Third Corps, Sumner's Second Corps and Franklin's Sixth Corps were drawn up in lines with forty guns and half the entire Union army. Magruder, the feisty Confederate, was always willing to fight, whatever the odds and he went in to attack the Union rear guard, confident that Jackson was right behind him.

Jackson failed Lee again. He was nowhere to be found. For the third time in five days he was late so Magruder made his assault without Jackson. The Union forces held fast. Magruder's outnumbered troops finally had little choice except to pull back and wait for Jackson's 18,000 men.

The Union troops could have counter attacked and done so successfully... but they had their orders, unpalatable as they were, to *'hold the ground until dark, and then join the retreat.'* Lee's chance to capture the Federals had been bungled again. By the time Jackson arrived and fighting resumed, there was some hand-to-hand fighting but again the rebels were held. It hardly mattered; the Yankee artillery and supply wagons were well on their way to safety. The fight at Savage Station turned into a bloody mess. Without leadership, some brigades suffered heavy casualties. One Vermont regiment lost half their men. Even so, the battle ended in a stalemate and the Federal retreat continued.

One of the unpardonable results of McClellan's failures in leadership was the lack of care for his wounded. More than 2500 wounded Federal soldiers were left on the battlefields to the mercy of scarce medical attention and, if a wounded soldier survived, the miserable accommodations of a Confederate prison.

Lee must have been furious; for the *fourth time* Jackson had failed to do his part in the attack. The probable reason was just that Jackson and his men were worn to a nub from the constant fighting and marching with very little rest. After the battle, some of the Federal prisoners, taken by D.H. Hill's men, spoke to their jailers as they sat around the fire that night, chatting away. An episode told by a man who was there will give some idea of the closeness between the Confederates and the Federal soldiers as fellow countrymen... and not enemies... in better times. The subject of the present campaign was, naturally, a taboo subject. The talk was something like this:

Confederate soldier: "Do you know Old Man Billings in Chicago? He is a cabinet maker; he used to have a place at the corner of State Street."

Federal prisoner: "Oh yes, I know him very well. He is in the same place still. I have a brother who worked for him. One of his sons went south about two years ago."

Confederate: "Yes, that was Stephen. I knew him in New Orleans. He joined the New Orleans Cadets and went off with the Second Louisiana."

Federal: "He has two other sons; one of them is with us. The other is a Lieutenant in the 5th Illinois, and I think he is in Grant's army."

Confederate: "Does O'Malley and Robertson still carry on the foundry business there?

Federal: "Yes. Robertson is dead, but one of his sons carries on the business. Another of his sons is in the 7th Illinois... a Captain, I think."

A second man, a Confederate listening to the conversation, spoke out.

Confederate eavesdropper: "Do you know old Peterson that has a large gas fitting establishment in St. Louis? I think it is on Pelham Street."

Federal: "Yes. Some of his sons went down south a while ago."

Confederate: "Yes, two of them came down and started a branch business in St. Louis as agents for their father. One of them is now in our regiment... that is Donald Peterson. But the other one, Bernard, I think, went North in the Spring and could not get back, as the blockade has been put on Cairo.

Federal: "Well, I knew them both. Bernard joined the 7th Missouri, and is now with us in Curtis' division.

Confederate: "Are you not with Siegel's?"

At this point the Federal shook his head in warning to his comrade. The conversation was nearing a forbidden subject; the present campaign. Just then the order to move came. The prisoners were sent to the rear and the Confederate went forward to march to another position. The prisoner, the conversation over, bid goodbye.

Federal: "Well, goodbye, boys. Good luck to you and take care of yourselves."

Confederate: "Alright. We will try to do so. These great coats of yours are warm and comfortable, good for this weather."

Federal: "Yes, they are very warm, and they are needed for this weather. Goodbye."

The writer mused.

"I could not help reflecting on the manner of the conversation I had been hearing. What a strange thing was war, and particularly such a war as this. Here was a man in our company who had a brother who a year ago had been a member of our company. Now he was in the army opposed to us and with whom we would engage in deadly conflict within a few hours."

Another rebel soldier explained why the prisoners were forced to give up their coats to their captors.

"I could not blame our poor fellows for securing clothing of some kind. The greater numbers of us were ragged and dirty and good apparel could not be purchased for any price in Richmond."

GLENDALE AND FRAZER'S FARM

By the end of June, the bulk of the Union army had bivouacked on a field near the village of Glendale. Slocum's division of Confederates had come up within a mile of the Union army. He was ordered to attack the Federals. Instead of attacking, for reasons not known, Slocum's men spent an entire day hacking their way through dense woods to open a way for his troops to march to Glendale although they might have much more easily marched them *around* the woods.

Jackson also delayed an attack. He had his men repairing a bridge not far from Glendale when his men could have more easily forded the shallow stream below the burnt-out bridge and reached the Union army much sooner.

The Battle of Frazer's Farm, near the crossroad village of Glendale, finally began and was an example of one of those strange tricks of fate. Any science fiction writer might have found Slocum's and Jackson's needless delay a perfect excuse to wander off in fancy to an alternate reality, a world of 'IF.' Huger had Slocum's men spend hours in what became known as the 'Battle of the Axes,' when Huger might have taken an alternate route around the woods. Jackson made only feeble attempts to force back Federal troops who were on the other side of the river, so he could repair a bridge with an artillery duel that accomplished nothing.

IF the men of General Slocum's division had not spent hours felling trees to chop a road through thick woods to reach the battleground and IF Jackson had not wasted all day rebuilding a destroyed bridge when he might have easily forded the river, with Lee's army, Slocum and Jackson might have destroyed the Union Army at Frazer's Farm and won the war then and there.

Brigadier General Edward Alexander, commanding one of the rebel brigades, wrote, *'Never, before or after, did the fates put such a prize within our reach. It is my belief that on two occasions in the four years of the war, we were within easy reach of military successes so great that we might have hoped to end the war with our independence... the first was at Bull Run in July, 1861... The second chance we had (Battle of Frazer's Farm) impresses me as the best of all.'*

By noon of June 30, most of McClellan's army had crossed White Oak Swamp Creek. A third had reached the James River but the rest, except for Porter, were still marching between White Oak Swamp and the tiny community of Glendale on a road that led over to Malvern Hill and then to the James River.

Robert E. Lee was hard on the heels of the scattered Union army. He planned to attack the ragged, discontinuous lines of Federal troops, while they were bottle necked on the poor roadways leading to Harrison's Landing. Stonewall was ordered to press the rear guard at White Oak Swamp crossing. Then the rest Lee's army, 45,000 men, would attack at Glendale, two miles away. That would split the Union army in two. Lee would strike after Huger's division three miles out, as they came up to the Federals at Glendale. Longstreet and A.P. Hill, seven miles away, would follow Huger's attack with a massive second attack. Meanwhile, Confederate artillery would keep Porter busy on Malvern Hill before he had the time to set up a defense line.

Lee badly misjudged Fitz John Porter.

It was a good enough plan. The strategy was another chance for Lee to end the war—if it had worked—and Porter cooperated. Jackson's and Huger's late arrival changed the odds even more in the Confederate's favor.

There was plenty of hard fighting when the first rebels arrived and began to harass the Federal soldiers. There were breaks in the hurried Union defenses. But the Union army managed to resist the rebel onslaught with vicious up-close fighting that killed and wounded more than five thousand men. It was a bitter battle. Five generals were wounded. There was bitter hand-to-hand combat with bayonets and rifles used as clubs, and officers fought with their *(normally ornamental)* swords. Artillery was captured and retaken. More than anything else, it revealed in harsh reality the timber of the commanding general, George McClellan, who should have been with his army.

When it was over and the Confederates withdrew, the Federals kept on marching. Lee had failed to stop the Federal's *'change in position,'* as McClellan euphemistically phrased the retreat.

Three Civil War historians and writers expressed their opinions of McClellan's actions that day.

After McClellan had supervised the deployment of three corps near the Glendale crossroads, Ethan Rafuse wrote, 'What McClellan did next *almost defies belief.'*

While the fierce battle was going on, General George McClellan spent the afternoon on board the gunboat, *Galena,* dining on roasted fowl with Galena's captain and sailing briefly up the river to watch the gunboat shelling of a Confederate division that had been spotted marching toward Malvern Hill.

Brian K. Burton wrote that, *'More than any other day… McClellan's judgment on the thirtieth is suspect. He had arranged for signal communications between Malvern Hill and the river but that was a poor substitute. To leave the units of five different corps at a vital point with no overall commander was to court disaster.'*

Steven Sears wrote, 'When McClellan deserted his army at Glendale and at Malvern Hill *(Where Fitz John Porter might have turned the tide entirely in the Union's favor had he had his way)* during the Seven Days, General McClellan was guilty of dereliction of duty.'

McClellan, who had not been a witness to any of the fighting, in spite of the chaos and confusion going on around him, sent a *triumphant wire* to the War Department in Washington. McClellan's message ignored any reference to what most men would have regarded as a flat dereliction of duty; his absence from the battlefield.

'My army has behaved superbly and have done all that men could do. If none of us escape, we shall at least have done honor to the country. I shall do my best to save the army.'

It was a self-serving, flat out fabrication (except for his reference to the courage of the fighting Federals, which deserved acclaim). *McClellan* then had the chutzpah and a further revelation of his blind ignorance of the enemy's true strength, or lack thereof. He asked for something he knew he could not have: *'I need 50,000 more troops. Then I shall retrieve our fortunes.'*

Part of the Union army's good fortune in escaping destruction at Glendale was the fault of the rebel commands. After the battle, Lee wrote, *'Could the other commands have cooperated in this action, the result would have proved most disastrous for the enemy.'*

D.H. Hill said, 'Had all our troops been at Frazer's Farm, there would have been no Malvern Hill.'

Lee joined Jackson as they pursued the Federals. Jackson was in the vanguard and Lee, still bitter, although he kept his anger hidden, spoke up. Once, when one of his officers voiced his concern that the enemy might get away, Lee's comment was short but meaningful: *'Yes he will get away because I cannot have my orders carried out.'*

❧ 20 ❧

Malvern Hill

Malvern Hill is not a hill. It is more of a plateau a mile-and-a-half long and three-quarters of a mile wide. The crest is more than a hundred feet high. On the south there is the swampy ground next to the James River. High ravines and creek runoff separate the Hill from the land below. If the Federals were looking for a good place to defend against an army, Malvern Hill was such a place.

Major General Fitz John Porter was at Malvern Hill, three miles ahead of Lee. Taking Malvern Hill and crushing Porter's men was another chance for Lee to smash the Union army. However, this time Lee was up against Fitz John Porter and Porter was a different kind of soldier from George McClellan. Porter stood in his way and held the 150-foot-tall eminence known as Malvern Hill. He was not about to give way easily to anyone without a good fight.

This time Jackson was on the scene. He was more ready for battle than he had been for several days.

Lee was overheard to say before the battle, "This battle will be *the opportunity of my life.*"

If he could destroy Porter's corps, he would be in position to overrun the remaining leaderless, disorganized Union forces as they struggled away from Glendale on their way to the defenses on the James River. Victory and recognition for the Confederacy was in sight.

One last obstacle to overcome would give Lee and the Confederacy that victory. That obstacle was Major General Fitz John Porter. Porter and his men had the assignment of holding Lee and the Confederate army. He had stopped on Malvern Hill and he had made his place secure against the coming enemy forces. Then he waited for Lee.

During the early days of the Civil War there were turning points for the North as well as the South. There were times and battles when an inept general fighting an enemy, who did all the right things, might have ended the war.

The battle of Glendale was such a place and a time. Gettysburg was another. Had General Lee listened to Longstreet at Gettysburg, and gone *around* the Union army instead of a hopeless direct attack up a hill covered with scores of accurate Union cannons, Lee might have reached Washington and forced a peace. The Battle of Malvern Hill was another such turning point... if Porter had been in charge of the Union strategy instead of McClellan.

The Battle of Malvern Hill didn't work out that way for Lee. Porter's men, holding the Hill, nearly destroyed *Lee's army*. They would have changed the tide of the war if McClellan had not completely lost his nerve. His frightened insistence after the fight to continue the retreat closed any remaining possibility of a Northern victory. He had turned his back to a speedy end to the war when he chose *not* to follow up Porter's advantage at Malvern Hill.

Malvern Hill was the last battle of the Seven Days. It was also the first time when the Union army occupied good ground. The broad plateau had excellent visibility, Porter had cleared the slope of timber and the open fields to the northern side could be swept by the deadly fire of Porter's 250 cannons. He was further supported by three gunboats and the navy guns on the nearby James River. Porter had arranged his defensive lines in a wide semi-circle all along the northern rim of the plateau. Morell was on the right with his division and Kearny and Hooker, from Heintzelman's divisions were on the left.

By Monday afternoon on June 30, McClellan's army stretched for a dozen miles with its head resting on Malvern Hill and the remaining Federal troops coming up fast. Three divisions, 16,000 men and nearly a hundred guns, farther to the rear behind the front line infantry, were primed and ready. Another 13 huge siege guns had been hauled up the hill and more guns were here and there to meet any attack from any direction.

Lee formed a crescent of men a mile wide, ringing the base of the plateau. To shake up the Union defenders on Malvern Hill, Longstreet planted forty cannon on a smaller hill not far away. When they fired, the Confederates would charge up the slopes screaming the fearsome rebel yell. So sure of victory, Lee elected to attack Porter directly, instead of a flank attack.

Despite the opposition of Lee's general, D.H. Hill, Lee mounted a direct attack at Malvern Hill. Lee was mistakenly confident that one final push would work. Later, in a tragic replay at Gettysburg in 1864, Longstreet counseled Lee against another direct attack to no avail.

Once again, things went wrong for the Confederates. Jackson was late. His guides had sent him on the wrong road and away from the battlefield. Huger's division and D.H. Hill's division were sent forward instead. They waited for the rebel artillery to soften the enemy on the plateau. The Confederate guns blasted off but, unfortunately, Porter's artillery opened first. From 1 PM to 2:30 PM that afternoon, Hunt, Porter's artillery chief, launched the greatest artillery barrage of the war.

The Union gunners were good. The Confederate guns had been placed close together on a hill and the Union guns quickly disabled most of them... along with blasting the advancing rebel troops. Huge 50-pound shells were lobbed from the three gunboats a mile away on the James River, further spreading havoc and destruction in the ranks of the rebel attackers. Nevertheless, D.H. Hill and 18,000 men started forward.

At 4:30 Porter saw their dust drawing near and sent 30 guns firing at the approaching rebels. At the same time, on Porters' signal, US Navy gunboats sent 100 pound missiles screaming through the air. The frightful missiles were so huge the rebels called them lampposts as they fell like the fingers of God with dreadful damage on the Confederate troops.

The next day was nearly a repeat of the day before; the Confederates were on open ground and the Federals were higher up, on the plateau. During the night Porter had taken more steps to build a stronger defense line. Lee knew this of course but he expected Longstreet any moment on his right, and for Jackson and D.H. Hill's brigade to arrive shortly.

At half past two in the afternoon A.P. Hill sent his brigades on a half-mile wide front to strike hard at the center of Porter's line just as the Federal cannons opened up. The Union riflemen sent a sheet of flame at the attackers. The beleaguered attackers, their view of the terrain blocked by smoke, struggled through the mire of the marsh and mud up to their ankles. Hampered by the dense pine trees on the banks, the rebels lost all order and struggled blindly in all directions. Those few that got through and reached the top of the ravine clashed with Sykes' *'Death before Dishonor'* Zouave troops.

Some said there never was a hotter fight. The musket fire was so intense that saplings and brush were cut down as though with a mower. Tremendous crashes of the artillery made the ground move like an earthquake. Soldiers on both sides ran in panic for shelter from the destruction of the muskets and the artillery.

At sunset there was a lull. The Union's men hoped it was over, but Stonewall Jackson sent one last overpowering massive attack at the Northern troops. The Union's senior engineer, Brigadier Barnard, had been scouting the country to the west of the fighting while the attack at Beaver Creek Dam was going on. Brigadier Barnard saw Jackson coming with 55,000 rebel troops about to take Porter's flank. Porter's supply line of 35,000 men was threatened. Barnard had one of his men ride to tell Porter what was coming.

'It was the most desperate charge I ever saw,' one Confederate soldier, who had survived and witnessed the charge wrote. Sixty percent of the rebels never escaped the fire. Nearly a third of Sykes' front line defenders suffered as well in the hand-to-hand clubbing and fighting. The fight went on for more than an hour and a half until, for a time, it ended.

A.P. Hill said of his men, "Brave men had done all that any soldiers could do."

Some of the Alabama boys of Ewell's division reached the stream and sank to their shoes in the mud of the marsh. The red-legged Federal Zouaves sent a wave of musket fire down on them. The Alabamans tried their best to reach the three-tiered Federal line but failed. Regiment after regiment rushed back to the Confederate lines in total disorder and confusion. Porter's men killed or wounded twenty percent of their attackers.

Two of the best Union divisions, led by Hooker and Kearny, were the first hit. Some broke through with hand to hand fighting and bayonets. Fresh Union troops staved off the charge and Kearny mounted a counter attack that restored the lines. By nightfall the closest that any of Lee's men had reached to the center of the

Union lines was no more than 600 feet.

Even Jackson was impressed.

He said to Trimble, who wanted to try once again to stop the Union artillery, "General Hill has just tried with his entire division and been repulsed. I guess you'd better not try it."

D.H. Hill wrote afterward, *'It wasn't war, it was murder.'*

The Union line broke but reformed, filled in the gaps, and held. A.P. Hill and his Confederates followed on Jackson's heels. What saved the faltering Union forces was that Jackson's attack had been late for the second time. Lee had struck Porter's line with everything he had.

By mid-afternoon the battle rolled around Boatswain's Swamp. Twilight in the ravines trapped smoke and made a fog that dropped visibility to zero. The unending din of cannon stabbed at the darkness with 15-foot flames. Rebel casualties filled the two acres of the broad plain leading to the crest of the hill in no time. McClellan, at his headquarters, could not hear the sounds of the battle and without messengers he was unaware of the action.

A bitter tale it is to tell, and there is no doubt that it happened that day at Malvern Hill. It was a story so heart-breaking and so much a poignant reminder of the depths of human misery that was possible during the Civil War that the story was retold later. A Confederate Irish officer, who fought that day, was there. Captain D.P. Conyngham tells the story of a father and a son typified one of the greater tragedies of a Civil War where brother fought brother, and father fought son:

"I had a Sergeant Driscoll, a brave man and one of the best shots in the brigade. When we charged at Malvern Hill, a company of the enemy was posted in a clump of trees, and kept up a fierce fire on us. Their officer seemed to be a daring reckless boy, and I said to Driscoll, *'If that officer is not shot down, many of us will fall before we pass that clump of tree.'*"

"Driscoll raised his rifle, and in that moment the officer exposed himself. Bang went Driscoll and over went the officer, his company at once breaking away and falling back. As we passed the place I asked Driscoll to see if that officer is dead; he was a brave fellow."

"I stood looking on. Driscoll turned him over on his back. The wounded officer opened his eyes for a moment, and faintly murmured, *'Father.'* Then Driscoll's son closed his eyes forever. I will forever recollect the frantic grief of Driscoll. It was harrowing to witness. The dead officer was his son who had gone South before the war."

"And what became of Driscoll afterward? Well, we were ordered to charge, and I left him there; but as we were closing with the enemy, he rushed up with his coat off. Clutching his musket, he charged right up to the enemy, calling on the men to follow. He soon fell but jumped up again. We knew he was wounded. On he dashed, but soon rolled over like a top. When we came up to him he was dead, riddled with bullets."

On July 2nd, Lee was as close to defeat as it is possible to be without declaring surrender. When he realized Malvern Hill could not be taken he asked for a truce so that the five thousand wounded and dead could be cleared away.

That statement of battle casualties and what happened to the wounded men afterward, in this fight and in all of the battles of the Civil War, is the sad story that was never told in all its sorry detail to the mothers, fathers, wives, and friends at home. Later in the war, women were used to assist the medical teams at the hospitals. Louisa May Alcott, the author of *Little Women*, volunteered as a nurse, along with many women, North and South. Alcott told of her experience:

"After receiving the Governor's approval and the necessary passes to one of the military hospitals in Washington, I traveled by steamer, by train and by carriage from Boston to Washington. When I arrived I asked the woman in charge, *'What am I supposed to do?'* She instructed me, *'You will wash, dress, warm and nurse them for the next three months. You will count yourself fortunate if you get to bed by midnight.'"*

"The first thing I met when I entered the wards was a regiment of the vilest odors that ever assaulted the human nose. Armed with lavender water, I besprinkled myself that I became known to the patients as the *'nurse with the bottle.'*

"When I reached the main hall I paused to take my breath and survey. There they were, our *'brave boys'* as the papers justly called them... cowards could hardly have been so riddled with shot and shell, so torn and shattered, or have borne the suffering for which we have no name. Each bore his injuries with such uncomplaining fortitude, which made one glad to cherish each like a brother."

"In they came, some on stretchers, some in men's arms, some feebly staggering along propped up on rude crutches, and one lay stark and still with covered face as a comrade gave his name to be recorded before they carried him away to the dead house. The sight of several stretchers, each with its legless, armless or desperately wounded occupant admonished me. I was there to work."

The men Louisa May Alcott wrote about were men from the Battle of Fredericksburg. But it was like this in every battle of the Civil War. For every man killed two died of disease, bad drinking water, poor clothing or mosquitoes and malaria. Most doctors didn't wash their hands and often the wounded man died of infection. The only treatment for a broken arm or a broken leg was to amputate the limb.

On the battlefield the wounded men often had to lie on the battle ground for several days before a horse-drawn ambulance could come to carry them away to a field hospital. The field hospital was usually no more than a tent or a cattle barn, and the surgeon worked on manure-covered floors.

On Malvern Hill, by afternoon, the sounds of the Battle had fallen away. A courier rode up to Porter's headquarters, dismounted, saluted, and handed General McClellan's orders to Porter. The courier recalled that moment.

"General Porter read the dispatch. I saw a frown on his face. When General Porter received the order to retreat he turned to his adjutant with the greatest reluctance. *'Lieutenant,'* he said, *'Give the order to bring our guns off Malvern Hill after dark. Then start toward Harrison's Landing.'"*

After winning a smashing victory, Porter did not want to retreat. McClellan was unaware that Robert E. Lee had gone to bed that night believing he'd been defeated and that Richmond was in even greater peril from the Union army. Porter had ample reason to guess that was the case for the beaten Confederate General. Once again, if McClellan had followed a fighting General's sureness of victory, the tide almost certainly would have turned for the Union. Instead, McClellan had chosen to retreat.

McClellan heard the news of Porter's fight on Malvern Hill. After refusing to reinforce Porter with more of the 60,000 troops he had available, McClellan sent a telegraph message to Secretary of War Stanton. *'If I save this army now, I tell you plainly that I owe no thanks to you or any other persons in Washington. You have done your best to sacrifice this army.'*

The military supervisor of telegraphs censored the most egregious part of the communique but Stanton heard of it. Not only had George McClellan made a bitter enemy of Stanton *(who never forgave a slight)*, but worse yet President Lincoln had been insulted. McClellan's words would come back to haunt him. And, his words may have been a direct cause for Secretary of War Edwin Stanton's vendetta for all things *'McClellan.'* After Second Manassas, to Porter's great misfortune, Stanton's bitter hatred of McClellan came to include McClellan's favorite General, Fitz John Porter.

With the darkness of the coming night, the firing of muskets died away. The only sounds from the battlefield were the moans and cries of those who were wounded and still alive. Lee had lost 20,000 men and Porter had saved McClellan's army. Lee had enough. He no longer wanted to destroy the Union army. All he wanted to do was to take his tattered forces back to Richmond and begin the repairs and rest they badly needed.

Watching Porter follow the bulk of the army to Harrison's Landing, it is recorded that Lee said, *'In view of the condition of our troops who have been marching and fighting for seven days under the most trying circumstances, it was determined to withdraw, in order to afford them the repose they so badly needed.'* Much later, Lee also said, *'General Porter's defense at Malvern Hill was an extraordinary arm of McClellan's army.'*

Although persistent caution ruled all his decisions, General McClellan relied on Porter more than any other of his officers. Whenever McClellan was away to Washington or other places as a part of his military responsibilities, it was Fitz John Porter who took up the slack and acted as his surrogate. Porter acted boldly and bravely on Malvern Hill.

That single victory cemented Fitz John Porter's reputation as a man ready for a fight and never to retreat without good reason. Porter's guns had slaughtered General A.P. Hill's gray-shirted rebels by the hundreds. Lee and Jackson had been repulsed with great losses.

Confederate D.H. Hill said later that with Yankee artillery and Confederate infantry he believed Porter could whip anybody on earth.

AFTERMATH

The numbers of the casualties of the wounded and dead after the Peninsula Campaign and the Seven Days of fighting that followed was appalling. By the end of the Peninsula Campaign, from June 25 to July 3, 1862, thirty thousand men died or were wounded. The total number of casualties for the first half of 1862 was the equal of all the battles in the western theater, including the terrible battle of Shiloh. The numbers, read as cold statistics, makes one numb to their meaning.

Even to be wounded meant probable death or dismemberment at the hands of the overworked medical people. There were anesthetics, but the causes of infection were not yet understood. The chances for a wounded soldier to recover from any serious wound were seven to one. And, if you lived, you were nearly certain to face a long period of infection. One man in fifty was discharged with one or more missing or useless arms or legs.

Most of the casualties were from bullets. Only one man in twenty was injured from artillery fire. Although there were some bayonet charges, only one man in two hundred was wounded by a bayonet or a saber. Bullets were bad enough. The Civil War muskets fired a soft lead pellet that weighed about one ounce and was the size of the end of your thumb. When the bullet struck flesh the lead flattened and lost shape on impact and made a huge ugly wound. When a minie ball struck bone, the ball shattered bone fragments like spaghetti and carried bits of bone fragments into the body to lodge in the soft tissues, increasing the likelihood of sepsis and amputation. For the wounded prisoners it was worse, especially the Northerners that were captured. The South was fighting hard just to keep their fighting men fed and clothed. The war for everyone, still in its early stages, was already becoming a hard row to hoe for everyone.

After the Federals had left the field as the rear guard under orders of retreat for McClellan's *'change in position,'* the rebels swooped over the battlefield. Rich in spoils, the Confederate soldiers gathered up cannons, brass and bronze field pieces, caissons, horses, camps, clothing, small arms, banners and the insignia of war. All fell into their hands and the Union dead and wounded were stripped of clothing. Malvern Hill was the end of the Peninsula Campaign. McClellan was sent to Northern Virginia to reinforce Pope while Lee turned his eyes on Washington.

Union General
John Pope

❧ 21 ❧

Chess Game

General George McClellan, like a little Napoleon, had started with such high hopes. Now he was finished. Sadly, he lacked the fighting spirit that Lee, Longstreet and Jackson possessed. A strong fighting spirit was essential for any general in any war. Lincoln was fed up with McClellan's perennial 'case of the slows,' and his extreme caution and unwillingness to take chances when the potential benefits were great enough to outweigh the perils. The lack of that quality in the Union's most important military position was losing the war. McClellan had lost Lincoln's support and the president was convinced McClellan had to be replaced. The North and President Lincoln needed a man who would show more fight.

McClellan heard the rumors. He saw the handwriting on the wall of his future replacement and McClellan made what was for him a herculean effort to move a little faster than his usual pace. McClellan looked to Burnside for help. General Burnside had been in a few battles and he had a reputation as a fighter. General Ambrose Burnside was supposed to join McClellan soon. Then, with Burnside, he would advance on Richmond and prove he possessed the warlike belligerence needed to win the war.

Despite Little Mac's sudden conversion to fierceness, Abraham Lincoln had already made other plans. What McClellan intended wasn't good enough. On July 1, Lincoln turned to another man of Kentucky, like himself, who might give him the fight he needed as major general: John Pope.

General John Pope was a friend and a fellow Republican and he had been in Lincoln's escort at his inauguration. After some minor victories in the west Lincoln believed that here was a general who would fight and Pope was chosen to replace George McClellan.

Lincoln was also painfully aware that the Union armies lacked coordination. A strong general-in-chief was imperative. Until U.S. Grant came to the fore a year later to claim the job, Lincoln had few generals to choose from. Until one could be found, he gave Henry Halleck the job.

Halleck was an old general in semi-retirement. He was taken from his office and his papers and ordered to take field command of the *United Northern Armies*, coordinating the effort of the Federal forces and a dozen separate armies for the first time. A bureaucrat more than a soldier, Halleck's cold abrasive personality alienated his subordinates. One observer described Halleck as a *'cold, calculating owl.'* Lincoln rated him as *'little more than a first-rate clerk.'* He was no man for that job and other men like Burnside and McClellan, when given orders, did not always obey and mostly ignored Halleck.

General McClellan was still a man with powerful friends in high places in the Democratic Party. To lighten the blow of demotion, he was told that he would continue to direct the operations in Virginia but John Pope was given the reins for a new assault against Lee.

Halleck looked over the confused military situation and decided the best move was to bring McClellan home to Washington. With a combined army of 150,000 men, McClellan and Pope, together, could march down the Peninsula like a steamroller and finish off Lee.

Pope, in his new (yet unofficial) position, was assigned three jobs: to make certain the capitol was not threatened, to protect the Shenandoah Valley, and to go after Lee. Pope was given General Irvin McDowell's army, which had been guarding Washington D.C., and Porter's powerful Fifth Corps of battle-trained regulars. A third army was promised. Franklin's corps never arrived, thanks to another attack of McClellan's 'slows,' until after the Battle of Second Manassas was over. It was a little too late to help.

A total of 20,000 men were taken from McClellan's command and given to Pope. With McDowell aboard and Porter and Banks joining him soon, on July 14, 1862, Pope started toward Gordonsville with 50,000 troops to find Robert E. Lee.

Lee was a canny strategist, He knew the odds and he knew he was in trouble again. Confederate spies had informed General Lee of Union plans to beef up the Yankee forces to a size *(if it was at all handled well)* that might spell out the demise of the Confederacy.

At the moment Lee's army was camped between two Yankee forces. Pope was coming down the Peninsula from Washington, and McClellan was holed up with his fifty thousand troops at the Union Base of Harrison's Landing on the James River, twenty miles from Richmond.

Lee reasoned, being the aggressive fighter that he was, that if he could finish off the lesser of the two armies, the force headed by John Pope *(not yet reinforced)*, he could handle McClellan at his leisure. Robert E. Lee's bedrock strategy of operating against a larger enemy was his method to strike hard at parts and pieces before the enemy could set its full strength against him.

General Lee, stationed with most of his army near Gordonsville, decided to go for Pope. His Confederates, like a wolf pack hunting down the weaker prey, would peel off the weakest part of the enemy, starting with Pope. General James Longstreet and General Thomas J. 'Stonewall' Jackson, his left and right wings, were instructed to begin the new offensive and hit Pope hard.

James Longstreet, tall, bearded, taciturn, commanded the First Corps. Lee called him *'My old war horse,'* an indication how much Lee depended on him.

His enemies were soon to learn a fact about James Longstreet; in spite of this less-than-perfect offensive against Porter's Federals at Malvern Hill, General Longstreet was no man to be treated with indifference. In the words of biographer and historian Jeffrey D. Wert, *'Longstreet was the finest corps commander in the army of Northern Virginia. He was, in fact, arguably the best corps commander in the conflict on either side.'*

James Longstreet was a superlative general and fighting man. However, Fitz John Porter, given the time and the opportunity, might have proved his superiority to nearly any general, North or South. Porter never had an opportunity to prove his standing because of his trial, conviction and the early end of his career.

After the First Battle of Manassas (Bull Run), Longstreet's trusted staff officer, Moxley Sorrel, wrote of Longstreet's occasional flares of temper.

'When the Confederate army at the First Battle of Bull Run (Manassas) defeated McDowell and the Federals were running from the field in confusion, Longstreet and the other commanders had been ordered not to pursue the enemy. Longstreet was in a fine rage; he dashed his hat to the ground and stamped. Bitter words escaped him. Longstreet said, 'Retreat? Hell, the Federal army is broken to pieces.'

At the Battle of Gettysburg, Longstreet disagreed with Lee but, nevertheless, sent Pickett against the Federals in a disastrous charge. That, and the fact that Longstreet joined the Republican Party after the war and served with his old friend Ulysses Grant, made his name anathema to his old friends in the South.

Thomas *'Stonewall'* Jackson commanded the famous 'foot cavalry' of the Second Corps; named for their ability to cover the land rapidly by marching for long periods with little rest when speed was called for. Humorless, gawky, with a killer's blue eyes, Jackson was a fire and brimstone Presbyterian. A teetotaler, Jackson never drank and a story was told of Jackson by a friend.

Colonel A.R. Boteler said, "It was after ten o'clock at night, *May 30, 1862*, during the Peninsular Campaign, when I returned to headquarters for final instructions for our move against the Federals. Before going up to the General's room I ordered two whiskey toddies to be brought up after me. When they appeared I offered one of the glasses to Jackson, but he drew back, saying, *'No, Colonel, you must excuse me; I never drink intoxicating liquors.'*"

"I know that, General," says I, "But as you habitually abstain, as I do myself, from everything of the sort, there are occasions, and this is one of them, when a stimulant will do us both good. So you must make an exception to your rule, and join me in a toddy tonight."

"He again shook his head, but took the tumbler and sipped its contents. Presently, putting it on the table after but partially having emptied it, he said, *'Colonel, do you know why I habitually abstain from intoxicating drinks?'*"

"On my replying in the negative, he continued: *'Why, sir, because I like the taste of them. And when I discovered that to be the case, I made up my mind at once to do without them altogether.'*"

Jackson hardly looked the part of the sharply uniformed military man. He always wore a mangy broken-visored cadet's forage cap he had acquired during the Mexican-American war. Yet there was no man with more fight and determination to win. He was a disciplinary martinet, taciturn, humorless and a man of secrets. Jackson's first rule of strategy was always to mystify, mislead, and surprise the enemy.

Lee sent his two best generals to crush Pope before Pope could join McClellan and before McClellan could send Pope the promised reinforcements. That was a move neither Pope nor McClellan expected.

22

Cedar Mountain

"I want Pope suppressed."

Those were Lee's angry words when he learned that Pope had taken charge of the Union Army. Lee had no use for Pope. He considered Pope a braggart and a man without principle. Pope's war on civilians, his threats to shoot civilian hostages if guerillas attacked him, John Pope's promise of an all-out war, especially on the Southern civilian population, enraged Lee as few other matters could.

The three General Orders Pope had given to his troops that enraged Lee, were especially horrendous to all Southerners. They were Numbers 5, 7, and 11. These three orders were hard examples of Pope's determination to make the war a no-quarter-given conflict. To the Southerner, used to a polite sort of old-world military exchange, Pope's dictates were insulting and ungentlemanly to the extreme.

It is easy to understand the Southern view; Southerners believed in the total rightness of their cause. If you were to ask any Southern man or woman, who read the papers and knew what the war was about, he (*or she*) most probably would have answered, "We have the legal right to secede."

The South saw the rules as a license for Pope's troops to wage total war against civilians and word of the Orders spread through the South like wildfire. Pope was hated as few Northern generals had ever been hated and the Southern newspapers labeled him an 'uncivilized brute.' What were these heavy rules that raised such a hue and cry of outrage among the citizens of the Confederacy?

Order Number 5 was a license for any soldier in Pope's army to take food and property from the civilian population as they wished. The hollow promise of 'vouchers' payable after the war *provided* the victim was somehow able to prove his *'loyalty,'* meant next to nothing to the victim of theft.

Order Number 7 punished civilian attacks against the Union army. The order went far beyond that. If your neighbor was proven to be a guerilla, acting to sabotage the Union army, the perpetrator, his family and all *'citizens within a five-mile radius of the guilty person were held equally responsible'* for the sabotage. The guilty person (*and his innocent neighbors*) were required to pay an indemnity to offset the cost of the damage or the loss. The perpetrator could be shot on the spot and his house could be razed to the ground.

Order Number 11 forced all Southerners in the path of the army to swear allegiance to the United States. If they refused *(remember, these Southerners were as loyal to the Confederacy as any Federal citizen was to the Union)* they would be uprooted from their home and *'sent beyond the extreme lines of the army's pickets.'* If any of the dispossessed tried to get home again they would be shot as spies.

General Orders 5, 7, and 11 were the same as if a criminal band of marauders forced their will on any Southerner caught by Northern soldiers. A fourth order, Order Number 19 made a weak attempt to smooth over the harshness of the first three orders but without success.

Jefferson Davis had his innings. When he learned of Pope's orders Davis ordered that all captured Union officers to be imprisoned and charged as felons. These harsh attitudes by both sides toward a stubborn enemy was as old as recorded history. In Pope's defense he applied what he believed was a necessary military maxim against a determined and dangerous enemy. In fact, later in the war Grant authorized his Deputy, Sherman, to lay waste the land as he marched to the sea. It was still early in the war. Neither the South nor the North had yet come to accept the bitter truth: they were in a fight to the death.

The Seven Days Battle had ended. McClellan had pulled in his horns. He was no longer a threat to Richmond. Pope's forces, along with Nathaniel Banks' and Franz Siegel's corps, had deployed their troops in a wide arc across Northern Virginia. Pope waited for reinforcements from McClellan and he would soon have Porter's, Heintzelman's and Franklin's corps. They were to join him on the Rappahannock River line. Once McClellan caught his wind Richmond would be in trouble again.

By the middle of July, Pope was on his way to link up with McClellan's 80,000 troops. Contrary to good strategy, Pope divided his army along the Rapidan River. Lee knew this and Lee's plan was simple. Since McClellan wasn't doing much of anything near Richmond, Lee took a calculated guess that 'Little Mac' would stay where he was. Lee also knew that Pope had sent Banks' corps out in front of the other parts of the Union forces and was near Cedar Mountain. From all the reports he was getting from Stuart's cavalry and from a host of his rebel spies, the Union forces were spread pretty thin.

Lee decided to attack Pope's lead unit before it could retreat or be reinforced. That was General Banks' corps, which was riding shotgun as Pope's army moved south. Lee sent Jackson's three divisions to Gordonsville with 12,000 men to isolate that part of Pope's army near Culpepper. Lee reasoned that after Jackson had eliminated Banks with his larger force, Lee and Longstreet would follow Jackson and attack Pope's center.

No Confederate general had more fight in him but Jackson's failing was one that the astute Lee recognized; Jackson kept his battle plans a secret that was known only to Jackson. For a commander, who faces a major emergency and has not been informed about his superior's plan of battle, the decision he is forced to make can be the wrong one and might even lose the battle. Knowing Jackson's habit of keeping his officers too often in the dark about his plans, Lee's letter to his left wing included some helpful hints. In his letter to Thomas Jackson, Lee wrote, *'Allow me to advise you to inform your division commanders of your movements. You will save much trouble in arranging details and they can act more intelligently...'*

Sad to say, Jackson did not always listen. His habit of secrecy caused trouble for him at Cedar Mountain. Whatever Stonewall Jackson's failings, when the chips were down and there was an enemy before him, the crusty general was not a man to quit a fight no matter the odds.

The Cedar Mountain fight with Nathaniel Banks was a prime example of the worst of Jackson's failings. His forces were sent into the fight piecemeal fashion. He lost more men than he would have lost otherwise if he had gone against Banks with all his force at once. Not only that, but Jackson's problem of secrecy from his officers caused a delay when Ewell and A.P. Hill's divisions, coming to Gordonsville on alternate routes, got mixed up and they were late getting to the battlefield.

Stonewall Jackson was always ready for a fight. His opponent, Nathaniel Banks, was also ready and quite willing to fight. Before the battle at Cedar Mountain, Jackson told his staff physician, Hunter McGuire, *'Banks is in our front and he is generally willing to fight, and he generally gets whipped.'*

Banks did not intend to allow Jackson to whip him again. General Nathaniel Banks, self-taught from boyhood, had started as a bobbin boy in a cotton factory and worked his way up to editor of a newspaper. He became a congressman and then Speaker of the House of Representatives. The officer facing Stonewall was not only willing to fight, but General Banks was an angry man with something to prove. He had been beaten badly by Jackson in June at the Rapidan River and now he intended to set the record straight.

In blistering heat the order came down to the Federal troops, *'Get ready to march on five minutes' notice with two days cooked rations and 150 rounds of ammunition per man.'* Within an hour they were on the march and, in the heat and loaded down with the heavy load of equipment, ammunition and rations, the men began to fall by the wayside.

As Banks' men passed through Culpepper, secessionist citizens who favored the Southern split with the North and knew Jackson was on his way to fight Pope's men, called out from the sidewalks and houses to the soldiers, *'Old Jack will give you all you want'* and *'You'll come back double quick if you come back at all.'*

August was unusually warm and marching with a heavy pack was hot work. By the morning of August 9, Jackson had closed on Banks' division on Cedar Mountain and the fight began not far from the Culpepper Courthouse. Banks with 8,000 men was reinforced with Ricketts' division and King's division was on the way to help.

Jackson was on the way as well and it was hot going. Choking dust followed the line of march for the Confederate soldiers. Jackson, always ready to go to the attack, sent Brigadier Jubal Early's brigade (Ewell's division) against the vanguard of Banks' skirmishers south of Culpepper Road near the Crittenden farm.

It was late afternoon when the two sides met in the shadow of Cedar Mountain. Jackson's men came up against Banks' skirmishers and the Federals attacked three brigades of Jackson's tough fighters. The men of Bank's brigade were painfully aware of the loss they suffered earlier ten miles away on the Rapidan River just a month before. These men were eager to face Jackson again. Lacking reserves, since the rest of the Federals had not arrived, and battered by Jackson, Banks' men reluctantly were forced to withdraw when night made it too dark to see the enemy.

On the following day, with the odds stacked against him, Banks made skillful use of the terrain to mask the true size and the position of his smaller force. Major General Christopher Auger's division was posted south of the road. Auger's men were hidden by a large cornfield. Major General Alpheus Williams' division found cover in the thick woods north of Culpepper Road. An hour or two after noon the artillery duel began.

Confederate Private John Hatton, working as part of the gun crew of one of General Ewell's batteries wrote,

'The fight was raging. Our gun became so heated by rapid and constant firing that applying water on the sponge head would fizz when I swabbed out the gun barrel. We had to cease firing a while to allow the gun to cool. I rested the sponge staff against the wheel (of the gun carriage) and drew my sleeves up, right and left, across my face to wipe off the perspiration that was trickling into my eyes. I turned my canteen up to my mouth to take a drink of water but it was empty. A ball of some sort had made a hole in the bottom.'

'I resorted to the sponge bucket to quench my thirst and I drank heartily. The water was mixed with burnt powder washed from the sponge head. The sponge bucket was a small iron bucket that held about one-and-a half gallons with a mouth just large enough to insert the sponge through the sliding top of iron. It was used to carry water on the battlefield to dampen the sponge to quench the sparks remaining in the barrel of the gun after each charge was fired.'

'During this fight our sponge bucket was sent to the branch (creek) twice to be filled to quench our thirst as well as the gun. It was a very warm day. While we were waiting for the gun to cool off, the cannoneers squatted around the gun to protect ourselves as well as we could from the firing missiles. One time a solid shot came flying over the field like a rabbit. It bounced off our gun missing everyone. The gun was cool in five or six minutes and our work commenced.'

From a ridge above the Grays, Yankee cannons rained shells upon Jackson's men as they deployed on Culpepper Road. To counter the barrage, the Confederates brought up two Parrott guns and a gun from the cavalry in the road and exchanged fire with the Union guns. Up until that time the Confederates were unaware that Banks had a division of Union troops waiting behind the cornfield. After two hours of trading fire, General Winder, standing near the Confederate guns, was felled by a shell fragment. His wound was severe and proved to be mortal. Taliaferro, and other brigades, were without the benefit of Winder's leadership, and began a belated attack on Banks' forces at about half past five in the afternoon. A private in Ewell's division wrote about the battle of Cedar Mountain:

'We made a dash for the crest of the hill, [our guns] unlimbered, and commenced a rapid firing. The enemy's cannon balls and shells kept the air torn with a deafening roar and buzz, while there was a terrific storm raging on our left and in front. In our rear under the hill on a level spot, was located the dwelling house of a lady by the name of Crittenden. Farther across the valley, some distance up the side of Cedar Mountain, was stationed a rifle cannon, the balls and the shell of which passed nearly over our position.'

'As I raised my right arm with the rammer in hand in the act of servicing my gun, a fragment of a prematurely exploded shell from the rifle piece passed under my arm. The sergeant who

was standing near our gun directing the fire was struck down by a fragment of matter striking him in the face. He was picked up by the ambulance detail and carried from the field, the blood flowing freely from his wound. Many shots were heard striking Mrs. Crittenden's house; and I was told the lady was in the house all the time.'

An hour before sunset, General Banks pre-empted Jackson's belated attack with an attack of his own. A private of the 21st Virginia infantry saw the fight, and later wrote:

'The enemy was not only in our front, flank and rear, but had the brigade surrounded. The road was full of Yankees. There was such a fight as was not witnessed during the war; guns, bayonets, swords, pistols, fence rails, and rocks were used all along the line. I have heard of a "hell spot" in some battles, this surely was one. Our color bearer knocked down a Yankee with his flag staff and was shot to death at once. One of the color guard took the flag and he also was killed. Another man bayoneted a Yankee and was immediately riddled with balls, three going through him. Four color bearers were killed with the colors in their hands. The fifth man flung the riddled flag to the breeze, and went through the terrible battle unhurt.'

'Colonel Cunningham (who led a 21st Virginia regiment) had crossed the road leading his horse. He pulled down a fence and passed through the gap into the field. He started to mount his horse, his foot in the stirrup, when he was struck by a bullet and fell back dead, his horse receiving his death wound at the same time.'

'It was a terrible time… nearly half of my regiment lay on the ground dead and wounded, while the remnant was still fighting hand to hand.'

The Confederates, still confused in the wake of General Winder's death, were thrown back. The Southern line was pierced. The fighting between Jackson and Banks teetered back and forth for several hours until the entire Confederate line was in jeopardy. General Jubal Early, commanding one of Jackson's brigades, found his flank disintegrating under Banks' attack.

Reporting to Jackson, he said, "Unless I hold my position I cannot rally my retreating men."

These rebels did not lack for courage.

Ordering Captain William Brown to open fire on the advancing Federals, Brown answered, "General, my ammunition is nearly out. Don't you think we had better charge them?"

Brown was 65 years old and had a son in his company. They held their position until the retreating men were rallied to hold on. At the critical moment Jackson mounted his horse and spurred his mount into the chaos. Imploring and cajoling, he called to his men to stand fast. The Southern ranks steadied and countered the attack.

Banks had no more reserves and, with half his men down, Crawford division was forced to beat a hasty retreat. After a mile Jackson called off the chase. With night approaching, the fighting grew less active until it ended completely.

When night came, Banks was lacking reserves since the rest of the Federals had not arrived, and battered by Jackson, Banks' men withdrew. Each side counted its losses. Banks suffered casualties of a third of his men. The bloody battlefield of Cedar Mountain was a scene of carnage. With more of Pope's troops arriving at Culpepper every day, Jackson abandoned the hard won field at Cedar Mountain and pulled his army back across the Rapidan.

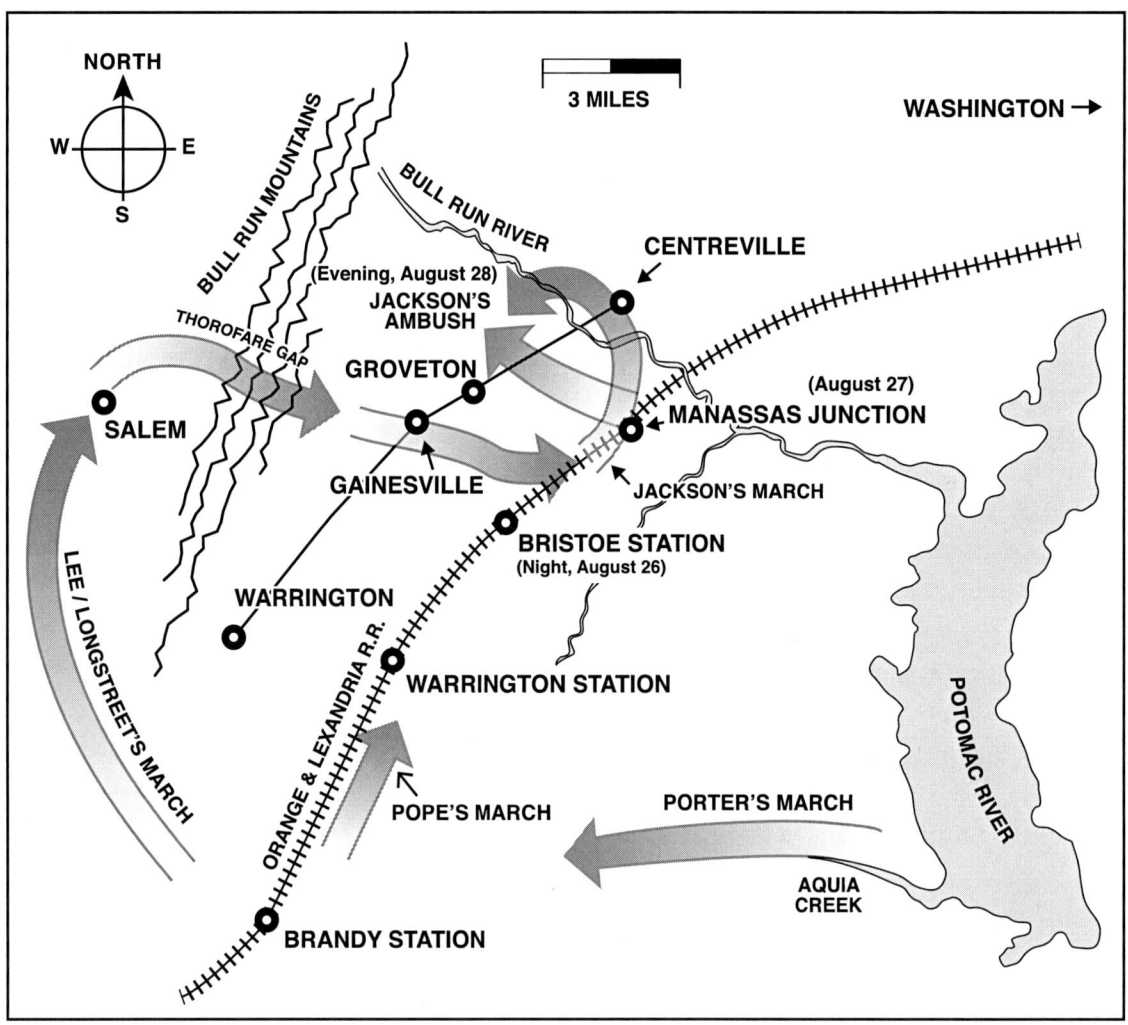

BATTLE FORMATIONS — AUGUST 25-27, 1862

As men gathered for war, Confederate General Stonewall Jackson marched non-stop from Richmond. His army moved north in secret behind the Bull Run Mountains and through the Thoroughfare Gap into the Plain of Manassas. Once through, Jackson headed for Gainesville, then toward the Orange and Alexandria Railroad. Going north, his next stop was the Union Supply Depot at Manassas. After his men had satisfied themselves on the Union provisions, the stores of shoes, and the plunder, Jackson separated his forces. One arm marched toward Centreville, while the other was sent directly toward the abandoned railroad above the Warrenton Turnpike. Once there, on the slopes of Stony Ridge and safely behind the abandoned railroad, Jackson's forces watched in ambush for General Pope's Union army.

Pope, who had been on the Rappahannock River preparing to attack Richmond, was drawn away to go after Jackson. Union General Porter, whose army had helped General McClellan on McClellan's ill-fated attack on Richmond, left Aquia Landing on the Potomac to join Pope. Generals Lee and Longstreet, following Jackson's trail through Thoroughfare Gap, entered Manassas Plain. Jackson was ready to join Longstreet for the final attack on Pope and the stage was set for Pope's mammoth blunder which delivered Pope's Union army into Lee's hands.

❧ 23 ❧

War on the Home Front

In the summer of 1862 the North still hoped for glory and easy victory but Lincoln knew the temperament of the rebellious Southerners. Other men, less starry-eyed than the optimists of a quick resolution to the conflict, saw the same ghosts that Lincoln saw upon a far horizon. They knew the misery that lay ahead for the country.

Life went on. The business of the country continued despite the war. The president signed the Pacific Railroad Act that opened the way across 3000 miles of unexplored land to California and Oregon. America was introduced to the pleasantries of the income tax. Anyone who boasted an income of more than the munificent annual sum $700 had to pay 3% of their income. America decided they needed a Federal Bureau of Printing and Engraving along with a better way to standardize printed money.

There was a bloody revolt of Sioux Indians in Minnesota over living conditions on their reservation. Three hundred whites were massacred and Lincoln sent General Sibley and Federal forces to deal with the uprising.

Secretary of State Seward thanked the British for their willingness to help and politely declined their offer to 'mediate the war' between the Confederacy and the Union with what I imagine might have been a frozen smile of thanks.

Northern Democrats continued to press the Union government to allow the South to keep their slaves, becoming an irritation to the Republican administration. For the first time, the term, 'Copperhead' was used by the *Cincinnati Gazette* to label persons who would not admit they were Southern sympathizers and 'Peace at any price' Democrats.

President Lincoln went to Congress to ask for the legal authority to pursue the war. He needed more money and more men. The war cost money; lots of money. By the first of July the public debt was over $500 million and Congress, now heavily weighted with Republican Abolitionists, voted to throw nearly half a billion dollars at the war problem. This amount of money in 1862 was an astronomical figure never before imagined by the young nation. The growing Union army was expanded by another three hundred thousand new recruits, but they, along with most Americans, had no clear idea of what they were headed into. The enlistment period was for less than most summer vacations; a short ninety days.

James Sloan, a music writer, wrote a marching song that was printed in *The Saturday Evening Post* to help raise volunteers. It began with the almost biblical appeal, *'We are coming, Father Abraham, Three hundred thousand more.'*

A second request to Congress two weeks later was for another five hundred thousand soldiers; the truth slowly made itself known in the grim numbers. Lincoln knew he needed an army of over a half a million fighting men.

When the news for the enlistment levies was published, the recruits, farm boys and city boys, crowded the enlistment centers, laughing and joking over the expectation of adventure and quick glory. The short period of service made them all the more eager to be a part of the *Grand Excursion,* to get in quickly before it was over. So little time remained to win the glory they expected. Men were troubled that the war would be over before they saw any real fighting. In three short months the rebellion would surely be at an end and the uppity Southerners would have been put in their place.

Recruiting posters could not be said to be false advertising but no one can doubt today that the rosy pictures they painted did not exactly reflect the truth. One popular poster offered an enticing prospect for the new soldier.

EXCURSION PARTY
FOR THE SUNNY SOUTH
NINE MONTHS
VOLUNTEERS RECEIVE up to $50.
Don't let the 30th of December find you
Still EXPOSED TO THE DRAFT.

The South saw things more clearly. They were not fooled by a vision through rose-colored glasses. The men and their women knew full well the hell that was ahead. In early 1862, came word that the Union had decided, once and for all, to end this foolish rebellion and a new Union army began to organize. Soon they would come again to invade the capitol of the Confederacy.

For the moment, like the calm before the storm, all was quiet on the rolling land of the Virginia Peninsula, where both capitols were situated. They were close neighbors indeed. Barely a hundred miles separated Washington D.C. and Richmond. McClellan had been stopped once from invading Richmond; it had been a close call. Then Lee had driven the Federals back and away. Southerners scanned the Richmond newspapers closely. McClellan had been ordered to pack up in retreat to Harrison's Landing. Ships were being loaded with troops and they were going back up the Potomac to Alexandria and Washington. What would happen next?

George McClellan didn't know it yet and he wouldn't find out for a few days. He would not be the man to lead the next assault. Someone more aggressive, bent on a Confederate defeat, would be chosen. But it would not be the soft-on-slavery George McClellan no matter how popular a figure he might be for some in the North.

Republicans and Abolitionists believed McClellan's unwillingness to fight aggressively was a thinly disguised desire to let the South remain a separate country and keep their slaves. Many Northerners went so far in their criticism of McClellan as to consider him to be a traitor. One popular cartoon of the day blazoned the headline:

McCLELLAN IS PRIVATELY PLEDGED TO MAKE PEACE

Frank Bellew's bitterly satiric cartoon from that year's *Harper's Weekly*, showed McClellan with his fellow Copperhead Democrats, who were running McClellan for president in the 1864 election. A figure, representing McClellan, begged a Confederate figure to come back to the Union:

'WE ARE VERY HUMBLE, PLEASE COME BACK.
WE WILL DO ANYTHING YOU WANT.'

There was some truth in the insinuations. Many felt that McClellan was not *entirely* loyal to the Union. Professor Allen C. Guelzo, Director of the Civil War Studies Program at Gettysburg College, wrote about a side of McClellan's politics that revealed more of the man than simply a petulant general that would not fight.

Professor Guelzo pointed out, and his remarks are paraphrased, that *'Major General George McClellan was a partisan anti-Lincolnite with a General Douglas MacArthur view of his own importance. To many Democrats who still clung to a vision of a Union which included a slaveholding South, McClellan was a hero. During the first years of the war, it was rumored McClellan had opened his own back-channel negotiations with Confederate officers.'*

'McClellan encouraged men among his own officers to talk loosely about staging a military coup. He made it known that if he seized power, any possibility of emancipation would disappear. Fugitive slaves would be fair game for rendition to their owners as a part of the peace settlement… so Lincoln decided to strike first (with the Emancipation Proclamation). It is ironic that the victory Lincoln needed was provided by George McClellan at Antietam. Lincoln had out-maneuvered McClellan and his fellow Copperheads.'

John Pope's military career was not marked by shining accomplishments. He did, however, capture New Madrid and take Mississippi Island Number 10 the year before in April. That was no mean accomplishment. It opened the entire Mississippi to Northern commerce and military travel.

Pope looked good. He graduated high in his West Point class, he served with credibility in the Mexican war and, to add to his laurels, like the president, he was a staunch Republican and a fellow Kentuckian. He had even ridden with the president during Lincoln's inauguration.

Pope was not an empathetic man; he had more than his share of blind spots. In his first address to the troops Pope boasted, *"I have come to you from the West* (where he had won a few small fights against the Iroquois Indians), *where we have always seen the backs of our enemies."*

That unfortunate expression of bravado would come back to haunt General Pope like any empty boast.

John Pope's exalted view of himself prompted an officer that had had known him at West Point say, "Pope is a Blatherskite, who has a habit of exaggerating his own accomplishments."

Pope's blown up sense of self-importance made him fix so firmly on his own beliefs that he often closed his mind to dissent. That, too, would come back to bite him. Pope was not inclined to listen to his officers when they disagreed, and that trait would be his undoing during the Second Battle of Manassas.

One tale that revealed something of Pope's arrogance was told after the battle of Cedar Mountain. The surgeon for the 82nd Ohio Regiment, Colonel Cantwell, learned that his brother, Lieutenant Colonel James Cantwell, had died in battle while leading his regiment. Surgeon Cantwell asked General Pope for permission to go under a flag of truce to recover his brother's body from the Confederates. He later wrote of his meeting with Pope.

'I went to General Pope, and made the request for permission to take the body of my brother home. With a pompous mien, such as only heartless, brainless fools assume, he turned on his heel. His reply to my request was to say, "I'll think of that hereafter."'

John Pope brought much of the antipathy on himself. Criticism came from all quarters. He was generally considered to be a braggart and a bumbler by many of his own officers. Nevertheless, Pope had a reputation with the Lincoln administration as a 'solid' man and a soldier who was willing to fight. Lincoln and Secretary of War Stanton had had enough of McClellan's indecision and super-caution.

Pope's first order of business was to defend the capitol and Jackson was a threat to Washington. A part of Pope's army, Banks' corps, had met and fought Jackson on Cedar Mountain so Pope requested permission to chase after Jackson. Lincoln disagreed. He did not believe Jackson was a genuine threat. Besides, McDowell was capable of defending the capitol.

"I want no more defensive fighting," Lincoln reminded Pope. "I want you to go after Lee."

The President was fed up with allowing Robert E. Lee to call the tune as Lee had with George McClellan. Enough was enough. All the while, to spare McClellan's feelings, Pope's elevation in rank had been a carefully kept secret, even from John Pope. Five days later the cat was out of the bag. McClellan knew he had been replaced.

The President was a man who could size people up pretty well. McClellan was an important man in Northern politics and he had plenty of Copperhead supporters. Lincoln, always the shrewd politician, did not wish to let the thin-skinned George McClellan know about the change in command any sooner than he had to. However, Pope had to know to do his job. He was finally told he was in charge.

Pope had been promised Heintzelman's, Franklin's and Porter's corps. When he went against Lee he would have a force of 60,000 troops in the new Army of Virginia. George McClellan was left with an injured ego and the empty honor of nominal command of the Army of the Potomac.

General Fitz John Porter, as well as all of McClellan's officers, had been kept in the dark about the administration's decision to have General John Pope carry the war to the South. Until that time, in each of the several battles he had fought for McClellan, Porter had followed McClellan's philosophy of caution toward the rebels. McClellan still hoped for an easy solution and an end to the war. Even at Malvern Hill, during the Seven Days campaign, when Porter might have defeated

Robert E. Lee and gone on to capture Richmond, Porter had been ordered to continue a rear guard action.

Now Porter had a new boss, and John Pope was a man Porter didn't much care for. Nevertheless, he accepted the change in command and made ready to obey. Porter was not a man to keep irritations buried inside. He revealed his feelings to his friend, General Burnside, in a letter. Unfortunately for Porter, his writing came to light after Second Manassas. Edwin Stanton, Secretary of War, considered Porter's statements damning and Porter was known as McClellan's friend and a fellow Democrat. The statements in Porter's letters were conceived as a clear indication of Porter's disloyalty to Pope and to his country by the Republican court martial.

The letters *(and several others he had written to Burnside)* were made public in court and helped to weigh the circumstantial evidence to convict Porter of the charges of disobedience to Pope's orders.

One of Porter's letters to his friend, General Burnside said, *'I regret to see that General Pope has not improved since his youth and has now written himself down as what the military world has long known as an ass.'*

That was not a wise thing for Porter to say, especially since Pope was now his superior officer. Despite his change in command from McClellan to Pope, it is likely that Fitz John Porter, as much as he liked and admired McClellan and as much as he did not care for Pope, might have welcomed some aspects of the change. He was a man that did not care to always be on the defensive as McClellan had forced him to be. This assessment is based to a great degree on his statements to other officers after his powerful defense at Malvern Hill, as well as his natural inclination to take the fight to the enemy whenever circumstances permitted.

George McClellan had received his orders from new General-in-Chief Henry Halleck, to leave Harrison's Landing. He loaded his men aboard the ships for Alexandria. From there he was to send some of his men to join Pope's Army of Virginia. Together the two forces of Pope and McClellan would begin a new and hopefully final assault on Lee and Richmond.

In early August, McClellan's troops marched through the streets of Culpepper on their way to Aquia Landing to board the troop ships for Alexandria. The men were stifled by the suffocating heat and choking dust. All the while, as they marched, they were serenaded by a small Confederate girl. A dark-eyed child, swinging her bonnet and sitting on her wall before her home, sang a ditty of her own making, to the hurrying Federal soldiers as they passed.

"Goodbye Yankees, I'm glad you're going. Goodbye Yankees, I'm glad you're going. Good bye, goodbye."

$\backsim$ **24** $\backsim$

The Gamble

It wasn't long before Lee guessed that Halleck's plan was to combine the Union armies under John Pope's command. That was bad news. Not so much that Pope was feared, but because of who he was. Pope's general orders defined the man and he was hated.

When the news spread there was consternation. The North had the manpower and the military resources to do almost anything. Pope and McClellan, together, could move south down the Peninsula like a steamroller. Their combined forces far outnumbered Lee's smaller army. McDowell had arrived on the north side of the Rappahannock River. About to join Pope, McDowell had his army sitting, half and half, on both sides of the Rappahannock. In the process of moving his corps to the south side, his left flank was weak and exposed to attack. Lee did what was natural in war, and what the Northern generals were too blind to see: he sent Jackson to strike McDowell's flank.

A few hours before the planned attack, fortune smiled on John Pope. General John Buford, head of Union cavalry, on Pope's order, sent two of his horse regiments to Raccoon Ford to pinpoint Lee's exact location, so he could pre-empt any possible rebel strike. Buford's New York Cavalry crossed the Rapidan and raided Jeb Stuart's headquarters. During the melee of Buford's raid, Lee's battle plan for Jackson to attack the lagging tail-end of McDowell's Corps on the wrong side of the river was discovered among the captured papers.

There was nothing wrong with Lee's plan except that Jackson had been delayed two days by bad weather and poor roads. Pope had already moved McDowell's remaining troops across the Rappahannock and his army was firmly established on the northern side along a nine-mile front. There were few good fords and it was an excellent new defensive position. Also Franklin was on his way, although he was not expected for a week. Now Pope could wait in relative peace with less fear of a surprise attack.

General Jubal Early's brigade, in Stonewall Jackson's corps, had returned that day from raids on Union supplies. Early's men, trying to cross the swollen river (it had been raining hard), got bogged down. His troops were stranded on the wrong side of the river. Pope found out and sent John Reynolds' division and some cavalry to capture Early's men.

General John Fulton Reynolds was a good man to send after Early. He was one of the most highly esteemed of the Union commanders. Forty-seven years old, a West Point graduate and veteran of the war with Mexico, Reynolds had won two brevet commissions for bravery. Reynolds might have captured General Early and his brigade but Early's troops, knowing they stood a good chance of spending the rest of the war in a Union prison camp unless they moved quickly, managed in a move of desperation to cross the river and escape.

While Pope waited each evening the troops were serenaded by the regimental brass bands well into the night. When *Home, Sweet Home* was played, and as the strains of the tune drifted across the water, men cheered on both sides of the Rappahannock. That nostalgic song was followed with *'Maryland, My Maryland.'* Both Confederate and Federal bands played each evening but the lyrics were slightly different from those sung by the Southern soldiers.

At taps, the sad sentimental strains of *'Lorena'* were heard from the northern shore. Some of the soldiers that heard the tune suddenly became so homesick they wondered for that long moment why they were fighting and not home with a sweetheart.

Many men knew the story of Lorena. Written by Reverend Henry Webster, the lyrics came to Webster after a broken engagement. Lorena's wealthy father forced an end to the engagement. When they parted for the last time, Lorena gave Henry a letter. The line in her letter, *'If we try we may forget,'* made such an impression on Henry's broken heart he used the line in the song he wrote for his lost love.

> *The story of that past, Lorena,*
> *Alas! I care not to repeat,*
> *The hopes that could not last, Lorena,*
> *They lived, but only lived to cheat.*
> *I would not cause e'en one regret*
> *Rankle in your bosom now,*
> *For 'if we try we may forget,'*
> *Were words of thine long years ago.*
> *It matters little now, Lorena,*
> *The past is the eternal past;*
> *Our heads will soon lie low, Lorena,*
> *There is a future! O, thank God!*
> *Of life this is so small a part!*
> *'Tis dust to dust beneath the sod;*
> *But there, up there, 'tis heart to heart.*

On August 26, giving Pope an added boost in his fortunes, Heintzelman's corps, another part of McClellan's army which Halleck had given him, arrived from Alexandria. Heintzelman was overdue but he came just in time to ensure Lee's army could not easily defeat Pope.

Heinzelman's Third Corps should have arrived sooner. McClellan, always with an eye to political maneuvering, had delayed sending Heintzelman's eight thousand men because of his suspicion *(still a secret)* that Pope might replace him as Commander of the Northern armies in Virginia.

Lee sent Major General James Ewell Brown (J.E.B.) Stuart and 1500 experienced cavalry to loop around the Federals and hit the Orange and Alexandria railroads. The main rail connection was Pope's main supply line from Washington sixty miles to the north. Ripping up the tracks and burning the boxcars would slow the movement of troops, food, ammunition and the other needed supplies the army must have to fight.

When Pope heard of J.E.B. Stuart's raids he sent Major General Franz Siegel's Tenth Corps across the river to find and attack Stuart. Franz Siegel was a German ex-patriot from Austria. He was a favorite of the German-American population in the North and there were a lot of them. He had rallied many Missouri Germans to the Union cause, and at the Battle of Wilson's Creek in 1861 the German-American soldiers had performed well.

General Siegel's First Corps consisted of three divisions. Many of his troops were of German descent and Siegel was able to rally the German population in the Union cause. Some could barely speak English and the native-born American troops didn't think much of them, mostly because of their foreign ways. There was an opinion by some that the German soldiers did not always perform as they should. That was not true; they fought and died hard. General Siegel was a mediocre general but Siegel had a good side; the German troops worshiped him and he commanded their loyalty. It was common to hear German recruits declare proudly, '*I fights mit Siegel.*'

Such pandering was not unusual. Lincoln needed the German-American soldiers and, almost to a man, they were anti-slavery and loyal Americans. During the war the Irish immigrants were given the same recognition.

General J.E.B. Stuart's '*go for leather*' horsemen were jubilant; his cavalry had eluded Siegel and cut all the way across Pope's rear until, by mid-morning of August 13, Siegel's men had caught up with them. When Stuart found out the Federals were hot on his trail he had his artillery regiment unlimber their gun carriages and they set up their guns, ready to defend against the Federals. One of the men in Stuart's battery told what he had experienced.

"We drove our horses into a large hilly field that sloped to the river. There was a knoll and a Captain told us, '*Put some of your guns here and fire a few shells into that piece of woods you see yonder on the other side of the river. I think perhaps there is something in there.*'"

"There was nothing I could see but we unlimbered the first gun and landed a shell near the center of the woods. That woke up the lion sure enough. The shell we fired was a twelve-pounder percussion ball and it exploded with a crack right near the enemy's lair. The Yankees were there alright. They had a battery of six or eight guns in position in those innocent looking woods and they let go right after our shell exploded. I saw six or eight white piles of smoke rising from the brush and I heard the thunder of the guns and the terrible screaming of the shells passing overhead. For two hours we fired as fast as we could and so did the Yankees."

Siegel's men were in the woods. When the rebel artillery opened up, a Union lieutenant who was on the receiving end of the Confederate artillery shelling gave his first-hand report of the killing.

"From the first firing, every shot of the enemy's guns passed over us very low, or in some cases, hit among us. Our makeshift houses we had built, while we waited for the rest of Pope's army to gather, were completely riddled and torn to pieces. Many of our men were hit. Strange to say only one man was killed."

"Poor fellow, he raised his head to change his position and a shell came crashing through the bushes. It took his head clean off from his shoulders. His face, with the nose, eyes, mustache, chin and everything perfect; was blown directly past Levi's company. His head landed in the grass in front of Captain Miller's Company. The eyes were wide open and staring at the men as they lay watching in the ranks."

After the fight General Jubal Early, a part of Ewell's division in Stonewall Jackson's corps, got bogged down and stranded in the heavy rain on the wrong side of the river so Pope attacked Early's brigade. General Early escaped and the fighting ended in stalemate.

It was time to take the offensive. Lee had weighed his options carefully; the South had neither the production capability nor the manpower to defeat the North. The Confederacy needed time to discourage the North into allowing the Confederacy and their slave monopoly to exist. A few rebel victories might even bring the British and the French to recognizing the Confederacy. Lee had to find a way to force Pope away from Richmond. He made a very risky decision. His decision took courage; it reflected the kind of military judgment that separates the mediocre generals from the great commanders. Lee decided to *split his forces.*

Lee had another large problem that he must fix first; he had to re-organize his forces. The army was organized poorly and in a slip-shod manner. Lee was going to attack fast and hard with a smaller force. His nine separate divisions had to stop operating as nine independent armies. That had been the Union's problem and Lee could not afford that luxury. Lee's army had to operate like a well-oiled machine and no longer like a rabble.

His solution was simple. He combined his forces into two corps. Lee placed five divisions, 30,000 men, under James Longstreet's command. Longstreet, like Lee, was a fine tactician and as dependable as a workhorse. Thomas 'Stonewall' Jackson was given two divisions totaling 24,000 men. Jackson's was the smaller force because Lee could not quite depend on Jackson when push came to shove. Often, for reasons not always clear, Jackson was sometimes laid back and not always on time for the job. However, when the chips were down when Jackson *did* decide to fight, he was unstoppable.

Jackson was referred by others, North and South, as 'Stonewall' Jackson for his unrelenting stonewall-like defense at the First Battle of Manassas. Jackson commanded the famous *'foot cavalry'* of the Second Corps; so named for his troops ability to cover ground fast, marching for long periods with little rest when speed was called for.

Humorless, gawky, and a killer, Jackson was also a man of secrets. Jackson's first rule of strategy was always to mystify, mislead, and surprise the enemy. Longstreet was a tall, bearded, taciturn man. Lee called him, *'My old war horse.'* And the affectionate aphorism was an indication how much Lee depended on him. Jeffry D. Wert wrote that *'Longstreet was the finest commander in the Army of Northern*

Virginia. In fact, he was arguably the best corps commander in the conflict on either side.'

One of the few options that remained for Lee *(and the Confederacy)* was to divide and conquer the smaller parts of the Union armies. Lee leaned on the element of surprise. A surprise move that he planned to make was one that no one in the North would expect. To execute his plan, Lee first had to keep up the pretense that his entire Confederate army was still holding their defensive position across the Rappahannock River in front of Richmond. Without McClellan or Pope any the wiser, Lee slipped most of his army across the Rappahannock and left behind a shadow force. The man in charge of the skeleton force was General John R. Magruder, the same man who had bamboozled McClellan. Magruder had proven his skill at military legerdemain at Yorktown with wooden cannons and by sending his same brigades marching again and again just out of cannon range.

The Confederate army was still pretty much a match for Pope's army, at least until Porter's Fifth Corps and Heintzelman's Third Corps joined Pope. For Lee that meant he had pretty good odds. Besides, Robert E. Lee could move quickly when it was necessary. The risk Lee took was this: if he had made a wrong decision to send most of his army away from the defenses of the Confederate capitol, all McClellan had to do to capture Richmond was to march full steam ahead and walk right over Magruder's skeleton force. Richmond would most surely fall. Then and there the South would lose the war.

On August 24, 1862, Lee called his two wing commanders to his tent. He proposed a bold new strategy. Longstreet was to keep Pope occupied while Jackson made an end run around Pope to destroy Pope's base of supplies at Manassas Junction. Longstreet would keep a token force of 25,000 men to defend Richmond. That would be just enough men to fool McClellan and Pope into believing that Richmond was still well defended.

Lee's move to split his forces, the strategy he planned, was a dangerous gamble and he risked disaster; Pope might attack Richmond and Longstreet's smaller army. However, by sending Jackson to raid Pope's supply depots in Pope's rear, Lee counted on the threat to Pope's force and to Washington. Pope would then have to move his forces north to protect his flank and the Northern capitol, which was only a two days' march away.

There was more to Lee's gamble. Pope might try to capture Jackson's force but Pope had no idea that Jackson's division had been increased to 20,000 men. If Pope tried, Lee was certain that Jackson could hold his own against nearly anything Pope might throw at him.

Robert E. Lee had taken the measure of the political climate in the North. A threat against the Northern Capitol would shake them in their boots and remove the threat to Richmond. Everything in Lee's planning depended on whether Jackson could move fast enough and smartly enough to carry out his part of Lee's dangerous strategy.

❧ 25 ❧

Foot Cavalry

Just after midnight on the morning of August 25, 1862, Lee outlined his plan to his two generals, a plan that might crush John Pope. He ordered Jackson to take his 25,000 troops north toward the Manassas supply depot. Longstreet was to stay near Richmond for a short time before leaving to join Jackson. That ploy was to deceive Pope into believing the entire Confederate forces *(not just Magruder's token force)* were still defending the capitol. It would be one of the great strategic battle plans of the war... *if it worked.*

One of Jackson's officers overheard Jackson's reply to Lee's order to march early.

Jackson's answer was quick. "I shall leave this morning."

For Jackson that meant his army would march in darkness, just after midnight. There were no complaints; they trusted their commander.

A soldier said, "We were told to take our half-eaten victuals and get packed. Some of the men had not even cooked their rations and had to take them raw."

Jackson's aim was to head north, go up the Shenandoah Valley and turn east to Thoroughfare Gap through the Bull Run Mountains. He would end up in Pope's rear. Once on the Manassas plain, his men would hit the Union supply depots. There were several of them but the main Union supply depot was at Manassas Junction, a mile or two from the Bull Run Creek and closest to Washington. At the same time, he would harass any Union troops on the way.

Jackson's march was being made to fool Pope into believing that Washington was under a new threat. That uncomfortable fear would make Pope believe he had a very dangerous enemy behind him and it would draw Pope into the Manassas plain. Once there, Lee would send Longstreet and his two commanders to attack Pope in force and eliminate a large part of McClellan's army.

Lee sent Stuart's 1500 cavalry riding that same morning to spearhead the move and to scout out the opposition. Longstreet was to follow in Jackson's footsteps. When he made contact with Jackson the two wings of the Confederate army would launch a smashing unified attack on Pope. The battle would be fought on the very same ground where less than a year before the Union army under McDowell at the First Battle of Manassas had been beaten so badly.

The Confederate bugles sounded reveille early but Stonewall's men were used to marching at odd hours. There was murmuring, not from criticism but from curiosity.

"What was up?"

"Where were we headed so early?"

Stonewall had not confided to anyone where they were going. Such secrecy by their commander was a fact of life his division commanders had learned to live with. There was a hasty breakfast, each man was issued 60 rounds of ammunition and knapsacks were gathered up and sent to the rear. They were marching light… and fast.

"No straggling," the order came through the ranks.

"Close up. Close up," Followed the unceasing call from the sergeants.

"Keep your shoes and trousers dry on crossing the streams."

There was in the air, a sense that something important was about to happen. What it was, knowing the general these tough rebels were used to, the march would end in a fight; a fight that might make all the difference to the Confederacy. Officers were assigned along the column to make sure there was no straggling. This army had to move as fast as possible. When they came to a stream, and the country in Virginia had plenty of streams, big and small, they were expected to take them in their stride without slowing the pace. The men splashed across streams the same way they met and passed every fence, hill ravine or obstacle of any kind in the same determined way without comment. There were no songs and few jokes. Breath and muscle had to be conserved. Not a man doubted this would be one of those super-fast marches that had given Jackson's army the title of 'foot cavalry.' On they came through the early hours of night into brightening dawn like grim harbingers of death.

As they headed up the Shenandoah Valley most of the marchers were on the lookout for Federal troops thinking that they might be repeating their earlier experience of finding more scattered Northern generals and frightening the citizens of Washington. The Shenandoah campaign had been the scene of a series of battles when, the month before, Jackson's men had met and defeated one Union force after another: Banks, Fremont and part of McDowell's rear guard.

The killers sped through the early dawn, stopping hardly at all except when some of the men took advantage of a delay for a quick bite at a friendly farmhouse, or while the artillerymen struggled to get the heavy wagons and guns across and up the sides of muddy creeks. During the few times they were able to take a quick rest someone always had the get up and go to forage the countryside.

One lucky forager said later, "I was able to buy a cake of cornbread from a farmer's wife. It was moldy, but after I trimmed the edges, my cornbread was the envy of the company."

First in Jackson's columns, as they were quick-marching through the warm August Shenandoah Valley morning, was Major General Richard Ewell and his division. Dick Ewell, sometimes affectionately referred to by his men as *'Old Baldy,'* was a man who had spent his whole life in the army. Dick Ewell was a soldier upon whom Jackson could depend.

Historian Larry Tagg described him: *'He was short with a fringe of brown hair on an otherwise bomb-shaped bald head. Bright, bulging eyes above a prominent nose made him look like a bird. He had a habit of uttering strange remarks in his shrill stuttering lisp. In the middle of a conversation, he would make odd remarks like, 'Now why do you suppose President Davis made me a Major General anyway?''*

Ewell was a hypochondriac who had convinced himself he had some mysterious internal 'disease.' He subsisted almost entirely on a dish of hulled wheat boiled in milk and sweetened with sugar. Richard Ewell was the reigning eccentric of the Confederate army. Even so, his men knew at first hand of his bravery and generous spirit and loved him all the more despite his odd ways. Ewell's four brigades were made up of men from Georgia, Louisiana, Virginia, and a regiment or two from North Carolina and Alabama, all hard fighting country boys that had seen action before.

A.P. Hill's 'Light' Division followed. Hill's fast moving soldiers were led by a young hotheaded officer whose one-time sweetheart had married George McClellan. All matters Northern made him surly. As for John Pope, Ambrose Hill had written to a friend that he would *'Welcome the chance to paralyze this western bully Pope.'*

Brigadier General William B. Taliaferro, leading Jackson's own division, brought up the rear. Taliaferro had grown to be a better soldier in Jackson's service. He did well at Cedar Mountain but he was known to complain that Jackson's penchant for secrecy was *'sometimes carried too far.'*

Stops for rest were rare. As soon as the order to halt was heard down the lines, the men fell where they stood like collapsing jackstraws. Some reached in haversacks or drew some piece of stale flapjack from a pocket; a dirty brown mixture of fried flour and lard or bacon grease. There was no time to cook or fry. The men ate their hard tack or whatever had been foraged on the march; green corn, apples, persimmons. Then, all too soon came the order to "fall in" and continue the march.

Up the Shenandoah Valley they went, as swiftly as only Jackson's foot cavalry could. Then they turned east toward the Bull Run Mountains. Jackson's army, hidden from detection by the mountains, reached the small village of Salem a few miles from the entrance of Thoroughfare Gap. The gap was the favorite pass through the Bull Run Mountains into the peninsula and to the plains of Manassas.

By afternoon they passed into the narrow cleft of the gap, a natural formation that split the Bull Run Mountains like a giant cleaver had cleft the stone. Going east, the long gray columns followed beside the Manassas Gap railroad, barely wide enough for the single railroad track that ran through the gap to from Salem to Gainesville. Next to the road, a sorry excuse of a narrow stream snaked its way through the bulrushes. The narrow dusty roadway paralleled the stream only wide enough for a single column of soldiers to pass on their hurried journey toward the Manassas Plain.

Jackson's forward scouts reported the good news: *'Pope has no guard at the exit.'* That Pope had left not even a small contingent of men to watch his back door at the rear of his army was nearly inconceivable. Such reasonable caution was a detail of good generalship that a novice general would not have neglected.

"Keep your eyes open," the sergeant repeated to his skirmishers as they moved ahead.

The gap was a perfect place for an ambush and a pass that any wide-awake general would certainly have guarded.

No one saw the enemy slip through the gap. By the second day Jackson's 24,000 troops were on Pope's rear. Neglecting to guard the gap was one more piece of evidence of Pope's deficiency as a leader. Along with a series of other mistakes, these blunders would prove fatal to Pope's ambition.

Jackson's army followed the Manassas Gap railway east through the narrow wooded canyon, then out past the villages of Haymarket and Gainesville, swinging east against a rising morning sun. By August 26, Jackson's men had marched fifty-four miles with short stops and little rest for thirty-six hours. The Confederate army had moved fast.

As part of Lee's plan to confuse Pope, Stonewall directed J.E.B. Stuart's cavalry to race ahead of the rebel infantry to Bristoe Station, a smaller Union supply dump. Bristoe Station on the Orange and Alexandria Railroads was twenty miles behind Pope's line on the Rappahannock River.

Union soldiers, guarding the station, hardly expected an attack and Stuart's cavalry easily overwhelmed the two Federal companies guarding the small train stop. The Federal trains that came up, not aware that unfriendly troops held the station, did not expect trouble. They did not look for rebels so near Washington.

One train got through the logjam on the tracks by smashing through the timbers but that was all that passed that day. Sadly, for the hungry Confederates, the trains carried no food. Jackson's men managed to smash three more trains. Tearing up the tracks derailed the next three trains.

Stonewall Jackson was fast becoming a figure of fear and admiration by the Northern troops. One captured Union soldier, whose leg was broken, asked to be lifted from his pallet so that he could see General Jackson. Silhouetted against the fires, Jackson's gaunt figure in dusty uniform and old forage cap drawn down to his nose, stood a hundred feet away. The injured soldier groaned in amazement to see the man, who was the *'scourge of the Federal army.'*

His awed and bewildered comment when he saw Jackson was to whisper aloud, "Oh, my God. Lay me down, lay me down."

When times were harder than usual for the men in Jackson's army, that injured Federal prisoner's bemused remark was often repeated in humor to lighten the misery.

General Richard Ewell remained behind at Bristoe Station as Jackson's rear guard. The bulk of the army, not stopping or slowing their pace, moved at top speed across the hilly plain four miles north toward Manassas Junction. Only a hundred men held the base. By the time the rebels poured over the Yankee's thinly held defenses, the Federal guns had no time to aim and the few shells that were fired flew safely over the rebel's heads.

When Pope tried to call Washington he found that the telegraph lines were dead. Reports came in of the raid on Bristoe Station; a small force of Federal troops near Bristoe Station had spotted some of Jackson's men. Their messenger rode off to send word to Pope that *'a large Confederate force has been seen forty miles from Washington.'* If Pope realized that Lee's army was now split, he could destroy Jackson before Longstreet joined him.

The report raised a ruckus and a storm of conjecture in Pope's headquarters. Where was Jackson going? Why was he there? Was this a new invasion of Washington? Pope had to make sure. He decided to pull his troops back from the Rappahannock and go after Jackson. While he debated Jackson's fate, Stonewall's busy marauders went about the pleasant task of destroying Union trains and raiding Union supply dumps.

Manassas Junction was Pope's main supply base. That was Jackson's target. There was, at that important rail station, dozens of train cars sitting on the sidings loaded to the ceilings of the box cars with all matter of army supplies. Scattered around the large train depot there were also five large well-stocked warehouses filled to the rafters with tons of every possible kind of food; canned meats, hams for the officers, rations for the troops, shoes, clothing, barrels of whiskey, uniforms, arms, ammunition, blankets and all the things an army must have on the march.

Just after daylight, Jackson's men occupied Manassas Junction with Taliaferro and A.P. Hill's troops. They raised hell, putting new shoes on their bare feet and feasting on Pope's supplies. Stonewall's men had a picnic. Finished with their scavenging, they set ablaze every supply they could not take with them. It was time for Jackson to move closer to where he expected Lee to meet Longstreet and make ready for the battle. When his men had eaten, drank or carried all they could take away from the still smoldering depot they headed toward Gainesville. It was during this wholesale devastation to Union supplies that the rebels captured a prize.

One of Pope's dispatches to Washington was discovered in the debris. It was a lucky find; the dispatches laid out important facts Lee needed. The papers named the size of Pope's army and the news that Porter's Fifth Corps with his 30,000 veterans was on its way to join Pope. Beside that good fortune, Stuart's earlier acts of sabotage and destruction at Bristoe and Manassas had stopped the trains that were meant to reinforce McClellan and bring troops to Pope. Lee's strategy had worked to perfection.

The flames at Manassas, burning boxcars and unusable supplies, burned so high the men of Pope's forces saw the light in the sky all the way from the Rappahannock River forty miles away. Pope sent his troops after Jackson, the light show in the dark August night, the first hint Pope had of the Confederate attack. In his delusion that Jackson was running, Pope took the flames as a good sign. To John Pope, ready to grab and accept any evidence that supported his already decided opinion, the flames represented a sign of desperation by the fleeing Jackson.

Jackson was always a master of deception. After raiding and burning the Union supply depot at Manassas Junction, he sent each of his divisions away from the Manassas supply depot in a different direction. Taliaferro's men went directly toward Bull Run. Ewell and Hill's divisions got lost for a while and Ewell headed toward Centreville, by mistake, then backtracked toward his destination at Bull Run. The roundabout marches fooled Pope again. Various reports from his scouts persuaded John Pope that Jackson was no longer at Manassas but was, instead, near Centreville, five miles from where he was.

The next day, Jackson followed Stuart and Trimble with the rest of the troops. Jackson made a loop around Manassas to confuse Pope, moved toward Centreville, then turned west along the Warrenton Turnpike. He stopped at last to take a strong position on the hills above the pike roadway behind an unfinished railroad. Ewell and Hill were soon back on track, their meandering having only confused Pope's scouts more than ever.

Jackson, meanwhile, after razing the Manassas depot, went to ground behind an abandoned railroad. That rail line, at one time, would have been a railroad built to compete with the Orange and Alexandria railroads. The money for the rail line had run out. All that was left were mounds and ravines of the unfinished work. It was a perfect place to defend against an enemy. There Jackson and his army would remain to hold off Pope until Longstreet arrived with the rest of Lee's army.

Pope followed his fantasy. His advance forces reached Warrenton a mile from Gainesville and seven miles from the big Union depot at Manassas Junction. Pope had worked out a foolproof plan. His plan was simplicity itself. He would crush Thomas Jackson's men in a vice between the jaws of two of his corps.

Porter was on his way from Aquia Landing, due at Bristoe Station the next day. Porter's corps would advance north along the Warrenton Turnpike from Gainesville and stop Jackson before the rebel had a chance to escape through the Thoroughfare Gap into the Shenandoah Valley. The rest of Pope's army would press hard at Jackson as he fled from Centreville where Pope thought he might be after his pillaging. After Pope had defeated Jackson he would go for Lee, take Richmond and end the war; a sure and certain solution to Pope's problem.

Pope had not counted on General Robert E. Lee, who was going to make sure that Richmond's defeat did not happen. Longstreet's thirty thousand men knifed northward through the Shenandoah Valley following hard on Jackson's footsteps.

Thomas 'Stonewall' Jackson was the key to Lee's strategy. Jackson's career was colorful but had begun with political problems. November 6, 1861, a month after receiving his new commission as a Brigadier General, Stonewall Jackson was ordered to destroy the Baltimore and Ohio railroads and a couple of dams near a Union army under General Hancock.

October was wet, rainy, and bitter cold. There was plenty of snow, rain and sleet. Jackson's second in command, Brigadier General Loring, was told to set up camp and wait for orders at the small hamlet of Romney.

Romney was about as cheerless and exposed a place as anyone might imagine. It lay on the south branch of the upper Potomac. There was no housing and nothing much else but a few dilapidated old buildings with leaky roofs.

General Loring objected to the less than first-class accommodations. Loring had political pull with Jefferson Davis and Secretary of War Benjamin for the Confederacy. Jackson would not change the order. Romney Village was where he wanted Loring's 10,000 men to set up shop.

Loring raged to his officers. He sent a dispatch to Benjamin, voicing his unhappiness with his lot and with Jackson's impossible order.

"I will not take up quarters in this godforsaken cheerless pest hole," he wrote to Benjamin.

The War office got his letter and granted Loring's request to take better quarters in a more amiable location. When Jackson discovered what the War Office had done, *over his orders,* he quit. When Jackson's resignation reached his attention, President Davis was forced to rescind the Benjamin order and to apologize to Jackson. The Confederacy was learning the sort of man Stonewall Jackson was.

That same winter in 1861, Jackson endured what his men were forced to endure. The story is told that as the men shivered from the bitter cold, one of the men crawled out of his blankets in the morning after a heavy snowfall. Half frozen and cursing the cold, nearby, under a tree, another man crawled out of the snow.

"Damn, if it isn't colder than the hind leg of a snowshoe rabbit." he said to the men near him.

The complainer was General Jackson. He had ridden up in the night and lay down in the snow beneath a tree among his troops. Hours afterward, the incident was talked about throughout the camp. It firmly established Stonewall's popularity with his hard-bitten troops.

Jackson's military operations were almost always unexpected and baffling to the enemy. In the early part of the war, he explained himself to John Imboden, a brigadier general.

"Always mystify, mislead, and surprise the enemy if possible, and when you strike and overcome him never let up in the pursuit so long as your men have strength to follow. An army routed, if hotly pursued, becomes panic-stricken and then can be easily destroyed by half their number."

"The other rule is never fight against heavy odds. If by any possible maneuver you can hurl your own force on only a part, and that part is the weakest part of your enemy, then crush it. Such tactics win every time. A small army may thus destroy a large one in detail, and repeated victory makes it invincible."

PART THREE

Second Manassas

❧ 26 ❧

Old Ground

In late August of 1862, on the eve of the Second Battle of Manassas, a young news reporter traveled by train through Virginia. His train passed over the same ground where eight months before, the First Battle of Manassas had been fought. That battle had been referred to by one writer as a *'Battle of Blunders.'* The battlefield that the news reporter saw lay between Washington and Richmond stretching from Manassas Junction to Thoroughfare Gap and along and around the hilly land beside the Warrenton Turnpike.

George A. Townsend, a 21-year-old reporter for the *New York Herald*, traveled by train on the Orange and Alexandria railroad between Washington and Warrenton. He had been told to report about what the *Herald* believed would very soon be the scene of a second great battle between the armies of John Pope and Robert E. Lee. The clash would take place here on the hilly plain of Manassas, around Groveton and south of Bull Run Creek.

As Townsend sat in the shaking, rattling, bare, filthy passenger car, looking out the window of his car, he must have felt some sense of history and powerful emotions about the tragedy of war. He must have had a sense of the misery that had been the legacy of the first battle fought here once before on this same bloody ground.

Did the reporter, at twenty-one years of age and not yet hardened to the vagaries of life, have a disturbing sense of déjà vu? Did he hear, somewhere just beyond the range of human hearing, the wails and cries of those dead men calling from their graves? Was a second human catastrophe about to be repeated?

Going due south on the Orange and Alexandria railroad, a rail line that stretches a hundred miles between Richmond and Washington, Townsend's passenger car clicked and clacked the miles away as he moved over the iron rails. He passed small hamlets and villages, rail stops, farms and the ruined aftermath of war. The small crossroad villages and train stations were occupied; manned not by the occupants, but once more by Union troops. He might have recalled Mathew Arnold's words;

> *And we are here as on a darkling plain*
> *Swept with confused alarms of struggle and flight,*
> *Where ignorant armies clash by night.*

Sixty thousand men had fought here in 1861. That First Battle of Bull Run ended with a Northern defeat and left the Confederacy with hopes for a quick end to the war and a permanent separation from the North. The Herald reporter passed Manassas Junction, then Bristoe Station, Brandy Station, and Warrenton Junction. He was headed south, going toward the Rappahannock River, where the Union forces waited for Robert E. Lee.

As his train bore him southward, he passed Culpepper. Culpepper was followed by Cedar Run (Catlett Station was there), then Gordonsville, and Orange.

George Townsend wrote of that day. He chronicled his experience in language that was as fresh and true as if it was yesterday as he went on his way to see the war.

'The towns I passed looked like ruins in a vast desert... the wretched denizens, sympathizers of the Confederacy, had fled in cold and poverty to a doubtful hospitality in the far South. I saw no fences or any living animals, save the braying hybrids, which limped across the naked plains to eke out existence upon some secluded patches of grass. These poor mules had been discharged from the army. They added, rather than detracted, from my feelings of lonesomeness.'

'As the train passed Manassas Junction, heading toward Cedar Run and Culpepper, the few dwellings I saw that seemed to be occupied were no longer tidy or cared for. The few women I saw looked up as my train passed. They were sun burnt, hair unbraided, clothing worn and hands hardened by toil. There was not a Negro left to till the fields. The women were the hewers of wood and the drawers of water; hands callused from the hoe and the shovel. There were no men. Not a son or a brother or a husband remained. They had gone to join the war.'

'At last I came to Bull Run, the dark and bloody ground where the first grand armies fought and bled soon to be consecrated by a baptism of fire. The railway crossed the gorge of the river below on a tall trestle bridge. The turgid currents of the Bull Run River flowed between gaunt hills, lined with cedar and beech. Here and there, as the train went on toward my destination, there were fords for crossing.'

'Directly beyond the wide plains of Manassas Junction, stretching to the far horizon were the undulating lines of the Bull Run Mountains. To the north, there was a line of telegraph poles going westward toward Manassas Gap. Ahead of the train, 20 miles farther, was Thoroughfare Gap through the Bull Run Mountains.'

In between the 20 miles of railroad and where battles took place, traveling from north to south, Townsend would pass the sleepy town of Warrenton with its several wooden buildings. He would pass Bristoe Station, Brandy Station, and the small village of Cedar Mountain.

Lining the western edge of the Manassas plain, like a sloping wall, were the Bull Run Mountains. This small range of high hills *(a small mountain range as such things go)* separates the Virginia Peninsula on the Atlantic Coast from the Shenandoah Valley and the Blue Ridge Mountains farther westward.

There are only a few ways to get through these hills. One of the widest and most used passes is Thoroughfare Gap. The Gap is no highway; it is a raw gash in the mountain, barely wide enough for a single train track and a dirt and gravel path that will hardly accommodate the passage of a cannon carriage and the horses pulling the carriage or a single column of infantry.

To get through the Gap requires about two miles of climbing from the western side and a gradual descent at Salem on the eastern side. When you reach the end, the way opens into the road leading to Haymarket and Gainesville.

At Gainesville the traveler will enter the wider road where most of the fighting occurred at the end of August in 1862; the Warrenton Turnpike.

The country around Manassas, Virginia, is as typical of rural America as any part of the Eastern United States. The rolling hills and grassy plains are covered with farms, clumps of thick woods, small streams, cuts, ravines, deep ditches, country lanes and tiny villages. The Warrenton Turnpike is a main roadway that runs from Centreville to Warrenton.

Every couple of miles along the Turnpike the way is intersected at right angles with smaller roads and lanes. First of these smaller roads on the western end of the Pike and two miles from Gainesville is Pageland Lane. That is the best way to Manassas Junction. Next, going east from Groveton is Sudley Road. Another two miles east on the Pike is the Manassas-Sudley Road. Twenty minutes more of fast walking will carry you along the Turnpike to the Bull Run River where a stone bridge gives the traveler a way across the wide stream. Beyond lays the village of Centreville three miles away.

Bull Run is not a creek or much of a river. At places, it is twenty or thirty feet wide but a person can wade across and hardly get his shirt wet. Manassas Junction and the town of Manassas are three miles south of Centreville and placed at the junction of two rail lines: The Orange and Alexandria Railroad and the Manassas Gap Railroad. Manassas Junction was a main supply base for the Northern armies. A little more than a mile or two from Gainesville, traveling northeast on the Pike, is the hamlet of Groveton, another place where much of the hottest fighting occurred. Groveton is a key location and a mile from Bull Run Creek. It is at the crossroads of the Pike and Sudley Springs Road.

A half dozen country villages and tiny hamlets are scattered about in a roughly twenty-square-mile rectangle sitting between the Atlantic Coast and the Bull Run Mountains. Some of the aged brick and wooden dwellings are still standing and sprinkled about the countryside, and are landmarks of two famous battles.

Stone House, another battle landmark, is at the junction of Sudley Road and the Warrenton Turnpike. Before the war Stone House was once a tavern. Later it was a hospital for the wounded. Brawner Farm, School House, Chinn House and Henry House are more of the small farms around which so many men fought and died.

Several other narrow country roads split off from the Warrenton Turnpike at intervals of a half-mile or so. Most of them go east toward the Orange and Alexandria railroad line; important because that railroad was a mail artery which supplied the Union troops with everything from more troops to provisions such as blankets, shoes, guns and bullets.

Crossing over to the Orange and Alexandria rail line, you might travel the same route and pass by the same scenes and railroad stations that George Townsend passed. It was at Manassas Junction, the largest army depot, that Jackson's men began their destruction of the trains and Union supplies, heaped in piles and filling the box cars after they took shoes for their bare feet, blankets, and all the canned hams and fine officer's provisions they could carry.

To better understand where the several smaller bloody battles happened at Second Manassas, picture a map of the battlefield in your head. Use as reference point the Orange and Alexandria Railroad. The railroad runs approximately northeast and southwest a hundred miles between the two capitols. The rail line, curving slightly to the east, goes all the way to a point a few miles from Richmond.

Most of the fighting took place on the small triangle of the towns of Gainesville, Centreville and Manassas Junction. Imagine a line between Centreville and Gainesville. This line is the Warrenton Turnpike; nearly four miles long. A few hundred feet west of the Warrenton Turnpike, and several hundred feet higher up the side of the Bull Run Mountains, is an unfinished railroad. Behind the heaps of dirt, earth, and debris from the leavings of the abandoned railroad, is the place where the Battle of Second Manassas began. That is where, behind the refuse and ruin of the unfinished railroad, Stonewall Jackson's men opened up with their muskets and artillery upon General Rufus King's unsuspecting troops as they marched along the Warrenton Turnpike on that hot August 28 afternoon.

All four of King's brigades were there… Doubleday, Patrick, Gibbon, and Campbell. For the Confederacy, Jackson's position was a good one. From behind the ramparts of the unfinished railroad on Stony Ridge, with its natural defenses of unfinished excavations, ditches, gullies and ravines, the Federals became excellent targets. When General King's unsuspecting Union brigades came near, Jackson's rebels opened fire with a sudden avalanche of minie bullets and artillery shells.

Centreville to Manassas Junction is the vertical, shortest part of our imaginary triangle. It is five miles in length and goes due south on the Manassas-Sudley Road, which butts into the Turnpike at Groveton.

The Warrenton Turnpike is bisected like a cross with the road to Manassas Junction. That's another three miles distant.

Thirty-five miles to the northeast, beyond Manassas, is the wide Potomac River. Sailing ten miles south down the Potomac you will arrive at Aquia Creek. Aqua Creek is where Major General Fitz John Porter began his march to reinforce John Pope before the battle. On McClellan's orders, Porter had brought his Fifth Corps from Fredericksburg, southwest five miles away, with 8000 battle-trained regulars.

In 1862, the capitols of Washington and Richmond were like two goalies watching a soccer game. They stood directly north and south from each other. The battlefield lay forty miles from Washington and sixty miles from Richmond. The graves of the dead soldiers from 1861, not a year old, still remained from the First Battle of Manassas.

Now a second battle was about to be fought, a great fight that would end in a bitter defeat for the Union, just as the first battle ended. More important to our story, this coming battle is where Major General Fitz John Porter would face the dishonor of a court martial that would convict him of cowardice and disobedience and began his fall into hell.

❧ 27 ❧

John Pope

Major General John Pope had rough edges, and he was pompous. Tall and burly, he spoke rapidly and often. Inclined to obesity, Pope was a heavy smoker. In appearance, his look was fiery and black eyed. He wore a luxuriant beard and his hair was thick and dark. With a string of minor victories in the western theater, he had replaced McClellan with Lincoln's hopes riding on his shoulders.

In his first address to his new army he boasted, "I have come to you from the West, where we have seen the backs of our enemies," meaning he was so fierce that they ran from him.

That bombastic claim did not have the inspiring effect Pope might have wished.

August 25, 1862, Chief of Union Armies, General Henry Halleck instructed Pope to take the offensive against Lee. The change placed Pope in command of the Army of Virginia. Pope was now in command of 60,000 fighting infantrymen and fifty cannons of artillery. John Pope may have guessed, but what he wasn't told by the aging Halleck was that Lincoln planned to replace McClellan and he, John Pope, would be given the reins.

General Pope was also instructed in clear terms by Abraham Lincoln to begin an active campaign against Robert E. Lee, and without waiting for McClellan's army to help him. That imperative from President Lincoln and the promise he would be in charge of a very large army might have been one of the reasons John Pope refused to accept any of the negative reports of a Confederate offensive. Nevertheless, what should have been plain to Pope before the Battle of Second Manassas, and as early as three days before the full-scale fighting began, were the ominous signs. Clear information came to Pope from two of the Union army's most reliable officers, John Reynolds and John Buford. They reported a very large Confederate force was coming fast. What they reported was not just a very large force. That force was quite a bit more than that. What was coming fast was Lee's entire army.

Instead of accepting and planning for Lee's appearance on the battlefield, Pope lurched forward with single-minded purpose to destroy Jackson, the elusive enemy before him. To add insult to the injury of Pope's high hopes, he was totally unaware that, when he found Jackson, it would not be a small raiding force. Pope would be facing half the Confederate army.

Some of Pope's men had a poor opinion of their commander. They had been given the freedom to forage off the land as they moved about. Rebel citizens, fighting for their homes, tried to thwart him by word or deed, and were ruthlessly punished. So severe were Pope's actions that many of his less bloodthirsty officers branded him a demagogue. These men objected to Pope's exploitation of the land and people. Pillage, arson, and rape by Pope's own soldiers had ceased to be considered crimes. Less principled soldiers that needed an excuse for their harsh treatment toward Southerners used General Orders Number 5, 7 and 11, written by General Pope, to bear down on all civilians whenever they had opportunity. Pope's ruthless approach sickened some of his men.

One of them, Lieutenant James Gillette of the 3rd Maryland infantry, witnessed the result of Pope's orders. Gillette later wrote, '*On one of the larger Maryland farms, the Scott farm, all of the crops and means of cultivation was gone. Mrs. Scott had 20 horses but not a kernel of corn to feed them. The Negros had absconded and her cows were shot, sheep and chickens gone. She hardly knew where she was going to obtain sustenance for her large family. Although Mrs. Scott's husband opposed secession, he was shot by a Northern deserter. The lawless acts of many of the soldiers are worthy of worse than death while the villains use as their authority, General Pope's order.*'

Captain William Lusk, leading New York Infantrymen, expressed similar feelings.

'*Pope's orders are the last unabatable nuisance. His practice means to force from the widow her cow, which is her only source of sustenance. It means the poor, and the weak, and the helpless are at the mercy of the strong... and God help them.*'

Comments by his men and officers about John Pope's character as a man and as a leader of men were unflattering:

"Pope is a blusterer."

"He is a braggart and a perverter of facts."

"He was out-generaled entirely."

"A more unfit man than Pope has never been seen."

"He was supercilious, ignorant and pretentious."

"He has not a friend from the highest general to the lowest drummer boy."

"Pope is a dunderpate. Never was a general and never will be."

Some had a poor opinion of Pope's style as a leader. An anonymous Union officer, who observed Pope on August 18 as the army retreated through the village of Culpepper, wrote of Pope, '*As our poor, dust-covered, foot-sore boys entered Culpepper they were greeted during nearly the whole night by a salutation from their commander-in-chief... His profanity was of a style that would have graced a Mississippi stevedore much better than a major general of the United States Army.*'

The writer may have been prejudiced. He was a staff member of Siegel's Corps, one of the many generals Pope blamed for the debacle and was out of favor with Pope after the Battle of Second Manassas.

A window into John Pope's mindset and his desperate search to excuse his shortcomings and mistakes was a statement he made after the lost Battle of

Second Manassas: "My misfortunes are owing to the persistent determination by McClellan, Franklin, Porter, Ricketts and Griffin, and some others, who were predetermined that I should not be successful. They more preferred that the country should be ruined than I should triumph."

Pope's harsh disregard for Southern civilians offended Lee. When Robert E. Lee heard of Pope's order to his men to deal severely with all Southerners, including those who suffered most, the widows, wives and children of the Southern men who were away fighting, Lee said, *'I want Pope to be suppressed.'* Lee spoke of Pope as if he was speaking about a common bully rather than a general. Second Manassas gave Lee the chance to 'correct' Pope and he made the most of his opportunity at the Battle of Second Manassas.

Another indication of John Pope's character was that he placed the blame for the loss of the Battle of Second Manassas on one of his finest corps commanders, Major General Fitz John Porter. Pope's allegations of *'cowardice in the face of the enemy and disobedience of orders'* were made after the battle had been lost and the army had retreated in panic to Washington's defenses. In light of the truth, which was determined by a rehearing twenty years later, the criminal allegations and charges that destroyed Porter's career were despicable.

The *true cause* for the loss at Second Manassas lay directly on the shoulders of Commander John Pope and his second-in-command, Irvin McDowell. General Fitz John Porter was blameless. He was innocent of every false charge that Pope brought against him. By his own courageous action, Porter actually saved the army from total destruction.

❧ **28** ❧

Porter Arrives

With Lincoln's directive foremost in his mind, and knowing Jackson was somewhere on the Plain of Manassas, in single-minded purpose John Pope was determined to find and destroy Stonewall Jackson's army. During the next two days, August 27 and 28, the only thing Pope managed to do instead was to wear out his troops with meaningless maneuvering and marching their shoes off without ever finding his enemy.

General Pope intended to start off his new assignment with a bang. Bristling with awesome new responsibility to save the Union, Pope was not about to allow Jackson or any other rebel army get near Washington. As the commander of the largest and most powerful force the North had been able to muster against the stubborn Confederacy, he planned to utterly destroy half of Lee's army by crushing Stonewall Jackson.

Pope was confident and believed that the odds were all in his favor. He had far more troops than Jackson, and Jackson was isolated from Lee's army. Pope erroneously believed Jackson was running for cover. He thought he would catch Jackson before he could get away, and crush him.

Pope set up his headquarters at Warrenton Junction, central to his gathering armies. Warrenton was a point from which he could shoot down Jackson no matter where the rebel chieftain tried to run.

At 8PM on the night of August 26, Major General Pope got word Jackson had raided Bristoe Station. Until then, he had been busy collecting his army, which was scattered all over the Peninsula, and bringing them to Warrenton Junction. Convinced Jackson was cornered, John Pope sent an order at 4:30 the next afternoon, to General Porter, who was at Warrenton. Pope wanted Porter and his corps to march to Bristoe Station, ten miles away and be ready by morning to fight Jackson.

That was an impossible order. Porter *did not receive the order until nightfall so that he could not march to Bristoe station and reach his objective by morning. It was impossible. To march his 10,000 men that ten-mile distance during the night, without a moon and over a road filled with pitfalls and debris would be a catastrophe.* Porter's inability to follow Pope's order was the basis for the first charge of 'disobedience to a lawful order,' the first of three charges under the *Articles of War* that were filed by Pope after the battle. The 4:30 Order was one of a number of odd orders from Pope.

Pope's battle report on August 25 and 26 reflected his uncertainty of Jackson's position. Pope wrote, *'What the enemy's purpose may be is hard to discover.'* Nevertheless, he sent his men looking for Jackson wherever he thought he might find his elusive enemy.

To better understand the logistics and insurmountable problems Pope was demanding of his two generals, the situation that morning should be made clear to the reader. The forces of Pope's new Union army were a combination of McClellan's army of the Potomac and Pope's force. Porter's corps and Heintzelman's corps had been the major part of McClellan's army.

On August 26, General Fitz John Porter had just come up from Aquia Landing after McClellan's retreat from Richmond. His Fifth Corps was on the south side of the Rappahannock River at the left of a broad semi-circle facing Lee's army. Major General Nathaniel Banks stood with his force on Porter's right, six miles away. Pope had placed Banks' division in the center, on the Orange and Alexandria Railroad. On the right, two miles from Banks' 8000 men, Major General Franz Siegel and his unpopular German-American troops looked across the Rappahannock at Longstreet. Major General Samuel Heintzelman's Third Corps was six or seven miles behind Banks and close to Pope's headquarters at Warrenton. Pope needed Heintzelman's corps nearby, in case the aggressive Jackson attacked his rear before the rest of the army arrived.

Major General Irvin McDowell was given charge over Major General Jesse Reno's smaller Ninth Corps, and along with Banks' and Siegel's men he held the right flank spot of Pope's army. McClellan's reluctant contribution to Pope's 60,000-man Union force was to bring the two largest corps in the Union. Each corps had about 9000 men; one headed by Porter and the other by Heintzelman.

McClellan had promised Washington he would send two smaller corps: the Second Corps headed by General Edwin Sumner, and a corps headed by Major General Franklin. No thanks to McClellan's perennial foot-dragging, these two corps never reached Pope in time to be of any use.

The attitude of Pope's dependency on McClellan's help was typified by Colonel Orlando Poe, *a brigade commander who wrote his wife a* letter on August 23rd stating, *'Pope's army is begging intensely for McClellan to take care of him.'* McClellan's reluctance to see his army evaporate around him and lose them to Pope took shape early. Although Porter had arrived, McClellan made sure Sumner was slower than molasses in January getting started. Halleck ordered General Franklin on August 4, to join Pope. But that order was countermanded by McClellan and Franklin never did reach Pope after McClellan had argued with Halleck, and other delays.

What about Jackson, Pope's target? To gain a better idea of where Stonewall waited for Pope and how he arrived at his position to ambush the unwary Pope, we must follow Jackson's line of march as he destroyed railroads and Union supplies before running for cover to wait for Longstreet.

Recall the description of the land around Manassas; it was a hard place to track an enemy who refused to follow a straight line as he plundered and razed the many small supply depots and stations. The Orange and Alexander rail line ran southwest to northeast between Warrenton and Manassas Junction. Manassas Junction was twenty-five miles north. Passing Warrenton, a traveler would pass a series of train stations and junctions. Some of these, Catlett's Station, Bristoe Station and Manassas Junction, were the first targets Jackson razed. The supply depots were placed along the Orange and Alexandria Railroad like dots on a long straight pencil line. Two miles north of Warrenton Junction *(Pope's headquarters on August 27)*, a traveler on the O and A rail line would arrive at a huge two-story wooden building. That was all there was of the train station at Catlett's Station other than railroad cars on a siding filled with army supplies. Six miles north from there brought the traveler to Bristoe Station *(another one of Pope's temporary headquarters during the battle)*. Four more miles from Bristoe Station was Manassas Junction, the main supply depot for Union supplies of all kinds, where Jackson's men held a celebration of destruction.

By August 28, Longstreet and Lee were on their way. They followed Jackson's route and had passed through the Gap to Haymarket, a sleepy village of a few wooden buildings, and then to Gainesville, where they made bivouac for the night before beginning their offensive against Pope.

Pope's excuse for failing to prepare for Lee's surprise arrival on the scene of battle was the sad commentary of a forlorn general looking for forgiveness despite being entirely to blame for his mistakes. After the Battle of Second Bull Run at Manassas, when the dust had settled, Pope wrote for the record, *'I have done all that I could to prepare, in case Jackson came through Thoroughfare Gap to threaten my rear.'*

In an effort to save his reputation and avoid blame in the post battle furor Pope wrote, *'I sent Colonel Hauptmann to direct one of my strongest divisions being sent forward to take post in the works at Manassas Junction. I ordered Kearney at Warrenton Junction to see that sufficient guards were placed all along the railroad to his rear. Another officer was told to post strong guards along the railroad from Manassas Junction to Catlett's Station.'*

*The truth is that t*he guards Pope stationed there were a minimum of troops… and they were asleep at the switch when Jackson's men appeared. In his report, Pope claimed that he had sent cavalry from Manassas to Thoroughfare Gap, to *'Watch for any movements the enemy might make in that direction.'* Pope further argued in the belated report that he *'fully expected Franklin's corps would be at his rear at Gainesville by August 26. Pope's expectation that Franklin would be at the Gap ready for Lee was hollow.*

General Franklin was part of McClellan's army. As with all of McClellan's corps and divisions sent to Pope, Franklin's corps, coming from Alexandria, was late getting there. During his rehearing, General Porter revealed that a *letter Porter had received from Pope admitted, 'No men had been placed in position to protect the Manassas area.'* Banks' brigades discovered Jackson for the *first time* when McDowell, on his own initiative, sent that force to check for the enemy in the Gap.

John Pope's claims of trying to be prepared and blaming others did not jibe with the facts. The embarrassing truth was that General Pope lied through his teeth. If what Pope claimed in that belated report to justify his mistakes was true he might have had a reason to blame others for the debacle that followed. The fact was that Pope was certain his rear echelon was secure although he had not a shred of solid information to back up his conviction. Not only did Pope know Franklin was *not* protecting his rear at Gainesville, he admitted to General Porter at 7 AM of August 26, *'I hope Franklin will be here by day after tomorrow.'*

The events leading to the three days of the historic battle of August 28 thru 30, have been chronicled here as they bear upon Fitz John Porter's unjust conviction. Pope and his friend McDowell should have been the ones to face the court martial for the loss of Second Manassas.

❧ 29 ❧

Bristoe Station

By the evening of August 26, disturbing reports kept coming in to John Pope at his Warrenton Headquarters. Large numbers of Confederates were moving toward the small town of Salem, in the Shenandoah Valley. That news should have cost Pope a few hours' sleep. Salem was not much of a town but it was the only way through the Bull Run Mountains into the Manassas Plain. It just happened as well to be the perfect place from which to send a Confederate army to strike at the Union's rear.

Had you or I been in charge of Washington's high hopes for a speedy end to the rebellion and knowing that getting rid of Lee's army was the way to do that, we might have sent a few troops to guard the pass... just in case. But not John Pope. He had grander ideas. With myopian singleness of purpose Pope was focused on Jackson. Once Jackson was in his sights, he would dispense with that threat in short order. Then, wherever Lee was, he would take care of the rest of the Confederates and go on to Richmond.

Pope's first inkling that Jackson was in the Manassas area was a report that came like a thunderbolt to Federal headquarters at Warrenton: *'rebels have attacked Bristoe Station.'* Pope was certain the insurgent assault was nothing more than a small cavalry raid, which probably didn't amount to much. He decided a regiment could handle the problem. Not wishing to delay *(he was nervous over other reports of troops near the Gap)*, Pope sent General Samuel Heintzelman an order to *'Put a regiment on a train of cars and send it to Bristoe Station. See what the cavalry raid at Bristoe Station is all about.'*

Early the next morning, General Hooker sent the 72nd New York Regiment on a train to drive the rebels away from Bristoe Station. The regiment piled into several box cars at Warrenton and rolled down the tracks to Bristoe. When the rail cars got within sight of the station, their commander looking out the window saw more than a small raiding party. The regiment he sent needed help.

Captain Bliss, in charge of the regiment, saw the danger and shouted the order to the engineer to reverse the train and pull back. The rebels were heavily employed about the station, busy with the destruction of all things they could not steal. Bliss was seriously outnumbered. This was a situation that was for more than he had bargained. Once safely out of range of the enemy guns and safely away down the track, Captain Bliss sent a rider back to General Hooker: *'Enemy in heavy force. Do not deem it prudent to go on without further orders.'* When General Pope got the word he was more convinced than ever that he had found General Jackson at Bristoe Station.

He ordered Generals McDowell and Siegel, and their 20,000 troops to go post haste to Bristoe Station and take care of the rebels. Pope suspected Jackson, after throwing a scare into Washington and burning up the supplies at Bristoe Station, might be returning to rejoin Lee and Longstreet at the Richmond defenses. This was his big chance to catch Jackson.

Hooker's division had arrived at Bristoe Station first. Confederate General Ewell's division was waiting. At first, Ewell held Hooker's Federals. *"Bullets whistling around very thick,"* one Yankee said later.

More of Hooker's men and reinforcements were added to the fight and the rebel general, Richard Ewell, seeing he was out-manned by the growing Federal forces, pulled back and went to join Jackson at Manassas Junction as planned.

Pope still had a hard time believing Lee had split his army. Such a move was too incredible for Pope to accept. It just wasn't done. He was sure that Jackson and a small force was retreating back toward Gainesville as fast as he was able to rejoin Lee's forces. All John Pope had to do was to block Jackson's escape before he got back into the Shenandoah Valley and catch Jackson in a vice. The only trouble was, by August 26, Jackson's whereabouts was a complete mystery and Jackson wasn't retreating. He was waiting to attack Union forces from ambush on Stony Ridge behind a well-defended abandoned railroad track. Furthermore, Jackson was about to be reinforced by 30,000 men, most of Lee's entire army. This was something Pope neither believed nor thought possible.

Pope made Bristoe Station his new headquarters. He arrived at Bristoe Station as dark was setting in still believing Jackson's main army was close at hand and he would still be able to catch up with him on the morrow.

That same night Pope and his staff watched the sky over Manassas Junction four miles away. They saw the red glare of fires reflected on the scudding clouds above the plain. Someone said, "Jackson is there. The arrogant bastard knows we're here and he thumbed his nose at us by burning our supplies at Manassas Junction."

Pope was not the least disturbed. Supplies could be replaced. He had Jackson in his sights.

"We'll catch him tomorrow before he can get away and run back to Lee," he said to Ruggles, his chief of staff. "Porter will be here in the morning with the Fifth Corps and with Heintzelman's and Siegel's corps we will end Jackson's fun."

General John Pope was delighted with the way things were working out. Surer now that Jackson's army was retreating, as he had surmised from the beginning, he was determined to cripple Lee by finishing off a part of Lee's army before another two days had passed.

Hooker's regiments had been hit pretty hard by Ewell at Bristoe Station and his troops were low on ammunition. Also, all of Pope's troops had not yet arrived so he planned his attack on the next morning, a day that would be nothing like Pope had hoped or planned.

❧ **30** ❧

The Drama Begins

On the evening of 27 August, 1862, General Pope intended to gather his army for an all-out assault on Stonewall Jackson, whose Confederate army, Pope believed, was in retreat and heading south. At 6:30 PM, Pope notified Colonel George Ruggles, Pope's chief of staff, to send General Porter his marching orders for the next day of 28 August. General Porter received Pope's orders at 9:50 PM that night to be at Bristoe Station by sunrise of August 28. This was a nearly impossible task. The orders indicated Porter should begin marching to Bristoe Station at 1 AM and arrive there at daylight. The orders also included instructions to Porter that he must find and direct Morell and Banks to bring their troops as well.

The order was confusing. Porter understood well enough what Pope wanted him to do. But there was a problem, which Pope could not know. Porter had about 10,000 men and they were tired. General Sykes' division had marched more than twelve miles that day and Morell's troops had covered nearly nineteen miles. There had been few rest stops for the last two weeks and they were worn with fatigue. The heat, the dust and a shortage of food and water had not helped. The troops were living on a short supply of coffee, hard tack and sugar and foraging parties continually went out to gather what they could find in the corn fields and orchards that they passed. Most of the marchers had not been able to bed down until ten o'clock that night.

Bristoe Station is ten miles from Warrenton. There is only one road and that road is crooked and narrow. In the widest places, the road is no more than ten feet across. Much of the road passes by the edge of dense woods and the path at these places is strewn with stumps and broken branches. It was a freshly made military road and the road crossed a dozen small streams, some of which were swampy, filled with quicksand and fringed with thick shrubbery. Two or three thousand supply wagons were crowding the road for much of the ten-mile distance. There was a railroad track, which crossed the road at several points but it was no place for marching because many of the rails and cross ties had been torn up. There were no open fields in which to march and, to cap off Porter's dilemma, the night was pitch black in heavy darkness.

In spite of these difficulties, Porter did his best to comply with Pope's order. After thoroughly investigating all possible ways of best complying with the order, calling a midnight staff meeting of his generals and seeing for himself the obstacles he faced, he made a decision. He sent his men marching at 3 AM, instead of 1 AM, to give the troops some minimum of rest and so that they would still arrive at daylight as ordered and in condition to meet the enemy.

The march began. Even so, several regiments still strayed and got lost, stumbling around in the dark. His officers contended with the added trouble but lost much time finding the stragglers and bringing them back to the column.

Major Alanson Randol, then an artillery captain in Sykes' division, said, "With all the ingenuity I could use in cutting my way and trying to cross one stream, it took me two hours to get my battery across." Pope's order did not reflect plausible reality.

As soon as Porter's brigades had begun their march, they came upon the wagon trains. Wagons and artillery blocked the road on both sides, sometimes several wagons deep. General Warren described the state of affairs, *'The wagons were parked pell-mell, like a lot of ice blocks jamming and blocking the way.'*

The road and the night were so dark one could not see fifteen feet off. The teamsters had no team master and were moving the wagons on their own. When the troops tried to make way for the marching, the teamsters were surly and unwilling to move without heavy urging, as it was the middle of the night. General Sykes had to station officers with drawn swords to keep the wagons back and one officer was forced to threaten the teamsters with a loaded pistol.

General Sykes later said, "I never had so much trouble with wagons in my life. Little progress would be made in the dark."

A march of ten miles in three hours, fighting so many difficulties, was remarkable. Many of the men had to remain under arms from two o'clock until first light, waiting to take their places in the column. A fair comparison of the obstacles Porter faced and how he overcame them is shown by the same march on the same dark night by two mounted men. Two officers of General Pope's staff, on horseback and with a guide, left Warrenton at midnight, lost their way and did not reach Bristoe Station until seven o'clock the next morning.

Porter arrived ahead of his troops at Bristoe Station at eight o'clock in the morning and his corps was fully up by 10 o'clock on the morning of 28 August. His troops were dragging with fatigue and no rest. Pope talked with Porter and made no complaint about the delay nor did he say anything about *'disobeying or obeying'* his order to move at one o'clock. Yet during Porter's trial a few weeks later, in response to the judge advocate's question to Pope, *'Did General Porter disobey your order?'* Pope's uncertain testimony was that Porter *'partly obeyed and partly disobeyed my orders.' At the court martial, Pope tried very hard to use Porter as a scapegoat for Pope's disorganized and impossible instructions. And sadly Pope was successful at the blame.*

Despite the wrongful finding by the court martial that Porter disobeyed the 1:00 AM marching order, it is a settled maxim in military law that *'An order requires strict obedience only when the order is given on the spot by a superior, who is present when he gives the order. In the absence of the superior officer, an officer is justified in using his discretion,* (as Porter did) *as long as he complies with the spirit of the order* (which he also did).'

After the harrowing march by the Fifth Corps, on Porter's arrival at Bristoe Station, General Pope informed Porter, "The necessity for the fast night march and early arrival has passed."

Pope had committed the first and the most fatal error he could have made in ordering Porter away from Thoroughfare Gap to Bristoe Station. At that very moment Robert E. Lee, Longstreet and 27,000 Confederate troops were about to enter the Gap and descend on Pope's army.

31

To Ground

All was peaceful around Bristoe Station. Porter's men were still weary from the long marches and very little rest. They fell where they were to catch some much needed sleep and Porter attended his superior to find out where he would be needed next. Events were changing fast and Pope was leaving for Manassas.

Before his departure, he briefed Porter: "Hooker's division was already in a fight last night and his casualties were heavy. His division is near the railroad at Bristoe but Jackson's men retreated several hours ago... probably toward Centreville on the Warrenton Turnpike. I have a report, and it seems reliable, that General Hooker was fighting General Ewell, Jackson's own First Division."

As Pope explained what he believed was the battle situation, Porter could not help but wonder why Jackson had sent an entire division at Hooker. If Jackson was bent on a fast getaway to the Gap, one would think Jackson might have deployed a strong rear guard and taken his army south as fast as possible.

John Pope's next sentence might have been a confirmation of Porter's speculation. What Pope said did not convince Porter entirely.

"Siegel's corps are moving on Gainesville. They will join the fight, along with Heintzelman, Reno and Banks. When Jackson tries to escape through the Gap they will be there. Your corps will go there also. Together, you and Banks will be the anvil and McDowell and Heintzelman, with Siegel's assistance, will be the hammer."

Porter kept his misgivings to himself. In Porter's experience, most of the time Jackson knew exactly what the enemy was doing. There was little doubt that Jackson must have known Pope would have a large part of his army waiting for him at Gainesville. Yet, he had not run for cover. Instead, General Jackson was fighting as though he was about to begin a major assault. Porter's uneasiness grew.

The relationship between Pope and Porter became strained. As much as Pope disliked McClellan, who had sent the Fifth Corps to him three days ago, still, he was happy to have General Porter. Porter was a first-rate commander and he led a tough, seasoned army. The problem in their relationship was that Pope did not like George McClellan and Porter was known to be McClellan's favorite general. Porter's loyalty to McClellan carried a heavy price.

It did not help McClellan's reputation during Porter's court martial when it came to light that McClellan had written a letter to his wife on August 29 and had complained, '*Two of my corps will either save that fool Pope or be sacrificed for the country. I do not know whether I will be permitted to save the Capitol or not. I am heartsick with the folly and ignorance I see around me. God grant that I may never pass through such a scene again.*'

From the several times Porter's old commander, McClellan, had run off at the mouth, it appeared to the president that McClellan wanted Pope defeated. Such remarks and utterings gave ample reason for some to hold the belief that McClellan could be a traitor. As a result, Porter, McClellan's friend and favorite general, was tarred with the same brush.

Porter may have shared McClellan's unrealistic political philosophy. Porter, for his part, made no bones about his dislike of Pope as a leader. Regardless of his politics Porter was, first, last and always, a loyal Union man and a brave soldier who followed orders.

Pope's final word to Porter, before he left him at Bristoe Station, was to '*wait for orders.*' He ended the meeting with, "I must see to what is happening at Centreville and along the Turnpike."

Pope's tardiness in giving Porter any directive would help lose the battle. Pope's lack of clear leadership and his lies about that morning at Bristoe Station would bring Porter before a military court martial.

Pope and his staff rode off to his new headquarters at Centreville leaving Porter to mull over the unanswered questions he had been left with, and with no new orders. Just after dawn Pope and his staff rode along the turnpike toward Groveton. Lieutenant Colonel David Strother, a part of Pope's staff, testified later at Porter's years-later retrial in 1878, to the events of that morning.

Strother testified: "The anxiously awaited order to mount was given. We rode rapidly by way of the Warrenton Turnpike toward the field of battle. At length we saw quite a large body of men approaching us on the hot and dusty road. They were unarmed and marching in a disorderly manner. I was quite shocked. Equally bewildered, General Pope halted the column. In a stern voice he called, '*What does this mean?*'"

"He was answered, '*We are on parole. We are prisoners taken by Jackson at Manassas Junction. We are now liberated on parole and we are going home.*' The answer stunned Pope. Although it was normal at that early part of the war to parole soldiers; obtain their pledge to fight no more and go home, the vast numbers of Union soldiers on parole stunned Pope and his officers.

There were between five and six hundred men, chiefly officers who had charge of the supplies at Manassas. With their train of clerks, assistants, sutlers, invalids, and bummers, the cavalcade passed us, cheering and shouting that they hoped we would make a finish of Jackson."

Here was some evidence that Jackson had more than a small force of irritating rebels. Nevertheless, on his way to his new headquarters at Groveton, Pope rode on still clutching his belief that once his forces were gathered at Groveton, the entire Union army would be in position to carry out his Grand Strategy; to stop Jackson, no matter the size of his marauders.

The fallacy in Pope's plan should have been obvious to him even then. Pope had been given plenty of evidence that Jackson was *not retreating*. Pope's troops had struck twice in force; first at Manassas Junction, losing hundreds of Union soldiers that were made Jackson's prisoners. The second time, when Jackson had every opportunity to escape through Thoroughfare Gap and join Lee, instead he dug in his heels and remained on the Plain of Manassas. On Stony Ridge, Jackson initiated a strong attack on King's division, mauling King and his Union force. An entire Union division was forced to withdraw from the area of the Turnpike. Third and lastly, Longstreet and the rest of the Confederate army were coming. Ricketts had confirmed that fact. Longstreet was not coming to help Jackson in a retreat, but to support Jackson in a major attack. If Pope had studied his enemy as Lee studied his, Pope would have had no doubt he was in for the fight of his life.

Pope's single-minded determination to 'get Jackson' was about to get him into more trouble. It is hard to believe or understand but Pope still did not know Longstreet had already arrived. After a retreat from fighting in Thoroughfare Gap, General Ricketts gave McDowell that news. The question remained, why didn't Pope's second-in-command, McDowell, inform Pope about Longstreet?

Now that Pope had found Jackson at Manassas Junction (the flames were still burning from the destruction), Pope changed the orders. To Generals Siegel and Heintzelman he said, '*Send your troops to Manassas Junction.*' The same command was issued to Kearney's division and Reno's corps. With six divisions totaling 30,000 troops, Pope was satisfied he would be ready to go for Stonewall Jackson.

Pope's plan took on a more detailed form. McDowell's corps would remain at Gainesville, soon to be joined by Porter's corps. This was Pope's statement at the Porter court martial; that he '*expected Porter to march to Gainesville.*' Yet, before he left Porter at Bristoe Station, he gave Porter no direct order except to say, "*Wait for orders. I must see to what is happening at Centreville and along the Turnpike.*"

Heintzelman was slow getting started. Meanwhile more and more messages kept flooding Pope's headquarters. Civilians reported more troops and trains loaded with soldiers were on the other side of Thoroughfare Gap in the Shenandoah Valley near Salem. Scouts reported large numbers of troops coming through the Thoroughfare Gap. John Buford, with his cavalry, backed up the reports to McDowell in person.

By every possible rule of war and good generalship, Irvin McDowell should have immediately forwarded Buford's news to Pope. But, for some reason never explained or justified, that did not happen. Much later, when Longstreet's appearance on the field had become a certainty, did McDowell then report this truth.

Jackson's main force was five miles away at Manassas. Now Pope had something he could sink his teeth into. Pope reasoned that 'If Jackson's able commander General Ewell had been at Bristoe Station and Jackson's men had set fire to Manassas Junctions' supplies, then Jackson must be at Manassas.'

It was almost noon before Kearney's troops reached the Manassas supply base. The sight that greeted the hungry tired soldiers was disheartening. All around on the ground of the Manassas Junction supply base as far as they could see there were empty boxes, broken barrels, empty cans, and the refuse of what Jackson's men could not take or burn. As a final insult, some of the empty boxes had served as toilets for some of the men.

Military supplies had broken down, partly due to poor organization and a lack of proper coordination between the army and the suppliers. The buck stopped with the commanding officer and Pope had his problems delegating responsibility. Many of the men had been eating green corn and apples. What they saw made them feel all the worse.

"Lord, Lord, they ain't left nothing but their shit," one dejected soldier said.

His companion remarked miserably, "This marching and sleeping on the ground without blankets and starving is beginning to tell very severely."

That evening John Pope was still filled with confidence. He was about to pounce upon Stonewall Jackson's army. His logic was plain. Jackson was somewhere between Manassas Junction and Centreville... or on his way out of the trap to the Gap.

John Kearney's division had come to Manassas Junction to find smoking piles of rubble. Phil Kearney's report to Pope and his staff was short, to the point and encouraging.

"General Pope, Jackson was at Manassas yesterday. Some of the fires were still smoldering. The meat and perishables scattered on the ground have not had a chance to spoil. He cannot have marched very far."

Pope was jubilant. "I agree. Jackson cannot be more than ten or more miles from the Junction. We shall catch him now."

Kearney's news gave the finishing touch to Pope's plan. If Jackson's army was at Manassas Junction one day ago, he could be easily found and overtaken. More than a chase, Pope expected Jackson would shortly head to Centreville or along the Warrenton Turnpike south toward Thoroughfare Gap and safety. Jackson's army would be in a vice from which he could not escape.

Pope wrote out new dispatches and orders for the chase and the coming fight. He was not sure as to where Jackson had vanished. By mid-morning Jackson might have slipped away to be anywhere within a radius of ten or fifteen miles from Manassas Junction. Pope was not the least dismayed. He 'knew' where Jackson was headed; he was headed for a fast getaway back to rejoin Lee's army.

"He has to be on his way to the Gap," he told his staff officers pouring over a map of the Manassas plain. "He is on his way to Centreville."

Fitting nicely into General Pope's delusion, a large Confederate force (A.P. Hill) had been spotted not far away from the crossroads hamlet of Centreville. The scout's report had reached Pope only an hour ago. Jackson's way of confusing the enemy was paying off.

That Confederate forces present at Centreville had never been an intentional ploy by Stonewall. General Ambrose Hill's Light Division, on their way to Stony Ridge to join Jackson, had simply got lost. It was A.P. Hill's rear guard the Union scout had seen. Once General Hill found out where he was, he turned his march in the right direction and went on his way toward Stoney Ridge to join Jackson. The mistake fooled Pope.

Pope made another mistake in his comedy of errors. Without waiting to check out the report more thoroughly, General Pope countermanded all previous orders. Hot on Jackson's trail, he ordered his weary army to gather at *Centreville* instead of Manassas. The infantrymen, marching in the ranks for hours, had been scorched by the sun, breathing the dust of the road until they were suffocating, hungry and tired and beginning to doubt the marching would ever end. Like a tick on a dog, Pope hung on to his conviction. Pope was determined to catch his prey before he ever reached the Gap.

Pope's Grand Plan was rushing to a victorious climax. Once he found and defeated Jackson, he would face Robert E. Lee. Besides his four corps, Pope had two of the more experienced corps in the Union army; Heintzelman's Third Corps, which boasted Hooker and Kearney's divisions, and now he also had Porter's strong Fifth Corps.

Major General Samuel Heintzelman was 'old' army, hesitant to attack and liable to fail in a pinch. However, his division heads were remarkable fighters, Joe Hooker and Phillip Kearney. General Hooker would one day lead his own corps. Kearney would have done as well in the army, had not a Confederate bullet brought him low at Antietam a few weeks later. Also, Major General Fitz John Porter had proven his mettle at Gaines' Mill and again at Malvern Hill during the Seven Days of fighting in July. Porter could be depended upon in a pinch.

In his After Battle Report Heintzelman noted, *'At 11 PM, August 28, I received instructions that the enemy's retreat had been intercepted. I ordered General Kearney's division to advance at 1 AM until he met the enemy's pickets… and for me to follow General Kearney at daylight with Hooker's division.'*

Hooker's division was to depart at 3 AM. Heintzelman's notes read, *'Hooker will act as a reserve for Kearney. I shall place him on the road 1 and ½ miles beyond Centreville.'* McDowell, Siegel, Reno and the rest of Heintzelman's corps headed for Centreville. The rest of the divisions were issued a string of orders directing them to assemble near Gainesville.

General Nathaniel Banks' division, still recovering from the losses of so many of his men in the fighting with Jackson at Cedar Mountain the week before, was given the easier task of covering the army's rear. He was told to march his men below Warrenton Junction and guard the trains as they moved more Union troops toward Manassas Junction. Porter's corps was at Bristoe Station ready to be launched to strike like a spear at Jackson as he tried to escape on the Pike. Despite these dreams of a glorious victory, for reasons never explained, Porter received *no orders* from Pope that day.

Jackson's strategy and elusive maneuvers were telling on the over-marched foot-sore Federal infantry. They were growing weary with the changes in position, little rest and the constant marching. Food supplies were running low and provisions had been badly managed. It did not help that the tons of foodstuffs at the Junction were now rotting garbage. The various divisions and brigades had their orders.

In letters sent the night of August 27 to each of his corps commanders, General Pope urged haste. Certain he was about to capture Jackson, his dispatches bubbled over with enthusiasm. The orders in their flowery wording reflected an optimistic forecast.

To Kearney, he said, "At the earliest blush of dawn push forward."

To Reno, "As you value success, be off at the earliest blush of dawn."

To McDowell, his second-in-command, he wrote, "If you march promptly and rapidly at the earliest dawn of the day, we shall bag the whole crowd. Be expeditious and the day is our own."

Pope followed his first gaffe, misreading Lee's intentions with another grave error. This time his miscalculation was monumental. John Pope was caught up in his own idea of great success. Reports continued to come in to Pope's headquarters about a *'large body of troops'* near Gainesville, yet Pope refused to act on this troubling information.

His friend and confidant, Major General McDowell, had some military skill and McDowell was a more pragmatic soldier. McDowell had a pretty good hunch what that mass of rebels sighted in the Gap and around Gainesville might mean. It could be trouble. His own cavalry, under John Buford's reliable command, had reported a clash with a larger than expected bunch of rebels west of the Gap. From Buford's report it was easy for McDowell to guess that Longstreet's army just might be closer than Pope... or anyone... suspected.

On his own and without waiting for Pope's say-so, Irwin McDowell followed up on his hunch. He sent Siegel's First Corps, along with some of his own troops to watch for the enemy at Gainesville. Brigadier General James Ricketts was directed to push forward with a couple of brigades, past Gainesville west and into Thoroughfare Gap just in case.

Ricketts' troops of New York, along with the Pennsylvania and Massachusetts infantrymen, were tough soldiers and had seen their share of action. McDowell hoped they could block any large force in the narrow canyon and keep them from pouring into the Manassas Plain and attacking Pope's unsuspecting rear guard.

General McDowell for some reason did not like to share information and continued to neglect to inform Pope of this vital piece of information. Furthermore, Longstreet's unreported position would become the linchpin of a debacle. Unaware of the threat from Longstreet, Pope tightened his *'circle of destruction'* on Stonewall Jackson. Single-minded and with a military myopia, Pope pursued that one purpose.

The sun was rising over the horizon when Pope broke headquarters at Bull Run on the morning of August 29. He moved with his staff along the Warrenton Turnpike to Centreville. Centreville was where he expected Jackson would be next, and would hopefully be destroyed.

When Pope arrived at Centreville, he got word *(for the first time)* that King's division had withdrawn from the Turnpike on the previous day. Pope had not expected such a move and he was in the dark as to King's reasons for the withdrawal. At that hour Pope was totally unaware that Jackson was strongly established above the Turnpike and that Jackson's division had driven King's brigades from the Turnpike.

If Pope had known Robert E. Lee's position, his normally florid complexion might have turned gray. Lee and Longstreet were out of the Gap along with 29,000 ready-to-fight Confederate soldiers. They had turned left at Gainesville. By 8:45 AM the long gray Confederate columns were marching north.

By 10 AM, General Hood, in the lead of Longstreet's column, neared Jackson's position on Stony Ridge. The remainder of the Confederate forces under Longstreet's direct command spread out along the Gainesville Road and made ready to roll forward into battle.

The pace of battle was accelerating fast.

News came to John Pope of King's move away from the Turnpike on the morning of 29 August. As Pope wrote later, King's withdrawal *'made an immediate change in the disposition and proposed movements of the troops for the succeeding day necessary.'* To further make his day miserable and compound the crisis, Pope was completely in the dark about the threat that was looming like a grim hurricane on the horizon from the 29,000 Confederates three miles away.

Still in the dark, Pope's first priority remained unchanged: to reclaim the position yielded by King and Ricketts on the Warrenton Turnpike near Gainesville. That position was crucial, Pope believed. The spot was a jumping-off place for the Union troops to make a rapid advance along the easy passage of the Warrenton Turnpike against Jackson's fleeing forces. The plan was, most unfortunately, a total fantasy and minimized any possibility of success.

Pope was a hard taskmaster, whose treatment of his officers could not help but cause dissatisfaction when total loyalty to orders was crucial. Once before, Pope had given Colonel A. Sanders Piatt, his staff officer, a scalding criticism for Piatt's retreat before a Confederate cavalry force after only two of the men in Piatt's brigade had suffered wounds.

Now, with Piatt the man he badly needed, Pope gave him a verbal, rather than a specific written order, to deliver to General McDowell: *"Tell McDowell to turn over King's division to General Porter and see that Porter and King march to Gainesville."*

Now, here was a puzzle. It was not the first of the odd circumstances that occurred during the battle, but Pope's orders all had a commonality. Often they were vague, too general, and confusing. This order, which Piatt carried to McDowell, was just such an order. The order required McDowell to order Porter to go to Gainesville… along with King. Therefore, logic tells us that King, subordinate to Porter, would be under Porter's command. Further, this was the *first time* Porter was given any kind of order, much less an order to march his 9,000 men to Gainesville. At Porter's court martial, McDowell *never admitted* he had been given that order.

Second, according to his trial testimony, Pope claimed that he had assigned Piatt and his brigade to Porter, yet he kept Piatt at headquarters instead of sending him and his brigade to assist Porter. Porter was never told Piatt was assigned to him, and he did not learn of this until many years later at the rehearing that found him innocent.

Pope's order implied John Pope knew Longstreet was near. Yet, he claimed ignorance of Longstreet's arrival, or that the Confederate army was anywhere near the battlefield. This curious chess game of Pope's receiving and denying receipt of such orders between the generals was used to find Porter guilty at his 1862 trial a few weeks later.

Following Pope's message for McDowell regarding General Porter, who was still at Bristoe Station, Pope wrote a conflicting dispatch for Porter.

'Push forward with your corps and King's division, which you will take with you, upon Gainesville. I am following the enemy down the Warrenton Turnpike. Be expeditious or we will lose much.'

By this order Pope committed a basic military strategy error. He ignored a well-established military maxim that requires a commander *not* to send converging and separate forces upon a point, which the enemy can reach first. In such a case, the enemy can attack and destroy the separate converging forces piecemeal. Unfortunately for the Union armies, at 8:45 in the morning of August 28, Longstreet was *already marching through Gainesville.*

❧ 32 ❧

Armies in Collision

Lee's plan to destroy Pope was taking shape. The drama was unfolding and four armies were about to collide. To make more clear the growing clash of events that lead to the battle, we shall go back to the day of August 27 before Longstreet's 30,000 troops had entered the Manassas Plain. While the competing forces were yet miles apart, rebels and Federals were enroute toward a conflict that would include a hundred thousand men... and the culmination of one other tragedy, the stolen honor and ruin of a good and needed Union major general.

By the afternoon of August 27, Longstreet was still in the Shenandoah Valley ten miles from the western entrance to Thoroughfare Gap. He had followed Jackson's march. Longstreet and his 30,000 gray-shirted Confederates were on their way to join Jackson's 20,000 troops.

Jackson, already at Manassas, had just finished smashing up the trains at Bristoe Station. He had looted and ransacked, then burned what was left at Manassas Junction and its mountain of Union supplies. Stonewall Jackson aimed to go next to take ground on Stony Ridge to wait for Longstreet.

Surprise and speed is everything. 'If' Longstreet could get through the Gap in time to join Jackson and 'if' Jackson's rebels could withstand Pope's three times larger forces, then Lee, together with his two wings, would be a match for Pope. Lee would have the fight for which he had planned.

By evening of August 27, Lee and Longstreet reached Salem on the west side of the Bull Run Mountains a few miles from Thoroughfare Gap. As they prepared to march through the Gap, a messenger from General Jackson arrived to inform Lee where Jackson had settled in to wait.

"Jackson has taken a position on Stony Ridge. He has not been discovered by the enemy and he is watching the Warrenton Turnpike below his position while he waits for you. He believes Pope thinks he is yet at Manassas Junction or at Centreville."

The courier added, "The Gap, until now, has been clear of the enemy."

That was the best of news. Pope suspected nothing. Lee called Longstreet to his side.

"General Longstreet, the morrow will bring a hard march through Thoroughfare Gap and, possibly, fighting. Have the men rest as soon as evening comes."

Mindful of Jackson's needs, Lee added, "We must seize the Gap. Send General Jones' division forward for the job. Then send Jackson a message: *'Longstreet is just west of the Gap and he will pass through in the morning'*."

Thoroughfare Gap is a natural curiosity. The mountain range has the appearance of being pulled apart by a giant hand into two parts separated by a little space, just wide enough for a creek, a country road and a railway to pass side by side through the Bull Run Mountains. The distance through the pass was not far, no more than three miles. Longstreet's fast moving troops, providing nobody held them up, could make the trip in a couple of hours. His men knew where they were going: toward the sound of Jackson's guns.

Robert E. Lee lagged behind. He was a good enough general that he allowed Longstreet, his dependable "Old Warhorse" to have his way. Longstreet knew exactly what to do. As the light faded at sundown, Lee climbed a small hill. He wanted to observe the Gap first hand. After a few moments he calmly rode back to the rear of the column, easy in his mind. Having received a dinner invitation from the owner of a nearby estate that was sympathetic to the rebel cause, Lee retired for the night. Lee spent the night near Avenal, a village on the west side of Thoroughfare Gap, at the home of Mr. William Beverly, a Southern sympathizer.

The Federals were not asleep. Union cavalry, scouting on their own from the eastern end of Thoroughfare Gap, reported the presence of rebel scouting parties in the Gap. General John Buford, a wide-awake cavalry commander, rode to headquarters and reported the news to Irvin McDowell, Pope's second-in-command.

Buford was a credible officer. Born in Kentucky, John Buford had seen action before the war fighting Indians along the frontier. By the age of 35, Buford had risen to the rank of major general in command of Irvin McDowell's Second Division Cavalry Brigade.

McDowell took Buford's report to heart. However, he was not overly concerned. The force Buford's men had seen might be merely a raiding party or a small force meant to harass the Federals while Jackson escaped. However, Buford's report worried him some. There was always the possibility of a second Confederate force coming through the Gap.

McDowell assigned General Ricketts the job of checking out the potential threat. Up to that time Ricketts had been working at the job of making sure the trains were running from Warrenton. They were necessary to transport Pope's reinforcements from Warrenton and the Rappahannock River.

Historical Note: General Ricketts was no stranger to war or Confederate musket fire. He had been shot five times and he had two horses shot from beneath him. He was a brave soldier. Ricketts' bravest act was the part he played a year after the Second Battle of Manassas. Following the Second Battle of Manassas, Ricketts was picked to be one of the men appointed as a judge in the General Porter military court martial. It was a trial created to intentionally convict Porter of the charges brought against him for the loss of the battle. To make sure Secretary of War Edwin Stanton got the conviction he wanted, Stanton picked every judge on the panel and every man was beholden to Stanton for tenure or for promotion. The majority of the judges voted for Porter's conviction but, alone of the judges, James Ricketts voted for Porter's acquittal. As a result of his honesty, *Ricketts lost his tenure.*

Whatever his reasons, McDowell chose not to send a dispatch to Pope, informing him of Buford's disturbing report. Instead, on his own authority, McDowell sent Ricketts' division to plug the hole in the narrow Gap and hold the enemy 'raiding party' at bay until Jackson was beaten. Perhaps McDowell reasoned he would have time to let Pope know and Ricketts would destroy the enemy in the Gap, whoever they were, at leisure. McDowell's failure to tell Pope until it was too late would cost Pope dearly in the three-day battle to come.

McDowell instructed Ricketts, "If Longstreet does not appear, you are to join King on the march toward Manassas."

Ricketts' main force, which had been heading from Warrenton, immediately changed their line of march with a shortcut across byroads and fields. By that afternoon and evening, his men had started the upward climb into the narrow defile to find the unknown force of the enemy.

As Longstreet marched toward Salem and Thoroughfare Gap on August 27, Pope searched for the elusive Jackson, always a few miles behind his prey. Stonewall Jackson had managed to slip his fast moving 'foot cavalry' in a rapid march around and behind the Union army. After leaving the plundered and burned supplies in smoking ruins at Manassas and Bristoe Junctions, Jackson went to Stony Ridge. There he waited for Lee and Longstreet behind the ramparts of the unfinished railroad above the Warrenton Turnpike.

Ewell and Hill followed Taliaferro, Jackson's lead division, toward what they believed was the way to Stony Ridge. Then Ewell and Hill made a mistake; they lost their bearings and ended up near Centreville instead of Stony Ridge.

That error in direction couldn't have worked out better to fool Pope than if it had been planned. Union scouts spotted the rebels and reported to Pope. Pope assumed he had found the fleeing Jackson and immediately ordered the scattered parts of his forces to assemble near Centreville for an attack on Jackson.

Ewell and Hill soon discovered their error and reached Stony Ridge to join Jackson. On their way, Hill's men were seen again, this time crossing a ford over the Bull Run Creek. Pope drew from the report of that siting as further proof Jackson had left Centreville and was running south toward Thoroughfare Gap to escape. All Union troops were ordered to change their lines of march and go to the Turnpike where Pope believed they would catch the rebel force.

This new mistake accomplished two things that helped the rebel cause greatly. First Pope was misled into believing Jackson was at Centreville and further wearied his already tired troops with another wasted march. Second, Union spotters seeing rebels crossing the Bull Run River and heading south bolstered Pope's certainty that he was hard on Jackson's heels and that Jackson was running for his life toward Thoroughfare gap and escape.

Late afternoon of the following day, August 28, while Longstreet was drawing ever closer, Rufus King's division marched into Jackson's path on the Warrenton

Turnpike. Pope had been looking for Jackson, but it would be more accurate to say that Jackson found Pope first.

Not planning to start a fracas without Longstreet, Jackson began the fight anyway. King's four brigades on the Turnpike were too inviting. Jackson's eager Confederates fired on the unsuspecting brigades marching on the Turnpike below.

On the Warrenton Turnpike, near Brawner's Farm, three miles away from the Gap, late afternoon fighting and skirmishing between Jackson's and King's brigades began. It lasted until nightfall when the fighting simmered down to an uneasy quiet. King's forces were out of ammunition and out of provisions so they withdrew to Manassas.

Pope, still at Centreville, had spent all day ordering his army to chase after Jackson; first to Bristoe Station, then to Manassas, and finally toward Centreville. When Pope and his staff saw the smoke of the combat from Chinn Hill a mile away, where King's men were fighting Jackson, Pope did nothing. Instead, he watched and waited for the rest of his army to assemble near Groveton.

It was not until after midnight of August 28 that he finally learned King's brigades had left the fighting on the Turnpike and gone to Manassas Junction to gather more ammunition and get something to eat. When Pope learned that King had withdrawn his forces from the Turnpike, Pope filled the empty space with Siegel's division. Pope's order to Siegel was *'Attack Jackson in force at first light.'*

Meanwhile, Longstreet was coming hard. Brigadier General Cadmus Wilcox, Longstreet's Third Division, wrote in Wilcox's After Action Report:

'After a tedious and fatiguing march we reached the Gap at 10 PM (August 27). Halting the column, I detached a company, followed by a regiment with instructions to approach the pass cautiously with a view to ascertaining if it was held by the enemy, and if so, as to his strength. In one-half to three-quarters of an hour, General Pryor reported that he had threaded his way through the pass as far as Antioch Church, near a mile beyond (the pass). No enemy was found.' The rest of the division followed and Wilcox bivouacked by midnight.

Longstreet called his brigade head to his side, "General Jones, send your division forward. Keep a ready eye out and alert your skirmishers to go forward. We must hold the Gap."

The division had reached the midpoint of the Gap and it was growing dark. Longstreet sent down the orders to *'have the men to rest for the night.'* By nightfall, General David Jones' division, the lead division in Hood's Right Wing, was well into the Gap. Jones' brigades were followed by Hood's First Division, then Wilcox followed and finally Kemper's divisions took up the rear. At this point, they had met no opposition. The Gap appeared to still be open and free of the enemy. Jones' skirmishers had gone forward a hundred yards deeper into the defile to reconnoiter the path ahead. They had not yet encountered any signs of the enemy so they too bivouacked for the night.

It seemed too good to be true to Longstreet. No general, even John Pope, would leave the Gap unguarded. It was after dark when Brigadier David Jones' cavalry scouts spotted Ricketts' Union troops. They reported, 'A large body, perhaps several brigades, is marching from the eastern side of the Gap.' Skirmishers sent word of the unexpected obstacle in the Gap. The remaining columns of the army were up and formed into columns. The men had had their rations and were ready to march behind Kemper's brigade with Lee riding beside the column into the Gap. While Longstreet's divisions were marching, their cavalry scouts rode ahead to watch for the enemy.

Longstreet's immediate concern was getting through the Gap. Was there a strong guard in the Gap after all? John Bell Hood's lead scouts moved ahead into the Gap and reported '*a large body of Federal troops.*' This was General Ricketts' division, which McDowell had sent. The way ahead was securely blocked against any Confederate advance. Within the hour Hood's search parties went north, scouting for another way through the mountains. There was none. The only way out was the Thoroughfare Gap.

Confederate Evander Law's division had come forward, along with more of Hood's own first division, but the narrow pass made mass attacks difficult. A flank attack… or some way to get behind the Federal enemy was necessary. More men were sent climbing the rocky mountain slope to find a path where a small group of snipers might harass the Federals while Hood went forward with troops and artillery.

General Jones immediately ordered forward three rebel regiments to meet the threat. The Ninth Virginia regiment, under General L.A. Armistead's leadership, placed his men in the hills to the right of the narrow pass. General Toombs' two regiments, part of Jones' division, were held in reserve to wait for Ricketts.

As one man described it, "The gap is a narrow defile in the Bull Run Mountains. It is just wide enough for the railroad, the creek and a public road to pass through. The mountains consist of three ridges. The Eastern ridge is low with the sides cleared and the crest covered with small timber. The western ridge is the highest and is rough and almost inaccessible. In the narrow Valley between the eastern and the western ridges stands an old gristmill. To the left, farther down the creek stands a large stone plaster mill."

The Gap was a bad place to fight.

Confederate General Robert Toombs later reported, '*We had just gotten well into the defile, when the bullets began to sing through the ranks and some men fell. They had no idea of danger until then.*'

Private Zettler, an infantryman in the 9th Virginia Brigade, recalled, "Our first warning that Ricketts' troops had arrived to challenge us was the sound of jingling canteens in the bushes just below where we sat in the darkness. 'Who's down there?' a man near me called out in the darkness. I saw his finger on the trigger of his rifle. I said to my friend, Baldy, in a low tone, 'Don't shoot. They may be one of our men.' Baldy replied, 'No. I see him. It's a Yankee.' Then Baldy called out, 'Say is that Company A? What regiment are you?' I heard the Union soldier reply, 'Eleventh Massachusetts.' Baldy fired. The line of blue Union soldiers rose up in the dusk, aimed their muskets toward us and fired."

The fight at Thoroughfare Gap had begun.

Bullets were flying thick and fast. Ricketts had made contact with General Jones' skirmishers. Confederate skirmisher, Private Randolph A. Shotwell of the 8th Georgia infantry, Hunton's brigade, was one of the lookouts. He was looking at

The Porter Conspiracy | *Gene Paleno*

the sky when the Union soldiers arrived in Thoroughfare Gap. All had been quiet and later he recalled the moment in a letter home.

'It was a picturesque spectacle in the narrow gorge… the great white moon looking through the notch on the camps of the blue coats at one entrance, and upon masses of the gray coats, or no coats at the other.'

'Suddenly, out of the darkness in front came a dazzling sheet of flame, with a deadly hail of bullets. The Yankees had taken post across the path at an old mill where there was a stone fence and great ledges of rock, behind which, they were not only safe but concealed. This was an ugly place to stumble into.'

For several hours the tough Union forces of Buford's cavalry and Rickett's obstinate infantry held Longstreet's divisions at bay. None of the leading regiments could come to grips with the enemy's skirmish line in the narrow pass.

Longstreet rode up when the fight began.

When he saw the bottleneck that had stopped his advance through Thoroughfare Gap he told Jones, his division commander, "We must clear them out. Jackson needs us."

Ricketts had found the rebels but he had found more than he had bargained for. As Jones' regiments came forward, Ricketts was waiting and his men fired first. The Confederates were surprised; Ricketts' defense was unexpected. There was more fighting with both sides fully involved. Ricketts' men suffered severe losses but they held their ground. The rebels could not pass the Union defenders.

Colonel Evander Law, another brigade commander in Hood's division who had been near the tail-end of the rebel column, reached the pass. As he rode up, General Hood was waiting for him. Hood had ridden from the direction of the Gap and knew the situation and the fighting with the Federals that was going on.

"The other side is held in strong force by the enemy," he told Law. "General Jones' division is fighting now in the gap. He is unable to force a passage. You must find another way through the Gap and reinforce General Jones."

Colonel Law turned to a man, a farmer who had lived in the vicinity for several years, and now the farmer spoke up. "I know these mountains," he said. "I'll guide you across the mountain by a trail nobody uses. It ain't an easy trail but it is only a short distance above the Gap."

Hood nodded agreement then turned to Colonel Law. "My brigade will follow yours, once you have found a way across."

Law began the ascent following his guide. Halfway up the mountain his guide began to stumble. He seemed uncertain. The guide had either missed the trail or the trail had run out.

"I apologize, General," he said. "I can't guide you no further. It's been years since I was here and it's grown over and maybe there's been a rock slide or two. It looks a lot different."

Colonel Law was sure the man was being honest and he decided to go on. Moving on through the tangled woods and huge rocks, he and his men reached the crest. Here he was confronted with a wall of rock, which seemed impassable. After a search on either side a crevice was found. The men passed through one at a time and, as soon as Colonel Law stood on the crest, he could hear, very clearly, the fighting in the Gap between Jones and the Federals down below. He could also hear the distant thundering of Jackson's battle at Manassas. To Colonel Law each gun was a call for help. One by one, his men passed through to help the beleaguered rebels in the Gap below. Flanking the knot of Union defenders, the rebels poured forth.

Longstreet's divisions raced out of the eastern entrance of Thoroughfare Gap. Longstreet had knocked down Ricketts' defenses and was marching to Gainesville. John Buford's cavalry was near and passed the news of the rebel breakthrough and their approach to General McDowell, as the first seventeen brigades passed through Gainesville at 8:45 AM on the morning of August 28.

The rebels were on familiar ground. Men, Union and Confederates, were still buried here and the land was yet littered with the detritus of war. The First Battle of Manassas, a year before, had been fought here. The Confederates must have felt some sense of history as they entered the Manassas Plain, and likely had a renewed determination to destroy Pope with a sense that what they were about to do would change the course of the war once and for all.

In spite of the importance of Longstreet's arrival, McDowell still failed to notify his superior of Lee's approach. We do not know why. Perhaps it was because McDowell had been humiliated in the First Battle of Manassas, when he led the Union army the year before and he hoped to correct the situation by himself.

Soon the Thoroughfare Gap was clear of Federal troops. Major General James Longstreet and his staff spent the night in a small cottage on the western edge of the Bull Run Mountains on the edge of the Plain of Manassas. Ricketts' infantry had been driven off but Ricketts' artillery kept up a merciless fire, so before nightfall Drayton's brigade went forward to attack the Yankee guns. Shortly after, Ricketts' artillery pulled up stakes and departed before Drayton had the chance to attack.

Major General Fitz John Porter was about to play his part in the unfolding drama. By 10 AM of August 28, Porter and his corps of 9,000 men had arrived at Bristoe Station as he had been ordered. He received no further orders except to stand and wait for more orders. Without orders from Pope and seeing the signs of rising dust near the Manassas side of the Gap, which Porter knew signaled the marching of a large body of men, Porter marched his men westward toward the enemy.

Two miles from Bristoe Station on the Manassas-Gainesville Road and yet several miles from the Gap, Porter came to a place where a sluggish stream called Dawkin's Branch crossed the road. Porter's advance party of skirmishers reported that they had seen enemy rebels. Shortly after the sighting, Morell's advance division came into contact with Longstreet's right flank.

The events of the next three days were a hundred small vicious fights, thousands of battle casualties, remarkable heroism, and equally remarkable ignorance by top commanders. All of which led toward... and ended with... the humiliating Union defeat.

❧ 33 ❧

The 1:00 AM Order

Now we shall examine Pope's August 27 order in detail. General Porter marched his Fifth Corps to Warrenton, after moving almost non-stop. He was going, as ordered, to support John Pope and his Army of Virginia. His 9,000 troops were tired; hungry and ready to drop from fatigue. Some of his divisions still had not arrived at Warrenton Station by midnight of August 26. They were coming, arriving by companies and brigades in a snaky column two miles long.

Two hours earlier, close to 10 PM, a messenger had ridden up to Porter's headquarters at Warrenton Station with an order from John Pope. The new order from the Commanding General instructed Porter to move his men to Bristoe Station, eight miles away. General Porter was directed to begin the march no later than 1 AM, three hours from that time.

It was a hard order to follow but, from the information he had been given, his men were badly needed at Bristoe Station. Normally, a well-disciplined military force of infantry can march an eight-mile distance in three or four hours, but the men were fatigued, the road was in poor condition, and they would have to deal with the darkness of the night.

Ready to obey, Porter read the order to his division commanders:

HEADQUARTERS ARMY OF VIRGINIA,
Bristoe Station, August 27, 1862 – 6:30 PM
By command of Major-General Pope
Maj. Gen. F. J. Porter,
Warrenton Junction:
GENERAL: The major-general commanding directs that you start at 1 o'clock to-night, and come forward with your whole corps, or such part of it as is with you, so as to be here by daylight to-morrow morning. Hooker has had a very severe action with the enemy, along with a loss of about 300 killed and wounded. The enemy has been driven back, but is retiring along the railroad. We must drive him from Manassas, and clear the country between that place and Gainesville, where McDowell is. If Morrell has not joined you, send word to him to push forward immediately; also send word to Banks to hurry forward with all speed to take your place at Warrenton Junction. It is necessary, on all accounts that you should be here by daylight. I send an officer with this dispatch, who will conduct you to this place.

P.S. – Be sure to send word to Banks, who is on the road from Fayetteville, probably in the direction of Bealeton. Say to Banks, also, that he had best run back the railroad trains to this side of Cedar Run. If he is not with you, write him to that effect.

If Banks is not at Warrenton Junction, leave a regiment of infantry and two pieces of artillery as a guard 'til he comes up with instructions to follow you immediately. If Banks is not at the junction, instruct Colonel Clary to run the train back to this side of Cedar Run, and post a regiment and section of artillery with it.

Major-General Pope

Union General Hooker's division had been in a hard fight. According to the dispatch, three hundred of his men were casualties. After a minute or two, by the light of a lantern, Porter walked outside and looked at the road to Bristoe Station and deliberated as the columns of his men kept arriving. There was no moon and there was a slight drizzle of rain. It was so dark he could hardly see his hand before his eyes. Since he had never traveled the road to Bristoe Station, he called two of his Staff officers to make a reconnaissance of the route he had to take.

"Ride out and determine the state of the road. Go as far as you can but be back with a report within the hour. Is the road clear for a fast night march? What are the obstructions, if any?"

His men rode off, quickly disappearing like unreal ghosts into the mist and darkness. While he waited for his division commanders to come, he thought about the best way to obey the order... or at least, the *spirit* of the order. Despite the obvious difficulties of obeying the order exactly, at all costs he had to have his troops to Bristoe Station by daylight... and in condition to fight.

Before the hour was up his two staff officers returned and gave their report to the group of waiting officers. The report was about as bad as it could be for an army marching in a hurry.

"The road is filled with wagons and teams. Most of the way we had to pick our way carefully through the thick darkness. We encountered several muddy streams that would hamper the movement of our heavy artillery. There is an old rail line next to the road but it was filled in many places with ties and sections of broken rails. That is not an alternate means of travel."

The second staff officer muttered, "It doesn't look good for a night march. Some of the regiments are bound to get lost in the woods. They'll lose their way in the darkness."

The discussion went on for a few minutes more, and all of his officers were in unison. Generals Morell, Butterfield, Sykes and Sturgis agreed that nothing could be gained by marching at 1 o'clock.

"We would lose much," one officer said. "If we start at 1 AM the men will be falling over their feet in the darkness as tired as they are."

Another officer, General Butterfield, suggested, "Let's wait until morning before we start.

"We can't wait," Porter said.

He read the order to his men once more.

"We *must* start as soon as possible and we must be at Bristoe Station by daylight to support General Hooker."

He paused, seeing their faces and reading their thoughts.

"It will be difficult in the thick darkness on a road that is obstructed with wagon trains. The troops are tired. Marching without rest for fourteen hours adds problems."

General Porter weighed all the pros and cons... after he had listened to his officers.

"Therefore, I shall delay the march for two hours. That way the men will be in better condition to fight when we arrive. Daylight will come after 4 AM and the men will be able to see their way without straying off the road and getting lost in the woods next to the narrow road. Let us sleep while we can and start no later than 3 AM."

The march through the darkness of the moonless night began at three o'clock. With grunts and groans, and some muffled curses, the men of the Fifth Corps roused themselves to wakefulness, fell into ranks and set out for Bristoe Station eight miles away.

Nine thousand men, the many pieces of artillery, limber wagons and the driving teams and supply wagons, felt their way through the darkness and stumbled past the countless obstructions. Still blocking the road in many places, Pope's several hundred army supply wagons and their teams lined part of the way and blocked parts of the road. The obstacle of the wagon teams was so great that at times Porter's officers had to force these wagons and teams to the side of the road with drawn sabers.

At 10AM, August 28, the last of Porter's brigades marched into Bristoe Station after a horrendous seven-hour march. When Porter arrived, at the head of his lead column, at eight o'clock, he learned that Hooker's men were no longer fighting the rebels. The rebels had retreated and General Hooker was in pursuit of Confederate Richard Ewell's troops, who were fleeing north along the railroad toward Manassas Junction, the main Union supply depot.

General Pope accepted Porter's explanation for delaying the start of the march by two hours without criticism or comment. After a brief conversation about the status of the several corps under Pope's command and their disposition, he left Porter at about 11AM. His final word was for Porter to *'remain where you are and wait for orders.'* There General Porter would wait as the battle on the Turnpike grew hotter and Longstreet grew nearer.

Despite the extreme urgency Pope had indicated with his 1 AM order, now Pope had no use for Porter's corps. Porter remained at Bristoe Station for the rest of the day and the night of August 28. Twice, during the day, Porter sent messages to Pope asking for orders. Pope's answer was, *'Tell Porter to stay where he is. When he is wanted he will be sent for.'* It was not until morning of the next day, August 29, that General Porter received orders to move.

⤛ 34 ⤜

The Chase Ends

Events moved swiftly. As Porter waited for orders at Bristoe Station, by August 28, nine o'clock that morning, five miles west at Thoroughfare Gap's eastern exit, Longstreet and 29,000 Confederate troops were spilling onto the Manassas plain through a narrow passage of the Bull Run Mountains.

Later that afternoon, five miles north of Thoroughfare Gap, a battle was about to begin. As the sun fell behind the Bull Run Mountains near Brawner's Farm on the Warrenton Turnpike, Lee's left wing waited on Stony Ridge. Stonewall Jackson's 20,000 Confederates were about to ambush Rufus King's four brigades as they marched toward where they had been told Jackson was.

Meanwhile, during the next forty-eight hours the two separate parts of a larger battle were coming together; one at Dawkin's Branch between Porter and Longstreet and one on the Turnpike between Jackson and King.

The fight on the Warrenton Turnpike began with Stonewall Jackson's crash of artillery and musket fire in the afternoon of August 28, near Brawner's Farm. It continued far into the night and it would continue the next day of August 29, until the entire forces of the two contesting armies, Union and Confederate, came together in one cataclysmic battle on August 30.

Farther south near Gainesville and the Thoroughfare Gap, during the dark early morning hours of August 28 General Ricketts' Federal forces tried to keep the cork in the bottle. They fought well and hard to keep Longstreet from coming out of the Gap into the Manassas Plain to join Jackson. After several hours of being hammered by Longstreet's vastly superior force fighting in the narrow defile, when the sun rose that morning Ricketts and his men were forced to retreat.

Ricketts continued to fight a desperate rear guard action but Longstreet's steamroller was relentless. The Confederate right wing, 29,000 gray-uniformed troops with Longstreet at the head and Robert E. Lee calling the tune, poured into the Manassas plain like a tide. As they passed Haymarket, Lee's men could hear, quite clearly, Jackson's guns five miles away on Stony Ridge.

Ricketts' retreat had been orderly. He was covered by John Buford's strong force consisting of Bayard's thousand saber-swinging cavalry fighters plus a good showing of artillery. As day came on, Ricketts' troops broke their temporary bivouac and continued their retreat to Manassas.

Beardsley's mounted fighters, the Union's Third Cavalry Brigade, was also busy. Beardsley and his cavalry guarded the trains of Union supplies at Warrenton Station, the main stop on the Orange and Alexandria Railroads. Nobody wanted a repeat performance of the damage Jackson's men caused when they razed the Union supply depot at Manassas Junction.

As Ricketts' men retreated toward Bristoe Station, Buford's cavalry waited, out of range of enemy muskets, observing the gray-uniforms passing through Gainesville. By nine AM, Buford had counted the size and strength of this new force. As the head of the Confederate column closed up behind their small squad of cavalry, Buford counted the flags and estimated their numbers. Then he dispatched one of his men with a note to General Ricketts.

'Seventeen regiments, one battery, five hundred cavalry passed through Gainesville three-quarters of an hour ago on the Warrenton Turnpike. Please forward this report.'

He knew it was important to get word to headquarters as soon as possible so that Pope would know they were up against more than just a small harassing force of rebels. The entire Confederate army was coming.

By one o'clock that afternoon Longstreet had begun his deployment south of the Manassas-Gainesville Road. Lee waited for Anderson's division, Longstreet's rear guard. When Anderson's forces arrived, he would begin his assault on Pope.

To that hour, neither Porter nor Pope nor any other Federal commander, except Ricketts and Buford, had any idea Longstreet had arrived. The assault was only hours away.

At Bristoe Station, General Fitz John Porter continued to wait all that day of August 28 for orders from Pope. Then, finally, the morning of August 29, General Porter received orders to march. General Ruggles, Pope's chief of staff, rode up to Porter's headquarters at Bristoe Station with the orders Porter had been waiting for. Porter was sent to join the rest of Pope's army to corner and crush Jackson.

'Move on Centreville at dawn of day with your whole command, leaving your trains to follow. Upon arriving at Centreville you will take the Turnpike toward Warrenton and push forward rapidly. You will find the whole corps of Heintzelman in front of you. Pass his stragglers and keep well up with his command, pushing rapidly toward any firing you may hear.'

The order troubled Porter. Porter knew, as anyone might have suspected, something big was happening a few miles north. From the north, near the Turnpike eight miles away, he could hear the unmistakable booming of artillery from King's battle with Jackson. Neither Porter nor Pope knew that Jackson's entire force had holed up at last on Stony Ridge above the Turnpike.

General Porter later testified at his trial, "That order to go to Centreville surprised me. I believed that order would carry me *away* from the likely scene of action."

Porter's perplexity was justified. He had seen the dust and the far-off sounds of a fight coming from Jackson's attack on King's brigades in the direction of Groveton on the Warrenton Turnpike. When he asked General Ruggles, Pope's chief of staff, who should know what the artillery fire was about, Ruggles appeared to know nothing more. With no better alternative but to obey orders, after eating breakfast, Porter put his column on the road to Centreville.

John Pope was oblivious to Longstreet's approach at Gainesville. He continued directing his forces to chase after the elusive Stonewall Jackson from Bristoe Station to Manassas Junction and to Centreville. He had kept them chasing a ghost from one place to another until the troops were dragging with fatigue.

Pope intended to trap Jackson at Centreville in a pincer's movement between his converging forces. He sent Joe Hooker's and Jesse Reno's forces to Centreville first. Once on station, Hooker's division was to act as a reserve force for Kearney's division. Reno's ninth corps was to follow Hooker's men and when Hooker's men were in position, a mile or so beyond Centreville, they were to wait in ambush until Jackson showed up and then spring the trap.

❧ 35 ❧

Ambush

To better understand the unfolding drama of the battle, the reader is taken back to the start of Jackson's ambush of the Union force. At about five o'clock on August 28, King's division was on the Sudley-Groveton Road, about to enter the Warrenton Turnpike on the way to Centreville. As the four brigades drew nearer, Jackson saw a target that was hard to resist.

At the moment Jackson's men opened hostilities on the unsuspecting Union troops, no one, least of all John Pope, except perhaps Buford and Ricketts, had any idea that Longstreet's 29,000 Confederates had come to the battlefield. John Pope had been blindsided. The sorry truth was that for the next two days he simply had refused to listen to his officers when they warned him that a large body of enemy troops had been seen coming through Gainesville. These reports had come both from General Ricketts and from General Buford, and later from General Porter and General Reynolds. None of these senior officers were prone to exaggeration or making false reports. Yet, when they told general Pope, in their words, *'he paid no attention.'*

Looking back in hindsight, it is hard to know why Pope did not accept and act on their reports. His mind was fixed on capturing Jackson. Perhaps it was part of John Pope's character; a bragging, blustering man who did not take advice easily and did not like to consult with his officers. Once fixed on an idea it was difficult for John Pope to change.

Some of the blame for the failure to act on the news of Longstreet's coming must go to Irvin McDowell, Pope's second-in-command. He also had received an early warning from Buford. Certainly, he had an indication of a powerful new force entering the plain of Manassas. Yet, when he was told about it, he failed to give that important news to Pope until the next day. Since his embarrassing loss the year before at the Battle of First Manassas, McDowell's penchant for acting alone and his self-serving efforts to manage the other generals may have been a reason for his oversight.

At five in the afternoon of August 28, King's four brigades marched toward Centreville with the rest of the army to help finish off Jackson. Instead, on the way not far from Brawner's Farm he ran into Jackson's ambush.

Pope had set up his headquarters near the Stone Bridge over Bull Run Creek three miles from the Brawner Farm. He waited there for the show to commence near Centreville supremely confident of snaring his prey. If he had any worries, it might have been that Jackson might escape his trap and flee south to Thoroughfare Gap. If that happened, Jackson would get away and his neat maneuvers would have been for nothing.

By late afternoon, with no word of any fighting at Centreville, Pope waited. Yet, when Pope and his officers mounted the nearby hill they could see smoke. But the smoke was not coming from Centreville; it was coming from the Warrenton Turnpike two miles away near Brawner's Farm. After it got dark, the flash of the muskets was visible as pinpricks of light. Yet, strangely, no one at Pope's headquarters placed any special significance on the light show and the gunfire. Pope was *so sure* that Jackson was at Centreville he concluded the smoke and musket fire signaled only a minor fight between King's men and some small force of Confederate cavalry or scouts. What else could it be?

General Irvin McDowell was Pope's second-in-command. Pope had been trying to find McDowell so that he could direct that commander to block Jackson's escape through Thoroughfare Gap... should Jackson slip out of his trap. McDowell's fleeting presence, which made him hard to find, was irritating. It can be explained. McDowell had ridden off in the night to Manassas, a Union headquarters. Things were so unsettled that McDowell had to find out for himself what was going on. McDowell was the senior officer on the field after Pope, but at times, he seemed more like an independent force, bound by his own rules.

Matters went from bad to worse for Pope. When he sent a messenger to find McDowell the staff officer was unable to find neither hide nor hair of General McDowell. McDowell had slept that night at Haymarket. By the time the messenger came to Haymarket McDowell was gone again. McDowell and his staff had ridden away to speak with General Porter, who was at Manassas Junction and soon to continue on his way to Centreville.

At that same late hour of August 28, Pope received an encouraging dispatch from Kearney at Centreville. Kearney had given Pope good news and bad news. The bad news was that Jackson was no longer at Centreville. The good news was that now Pope knew Jackson was running south toward Thoroughfare Gap and escape. It ended any possible concern Pope might have had about Jackson's whereabouts. Kearney's report said that his advance guard had *'driven Jackson's rear guard from Centreville.'*

Kearney had been fooled. A.P. Hill and Ewell *had* come near Centreville that day. That happened only because they had temporarily lost their way as they followed Jackson to Stony Ridge. By the time Kearney came upon their rear guard they had gone on their way to join Jackson. Pope was not disappointed. It was true that he hadn't snared Jackson at Centreville as he had hoped but now he 'knew' Jackson was in retreat, running toward Thoroughfare Gap. He would still catch him.

With the coming of nightfall, the troubling sounds of musket fire from the direction of Groveton on the Turnpike died away. Pope thought no more of the smoke and muskets near Groveton. His focus of attention was still on catching Jackson before he reached Thoroughfare Gap. No longer needed at Centreville,

Pope sent Porter orders to change his line of march. Now he must go to Gainesville to cut off Jackson's retreat. Porter had stopped at Manassas Junction, on the way to Centreville. When the order came to go Gainesville he turned his men around for the new destination at Gainesville. Porter's mission was to keep Jackson from escaping into the Gap.

The order to keep Jackson from escaping into the Gap was a *Mission Impossible*. Despite Pope's fear of an escape by Jackson, Jackson never intended anything so foolish as a retreat; he was waiting for Longstreet. Instead of the mission Porter had been given, before one o'clock that day he was to suddenly come against an entirely unexpected large force of rebels three times his own force (Longstreet). It was soon after that he received Pope's notorious Joint Order.

On the Warrenton Turnpike near Groveton, miles from Manassas Junction or Porter's march to Gainesville, Jackson's forces had settled on Stony Ridge. He was firmly established with his lines of Confederates behind the natural defenses of the abandoned railroad above the Warrenton Turnpike not far from Groveton.

Historical Note: The half-mile stretch of earth mounds along the half-finished construction of the abandoned railway, the cuts and ditches, were all that remained of the dream of the 1850 Manassas Gap Railroad Company. Meant to compete with the steep shipping fees of the much larger Orange and Alexandria Line, it had been abandoned after ten years of work when they ran out of money. Now it was a perfect place to wait for Longstreet.

Jackson's choice of position behind the abandoned railway had another plus. From his excellent vantage point half a mile from the Turnpike, and a hundred feet higher with a gently sloping, rock-strewn meadow in between, the rebels had an excellent view of the road within his artillery range.

The battle of Brawner's Farm was about to begin on the Warrenton Turnpike. The Turnpike runs roughly northeast to southwest between Washington and the several towns and villages farther south in the direction of Richmond. That country highway goes all the way from Centreville on the northeast end, to five miles away with Groveton at midpoint, to Gainesville eight miles away with Warrenton at the southernmost end.

The Turnpike is a good solid country dirt road. The pale yellow soil is hard and fast in August and the roadway is wide enough for four columns of marching soldiers to pass abreast of one another. With little rain and plenty of hot sun, thousands of military boots kick up plenty of yellow choking dust that could be seen from miles away.

Lewis Lane and Pageland Lane are smaller side roads that intersect the Turnpike near Groveton. Along the Turnpike, a thick grove of trees covered the hillside near where King's brigades were approaching that afternoon. The trees grew close together and cast black shade in summer. There was oak, maple, walnut, elm and dogwood. The woods that King's men were about to pass was about a third of a mile in diameter and straddled the Turnpike. Passing for a half hour through the shady grove made marching a bit more pleasant for the Union soldiers.

The men in Brigadier General John Hatch's four brigades were weary from constant marching. They had marched first from Bristoe Station, then to Manassas Junction and now they were headed to Centreville. Changing direction for the *third time* in eight hours, General King left Pageland Lane and entered the Warrenton Turnpike.

King was headed east in a mile-long column of four brigades. Hatch's brigade was in the lead, followed by Doubleday, Gibbon and Patrick. A red Virginia midsummer sun was dropping low in the west, beginning to touch the Bull Run mountaintops. At five o'clock, evening was not far off.

Their Commander, Rufus King was especially weary. General King was a sick man, subject to epileptic seizures. He had a seizure only the week before at Rappahannock Station and he was still recovering from the effects: weakness, disorientation and unsteadiness. The grind of marching since then had worn him to a frazzle and he rode in an ambulance. In spite of McDowell's concerns that King might be too sick to command his division, and because King was a close friend, he let General King keep an active command.

When King had a seizure, it would come without warning. The bone jerking, muscle spasms would incapacitate the general for nearly a quarter of an hour. Afterward, for several hours, he would be unable to command or give orders. Out of necessity, he had allowed his second-in-command, Brigadier General John Hatch, to handle many of the divisional details. As a result of his illness General King's brigade commanders were left to make their own decisions and forced to act on their own. Essentially, they were leaderless. Unfortunately, King was incapacitated at the same time Jackson gave King's four brigades his surprise.

Jackson's men had a great birds-eye view of the Federal troops that passed below that afternoon. Jackson had been prepared to wait quietly and wait for Longstreet but the brigades slogging through the afternoon dust was a target he couldn't resist.

Hatch's brigade was in the lead. He was followed a hundred yards behind by Gibbon's 'Black Hat' brigade, then General Marsena Patrick's untried raw recruits who had yet to see action, and in the rear was General Doubleday who would one day make baseball famous.

Jackson's guns and wagons got ready as the blue-suited Yankee brigades marched along oblivious of the threat above them. None of the several hundred infantrymen and officers expected trouble, much less a sudden attack by a large rebel force. Pope had convinced his officers that Jackson was near Centreville... or retreating toward Thoroughfare Gap. Surely no one, Pope least of all, imagined Stonewall Jackson was standing at their very elbow about to strike.

General Jackson watched the Turnpike like a keen-eyed hungry hawk; his long lean features a study of attention. When he saw the Yankees below on the Turnpike he was on his feet in an instant. Buckling on his sword, Jackson mounted his horse and galloped off. He had to see the enemy column for himself at close range.

Riding to a small hill above the Union army, he was in easy musket range of the Union soldiers and, had they known who he was, he might have been killed then and there. Trotting his horse back and forth, Jackson studied the Federal column. The soldiers were tired; you could tell it from the way they marched and their drawn faces. More importantly, they were in the open with no shelter or defenses. Jackson took a last good look. Satisfied, he turned and rode back up to the ridge to the assembled officers waiting for him.

Jackson *had been seen* by one Federal officer. That man was General Abner Doubleday. He recalled that moment when he spied the lean figure astride his horse watching.

"I led my brigade along a country road which came out upon the Turnpike about three miles from Gainesville going east toward Centreville. As I passed Patrick's Brigade, I paused to converse with Patrick. While we talked, I spotted an officer on a small hill a short distance away. He was watching our troops and he must have been there for some time. At once I came to the conclusion that he must be a rebel officer. I pointed him out to General Patrick and he looked toward the same hill for a moment to study the lone officer. Turning to me, General Patrick made the reply, '*I disagree, sir. That is not a rebel officer. McDowell himself has been on that hill. That hillock has been thoroughly scouted by Hatch's skirmishers only an hour ago.*'"

"Our conversation was hardly over when the officer on the hill turned around. He beckoned to someone in his rear and disappeared into the trees. I learned later from prisoners that the officer who had been reconnoitering our movements was General Jackson."

When Stonewall was back in his lines his men knew in an instant what his order would be.

Captain William Blackford, a staff member of Jackson's cavalry, said to General J.E.B. Stuart as Jackson rode back to his men, "Here he comes, by God."

Every man knew an attack was imminent. Jackson had seen fifteen regiments coming along the Warrenton Turnpike, twice the men he had close by on the ridge. Yet, despite their numbers, Jackson appeared relaxed. Captain Blackford later wrote of Jackson's composure in a letter home. '*Jackson was as calm as a May morning. He touched his hat in a military salute to the assembled officers and in a soft voice said, as if he had been talking to a friend in ordinary conversation, "Bring out your men, Gentlemen."*'

His men knew what Jackson's simple five-word order meant. His mounted officers wheeled and dashed toward the waiting infantry. From the woods on Stony Ridge, there rose a hoarse cry like wild beasts scenting blood.

"Fall in," the call came.

Rank on rank, the Confederate troops stood ready in minutes. The brigades came forward into the open field and spread out on the gentle slope below the unfinished railroad and deployed their lines for battle. Bayonets sparkled in the light of the setting sun. These were not raw recruits who did not know what to expect. These were men who were going into action as though they were going to a dance party. They were all seasoned veterans of many battles. These were men who had won every battle they had fought. The first fight of Second Manassas was about to begin, the Battle of Brawner's Farm.

❧ 36 ❧

Trial by Fire

On the Warrenton Turnpike, where the action was about to begin, Union General Gibbon's brigade followed Hatch's column. His four regiments led off with the 6th Wisconsin in front, followed by three Indiana regiments. The 2nd and the 7th came first and the 19th. Indiana regiment was last in the column. General Campbell's battery of four three-inch Napoleon rifles brought up the rear.

Hatch's four brigades turned right at the intersection into the Warrenton Turnpike. They moved east on the larger, more traveled Turnpike, which would have taken them over the old Stone Bridge, three miles away, across Bull Run Creek. Another mile farther was Centreville, where they expected to pounce on their prey, Stonewall Jackson and a small force of rebels.

The five hundred men marched, passing a hill and several farm buildings; John Brawner's white two-story frame farmhouse, his barn, and several smaller buildings. Before them half a mile farther, a few wooden structures and a couple of houses marked the village of Groveton.

Gibbon's Black Hat brigade had moved no more than a quarter of a mile when they came upon a thick stretch of woods. The trees grew up densely on both sides of the road for a hundred yards or so. The Turnpike highway at this point rose over a small hill. Hatch's brigade, three hundred feet in front of Gibbon's men, had just disappeared over the rise.

General King and his staff usually rode at the head of the column but today, that place was taken by Brigadier John B. Hatch and his staff officer, Colonel Timothy Sullivan. Rufus King was still recovering from his attack of epilepsy.

General King had ridden with his escort to a small hill a few dozen feet above the road where he could observe his column of brigades. It was a warm summer day. King must have been almost into sleep with the unending sounds of the rattling limber artillery wagons, squeaking wheels of the artillery pieces, cadenced boots striking the earth of the road, the restless whinny of a horse now and then, and a sergeant's harsh occasional reminders to some weary recruit to *stay alert.* The sound of hundreds of boots plodding through the hard-packed dust of the country road trampled the quiet of the August afternoon. Until that minute, no one had seen the enemy.

At the edge of the woods just ahead, some nameless private spotted movement. He shouted out a warning. A sergeant confirmed the sighting and repeated the warning to an officer.

"Enemy on the hill."

Colonel Sullivan, riding next to General Hatch, trained his binoculars at the woods where the officer pointed. On the edge of a ridge of trees, rising in a dark bank against the hot dusty yellow sunshine a half-mile away, he saw men. They were moving about busily intent on some task. He and Hatch discussed what it might mean.

"They could be rebels. Perhaps part of a cavalry force," Hatch remarked.

He was concerned. As he watched, heads turned in the ranks. The troops had seen them.

The scene took on more significance as a rebel gun was wheeled out of the trees. More gray shirted men appeared. The artillery piece was set into firing position and the distant rebel gun crew went to work doing what gun crews do.

Hatch roared out an order, "Get Colonel Reynolds here with a battery... fast."

The regiment was given the order, "Break ranks and take cover."

The regiments fell out and looked for some sort of cover. Following a well-rehearsed drill, the first squad ran to the ditch at the side of the road. Shouting for courage, they tore down the split rail fencing that separated the road from the field beyond. The heavy posts were torn from the ground. In the space of three minutes, they had made a way across the shallow ditch into the field for the passage of the artillery teams and the limber wagons, already on their way.

The 1st New York light battery came forward at a gallop, the teamsters lashing the horses to make speed. The wagons tore across the makeshift planking and unlimbered the Parrott field piece under an embankment. More broken posts and rails were heaped before the guns to protect the gun crews from the fire of the rebel muskets. The entire brigade dived for cover against the enemy shelling that was shortly expected.

A moment later there was a puff of white smoke from the woods. The Federal crew aimed their weapons, loaded shells, touched fuses and returned the rebel fire. Other men found more fencing and piled posts before them, or dropped to the ditches as shelter. The duel was on.

The brigade commanders had been informed by General Pope that Jackson's main force was still at Centreville... or in full retreat toward Gainesville. When the enemy guns fired the men expected these guns were merely Jeb Stuart's cavalry artillery meant to harass them. Cavalry sometimes followed such a surprise attack with troops and the men in the Federal column watched and expected the Confederate infantry to appear any moment.

More shells landed. They were coming, not from a single spot on the hill, but from several hidden locations around the hills and from among the clumps of trees and bushes. Shells continued to fall on the brigades as every eye searched for the guns. The men had little cover on the open road and field and they were entirely exposed to the exploding shells.

The troops were already sweating in their cotton uniforms. Carrying fifty pounds in their knapsacks didn't help. Farther down the road an artillery shell exploded above Doubleday's ranks and a dozen men fell. The rest scattered, looking about wildly for the unseen enemy and diving for cover in the shallow ditches beside the Turnpike. For a few moments there was panic. Men were hit by shrapnel, and for a time, there was some confusion. The officers calmed the men, quickly brought order, and the men settled down to answer the attack.

The regimental chaplain for Hatch's brigade wrote about the start of Jackson's surprise.

'As we passed along the Turnpike, the men marched in good order along the road with the front of our column to the east. The land was open on both sides of the Pike. There was little cover and our troops were wholly exposed to any possible enemy.'

'Shortly after, shells began bursting among us. A Confederate battery of two guns appeared in an opening in the woods a few hundred yards away on the right of our column. Soon after they began firing on our troops. Within minutes, enemy soldiers appeared and began an advance toward us.'

Just prior to Hatch's brigade receiving enemy fire, John Gibbon tells of his moment of peace before all hell broke loose for his brigade. He caught sight of something near the enemy guns and his years as an artillery officer made clear what he saw. He recorded his thoughts.

'I reached a gentle rise on the Pike and looked around. Not a thing moved in my sight. Casting my eyes to the left, coming out of the timber a short mile away, I saw a number of horses. With no time to think whether they were friend or enemy, or whether they might be our cavalry, I was struck by a fact. The horses had presented their flanks to my view. My experience as an artillery officer told me what it meant; guns coming into battery.'

On Stony Ridge, a half-mile distance away and hidden in the trees and heavy brush, Jackson and the several officers in his staff watched the show. The Federal divisions on the Turnpike below Stony Ridge were exactly the target for which Jackson waited.

The dispatch that General Jackson handed his messenger was an order for Generals William Taliaferro's and Richard Ewell's divisions: *'You are to advance in the direction of the Turnpike and deploy your infantrymen in battle formation.'*

While the fighting grew hotter, more and more Confederate artillery shells and canister shards of steel landed among the Federals. The sounds of the heavy fighting on the Turnpike was loud enough that it could be heard by Union troops west of the battle near the Bull Run Bridge several miles away (and John Pope).

As the firing started, General King and his staff watched from their hilltop just west of Brawner's Woods. For reasons unknown General King chose to do nothing to deal with the crisis. Hatch, now in command, ordered the colonel leading the regiment near the hottest part of the firing to send skirmishers to take position on the right of the line. He was concerned that more rebels might try to flank his brigade before Gibbon arrived. Two dozen sharpshooter riflemen were dispatched into the field to watch against that possibility.

Patrick's brigade of untried new recruits brought up the rear of King's column. As they neared Pageland Road on the Turnpike, more Confederate artillery opened fire. As soon as Union gunners had silenced one rebel piece, a second battery opened fire. This time their shells fell upon Patrick's brigade, which had been singled out for punishment.

A witness said, "Patrick's men were new recruits, untried and had never faced the guns. It caused havoc. Wagons careened about behind spooked horses, men forgot discipline and ran for cover. The rest ran for the shelter of the woods south of the Turnpike."

Very soon, as Gibbon's brigade came near the Brawner Farm, it became obvious they had run into a sizable force of Confederates. His regiments left formation and hurried through the fields and woodlots of the John Brawner Farm to help Hatch's men. Minutes later Gibbon's artillery crews had unlimbered their guns and were returning the Confederate fire. While he watched the Federal shells flying, Gibbon, an ex-artillery officer, heard the sounds of more artillery, farther off south of the Turnpike. He noted in his Battle Report:

'From the direction of the Brawner Farm, I heard the sound of another battery. I supposed the second battery was firing at the rear of our column. Until then I had believed we were only facing Confederate horse artillery, probably J.E.B. Stuart. I could easily drive them off. Now I was not as sure; this force was too large.'

These were men from Stonewall Jackson's own crack brigade, tough men from Virginia, Alabama, and Louisiana, who could shoot the eye out of a squirrel at a hundred paces. Gibbon's Wisconsin boys, along with the 19th Indiana Regiment, blazed away at the rebels from eighty yards away.

The 2nd Wisconsin Regiment had not moved a hundred yards when they ran into a solid line of Confederate skirmishers. Seconds later more gray-shirted rebels left the woods and the battle was on in earnest. Even as more masses of rebels drove at Gibbon's brigade, they failed to smash through the gritty Yankees. Gibbon's fighters held their own against the best that Jackson's men had to offer.

Gibbon was hesitant to believe that Pope might be correct, that this was merely part of Jackson's cavalry. Pointing toward the woods where he suspected the Confederate battery was hidden, he instructed Colonel O'Conner:

"Move rapidly in that direction. Keep your men quiet and we can catch one of Jeb Stuart's batteries."

Gibbon knew the enemy. During his fifteen years since his graduation from West Point, John Gibbon had fought in the Mexican War, charged against the Seminoles in Florida, and served five years as an artillery instructor at West Point. At the age of thirty-five, John Gibbon had learned to be suspicious and careful. He smelled a rat. He and the other brigade commanders had been told Jackson was fleeing. Why should the Confederate general suddenly reveal his presence with such a bang?

Gibbon's estimation of events was different from that of General Pope's. Gibbon's suspicion proved to be right on the mark; the rebel force was Robert E. Lee's left wing and the whole of Jackson's army was on the ridge above the Turnpike.

Speaking his thoughts aloud to his staff officer, he said, "It's for damn sure Jackson, sure as hell, is *not* retreating."

Brigadier General John Gibbon commanded the two thousand men of the 'Black Hat' Brigade.' It was called that because of the full dress black army hats preferred by their commander. Like all of the regiments in King's division, Gibbon's brigade had seen no action so far; except for the 2nd Wisconsin, which had fought at the First Battle of Manassas eight months before. His brigade had been trained to perfection and they were facing the flower of Jackson's army, his hard-fighting Stonewall Division veterans.

The story has been told, and it is probably true, that at Turner's Gap during the Battle of South Mountain, just before Antietam and right after the Second Battle of Manassas, Gibbon's western men forced the Confederates all the way back to Turner's Gap.

McClellan, then in charge, had asked, "What troops are those fighting on the Pike?"

Joe Hooker, Gibbon's division commander, replied, "General Gibbon's western men."

McClellan said, "They must be made of iron."

The men, thereafter, adopted the name. They were called, *'The Iron Brigade.'*

The 430 men of 2nd Wisconsin were led by General Baylor. Neither gave ground. For three hours they battled in a fierce confrontation that Stonewall Jackson would later describe as, *'fierce and sanguinary.'* The fight was a bloody battle.

Lawton's brigade came forward. Three regiments of Georgians smashed into Gibbon's line and Gibbon countered this new Confederate assault by sending the 19th Indiana and the 6th and the 7th Wisconsin regiments against the Georgians. Jackson poured more and more of his 20,000 Confederates into the fight. Gibbon and his veteran troops knew from experience what was about to happen. Slowly but surely Gibbon's men were forced to fall back, fighting for every inch. Seeing that he faced a much greater strength of rebels than he had first supposed, Gibbon sent a request for reinforcements to Hatch, Doubleday and Patrick, his fellow brigade commanders. Only Doubleday responded.

Brigadier General Abner Doubleday had originally been earmarked to be the third brigade ahead of Marsena's raw recruits in the tramp to Centreville. There had been a delay in the delivery of that order and Doubleday had not received his assignment until General Gibbon's brigade had taken its second position in the column. Now, to find his correct position, Doubleday hurried his men double time to pass Marsena's brigade so his troops could assemble behind Gibbon.

Abner Doubleday, the mustachioed 42-year-old brigade Commander, was another Mexican war hero. He saw action at both of the battles of Monterey and at Buena Vista. At Gettysburg, Doubleday would fight a Confederate force nearly twice his number for five hours before he was forced to retreat.

In that fight his soldiers would inflict nearly sixty percent casualties on the seven Confederate regiments that faced them that day. A man of many talents and a broad spectrum of interest, Abner Doubleday is thought by many as the Father of Baseball. After the war he held patents for a cable car railway, and his wide variety of interests led Doubleday to become a follower of the well-known spiritualist Madam Blavatsky and convert to Theosophy and spiritualism.

When Doubleday received Gibbon's request for help he was uncertain whether or not to order his infantry to attack instead of defend without orders from headquarters. He rode over to Gibbon. Both Doubleday and Gibbon had been told by their officers what Pope had stated quite positively: that Jackson's main force was still at Centreville.

Doubleday recalled his conversation with Gibbon.

"General Gibbon and I supposed we had simply been annoyed by one of the batteries attached to Jeb Stuart's cavalry. Those guns could easily be captured or driven off by a small infantry force. However, General King was not to be found to order an infantry force. Since we knew that Jackson's force was at Centreville, General Gibbon and I supposed we had run onto one of Stuart's cavalry batteries. General King, however, was nowhere to be found to give the order."

Like John Gibbon, Abner Doubleday was a fighter. He did not hesitate to give Gibbon his opinion.

"General, I think you and I should attack those guns."

Gibbon's retort was swift. "By heaven, I'll do it."

Gibbon had been holding his position. Now he took the initiative to attack, not merely to defend their position, which was vulnerable. The bullets began to fly. Jaw set, eyes fixed on the hill, Gibbon snapped orders. Six twelve-pounder Napoleons came forward to return the Confederate's fire.

He wrote in his report, '*After several minutes, I determined to silence the rebel battery. Colonel O'Connor, leading my 2nd Wisconsin regiment, ordered the fifty or so men of his flank companies to deploy in the field as skirmishers.*'

More rebel infantry appeared. Hundreds of gray-uniformed men came running out of the woods, whooping the rebel yell. Harvey Dew was a member of the 9th Virginia Cavalry, attached to Jeb Stuart. He described better than any other the difference between the rebel yell and the yell of the Federals.

"*There was a marked difference between the yells of the opposing armies. It was a recognized fact and a source of frequent comment. The yells were well defined and led to their designation as 'Yankee' and 'rebel' yells. The 'Yankee' yell lacked in breadth, pitch and resonance compared to the rebel yell. This was because the soldiery of the North came from large cities and towns. People in close proximity to one another had no need for loud cries. Screaming and yelling became annoying to the neighbors. In the charge by the Federals their peculiar characteristic yell was, 'Hoo-ray, Hoo-ray, Hoo-ray.' This, the Federals called a cheer. The sound was all on the first syllable, if heard at all it was 'Hoo,' uttered with an exceedingly short, low and indistinct tone. The second part was 'Ray' with a long and high tone slightly defecting at the termination. In some instances, the simple interjection, 'Heigh' was given with the same inflection as the 'Ray'.*

"*The rebel yell is best explained by spelling it out: 'Who-who-ey, Who-ey, Who-who-ey.' The first syllable was low and short. The second 'Who' was very high and prolonged deflecting on the syllable, 'ey'.*"

In the thick of the battle, Gibbon hurriedly sent back for Campbell's battery to drive off the rebel guns. Within a few minutes the Federal battery was in position and firing; this helped relieve the pressure on his brigade. The 2nd Wisconsin Regiment pushed forward. Before they could reach the battery, heavy fire began. The right of O'Conner's regiment was being decimated.

The artillery fire ended. As the dust settled, the Federals rushed to the place to where the guns had been lashing at them. The guns were gone; the Confederate guns had limbered and pulled out.

Doubleday wrote in his battle Report, *'As soon as our guns began firing I moved off to the left to witness the effect of Captain Campbell's fire. My 56th Pennsylvania and the 76th New York Regiments formed a line of battle and pushed up through the woods to support Gibbon's men.'*

'The Confederates opened a fierce fire from the left. The men scurried for shelter in a hollow by the roadside behind a fence. General Campbell's Battery B and the 4th U.S. Artillery Regiment rumbled close behind along the Warren Turnpike. They went into position beyond the timber and opened fire against the enemy. While the artillery dueled, General Gibbon's 2nd Regiment waited under heavy fire from shot and shell.'

'I heard more shots. Not knowing the source and not having an immediate report to enlighten me, I rode back to meet my troops. When I arrived, I found the 2nd Pennsylvania Regiment had run into a line of Confederate skirmishers. The regiment drove them back but the troops soon confronted more of the enemy. It was clear to me that we had met the main Confederate line and the fight was on.'

'Realizing the 2nd Regiment had run into more than just Confederate horsemen, I ordered the 19th Indiana Regiment to support the 2nd Wisconsin and the 7th Wisconsin Regiment followed. The 6th Wisconsin moved into the firing line in front of Campbell's battery and, by 6:45 that afternoon, my entire brigade, all of the 1800 men of my four regiments was furiously engaged with the enemy.'

Colonel O'Conner's skirmishers, a hundred feet farther away and in the front of the advance, reached a piece of woods. They ran smack into the main line of Confederates and the sudden musket fire was mountainous. To avert certain slaughter for the much smaller body of men, the skirmishers hit the sod. After the war, Private Philip Cheek wrote about his part in the skirmish.

'The Colonel ordered us to lie down. We all dropped into place and the shells came thick and fast. We hugged the ground, and then we heard to our left a rip-rip of heavy infantry fire.'

'Adjutant General Wood of Gibbon's staff rode up and saluted our Colonel. He said it loud enough so our company could hear it, "Colonel Cutler, with the compliments of General Gibbon you will form your regiment by battalion front and advance and join the (Wisconsin) Seventh on the right and engage the enemy."'

'Our regiment advanced in a line of battle across the field. Soon we heard a rip-rip again but did not fully realize the situation until the boys began to fall around us.'

'"Halt! Right dress! Aim! Fire!" came the order.'

'The old 6th gave a volley that awoke a cheer from the other three regiments and a corresponding yell from the other side... and that rebel yell... there is nothing like it this side of the infernal region. The peculiar corkscrew sensation that it sends down your backbone can never be told. You have to feel it. If you say you heard it and did not feel it you have never been there.'

The fight grew hotter by the minute. John Gibbon and his 'Black Hat' brigades were a fearless lot of men that had lived through several fights. Until the very end, during the three days at the end of August at Manassas, John Gibbon escaped serious injury. Yet he was in the thick of most of the encounters next to his men.

General William Taliaferro, commanding Stonewall's own First Division, said of Gibbon's men, *"They stood as immovable as painted heroes in a battle piece. Although they could not advance, they would not retire. There was much discipline in this, but there was much more of true valor."*

Hundreds more rebels came through the trees toward Gibbon's men and General Gibbon was forced to call for an orderly retreat. His Battle Report continues.

'I decided it was best to order a retreat. By this time it was plain to all of us that regiment after regiment of rebel infantry was visible. We held our ground behind a small rise in the land and faced them to open fire. The Confederates returned the fire and advanced to within 80 yards of regiment. The 2nd Brigade was being slaughtered. Colonel O'Conner opened fire and fell mortally wounded. Lieutenant Fairchild took command and, though heavily outnumbered, the 2nd Wisconsin held on for another fifteen minutes.'

From the Confederate side Taliaferro had executed Jackson's orders and his Confederates were in the fight. Afterward, General Taliaferro gave his assessment of the terrible struggle that commenced.

'Our artillery opened a havoc-inducing fire on the blue columns. At this time our lines were advanced from the woods where they had been concealed and advanced into the open field. The troops moved with splendid gallantry and in the most perfect order. Twice our lines advanced until we reached a farm house and one edge of an orchard.'

Gibbon's brigade moved steadily into the field next to a nearby farmhouse and took positions among the apple trees growing at the side of the house. The Confederates appeared from the woods and were coming toward them. Taliaferro wrote in his battle report later:

'The enemy held the orchard next to the farmhouse. My troops were about 80 yards from what appeared to be a superior force of the enemy. Our men stood in an open field with no cover. The enemy never once tried to advance upon our position but withstood with great determination the terrible fire, which our lines poured upon them. In this fight there was no maneuvering and very little tactics. It was a question of endurance... and both sides endured.'

That Confederate general's words were a simple statement; the men in gray and blue endured a killing fire for many minutes without letup as men fell dead or from fearful wounds. That battle was another demonstration of a strange quirk in the acts of men under fire. During the fight the soldier takes no thought of his past or of his future. He becomes completely immersed in the moment. For that reason, most men will fight on while his comrade, firing his weapon next to him, may in the next moment be killed or wounded, yet he continues to fight.

Gibbon's 2nd Wisconsin Regiment, six hundred men strong, moved forward in battle formation. This was to be their Trial by Fire. In the clash that day, Gibbon's 2nd Wisconsin Regiment lost 276 men out of the 430 men that were engaged. Over half the men of the 2nd Wisconsin Regiment that engaged would be injured or never go home after the war.

War would prove to be a hard taskmaster for these men of the Iron Brigade. Gibbon's regiments lost more than three-quarters of their number to death and injury at Gettysburg. The 24th Michigan, another of John Gibbon's regiments, lost 397 men out of a total of 496 soldiers.

The Stonewall brigade that had attacked Gibbon's men also had fearful losses. Of the 800 men engaged, the Confederates lost 340 men. This first blood was a precursor to 10,000 men that would be wounded or killed in the three-day Battle of Second Manassas.

John Gibbon's testimony, during the 1862 Porter trial, gives an added dimension to a dry recital of cold battle statistics from his part in the history of the battle of Brawner's Farm. When Judge Advocate Holt called Gibbon to testify, the tall, dark-haired ramrod straight general, a man in his mid-thirties, rose from his place and walked to the witness chair beside the judge's table. Holt nodded slightly to acknowledge Gibbon. This was the man who had been one of the Union's most fearless fighters.

Gibbon's testimony, while not directly supporting Porter's innocence of the charges, did lay bare to the court *(who purposely shut their eyes to many facts)* the evidence of Pope's major failing as a commander.

Court: "What did the sound of the artillery coming from the Brawner Farm cause you to surmise?"

Gibbon: "I supposed the cannon were firing at the rear of my brigade. My interpretation of the cannon fire was that we were facing Confederate horse artillery. I believed it was J.E.B. Stuart's artillery."

Court: "What were your reasons for believing the artillery firing at you was Stuart's?"

Gibbon: "It had been positively stated to the brigadier commanders by Pope's staff that Jackson's main force was still at Centreville. Therefore, it had to be a rear guard action. In our estimation it was Stuart's cavalry and not a part of Jackson's main force."

Court: "From what source did you receive this impression?"

Before answering, Gibbons hesitated a full thirty seconds. His reply was damning evidence of Pope's malfeasance.

Gibbon: "General Pope's staff. Earlier, one of Pope's staff had passed on General Pope's belief that Jackson's force was in full retreat toward Gainesville."

To bring you back to the Brawner Farm Battle, Jackson was bringing more and more of his 25,000 men into the Brawner Farm and they were forcing the Black Hat men slowly backward. It was dark now and one could not see the enemy to fire a musket and hope to hit someone.

A rebel soldier, who survived the carnage, also wrote of that fight. His letters were kept and later read to tell of the fierceness of the fight.

'The enemy was shelling us. Several men were killed while I stood there. I was about to move away, telling Featherstone standing next to me that this was rather warm work. A spherical case shell came thundering through the wood. I heard it coming and I was sure it would strike near. In a second I felt the wind of it. It struck Featherstone, taking off the greater part of

231

his head, passing through one horse and into the body of the next. Then it exploded, tearing the horse to atoms. The horse fell upon Featherstone and it was some time before we could extricate his body.'

A lieutenant of a Union infantry regiment expressed what he experienced, in a letter to home, in cold, almost clinical terms that are at times almost lyrical. What that Maine lieutenant saw and heard was one of the most fierce fights of the Battle of Second Manassas.

'In the din of battle, sound of musketry and the common yells of friend and foe, it was bedlam. The men who were hit were most singular. There were so many of them it looked like a crowd of howling dervishes dancing and kicking in our ranks. A bullet often knocks over the man it hits. It rarely, by force alone, fails to disturb his equilibrium. The shock of the bullet, whether he feels the pain or not, causes the victim to suddenly jump or shudder.'

'The enemy was armed with almost every kind of rifle or musket. The various tunes of the bullets singing I shall never forget. I shall never confound them with any other sound I shall ever hear. The fierce zip sound of the swift minie ball was not prominent by comparison. The main sound, or the air of the tune, if I may be allowed that expression, was produced by the singing of slow, round balls. Buck shot fired from smooth bore do not cut or tear the air as the creased ball does.'

'Each bullet, according to its size, rate of speed and nearness to the ear made a different sound. They seemed to be going in sheets, all around and above us. In heat of this battle, every man, with hardly an exception, was either killed, wounded, hit in his clothes, hit by spent balls and stones or jostled by his wounded comrades.'

'We had a wonderful exhibition. Some men reeled round and round, others threw up their arms and fell over backward, others went plunging backward trying to regain their balance. A few fell to the front but the force of the bullet generally prevented this, except where it struck low and knocked the soldier's feet from under him. Many of the wounded dropped their musket and seized the wounded part with both hands, and a very few fell dead.'

A.P. Smith, a Union infantryman of the 76th, wrote later after surviving one of the charges, *'We ran over fences, through the bushes, around the trees, over logs… the bullets and the shells tearing through the woods like a hail storm through a wheat field. We rushed on and several of the men were killed before we left the woods. After another three hundred feet the regiment came out into an open field. Here was a real battle in earnest. Just in front of us, and a little to our left, were the gallant boys of the Iron Brigade. They were fighting and falling in a manner terrible to behold.'*

Private Umberto Burnham, who was in that fight with the New York 76th Regiment, recalled in his autobiography, *'After going about sixty feet through some woods, all the time bullets flying around them like hail, the Federals reached a rail fence and an open field. As they emerged, they were within fifty yards of the enemy separated by a mere slight rise of ground. With the placement of Doubleday's two regiments, the Federal line was complete and the fire fight raged with unprecedented fury.'*

Major Rufus Dawes of the 6th Wisconsin Regiment recalled, *'The conflict was too terrible and at too close range to last long. It was now quite dark. The charging lines of the Confederates came toward us, the men bending forward so our bullets would go above them… I feared our single line of battle would be broken but they never wavered.'*

Once the Federal line had been established after the fierce fighting during the afternoon, Brigadier General William B. Taliaferro's rebel division scouts spotted a weak link in the Federal line. The left flank was virtually 'in the air.' To take advantage of the mistake, General Taliaferro sent three regiments from Colonel Alexander's brigades to work their way around the Union flank. While Taliaferro's men moved, the Stonewall brigade kept the Federals busy in front, and Starke's artillery kept lobbing shells at the enemy until after dark.

During the night attack, Taliaferro was wounded. Command of Taliaferro's division fell on his second, Brigadier General William Starke. Starke moved his men across the field and engaged the Federals. After a short while the Federals fell back and his men went to sleep for the night next to the Brawner's barn.

Union Major Dawes recalled, *'The fighting continued and three times the Confederates charged our lines. Colonel Robinson seized the opportunity. He ordered his regiment to "wheel quickly to the left." The execution was with as much precision as ever executed in drill. This brought us within 30 yards of the enemy. The Confederates came on but our boys opened a deadly fire so terrible and certain they broke in front of us and fled in confusion, leaving their colors upon the field.'*

Colonel William S.K. Baylor, Taliaferro's first division head, had established his brigades along the northern edge of Brawner's orchard. In the face of tremendous fire from John Gibbon's 2nd Wisconsin Regiment, Baylor's Virginians held their ground.

Then followed an unfortunate error; a rebel regiment assaulting enemy lines in the gathering darkness fired by mistake at the 2nd Virginia regiment. When calls to stop the firing didn't work some men tried to run the gauntlet to warn their fellow regiment to stop their firing...and they were shot down to a man. The mistaken battle of rebel against rebel continued until darkness ended the mayhem mistake.

Major General Richard S. Ewell's only offensive, before it got too dark to fight, was fought by Lawton's and Trimble's brigades. It was not only unsuccessful, it cost General Lee one of his best division commanders.

As Trimble moved forward into the fight, Major General Ewell joined the 12th Georgia Regiment in the advance. As they moved forward the men were swept away in a murderous cross fire. Ewell took a quick look under some pine branches to locate the source of the musketry. A minie ball struck Ewell just below the kneecap, piercing the joint and following his leg down for several inches. His kneecap was split in two and his tibia was shattered. He lay on the ground in the pine thicket for thirty minutes before he was discovered.

"Amputate the leg now," Ewell ordered the doctor, who had come looking for the wounded general.

The doctor convinced him to wait until they could take him to a field hospital. He was brought to Sudley Church, already filled with rebel wounded. Because of the fighting nearby, they moved the general to Buckner House, four miles north of the battlefield and there his leg was amputated.

Ewell's relationship with Jackson, in the beginning, had been strained. Ewell privately referred to the cagey Confederate leader as *'a fool and an idiot and as crazy as a March Hare.'* Ewell was a man not easily convinced. By the time he had served with Stonewall for several months, he had changed his mind.

"Jackson is no fool. He keeps his council but he has a method to his madness."

That day fighting erupted all over the Manassas plain. On the afternoon and evening of August 28, as the fighting continued near John Brawner's Farm on the Turnpike, fighting broke out on the Manassas-Gainesville Road as well. Porter's columns had reached Dawkin's Branch. His forward skirmishers had encountered skirmishers of Longstreet's divisions.

On Warrenton Turnpike, as it grew too dark to see, there was one more final exchange of hostilities before darkness ended the fighting. Jackson's men, firing their muskets, pursued King's divisions. Men from the New York, Pennsylvania and Wisconsin regiments were ordered to hold the line until the greater part of King's regiments could complete their retreat in order toward Manassas. One of Gibbon's soldiers, who survived the baptism of fire that day, wrote home after the battle in the darkness.

'The Confederate line was a black mass not fifty yards away. We stood for an hour, laying down and firing back. My God, what a slaughter. Men fell all around me but we got no order to withdraw. Wisconsin men would rather die than fall back without orders. A Colonel in charge of the 76th shouted the order to his regiment, "By the left oblique, Aim, Fire!" The 76th let loose a deadly enfilade fire, catching the rebels from the side.'

A.P. Smith recalled the sight. *'No rebel in that column who escaped death will ever forget that volley. It seemed like one big gun. When the smoke cleared away a little, the few that were left of that mass of human beings, who had so rapidly left the woods a few minutes before, had disappeared. The ground was literally covered with their dead and wounded.'*

Men continued to kill each other in near total darkness. At times they were thirty yards apart. More Union troops came and the Confederates were outnumbered. However, the Stonewall Brigade, Alexander Lawton's Brigade, and the Isaac Trimble Brigade continued the fight. Troops on both sides came together in the fields, woods and hills around Brawner's Farm in bloody conflict. The fighting escalated all day amidst the unfinished railroad and in the fields.

One of King's sergeants wrote later, *'It was now quite dark. As the rebels fell back there was a lull in the storm, but it was short. The rebels rallied, and burst from the woods with volley after volley. Our men loaded and fired with the energy of madmen and a recklessness of death truly wonderful. Human nature could not long stand such a terribly wasting fire. It literally mowed out gaps in their line. Isolated squads would rally together, and rushed upon us right into the face of death. Still we were pressed back. The rebel line pushed up with their peculiar, "Whoop, Whoop," a continuous yell. I galloped down the line of our regiment crying, "Cheer, boys. Call out Bully for Siegel. Call three and a tiger for the reinforcements." Would to God they had been there.'*

'When I got opposite to Colonel Cutler I heard that chug so continuous in battle, but not a muscle of the man's face quivered as he quietly asked, "Where is Colonel Bragg? I am wounded and he must take command."'

'The fighting continued and three times the Confederates charged our lines. Colonel Robinson seized the opportunity. He ordered his regiment to "Wheel quickly to the left." The execution was with as much precision as ever executed in drill. This brought us within 30 yards of the enemy. The Confederates came on but our boys opened a deadly fire so terrible and certain they broke in front of us and fled in confusion, leaving their colors upon the field.'

Confederate Brigadier General A.R. Lawton, one of Ewell's brigades, ordered his regiments to advance against Gibbon's 2nd Wisconsin regiment and they fought until dark. Private J.S. Blaite, in the 26th Georgia regiment wrote home to his mother about that night.

'We were ordered in just after dark. We marched steadily across an open field about 400 yards, over which the balls were flying by the thousands. Occasionally a man would drop from our ranks, yet not a man faltered. When we reached the fence the colonel gave us an order to lie down and commence firing.'

'After we had fired several rounds General Lawton ordered us to charge. At the command every man went over the fence. Then the Yankees began a fearful execution.'

John Gibbon's 2nd Wisconsin, 7th Wisconsin, and 76th New York regiments poured in a withering fire at the Georgia regiment. The Georgians staggered and then yielded. Firing continued for several minutes until darkness brought it to an end.

Confederate Brigadier General Isaac R. Trimble, leading another of Ewell's brigades, at 7 PM ordered his brigade forward. He told afterward of what he saw as they advanced on the enemy.

"My brigade moved forward in a beautiful line of battle across an open field. Soon we met the fire of the enemy and returned it briskly but not effectively, because the enemy was behind a small hill. The position of the left part of the 15th Alabama was in a thick clump of bushes, covering a space of about four acres and covered with rocks. Our line of battle, preceded by skirmishers, led us through a clump of rocky woods. We reached an old dilapidated fence on the other side. The field in front was clear but the night had grown so dark that the 'boys in blue' could only be seen by the flash of their guns. They had our range and we had theirs. Their position was out in the open and ours was behind the old fence. We were not more than fifty yards apart. The noisy musketry battle continued for about an hour, until darkness brought an end to the firing and the Federals drew off the field."

Losses on both sides had been heavy. rebel casualties were staggering; the Confederates lost nearly a third of their force. Taliaferro, Trimble and Ewell were so wounded they were out of action for months. In one rebel company, the 21st Georgia, forty of forty-five men were lost. The fight ended in a stalemate at the Brawner Farm with each side losing more than a thousand men.

With the coming of darkness, the fighting subsided. Finally, except for sporadic firing, it grew quiet. Withdrawal seemed the best course. The men waited a short while, and then they went out to collect the wounded. Afterward they pulled back to an open field near the Turnpike and fell upon the ground to grab what sleep they could. At 3 AM, the men were roused and set off toward Manassas. The battle was finished for the day. It would begin at dawn with a vengeance.

⚜ **37** ⚜

The Joint Order

At 3 AM on the morning of August 29, Stonewall Jackson was lying down resting on Stony Ridge, a hundred feet or so above and a mile from the Turnpike. A dispatch came from Longstreet. *'Longstreet's through the Gap,'* the message read. Tomorrow the fighting would be worse and the good news lifted a heavy burden from Jackson's shoulders. The dispatch gave him the news he had been waiting for; the reinforcements he needed badly to continue the attack were coming. In only a few more hours Longstreet would relieve him.

"I reckon he is at Haymarket by this time," Jackson announced happily to the men around him.

Now wide awake, he jumped up, demanding, "Where is the man who brought this dispatch? I must shake hands with him."

"Who are the leading elements?" Jackson wanted to know from the messenger.

"The Texas brigade," he was told.

Jackson turned to a staff officer.

"Major, put the Texas brigade left of the Turnpike. Gallop, sir."

The Confederate forces were gathering...

At 3 AM, while Jackson happily read his dispatch, four miles away General King and his four brigades were on their way to Manassas Junction to nurse their wounds and get more ammunition and rations. Rufus King was not nearly as pleased as Jackson.

Manassas Junction, a main headquarters for the Union army, was where the Union's battered, bruised and bloody troops might rest and repair from the fight the day before with Jackson near Brawner's Farm.

The fighting had taken a heavy toll on King's division. John Gibbon's brigade, especially, had borne the brunt of the bloody combat. Gibbon's 6th Regiment of *Black Hats* had held their own against Jackson's best for hours until sheer numbers began to tell and they had been forced back.

All four of General Rufus King's brigades had been pretty badly mauled by Jackson's men. The beating they had taken from Taliaferro's and Ewell's divisions all afternoon and evening of the day had left the four brigades nearly out of ammunition, hungry, and badly shot up with heavy losses. It had been some of the bitterest fighting of the war. And General King was no longer fit to remain in command. Epilepsy had struck him again and his command had passed to General Hatch.

That same morning of August 29, an hour after King's division arrived at Manassas, Major Rufus Dawes watched Porter's troops as they went by. Dawes commanded the 6th Wisconsin Regiment for General Gibbon after its commander had been wounded. Major Dawes later testified at the 1862 Porter Court Martial.

"I was aroused from sleep by the heavy tramp of hurrying feet and got up for breakfast. Fresh beef ration had been issued and hot coffee was made. It was about nine in the morning. We could hear the sounds of cannon and an occasional ripple of musketry coming from the Turnpike. General Porter's corps was passing and, at the time, the cannons from the Turnpike were roaring so loudly that Porter's men fully believed they were marching directly to battle."

"Someone in Porter's ranks said, *'We are going to show you, straw feet, how to fight.'* Porter's red-pantalooned Zouave troops aimed a running cry of disparagement at us in the nature of remarks such as, *'Pope's soldiers are something quite inferior to the Army of the Potomac.'*"

"I remember one of our men shouting back, *'Wait 'til you've been where we have been. You'll get the slack taken out of your pantaloons and the swell out of your heads.'*"

The shouter in Gibbon's regiment had the best of reasons to say that; Dawes' regiment lost a third of their men in the Brawner's Farm battle on the previous day.

The night before, August 28, Pope, secure in his headquarters near Bull Run, still hadn't heard about the fighting at Brawner's Farm. That morning of August 29, was when he finally learned that General King's five hundred troops, some of them green recruits, had fought Stonewall Jackson's seasoned rebels. Pope's first reaction was to write an urgent dispatch to King to *'Hold your ground'* but by the time King received the order his four weary brigades were already halfway to Manassas Junction.

General Rufus King was a good enough division commander to know that Pope needed to be made aware as soon as possible that the force which had driven King's division from the Turnpike was no small part of Jackson's army; it was *all* of Jackson's army. Early in the morning John Gibbon went to Pope's headquarters to give him the whole story on the Brawner's Farm fight.

Gibbon was a soldier that had seen plenty of action. He pulled no punches and made a point of impressing on Pope how important the Turnpike position was. It must be held if Jackson was to be captured.

Gibbon's recollection of that meeting with Pope, to which he testified later, was that his report was the *first time* that Pope had heard that *all of Jackson's force* was spread out on the Warrenton Turnpike. Once Pope realized Jackson's entire army was cornered on Stony Ridge, he saw this as his *last chance* to defeat Jackson. He issued orders to all parts of his army to attack the enemy along the Warrenton Turnpike. His orders were based on a certainty that Jackson had fled *south of*

Centreville and was in retreat.

General King's division had left a hole on the Warrenton Turnpike. The hole had to be plugged with more Federal troops. If there was no one to oppose Jackson near Groveton, Pope feared Jackson would escape much more easily. In his battle report Pope noted, *'General King's withdrawal makes an immediate change in the disposition and the proposed movements of our troops for this day necessary.'* John Pope's first priority was to take back King's lost position as soon as possible and rearrange his troops to the best advantage in order to catch Jackson.

Pope ordered General Franz Siegel to take King's place on Henry Hill and continue the attack on Jackson along the Warrenton Turnpike *'as soon as it was light enough to see.'* Siegel's First Corps would take up the slack and fill the empty hole King had left.

Within an hour of sunrise Jackson was told that Siegel's troops had filled the breach left by King's departure. Siegel's division now occupied those same positions King's troops had left vacant during the night. By first light it became apparent to the watchful rebel scouts that the Federals were making ready to renew the attack.

On Henry Hill, considered to be closest to the center of Jackson's line, General Siegel had placed his guns and mortars on the left of the Union line and south of the Warrenton Turnpike. His first division, led by General Robert Schenck, held the high ground. By five AM Siegel began an advance on Stony Ridge with all his artillery fire in support and all his infantry going forward.

Siegel's four divisions and his artillery formed their lines. An hour after dawn broke over the plains and wooded hills around Groveton, Siegel sent skirmishers across the Turnpike, into the fields and up the slope toward Stony Ridge to feel out the enemy and lead the attack. Siegel described his activities that morning.

'I formed in order of battle at daybreak having ascertained that the enemy was in considerable force within sight of the hills we now occupied. The enemy was shifting his troops from the Gainesville Turnpike to his right. I sent cavalry scouts as far as they could go. After an hour my cavalry scouts reported that the enemy was moving against our left and I sent a messenger to headquarters. Shortly, Colonel Ruggles came to me and told me to occupy the 'Bald Hill' on my left, which General Schenck did immediately.'

Pope's next directive early that morning of August 29 was directed to General Heintzelman:

'At 1 AM move out from Centreville on the Warrenton Turnpike. March with all the men you can take but no more than 2000 men. Pursue the Turnpike from Centreville to Warrenton. Advance cautiously and drive in the enemy pickets. At early dawn attack Jackson vigorously.'

Heintzelman sent word to his first division commander, General Philip Kearny to move toward Groveton before daylight. Kearney's attack would take some of the pressure off Siegel, who had already replaced King and had orders to attack at early sunrise.

Note to Reader: Recall, Lee and Longstreet were coming in force from Gainesville. Of this hard fact Pope appeared and acted as if he had no knowledge. This despite a dozen signs and reports.

McDowell was sent along with Porter to move toward Gainesville. McDowell and Porter would be waiting there to finish Jackson's destruction (Pope foolishly expected) as Jackson's Confederates fled toward Thoroughfare Gap and safety. Reno was ordered to support Heintzelman and Siegel in the combined attacks on Jackson.

An example of the close ties and friendship of opposing officers before the Civil War was Reno's relationship to Jackson. Before the war, at West Point Jesse Reno had been Jackson's close friend. More than just their one-time friendship, Reno's ties to Jackson could be traced back to 1700, when their families came to the United States from England.

In another of the countless tragedies of the Civil War, like Stonewall Jackson, Jesse Reno did not have long to live. Less than three weeks later Reno was killed by a rebel bullet in the Battle of South Mountain, two weeks after the Battle of Second Manassas. Jackson would die in battle soon after.

General Kearney had a problem with Pope's order. Kearney was to be a supporting force for Siegel. The trouble was that Phil Kearney was still nursing a grudge against Franz Siegel. Weeks before, a supposedly confidential letter, written by Kearny to the Governor of New Jersey was not very complimentary of the German-American troops. Somehow the letter came to Siegel's attention and Siegel published the letter. Kearny considered Siegel arrogant.

Evidence of Pope's lack of support from his officers made itself plain early in the three-day battle. Kearney was a combative, tough sort and he also had a prejudice against higher authority. He was especially prejudiced when that authority didn't seem to know what it was doing. His men had seen much fighting, along with King, the day before.

When Kearney read the order he said, "Tell General Pope to go to hell. We won't march until morning."

And that is what he did.

Kearney, in uncharacteristic disregard of orders, was not in motion at daylight, four hours *after* the appointed time. His brigade commander, General John C. Robinson arrived on the battlefield on Siegel's right at nine o'clock in the morning of August 29, four hours late, and immediately came under heavy fire. The fighting continued all day until, finally at evening of the 30th he was relieved.

Instead of supporting General Siegel's divisions by linking up with General Schurz' right, Kearny dawdled as he had promised until it was too late to be of any help, and Siegel was forced to retreat. After the battle, he apologized to the officers he had pledged to support. Had Pope wished it, Kearney, instead of Porter, might have suffered Pope's wrath for the loss at Second Manassas.

That morning at Manassas, Porter's troops broke out provisions before continuing their march to Centreville. Their fare, as they ate their provisions, was typical of soldiers in 1862: biscuits, salt beef, and coffee. The soldiers had named the biscuits *'sheet iron crackers.'* The flour and water crackers were so hard the soldiers called them *'teeth-dullers.'* The rock-hard flour biscuits were soaked in water or coffee and eaten with salt horse, a common name for salted beef or salted pork. Some 'homespun' tobacco, twisted into forms that could be chewed or cut into small pieces and smoked, finished off the repast.

While his division rested and ate, Porter rode up to Weir House, Pope's headquarters at Manassas Junction. He was intercepted there by General Piatt. General Piatt had come to give Porter an order from Pope to change his line of march. Porter's corps was now to turn about and go to Gainesville to intercept the 'fleeing' Jackson. Pope believed that Porter would need a larger force to stop and capture Jackson *'as he fled toward escape through the Gap,'* and Pope ordered a re-assignment of King's division to Porter.

Piatt said, "General Pope wishes you to take command of King's division and move upon Gainesville with your whole command, leaving your trains to follow."

No sooner had Piatt ridden off when General McDowell rode up. Porter told him what Piatt had said. The two men talked, reviewing the actions of the last sixteen hours. There was much to talk about. Before long, Porter understood McDowell's *main* purpose in dragging out the conversation; McDowell was about as unhappy as a general could be. He had lost a good part of his command to a junior officer. The loss of King's brigades did not sit well with Irvin McDowell. His pride was stung to the quick.

By 9:30 that morning Gibbon had ridden back to Manassas Junction where he delivered a second order to Porter; a repeat of what Piatt had told Porter: *'Push forward with your corps and with King's division upon Gainesville. I am following along the Warrenton Turnpike. Be expeditious or we will lose much.'*

This second order, which McDowell overheard, was a painful reminder to Irvin McDowell that he had lost King's division. Hearing it again, as Gibbon reported to Porter, made McDowell fidget with unhappiness. As soon as Gibbon was gone, McDowell turned to Porter with a suggestion.

"When we face the enemy, please place King's division on your right. That way my three divisions will be better concentrated."

Porter agreed. He was willing to soften the blow to McDowell's self-esteem. He understood that for McDowell to lose an entire division to a junior officer was a large nut to swallow. Being a man to face facts, McDowell also knew that if a battle should develop near Gainesville, he would need King's added force near.

It is important to note that during this conversation at Manassas Junction, *at no time* did McDowell take command of Porter's regiments as martial law might require (which would have seemed logical according to later charges against Porter). It was not until later when the *Joint Order* was received by both men that McDowell claimed that right. As the senior officer in the field, and in the absence of the army general, this was McDowell's legal prerogative and both men knew it.

Whatever were his failings, John Pope was not a stupid man. From his testimony at the 1862 Porter court martial trial, it is certain that John Pope knew early that Longstreet was coming. Pope's actions were like the driver of a heavy truck speeding across a lake of thin ice, the cracking of the ice loud in his ears. Pope was obsessed with finding Jackson, like the truck driver, before the ice broke and the truck plunged to the bottom. John Pope was so involved with Jackson's capture that he refused to believe Longstreet would be a serious challenge in battle before Pope could defeat Jackson. Pope ignored common sense in order to validate his vendetta. Pope's own testimony confirmed this fact during the 1862 Porter trial when he was questioned by the judge advocate *(Pg. 38 of Pp.379, Porter Court Martial).*

Judge Holt: "Did you know on August 29, or sooner, that Longstreet's corps, in whole or in part, had joined Jackson's force?"

General Pope: "I had feared the junction of those corps at any moment, as I knew that Longstreet was pushing forward to join Jackson. I therefore expected that movement of Longstreet certainly *during* the afternoon of the 29th."

Even with the disturbing news of King's withdrawal, Pope was not in the least discouraged. The stiff resistance King's brigades had encountered near Brawner's Farm and on the Turnpike only proved to his mind that the rebels were fighting a desperate rearguard action and determined to escape his trap. He was determined not to allow that to happen.

Several hours earlier near midnight, Pope was anticipating such a move by Jackson and had ordered Heintzelman's command of nearly 8,000 troops to Groveton to attack the *'retreating'* Jackson. Generals Joe Hooker and John Reynolds were two of the best men General Heintzelman had. Those two seasoned veterans, 'Fighting' Joe Hooker and one-armed Phil Kearney, had bivouacked all night on the shores of Bull Run and they were ready to move their divisions at first light.

Pope's next order was to Irvin McDowell. Having decided to give the missing General King to Porter, he had to let McDowell know. That is why he sent Piatt to Manassas with orders for McDowell. At Porter's 1878 retrial, When Porter's name was finally cleared and his honor restored, Piatt testified about his search for the missing general.

"I could not find McDowell. While I searched for him I found General Porter and gave him the message intended for McDowell with Pope's request that Porter should notify McDowell of the order when he found him."

Contrary to Porter's testimony, at the 1862 court martial, McDowell's memory was faulty; he had no recollection of such an order. He claimed he might have 'misplaced' any such request from Pope and promised to search his papers. Contrary to military regulations that required *all* notes and orders must be preserved, it was never found. That note, had it been offered into evidence at the court martial, would have been more strong evidence in Porter's favor.

Just before Porter's corps started to Gainesville that morning, he corresponded with his friend, General Ambrose Burnside; perhaps Porter needed to work off his frustration with Pope's mismanagement and confusing array of orders.

He wrote, *'I hope Mac is at work and we will soon get ordered out of this. It would seem from proper statements of the enemy that Jackson was wandering around loose. But I expect they know what they are doing, which is more than anyone around here knows.'*

In another dispatch to General Burnside, Porter said, *'All that talk about bagging Jackson was bosh. That enormous Gap (Thoroughfare Gap), was left open and the enemy will have jumped through.'*

After Porter was arrested, Burnside testified he *'saw no harm in these letters.'* He sent them to the president to make clearer Pope's confusion and mistakes and to help his friend.

In spite of Burnside's good intentions, General-in-Chief Halleck learned of the letters and Porter's words were used against Porter. The prosecutor used the wording in the letters to support Pope's allegations that Porter's vendetta against him had led Porter to purposely disobey orders. None of that was true. Porter followed every order as much as any soldier could, despite Pope's mismanagement.

A few minutes after ten o'clock that morning, McDowell and Porter finished their conversation at Weir House. The meeting broke up and Porter turned his mind to the complicated maneuver of turning his column around for the march back towards Gainesville.

McDowell, still perturbed over Pope's order giving King to Porter, sent a dispatch to Pope. McDowell's dispatch implied his loss of King's division could not be permanent; *'Of course this arrangement is temporary,'* his note said. After waiting as long as he dared for orders from Pope to reinstate McDowell's command of King, McDowell took the loss and rode off to join his corps.

Within half an hour McDowell was informed that General Ricketts was no more than a mile away. McDowell knew that Longstreet had forced Ricketts out of Thoroughfare Gap. McDowell must have had a good idea that Longstreet's Confederates were coming. He also knew that Porter would need all the help he could get when he met that army. He gave Ricketts an order to 'follow King's division toward Gainesville,' leaving Porter short-handed.

As Porter marched to Gainesville, Sergeant Robert Hennessy, in Morell's brigade, wrote of a soldier's feelings. Hennessy survived the war and later became a writer. His prose reflects his sensitive nature but more importantly, in eloquent terms, Hennessy spoke for the unexpressed thought of all soldiers about to meet an enemy.

'Our regiment and our company was on the right. We marched out of bivouac and halted, waiting until the other companies were ready that we might form a column. The strictest silence prevailed. Not a word was spoken. While we stood in the darkness, the orderly sergeant of the left flank company, who was full of mischief and animal spirits and was a friend, left his place in the ranks for a moment.'

'Running over to where I stood, and pulling me by my sleeve, he said in a half-joking way, "Hennessy, you are a very good fellow, but better you than me to be on the right to-night. Good bye, old fellow."'

'It was true. My place on the right would be with the captain on the right of the company. We would be the first to advance and approach the enemy. Had the enemy become aware of our approach and had advanced one or two pieces of artillery down the road, or had infantry been waiting for us, we stood a fair chance of being the first to be swept off.'

'It was a few minutes after four o'clock. The column moved forward in silence. Not a sound was heard but the steady tramp of the troops. Never did I see them march so steady or soldier-like. Some clicking of canteens against the hilts of sabers was immediately checked and suppressed, and the silence and steadiness of that march in the dark of night up that solitary road, lined on each side with black frowning woods, seemed truly grand.'

'I could never lay claim to extra ordinary courage, and I could never be accused of exposing myself needlessly and recklessly to the fire of the enemy. I may say that I was always happiest when I was out of danger, but it seemed to me there are times when a man does not have entirely free will or control over his sentiments. His courage may be stirred up by some great circumstance or necessity of the moment. Every other thought or consideration is forgotten and, I thought, that night pervaded these men. It seemed plain from my position that I was going to almost certain destruction and yet, I marched with pride on that occasion at the head of the column.'

Taking the Manassas-Gainesville Road, by about noon General Porter's mile-long columns reached Dawkins Branch, a small stream that crossed the road beneath a small bridge half way to Gainesville. General Morell, leading Porter's First Division, brought news of enemy troops ahead. Recalling McDowell's reference to *'Seventeen divisions, cavalry and artillery coming through Gainesville'* at 8:30 that morning, Porter had a good idea of who that enemy was.

Pope had the bad habit of sending verbal orders to his officers. His written orders were often confusing or vague and his verbal instructions followed the same pattern. Porter was a stickler for accuracy when it came to an order, and he tried to correct the situation. He had received several conflicting orders during the last few hours. Some of the directives were verbal orders from officers he did not know. Porter had advanced about two miles on the Manassas-Gainesville Road when a member of Pope's staff, Robert Abbott, delivered to General Porter the infamous *Joint Order*.

August 29, 10:30 AM

"To Generals McDowell and Porter: You will please move forward with your joint commands toward Gainesville. I sent General Porter written orders to that effect an hour and a half ago. Heintzelman, Siegel, and Reno are now moving on the Warrenton Turnpike and by now must be not far from Gainesville. I desire that, as soon as communication is established between this force and your own, the whole command shall halt. It may be necessary to fall back behind Bull Run, at Centreville tonight. I presume it will not be so because of our supplies. I have sent no orders of any kind to Ricketts, and none to interfere in any way with McDowell's troops, except what I sent to his aid-de-camp last night, which was to hold his position on the Warrenton Pike until the troops from here should fall on the enemy's flank and rear. I do not even know Ricketts' position, as I have not been able to find out where General McDowell was until a late hour this morning. General McDowell will take immediate steps to communicate with General Ricketts and instruct him to join the other divisions of his corps as soon as practical. If any considerable advantages are to be gained by departing from this order, it will not be strictly carried out. One thing must be held in view: that the troops must occupy a position from which they can reach Bull Run tonight or by morning. The indications are that the whole force of the enemy is moving in this direction at a pace that will bring them here by tomorrow night or the next day. My own headquarters will for the present be at Heintzelman's corps, or at this place."

At about the same time that the Joint Order was given to Porter, Griffin's skirmishers made first contact with enemy troops on the Manassas-Gainesville Road near Dawkins Branch.

Griffin testified at the Porter court martial. "I had marched about two miles, having passed King's division in the road, when a countryman said, *'Look out, a trooper has been taken here, just in front a short distance.'* I asked him what forces were in front. He said none, except a few mounted men. I halted my brigade, threw four companies of the 62nd Pennsylvania to the front with instructions to move on in advance about half a mile. I then moved on until we came to a cleared space, where our skirmishers commenced firing with the enemy's pickets. At this point General Porter rode up and we halted. I also ordered the other eight companies of the 62nd Pennsylvania to the front to support those that were already out as skirmishers."

Porter gave the command and the entire Fifth Corps ground to a halt. Minutes later, McDowell arrived with *his* copy of the *Joint Order* in his hand ready to reclaim King's division as the Joint Order allowed him to do.

Separating the many parts of the Joint Order, the two generals determined what the order said was this:

1. Porter and McDowell shall move toward Gainesville.

2. As soon as communication is established with Heintzelman, Siegel, and Reno the whole command shall halt.

3. These orders shall not interfere in any way with General McDowell's decisions, except to require that he hold his position on the Warrenton Pike until General Porter falls on Jackson's flank and rear.

4. General McDowell is to assume command, where he chooses, of the other commands that are involved in the movement.

5. The order does not have to be strictly carried out, if any considerable advantages are to be gained by departing from the order.

6. The troops must occupy a position from which they can reach Bull Run tonight or by morning.

7. The whole force of the enemy is moving in this direction at a pace that will bring them here by *tomorrow night or the next day.*

What follows is this writer's clearer explanation and the meaning of each of the seven parts of the confusing order:

Point 4 of the Joint Order.

That part of the *Joint Order*, giving McDowell command, required Porter to give King's division to McDowell. Porter complied in an Action Statement later: '*I have sent no orders of any kind to Ricketts, and none to interfere in any way with McDowell's troops, except what I sent to his aid-de-camp last night, which was to hold his position on the Warrenton Pike until the troops from here should fall on the enemy's flank and rear.'*

As ranking officer, McDowell was entitled to command the entire force, his command *and* Porter's troops. This was understood by both men. That stipulation in the Joint Order was the best news McDowell could have had. It had the effect of reassigning Hatch's division back to him. Losing a division had been a blow to his pride and having it back made him happy. That reassignment of King's four divisions is what he had been waiting for.

McDowell's next words were to reclaim King's division: "I need King's division and I shall take him with me."

McDowell was told about the skirmishers. The gunfire near Dawkins Branch grew heavier as they talked.

"Have you any idea of the source of that fire?" McDowell asked.

Porter did not yet know they were the outriders of Longstreet's 29,000 Confederates. The sounds coming from the direction of the Warrenton Turnpike and close to Jackson's right flank were from the guns of Hood's division. Hood's division had split off from Longstreet's main force and Hood had come to rescue Jackson. The Confederates had encountered the opposition of Kearney's infantry while the rebels were driving the Federal troops back.

With no knowledge of the Confederate enemy's size, Porter told McDowell, "My skirmishers have encountered the enemy but I do not yet know whether they are in force or just a party of rebel raiders."

McDowell's next words, overheard by his staff and several other officers, that would later be denied, would become a bone of contention at Porter's court martial.

He said, "Porter, you are too far out already. This is no place to fight a battle."

Then McDowell and Porter rode off together across the railroad to discuss and review the situation. That was also the moment that Porter was informed about the dispatch Buford had given earlier.

McDowell took Buford's note from his pocket, held it out and said, "This note from General Buford stated that he observed an enemy force passing through Gainesville, at about 8:30 this morning."

By his total lack of emphasis on the note and its content, Porter was left with the impression McDowell placed little importance on the report. General Porter, however, had his own reasons to suspect that that strange Confederate force meant that perhaps Lee *had* arrived on the field.

When they had finished their discussion McDowell decided to modify his order to Porter.

He said, "Rather than pushing my command cross country to link up with Heintzelman on the Turnpike I will go north along the Sudley Road and move into position on Reynold's left. Your forces will link up with mine."

Point 5 of the Joint Order.

The wording was confusing. It gave McDowell (and Porter) substantial freedom of action. The provision stated, *'If any considerable advantages are to be gained by departing from this order, it will not be strictly carried out.'*

At General Porter's court martial, McDowell made clear his interpretation of that proviso. "I decided that considerable advantages were to be gained from departing from the Joint Order, and I did not strictly carry out a part of General Pope's order to attack the enemy at Gainesville."

These *'advantages'* McDowell spoke of were never made clear at the trial. General McDowell's decision not to *'strictly carry out the order'* might have been based on McDowell's need to help defeat Jackson quickly while Porter held Jackson's *'rescue force'* (Longstreet) in check.

Point 6 of the Joint Order.

This was one of the strangest parts: *'Push forward until connection is made with the forces, then halt; the troops must occupy a position from where they can reach Bull Run tonight or by morning.'*

That sentence signified that Pope was *aware* of Longstreet's approach. Pope believed if Longstreet's army threatened to overwhelm them, the better place to form the Federal forces might be behind Bull Run, which was easier to defend or launch a counter attack.

One other part of the order, conspicuous by its absence, was a clear directive for Porter to attack Jackson's flank on the Turnpike. Pope assumed that Porter would, somehow, *read his mind* that he must attack Jackson, although Pope had never thought to give Porter that order.

The two generals parted company. Porter returned to his command, preparing to move forward on the Manassas-Gainesville Road. General McDowell, returning to his command, had forgotten his most important obligation. He failed to send Buford's dispatch to John Pope. Instead, that all-important message remained in his pocket until evening and to this day McDowell's conduct has never been explained.

There is much disagreement what orders, if any, McDowell gave Porter before he rode off. McDowell admitted at Porter's court martial trial that he was vague. He could not remember the conversation perfectly.

McDowell testified at Porter's trial, "I said to Porter, you put your forces in here, and I will take mine up the Sudley Springs Road on the left of the troops engaged with Jackson."

During the court martial, and always afterward, Porter denied that was what McDowell said.

Porter testified, "McDowell said to me, *'Porter, you are too far out already. This is no place to fight a battle.'* Then we rode off across the railroad *(the Orange and Alexander Railroad)* and reviewed the situation."

Porter remembered that conversation much differently. Exactly what McDowell said was a point of great controversy at Porter's trial.

Porter testified, "McDowell modified my part of Pope's Joint Order. Discussing his plans, McDowell said, *'Rather than try to push my command cross country to link up with the forces along the Warrenton Turnpike, I will move my corps directly northward along the Sudley Road. From there you will move into position on Reynold's left where, theoretically, your forces will be able to link up with me.'* At that we parted and I returned to my command."

What *was* in evidence and *was overheard* by other officers, as McDowell rode away, was that Porter called out to him, 'What shall I do?' McDowell made no response, except to wave his hand, and was gone to join his command. Whatever McDowell may have said was, apparently, not understood by Porter. But it wouldn't have mattered, except that what McDowell claimed to have said was the basis for a *false conclusion* by the court martial and helped to convict Porter.

This above all is important to understand. *Whatever* McDowell said, or how the

246

court interpreted the remark, the instant that McDowell left Porter on his own it was not an order that Porter had to obey. McDowell had given up his command to direct Porter. Furthermore, if *whatever* McDowell might have said was *opposed* to the dictates of the *spirit* of the Joint Order, Porter was obliged to follow the *spirit* of the Joint Order.

One of the more serious charges made by the court martial was that Porter retreated and failed to attack the enemy. That charge was ridiculous.

From the beginning, the court was disposed to convict Porter. They could not have supposed *for any reason* that Porter, with 9000 men, would have been in his right mind to attack 25,000 rebels with one-third the force. McDowell had taken 15,000 troops from Porter's forces *(King's and Ricketts' troops)*. If McDowell *had* remarked, *'You put your forces in here,'* as he claimed, it *only* meant for Porter to stay where he was. It was *not* meant for Porter to fight a battle, or to attack Jackson.

Porter held that McDowell also said to Porter, *'This is no place to fight a battle. You are too far out already.' That* made sense. Pope's order allowed for a fallback position behind Bull Run. As the order stated in the last part, *'One thing must be held in view: that the troops must occupy a position from which they can reach Bull Run tonight or by morning. The indications are that the whole force of the enemy is moving in this direction.'*

McDowell knew it too. After taking two-thirds of Porter's force, if a battle was to be fought, it was *McDowell's duty* to stay and fight that force with Porter. Porter used good military judgment in holding a strong position while McDowell went for help.

There was another factor that colored Porter's reasoning. The mistakes and errors that Pope had made during the two days of August 28 and 29 were so numerous and glaring that they might have destroyed Porter's confidence in Pope's judgment. There were the futile marches, there was Pope's ridiculous proclamation of *'always seeing the backs of his enemies,'* there was the wasted order to march to Centreville when Porter *knew* there was no enemy there, and there was Pope's abandonment of Gainesville at the same moment Longstreet was marching through the Gap. All these left Porter completely uncertain of Pope's ability to command the army, and much less certain of Pope's ability to command Porter's actions in the life and death battle that was coming on fast.

The most glaring error of fact in Pope's *Joint Order* that made up Porter's mind was the part that claimed, *'The indications are that the whole force of the enemy is moving in this direction at a pace that will bring them here by tomorrow night or the next day.'* Pope *knew* it was not true; Longstreet was already here.

Porter had four choices:

He could attack the enemy, but Colonel Marshall, his scout, reported the enemy force was more than twice the number of his own and more were coming.

He could make a flank march to the right so he could reach the rest of the Union army. The distance was three miles over broken rocky ground with many ravines and marshy streams and through dense woods, impractical for moving his artillery. Besides, Porter's troops as they marched would be exposed to a *'ruinous attack.' These were Longstreet's words when, a later time after the war was over, he offered his opinion.*

He could retreat if he took the Sudley Road. That was the same road McDowell had taken. But now it was filled with McDowell's troops.

He could remain where he was and try to hold Longstreet in check. In fact, by remaining where he was, Porter made McDowell's march all the *safer from an attack* by Longstreet.

After Porter and McDowell had finished their conversation, Porter rode across the fields to rejoin his command. The presence of the enemy in his front was well established and to obey the Joint Order, to push ahead to the right and connect with the other Union forces he would need Hatch's division. He sent his chief of staff to McDowell with a request to once more place Hatch under his control.

McDowell's response was a polite but a firm 'no.'

'Give my compliments to General Porter. I am going to the right and I will take General King with me. I think you had better remain where you are but if it is necessary for you to fall back, do so on my right.'

Porter, knowing he could not have King's division, decided to push to the right anyway. He ordered Morell to *'Push over to the aid of Siegel and strike (Jackson) in his rear. If you reach a road on which King is moving and he is ahead of you, and let him pass and see if you cannot help Siegel.'*

Porter next made an attempt to follow Pope's order to move toward Gainesville and attack Jackson's flank. Griffin recalled his pickets and moved toward the right. His men had advanced about a third of a mile when they were stopped by obstructions; ravines and heavy brush; which they could not get through. At the same time, the enemy began tossing shells at them and Griffin placed his brigade in the rear as the artillery fire continued.

After Griffin's cross-country advance had been aborted, Porter had Morell send the 13th New Yorkers ahead along the Manassas-Gainesville Road as skirmishers. That regiment was under the leadership of one of Porter's toughest commanders, Elisha Marshall. The fifty-odd infantrymen of the 13th were New Yorkers and as tough as their commander. Colonel Marshall testified at the Porter court martial as to what his skirmishers found in the woods on the other side of Dawkins Creek. Marshall stated,

"I crossed Dawkins Branch following the Manassas-Gainesville road and we occupied the timber on the other side. My regiment had not gone a dozen yards when we found Confederate cavalry among the trees. They saw us, we attacked, and they quickly dispersed. I thought they were retreating. Soon, however, a column of Confederate infantry appeared and clashed with our men. Our artillery, on a small hill near Dawkins Creek, opened up on the rebels. The rebels replied for a short while and then fell silent. I immediately sent back a report to General Morell that the enemy was forming against us on the left."

Stuart's cavalry, guarding Longstreet's right flank, had galloped down the Manassas-Gainesville road. As Stuart passed near Dawkins Branch he saw clouds of dust from the marching of Porter's 9000 men. At the time General Stuart did not know it was Porter's Fifth Corps but General Stuart instantly grasped the danger to Longstreet. He knew his six brigades were hardly enough to stop this new enemy and sent word back for reinforcements. Longstreet was unable to comply. He was not yet ready to spare any troops. Stuart rode back to his waiting regiment and decided to try a bluff. He had his men cut saplings and brush and by dragging them behind their horses, he created his own clouds of dust. This act was followed by Colonel Rosser's 5th Virginia Regiment skirmishers, who moved toward the strange new army to hold them off a little longer.

Longstreet was still in the midst of deploying his troops. After the war, he wrote to Porter and told him how his troops were arranged near Dawkins Creek that afternoon and what he did when he saw signs of Porter's large force.

'I first had Brigadier Commander Montgomery Corse report on the situation. Throwing out my skirmishers, but not being aware of any troops on my right, I saw an enemy display a considerable force in my front. They moved at once to the cover of the woods. I deemed it prudent to fall back a short distance.'

After deciding that the force in his front was indeed Longstreet, and considering McDowell's opinion that he should remain where he was, Porter determined to take a defensive position. To Morell, he ordered, *'Move your infantry and artillery above the crest of the hill above Dawkins Branch. Conceal the guns behind the bushes and make ready to defend our position. Our artillery should fire at the enemy, but save your ammunition.'*

Still trying to decipher the huge force before him, Porter reached the conclusion that it *was* Longstreet's army. Considering that McDowell had said he should *'remain where he was,'* and taking into account that Pope did not know Longstreet's main force might have arrived on the battlefield, Porter decided to defend against Longstreet.

While Colonel Marshall's skirmishers were fighting rebels at Dawkins Branch, Porter could hear the steady rumble of Pope's guns on the Turnpike to the distant right, closer to Groveton. Those Federals were too far away to be of any help in his present predicament and Porter must have wondered whether Pope had *any idea* that this new huge force of rebels faced *his* men.

As Porter listened, the sound of the firing at Groveton began to change. Gradually, the sounds receded. With no word or a way to know what was happening in the battle to the north, he feared that Pope's forces might be falling back against a more powerful enemy.

In his front the sporadic skirmishing and artillery duels continued between Porter and Longstreet. Jones faced Porter's troops. Sometime before 4 PM Longstreet sent Wilcox's division to support Jones and the fighting continued, gradually increasing in intensity and violence as each side probed the other's defenses and strength.

Without guidance, and knowing only that a new large army had arrived at his front, Porter made an attempt to salvage what he could of the uncertain situation. He hoped his force might stem the Confederate tide in front while he moved his brigades closer to the Turnpike and the fighting to support the rest of Pope's army. He sent a message to McDowell and a duplicate message to Siegel to let them know what was causing the rising clouds of dust close to Gainesville.

'I found it impossible to communicate by crossing the woods to Groveton. The enemy was in strong force on this road, and, as they appear to have driven our forces back, the firing of the enemy and ours retired, I have determined to withdraw to Manassas.'

'I have tried to communicate with you but my messengers have run into the enemy. They have gathered cavalry, artillery and infantry and the advancing masses of dust show the enemy is coming in force. I am now going to the head of the column to see what is passing and how affairs are going. Had you not better send your train back?'

A little while after six o'clock Porter received word that the battle was going well on the Turnpike and the rebels were being driven back. This was good news and he immediately determined not to retreat to Manassas. Instead he would make an advance against the enemy.

Then Longstreet changed Porter's mind. Porter was convinced that Longstreet was not going all out to attack him. Porter saw gunfire on the Turnpike. *This signaled to Porter that fighting had renewed on the Turnpike.* Porter decided retreating to Manassas was not a good move.

On the other side of the Manassas-Gainesville Road, where Longstreet's divisions and brigades were massing, Robert E. Lee was considering an attack. He was anxious to join up with Jackson and make a massive smash at the Union army on the Turnpike as soon as possible. Longstreet was at his side and Lee usually made his wishes known to Longstreet as suggestions and not as a command.

"Why not make an attack against the Union left?" he asked.

Longstreet, always more cautious than the more aggressive Lee, explained his reservation. He was still unsure what Federal force faced him.

"General Lee, let me make a reconnaissance of the Federal force before me. I must have more intelligence on this *'unknown quantity'* before an attack can be made."

James Longstreet faced a twin dilemma; on his left Reynolds' division occupied a formidable position on the Warrenton Turnpike. On his front and right, and more worrisome, was the question of Porter's force, yet a mystery.

Porter's troops deployed for a fight. It became clear to Porter that Longstreet was just as anxious to hold off an attack as Porter was to initiate one. He decided not to retreat toward Bull Run because the situation had changed. Porter sensed from Morell's reports of the skirmishing that Longstreet did not wish to attack him. After the war, Longstreet admitted that *was* the case. Longstreet convinced Lee that the offensive should not begin until Longstreet knew exactly what Union force faced him.

Porter notified Morell, *'I wish you to push up two regiments, supported by two others, preceded by skirmishers, with the regiments at intervals of two hundred yards and attack the party with the section of artillery opposed to you. The battle looks well on our right and the enemy is said to be retiring up the pike. Give the enemy a good shelling when your troops advance.'*

Concerned about McDowell because Porter could hear the sound of heavy fire to his right where Porter supposed McDowell had gone, he added to his directive, *'We cannot retire while McDowell holds his own.'*

At his court martial Porter testified, "This movement was abandoned because our threatening attitude proved sufficient to hold the enemy to our front, which was the object to be accomplished."

Porter continued to wait for news from the battlefield near Groveton, but none came. At 6 PM he sent another plea for guidance from McDowell.

'Failed in getting Morell over to you. After wandering through the woods for a time I withdrew him, and while doing so, enemy artillery opened on us. My scouts could not get through. Each found the enemy between us, and I believe some have been captured. Please let me know your designs; whether you retire or not. I cannot get water and am out of provisions. Have lost a few men from infantry firing.'

Pope was back at headquarters and under the delusion that Jackson was his primary enemy. Pope waited for the sound of gunfire that would signal the opening of Porter's attack against Jackson's right. That wasn't to be. By the time the Joint Order came from John Pope, Porter had become so involved in a fight against both Longstreet and Jackson that he could not easily make the change. Some of Porter's men were already fighting Jones' division, the vanguard of Longstreet's forces.

Porter sent McDowell a dispatch to explain that he was unable to carry out his part of the Joint Order, at least until the outcome of his present fight with Jones had become clearer.

'I am being annoyed by Confederate fire and skirmishers. I have sent Sykes and Butterfield to strike the batteries, which are thinning my ranks. The enemy has six pieces in a battery on my right on the Warrenton road. Butterfield shall take the Confederates in their flank.'

This order, and McDowell and Pope's denials that they had ever received or seen such an order from Porter, was another example of *lost or misplaced orders*. And, by their unexplained disappearance, helped to convict Porter.

Porter sent a second dispatch to McDowell explaining the new turn of affairs and asking for King's division. His second dispatch to McDowell stated that he had decided *not* to retreat to Bull Run but to stay and hold Longstreet at bay. That is what Porter did for the next several hours, until he received Pope's 4:30 Order to attack Jackson's right flank.

Reverdy Johnson, Porter's lawyer, asked McDowell about Porter's second note.

Johnson: "Did you, after that time, and after the receipt of the first note, receive another note?"

McDowell: "I do not remember to have received another note."

Johnson continued to question McDowell.

Johnson: "Recollect, if you can, whether you received a note from the hands of one of your aids, after the reception of the first note, stating that the accused was there *(near Dawkins Branch)* and in position, and Porter could hold *(that position)*, and perhaps attack, if strengthened by the division you had taken from him, King's division or another?"

McDowell's reply was pure mendacity and prevarication.

McDowell: "I do not remember to have received a *(second)* note but I remember that my aid-de-camp told me that General Porter stated to him if he had King's division, he could make a dash, or something of the kind. Whether it came in a note or by word of mouth, I am not clear. I rather think it was brought to me by the aid-de-camp as near as I can remember."

Pope's original promise in the *Joint Order* was that King would support Porter on his attack at Jackson. Shortly after 1:45 PM, Butterfield let Porter know his skirmishers could not advance because King was not where he was supposed to be. Porter's right flank was now exposed to Longstreet's large new forces, which were coming up fast on General Porter's exposed right flank. Porter sent repeated requests to Pope to send Heintzelman to support his right but received no reply. With his men under an annoying fire from Confederate artillery and skirmishers, Porter sent word to McDowell that nonetheless he would do his best to conform to the new order.

In response, Porter received a note from McDowell telling him to *'proceed with the movement and Heintzelman will attend to the front and right. Reynolds has been pulled out of the column and put over on your left.'*

Anderson was the last of Lee's forces to come through Thoroughfare Gap and join Longstreet. By mistake, in the night, Anderson had marched his men too far along the Warrenton Turnpike. Longstreet cautioned him that he would be under the Union artillery in the morning so he turned his men around and they fell back to a safer position. Reynolds' scouts reported Anderson's movement and Pope (again misreading the signs) interpreted Anderson's reasonable change in position as *a retreat by Jackson's forces*. At Porter's court martial, McDowell testified about General Anderson's changes in position and the effect it had on Pope.

Shortly after 6 PM, Reynolds received word from Pope that the enemy was falling back, and to *'send Hatch's division right up the Turnpike after them.'* General Hatch's men came streaming down Sudley Road and Reynolds sent them forward in pursuit of the enemy.

Reynolds testified at Porter's Rehearing.

"I monitored the progress of the column for a short while and I was incredulous at what I saw. The men had run into a strong force of the enemy and the enemy was not retreating. By then the issue was no longer in doubt. Hatch's brigades were no match for the force facing them. After a bloody fight they fell back to near Dogan Ridge."

What happened to Hatch was one more powerful piece of evidence that Pope ignored information that was vital to his plans; he failed to see Jackson was not retreating and that this 'strong force' was part of a *new force*; a force that could only be *part of Longstreet's army*.

General Robert E. Lee, at the head of Longstreet's column, arrived on the field about 10 AM. He moved down the Turnpike ahead of the column with the 4th Virginia Cavalry Regiment to find Jackson's men. Ahead there were troops. Were they Jackson's men? Lee rode forward by himself to see for himself where Jackson's troops were placed and how Hood would best link up with them.

It was nearing noon. Longstreet's troops were deployed in position and ready to attack Pope. Once Jackson had circled around and behind the Federals, the Confederate army would be ready for a massive smash at the Union army on the Turnpike, which was still unaware of Lee's approach.

A story told of Lee illustrates his unshakable coolness under fire.

When he returned to where Longstreet waited, he remarked in the calmest of voices, to an officer at his side, Major Charles Venable, "A Yankee sharpshooter came near to killing me just now."

Venable said afterward, "We could see how near it was. His cheek had the mark of the bullet that had grazed him."

Longstreet finished his reconnaissance of the woods and the terrain near Dawkins Creek. When his deployment was complete he reported that news to General Lee. Lee recommended that Longstreet should make an attack against the Union troops on Pope's left immediately.

In the face of Porter's obstinacy and continued fighting Longstreet told Lee, "Conditions for such an attack are not favorable. The Federal position extends well left of the Warrenton Turnpike. If we slide farther right to attack the left side of Pope's forces at Groveton, it might be done. However, the large Federal force, which our skirmishers engaged this morning, is large enough that such a move on our part would expose our right flank to the Federal force."

All of this uncertainty could have been explained had Robert E. Lee known that the *'unknown forces'* approaching on their front was Fitz John Porter, and his 9000-man fifth corps was the same adversary that a month earlier had beaten the rebels so badly at Malvern Hill. When Longstreet finally discovered Porter's corps was in front of him he sent Jones' brigade to face the Union force, which had stopped his advance against Pope on the Turnpike. The fighting increased in severity and Longstreet found it necessary to back up Jones' troops with Wilcox's division to strengthen the Confederate attacking force in front of Porter. Thus, without sacrificing men, Porter had drained a part of Longstreet's planned advance force and delayed Longstreet's attack against Pope.

Porter said later during his 1878 rehearing, "I discussed the enemy situation with General Morell. By noon I had deployed our artillery and all four of my divisions were ready for battle. Our scouts reported that Longstreet's forces were on the other side of Dawkins Creek and in the timber beyond, across from the Manassas-Gainesville Railroad. I did not think, from the sounds coming from his forces, that James Longstreet had any idea what Union force faced him."

After the war, Longstreet wrote to Porter. He told him how his Confederate troops were deployed near Dawkins Creek that afternoon and the discussions he had with General Robert E. Lee about having Porter's troops in front of him and how Porter had delayed Lee's attack. *'I first had Brigadier Commander Montgomery Corse report on the situation. Throwing out my skirmishers, but not being aware of any troops on my right, I saw an enemy, who displayed a considerable force in front, which at once moved under cover of the wood. I deemed it prudent to fall back a short distance.'*

Longstreet spent the afternoon of August 29 overseeing the deployment of his troops. He ordered Hood's batteries into position. Hood's division of infantry were deployed on the right and on the left of Turnpike Road. Anderson's division of 6,000 troops under Longstreet, arrived on the battlefield at dark. Artillery from Anderson's division was placed on a knoll near the Brawner Farm to protect Jackson's left flank. They marched toward the Federal position but halted and returned when Longstreet warned them they had marched too far. By morning, if they remained there, they would be under the Federal guns. Anderson's retrograde

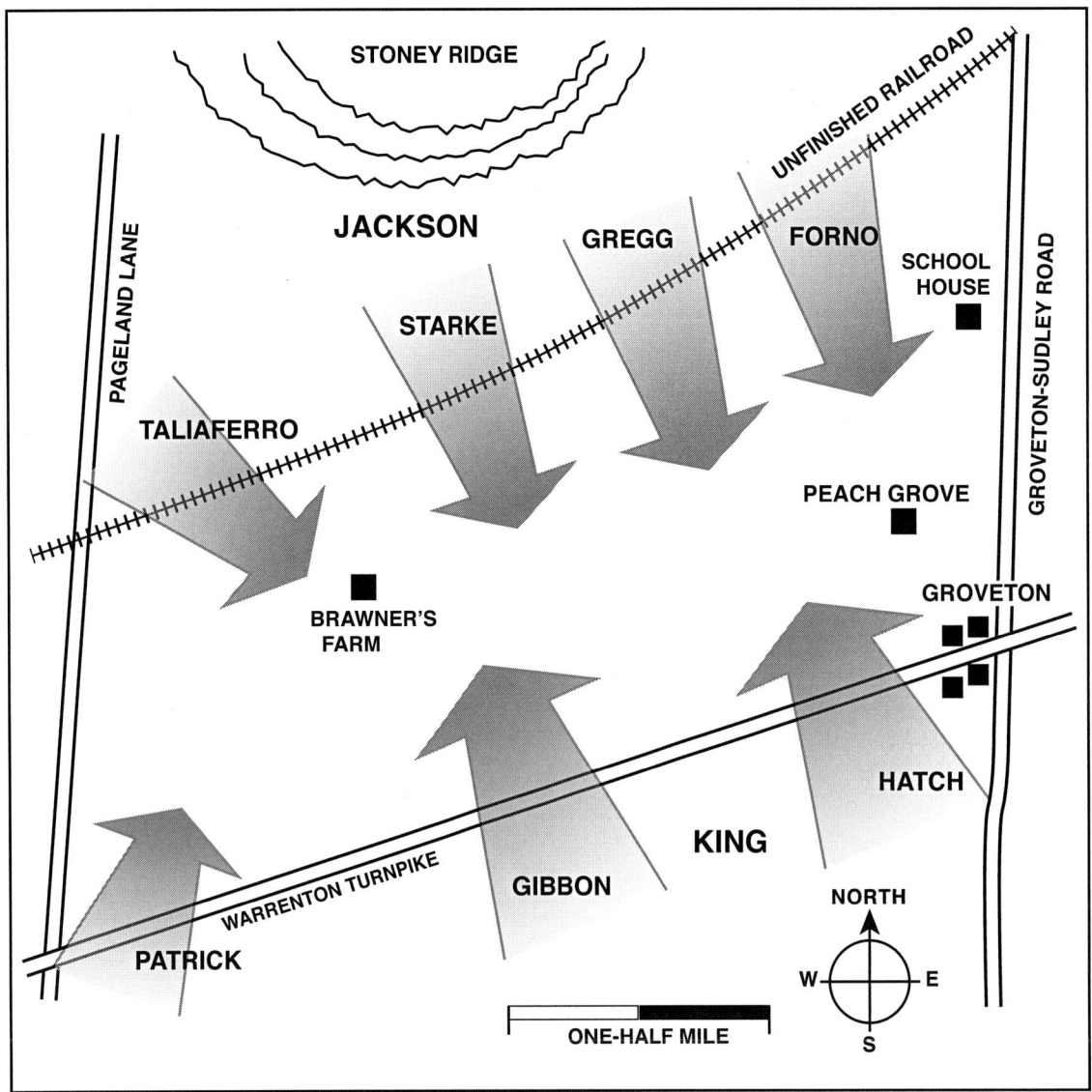

THE BATTLE OF BRAWNER'S FARM — AUGUST 28, 1862

Union General King's division headed north on the Turnpike following reports that General Jackson was at Centreville. When King became ill General Hatch took charge of the Union forces. With no idea Jackson was watching above and behind the abandoned railroad, Jackson launched his attack on Hatch's Brigade. Hatch sent General Patrick's brigade to oppose the rebels until General Gibbon could arrive to help.

As the battle grew hot, Gibbon faced Confederate General Taliaferro. Taliaferro's Rebels were Jackson's best. These were men who could shoot the eye out of a squirrel at a hundred paces and the two sides blazed away, separated by only eighty yards. They fought around Brawner's Farm, the ruined Peach Grove, and on the slopes between the Turnpike and the abandoned railroad. In that bloody fight a third of the men on both sides were lost.

Taliaferro said of Gibbon's men, "They stood as immovable as painted heroes in a battle piece... although they could not advance, they would not retire. There was much discipline in this, but there was much more of true valor."

movement that night caused Pope to misunderstand. He believed the rebel's temporary movement was one more indication of Jackson's retreat.

The night of August 29 was quiet. Nobody on either side was killed and nobody was being shot. Captain Waterman wheeled his Rhode Island battery of four Napoleons and two Parrott rifles into position and Robert's 1st Michigan Regiment moved next to the artillery in support. Morell's men and Sykes' corps went to sleep in their positions ready for the morning's business. Beyond that, the troops in all divisions settled in for the night in bivouac.

It must be emphasized that Porter's stubborn refusal to fall back *(as McDowell had suggested, and he had a legal right to do under the terms of the Joint Order)* but to face Longstreet, saved Pope's army from destruction. The delay it brought about allowed the Federal forces time to be *partly* ready when the Confederate assault came the next day.

Although the Federals were defeated in the battle that followed, because of Porter's defense they were able to retire to Centreville in good order instead of the entire destruction of the Union army that would have happened. That long delay of Longstreet's advance through Porter's efforts saved Pope from total disaster. It gave Pope the time he needed to retreat behind Bull Run.

❧ 38 ❧

Day 2: Turnpike

On the morning of August 29, Pope was still ignorant of many facts as he carried out the first part of his plan. Siegel's corps and Reynold's division would strike Jackson's right and center. Heintzelman's 3rd corps and Reno's 9th corps would move against Jackson's left flank and Siegel was to replace King.

During the previous evening, Siegel's troops, on their way to Centreville, crossed one of the fords on Bull Run Creek as they were coming to replace King. Just before dark, units of Siegel's corps brushed with more enemy troops. The rebels were on their way to join Jackson.

Siegel's report reassured Pope he was hot on Jackson's trail. Siegel's men fired a few rounds and the rebel skirmishers retired. Siegel, believing there were more rebels in the area, sent infantry units to Henry Hill. Henry Hill was one of the larger and higher prominences from which one could watch for the enemy.

Siegel remained on the hill. His troops settled in behind their defenses. Julius Stahel, First Brigade, had been fighting near the Robinson Farm and his four regiments, men of New York and Pennsylvania, found places to the left of the farm on a smaller hill, Bald Hill. Colonel Nathaniel McLean's brigade set up bivouac 200 yards from Chinn House and Milroy's brigade remained near Siegel's command post.

Siegel pored over reports of the wounded men and the fatalities when a messenger reported to his headquarters with Pope's order. *'Attack the enemy vigorously at dawn.'* He passed the word to his brigade commanders within the hour. On the morrow, his division would spearhead the entire Union advance against Stonewall Jackson.

General Siegel wrote in his report. *'I formed an order of battle at daybreak, having ascertained that the enemy was in considerable force beyond Young's Branch, and in sight of the hills we occupied. I therefore directed General Schurz to deploy his division to the right. General Milroy, with his brigade and one battery took the center near the Stone House. General Schenck's division formed our left. Schenck's artillery was planted on the hill in excellent range of the enemy.'*

Siegel, with Heintzelman's and Reno's assistance, made a much larger force than King's four brigades, and they moved against the rebels on Stony Ridge. On the

Warrenton Turnpike, near Henry Hill, at first light an artillery duel began with a bang between Jackson's and Siegel's artillery and continued all day.

By 9 o'clock, after the rising of the sun on Henry Hill, Siegel's attack on Jackson was underway with Milroy's and McLean's brigades. Siegel, coming from Henry Hill, spread his 9,000 men along a two-mile front and moved west. His divisions and those under Reynold's command, struck hard at Jackson's center and Jackson's right flank. Heintzelman's third corps and Reno's ninth corps, coming from Centreville, along with Schurz and Stahel, two more of Siegel's divisions, made their attack against a rocky crest on Jackson's left flank that was being defended by tough South Carolinians.

The Union soldiers advanced, crossed the Turnpike and began to move through the fields toward the hills above Groveton. General Stahel reached the Dogan House with his four regiments and reported, *'Here I found a number of dead and wounded soldiers from the fighting on the previous evening.'* These were men of King's division, who had not been taken from the battlefield from the fight of the evening before. Some of the wounded men were still alive.

To try to rescue and attempt removal of the wounded, while the enemy was firing at the rescuers, was hazardous business. The well-recognized courtesy by both rebel and Yankee after a fight was to make a truce to recover the wounded and dead.

A reality of war was that the first side to ask for a truce was admitting defeat. At the Battle of Shiloh, earlier that year in April, General Grant left his wounded on the battlefield for three days to keep from making the enemy believe he might be ready to admit he had lost that battle. After the tide turned and Grant prevailed, the wounded, those still alive, only then were brought to a field hospital.

That morning, a rescue party was sent out into the field north of the Turnpike with one of the horse-drawn ambulances. Within ten minutes the men carrying the wounded heard the sudden zip and the sound of muskets and bullets tore through the wooden planking of the ambulance, peppering the canvas with holes. They were under rebel fire. Forced to stop work, the ambulance driver and the two orderlies lashed their horses and returned post-haste to Federal lines.

An ambulance driver said, "I knew, from the groans and the occasional call for help that there must have been more than a score of wounded men still lying about. There was nothing we could do until the officers requested a truce, and that was unlikely for some time. One of the drivers was struck in his leg by a bullet."

A.P. Hill's and Richard Ewell's Confederate guns had been planted on a high ridge, nearly a mile away from Henry Hill. They were mostly concealed in brush and trees, which made it difficult for Schenck's batteries to find the Confederate cannons. On the other hand, Schenck's guns were clearly visible to the enemy, which made it hotter than it might have been for Schenck's gun crews during the fight. By 10 AM Jackson's men were in desperate combat with Siegel's men.

As the fight continued, Jackson rode up to a higher elevation of the ridge and trained his field glasses on a far off cloud of dust. It was the sign he had waited for; Longstreet's men were moving over Warrenton Turnpike in his direction. Stonewall had thought ahead. He had prepared for a good placement of Longstreet's artillery, as well as a plan for the best way for Longstreet to place Jackson's divisions for support. Just beyond the two-mile front above the Turnpike, where his men had been stationed, there was a higher spot in the terrain. That small plateau was an ideal location for Longstreet's 19 guns when he arrived and Hood would place his division on Jackson's left flank. It was a well thought out battle plan against General Pope, who was totally ignorant of the enemy's movement.

Siegel's divisions and artillery were mostly German. His three divisions were each headed by generals, who were of German descent: Schenck, Von Steinwehr, and Schurz. The brigades and regiments were filled with men with German names like Muhleck, Krzyzanowski and Schimmelfennig. Siegel also carried with him an independent brigade led by men with the more common names of Milroy and McLean.

Robert Milroy's Independent Brigade and Stahel's Second Brigade, led by Nathaniel McLean, were ordered to make the initial attack. The other two brigades soon joined the fighting.

General Robert Huston Milroy led Siegel's Independent Brigade under Schurz' division command. He was a citizen soldier and a volunteer. He hated West Point and most West Pointers.

Milroy once remarked, "I consider West Point, next to slavery, the great bane of our country. I have no faith the war will end in five years if the direction of our armies is left with Halleck and McClellan. But if put in the hands of good volunteer officers, it will be ended in 90 days."

Standing six-feet-three-inches tall, Milroy had piercing black eyes, an aquiline nose and long silvery hair. His men loved him and they dubbed him, affectionately, the Grey Eagle. In battle, there were occasions when Milroy would gallop up and down his front, fiercely shaking his fist at the *'rebel scoundrels'* and calling them all sorts of outrageous names.

As Milroy often said, "I fight for my country, the integrity of the Republic and for the freedom of the slave."

General Nathaniel McLean, leading Schenck's Second Brigade and part of Siegel's division, was nearly fifty and an attorney with a law degree from Harvard. He had been relieved of command twice for failing to satisfy another corps commander, but, like Milroy, he was a brave soldier.

From the start Schurz' men were under tremendous small arms fire. The sound of heavy musket and artillery fire could be heard in the fight against the South Carolinian rebels in the trees. Milroy heard the battle sounds and he could tell Schurz was having trouble. Without further thought, the excitable Milroy decided he had to jump into the fight and help his division commander.

It was poor judgment by Milroy and a bad move on his part. The attempt to help General Schurz was a disaster. General Milroy had only two regiments and he was going up against an entire battalion of Jackson's troops and artillery. Not only that, he had to march his men directly across Jackson's front to reach Schurz' troops. All the while his men were an easy target in range of the enemy's muskets, and dozens fell.

That action had the questionable distinction of being the first Union charge of the battle. Milroy's heroic gamble was not only a bad idea, but the thoughtless attack cost Milroy *a quarter of his troops*; more than 300 men were shot in the useless charge.

Milroy wrote in his battle report, *'We advanced until Siegel's whole infantry force and all his batteries were engaged with the enemy… they were on the same ground where King's brigade had fought so furiously. The ground was littered with wounded and the dead from the day and evening before and Schenck's men stopped to rescue the wounded before going on.'*

Siegel's line continued their steady advance. The few rebels that appeared offered little resistance. The forward advance was too easy; it was only the calm before the storm. One of the wounded rebel prisoners was overheard to say as the Federals passed, "There'll be the devil to pay ahead."

Minutes later the Union infantry found what they had been looking for… in a blast of firepower with muskets and artillery. Ewell and Jackson's divisions had been waiting and they opened up on the advancing Federals with a volley of minie balls and artillery grapeshot.

Alfred Lee, 82nd Ohio, an infantryman in one of Milroy's regiments that had been in the line of advancing Federals that survived the firestorm, wrote a letter home to tell his people what he had faced that morning.

'The Confederates rose and with a wild yell poured a deadly volley full into our faces. It shook our line and we fell back. Colonel Cantwell, our regiment commander, ordered us to counterattack. We tried again but before the counterattack had barely begun, Colonel Cantwell was shot in the head and killed.'

Without their colonel, the 82nd Ohio fell back. They were unable to hold their position near the unfinished railroad and were driven into the woods to escape the fire.

Milroy's Independent Brigade swept forward next in a wave, with Robert Huston Milroy the 'Gray Eagle' galloping at its head. They crossed the Groveton-Sudley Road moving at a run to strike at the 'Dump.' The 'Dump' was the name given to a thirty-foot gap in the unfinished railroad where enemy opposition appeared light and where Milroy's men had fought the day before.

Milroy's battle report said, *'I could only see the flank of our long battle line. They passed out of the woods as they approached the railroad line. In a moment or two, the men passed over the same ground where my boys had struggled so desperately the hour before. I held my breath as they reached that same fatal line which had struck down so many men.'*

'A volcano of fire opened from behind the railroad track. Hundreds of brave fellows in our long bristling line sank before that fire to rise no more. The still advancing line faltered but for a moment. An answering volcano followed the first and an instant afterward a great shout arose and a long line of Confederates surged rapidly across the railroad embankment at charge with bayonets fixed.'

'I ordered my reserve to open fire on the rebels, which they did. The volley caused much discomfiture and stopped the rebels. I ordered a charge. Colonel Latham's 3rd Virginia Regiment was composed of men from West Virginia, sympathetic to the North. They dashed out of the wood and down across the meadow at the fleeing rebels. I dashed ahead, cheering my boys.'

'I got nearly across the meadow when I noticed heavy masses of rebels in front of us. They were as far down the railroad as I could see and they were coming to support their fleeing comrades, who soon rallied and were coming back.'

The fight on the Turnpike got worse. Siegel's corps and Reynold's division struck Jackson's center and Jackson's right flank. Heintzelman's third corps and Reno's ninth corps attacked Jackson's left flank. 2500 Union soldiers struck the 500 men of the Stonewall brigade at the old Manassas railroad line while Milroy's Federals came in a double phalanx pouring musket fire into the Confederate ranks.

The rebels had to run and find a better position of defense than the one they had against the Federal onslaught, and scurried to reach a cut near the unfinished railroad. The Confederates called for help but they had to wait ten minutes because all of Jackson's men were already in the fight.

At the last minute when things were blackest for the rebels and the issue was in doubt, Jackson's massed artillery turned upon the attacking Union soldiers and finally took some of the pressure off the Stonewall brigade. That single small battle along the abandoned railroad between Milroy's men and Stonewall Jackson's own brigade was some of the fiercest fighting of the war.

At the other end of the Confederate line, a quarter of a mile away nearer the Bull Run Creek, General Early had been skirmishing with Kearney. The Texas Brigade, which had been held in reserve, came forward to help Early's troops and meet the Federals with an additional six hundred rebel fighters.

Just before 5 PM August 29, Kearney crashed into the left flank of the Confederate line on Stony Ridge. The attack had been in progress for nearly an hour and Kearney was gaining ground against the Confederate left. Kearney reported, *'Jackson is retreating toward the Pike from the direction of Sudley Springs.'*

General Kearny came under some heavy artillery fire next. Artillery often is a prelude to an attack and everyone knew it. Kearney's move, to be ready for such an attack by a Confederate force, was to send a brigade of 300 men, under Brigadier General John C. Robinson, to the extreme right. When they arrived, fifteen minutes later, the men fixed bayonets and waited for the expected rebel charge. One of Robinson's men chronicled his preparations for the expected attack.

'The Confederates began using their artillery. Their shot and shell went flying over our heads, falling far in our rear. Soon enough they shortened their fuses. The shot commenced to explode over our heads but closer by. General Robinson, anticipating the artillery fire was preliminary to a charge, ordered us to fix bayonets and lie down.'

When the rebels appeared coming out of the woods, Kearney's division of Red Badge fighters, and Robinson, Kearney's First Brigade Commander, met them head on. By afternoon, Kearney's division was battered after fierce hand-to-hand fighting and close contact musket exchange. By shear bravado and tenacity, they had forced the rebels back along the unfinished railroad but the fighting had been hard. They had suffered heavy casualties.

At 11 AM, Hooker's division arrived on the battlefield to support Siegel. General Hooker's orders had reached him during the night of August 28. Hooker's move toward the Warrenton Turnpike was part of the plan to catch Jackson in Pope's vice between McDowell's and Porter's forces. On the south end were Heintzelman's men. On the north end, Reno and Siegel would attack. Siegel's divisions were already near the Turnpike and in a strong position on Henry Hill.

Private Martin Haynes, part of Grover's First Brigade of the 2nd New Hampshire regiment, wrote to his mother after the battle about how close they were to Jackson's men.

'Our brigade marched down the Warrenton Road toward Groveton, past the Stone House and the crossing on Sudley Road. At length we filed into the open fields to the right of the road, when the 1st Massachusetts Regiment was sent to support Siegel's line. The remaining four regiments in our division (Hooker's second division) rested in two lines, sheltering from the enemy's artillery by a hill in the field in our front. We were near the edge of the woods and we were in clear view of Jackson's batteries.'

Hooker's New Englanders moved to attack on Stony Ridge. The rebels opened fire from behind the embankment on the abandoned railroad. The newest advance was led by Hooker's First Brigade leader, Colonel Cuvier Grover, while General Milroy's men stood near Grover's men as they made ready for the charge.

In a letter to his wife, Milroy wrote, *'I had made that same charge earlier when we tried to take that rebel stronghold that morning. Colonel Grover had a full brigade of fine looking fellows but he had no idea of the strength of the position he was about to attack.'*

Hooker's 1500 men were fighting again on the same ground where Milroy had tried and failed to break Jackson's line. General Cuvier Grover lead a brigade aiming his offense toward a cut in the unfinished railroad where there appeared to be few defenders.

Milroy was not shy about giving Hooker's brigade commander, Grover, the value of his painful experience against the rebel stronghold.

He told Grover, "The only way you can drive them out is to go forward with fixed bayonets and loaded guns. Fire when you get close and dash over the railroad embankment with a yell and drive them at the point of a bayonet."

General Grover's brigade led one of the few true bayonet charges of the war. His 11th Massachusetts Regiment charged Jackson's line at the abandoned railroad at about 3 PM. Colonel William Blaisdell had led the regiment and told of the grim and deadly charge.

"We advanced about a mile to the edge of a heavy wood, moving forward in a line of battle. When we were within range of the enemy's pickets, we halted and fixed bayonets. Again, moving forward, we drove the enemy pickets before us until we engaged a heavy line of the enemy's infantry. We drove them back and over a line of railroad where the road-bed was 10 feet high. Behind was posted another heavy line of infantry, which opened a terrific fire upon the regiment as we came out of the woods."

"We received the heaviest of the enemy's fire and that staggered the men a little, but, recovering in an instant, they gave a wild hurrah and over they went, mounting the embankment and driving the enemy before them at the point of the bayonet."

"Here for two or three minutes the struggle was very severe, the combatants exchanging shots with their muskets almost muzzle to muzzle and engaging hand-to-hand in deadly encounters. Private John Lawler, of company D, drove in the head of one rebel with the butt of his musket and killed another with his bayonet."

"The enemy broke in confusion and ran. Great numbers threw away their muskets. The regiment pursued them some 80 yards into the wood where it was met by an overwhelming force in front, at the same time receiving artillery fire, which enfiladed our left and forced us to retire, leaving our dead and wounded where they fell."

One lieutenant from the 11th Massachusetts Brigade standing near Grover wrote later of that charge: *'A member of General Hooker's staff rode up to the brigade and gave a verbal order to General Grover. The General formed the regiments and they marched to the right of the line and halted in the border of a thick forest.'*

Grover asked the general's aide, "What does General Hooker want me to do now?"

The aide replied, "Go into the woods and charge."

Grover asked, "Where is my support?"

It was a good question. Grover saw no troops near his position

"It is coming," was the aide's reply.

Grover dallied for fifteen minutes waiting for the promised support.

The aide returned and said, "The general is much displeased because you have not made the charge."

Grover immediately turned without a word and issued the order to his men. That grim directive was repeated down the rows and rank on rank, "Fix bayonets."

Led by General Grover, the men advanced upon a hidden foe, through the brush and tangled woods, which caught on their weapons and uniforms, constantly interfering and slowing their progress.

An exasperated private called to his colonel, "Colonel, do you know what we are going to charge on?"

"Yes, a good dinner," was his light reply.

Then there erupted a furious close combat fight; each side using every weapon they had, from bayonet to clubbing each other with the stocks of their muskets to firing their muskets at close range.

The fierceness of the fighting was described by Blaisdell in that assault.

"They reached an embankment of the unfinished railroad and the bullets began to sing. They seemed to create a breeze that made the leaves upon the trees rustle and a shower of twigs and small branches fell upon the ground. The balls penetrated the barrels and shattered the stocks of many muskets. Soldiers, who carried the ruined weapons, dropped them and picked up the weapons of the helpless comrades lying around them."

The railroad bank was gained. The column, with cheers, passed beyond. The rebel infantry, a Georgia brigade, had given way. Victory appeared certain when a crowd of rebels rose up, seemingly, from nowhere and delivered a destructive blast of muskets fired in a mass volley at the victors.

Jackson had sent more men to stop the break and Hooker had no reinforcements. What might have been a solid break in Jackson's defenses was a failure. A brigade that had already lost a third of its number was forced to retreat. That Confederate force they had met was led by Colonel Edward Thomas' brigade of A.P. Hill's division. A man of the 16th North Carolina remembered the terrible moment.

'About three o'clock the enemy made a vigorous attack on our left, plunging with great fury to our division and piercing the line with bayonets. It looked for a time as if the entire left wing of the Confederate army would be overwhelmed...'

General Pender, Thomas' superior officer, stated in his report, *'I ordered my brigade forward to support Thomas. My men moved forward very gallantly, driving the enemy back across the railroad cut, through the woods on the opposite side and beyond the batteries in the next field.'*

There is a true story told of that day. The story is probably the same as countless such tales of the Civil War. A Major Lang, who was only nine days promoted to command his regiment, was given an order by General Milroy.

Milroy said, "Major Lang, now is the opportunity to distinguish yourself. I want you to charge that railroad embankment just in front of our position, and see what is behind it."

For the new Commander there was but one reply to such an order. As Major Lang was arranging his companies for the charge, Captain Gibson, who knew Lang well and who would be leading the charge, came to Major Lang. The captain's face was as calm and as spiritual as if he was prepared to march to the bridal alter. His next words shocked Lang.

"Major, I shall be killed in this charge."

The major tried to quiet the captain's apprehension with a few pleasant words but the captain persisted.

"I tell you I am going to be killed. I knew it last night and I have known it all morning."

Captain Gibson was known to be as brave a man who ever drew a sword. Major Lang begged him *not* to make the charge but the captain would not listen to that. His mind was made up and the charge began. Halfway across the field a bullet struck Captain Gibson in the forehead and he fell dead, face to face with the foe.

The charging column continued with only a few scattered shots meeting the Federal advance. A hundred and fifty feet from the railroad embankment a deluge of blistering musket fire poured over the edge of the mound and sent such a crash of leaden hail into the ranks of the Union soldiers that they were forced to beat a hasty retreat, leaving many men dead and wounded on the field. They had met the Stonewall Brigade, Jackson's own.

The Union front held for several minutes against this newest onslaught of the enemy but, under the withering fire, Milroy's unit soon began to fall apart. The 3rd Virginia Regiment stood in the meadow alone, 200 yards from the woods. Although confronted by an overwhelming Confederate force they continued to fight on alone.

Milroy shouted, "Fall back."

In the rising din it was impossible for their leader to be heard. The 3rd continued to push forward to the foot of the railroad bed, which stood several feet above the meadow.

Milroy wrote, *'Finally, a storm of bullets convinced my little regiment. It was time to get to the friendly cover of the woods as soon as possible. The greater part of my 3rd Virginia*

Regiment started for the grove.'

To cover the retreat Milroy ran to find the battery he had sent for a half hour before.

'I knew that if I could get the battery in position on the hill at the edge of the forest bordering the meadow that I could probably check and drive the enemy back with canister. I met the first gun a hundred yards from the position where I wanted it. The gunners moved it frantically forward to the hill at the edge of the forest and unlimbered the piece. They rammed the canister into the tube and fired. The first shot had little effect. At the second charge their aim was better and produced a considerable commotion and some tumbling in their column.'

Milroy had no foot soldiers left to support his guns. The gun crews were unprotected and in a precarious spot without strong infantry to support them. He hurried in search of men but his own brigade was under so much heavy fire they were useless to him and he was forced to withdraw his guns. With the Confederates in hot pursuit, his brigade fell back to a hill three-quarters of a mile away. Milroy's situation was perilous. He sent an urgent message to Pope.

'If you do not send me fresh troops and batteries the rebels will soon be on me.'

Things grew worse still. Milroy's commander, Siegel, called for assistance from Heintzelman's corps. Heintzelman sent Brigadier Philip Kearney and Siegel's other three divisions forward with their regiments. Captain Dilger's battery reported, *'My batteries were ordered to support General Schenck's division. I advanced and took up a position on a hill just opposite a large battery of the enemy, which mounted ten guns. I engaged the enemy in a spirited duel.'*

While the fighting raged about the abandoned railroad, Pope was blind to the danger from Longstreet's powerful support and Hood's arrival on Stony Ridge. Pope was completely caught up in his own private war. He finished writing the orders that would gather the scattered parts of his army to Groveton and complete the job of crushing Jackson. Then he turned to the several of his officers standing around the map table. There was an unmistakable note of satisfaction in his voice.

"The game is in our hands, gentlemen. I don't see how it is possible for Jackson to escape without very heavy losses... if at all."

Giving the several dispatches to Colonel William Roberts, his chief of staff, Pope said, "I want to concentrate our forces on Jackson. Send these immediately."

Pope's army *was* indeed scattered. Like hounds hunting a prey they were spread over a thirty square mile area around Manassas. Jackson had confused Pope and led him on one fool's errand after another as his troops followed a scrambled trail.

After issuing the necessary orders to bring his army together at Groveton, Pope's next priority was to regain, what he believed to be, the position yielded by King and Ricketts near Gainesville against the *'rescue force'* that had come to help and save Jackson.

While Pope expressed his satisfaction over being about to pounce on Jackson, Siegel was in serious trouble. Siegel faced Jackson's entire force. Franz Siegel needed help desperately.

One of the last attacks by Union troops was by Kearney against Jackson's left flank. The Confederate Major General A.P. Hill's Light Division had fought and held the line earlier but now they were nearly out of ammunition. The dash was a surprise for the rebels; they were expecting a return volley and had not anticipated looking into the muzzles of the guns delivering the minie balls. Those rebels that tried to make it a fight were instantly shot or bayoneted. Some cried for mercy. Some played 'possum,' lying dead and making no sign, while others made a break to the rear. The men of the second division followed, gone wild with the red rage of battle. A private told of Kearney's charge.

"One fleeing rebel, slowed in his flight by three rolls of blankets *(probably from the spoils of Manassas)* fell in a heap. Quick as a flash my sergeant yanked a ferocious looking *'Yankee killer'* from the Johnny's belt, fashioned from a huge flat file, such as men carried as side arms. The poor fellow caught the glint of the steel and cried out, *'Oh, for God's sake, don't.'* The blow was suspended. *'All right Johnny,'* my sergeant said to the rebel. Pushing the weapon into his own belt, he rose and left the rebel as he lay."

A rebel soldier, on the other side of the old railroad embankment had his say about the same fight and about the back and forth fighting that followed Kearney's charge.

"We had a strong position behind the railroad embankment. We fought them Yankees for about an hour and drove them back. When they flanked us and both wings gave way, we were told to get out of there but we didn't get the courier's message. The men fought like heroes. Our regiment was in the center. When we were surrounded I stood on the embankment and fired right down amongst them just as they were charging up the bank fifteen ranks deep. I got out of there triple quick."

Jackson committed the last of his reserves, Early's brigade, and the Federals were repulsed.

A rebel private wrote to his wife, Amanda, about that day.

'They charged and the first thing I knew we were nearly surrounded. I stood on the embankment (the unfinished railroad) and fired right down among them just as they were charging up the bank about fifteen ranks deep. My regiment was getting away and I followed. They charged over the road but Branch's brigade met them and drove them back a mile to the other side.'

'I went where I fired last and three of the devils were lying there. I got me a good Yankee zinc canteen which fortunately was nearly filled with water.'

General Kearney, who had come up to assist Siegel with his division, reported, *'Enemy forces, in heavy columns, are bearing down on my right and we are forced to fall back. Siegel's other divisions have withdrawn with my troops.'* John Reynolds' division was close by. King didn't know where Reynolds' division was. General Ricketts was of no help; he was too far away. King's scouts reported the bad news that Ricketts' division had fallen back near Gainesville. They were three miles away in retreat from a mysterious new enemy.

Near noon Pope arrived on the battlefield to inspect his handiwork.

He recalled, "I found the two armies confronting each other, both considerably cut up by the sharp action in which they had been engaged since daylight. Heintzelman's corps occupied the right of the line, in front or west of Sudley

Springs Road. General Siegel was on the left, with his line extended a short distance south of the Warrenton Turnpike, and Schenck's division occupied the high ground to the left of the road. The extreme left was occupied by General Reynolds' division. General Reno's corps had reached the field and most of his brigades had been pushed forward into action, leaving three regiments in reserve and in the center of our line."

Meanwhile, as Porter held Longstreet at bay, Pope sat in his headquarters on Buck Hill, satisfied all preparation for Jackson's destruction were complete; the jaws of his vice was about to close on Stonewall Jackson. Pope surmised that Jackson was cornered on Stony Ridge behind the abandoned railroad and the chase would soon be over.

Pope's army was gathering and they were about to attack. Pope believed that if Jackson retreated for Gainesville, Porter and McDowell would be there waiting for him. Every means of escape had been covered and *nothing could go wrong*.

About 6 PM, Porter was near Dawkins Branch preparing for the attack against Longstreet's right flank, which was about to commence. But before Morell could place his troops in position and before General Porter could judge the effect of Morell's advance on Jones, the belated 4:30 PM Order from Pope had arrived.

❧ 39 ❧

The 4:30 PM Order

Major General George Morell commanded the first of Porter's two divisions and Sturgis' reserve corps, which included Piatt's brigade. George Morell in civilian life had been a lawyer, like his father before him. His father had served as a judge of the Michigan Supreme Court and was a good jurist. George Morell was also an honest man. Although George Morell escaped unscathed during the Civil War, Morell's personal integrity would cost him dearly. He was one of the few officers of Second Manassas who testified *in favor of* General Porter at his court martial. Because of his defense of Porter, Morell's military career was ruined. Soon after the trial Morell's appointment as a major general was not renewed and he left the service and became a farmer for the rest of his life, dying five years before Porter was cleared of all charges.

Morell's forward skirmishers returned from the forward position. They had brought two captured Confederate scouts to General Porter for questioning.

"These men told us that Longstreet is just ahead of us, General," Morell said.

Porter looked to the west and, above the trees in a place different from the fight near Groveton and he saw clouds of dust rising in the direction of the Turnpike near Gainesville. That was a sign that there was a new large enemy force, and it was not far off. Still intent on reaching Jackson's right flank, Porter ordered General Hatch, who was part of the battle conference with General Morell to "Push ahead upon Gainesville and prepare for action."

Just after 4 PM, Porter received word from Pope's staff officer that the battle on the Turnpike was going well.

Pope wrote to Morell, *'Push up two regiments, supported by two others, preceded by skirmishers, the regiments at intervals of two hundred yards and attack the party with the section of artillery opposed to you. The battle looks well on our right and the enemy are said to be retiring up the pike. Give the enemy a good shelling when your troops advance.'*

General Morell was about to lead one of the most fearful advances of the Battle of Second Manassas. Just as the sun was starting to sink in the west, on August 29, a dispatch ride brought an order to Porter. It was time-dated for 4:30 PM that afternoon but, because of the difficult terrain, the rider was not able to reach General Porter until it was nearly dark. The time of receipt of the 4:30 Order became a bitter dispute later at Porter's trial, and Porter was charged for disobedience for not following that order. The 4:30 Order read:

General Porter,

'Your line of march brings you in on the enemy's right flank, and if possible, on his rear, keeping your right in communication with General Reynolds. The enemy is massed in the woods in front of us, but can be shelled out as soon as you engage their flank. Keep heavy reserves, and use your batteries, keeping well closed to your right and rear, so as to keep you in close communication with the right wing.'

Porter gave orders to his lead division commander to comply and began the breakthrough to the Turnpike and Jackson's flank. From the tenor of Pope's order, haste was a necessity if his troops were to coordinate and support Pope's maneuver against Jackson correctly. Immediately he called Morell to his side.

"Attack immediately," he told him.

That attack order wasn't so easy for Morell. First the rebels before him had to be cleared out of his way and thrown back so he could carry out the order. Unless he could accomplish that there was no way he could move ahead to the Turnpike and reach Jackson.

Sometime earlier, after 4 PM, Longstreet had sent Wilcox's division to support Jones, who was having trouble with Porter's troops. The sporadic skirmishing and artillery duels continued between Porter's forces and those of Longstreet. The fighting gradually increased in intensity and violence as each side probed the other's defenses and strength. Already Morell's scouts had gauged the strength of the rebels on his front that blocked his way. To try to go forward would be suicide with the Confederate mass on his left. Neither Pope nor Porter knew it then but it was not possible for Porter to reach Jackson with Longstreet's entire army in the way.

George Morell was a good soldier. He was ready to obey the order. However, with so much at stake, he recognized an additional problem. It was late in the day and going forward in the dark would be a cat's cradle of confusion before they had halfway begun the assault. He sent Porter a note acknowledging the attack order and willing to obey. He did not wish to appear dogmatic about his reluctance to attack in darkness, saying that he *'believed that an attack might not be practical'* in the coming darkness.

Porter knew full well what Morell would face. He agreed. It was difficult enough in bright daylight for the infantry to pick their way across ravines, over boulders and through thick woods with a powerful enemy bearing down on his left flank, along with artillery shelling his men. In the dark of night, it would be a catastrophe. Not only would his troops lose their way and become disorganized, when they were attacked, by artillery or infantry, they would be sitting ducks.

So far he had kept the enemy from advancing so he gave Morell his reason for not canceling the 4:30 attack order completely and withdrawing too quickly.

"We cannot retire while McDowell holds. Send your scouts to determine whether there is a way to reach the Turnpike."

To better understand something of the distances involved and the difficult terrain one must know what Porter knew. Jackson's main forces were spread along the Warrenton Turnpike and Stony Ridge. As the crow flies Jackson's left flank was about six miles from Dawkins Branch.

That distant is a misleading number; men are not crows. The terrain between Porter and Jackson was an obstacle course of dense woods, gullies and ravines, streams and muddy marshes. It was not territory any army could pass over quickly.

After a while the enemy artillery died away. Porter ordered a stop to the Federal shelling.

As he later testified, "I was quite certain I was right. The enemy was hesitant about attacking us, not sure how large a force I was. Our threatening attitude proved sufficient to hold the enemy to our front, which was the object I wished to accomplish."

Porter waited impatiently for news from McDowell, Pope or from the battlefield. None came. He sent another plea to McDowell for guidance. He began by apologizing for failing to get through to aid him in his fight.

'I failed to get Morell over to you. After his scouts wandered through the woods for a time, they encountered severe obstacles and heavy artillery fire. I was forced to withdraw them. We suffered heavy casualties.'

Porter made it clear to McDowell that there was no way he could break through to the Turnpike.

Porter counted on one thing, and that was the Confederate army's continued hesitation with no aggressive advance or charge by the rebels, except for some heavy skirmishing. He kept his position because the enemy had no real intention of an all-out attack. Even though Porter's corps was out-manned three to one by Longstreet's right wing, Lee and Longstreet could only be waiting to start an offensive against Pope's army. He, Porter, was delaying that all-important move.

As he testified during his trial, "I became satisfied that Morell was right. By holding the enemy (Lee's army) before us, we were producing all the good effects of a battle and would get none of its evils."

As the firing at Dawkins Branch died down and night came on, at about 7 PM McDowell returned to headquarters on the Turnpike, after sending Hatch down the Pike. McDowell gave Pope a briefing on two dispatches he had sent during the day. First, he showed him Buford's dispatch, which until then, he had kept in his pocket.

The earlier dispatch from Buford, which McDowell held over a day and failed to pass on until this moment, reported the approach of the Confederate army and read, 'seventeen brigades of rebels, artillery and five hundred cavalry passed through Gainesville this morning.' With things going so well, it seemed like a good time for McDowell to show Pope the troubling August 28, 8:30 AM dispatch.

When Pope read the dispatch he did not seem to be worried. He paid only scant attention to news of a new enemy force.

It was news that should have put any commanding general on high alert. Pope was so cock-sure he was about to catch Jackson that day, not much else was important.

269

If he thought about Buford's dispatch at all, most likely he reasoned that the 'new enemy force' could easily be dealt with *after* he had captured Jackson. After all, to his thinking, that new force had come to *cover Jackson's retreat* through Thoroughfare Gap. Most surely, Robert E. Lee could not be daring to attack Pope.

Porter was on his mind. He was baffled and angry. Porter had still not started an attack. Where was Porter? Why had Porter's offensive against Jackson not arrived?

Pope's patience was exhausted. He called his assistant.

"Go see Porter. Bring me word why he has not attacked."

By this later hour it was quite likely that John Pope was well aware of Longstreet's presence… and that a part of Longstreet's force was intending to make a connection with Jackson. Circumstances and logic dictate that Pope rationalized. He might have reasoned that it meant Jackson's right flank was still probably vulnerable to attack from the direction of Gainesville.

McDowell next handed Pope a dispatch he had received from Porter. The message read, '*I failed in getting Morell over to you. After wandering through the woods for a time I withdrew him, and while doing so artillery opened on us. My scouts could not get through. Each one was captured. Please communicate the way this messenger came. I have no cavalry or messengers left now. Please let me know your designs, whether to retire or not. I cannot get water and am out of provisions. Have lost a few men from infantry firing.*'

Porter's dispatch was a desperate call for help, or at least some guidance from the officers that should have given him some help. Pope read the dispatch but his mind was on only *one subject*. Porter had not obeyed his 4:30 Order.

Pope's entire attention was focused on only the part of the dispatch, which read, '*Please let me know your designs, whether to retire or not.*' That made it clear to Pope that Porter had failed to even *begin* the attack on Jackson. He was livid with anger.

"I'll arrest him," he exclaimed and turned to his secretary to write out the arrest order.

McDowell's heavy guilt for his mistakes must have come back to haunt him and they made him speak in Porter's defense. Irvin McDowell was very much to blame for Pope's ignorance of the true state of affairs relating to Longstreet's presence on the field. To cover his own sizable incompetence, McDowell intervened in Pope's rage. At best McDowell's soothing explanation was a backhanded act of faint criticism that did nothing except to paint Porter as a misfit, and to direct criticism away from his own actions.

In defense of Porter, McDowell said to Pope, "Porter's action was not an act of disloyalty; merely incompetence."

McDowell's fatuous remark regarding Porter was a reflection of the man's lack of character and ineptness.

Later, McDowell was investigated by a court of inquiry for his part in the loss of the battle. General Schofield, chairman of Porter's 1878 rehearing, said of McDowell, "Porter's action might have saved the entire Union army from complete defeat caused by the ineptitude of John Pope and his second-in-command, Irvin McDowell."

Pope cooled down. At three o'clock on the morning of August 30, he sent Porter a second far more dictatorial order; one that was a peremptory, no-nonsense command.

To General Porter:

'Immediately upon the receipt of this order, the precise hour of receiving you will acknowledge, you will march your command to the field of battle of today and report to me in person for orders. You are to understand that you are expected to comply strictly with this order, and to be present on the field within three hours after its reception or after daybreak of tomorrow morning.'

Kearney's attack against Jackson's left had been in progress for an hour. He had gained ground and Kearney's success had given Pope one more reason to believe Jackson was retreating south toward the Gap. Pope sent McDowell in pursuit of the 'fleeing' Jackson and after deploying the rest of his troops along the Turnpike, Pope rode back to Buck Hill, which the Union general had made his headquarters.

Porter was a man of strong opinions and a good judge of men. On August 27, after fighting to get his army to Bristoe Station, Fitz John Porter had *his* first good look at John Pope. In a letter to his friend, General Ambrose Burnside, who was at Fredericksburg, Porter had said,

'Everything is at sixes and sevens and I find I am to take care of myself in every respect... all this talk of bagging Jackson & etc., is so much bosh.'

By the morning of August 30, Porter was angry and irritated and for good reason. Already he had seen and heard enough to know his worse suspicions were confirmed; Pope's lack of leadership had made itself evident time and again. Pope was indeed an ass.

Porter's note to General Pope acknowledging the 4:30 Order to attack Jackson's right made it clear to Pope that he had received the order as the sun was going down and darkness was coming on fast. He reminded the general that reforming 9,000 men would take at least an hour or more no matter how quickly the commands were given and passed down the line. Porter further explained to Pope that the lateness of the hour made such an all-out attack impractical until next morning. Marching was difficult enough in bright daylight, and near impossible in the dark of night. His troops could lose their way and if they were attacked by artillery or infantry, they would be focused on travel, not defense, and would fare poorly.

During General Porter's trial in 1862, Pope claimed to have *'misplaced the note* that Porter wrote that day.'

It is a military maxim and an absolute rule that all dispatches, reports, orders and notes written and sent during battle must be preserved. That critical and all-important writing was one more piece of vital evidence that would have made clear Porter's determination to follow orders. It would have explained the circumstances Porter faced and show that Pope's order was impossible to follow exactly.

The existence of that missing note was requested by General Porter but, contrary to the rules of military record keeping, Pope was never able to produce the missing note at the 1862 court martial or at Porter's rehearing in 1878. Nevertheless, the testimony of Porter's generals and the staff officer that wrote the notes, were heard at the 1878 rehearing. They were present when the note was discussed and written.

Had General Porter obeyed the 4:30 Order, and gone forward against Jackson with Longstreet's army at his left side, Porter's attack would have been a calamity. His men would have been under constant musket and artillery fire on his left side from Longstreet's guns. His troops would have been butchered with no chance of breaking through Longstreet's defense to reach Jackson. Besides that considerable problem, it was getting too dark to tell friend from foe. A night assault would have been foolhardy and pointless against the 29,000 Confederate troops.

Morell had something to say about Pope's 4:30 Order at Porter's trial. He protested the order. During the Seven Days Campaign, General Porter had held the Confederate attacks at Malvern Hill and Gainesville against the best Lee could throw at him.

Morell stated, "General Pope's *4:30 Order* must have been given under some misapprehension by General Pope. Pope was certain the enemy was in retreat. My scouts reported the opposite; the enemy was *not* in retreat along the Turnpike."

That statement by George Morell was a masterpiece of understatement. John Pope's understanding of the true state of affairs was completely off the mark and the tide was about to turn for Robert E. Lee. Pope's Army of Virginia stood on the precipice of total destruction.

Confirmation of the wisdom of Porter's decision came after the war from another source, Confederate soldiers, who were there. In 1867 Robert E. Lee wrote to Porter:

'The result of an attack against 25,000 men before noon of that day may not be certain, but it ought to have been repulsed if it was made after Longstreet had formed his troops. The probable result of an attack on Longstreet after twelve o'clock would have been repulsed.'

General Longstreet, in a letter to Porter said, 'We were all particularly anxious to bring on the battle after twelve o'clock, General Lee more than the rest. If you had attacked any time after twelve o'clock, it seems to me we would have surely have destroyed your army, that is, if you attacked with less than 25,000 men.'

In 1864, John Bell Hood, Longstreet's division commander, wrote to Porter.

'An attack made by you, with 9,000 men, it seems to me, would have been attended by a repulse, and, perhaps great, had time permitted it to have been followed up. It is almost certain, had you attacked at 11 AM, with your command as I supposed it to have been, you would have been repulsed. Had your attack been at or near two o'clock, you would have been used up, and those on your right might have, and probably would have, been overwhelmed, too...'

General B.H. Robertson, a leading army tactician and a combat veteran, wrote in 1870 about that day.

'I should say an attack with 25,000 men would have failed. After twelve o'clock and throughout the day, I believe an attack with 9,000 men would have been utterly disastrous to the Federal forces.'

Here is a puzzle. General Pope knew, or reasonably should have known, from the earlier reports of General Buford and General Banks that a 'large force of the enemy' had been sighted near the Thoroughfare Gap. That force was on its way toward the Manassas battleground. Pope even swore before the court martial when he testified that he *'feared Longstreet's arrival at any moment; certainly during the afternoon of August 29.'*

Pope's testimony and his battle reports gave the lie to his claim that he did not know Longstreet was not yet on the field. In his *August 30* Battle Report, Pope wrote, *'We fought a terrific battle here yesterday (August 29) with the combined forces of the enemy, which lasted with continuous fighting from daylight until dark.'*

At another time, in diametrically opposing testimony, Pope swore, "Porter had at his front no considerable force of the enemy. I believed then and I was very sure up until eight o'clock that night Porter might have attacked Jackson's right flank and rear before there was any possibility that Jackson could be reinforced."

❧ 40 ❧

Eighteen Cannon

It was a quiet night except for occasional almost halfhearted musket fire. There was not much activity on either side. With the coming of the August morning, there was plenty of bustle and commotion at Pope's headquarters on Buck Hill. His first courier appeared at 3 AM and he brought unhappy news that Franklin's 5,000-man corps was nowhere near. Pope had been waiting for Franklin to fatten his 50,000-man force. Franklin was days away.

General William B. Franklin's corps was one of those army units that Chief General Halleck had ordered McClellan to send to Pope, much to McClellan's unhappiness. George McClellan had been forced to part with most of his army, which went to John Pope's command; a most disagreeable choice for the self-important McClellan. Most of the others had shown up; Siegel's, Banks', Reno's, Reynolds' and Porter's corps; soon or late, depending on how slowly McClellan could drag his feet. Grudgingly, like an angry dog guarding his last bone, McClellan continued to fight the loss.

Franklin was not altogether enthusiastic about going, which was plain from his reply to Pope. The day before Pope had notified General Franklin, who had finally started on his way to Manassas, to carry extra rations for his men and forage for the horses. The courier's message from Franklin that greeted Pope at 3 AM that morning of August 30 gave a sorry answer to Pope's request; *'The trains of supplies that you request will be sent as soon as you send me a cavalry escort to guard my trains.'*

That surly answer was the last straw for John Pope. With all of the things going wrong General Franklin's reason was an obvious ploy for further delay. Pope was thoroughly frustrated and he later wrote of his disappointment: *'It was not until I received this letter that I began to feel discouraged.'*

Although Pope was not a well-liked person, one can understand his aggravation. Pope's carefully laid plans had gone wrong one after another. General Porter had not obeyed his orders and General McDowell was repeatedly getting lost or off somewhere so that good communication with his second-in-command was worse than chewing nails. Most irritating to the newly installed general of the Army of Virginia was Pope's conviction, that in spite of his belief that Jackson was about to be destroyed, his own generals kept annoying him with wild rumors of *another* rebel force coming on the field to further disrupt his campaign.

Things were not all bad for General Pope. That very morning he had personally questioned several wounded Confederate soldiers and rebel prisoners and took comfort from their answers. Pope was satisfied that he *had* been right all along; Jackson *was* retreating and the rumors were unfounded. When the prisoners had been taken away his cares left him and he became optimistic once more. Before the sun was up he penned a letter to General-in-Chief Halleck, his superior in Washington. In his letter he boasted, among other things, that *'the enemy has been driven from the field. We have made great captures and our troops have behaved splendidly.'* Certainly his last statement was true. McClellan's soldiers had been well trained and most of them had seen action. The Federal infantry had proved itself in the Peninsula and in the Seven Days Campaigns.

PORTER HOLDS LONGSTREET

In Confederate headquarters on the early morning of August 30, the day had also started out to be quiet. Lee waited, expecting Porter's strong assaults against his front lines near Dawkins Branch to continue. He was disappointed. Had Pope's forces attacked him, Lee was in such a strong position that he would have had the advantage. Further, with no evidence of activity other than Porter's force, Lee realized that Pope might *not attack at* all that day.

Robert E. Lee was becoming impatient. Trusting Longstreet's judgment, he had already delayed his planned offensive for eighteen hours. Porter's vigorous attempts near Dawkins Branch to break through Longstreet's troops so that he might strike at Jackson, as Pope had ordered, had forced Longstreet to expend more troops. Longstreet had sent first Jones', and then Wilcox's divisions against Porter's brigades. These were two large divisions the Confederacy needed for the main offensive and Porter's aggressiveness had thrown Lee's timetable into a cocked hat.

It was time for Lee to make a decision. Longstreet's lines were formed for battle and they were ready to roll. Yet, General Longstreet was still reluctant to start the offensive. He had not fully taken the measure of the Federal force before him.

The night before, Longstreet had promised his anxious chief, "Though I am more than anxious to meet your wishes, General Lee, as the day is far spent, at nightfall I shall send a reconnaissance in force to the immediate front of the enemy. If an opening is found for an entering wedge, then, at daylight, we shall have all things in readiness for a good day's work. If a weak spot is found, my right wing will push ahead or go *around* Porter's troops in the morning."

Now it *was* morning. Even so, Lee was willing to let *another* day pass without an attack, hoping Pope's other forces would attack first. Whatever happened, Lee was ready. He told his two wing commanders, Jackson and Longstreet, to allow the day to pass without a fight.

Lee instructed, "Let us make no aggressive moves. If by tonight Pope has still not attacked, we shall move around the Union right, parallel to Pope's lines, and go towards Bull Run and try to get between Pope and Washington," adding, "If Pope elects to fight we shall accommodate him."

Sixteen years later in 1878, when General Schofield was commissioned to rehear Porter's 1862 court martial conviction, testimony was offered from the same men who had been a part of the Second Battle of Manassas; both Union men and Confederates. Charles Marshall, Robert E. Lee's chief of staff, testified about Lee's words and probable thoughts on the morning of August 30, 1862.

"I think General Lee's wish was that we would be attacked. The fact we were not, caused General Lee to defer any action he might have taken that morning."

General 'Stonewall' Jackson had a busy afternoon the day before, August 29. That evening Jackson and his escort had ridden from Stony Ridge to Lee's headquarters where he spent a restful night. At the morning meeting General Lee outlined Jackson's part in the coming counter offensive.

"You are to make a diversion against the Union right near Groveton. At the same time, make an end run with your forces around the Union left and join your forces with those of General Longstreet."

The result of the maneuver would be that both wings of the Confederate army would be joined. Then, fifty thousand rebels would descend on the unsuspecting John Pope.

LEE'S ARTILLERY PREPARES

Good artillery can make or break any advance. It can turn any retreat into a demoralized route. Lee's artillery, while not as accurate as those of the Federals, was quite adequate for the occasion. This day the Confederate cannons were ready. At 2 AM, batteries including several separate artillery pieces were hauled by teams of horses and moved during the night to their positions. Limber wagons carried chests of ammunition and gunnery supplies and caissons brought canisters and shells for the long-range cannons. Tins were placed aboard the wagons, containing lead and iron balls that would shatter on impact and flail through the enemy targets like a hundred muskets firing at once.

The Confederate artillery pieces included dozens of long-range cannons called Napoleons. These were smooth bore muzzle loaders, developed under the reign of Napoleon III. They fired a 12-pound projectile and the men referred to the pieces as 12 pounders. The Parrott cannons were also muzzle loaders but, because of their rifled barrels, the missiles turned screw-wise as they left the barrels, which made them more accurate than the smooth bore Napoleons. Most Confederate cannons, including the Parrotts, were cast iron since bronze was in short supply in the Confederacy. A heavy band of wrought iron around the breech prevented the barrel from exploding or cracking apart in the heat of battle.

Some of the projectiles were explosive shells. These contained black powder that would detonate 15 to 20 seconds after the projectile left the barrel to blast apart shards and pieces of hot iron above the enemy's heads. Others projectiles were filled with grapeshot, so called because the internal mass was a cluster of small iron balls, usually nine to a cluster. On impact the grapeshot would break apart and scatter among the enemy troops and mow them down like a volley of minie balls.

A place for the guns had been chosen on the ridge above Groveton among Jackson's forces. The prominent knoll that had been picked was the perfect location to wait for Pope's troops, who were encamped and had spread out below, around the Warrenton Turnpike and in the nearby hills.

As it grew lighter the gun crews took their places. Rammers were ready to force the powder charge and the projectiles down the barrels of the cannons, whether shrapnel or canister, and to seat them firmly in the breech. Some of the guns would fire solid shot, with oblong-like bullets for the rifled Parrotts and spherical-like minie balls for the smooth bore Napoleons. Standing by each gun, a man stood ready with his sponge. In the heat of battle and with many firings, the barrel collected grime and detritus or smoldering cloth and, with each firing, a sponge was needed to clean the barrel. When the order came to fire, a man would place a spark to the vent, a small hole in the breech, through which the spark traveled to ignite the powder charge. The result was a mass killer of men.

Colonel Stephen D. Lee, General Lee's nephew, was in charge of the artillery battalion. He wrote of the morning's preparation for battle.

'I placed my 18 batteries on a commanding ridge. This ridge was about the center of the battlefield, Jackson's corps being on my left and Longstreet's on my right. It was an admirable ridge, generally overlooking the ground in front for some 2000 yards. Groveton Woods were 1300 yards in front. Four howitzers were placed on the extreme left of my line. Nine rifles (Parrotts) were spaced along the ridge to the right. Five howitzers were kept under cover of the woods.'

When he reported his artillery deployment at nine o'clock to his uncle, General Robert E. Lee, the rebel commander's response was brief. Lee was satisfied.

"You are just where I want you. Stay there."

The greater numbers of long-range artillery pieces would support Jackson on his right flank, where Longstreet's offensive would begin with John Bell Hood's division. Longstreet had sent scouting parties to where he thought the Union lines were located. He was still uncertain, and was unable to be sure of their exact position because of the darkness.

John Bell Hood had been sent to help Jackson more quickly, and the action began. By 9 AM Hood was hotly engaged with Porter's and Reynold's men near Groveton.

A.P. Hill continued to hold Jackson's left flank on the ridge. Because the morning had been quiet, his brigade went to the rear for their day's rations of crackers and meat, plus 100 rounds of ammunition.

THE CONFEDERATE PLAN

The Confederate plan for the main offensive against Pope was simple; when the order to fire was given, Colonel Montgomery Corse's brigade of Virginians from Kemper's division would go forward. Corse was to be followed by Jones' division, and when that infantry tactic was completed, Anderson's division of five thousand troops would follow. Jeb Stuart's cavalry battalion would gallop ahead, sabers swinging. Hopefully, the Federal enemy would be surprised and fall before the greater concentration of rebel forces like scattered leaves before a storm wind.

General Anderson was late. His division had been Longstreet's rear guard on the old Rappahannock line. On the way to join Longstreet, Anderson had lost his way. His infantry had marched too far in the soupy darkness with no guide because

Longstreet had forgotten to send a staff officer to show them the way.

Between three and four that morning, General Richard Anderson's three brigades of 4500 men had passed through Thoroughfare Gap into the Manassas plain and every man knew they had reached the battlefield. There was plenty of evidence of death and debris from the previous day's fighting laying in the fields around them and beside the Turnpike.

When Hood learned of Anderson's appearance on the battlefield, he was concerned. He knew that the Federals had thirty or forty cannons aimed on Anderson's spot where his men had decided to encamp beside the Turnpike. Longstreet spoke later of his worries for Anderson that morning, which he offered in evidence at Porter's retrial.

"I was prepared to lie down and rest for a few hours before dawn, until one of my aids told me about Anderson. I mounted my horse, rode off to find General Anderson and warned him to withdraw to a defensive position. I told him to move his division as soon as possible. I was certain that at daylight the Federals would, most certainly, open up on his men."

POPE: STILL UNAWARE

Anderson's men immediately moved back a distance. Soon enough they found their way. As they neared Brawner's Farm, they passed the grisly guideposts of dead bodies from the previous day's carnage which littered the fields and the road around them.

As they marched along the Warrenton Turnpike during the early hours of August 30, Pope's scouts were watching. When they saw the force of marchers halt and reverse direction, Pope's scouts rode to Buck Hill and reported the enemy move to Pope. Pope took the report and, instead of relating the large marching column to Buford's earlier report of '*17 regiments of an enemy coming through Gainesville,*' he interpreted the rebel movement to be another piece of concrete evidence for Jackson's continuing retreat.

General Patrick, of Morrell's fourth brigade, had just arrived at Dogan Hill. General Patrick peered into the faint light of the coming morning and he was treated to the far-off spectacle of enemy (*Anderson*) troops in column on the turnpike. His artillery sent a few rounds in their direction to send them on their way a little faster. General Patrick reported the sighting to McDowell but McDowell refused to place any special significance to Patrick's report, and what that interesting fact might mean.

At Pope's headquarters on Buck Hill, Pope was oblivious to the gathering forces of the enemy or the long-range guns that peeked over his head. He completed his plans for the day and wrote the necessary orders to his several division heads, confident he would capture Jackson. One of those orders would change the course of the battle.

THE PEREMPTORY ORDER

At 3:30 AM, while it was still dark at General Porter's headquarters near Dawkins Branch on the Manassas-Gainesville Road, Porter received Pope's *Peremptory Order*. The directive to Porter was arrogant and unconditional.

'Immediately upon the receipt of this order you will march your command to the field of battle and report to me in person for orders.'

Pope refused to accept any of Porter's reasons for his inability to obey the Joint Order or the 4:30 Order. All of Porter's explanations for not being able to reach Jackson's left flank fell on deaf ears. Pope was angry. His insulting no-nonsense peremptory order was a reflection of his disgust and fury with Porter and he was tired of fooling around without the results he demanded. He intended to make sure *this time* Porter understood him.

Porter complied immediately. He did what was necessary to carry out Pope's directive with dispatch and efficiency by marching his men in the only way open to his troops; the same back road McDowell had taken on the afternoon before. That route was directly *away* from the enemy that he had neutralized.

It was no small undertaking. To move 9,000 troops at night and in total secrecy required some difficult and delicate maneuvering. It was necessary to pull away from the rebel pickets with a maximum of silence and a minimum of notice to leave, without alerting the enemy.

Union Colonel Charles Roberts, leading General Butterfield's First Brigade, broke bivouac on the Manassas-Gainesville Road at 4 AM. Once Porter's troops had been extricated from their positions at Dawkins Branch, Porter sent the mile-long columns on their way toward Groveton. It was about a three-hour trip and by eight o'clock on the morning of August 30, Porter's columns reached Dogan Hill next to the Warrenton Turnpike. Porter's regiments, companies, brigades and divisions found a place to camp and they settled in the fields around the Dogan Ridge and Dogan house.

General Morell had not been as fortunate. After careful preparations to get Roberts' lead brigade into the three-hour march, and following with the remainder of his division, Morell lost his way. The error had not been entirely Morell's fault; his orders were to *'follow Sykes' division'* and by the time Morell got going Sykes' men were out of sight. Therefore, Morell followed Pope's *earlier* order for his army to *'go to Centreville after Jackson.'* But that earlier order had been superseded with new orders that sent everybody toward Groveton. Out of touch with the rest of Porter's command and assuming Centreville was his destination, General Morell took the road to Centreville. Butterfield thereupon took charge of Morell's remaining brigades and continued in charge until Morell got back. But that was nearly 4 PM, after the battle was nearly over.

All during the night of August 29, Jeb Stuart's cavalry had been busy guarding the flanks of the Confederate army and keeping tabs on Porter's large Federal force that was holding up the planned offensive. Not long before dawn had broken, it became apparent to Jeb Stuart that the last of the Federal forces that had been threatening Longstreet's right flank were moving off. They would be gone by sunrise. He rode at a gallop to headquarters with the news.

"The force, which has been in our front near Dawkins Creek, is moving away toward the Turnpike," he announced to Longstreet and Lee.

That was good information. Porter's fifth corps and Hatch's division, 9000 Federal troops, had held up Lee's offensive for a day and a half. Now they were gone and the way to Pope's unguarded left flank was wide open. Lee's offensive could begin without the troublesome large Union force on Longstreet's right flank. With his *Peremptory Order* to Porter, John Pope had very conveniently *removed the last obstacle to Lee's offensive and the near destruction of the Union army.*

❧ 41 ❧

Porter's Attack

Porter rode in with his staff to Buck Hill Headquarters about 7:30 AM. The first of his brigades and divisions were still arriving in long columns and while the officers saw to the placement of the troops in the fields and on Dogan Hill, Porter reported to General Pope. He was just in time to hear Pope giving his final directives for the day.

John Kearney's successful attack on the Confederate left flank near Bull Run Creek the afternoon before had decided for Pope that one more hard thrust against Jackson's left flank might tip the scales. One more strong push might be the last urging needed to hurry Jackson's retreat. At the same time Pope intended to catch the fleeing Jackson before he could escape into Thoroughfare Gap.

His General Order to his assembled officers was to, *'Hold the center near Groveton and mass our troops on the right closer to Gainesville so as to forestall Jackson's retreat to the Gap. McDowell will make an attack on Jackson's right flank, along with General Porter's Fifth Corps, General Reno's Seventh Corps and General Heinzelman's Third Corps.'*

As his officers listened to Pope's orders rumors of a large force of the enemy, *coming from Gainesville*, continued to rattle around in the officer's heads. Perhaps, for that reason, nobody at the staff meeting seemed to be very enthusiastic about the operation. Disturbing reports of a strong enemy presence had continued to come into headquarters all that morning; from Ricketts, from Reynolds, from Banks, from Stevens, and from Porter.

Later Porter spoke to his biographer, John C. Ropes, in 1887, about that meeting. Porter recalled, *'I reported to Pope and gave him my positive belief of Longstreet's arrival opposite his left. General Reynolds was present and he gave his convictions to the same effect. Reynolds added that the enemy was then turning to our left. General Buford had previously expressed this belief and Reynolds referred to his dispatch to General Ricketts of the 29th stating that he had seen a number of Longstreet's regiments passing through Gainesville. Our warnings were in vain. Pope put no confidence in what we said.'*

Kearney, who had been fighting Jackson's men since dawn near the Sudley Road at Jackson's far left flank, added to Pope's discomfort. Kearney's report was that, *'Ricketts and my positions are completely enfiladed by the enemy's three or four long range batteries.'* The long range guns were not all from Jackson's artillery; some of the guns belonged to the mysterious second enemy that Pope refused to acknowledge. Perhaps, with minds that were more suspicious and more open to the possible approach of a new enemy force, McDowell and Heintzelman requested time to make a quick reconnaissance of the turnpike. Since their quick look-see would not interfere with the planned noon offensive, Pope agreed.

General Jesse Reno's Ninth Corps had not attended the staff meeting but had remained bivouacked the night before, near Jackson's extreme left and not far from Bull Run Creek. When he heard the rumor that Jackson was running he was incredulous. Reno sent his aid, Isaac Stevens, riding to headquarters to tell Pope in person that for '*Jackson to be fleeing was ridiculous. For any member of the high command to give it credence was a mistake.*'

Pope's reaction to Reno's message and Steven's verbal repeat of Reno's opinion, was to blandly order Reno to '*make a reconnaissance of the woods at his front and report back.*' Reno did as he was told. Shortly afterward he sent Stevens back to Pope with the same warning: '*General Reno encountered strong enemy resistance.*'

Stevens knew the reconnaissance indicated a rebel force. Pope would not listen. When Stevens testified at Porter's rehearing, he stated, '*Reno's report had no effect on Pope's opinionated mind.*'

General Jesse Reno's relationship with his Confederate enemy, Thomas Jackson, was one more poignant reminder of the tragedy of America's Civil War. Reno's family, for generations, had known Jackson's forebears and Jesse Reno was a close friend of Stonewall Jackson during their West Point days. Yet now they faced each other behind a musket or a bayonet.

Before Porter left Pope's meeting, one of Porter's men brought in a wounded 'Federal.' The wounded man claimed to have escaped from the previous day's fighting and he had something to say. Porter thought the man a Confederate and placed small weight on the parolee's news. Porter later told his biographer:

'*The wounded man said he had been taken prisoner the night before and escaped. He said the enemy was retreating. I didn't believe him and I was sure the escapee was a Confederate plant. As Pope questioned the man, I gave a stout disclaimer that I regarded the man as either a fool or designedly released to give the wrong impression and no faith should be put in what he says.*'

Pope gave Porter's opinion no credence. Instead he accepted the escaped prisoner's claims as true. When he finished questioning the 'parolee,' Pope gave Porter an order.

"General Porter, I want you to attack Jackson immediately. General King will support you."

Minutes after Porter rode off to begin the attack against Jackson, McDowell and Heintzelman returned from their reconnaissance mission on the Turnpike with good news for John Pope. What they told him was exactly what Pope wanted to hear.

Heintzelman said, "All points held by the enemy the day before beyond Bull Run have been abandoned. When our scouts went over the Sudley Springs Road and west of the road, they saw no evidence of the enemy in force. All they found were some skirmishers and advance posts or rear guards."

The report confirmed for Pope that the Confederates were in retreat. By this time the idea of a Confederate retreat had infected most of Pope's officers as well. Even Siegel, on the front lines fighting Jackson's men, had come to believe Jackson was in retreat. It was untrue, of course. Jackson was following Lee's orders to make the Federals believe exactly that. He had already started to move his troops south and around behind Pope's farthest position on the Turnpike to join Longstreet in the massed offensive.

Porter went up to White House on Dogan Hill, where General Patrick had his headquarters. Porter then relieved General Patrick, who had been stationed around Dogan Hill. Once he had relieved Patrick, Porter's next task was to see to the business of deploying his men and those of Ricketts' and Hatch's brigades in Patrick's place, to carry out Pope's order to attack Jackson.

General Morell and General Griffin's brigades had gone, by mistake, to Centreville so General Butterfield had taken command of Morell's division. Colonel Charles Roberts led Morell's First Brigade. His men took time to wolf down some breakfast; his troops had gone many hours without food or water. They were interrupted in their hurried meal with new orders to *'move to the top of the ridge where the artillery was stationed.'*

By noon, Porter had sent Sykes' and Butterfield's divisions along with artillery to the south side of the Warrenton Turnpike. They were ready to cross Warrenton Turnpike to assault Jackson's right flank. The two men commanding Morell's two brigades, Colonel Roberts and Colonel Weeks, went about the business of sending out skirmishers and pickets against Jackson's Confederates, which they knew lay in wait a mile away on Stony Ridge beyond the woods and behind the fortified embankment of the abandoned railroad.

Butterfield ordered, "Advance your skirmishers into the woods and move your men to the top of the ridge."

Roberts' 25th New York Regiment and Berdan's First United States Sharpshooters moved across a field against the enemy. Butterfield's and Hatch's brigades led the charge with King's division on Roberts' left.

Roberts testified about that attack on Stony Ridge at Porter's 1878 rehearing.

"At 11 AM I received orders to advance my skirmishers briskly through the skirt of woods at my front. Following my command to attack the enemy, I deployed my skirmishers covering our front and went next to the third brigade. Connecting with General Ricketts' two regiments, we reached the brow of a hill. We had passed nearly through the belt of timber to our front when, upon the opposite edge beyond the wood, we received an exceedingly hot musketry fire. We were obliged to halt."

Colonel Henry Weeks assumed command over Butterfield's 3rd Brigade now that Butterfield had taken over the missing Morell's spot as division head. Weeks placed the 17th New York Regiment next to Roberts' 25th Regiment. After taking position, the 17th New York deployed six companies as skirmishers with Berdan's sharpshooters deployed on the left of the regiment and in front. Weeks then advanced with the 25th New York into the woods. Hatch's division was placed in the rear and Porter's and Hatch's troops moved against Jackson's line on Stony Ridge.

One of Berdan's sharpshooters recalled,

'At about 10:30, a skirmish line, in which our regiment formed the center, was deployed. We advanced slowly and cautiously, first across a field, then into a dense wood, without meeting strong resistance. Toward noon our advance was becoming more difficult as the enemy was showing opposition, yet he was slowly retreating.'

Sykes' division had arrived and his brigades took position. His 3rd U.S. regular infantry advanced toward a stone house and drove some rebels away, who were sheltered there, then moved toward the embankment in concert with Porter's forces. What the Federals did not know was that Longstreet had sent General Wilcox's division to reinforce Jackson's defenses, along with the heavy guns of Longstreet's batteries.

Colonel Elisha Marshall, of the 13th New York Regiment from Colonel Roberts' brigade, further described the battle.

'We advanced on the hills, crossed a meadow and went into the woods. The enemy had a strong force hidden in the woods and there were more Confederates waiting for us in a gap on an abandoned railroad where the bulk of Jackson's men were hidden. We tried to advance from the woods and we were repulsed by a terrible fire of grapeshot, canister and musketry which mowed down our men like sheep to slaughter.'

'The rebels had their batteries posted along the edge of the woods and they caught us in a deadly crossfire, while the railroad breastworks served as an excellent defense for Jackson's men.'

Colonel Weeks' 17th New York Regiment, following Roberts' brigade, pushed out of the timber to lead the third brigade's advance. Major William Gower, commanding the 17th, wrote in his battle report,

'The men were up in a moment. We advanced and crossed the road, the men scrambling over a fence and moving steadily forward in quick time. No sooner had we appeared in plain sight of the enemy than he opened a tremendous fire of artillery and musketry on our lines. Nothing could surpass the behavior of the officers and the men. Our troops closed the gaps in our ranks. I rode to the head and gave the word, "Double quick, charge." With a mad yell, the gallant fellows rushed up the hill to what was almost certain death. We now reached a sort of plateau; a battery on the summit was playing upon us. Another battery on the right opened with canister, completely enfilading our lines. The woods to our left were completely filled with the enemy's infantry. We seemed entirely without support, being some distance ahead of the brigade. I was compelled to halt. I ordered the men to lie down and commence firing.'

A letter, written to a friend by one of the men of the 12th New York regiment, stated, *'Like the other attacking brigades, Colonel Weeks' men locked in a savage firefight with the Southerners, keeping up a sustained musketry fire that staggered the rebels again and again. They could make no headway against the semi-fortified line.'*

A man of the 83rd Pennsylvania recalled in a letter home, *'The enemy was secreted behind a little hill a short distance in advance of us. Occasionally they would rise and pour in one deadly volley into our ranks, and then settle down into their hiding places. Batteries on our left were shelling us and everything was in confusion. Regiments got mixed up, brigades were intermingled, all was one seething, anxious, excited mass. Some officers were yelling, Fire! While others were yelling, Cease fire, for God's sake! You are shooting at your own men! In the midst of all this confusion there seemed to be no competent head to bring order out of chaos.'*

One reason for the confusion was that Colonel Weeks fell wounded early in the fight. Command devolved on a citizen soldier, James Rice of the 44th New York. The situation went from bad to worse. The column was crumbling. The position was impossible and for his men to remain any longer would probably end in being surrounded and captured. Rice ordered the brigade to fall back.

After 30 minutes the attack had failed. Each man knew they had done their best. The men of the third brigade fell back across the field but as they retreated there was a decided spring in their step. These were not beaten men. The rebels kept up a heavy fire and the last traces of confusion only disappeared when the men were back behind their artillery. All through the attack, Porter's artillery on Dogan Ridge kept working their pieces.

Stonewall Jackson, after his meeting with Lee much earlier that morning, had returned to his troops on Stony Ridge. At 8 AM, before Porter had received Pope's order to attack and while it was quiet in the fields around Dogan Hill, Jackson's scouts reported Porter's movements below.

After watching the concentration of Starke's division in front of the woods for a while, Jackson turned to Colonel Baylor who was in command of Jackson's old brigade and said, "Well, Baylor, it looks as if there will be no fight today. But keep your men in line and ready for action today."

Jackson wheeled his horse around and returned to his field headquarters next to a haystack near a battalion of Confederate artillery and caught up on his sleep. Within the hour Porter's attack began and Jackson was up in seconds wide awake.

When Joe Hooker came to the Buck Hill Union headquarters and reported in with General Heintzelman to receive his orders, he stopped to chat with his friend, John Reynolds. The two generals were friends. They often exchanged what information they had that the other might need. Reynolds told Hooker that which Pope refused to believe. Conversely, many of the officers were brainwashed by Pope's false optimism and did not believe that a major Confederate offensive was imminent. Reynolds told his friend,

"It is my positive belief that Longstreet has arrived on the field of battle."

Reynolds' new piece of information was something of importance that made Hooker pay careful attention. The information Reynolds gave him might be vital because Hooker knew that his division might soon have to face that same unexpected threat. As Reynolds mounted his horse and turned to leave for his command, he said something else to Hooker that Pope's entire army would soon have to deal with.

"I believe the enemy is turning to our left."

This stark warning and the many repeated warnings that Pope's officers had given to the commanding general had made as much impression on John Pope as the hole one's finger leaves when poked into a pail of water. Boiled down, all of the reports of a new force of the enemy on the field were repeats of Buford's first 8:30 AM report to Ricketts and McDowell of '*17 regiments, artillery and 500 cavalry passing through Gainesville.*'

Ricketts, Reynolds and Porter were not the only ones who had their strong opinions about a new enemy force. General Banks, under McDowell's command, had also spotted troops on the Turnpike early on the morning of August 27. Banks had sent a dispatch to Pope, which said, '*It seems apparent the enemy is moving upon the Valley of the Shenandoah.*' The Shenandoah Valley was, of course, the route toward Thoroughfare Gap from Richmond and the best way into the Manassas Plain.

Pope, from the beginning, continued to misjudge the importance of all such reports. Whatever his convoluted reasoning, from that moment and for the next seventy-two hours all of Pope's decisions were colored by his stubborn fixation on his self-deceptive myth of the enemy's retreat.

General Pope's order to his assembled officers during the early morning staff meeting had been to '*make an attack on Jackson*' and Reynolds had renewed his attack from the night before.

Of all the action against Jackson's left flank on Stony Ridge, on the morning of August 30, Reynolds' Pennsylvania Bucktails were the first Federals to renew hostilities. Before his brigades had moved a hundred yards through the woods, Reynolds' second brigade, led by General Truman Seymour, made contact with the enemy.

Colonel McCandless of the 2nd Pennsylvania Reserves reported, "*Under cover of the woods we crept up on some rebels, but the scamps were too wide awake to be caught. They skedaddled before we could flank them.*"

Minutes later, crossing a wide open field, McCandless' brigade came up against the Confederates they were looking for. A large force of the enemy was posted in some woods on the other side of the field and they were firing at McCandless' men from the protection of the trees.

The firing increased and the men found shelter behind mounds of earth and fence posts and a duel began. Reynolds had warned Pope of a massive rebel presence opposite himself. He had been ignored so he resigned himself and followed Pope's orders to continue the attack. His men made no progress during the next hour, so, in a vain hope at 9:30 AM, Reynolds asked once more for reinforcements. What Pope sent him was a drop in the bucket for the size of the rebel force that he faced; a single brigade, along with a single battery.

Siegel, who should have been near enough to support Reynolds in his hour of need, was too far away to the south on Chinn Ridge. He had already started his advance against the rebels and he was of no help to Reynolds. Siegel might not have been overly concerned. After all, like most of Pope's officers, Siegel had been infected with Pope's delusion of a Confederate retreat.

Pope's comfortable attitude with his denial toward any new enemy threat led to other omissions that might otherwise have saved the army. A demonstration of this was Pope's decision not to deploy his artillery. The Federals had many artillery batteries that should have been used at this critical turning point in the fighting. They were not. McLean and the 55th Ohio Regiment had a battery of six excellent Wiard rifled steel guns. They were the only ones on the field and capable of terrible damage yet Pope allowed them to remain unused.

Kearney's Red Patch Pennsylvanians had been under heavy fire that morning. Soon after dawn some of Ricketts' men moved up to relieve Kearney and give Kearney's men a chance to rest. Thoburn's and Duryee's brigades were given the job. They moved over to Kearney's right, next to one of the Bull Run River fords and took Reynolds' position to resume the offensive against the abandoned railroad defenses.

After relieving Kearney, Ricketts' brigades, those of Duryee and Thoburn, were confident they could continue the pursuit against the retreating Jackson and opened up on the enemy with a battery of 10-pounder Parrott guns. To their great surprise, within ten minutes Duryee's Parrotts were answered by a heavy killing barrage of shelling from Stephen D. Lee's battery of six guns close to their position.

The damage became so severe with so many men hit by shrapnel that Ricketts was forced to halt his advance. As Reynolds had been forced to do, Ricketts' men looked for a spot where the rebel guns couldn't hit them so easily.

As Kearney's men rested hoping for a little peace, without warning three or four of the same artillery pieces that had hit Reynolds now slammed into Kearney's men. They were forced to change position to avoid being hit. Kearney moved his men to a place near one of the fords on Bull Run but the change in position didn't help.

A man in the brigade reported later, *'The Confederate shot and shell went flying over our heads falling far into our rear. Soon they shortened their fuses and the shot commenced to explode over our heads. Anticipating a rebel charge, we fixed bayonets and lay down.'*

Ricketts' other two brigades, led by Tower and Stiles, commenced an assault on Jackson farther down the Pike. They were hit and hit hard with unexpected heavy artillery fire. Long range cannons rained down shells on Ricketts' men like deadly hailstones. No one knew it yet but the guns were Longstreet's. General Longstreet had placed his 18 long range cannons on the higher elevations above the Federals and they were shooting down Ricketts' men like they were fish in a barrel. William Davis of Ricketts' 7th Indiana Regiment gave details of the effect the rebel artillery fire had on the men.

"We advanced. Now came a volley, being behind piles of rails we were somewhat shielded, but soon came shells, grape, and canister. We moved out in order and formed a line in the field but we could not advance."

Ricketts was feeling the pressure. He sent probes all along the rebel lines and they were stopped cold before they had fairly begun. The Confederate artillery was unrelenting. At 9:30, Ricketts' infantry, unable to stand the fire and losing a good part of his attacking force, sent an urgent dispatch for help to McDowell. McDowell, who was at headquarters with Pope, told Pope that Ricketts' dispatch *'indicated an attack by a strong new rebel force on his men, south of Groveton.'* Ricketts' dispatch to McDowell called for help in no uncertain terms.

'We must have assistance. My brigade is engaged and we have no support.'

McDowell did not reply directly to Ricketts' message. Instead, wanting Pope to know what kind of resistance Ricketts was facing, he forwarded Ricketts' dispatch to Pope. Pope read Ricketts' message and by reply to Ricketts' call for help, sent his staff officer, Colonel Strother, with an order. The order directed Ricketts to *'Push into the woods and contact the enemy.'*

Pope, stubborn to the end, believed that if Ricketts got his men through Jackson's right flank and away from the killing artillery fire which he believed were Jackson's guns, then Ricketts, under the cover of the dense trees, could complete his assault on Jackson. When that had been accomplished, the rest of the Union forces would crush this newest Confederate enemy. Pope's own staff officer, Colonel Strother, later wrote about the strange scenario surrounding Ricketts' dispatch and Pope's reaction to the message:

'Pope's preconceived notions had already decided him on his course of action.'

Ricketts' reply to Pope's order to *'Push into the woods and contact the enemy'* was short, and Ricketts was probably very much irritated at the bland and useless responses he got from Pope and McDowell.

Had anyone read General Schofield's 1878 harsh assessment of Pope and McDowell years later at the Porter rehearing, their reaction would be grave disappointment toward the two generals' cataclysmic bluster. Inept commanders giving a poor response to Ricketts' terrific dilemma bluntly illustrated their incompetent leadership.

Ricketts tried again to enlighten the two men to his precarious situation.

'I have made that attempt but I have not been able to break their line.'

When Pope learned of Ricketts' failure, Strother asked Pope, "Shall I send Ricketts another order to advance?"

Even without an order Ricketts *had* tried a second advance, but to no avail. His men had fallen back after a bad fight. All four regiments of Duryee's brigade were badly cut up with many wounded and dead. Ricketts, with some heat, told Strother, when he appeared a second time, of his second attempt.

"We *made* contact with the enemy, but still there was no advance."

Still ready to try again, he said, "If Pope insists I will try again."

When the bewildered staff officer returned to headquarters and gave Ricketts' message to Pope, Pope's impatience with this ridiculous obstacle to what he thought would be an easy attack was plain. His angry retort was both stubbornly childish and without reason.

"No, damn it. Let him go."

Pope was still convinced the enemy's resistance was only a last ditch desperate rear guard action by Jackson.

His anger focused next on Fitz John Porter. Hoping Porter was ready to move against Jackson by this time, a thoroughly frustrated Pope sent word to Porter.

'Your corps and General King's division are to make an immediate full all-out assault against Jackson's right flank.'

General Porter, long after he had been convicted by the military court martial in

September of 1862, was at work to prove his innocence. He wrote in his private papers:

'John Reynolds had written to me. Reynolds had been assigned by McDowell to work beside my troops in the pursuit along the Warrenton Turnpike. He was posted on my left and he quickly became convinced the enemy was not retreating. Reynolds said to me, "I pushed through skirmishers to the edge of the woods on the left, gaining sight of the open ground beyond. Advancing into the open ground, I found a line of enemy skirmishers with cavalry behind them. They were not moving but they were masking a column of the enemy waiting for us to advance so they could fall on our left flank. The enemy opened fire on me and I was obliged to run a gauntlet of heavy fire to gain the rear of my division."'

'On the morning of August 30, McDowell was at headquarters. When I made the case that there was a strong new enemy presence on our left, McDowell demonstrated very little apparent concern. Although he knew that I had seen troops coming from the Gap that morning and reported that fact, General Pope did not seem at all cognizant of the seriousness of the threat.'

POPE GETS THE MESSAGE

What *finally* caught and held the stubborn general's attention was John Reynolds' news. Later that morning Reynolds rode into Buck Hill. His horse was covered with sweat from the ride and he gave John Pope information that *finally* convinced the obstinate Union leader.

"General Pope, I ran a *gauntlet of fire* to escape being captured," Reynolds said. "I have, personally, seen a large Confederate column of many troops. The column was made up of more than one division and they were *not* part of Jackson's force. They are south of the Warrenton Turnpike and they are marching toward us *now*."

As Reynolds spoke, John Buford, the chief cavalry officer for the army, was there. He listened carefully to Reynolds' report.

When Reynolds had finished, Pope turned to Buford. "Take your brigade of cavalry out beyond the left. Reconnoiter as much as necessary and report back as soon as you can."

Now, for the very first time John Pope acted as if he was fully aware of Longstreet's threat to his left flank and rear. He sent his chief of staff to General Siegel on the Turnpike for Siegel's take on the action. Siegel's battle report recorded the activities of that afternoon:

'I received repeated reports that the enemy is shifting his troops from the Gainesville Turnpike to his right. A strong force of several brigades of the enemy is moving against our left.'

Siegel's report got a reaction. Pope sent his chief of staff back to Siegel.

Pope instructed, "Colonel Ruggles, have General Siegel send a brigade to…"

The frustrated and somewhat harassed General Pope pointed vaguely in the general direction of a range of hills just south and next to the Warrenton Turnpike.

"… to that *Bald Hill*."

When Siegel received the order from Ruggles, still unclear, he sent a messenger to Pope's headquarters. Shortly afterward Siegel wrote *'I received an order to occupy the "bald headed hill" on my left, which I did immediately.'*

The blurred directions Pope had given Ruggles were perpetuated and made even more unclear when Ruggles repeated Pope's order to General Schenck. The unfortunate result of John Pope's penchant for a lack of specificity and imprecision of speech in giving orders would help in one more way to lose the battle. Schenck sent McLean's brigade to Chinn Ridge, *not to the west shoulder of Henry Hill* that Pope claimed to have been his intent.

Pope claimed later that Henry Hill is what he meant. By 3 PM, sending one of General Siegel's toughest brigades of 1,200 men to the *wrong* hill would become a massive problem for the Federal forces. Before the sun had set Longstreet's Confederates would roll in a flood toward Chinn Ridge.

The devil that haunted Pope's ability to communicate and this gross error in giving directions would be paid for in blood. Like the Joint Order and most of John Pope's directives, confusion and ambiguity would be the pitfalls of Pope's military demise.

Pope's careless reference to a '*bald hill*' should be remembered. That hill was actually Chinn Ridge. Pope had *meant* to send Siegel's division to the left slope of *Henry Hill*, which commanded a good view of the entire Union left flank and insured a strong defense against Longstreet's forces. The sloppy order illustrated Pope's carelessness and perhaps his ignorance of the terrain.

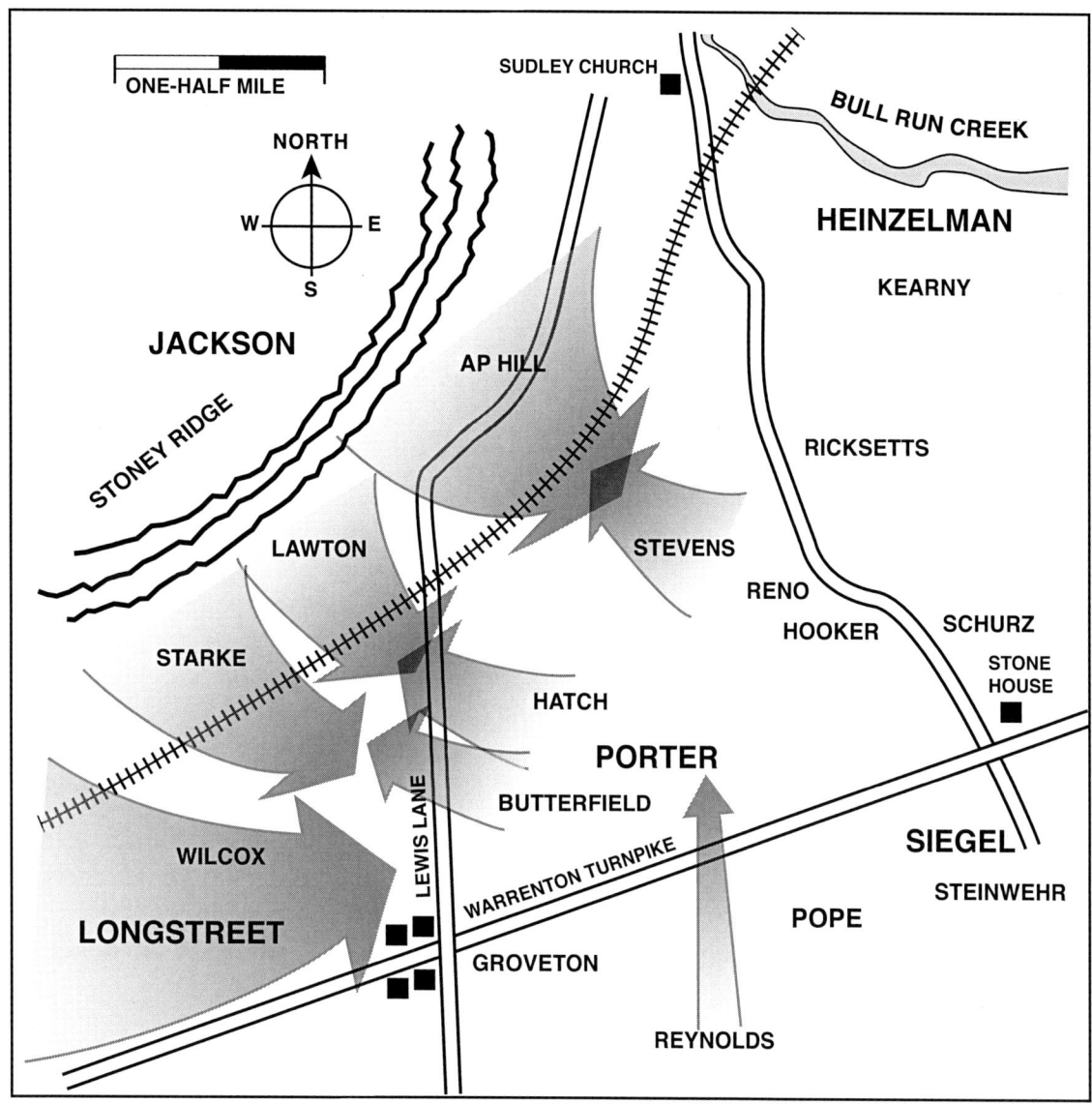

PORTER'S ATTACK — AUGUST 29, 1861

Union General Pope stubbornly refused to believe the reports from his officers of seeing a large enemy army approaching. So set on destroying Confederate General Jackson, whom he thought was retreating, he ordered General Porter to attack Jackson. Porter could not. Unable to reach Jackson to obey Pope's order, Porter fought off General Longstreet's army for several hours alone.

Porter knew the truth. He had seen the large force coming from Gainesville. He knew it was Longstreet. Porter's hours-long delay of the Confederate army knocked Lee's plan for a massive attack into a cocked hat, saving the Union. Porter's desperate fight delayed General Lee so the Union army was not destroyed and lived to stop Lee at Antietam two weeks later.

One of Porter's men wrote of the Porter attack: "Colonel Weeks' men locked in a savage fire fight with the Southerners. They kept up a savage sustained musketry fire that staggered the rebels again and again. The rebels could make no headway against their line."

❦ 42 ❦

The Pursuit

Pope's weak link, his left flank, was still unprotected. It was because of Pope's vague order to Siegel earlier to *'move to the bald headed hill.'* If, instead, Siegel's men had gone to the *left shoulder of Henry Hill* as Pope later claimed he had intended, that correct move would have insured the defense of the army's left flank. Pope had no one to blame but John Pope.

McDowell spoke with Pope again later that morning about the growing threat to the Union right. Pope listened to his second-in-command. McDowell's conversation is not recorded but something he said and the way he expressed himself may have *finally galvanized* John Pope to a more careful assessment of his wily enemy. Perhaps he decided a larger and more organized pursuit of Jackson was necessary to finish the job more quickly. He broadcast a new order to all his forces.

THE PURSUIT ORDER

'The following forces will be immediately thrown forward in pursuit of the enemy. Press him vigorously during the whole day. Major General McDowell is assigned to the command of the pursuit. Major General Porter's corps will push forward on the Warrenton Turnpike, followed by the divisions of Generals King and Reynolds. The division of General Ricketts will pursue the Haymarket Road, followed by the corps of Major General Heintzelman. The necessary cavalry will be assigned to these columns by Major General McDowell, to whom regular and frequent reports will be made. The general headquarters will be somewhere on the Warrenton Turnpike.'

McDowell forwarded Pope's directive to Porter to *'Pursue Jackson forward on the Turnpike.'* Porter was so involved with his movement against Jackson's main body of troops on the Ridge that he was unable to make the change easily. The two different efforts expressed in Porters first peremptory order and this latest order to *'attack Jackson,'* were *entirely different* and incompatible directives. Nevertheless, in the spirit of cooperation Porter wrote to McDowell:

'Your dispatch received. I have already sent Butterfield, who will be followed by Sykes, to strike at the batteries that have been thinning my ranks. The enemy has six pieces of battery on the right of the Warrenton Road, which Butterfield will take in flank, while artillery engages them in front. All will be in motion soon. I had these in motion too late to move on Warrenton Road.'

McDowell saw the problem Porter had been having in his assault against Jackson. He ordered Reynolds to take his division off Chinn Ridge and go to Porter's assistance. Reynolds' change of position from Chinn Ridge was another critical mistake by the Union High Command. The mistake would become apparent later that afternoon when Longstreet's Confederate divisions rolled toward and attacked the too lightly defended Chinn Ridge.

Reynolds, following orders, promptly moved out taking his infantry and batteries and leaving McLean completely alone on Chinn Ridge.

McDowell informed Porter what he had done:

'I will attend to the front and right. Reynolds has been pulled out of the column and put over on your left.'

THE MIX-UP

New problems were developing on Porter's firing line. At 1:45 PM Butterfield notified Porter that his skirmishers could not advance due to lack of support on his right, Butterfield noting that that was *'where Hatch's division should be.'*

A giant mix-up had occurred. Butterfield sent word that his forward line had been stopped cold by a strong rebel force. There were gaps in his line from heavy losses. Under the impression that McDowell's earlier verbal promise that *all four of Hatch's brigades* would support Butterfield, Porter learned that this sadly was not the case. Porter learned from a message that McDowell had changed his mind. Instead of sending Hatch's men to Porter's aid, he had sent Ricketts.

Ricketts never got there. On his way to support Butterfield, Ricketts had been stopped by another Confederate force. As a result, Butterfield was left with *no support*.

PORTER STRENGTHENS HIS LINES

Porter dispatched an order as quickly as he could to Hatch to *'come forward to my right.'* He notified General Roberts to *'wait until Hatch arrives and then push forward.'*

Porter took steps to straighten out his lines and fill the gaps. He sent Roberts' division to support Butterfield's weak spots and he ordered those of Hatch's brigades that had arrived to swing over and help Butterfield where help was still needed to strengthen his lines.

Porter's planned change in attack to *'pursue Jackson along the Turnpike'* drew near. Seeing how difficult the move would be after more and more of Anderson's and Wilcox's Confederates had emerged against the Federals, Porter then sent a courier to McDowell.

Porter asked for a part of General Siegel's corps, a division, which was placed forward a half mile, to reinforce his troops in the complicated maneuver he had planned. He received no response.

Moving another general's brigades along with Porter's force was a highly dangerous and delicate exercise. To really mess up things for Porter, as each of the regiments and brigades moved about to find their place in the complex pattern of attack, every one of the several units almost immediately came under heavy musket fire.

Porter got his troops into proper alignment and pushed forward. The fifth corps took the center position with Butterfield leading. Doubleday and Sykes were held in reserve. Hatch's division was placed on the right. Hatch's three brigades led by Gibbon, Patrick, and Sullivan were to step off with Porter's men. By noon, General Porter had all of his divisions in place and advancing with artillery: howitzers, 6-pounder brass guns and 10-pounder Parrotts, placed in positions overlooking the field. Porter's offensive on Jackson's right flank had started.

PORTER'S OFFENSIVE AGAINST JACKSON

Jackson had been sitting quietly on a fence post when the echoing crash of battle to his front told him that the Federals were attacking all along the Turnpike. He mounted his horse and rode into the woods to judge the seriousness of the attack. What he learned was grim news; the entire Federal force was moving against him. Jackson dispatched two couriers; one to Lee and one to Longstreet asking for help. Within a half hour Lee received Jackson's call for help. Jackson's line was hard pressed. He needed reinforcements.

Lee passed the word to Longstreet, who promptly took steps to give aid. He sent Anderson's division forward toward Jackson's lines and rode out from headquarters to better understand the attack against Jackson's left. As he neared the front, Longstreet heard the crash of fire that signaled the opening stages of Porter's furious assault.

General Roberts' six Union regiments left the woods and started across the field toward the embankment next to the abandoned railroad where the rebels were waiting. Colonel Elisha Marshall, who led the 13th New York Regiment, testified at Porter's retrial in 1878 how the attack began:

"As soon as we commenced scaling the fence along the Groveton-Sudley Road, the fire commenced. We started on a sort of double-quick step across the field and we got about half way across when the fun stopped."

Soon after, Marshall dispatched a courier to Union headquarters to alert them to new artillery and more enemy forces on the field.

'The enemy is in much larger force than I can see. From the officers, I should judge a brigade. They are coming in on our left and I had been advancing. Have also heard the noise on the left as artillery. They are quite close.'

Marshall heard rightly; Longstreet was on the scene. The artillery was his. Longstreet recorded his memory of that day.

'At the critical moment I happened to be riding to the front of my line, and I had reached the left of the Turnpike. I could plainly see the Federals as they rushed in heavy masses against the obstinate ranks on the Confederate left. It was a grand display of a well-organized attack, thoroughly concentrated and operating cleverly. So terrible was the onslaught that Jackson begged for reinforcements. I received the same order (to help Jackson) at the same time from General Lee.'

Colonel Stephen Lee, in charge of his uncle's guns, was eating his dinner when Porter began his offensive. A private, excited at the sight of the massed ranks of Porter's brigades approaching up the hill, yelled out to his captain, who was sitting at the camp table with Colonel Lee.

"Here they come, Captain! Here they come!"

Lee rose from his unfinished dinner and ordered his five howitzers to join the four smooth bore rifles already on the left of the ridge toward which Porter's men were heading and ordered the firing to start.

"Fire on the enemy flank and on the woods where their reserves are waiting," he ordered.

In minutes the 18 guns of Lee's battalion were sending sheets of fire at the Federals. Porter had massed his units in compact columns many ranks deep. As Porter's attackers came out of the fields near Groveton, the 18 Confederate cannons had a target they couldn't miss.

After the war, during a Union medal of honor ceremony, John Slater of Elisha Marshall's regiment spoke for the members of Porter's battle-shredded infantry survivors of that terrible afternoon.

"The air was filled with a tempest of zipping metal. Behind us we could see the field we had just crossed being cut and furrowed by the shells of the Confederate artillery. So frequently did the shells tear the earth the ground seemed like a mill pond in a shower. In front of us was a wall of Southern fire; a wall that seemed impenetrable. The rebel infantry poured in their volleys, and we were scarcely a dozen feet from the muzzles of their muskets. Scores of wounded were mowed down until a perfect windrow of our dead and wounded marked the farthest advance of our regent. For twenty minutes the bullets hummed like swarming bees, until those yet alive received orders to fall back."

Butterfield, leading Morell's division in his absence, had been the first to make the Federal advance against Jackson's fortified defenders. His battle report described what the 25th New York encountered.

'We had advanced but a short distance into the woods when we met the enemy's skirmishers. We drove them back until the left of our line came into an open field. Berdan's sharpshooters became mixed up with our skirmishers. Here we began to receive a sharp fire on our right. I found it impossible, with our small force, to drive back the enemy. I immediately reported the fact to Colonel Johnson (commanding the 25th New York regiment), who sent out two additional companies. Shortly, we were able to advance some yards under a severe fire.'

Captain W.H. Chapman, commanding the Dixie Brigade of Longstreet's artillery batteries, recalled the battle in a post-war letter he had written to General Longstreet about his action just before 3 PM that afternoon as Porter's men came forward.

'I had ridden to a position occupied by Featherstone's brigade. I was at the highest point on that prominence and I could see the enemy's infantry, about a mile distant. They were moving in large bodies to the left and disappearing in a body of woods in front of Jackson's right wing. I hurried back to my battery, which was on the left of the Turnpike, about fifty yards from it, and immediately behind Hood's division. On the way I passed you (Longstreet) as you headed toward the front. I told my gunners to be ready to move and in less than five minutes the order I expected came. It was the order to move and we did move--at a gallop. Soon we reached the point where we were on the left of the Turnpike, fifty or a hundred yards from it.'

'We went into the position where I was directed and we commenced firing at a heavily massed *body of infantry. (This was Butterworth's brigade). They were not more than 400 yards distant and we fired until their ranks were broken and driven back.'*

Major Edwin Gilbert led the 25th New York Regiment. His regiment had gone too far to the left and he was nearly alone. There were a lot more Confederates in their front than Major Gilbert had in his single regiment. Major Gilbert wrote:

'We had advanced but a short distance into the woods when we met enemy's skirmishers. We began to receive a sharp fire from our right. I soon found it was impossible to drive the enemy back with my small force.'

THE SHARPSHOOTERS

Major Gilbert sent word for help and reinforcements arrived. The First United States Sharpshooters, all crack shots, were led by the man that had created the Union Sharpshooter regiments, Hiram Berdan. These were experienced regular army men and they were armed with the latest and most accurate Sharps rifles.

George Albee, one of Colonel Hiram Berdan's Sharpshooters (Butterfield's artillery regiment), all of whom were armed with accurate Sharps rifles, wrote, *'We were deployed over an open field in the face of rebel sharpshooters and a rebel battery somewhere above us on a hill. They popped away at us pretty lively as we went across. Finally, we got into a dry watercourse that sheltered us a little, and engaged the rebel sharpshooters for about two hours at a distance of 2000 feet.'*

Historical Note: The appellation 'Sharpshooter, came from their use of the Sharps Rifle. They weighed thirty pounds and had to be loaded at the breech, one bullet at a time. During the Civil War sniping, or sharpshooting, was a recognized psychological weapon as well as an excellent way to cut down enemy officers from a half mile or more. Hiram C. Berdan, who raised the first Union regiment of Sharpshooters, was a champion marksman and a self-made millionaire.

The government gave Berdan the job of finding recruits. Hiram's men had to be good. To qualify, the marksman had to place ten shots in a ten-inch circle from 200 yards.

Colonel Berdan drew his men from nearly every state in the Union. There was even an all-Native American company of Indian sharpshooters. These were men from Northern Michigan, who came from tribes of the Ottawa, Ojibwa and Pottawatomie. At the start of the war and at the Second Battle of Manassas, his troops were equipped with Sharps Rifles. Later, they used a shorter, lighter half-stock Plains Rifle, known as the 'Dimick Rifle' after their maker, Horace Dimick.

By 1863, many of the men who were still alive bought themselves the new, more accurate 16-shot, lever action Henry Repeating Rifle out of their own pockets, for three month's pay ($40.00).

Sharpshooting was a risky business. After Gettysburg, of Berdan's original twelve sharpshooters, only Berdan and one other man was still alive.

BULLETS LIKE HAILSTONES

Another of Butterfield's divisions leading the charge for the Union was the 17th New York. Colonel Weeks had been struck down by a bullet and Major Grower, in command, reported the charge.

'We crossed the road, scrambled over the fence and moved forward in quick time. No sooner had we appeared in plain view of the enemy when they opened up a tremendous fire tearing huge gaps in the Federal line. Nothing could surpass the behavior of the officers and men, as the latter closed the huge gaps in the line. Placing myself at the head, I gave the word: Double, quick, charge! and with a mad yell the gallant fellows rushed up the hill to what was almost certain death.'

General Roberts, leading Butterfield's First Brigade, charged *Jackson's First Division*, which were under General Starke's Confederate command. As Porter's troops approached, William Starke made this report of the death of one of the Confederate officers.

'The Federal advance looked irresistible. They rose up in front of us as suddenly as men rising up out of the ground showing themselves at the old railroad line opposite our line in a double battle phalanx coming forward in slow time, pouring their shot in our ranks in unmerciful volume.'

'Colonel Baylor, leading one of the Confederate brigades, ran to the front of his men, grabbed the flag of the 33rd Virginia Regiment and dashed into the field screaming over the din, "Boys, follow me."'

'The men started forward and another fusillade tore into their ranks. Colonel Baylor fell dead and the brigade retreated back to the safety of the woods.'

The fighting grew worse. The rebels were sheltered by a well-fortified embankment of earth behind the abandoned railroad with plenty of cover. Now and then they would rise up and pour a deadly volley into the Federal ranks and then settle back behind their defenses. With an avalanche of rebel fire smashing into the masses Union attackers sometimes from ten feet away, Butterfield's regiments were decimated and finally had to retire.

Doubleday's three regiments held their place as support in the woods. When the fight began the trees were not much protection. A.P. Smith, a member of Doubleday's 76th New York Regiment, wrote after the battle, *'The grape, shells, and solid shot came through the woods like hail. After twenty minutes the order came for us to retreat, the attack on our left having failed.'*

One Federal fighter described the fighting, *'The bullets flew as thick as hail stones.'*

The Confederates were helped when rebel cannons began lobbing shells into Butterfield's men and the Federals fell back to the shelter of the trees. The rebels thought they had stopped the attackers but these were regular troops of the U.S. 1st Sharpshooters. Berdan's men had remarkably accurate smooth bore muskets and they were much better shots than the Southerners which made the fight equal and the battle continued growing fiercer all along the line.

Another of Jackson's men remembered that moment.

'We halted our brigade under the shelter of the cut, where we were able to hold the enormous force of Federals pressing up the hill. When they appeared in front of us the first wave met a blinding fire. When the smoke arose, the line of Federals was almost swept away. The second wave met an even hotter reception as the Louisianans pumped bullet after bullet into them. But the Federals came in such force that help was needed.'

While all of this was happening on the slopes below Stony Ridge, Jeb Stuart watched the drama from afar. His cavalry was no longer needed, so he climbed an enormous Walnut tree. Stuart had a wonderful view of the entire battle ground in his ring-side seat hidden among the trees. The Confederate cavalry general watched the spectacle unfold as his troops waited for him below.

❧ 43 ❧

The Last Battle

Porter made his last charge against Jackson's line that day. The several charges his infantry made were of such a desperate and heroic character that many men, survivors of this holocaust, soberly remembered and spoke of that fight.

Union Captain Mason Burt, leading the 22nd Massachusetts Regiment, was one of those men. He testified about that day during Porter's 1878 retrial, to a basic truth that gave the lie to all of Pope's claims and all of the charges against Porter.

"I watched as the wounded returned from the charge. Neither their captain nor the wounded returning yet realized that Longstreet's fifty thousand rebels had arrived on the battlefield. No one in the Union army, least of all their general, expected that the overwhelming forces of Robert E. Lee's army were there. Such a great mass of Confederates troops stood between General Porter and Stonewall Jackson that any successful completion of our (Union) offensive to attack Jackson's right was an impossible task."

An excellent reporter and the commander of one of Longstreet's divisions, Confederate General Cadmus Wilcox was on a small hill that afternoon watching Porter's attack. Afterward, he wrote about what he had seen.

'I rode to the front to witness the drama. Seeing the advance of the enemy, I repaired at once to the interval between Pryor's and Featherston's brigades. From this point there was an excellent view of the field not more than 440 yards distant. The first line of the enemy advanced in fine style across the open field. There was but little to oppose them. They were fired upon by our pickets and skirmishers, but they continued to advance. Ascending the rise, they came into full view of Jackson's line and were received with a terrific fire of musketry at short range.'

'They hesitated for an instant, recoiling slightly, and then advanced to near the embankment. A second line issued from the woods upon the field and one of our batteries (Chapman's Dixie Artillery) fired upon them. The battery, being near the Turnpike in an excellent and commanding position, was most opportunely delivered upon the advancing line of the enemy. They were caught in an open field. The effect of every shot could be seen. As the shells and spherical case would burst over in front and near them, their ranks would break, hesitate and scatter. At length the front line of the enemy broke and fell back with great precipitation and disorder, followed by a portion of Jackson's troops.'

RAW RECRUITS BECOME BLOODED VETERANS

When the Union infantry fell back the Sharpshooters were determined to hold their ground. The precision riflemen had a good range on some of the rebel batteries that were tearing the Union lines into shreds and they tried their best to blunt the attack against the Federal infantry. Sharpshooter Charlie Champis wrote home afterward of the Sharpshooters' part in the attack.

'We lay in a ditch until three or four o'clock, then our columns charged. We advanced at the same time. The enemy opened up their batteries on us. We had a position on the left of our division and a very dangerous one it was. Our troops began to fall back in good order to the hill where our artillery was planted.'

General Hatch tells of a single charge by the Federals against Jackson's line behind the abandoned railroad. He saw that all four regiments of Butterfield's first charge had failed to break through the rebel lines on the embankment, and he sent Sullivan's 24th and 30th New Yorkers forward. The 24th and the 30th were followed by regiments in Patrick's brigade; the 21st and 35th New Yorkers. These two regiments were a part of General Marsena Patrick's brigade. They were men that had been raw recruits the day before during the Brawner Farmhouse debacle. Now they were blooded veterans.

General Marsena Patrick described the fog of war when even with the greatest of courage and the best of planning goes wrong:

'My two regiments moved steadily forward, impeded by the retreating regiments. The 35th reached the edge of a wood near a cornfield. In the cornfield a strong body of the enemy appeared. The New Yorkers suffered terribly from the galling fire that was impossible to return.'

As the 21st and the 35th Union regiments struggled forward, the field became a tangled sea of blue. A rebel defender, watching from the fortified embankment, later described what the Confederates saw and what they did.

'My regiment fired into the mass. They were simply jammed up against the embankment so thick it was impossible to miss them. Cicero Kirkland, of my regiment, mounted to the top of the breastworks and poured buck and ball into them as fast as one of the boys could load and hand him a musket. What a slaughter.'

TOO FAR TOO SOON

General Patrick saw what the enfilading fire from the rebel artillery on the embankment was doing to his two regiments. He sent in the 80th New York next. However, their officers had misread the order. The 80th advanced too far from the cornfield and the edge of the woods where they were supposed to go to join with and support the other regiments. As a result, the 80th came to the rebel lines all alone. General Patrick wrote,

'Three times the 80th New York Regiment charged the embankment and three times they fell back. Six color bearers were shot down and Colonel Pratt fell mortally wounded. The fire was too heavy and there were too few of the men left to continue the assault. Orders came to "Hold the position. Support is on the way!" but no support came. Without reinforcements the battered regiment had to fall back to the rear.'

Sargent David Hamer described Sullivan's advance.

'The New Yorkers could not follow. We were too few to drive out the enemy troops on the other

side so we lay flat near the top, occasionally holding muskets over our head to discharge the weapons in the direction of the rebels, hoping to hit someone on the other side. After holding our position for nearly an hour we were obliged to fall back.'

Sargent Hamer recalled one of the many tragic fatalities from the charge that day.

'As we crossed Schoolhouse Branch the Confederates loosed another volley but not with the same deadly effect as before. Soon the two decimated regiments reached the embankment. Major Barney spurred his horse to the top of the hill, and, for a few brief moments he towered above all, a solitary figure, beckoning his men to follow. In a flash of musketry, his horse reared and Barney fell dead upon the embankment. The New Yorkers did not, could not follow.'

Men in battle are transformed by the nearness of death and destruction. They become something not quite human. Led by Major Andrew Barney, the 24th New York pushed on against a withering fire. One of Barney's men, who was a part of that charge, wrote later of his experience.

'The fight seemed like the popular idea of pandemonium made real, and indeed it is scarcely too much to say we were transformed for the time from a lot of good-natured boys to the most bloodthirsty of demons.'

ROCKS FOR BULLETS

Lieutenant Theron Haight, an officer of the 24th New York, added his comments to the wild bloodbath against Jackson's defenders, *'The enraged men pushed across the plain. There was some firing on our part as we crossed the field because the line did not move fast enough to keep us busy otherwise.'*

When the 24th New York reached the embankment something new occurred. Haight recalled, *'There came a not-looked-for variation in the proceedings. Huge stones began to fall upon us with very unpleasant effect.'*

It was no wonder. Haight's comrades were being hit with rocks. The rebels on the embankment had run out of ammunition. Colonel Leroy Stafford, the Confederate officer, who led Starke's 9th Louisianan Regiment, told the story of what the desperate defenders did when there was no more ammunition.

'At this point our ammunition began to run low. We scrambled and procured some from the dead bodies of our comrades but the supply was insufficient. There was no time to send to the rear for more. As the Federal line neared, the command "fire" echoed all along the line. Many men dispatched their last rounds. Then an Irishman of the first, M. O'Keefe, jumped up and hollered, "Boys, give 'em the rocks."'

'The Louisianans sent a shower of stones into the remains of the Federal ranks. But the need to throw stones was soon dispelled as Brockenbrough's brigade arrived and opened fire.'

Rebel reinforcements arrived and the Federals were hit with bullets instead of rocks. Haight continued his gory recital of that afternoon.

'Many of the men held their arms before their faces, as though to keep off a storm. Bullets poured into them from the rebel infantry. Worst of all, Longstreet's batteries, freshly posted on a rise of ground a mile or so to our left, were enfilading the approaching troops with solid shot and shell. The second line gave way before this storm and ran back to the cover of the woods.'

Private Fisher Baker's testimony at Porter's retrial was grim.

"Slowly at first, and then more rapidly, the shattered ranks of Roberts' Maine,

Massachusetts, Michigan, and New York Regiments fell back across the field. As we retired, the rebel artillery was immense. For the men who were left and still able to walk, the cannon fire was a gauntlet of hot whizzing iron. Our losses were heavy but the survivors rallied by, with other regiments. General Porter himself was there among us and we left the field in reasonable order."

☙ 44 ❧

Beginning of The End

Porter's troops were never to succeed against Stonewall Jackson. His infantry would be driven back with his men in chaos. The hour when Longstreet had arrived heralded the beginning of the end for Pope's grandiose plans of victory.

Union Captain Mason Burt, who led the 22nd Massachusetts Regiment that day, said afterward, *"The wounded from General Porter's ill-fated charge toward Jackson's right flank streamed past us. At first the troops were all very jolly and full of enthusiasm. A wounded man said, 'Look at that,' as he held up his arm, which showed a clean bullet hole. 'That's good for thirty days. It is just the prettiest of wounds a man could ask for. I wouldn't take a hundred dollars for it.'"*

"Then came a fellow with a very slight hurt, but with the bloodiest face you may imagine. This soldier with a bloody face had seen the truth and the future outcome of the charge, and the battle. He mopped at the crimson gush and said, 'No show for you boys today.'"

Union Captain Burt had seen the unwinding and the preface of the mayhem to follow for all of Pope's army.

"At first they were filled with the expectation of victory. But as the hour passed and the fighting continued, more and more men realized what was happening. The boys were all merry at first as they came limping by, swearing very cheerfully and sure it was all up for the 'Johnnies.'"

"As the soldiers multiplied the Union offensive began to look more dubious. When I saw the broken squads of the unhurt men and I saw their faces and heard their exclamations, I knew the Johnnies had not been dislodged."

They would not be dislodged. By that hour Hood's divisions were in close support. The 2000 troops from Texas, Georgia, Alabama, Mississippi and South Carolina poured death into Porter's ranks.

A private in a Zouave Regiment from New York's Fifth watched the destruction of a brother company of Union skirmishers as they fled from the murderous crossfire emitting from the newly arrived reinforcements of Lee's army.

'I heard one of them cry "The enemy is coming and they are right on top of us." Before orders could be given to change position, the balls began to fly from the woods like hail. It was a continual hiss, snap, whiz, and slug. A man fell near me without a sound. He was the first one hit and he was dragged to the rear to be out of our way. We commenced to fire but the rebel fire

was murderous and men were falling on either side of me.'

'The 10th New York Infantry had broken and they were flying to the rear. We had not fired two rounds before the rebels were on us in front and in the flank. Their object was to surround us. The order was given to retreat and save ourselves. It was every man for himself. But we did not hear the order.'

'The newer recruits gave way and then the whole regiment broke and ran for their lives, the rebels after us with their yells, like Indian war whoops. They were the Texas and Mississippi Riflemen and they were six to one of us. They were in shirt sleeves and came charging and yelling for Jeff Davis and the Confederacy. While I ran down the hill I saw men dropping on all sides.'

At around four o'clock, General Morell finally arrived on the battlefield after going to Centreville in error. He was just in time to witness the retreat of his shattered division. Immediately, he took command from Butterfield and did what he could to restore order.

After falling back, General Butterfield reformed his regiments in the open field behind Groveton Wood. The brigade moved to the hills, where the Federals had plenty of artillery planted. The rest of Porter's divisions, Butterfield and Sykes, kept on going to the rear past the Stone House and there they halted and waited for about an hour.

Artillery did their best to cover the retreat. The gunners used every sort of ammunition they had. Shrapnel, nails, iron junk and pieces of iron in casings that burst above the target, all of which were effective for the short range work. The ammunition that they used was especially effective to stop the enemy infantry who sheltered in the trees to escape the hot Union fire.

Confederate Colonel Leroy Stafford, part of Jackson's division, spoke after the war before a Southern audience about Porter's assault.

"The first wave of the Federal attack was met by a blinding fire. When the smoke arose the line of the Federals was almost swept away, with the exception of a gallant band, which had advanced and secured protection on the opposite side of the embankment. The second line of Porter's men met an even hotter reception as the Louisianans pumped bullet after bullet into them. But the Federals came in such force that help was needed. Jackson saw this and ordered Stafford's second line to come forward into the fray. With a great yell the troops charged down upon the Unionists and the battle reached its climax. Yet a third Federal line appeared."

For the Confederacy, Brockenbrough's Virginians were the first of the reinforcements Jackson had requested to hold back Porter's charge. Robert Healy, a man of the 55th Virginian Regiment, wrote *'We moved ahead double quick and when we saw the enemy we were saluted with cannon. We pushed on to the old railroad track. The troops were out of ammunition and they had been throwing rocks, which they had picked up out of the blasted bed of the railroad, chips and slivers of stones, which many were collecting and others were throwing.'*

'We opened fire and the Federals made but a feeble resistance. Soon they were in headlong retreat and the blue-clad survivors rushed rearward toward the woods.'

By 4:30 PM, scores of Federals had been mowed down until a windrow of the dead and wounded marked the farthest advance of the regiments.

Wrote another man, *'Flags fell, only to be scooped up by another pair of desperately anxious hands. For twenty minutes the bullets hummed like swarming bees, for twenty minutes, and those yet alive received orders to fall back.'*

In a letter home, Private Fisher Baker described the terrible aftermath of the charge.

'Slowly at first, then more rapidly, the shattered ranks fell back across the field. The artillery fire (by the enemy) was by now immense; a gauntlet of hot whizzing iron. Losses were heavy but back by the road the survivors were rallied by General Porter himself, among others.'

By five o'clock, Pope realized the peril that faced his army. Porter needed support on his left. He dispatched Colonel Strother, his staff officer.

'I was ordered,' Strother wrote, 'to ride with all possible speed to General Heintzelman on our extreme right and bring over two of Ricketts' brigades. I found Heintzelman, who said that Ricketts could not move as he now occupied a most important position. He said there was a whole division of Pennsylvania Reserves disengaged. So I took the discretionary power of ordering them over double quick.'

The only large Union body that was not a part of McDowell's ill-fated 'pursuit' operation was Siegel's First Corps. That was because General Siegel had been designated as a reserve unit. Stahel's three regiments, atop Dogan Ridge, could do little beyond act as a net for Porter's rapidly retreating regiments.

McLean's Ohioans looked on helplessly as Warren's and Hardin's brigades were cut down and scattered in front of them. McLean could see the Confederates advancing, driving a regiment of Porter's Zouaves before them like a giant push broom.

McDowell was aware that Porter's attack had stalled because Porter's troops had come up against a vastly superior force. He sent an order to Siegel to send a reserve brigade to assist Porter. The situation was changing fast. Siegel's *own* troops were in trouble. McLean's three regiments, who had been on Chinn Hill, found themselves entirely alone. One brigade had gone to help Porter and his other brigades were yet on the Turnpike fighting Jackson.

McLean, leading Schenck's Second Brigade, caught sight of Reynolds as he marched with his troops across McLean's front. McLean rode out to intercept Reynolds.

When he stopped him McLean asked, "What are your orders?"

Reynolds, knowing that a serious crisis was developing, was in a hurry and his response was curt. "Take care of yourself, General McLean," he replied. "The enemy is approaching in heavy force."

Reynolds had good reason to reach his own division quickly. His brigades were under heavy Confederate fire. John Reynolds was witnessing Robert E. Lee's main offensive.

After the first charge, Major William Lamont, leading the 83rd Pennsylvania, of Butterfield's brigade, recalled the moment of Porter's main attack that day in a talk after the war, which was almost lyrical in its description. Lamont was one of the men who were wounded in that charge.

"Forward we went across a green meadow, where children had played and sheep had gamboled in the peaceful past, into the dark and dreadful woods, reeking with blood and sickly with the scent of death. Every mouth was firmly set, every heart beat faster and, perhaps, across the war-worn faces there came a shadow, and maybe a little prayer just whispered its half-forgotten mutterings in some sinful ear."

"On we went. One man fell. We were in the midst of it. Above the deafening roar coming from every quarter, the voice of the Colonel *(Colonel H.S. Campbell was also wounded that day)* sounded clear and full, *'Fire!'* We sent a volley into the enemy's front so sure and steady that afterward we heard it was the settler for the day."

"Their fire slackened. The Colonel went right in front, waved his cap and shouted, *'Forward boys, we're driving them.'* On we went at the double through the brushwood toward the railroad cutting, on with enthusiasm and excitement of Lord knows what. A faint cheer came from a wounded blue coat and the bullets whistled past my ear with a peculiar 'fizz' as I rushed up the bank on the other side. There we stood and let them have it hot and heavy until their fire ceased."

"We lost a good many men. As shadows gathered over the tall pine trees, the order was given to retire. Short as the affair appeared from the time we entered these woods until we fired our last shot, an hour must have elapsed. It did not seem like five minutes."

❦ 45 ❦

Hell's Vortex

Twenty-nine thousand cheering shouting Confederates swept down on Porter's shattered left flank like a juggernaut. With Hood foremost, the Texas brigade spearheaded the charge and the 1st, 4th, and 5th Texas Regiments along with the 18th Georgia Regiment collided against Roberts' 10th Regiment with a force difficult to imagine.

Just before four o'clock Jackson saw that Porter's Federals were giving way. He passed the news to General Lee. Kemper's and D.R. Jones' divisions moved ahead with Hood's Brigade leading the advance against Porter's exposed left flank. The nearly fifteen hundred infantrymen of Roberts' four regiments and Sullivan's and Patrick's eight regiments fell back to the open field behind Groveton Wood where there was plenty of Federal artillery planted. The Federal gunners hammered the Confederate pursuers as best they could to slow them down and protect Porter's men, firing shrapnel at close range and raining iron on the enemy.

Butterfield's 5th New York was nearest the rebel front line. That company had been waiting at the edge of Groveton Woods for orders to advance against Jackson. When Longstreet's offensive began the men of the 5th were too far from the action to know what had happened. As they waited in battle formation it was quiet. Then, all at once, from out of the woods before them, the men of the 10th New York regiment, who had been one of the first companies to clash with Longstreet's infantry, came running through the trees of Groveton Woods like the devil incarnate was on their heels.

Private Alfred Davenport of the 5th wrote, *'It struck me that some mischief was brewing when skirmishers of the 10th New York, our sister regiment in Sykes's division, came tumbling back out of the woods shouting and running for their lives. They piled up on the left of our line in a heap, the men much scared. "The enemy is coming," they yelled as they came.'*

Another soldier of the 5th New York, Andrew Coats, recalled, *'Our officers hollered, "Attention Battalion" and then, in the next second, bang! bang! bang! came the sound of shots from the woods directly at our front. There was a terrific volley of musket fire and the balls began to fly through the air like hail. It was a continuous hiss, snap, whiz, and slug.'*

'At first we couldn't see the Confederates. There were only streaks of smoke in and among the trees. Then all at once, there they were; hundreds of men in gray uniforms. Someone, thinking

*they were the remnants of fleeing Federals, shouted "Don't fire. Those are men of the 10th."
It wasn't so. They were Confederates but we did not know that. The new arrivals of the 10th
hid them from our view as they came from the woods.'*

*'The Confederates loosed a volley at us that was devastating. We returned a ragged volley of
musket fire but the rebels cut us down as if at the hands of an executioner. As we fought on,
our color guards were nearly all downed, yet the colors still flew in the wind. Sargent Andrew
Allison, bearing the flag, had his wrist smashed by a rebel bullet but held on to the flag. A
moment later he fell dead with a bullet through his heart. There was no hope of holding the
line and the men ran for their lives.'*

Corporal Daugherty of the U.S. Regular Army was another witness who related
the carnage and destruction around him with clear and heart stopping objectivity
during his precarious flight.

*'I saw men dropping on all sides, canteens struck and flying to pieces, haversacks cut off and
rifles knocked to pieces. It was a perfect hail of bullets and I expected to get it at every second.
On, on I went, the balls hissing by my head. I felt one strike on the hip, just grazing me and
cutting a hole in my pants. I crossed the run in the wake of Colonel Warren, our commander
being about 100 yards ahead of me, with his red cap in his hand (a Zouave officer), his horse
running at the top of his speed. I turned to look once, and only once. That was enough to let me
know there was no time to stop. We ran like dogs.'*

Corporal Daugherty passed Colonel Warren, One of Porter's Brigade Commanders.
The survivors of Warren's brigade streamed back over the fields until they reached
Chinn Branch where the officers rallied them. Warren watched the retreat of his
men from horseback, seemingly dazed by the utter mayhem that had been visited
upon his fleeing troops. Corporal Daugherty recounted:

*"Colonel Warren sat immobile on his horse looking back at the battle as if paralyzed. A handful
of men had formed near him in files of four. They were blackened with dust and smoke and they
stood under the colors silent as statues, gazing vacantly at the tumultuous concourse trudging
by. A murmur of surprise and horror passed through the ranks of the watching Regular Army
troops at the fate of the brave regiment."*

For the Confederacy, John Bell Hood brought up his three brigades, along with
Wilcox's, Anderson's, and Jones' divisions. Hood struck Porter's infantry while
the Union forces were still battling Starke's Louisianans, Jackson's men. No troops
fought with more fury and determination than Porter's men. In ten minutes what
remained the Federal troops were nearly wiped out to a man.

Daugherty said, *"After nearly a half hour in the vortex of Hell, the Federals were forced to
fall back before the full weight of the Confederates. Confederate gunners continued to let loose
a hail of grapeshot, cannon balls, shells and rifle balls on our retreating Federal troops. Some
of the men, hopeless they could make it to the other side of the field alive, gave themselves up
as prisoners."*

The measure of the destruction perpetrated by the thousands of rebel muskets
fired and the large numbers of artillery that fell upon Porter's infantry may be
measured by the incredible loss of life during that few minutes. The 5th New York
Regiment lost more men killed in five minutes than any other infantry regiment
of the Civil War.

Longstreet's and Jackson's divisions reformed at the edge of the woods. Once more they advanced. Only a thousand of Porter's soldiers still opposed the masses of four Confederate divisions. The 5th Texas, Hood's brigade, sensing victory, ran forward. Their Colonel, J.B. Robertson, described the speed and the power of the relentless Confederate army attack.

'As my brigade moved across the field held by the enemy skirmishers, I moved my men at a run. The enemy skirmishers were encountered and driven back. I ordered the regiment to fire on and charge them. They broke and we pressed them back. The 18th Georgia overcame the Zouaves so quickly that no halt was perceivable in the line.'

POPE FACES THE TRUTH

Word of the powerful Confederate assault on Porter's men reached Pope quickly. For the first time, since his mistaken pursuit of Stonewall Jackson had begun two days earlier, John Pope was forced to come face to face with the truth. Under the avalanche of four Confederate divisions, Porter's left flank was collapsing. The rest of the Union army, Heintzelman's, Reno's, Hooker's and McDowell's divisions, being most of Pope's force, were all more than a mile away and still deep into the assault on Jackson's no-longer-existing right flank.

McDowell, getting word of Porter's troubles, sent some of Reynolds' men, who had been on Chinn Ridge with Siegel's division. Reynolds' help was a matter of too few men sent too late to make a difference. McLean, Siegel's lead brigade on Chinn Hill, had been left without the forces he would soon need to hold the line on that important defense point.

Porter's forces gave way under Hood's attack. Without waiting for orders from Lee, Longstreet moved forward against the Union left. His order to Hood was to *'push for the plateau at Henry House, in order to cut off the enemy retreat at the crossing of Young's Branch.'*

General Jones' Georgians pushed forward and Jackson's artillery joined in on the Union left, raking the tightly packed formations with shot and shell, and tearing gaps in the Yankee lines. General Porter's and General Hatch's infantry, tightly packed, were massacred with shells and musket fire. Half of Hatch's division was shattered as they streamed back across the fields, with Sullivan's New Yorkers following close behind to the cover of the batteries on Dogan Ridge.

Abner Doubleday was now in command of Hatch's division. On orders from Porter he moved his brigades, as if on parade, to a position behind a line of batteries where they waited, crowning the summit of Chinn Ridge. There they stayed for a half hour before the next onslaught began.

Porter assembled Butterfield's and Morell's battered survivors and brought their tattered brigades back an eighth of a mile to the rear behind Stone House, where there was plenty of Union artillery planted. After covering Porter's withdrawal from the field, Sykes' brigades were withdrawn from the woods in good order and took a position near Dogan Ridge.

Lieutenant Colonel Chapman's Sharpshooter brigade was ordered to *'retire in line of battle,'* to be ready for action, near Bull Run Hill. One of the U.S. Regular Army soldiers, a Sharpshooter, told of the moment.

"Our division passed over the southern slope of Dogan Hill in the finest order. We passed into

a lane that ran along the foot of the hill and led to the Turnpike some distance beyond. We encountered the most awful confusion there. The narrow space was packed with Butterfield's and Roberts' broken brigades and many were wounded."

"In the midst of this throng were several ammunition wagons and Snead's battery. The infantry, obliged to halt to maintain its organization, was delayed several minutes here. Then our brigade moved along with the mass into the road and down to the tollgate at the foot of Henry Hill."

CHINN RIDGE

On Chinn Ridge a mile north of Longstreet's initial assault, Siegel's men had ringside seats to the unfolding drama. As Porter's smashed brigades fell back, Siegel was the first to bear witness to the Federal retreat and to the advance of Longstreet's Confederates. To add insult to injury, the *'fleeing'* Jackson had slipped around Pope's army and had joined Longstreet to help in the assault. Fifty thousand rebels were in the process of demolishing half of Pope's army.

As the full force of Lee's army surged ahead, there remained three points which had to be held long enough to allow the Union army to escape over Bull Run Bridge to safety at Centreville and the Washington defenses. These landmarks were Chinn Ridge, Dogan Ridge and Henry House Hill.

Chinn Ridge is topped by a large flat plateau. The trees were gone and the hilltop commanded a view of the approaching enemy forces as well as the route of retreat for the Federal army, down the Warrenton Turnpike, over Bull Run Bridge, and on to Centreville. The *only* way to avoid total destruction of the Union Army was for the Chinn Ridge defenders to hold the Federal lines against the rebels until dark. Such a defense would enable Pope's men to reform and begin the retreat toward Centreville. Pope ordered McDowell to send what units he had to reinforce Porter's line and establish a new defense line around Chinn Ridge.

Lee's strategy was plain. Capturing Dogan Ridge, smaller than Chinn Ridge and a thousand feet west across the Turnpike, was the next place the Confederates would charge. After Dogan Ridge came Henry House Hill. Henry House Hill, farther north, was a bare hill and would be the Union army's last line of defense.

On Chinn Ridge, Colonel Nathan McLean and his Ohio regiments were barely holding the worsening Federal left. They needed help badly. General Siegel sent Milroy. Colonel John A. Koltes' brigade followed. Dogan Ridge was also being held against the swarming Confederates by the three regiments of Julius Stahel's first brigade. His fourth regiment, the 41st New York, had gone to McLean's assistant on Chinn Ridge.

Hood's division followed D.R. Jones toward Chinn Ridge. The 10,000 Confederate attackers were descending on a mere 1200 of McLean's remaining Federals, but McLean had artillery. A battery of three guns hurled shells and grapeshot at the charging rebels tearing great holes in the rebel lines. Hood's men were thrown back, but only for the moment. As Chinn Ridge's defenders fought to hold on, Wilcox's division advanced on Dogan Ridge from another direction in a relentless mass of shouting gray uniforms.

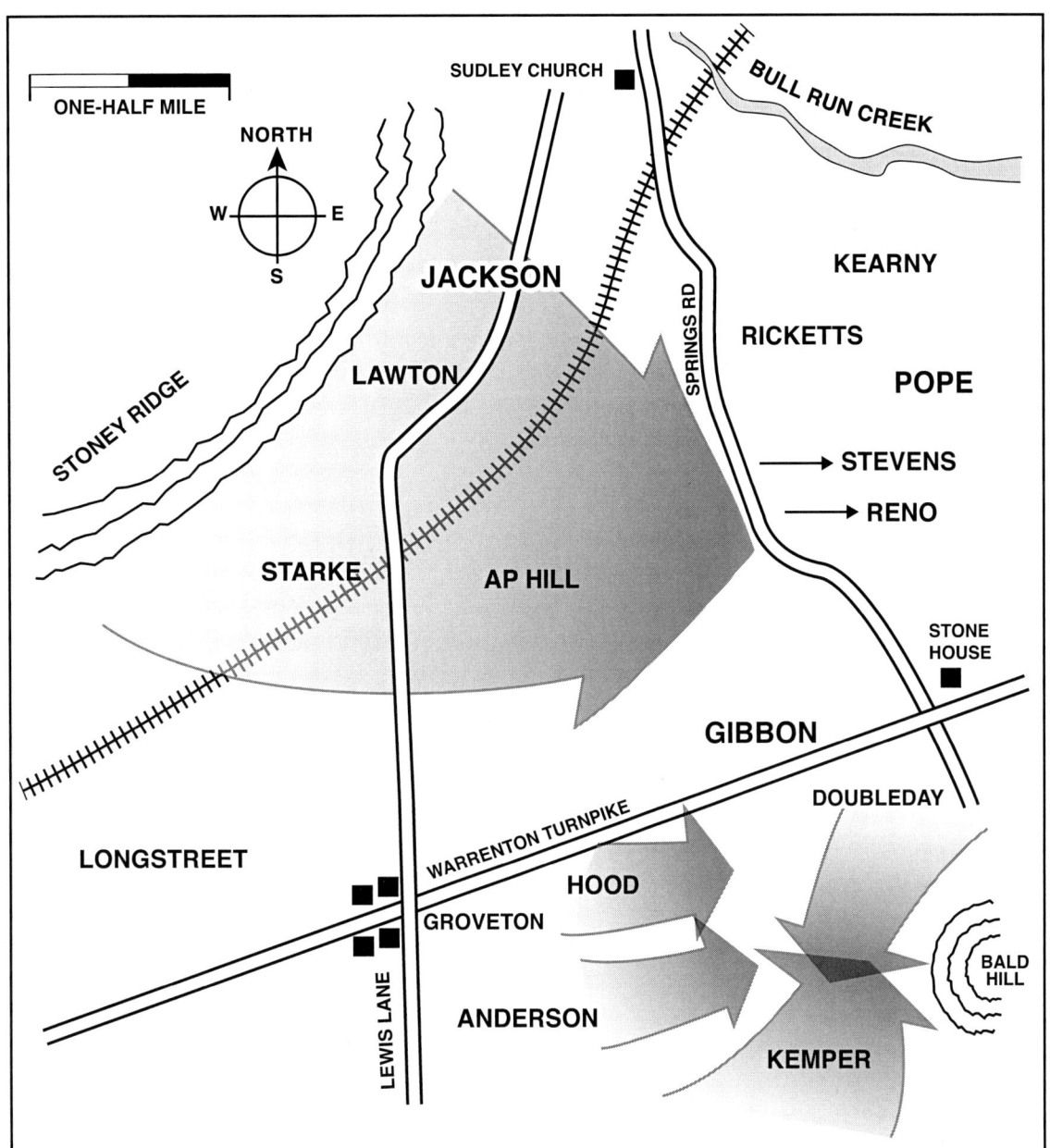

THE FINAL BATTLE / 5:00 PM, AUGUST 30, 1861

Union General John Reynolds' news finally caught and held stubborn General Pope's attention.

"General Pope, I ran a gauntlet of fire to escape being captured," Reynolds said. "I have, personally, seen a large Confederate column of many troops. The column was made up of more than one division. They were not part of Jackson's force. They are south of the Warrenton Turnpike and they are marching toward us now." General Lee attacked. One Union position after another was taken, until Pope pulled his forces over the Bull Run Creek to Centreville to reform. Porter's attack saved Pope's army from destruction.

'FRIENDLY' FIRE

Then occurred one of the most unfortunate mistakes of war that sometimes happens in the heat of battle. Lieutenant Colonel Holmstedt's men of the 41st New York fell under 'friendly' fire.

As Colonel McLean's battle report tells, *'Someone called my attention to a large body of troops behind my left. I supposed they were enemy troops and I ordered two artillery pieces turned on them. Almost at once I was assured the body of men was friends coming to our assistance. So I countermanded my order to the battery. However, that was a mistake. At that same moment a second heavy force of enemy troops came out of the woods. In the confusion and the fog of war, a second mistake was made. These troops, which I had mistakenly thought were friends, now combined to attack my left flank. My two regiments and my artillery were overpowered and driven back over the top of the hill. I ordered the men on my right flank to charge the enemy and the enemy advance was checked at once.'*

'My men cheered to stop the rebel assault,' McLean wrote later. *'We advanced once more, but then a new force appeared on my right flank. I felt if they reached us, it would result in our defeat so I gave the order to fall back slowly.'*

A few hundred yards away, the red and blue Confederate flags of Longstreet's advancing columns were plainly visible to the watchers on nearby Henry and Dogan Hills. As Kemper's three brigades advanced through the fields south of Chinn House, for a few moments more, the regiments of Siegel's brigades tried to stand against the rising tide of massed Confederate troops but the defenders were beaten back. The fire was so terrible and the noise of battle was so great it was impossible to be heard or give orders and the Federals retired in confusion, running to the small safety of the woods.

As the valley filled with the remnants of Porter's command, Pope realized he was in deep trouble. The left of his line, McLean's brigade on Chinn Ridge, was crumbling and Nathan McLean badly needed help. Pope called Colonel Strother to his office.

"Ride with all speed to General Heintzelman. Tell him to bring two brigades of Ricketts' division; Duryee and Thorburn."

"I found Heintzelman," Strother testified during the Porter trial. "But General Heintzelman said Ricketts could not move. Ricketts now occupied a most important position. General Ricketts said there was a whole division of Pennsylvania reserves that were disengaged. I took the discretionary power of ordering those idle troops over to the battle double quick."

More evidence of Pope's increasing anxiety was made plain. Pope was riding along the Warrenton Turnpike when he came upon a column of infantry marching toward the crest of Henry Hill. He stopped the column and demanded an explanation of Lieutenant Colonel William Marston, the officer leading the column.

"What troops are these and where are you going?"

"We are the regulars of Chapman's brigade. We have orders to proceed to the rear and cook rations," Marston replied.

These men were regular troops of General Chapman's brigade. Marston had been given orders to take his hungry men to the rear and cook some rations. Pope flew into a fury. He lashed out at the officer.

"Damn you! Where the hell do you think you're taking these men? The battle is over there," he shouted.

Pointing to the smoke and sound of gunfire on the left of the Pike near Chinn Ridge, he said, "You stay right where you are and don't you move until you receive further orders."

By this time Ricketts' division of Pennsylvania reserves had reached the fighting and were trying to stop the rebel onslaught. It was no more than a half hour that the Ohio men were able to withstand the rebel onslaught but it gave McDowell time to rush Styles' and Tower's brigades onto Chinn Ridge. Just as the Ohio men had given their best and were forced back or had fallen, Tower's regiments came at a run to hold Kemper's division. The Union guns opened up to batter at Hood's brigade, but the Confederates fought through Tower's line who gave way in a melee of hand-to-hand fighting.

General Nathan Evans' four regiments of South Carolinians and John Bell Hood's independent brigade, opened a vicious attack against McLean's left flank. New crises developed everywhere on Chinn Ridge.

General Tower, Ricketts' second brigade commander, fought with his men on the crest of Chinn Ridge desperately trying to stem the onslaught against their fellow brigade, led by McLean. The rebels had sent so many men against McLean that when Ricketts' gunners tried to lob shells at the Confederate attackers, the gunners stepped on their own troops lying on the ground around them.

So furious was the fighting as Ricketts' regiments hurled themselves into the fray that the officers were in the middle of the fighting. General Tower fell wounded and command passed to Colonel Coulter of Stiles' 11th Pennsylvanians. The regiments retreated at the edge of the woods near the crest but those that remained were under a tremendous fusillade.

As the troops of the 26th New York disintegrated and fell back, Sargent Charles McClenthen wrote of that moment.

'We were under as heavy and as galling a fire as had been poured into any body of troops during this war; shot, shell, grape, and canister with a heavy enfilading fire of musketry.'

They tried to save their guns but, McClenthen wrote, *'As the bullets shot across our rows of defenders they fell like wheat before a thresher. No troops in the world could stand that fire and we commenced falling back.'*

The full force of the Confederate wave slammed into the Chinn Hill defenders, but they continued to hold somehow. Thousands of muskets blasted at the gray uniformed attackers as they continued to surge forward. Wounded men were everywhere trying with all their strength to get away from the hellish fire.

Austin Stearns of the 13th Massachusetts Regiment recalled, *"One wounded man fell next to me. He tried to speak. But the blood filled his mouth and he would blow it in all directions. He was the most dreadful sight I ever saw. We could not help him for it was no use."*

Franz Siegel's corps was closest to the fighting on Henry Hill. When he saw the trouble McLean was having on Henry Hill he had Schenck order two of his brigades; Milroy's and Koltes' troops, to McLean's aid. At Dogan House, Stahel's brigade continued to hold their important opposition on the heights of Dogan Ridge.

Shortly after 5 o'clock Stahel sent his 41st New York Regiment to jump into the fight against the rebels. Moving the men wasn't easy. They had to cross an open field, a deep ditch and climb the high rocky side of the Hill. Once there it was just as difficult to reform the regiments in lines of battle; a thick patch of trees covered the top of the hill where they were. At the same time the men of the 41st Regiment were under heavy Confederate fire.

HOLDING ON

McDowell worked frantically to secure an all-important position for the Union army on Chinn Ridge. The 55th Ohio was thrown into the battle, fighting gamely, but were forced to retreat. The 2nd New York Light Battery continued to fire at the enemy from Dogan Ridge. Schurz's division endured heavy artillery fire, while Koltes' brigade was ordered into the fight on Chinn Ridge. Roemer and Dilger's 6-pounder and 10-pounder rifles continued to fire at the advancing enemy, but those guns were subjected to heavy enemy artillery fire and several more guns were hit.

By this time, McLean's men had fallen back and were out of the way of artillery. Colonel McLean gave the order and Weiderick's artillery opened up on the rebels, driving them back. McLean told his story of that hour to an historian long after the battle.

"They fell back more rapidly than they had charged my men. While the batteries were pushing the rebels back, I noticed a newer body of rebels to the rear of the left flank of my regiment. Thinking they were the enemy, I ordered two pieces of artillery to be turned on them. Someone yelled, 'We are friends,' so I countermanded my order."

"That was a mistake. A heavy force came out of the woods and they were joined with the troops I had thought to be friendly. Both bodies attacked my left flank. We were overpowered and my regiments retreated over the hill, managing to limber up and take my batteries with them. The fighting was severe but the men held their ground and the enemy's advance was checked. For the moment the tables were turned; the enemy continued to retreat before the determined advance of my men. I saw another heavy force on my right flank. I knew that if they reached us it would result in my defeat with a great loss of men. I gave the order to fall back slowly."

Colonel Orland Smith, leading the 73rd Ohio Regiment for Colonel McLean, reported, 'The situation was now critical. The Confederate flags of the column bearing down on us were clearly visible. A battery on our left opened up on us and the shot and shell came plowing down our lines. For a few moments the 73rd tried to stand but were soon overpowered. There was no alternative but a retirement.'

Now it was the turn of the 73rd Ohio to halt the rebel advance.

Major Robert Reilly lead the 73rd and wrote in his battle report, *'We were advancing on the enemy confident of victory. We were hailed, stunned, and surprised by a terrible crash of musketry, grape-shot, and shell from a very large force of rebels who had marched upon us. This stopped our progress immediately and we fell back.'*

The Union troops could do nothing except to load and fire, load and fire, load and fire, after these men believed they had been so close to capturing Jackson and victory. The incredible mass of rebel infantry was a sight that few of those who survived the battle could believe possible.

One of the Confederate men admitted, *"We were a mere mob. There stood the enemy in a beautiful line. Had they only advanced on us they would have routed and captured us. Not only did the Federals not advance (Siegel's men), they allowed us to turn to their right and we fell upon their left flank. The Yankees did not wait to lock bayonets with us but turned and fled."*

More of Longstreet's men entered the fight in the fields around Chinn Ridge. John Bell Hood's brigades, Evans and Kemper, poured fire down upon the Union troops. What happened next was told by Private Alexander Hunter of the 17th Virginia Confederate brigade.

'We advanced until we reached a small outbuilding. Suddenly a regiment of the enemy sprang up behind a wall and let loose a withering volley at point blank pistol range. We were not expecting it and it came upon us with the suddenness of a thunderbolt. Our Colonel fell, his leg fractured by a bullet and many were killed in that volley. All discipline was at an end and only individual bravery made up for the deficiency.'

'We all sprang forward with one ringing yell, the officers waving their swords and the men standing only long enough to fire off their guns. Every man took aim before his finger pressed the trigger and the ground in our front was literally lined with blue. Still they stood their ground. Our foes were a Western regiment from Ohio who gave and received and asked no odds.'

HENRY HILL

The fighting grew heavier near Henry Hill and Union Major Ames told of the fight.

'We went over hill and hollow, running till we panted like dogs. I thought we should fall from sheer exhaustion. Stumbling over the remnants of a fence, we found ourselves, finally, in a country lane and came to a halt.'

'There was a partial lull in the firing just then. For a few minutes we thought we had found a quiet retreat in that lane. Good luck or skill had taken us into a first-rate position for defense. The lull in the battle gave us time to dress our line back to the roadside. Somehow the run had cheered us up. In spite of the defeat we now had a feel of a contagion of confidence. Our fear we had was all gone. We examined our musket locks, shoved cartridge box rounds to the front of our belts and picked out such slim shelter as the shallow little roadside ditch could afford.'

'The lull didn't fool us a bit. We knew it was coming harder in a minute. Half a dozen brass Napoleon guns came up behind us and took position on a slight rise in the ground. I am afraid to say how near; we could look into their open mouths. There was a minute or two of silence, in which we stood expectant and looked across the road into the pine woods in front. Then came a rattling crash of musketry, a screaming yell of men, and the tramp of advancing lines coming through the woods. The Napoleons opened and we opened too. It was the first shot we had that day.'

'We must have made it lively for the Johnnies; they never made it through the fence. In front I saw but one man all the rest of the day. A big fellow, in full gray to his blanket, climbed to the top of the fence and sat there astraddle swaying back and forth, till he fell heavily inside.'

'But oh, the brass guns behind us. How the gunners did dance with excitement as they poured in their fire. Bully guns for short range fighting. Every time they fired we had to duck down and even so, we got covered with grains of powder and burning bits of flannel and great puffs

of hot smoke. I saw the gunners putting in the powder bags when you could not beat your hand on the hot press.'

'We got our confidence and our courage and seasoned the woods with the liveliest kind of firing whenever the rebs came marching up again, for they came back two or three times before they gave it up. But they made their mark on us, you can bet on that. The wounded fell down just where they stood. One fellow wanted me to turn him over so that I might get at his cartridge box when my own should be empty as he wouldn't want it himself. The poor fellow was dead before we left.'

❧ 46 ❧

End Game

The fight for Chinn Ridge had been a disaster. McLean withdrew. The 8th and the 27th New York Regiments left Dogan Ridge. Morell pulled back to the top of Bull Run Hill near the Robinson House. The rest of Porter's divisions assembled to the rear of the Robinson House below Henry Hill and by 6 PM it was clear to Pope that the battle was lost.

The end was in sight. Longstreet's main force was driving ahead to victory. Henry Hill, Chinn Ridge, Dogan Ridge; all key positions, one by one were being lost. During the next forty-five minutes nearly eight thousand men clashed in a life or death struggle. There were advances and retreats; men fought until they ran out of ammunition. Guns fired until the barrels and the breeches were so hot they could not be fired. Thousands were wounded and hundreds fell on the small patch of ground around Chinn Hill and Henry Hill that brief hour never to rise again.

Pope moved his command to Henry Hill, still held by the Federals. From that vantage point he watched the battle's progress and, just before 6 o'clock he dispatched a number of his staff officers to the various parts of the battlefield. The orders were, *'Begin a gradual withdrawal.'* By 5:15 PM, the climax had been building. By 6 PM it was clear the battle was lost. Banks was told by Pope to destroy all public property at Bristoe Station and fall back to Centreville.

The entire left side of the defending Union army was being broken. Now all efforts were made to keep the Confederates from moving to the Union rear and breaking the back of the Federal defense. The brigades and regiments, one after another, fell back to reorganize near the Stone House. Crossing the Bull Run Bridge, men continued to move east and Milroy continued to fight to hold the western slopes of Henry Hill.

Responding to the deepening crisis on the left, Porter moved Buchanan's division next to the ruins of Henry House. Chapman waited for the enemy on Sudley Road. Warren placed what was left of his troops in the rear side of the Henry Plateau and east of the Stone House.

A private of the Confederate 9th Georgia Infantry, charging the summit of Henry Hill remembered an impromptu speech their brigade commander had given them before the charge. He reminded his men of another time, a year earlier when the

North and the South had fought on this very same ground.

"Sergeant Anderson shouted *'Attention.'* The boys shouldered arms. Our Colonel, Billy Johnson, of the 7th Georgia, rode out in front. *'Boys,'* he said to us, *'We have come back to our old stamping ground. If any of you bastards kill a Yankee, put on his shoes quick. If you get to a sutler's store, eat all the cheese and crackers that you can possibly hold and if you get any good cigars give old Billy two. Forward.'"*

"The boys raised a yell. By the time the brigade marched through the old fields and struck the woods *(near the crest of Henry Hill)*, Colonel Billy was killed. If he got his cigars I did not see him smoke them."

The rebels were not above using psychological warfare when the opportunity arose. Theron Haight, a Corporal the 40th New York Regiment, recollected the Union's fight.

"Men were falling on all sides. Our line formation was practically lost. We were a mere mob whose only unity was in blazing away at the line of fire in our front. The officers tried to reform the men and all of them were giving orders at the same time."

"Suddenly, a body of troops was seen moving toward us from the trees along the lane to our left. We were in doubt whether they were friends or enemies. They shouted, *'Don't fire at us boys. We're coming to help you.'"*

"Some of us felt reassured while others, incredulous, cried, *'Don't believe 'em; they're rebels,'* and ran toward the rear. Then a shattering volley lit the gathering darkness, revealing the gray uniforms of a strong Confederate line. The bullets slapped into Sullivan's men like hailstones against a window."

McDowell worked to secure a last-ditch position on Henry Hill. At 5:15 one of McDowell's staff officers galloped up to Battery 'D' near the Dogan House.

Pointing toward the Lewis House, he cried out to the gun captain stationed there, "For God's sake, hurry up. They are massing in our front over there."

McDowell ordered Gibbon to deploy his Black Hat troops. His brigade was placed in position near Robinson House, his batteries were unlimbered and he prepared for action. Reynolds' division watched for nearly an hour as their comrades were pushed off Chinn Ridge. Disaster loomed but Reynolds hurried back to his men who were resting just north of Henry House ruins.

He bellowed to his two brigades, "Now boys, give them the steel. Charge bayonets, double quick." His men crossed the field.

As an historian chronicled the clash, 'The contest became hot and desperate. Greatly outnumbered, still they were able to hold the rebels in check for the moment. It was hand to hand encounter. Reynolds, in the thick of the fight, grabbed a shattered staff from one of the regiments and rode up and down the line, waving the flag about his head and cheering on his men.'

"The effect was electrical," one man said.

The reserves held.

After his failed attack on Jackson's line, General Porter repaired to Henry Hill and personally placed his troops for the fight on the prominence. By evening of the

30th Longstreet's army hurled itself at the Federal line on Chinn Ridge. An hour later Jackson's attack drove into the center of the Federal line. Furious defense held the Confederates at bay and only the coming of night saved the Union forces. Pope's troops made an orderly retreat and fell back on their defenses in Centreville. There had been a total of 25,000 casualties.

UNION RETREAT

Now it was Lee's turn to make a mistake. If Jackson had moved from Stony Ridge he would have prevented McDowell from sending Siegel's brigades to Porter's assistance. However, one can understand, no matter how necessary, Jackson's men had been decimated by the earlier Union attacks. Once more the Yankees held; but only for a moment. Once more the Federals were flanked on the left and thousands of soldiers streamed in retreat. Pope's left wing was no more. It was Jackson again who saved the rest of the Yankee army from total disaster because he did not press them from his place on Stony Ridge.

For two hours the Union forces held in a new line at the crest of Henry Hill. The brigades of Reynolds, Sykes, Milroy and Schurz joined what remained of the left wing, repulsing a series of rebel attacks. As it grew dark, Pope was able to withdraw his defeated army toward the banks of Bull Run. The Yankees yielded finally on Henry Hill but Lee's opportunity had passed.

It wasn't over. General Robertson's cavalry threatened to break through the Union retreating columns but Buford resisted with all his forces and the rebels ended their advance. The Federals destroyed the bridge and fell back on stronger defenses at Centreville.

An orderly withdrawal of the Federal forces was underway. The mass of troops and wagons struggled eastward across the Stone Bridge, over the Bull Run Creek and along the Warrenton Turnpike. The Union army began the melancholy journey to Centreville. Porter withdrew to organize the remnants of his corps in the march eastward along the Turnpike to Centreville. The drizzling rain and leaden skies were a reflection of the sadness and the melancholy that pervaded the mind and hearts of the survivors as they trudged along the road. 13,000 Union soldiers had been wounded or had been killed during the three days at Manassas. Stragglers were still coming in. Franklin's Sixth Corps and Sumner's Second Corps had finally arrived. Their fresh troops more than made up the losses but there would be no more fighting for now.

Next day Pope decided to retreat to the defenses of Washington. His troops marched eastward on the Warrenton Turnpike while Pope remained behind with his strong rear guard commanded by Reynolds' and Buford's cavalry.

General Gibbon was designated to act as the army's rear guard. Gibbon rode over to Henry Hill where he met General McDowell. Gibbon placed his brigade on a ridge alongside the Warrenton Turnpike where the road climbed a hill near the Robinson Farm. He unlimbered the pieces of Battery 'B' and prepared for action. Reynolds' battery was still under heavy fire and he was in danger of being flanked so Reynolds passed an order to move the cannons to the rear.

Lieutenant George Breck wrote, 'We opened a brisk fire. While here, a rebel regiment charged our battery. They came down through the woods in line and good order and they were within 250 yards of us when our guns opened up with canister. Our captain was on his horse telling the boys to give them canister, give them canister and stick by the guns.'

'Well, every gun soon shot out with canister, the command to fire being given, and when the smoke drifted away all that remained of that Southern regiment were scampering up the hill as fast as their legs could carry them.'

On the Sudley Road, Sykes' division of the second brigade under General Chapman was the last to become engaged with the advancing rebels. Once engaged, the fire fight was furious. The regulars held for a short time until, as an officer conceded, it was time to withdraw and the brigade fell back. At 8 o'clock that night, Pope issued the formal retreat orders. Feeling there was nothing more to be done, Pope began his journey to Centreville.

Lee's last chance had passed. Jackson began moving against the Yankees but by this time Pope's forces were retreating in good order. Crossing Bull Run the defeated Union army found defensive positions at Centreville while McClellan's men jeered at Pope for his stubborn failure to call up the waiting Army of the Potomac.

As the beaten army retreated, Brigadier John Gibbon, commander of the Army of Virginia, formed his Black Hat Brigade in a battle line as a rear guard force for the retreating Yankees on the Warrenton Turnpike east of Henry Hill. It was there, late in the afternoon, he met his friend, Phil Kearny.

Gibbon said, "I heard someone inquire in a quick tone, 'Whose command is this?' Turning to look, I recognized General Phil Kearny. I walked up to him and told him I was directed to act as a rear guard."

"He was a soldierly looking figure as he sat, straight as an arrow, on his horse, his empty sleeve pinned to his breast. He turned to me."

"In his curt way he said, 'You must wait for my command, sir.'"

"Yes," I replied, "I will wait for all our troops to pass to the rear. Where is your command, General?"

"Off to the right, don't you hear my guns? You must wait for Reno, too."

"Where is he?"

"On the left; you hear the guns? He is keeping up the fight and I am doing all I can to help."

"Then in a bitter tone he spoke out with, 'I suppose you appreciate the condition of affairs, here sir?' I did not understand his remark and only looked inquiringly at him. He repeated, 'I suppose you appreciate the condition of affairs. It's another Bull Run, sir. It's another Bull Run.'"

"Oh," I said. "I hope it's not as bad as that, General."

"'Perhaps not,' he replied. 'Reno is keeping up the fight. He is not stampeded. That is about all, sir. My God, that's about all.'"

"It is impossible to describe the extreme vehemence with which he uttered these words as he rode towards his command."

❧ 47 ❧

Chantilly

The worst was over for a while, but Lee hadn't quit by a long shot. Pope's army continued to trudge its weary way into Centreville's better defenses. All that night and the next day the defeated Union Army marched discouraged but reasonably well organized, muskets at the ready. The army was still very much a fighting body thanks to the desperate last ditch defense against Longstreet by its heroic fighting men.

General Porter had played his part; his twenty-hour delay of Longstreet at Dawkins Branch, and the final battle against Lee's entire army had made the difference between an orderly retreat and total destruction of Pope's forces. Pope's army had neither been captured nor destroyed. Bitter with disappointment as they were, they would fight again, near the Chantilly Plantation, in the South Mountain passes and on Antietam Creek.

Now in the clammy cold of the rainy August night the fifty thousand Union troops marched away from Bull Run and to a national humiliation. There was little time to blame anyone for their loss on the Plain of Manassas. Yet every man in the Federal army knew *something* had gone terribly wrong at the high command.

The victorious rebel soldiers wasted no time in taking full advantage of their success. When they no longer had any instant expectation of overtaking and destroying Pope's forces, the hungry battle-worn rebel soldiers poured into the empty scattered Union camps and supply stations to find a cornucopia of coffee, sugar, food, wines, clothing, shoes, blankets and all manner of the kind of supplies a soldier needs most.

Some of the rebels rushed into the camps, fires still burning and coffee on the stove, while John Pope's men were retreating across Bull Run Creek and heading toward Centreville two miles away. The famished Confederate troops found coffee still hot, sugar at hand ready to be dropped into the coffee cups, bread in the oven, crackers by the box, fine beef ready cooked and desiccated vegetables by the bushel. The officer's tents yielded canned peaches, lobsters, tomatoes, milk, barrels of ground and roasted coffee, sugar, and everything a hungry soldier craves. There were cases of liquors and wines, boxes of cigars, and tobacco in the supply wagons.

Men on both sides of the battle who had fallen suffered what casualties in the Civil War were common. Some of the most badly wounded lay in the fields until their wounds festered and they died. A few had lasted long enough for rescue parties to find them, sometimes days later. The Confederates filled the nearby homes with the wounded. Eventually, both sides buried their dead and turned their thoughts toward tomorrow's fighting.

The weary rebels had achieved a tremendous victory and the spoils made the victory all the sweeter. Lee had beaten a large Union army, the way north was open to Washington and Virginia and the Southern capitol had been saved.

Franklin's division arrived in Centreville on August 31. The Union army, weary and shot up as they were, was still a powerful fighting body and Franklin's five thousand troops more than made up for the casualties. John Pope had lost control of his army. He hesitated between a rock and a hard place, uncertain what he should to do next and delayed any action for more than twenty-four hours. Pope's irresolution gave Lee time to assemble and keep the offensive.

Pope did something he hated to do; ask advice. He called a conference of his corps commanders. As a result of that uncomfortable discussion, although some of the officers were in favor of a counter offensive, Pope decided the army must head back to the safety of the Washington defenses.

A dispatch from General-in-Chief Halleck changed his plans. It was an order he could not ignore. He was told to attack Lee. Pope, reluctantly, ordered an advance on the enemy's lines.

Lee was two steps ahead of John Pope. While Longstreet remained conspicuously in front of Pope's forces, the wily Stonewall Jackson, with Stuart's cavalry scouting for him, looped around north of Centreville to strike at the rear of the Union army. Luckily for Pope, Jackson's troops were worn out from the battle and they moved slowly, unlike their usual fast-moving pace that had given them the name of 'foot cavalry.'

Before the main part of the Confederate Left Wing reached their objective, Federal scouts sighted Stuart's cavalry. When Pope got the report, which was an old habit of his, he rejected the idea they were forerunners of a Confederate attack and dismissed the report as only a Confederate patrol. An hour later, Union cavalry patrols brought more news. They had seen Jackson's entire force coming along the edge of the Little River Turnpike north of Centreville and marching toward Pope's rear.

Southeast of the old Chantilly Plantation that sprawled over the Virginia countryside north of Centreville, Jackson's tired troops were resting while Jackson took a nap before the strike he was about to make on Pope's army. It began to rain, and it poured down in a flood. It was the last day of August 1862, and the cold summer rain was a sad epilogue to a sad and bloody battle.

The news his scouts had brought him about Jackson woke up Pope. Not waiting for Jackson to attack, at three o'clock that same afternoon Stevens' division, a part of Reno's corps, was sent to attack Jackson.

Stevens' division wasn't large or strong enough to stop Jackson and Phil Kearney's men raced into the rainstorm to support him. The downpour was so heavy the wet ruined the black powder so that the muskets could not fire. With soaked ammunition the battle became a bayonet man-on-man brawl in the blood-soaked mud and rain. Like most of the battles of the Civil War, officers were spared no more often than the foot soldiers. General Stevens was struck in the head by a bullet and died on the spot. General Kearney, who liked to lead his men into battle, made the serious mistake of riding so far into the melee that he rode into Confederate lines. Before he could escape, he was also shot and died within minutes.

Several stories have been told about the way Kearney died. The story most plausible was one told after the battle by one of the Confederate officers, who had witnessed General Philip Kearney's death. Major Grice of the 45th Georgia Infantry brigade told this version:

"The battle was over. Darkness had ended the conflict and the firing had ceased. General Kearney rode alone to the front of the 49th Georgia. He had lost his way in the darkness and he had to know whether these men were friends or enemies. When he got close to the line, he asked, 'What troops are those?' A man of the regiment answered his question with one of his own and Kearney answered."

"Some of the men thought he said, 'Confederate.' Others thought he said 'Federal.' Kearney, discovering his mistake, wheeled his horse around and started to gallop away to safety. Captain Pate gave the order, 'Fire on him.' Kearney bent low in his saddle, head on the neck of his horse. As he did, the bullet entered his body directly from the rear. He fell from his horse and died in a few minutes."

The next day, when General Lee learned of Kearney's death, he sent Kearney's body back to his men under a flag of truce.

The Chantilly fight was over but Jackson's half-hearted pursuit continued on to the gates of Washington. That one-day fight hadn't settled anything except to cost the Federals a few more casualties and two of their generals.

Lee had accomplished another of his important objectives with Jackson's pursuit; Lee had forced Pope to fall back upon the Potomac. Because the Union army was no longer a threat, it cleared the way for Lee to begin the Maryland Campaign. As was Robert E. Lee's aggressive style, he immediately invaded Maryland. Jackson captured Harper's Ferry and all the Union supplies, and 11,500 Union soldiers were sent to Southern prison camps.

**Union General
Ambrose Burnside**

❧ 48 ❧

Antietam

The Battle of Antietam was fought two weeks after the Battle of Second Manassas, and was a victory for the North. Slim as that narrow victory was at Antietam, it gave President Lincoln enough political clout to sign the Emancipation Proclamation. On April 8, 1864, it was passed by the Senate and a year after that the House passed the amendment by a skin-of-your-teeth narrow vote, passing by a majority difference of two on January 31, 1865. On December 6, 1865, the Amendment was adopted. The Thirteen Amendment outlawed slavery and involuntary servitude, except as punishment for a crime.

As Lee marched north toward Washington, the Lincoln administration, with little choice to do otherwise, once again picked George McClellan to stop Lee.

McClellan had skill as an organizer. Single-handedly, he had built a powerful Union army from scratch. His troops loved him and he was popular at home. After his sorry performance during the Peninsula Campaign in the summer of 1862, he lost favor with the Lincoln Administration. McClellan was brought forward once more and for the last time in the Civil War.

As it turned out, McClellan won the Battle of Antietam in spite of his many mistakes. Antietam was, in fact, the *only* battle of the Civil War that McClellan ever fought from start to finish.

That battle could have made or broken George McClellan. If he had followed up Lee's retreat with an offensive, which he could and should have, he might have ended the rebellion. Instead, in spite of having an army twice Lee's force, he barely managed to stave off another defeat and hold Lee at bay for what the North chose to call a victory.

Robert E. Lee kept coming. Following the route of the Union army from the Plain of Manassas and John Pope's humiliating defeat, Lee intended to invade the North and force a peace once and for all. A copy of Lee's battle plans, Order Number 191, fell into McClellan's hands. From this McClellan learned Lee had split his forces. McClellan hoped to destroy these isolated parts before they could join and concentrate against him. What followed was called the Maryland campaign.

South Mountain is a part of the Blue Ridge Mountains after they enter Maryland.

It separates the Hagerstown Valley and the Cumberland Valley from the eastern part of Maryland. Three South Mountain passes (or gaps) must be crossed to move from the Hagerstown Valley to reach the Cumberland Valley. They are Crampton's, Turner's, and Fox's Gaps.

McClellan was tardy in his pursuit of Lee, as was McClellan's style. He had to pass through these three gaps to catch up to the Confederate forces in order to catch and defeat Lee. From the start, even after Lee's strategic victory, the rebels had been heavily outnumbered. Still, in the first of these confrontations at the Battle of South Mountain, also known as Boonsboro Gap, McClellan's advance had delayed.

In McClellan's planned offensive to prevail against the Confederate army, he waited a full day before beginning his pursuit of Lee. This gave Lee just time enough to gather up his forces and meet McClellan at what became the bloodiest battle of the Civil War, Antietam. In the South, the battle was known as Sharpsburg.

The Battle of Antietam was historic for several reasons. Antietam was the only battle George McClellan engaged in to the finish. General Ezra Carman was present, and wrote '*More errors were committed by the Union commander than in any other battle of the war.*' Also, two future presidents fought during these battles, William McKinley and Rutherford B. Hayes.

The battle began with a challenge. Lee, in a defensive position west of Antietam Creek, challenged McClellan to attack him. In answer to the challenge, McClellan displayed his usual caution. When he did attack it was piecemeal. He sent no more than three-quarters of his army against Lee, instead of concentrating his forces where he should, while Lee used all his army. Though greatly outnumbered, once again, Lee had convinced McClellan he had a far larger army than he did.

McClellan struck Lee's left flank with Hooker's First corps. Mansfield's Twelfth corps crossed the Antietam behind Hooker in support. The rest, the Second, Porter's Fifth and the Ninth Corps remained behind east of the Antietam. Franklin was sent to help out but only after the battle was half over.

At this point in the fight, McClellan's penchant to play politics took over. McClellan, being afraid that the powerful generals, Sumner and Burnside, might take credit for a victory instead of himself, kept those two corps on the east side of the Antietam—after taking half of Burnside's command and leaving Sumner with only his Second corps.

McClellan followed these mistakes with other errors. Burnside was finally sent to join the fight but it was three hours too late. When Hooker got into the fight at Dunker's Church cornfield, Mansfield was late in bringing Hooker the support he needed. The result was that Hooker and Jackson shot each other to pieces without any help for Hooker from the forces McClellan had in reserve. Sumner and his 15,200 troops advanced finally, but they were two miles away from the action. McClellan allowed only two of Sumner's three divisions to cross the Antietam and General Sumner marched into an ambush. In fifteen minutes he lost 40 percent of his men.

The 'nail in the coffin' for General McClellan was when he listened to a demoralized General Sumner, who insisted they were on the verge of a total defeat if they took the offensive. When McClellan looked to the one man he trusted, Porter, McClellan decided that his only reserves could not be spared for a final all-out offensive against Lee.

Lee was near defeat and he sent his forces back toward Richmond. McClellan would not renew the battle and follow Lee. Had he done so, would have destroyed Lee's army, and probably ended the war. One can only imagine President Lincoln's despair and frustration.

One of McClellan's greater problems was his failure to communicate his plans with anyone. The one man with whom he consulted was General Fitz John Porter. At one crucial point in the battle, when the outcome was in doubt and another massed assault would have won the day for the Federals, McClellan held back his reserve, Porter's 5th corps, the same way he had done at Malvern Hill. As a result, Lee got away to fight again. McClellan trumpeted what was truly a strategic loss for the Union and his delusion of such in a letter to his wife, writing *'I fought the battle splendidly and it was a masterpiece of art.'*

Lee was stopped; no thanks to McClellan. How then was the Union army able to stop Robert E. Lee? On the eve of the fight McClellan claimed, *'I face a rebel army amounting to not less than 100,000 men. They outnumber my own army by at least twenty-five percent.'* Except it wasn't true.

The facts were that McClellan had more than two times as many men than Lee. The difference was that Lee used *all of his men* in a master's fine battle strategy. McClellan's perennial fear of losing, instead of fighting to win, caused him to send men in piecemeal lots against the Confederates.

There were only two generals that McClellan trusted and in whom he confided; Joe Hooker and Fitz John Porter. The other corps commanders, Sumner, Franklin, Burnside, and Mansfield, were not consulted as to battle plans. McClellan called no council of his generals, he issued no plan of battle and conferred only with Porter.

McClellan's loss of reputation after Antietam left its mark on Fitz John Porter, to Porter's ultimate destruction in the court martial. The trial and the accusation of Porter that followed soon after Antietam were a condemnation aimed as much at McClellan as they were at the innocent party, Fitz John Porter.

After the battle, Porter remained in command of the Fifth corps and was given charge of the defenses of Washington, but not for long. In November of 1862 Porter was arrested and faced a military court martial. He was convicted of cowardice and disobedience at the Second Battle of Manassas, and cashiered from the army in disgrace.

Three events followed the Battle of Antietam and the Battle of Second Manassas. The first was that two top Union generals were found to be inept for command. John Pope and Irvin McDowell would no longer be allowed to decide life or death for thousands of men.

The second event was the Battle of Antietam a week later and gave the Union a slim victory over Lee. Slim as it was, it was enough of a victory to give President Abraham Lincoln the excuse he needed to proclaim the Emancipation Proclamation.

The third event was less noticed and would be hardly remembered. Yet that affair was the most important military court martial of the century, the conspiracy that led to the trial and conviction of Union Major General Fitz John Porter.

PART FOUR

Defeat and Victory

❧ 49 ❧

The Court Martial

The Republican administration had long been searching for a way to bring down the egocentric but powerful Democrat, George McClellan. Even long-suffering and patient President Lincoln had had enough of McClellan's 'slows.' John Pope, who boasted that his men *'had always seen the backs of their enemies,'* had been charged to take over and win the war but that didn't work out well. Pope's performance at Manassas had been no better than during McClellan's Peninsula Campaign. Lee, Longstreet, and Stonewall Jackson had out-thought and out-fought Pope in both campaigns. Not only that, Lee came within a nit's hair of destroying the Northern army and invading Washington.

Major General Fitz John Porter, who had the misfortune to be McClellan's close friend and protégé, became the target of the rage of the Democrat leaders in Washington. McClellan was considered untouchable, but Porter, who had played an important part in the Battle of Second Manassas, was the perfect scapegoat after the ignominious loss at Manassas to the Confederacy. Porter became the symbol of all the Republican's hatred in 1862. Furthermore, Porter's intemperate personal letters to his friend, General Burnside, were openly critical of General John Pope's fighting abilities.

John Pope had been the Republican administration's Poster Boy. Secretary Stanton and the President had hand-picked John Pope for the fight at Manassas. Pope's loss rocked the foundations of the Republican Party's hold on national politics. Someone had to pay.

Porter's court martial and conviction accomplished one of the administration's most important objectives. They had to send a crystal clear message to all Union generals and officers no one would misunderstand. Any general or officer, who mixed Democratic pro-Southern politics with military duties, would be speedily dealt with in a similar way. The angry cry went out from Washington and the Republican administration: *'From this day forward there will be no disobedience. The Civil War will be fought with single-minded purpose until the South is defeated.'*

It was on the steps of Fairfax Courthouse on September 5 that Porter spoke to Pope. This was *before* he was arrested for disobeying orders at the Battle of Second Manassas.

As they talked to each other that day Pope declared to Porter, in the hearing of Colonel Ruggles, a member of Pope's Staff, that his (Porter's) conduct during the battle was, in Pope's words, "Entirely satisfactory."

Five days later all that changed.

After Pope went to Washington and spoke with the president, Pope stated, "I came to Washington and there I saw Porter's military conduct during the battle in a new light."

What or who changed Pope's mind? Stanton? What happened in those few days that *opened Pope's eyes* to new facts? What conduct of Porter's was told to Pope that Pope had not seen before? Pope stated that his eyes rested on *'certain telegrams'* by which Porter's guilt was determined. These telegrams were from Porter to Burnside. In some manner these letters got to General Halleck, then to Secretary of War Edwin Stanton, and finally to President Lincoln.

Burnside, Porter's good friend, said later that he forwarded Porter's letters as evidence of Pope's inability to lead and the cause of the defeat at Manassas. The letters were made public and the public press responded to their contents with charges of *'doubtful loyalty'* and with such epithets as *'traitor'* or *'semi-traitor.'*

When President Lincoln showed Pope these letters, it was only then his *'eyes were opened'* to Porter's guilt. Porter found it impossible to believe that Lincoln had planted the thoughts of Porter's disloyalty against Pope personally. Porter's relationship with Lincoln to that point had been cordial.

Not only were the letters made public, but Army General in Chief Halleck demonstrated a disturbing level of unfairness and injustice by his actions that followed. Before Porter was even found guilty, Halleck disclosed his personal bias and comments regarding Porter to the public press, an act that was illegally commenting on an ongoing trial and investigation; comments that were also unfair and prejudicial. Added to that miscarriage of justice, Brigadier General B.S. Roberts, a member of the court, later testified *for the prosecution*. Roberts was no less than a senior member of the court martial and it was Roberts who read the charges against General Porter.

A few weeks after John Pope came to Washington, President Lincoln met with General Porter. Lincoln told him that he had seen several dispatches or letters from Porter to General Burnside. The letters were dated a day or two before the battle of Manassas. The President summoned Porter to his office and spoke with Porter about the Burnside letters.

"These letters were most critical of Major General Pope. It is these letters, which have given me grave apprehensions about your willingness to sacrifice the army and betray its cause. Your words have raised a reasonable suspicion that you failed your commanding general," Lincoln told Porter.

Porter answered Lincoln.

"Mr. President, when I wrote those letters they were private thoughts, intended only for the eyes and ears of a fellow officer and friend. Any impartial investigation will let my countrymen be convinced that the confidence reposed in me was not misplaced. By such an investigation, the government will do justice to our country and to those engaged in fighting her battles. I was and I continue to be a loyal officer to the army of my country. No matter my private concerns and reservations about the conduct of General Pope, at all times I obeyed his every order to the limit of my ability and without reservation."

These letters, the evidence seems to imply, were the primary reason that President Lincoln and Secretary of War Stanton were determined to punish Porter, and did so with a court martial. On September 10, 1862, Porter was accused and tried for high crimes.

What was the damning content of these letters? There were the parts that were read during the trial:

'Pope went to Centreville having Heintzelman and Reno as bodyguards, at the time not knowing where was the enemy, and where Siegel was fighting within eight miles of him and in sight. Comment is unnecessary.'

That was the absolute truth.

Porter's implication that Pope was more worried about his personal safety by taking several thousand troops with him to Centreville, while at the same time Siegel was fighting Jackson's main army, reveals a lack of leadership by Pope. That was considered by the court to be disrespectful for the army's command by General Pope. The court claimed Porter's phrase, *'comment is unnecessary'* tells it all.

Farther on, in Porter's letter to Burnside, he says, *'I hope McClellan's at work and we will soon get ordered out of this. It would seem, from some statements of the enemy that he (Jackson) is wandering around loose (regarding Confederate Jackson's movements); but I expect they (Confederates) know what they are doing, which is more than anyone here (Pope), or anywhere knows.'* Note: Parenthetical words are added for clarity.

That was certainly the truth, although Pope claimed he had mountains of evidence to the contrary.

Another dispatch to Burnside said, *'There is a report that Jackson is at Centreville, which you can believe or not. The enemy destroyed an immense amount of property at Manassas. I expect the next thing will be a raid on our rear by way of Centreville, by Longstreet.'*

Simply put, Porter was fed up with Pope's clear and obvious incompetence.

These letters from Porter, meant to be private thoughts to a friend *and all true*, were taken as proof of a clear mark of Porter's disrespect for Pope. That was also true but, at no time did it interfere with Porter's duty. Pope was in command but appeared to be the last man to know Longstreet was coming.

Because of the letters, *and from whatever urging he had from Secretary of War Stanton*, Judge Advocate Holt made no bones about his personal prejudice for Porter. During the court martial, Judge Holt said, "The purpose *(of the letters)* was very obvious, to show the animus of the accused towards his commanding officer at or about the same time the alleged acts of disobedience took place. These dispatches enabled the Court to give a true interpretation to these acts and understand the spirit of these acts." *(Court Martial Record, Pp.221-224, 301)*

COURT MARTIAL

The court martial convened in the city of Washington D.C., in the large conference room of the Justice building on 10th Street in a downtown part of the Capitol, except for the one day when Colonel Elisha Johnson testified for the defense. On that day the court members and the attorneys crowded into the sick room where Johnson lay recovering from a frightful battle wound he incurred at the Battle of Antietam.

The trial began on December 2, 1862, and continued for *only* 13 days. The nine members and the judge advocate heard the charges. The hearing was to determine the guilt or innocence of General Fitz John Porter, a member of the Union Army.

The FIRST CHARGE was a violation of the Ninth Article of War, disobedience to an order. The charge listed five specifications; separate acts of misconduct. The FIRST THREE SPECIFICATIONS were, allegedly, Porter's disobedience to each of three different orders from Pope.

THE FOURTH AND FIFTH SPECIFICATIONS OF THE FIRST CHARGE not only alleged disobedience of orders, it claimed that Porter *permitted* Brigadier General A.S. Piatt's brigade to march out of action to Centreville, instead of marching with the rest of his troops to Gainesville.

The SECOND CHARGE was a violation of the Fifty-Second Article of War, refusal to attack the enemy. The SECOND CHARGE carried three specifications of misconduct. THE THREE SPECIFICATIONS were all similar in wording but with minor differences. Essentially, the three specifications charged that Porter disobeyed orders to fight while in the face of the enemy and that he shamefully retreated causing the loss of the battle to the enemy.

On the basis of these charges, Fitz John Porter was blamed for Pope's defeat at the Second Battle of Manassas. Yet, Porter informed the court that day, that earlier he had conversed on the steps of the courthouse with Pope, and Pope had 'Preferred *no charges* whatever against me.' Evidently, before these proceedings had commenced, someone had perpetrated an intricate web of lies meant to take all the ineptitude of Pope and shift it over to blame the innocent General Porter. This horrid mistake was so extraordinary and unusual that it went beyond a mere blunder.

The makeup of the trial court was bizarre. Two Generals, King and Ricketts, were fighting in different parts of the battle five miles apart at the identical moment when Porter was accused of doing, or failing to do, certain acts that affected King and Ricketts. Ricketts was fighting at Thoroughfare Gap and King was fighting on the Warrenton Turnpike. Yet, these two men were appointed as members of the court and held a deciding vote in the court that judged Porter. Further, adding insult to injury, King was called by the prosecution *as a prosecution witness*. His testimony helped make out a case for the prosecution.

MEMBERS OF THE COURT

It soon became clear that the nine members of the court martial against General Fitz John Porter were chosen carefully for a specific task: find Porter guilty. Major David Hunter, President of the court, was a close political ally of Lincoln and a veteran of the First Battle of Bull Run. Major General E.A. Hitchcock had advised Lincoln during the time when McClellan had repeatedly failed to go on the offensive against Lee. And everyone knew Fitz John Porter was McClellan's protégé and fair haired boy.

General Napoleon Bonaparte Buford, another member of the nine-man court, was the half-brother to John Buford, the cavalry officer who reported to Irvin McDowell, *'Seventeen divisions, five hundred cavalry and artillery passing through Gainesville'* on the morning of August 28. This information had provided a clear warning as to Longstreet's arrival on the battlefield, and was news McDowell had failed to forward to Pope.

Other members of the court included Brigadier Benjamin Prentiss who had served with Ulysses S. Grant. Prentiss had been recently released from Confederate hands in a prisoner exchange.

Brigadier General Rufus King, who had commanded a division during the battle, was Lincoln's former emissary to Rome. During most of the battle, King had been absent because he was suffering from epilepsy and General Hatch had taken command.

Brigadier General James Ricketts, another of McDowell's commanders, was the man that had tried in a night-long battle at Thoroughfare Gap, unsuccessfully, to prevent Longstreet from coming to Jackson's rescue on August 29.

Brigadier Silas Casey was a career General and an author of several military books on tactics.

Brigadier General James Garfield was a hero of the battle of Shiloh. He had recently returned East because of poor health. Garfield had been elected to the House of Representatives for Ohio.

Brigadier General John P. Slough was the military governor of the City of Alexandria.

Each of these men were depending on promotion from General Halleck. Each of these men, who voted for Porter's conviction, were promoted. The one man that did not vote for Porter's conviction, General James Ricketts, *was not promoted.*

PORTER'S CHIEF COUNCIL

Reverdy Johnson, who was Porter's chief council, was a powerhouse in Democratic politics in 1862. Unfortunately, with the rise of the Republicans and with Abraham Lincoln as President, Reverdy was swimming against the tide when he agreed to argue for Fitz John Porter. It didn't help that Reverdy had represented the slave owner in the Dred Scott case. That role, defending slavery, placed a black mark on his career with the Republican army leadership. However, his staunch support for the Union during the Civil War helped to redeem him. Personally opposed to slavery, like the defendant, Reverdy Johnson fought to keep Maryland in the Union. After the Civil War he served in the administration of President Zachary Taylor with honor.

DEFENSE OPENING STATEMENT

Porter was given the opportunity of an opening statement.

He began by saying, "Pope has preferred no charges whatever against me. Evidently, thereof, at the very onset of these proceedings, and even before these proceedings commenced, someone in connection with these proceedings had perpetrated a mistake so extraordinary and unusual that it should rather be called a blunder. I ask the court to consider whether this mistake or blunder does not cast a strong and strange suspicion over the origin and the inception of this whole accusation."

RUGGLES' TESTIMONY

According to Ruggles' testimony, Pope held a conversation with Colonel Ruggles on the fifth or sixth of September, two or three days after his conversation with Porter at Fairfax Court House. When Colonel Ruggles was cross-examined by the judge advocate about Pope's declaration *(that Pope was entirely satisfied with Porter's explanations)* on 2 September, Ruggles made this statement:

"General Pope told me that he did not wish to appear as a witness against General Porter. He told me that I should appear as the principal witness. I told him I was not acquainted with the circumstances of the case. Orders had been issued by General Pope that day that I knew nothing of. General Pope said to me, *'You know that such orders were given?'*"

"I answered, *'Yes, sir.'*"

"He said, *'And you know they were not carried out?'*"

"I answered, *'That is what I had been told; that was my impression.'*"

"He said then, *'That is sufficient.'*"

"He said that I would be summoned as the principal witness. I reminded General Pope of that conversation. I felt I was not sufficiently conversant with the case. I reported this conversation to the adjutant general of the army, and to Colonel Kelton, his assistant. I requested that General Pope should be summoned as a witness in the case."

QUESTIONS

Porter next objected to the *legality* of the trial. Porter questioned who, exactly, *had* proffered charges against him. Was it John Pope? Or did some other agency or person bring the charges *illegally?* General Porter posed an intriguing question to the Court.

Porter: "I desire to be informed whether the charges were signed, since the signature to the charges appears to be signed by an *officer of Pope's staff (General Ruggles, Pope's chief of staff)* for General Pope. If that is true, and this court was convened by John Pope, or any other officer, then *this is not a legal proceeding* under the 1830 provisions of the Statute. That law requires the court *must be convened by the president* and not by order of General in Chief Halleck."

"It appears that this general court martial was convened by a general order, which dissolved a military commission *(an illegal tribunal)*, as the order convening it recites, to investigate and report on certain charges proffered against me by Major General Pope."

"If the charges were made by General Pope, then this court is not legal. The provision of the Statute of 1830 requires a court, such as this, to be convened by the president of the United States, and not, as this one is, to be convened by General in Chief Halleck."

Judge Advocate Holt and Halleck, his boss, had made a serious legal error. Porter was right. It was an illegal court martial. Holt squirmed a little and then, after a closed door session, replied to Porter's objection.

Judge Advocate Holt: "The accused refers to the order, which appointed a military commission. It is true that it was said that the charges were proffered by General Pope. That was an error. In fact, no charges were proffered by Pope. That commission has been dissolved. This general court martial has been appointed by a special order from the headquarters of the army *(Which in fact was illegal. Only the president could convene the court martial)*. The new order makes no charges and General Pope is not the prosecutor in this case."

With that long-winded slippery statement, the judge advocate cleared the room. The doors were closed and the commission retired to decide what to do about Porter's objection. After some time, the doors were opened. The judge advocate had found a crafty way around the law, by ignoring the law.

Judge Advocate Holt: "The objection is overruled. The court is properly organized and the accused shall plead to the Charges and Specifications." *(Trial Record, P. 11:379)*

The trial *was* illegal. In violation of the sixty-fourth, sixty-fifth, and seventy-fifth articles of war, the trial court, as it was constituted, was illegal.

The Articles of War, the sixty-fourth article reads: *'General court martials may consist of any number of commissioned officers from five to thirteen, inclusively; but they shall not consist of less than thirteen when the number can be convened without manifest injury to the service.'*

This rule applies for even the most trivial offense. Washington was filled with high titled military men and Fitz John Porter's honor and his life were at stake. Couldn't Halleck and Pope have found more than nine officers?

The sixty-fifth article reads: *'Whenever a general officer, commanding an army, shall be the prosecutor or the accuser of any officer in the army of the United States under his command, the general court martial for the trial shall be appointed by the president of the United States.'*

The seventy-fifth article reads: *'No officer shall be tried by officers of lower rank if it can be avoided. Nor shall any proceeding be carried on except between the hours of 8 in the morning and 3 in the afternoon.'*

Of the nine officers appointed by the court only two held commissions of the same grade as Porter. There were, at this same time thirty officers in the army who were superior in grade to Major General Porter. Also, the proceedings of the court show that its sessions were held regardless of the time parameters.

Porter had a decision to make. He had the law on his side. He was so certain that the court, after hearing the evidence, would find him innocent and his name would be cleared that he did not pursue the matter. He pled *'Not Guilty'* to all charges. The trial commenced. The judge advocate was impatient to get the trial over with.

When Porter asked *(as was his right)* for the judge to prepare a written reply to Porter's defense, Judge Holt said to the court, "To prepare a written reply to the argument of the accused would require several days. It would involve a delay, which it is most important to avoid."

This was almost an unvarnished admission that the court was a 'pro forma' assembly. It was for show. The sentence had already been decided.

One of the members of the court, General B.C. Roberts, testified for the prosecution and against Porter. This sad state of affairs at Porter's court martial was contrary to all the laws of justice and the laws on the books in 1862. The secretary of war, Edwin Stanton, instructed the court on January 5, 1863, to finish its business quickly. He had sent the president of the court, General Hunter, a notice the month before, on December 5, 1862. Secretary Stanton was brief but his message was clear. He wanted the *'Porter matter'* finished, and quickly. *'The proceeding should be brought to a close speedily.'* *(Trial Record, Pp. 269:379)*

The administration touted the thoroughness and length of Porter's examination as lasting 45 days. In actuality, it took only 13 days. General Schofield's later condemnation of that trial during Porter's rehearing many years later, was to the point:

"A judge, who has in his hands the life of a human being, is not permitted to be in a hurry. He may grow weary listening to the evidence and in examining facts, but when he reaches the solemn moment of judgment he must deliberate unembarrassed by the hurly-burly of the outside world."

General Schofield added a sarcastic line of English poetry to his denunciation.

"Men must hang that jurymen may dine."

As the trial opened, Porter stood up and took the witness chair. Tall and handsome, he carried himself proudly. He wore the dark blue uniform, epaulets and the stars of a Union major general. Head up, shoulders braced, he was the epitome of a leader and a soldier in the Union Army of the United States. Fitz John Porter, commanding the army's fifth corps, was General George McClellan's most trusted subordinate.

Porter had served in the war with Mexico from 1846 to 1849, when he was promoted by Generals Zackary Taylor and Winfield Scott to the rank of captain and then to major for *'gallantry in action'* in the storming of Chapultepec. He was an instructor at West Point for six years and part of the Utah Expedition as chief of staff to Albert Sidney Johnston. In 1860 and 1861, with the Civil War looming, Porter supervised the withdrawal of troops from Texas and was placed in charge of protecting the railroads between Washington and the North.

When McClellan picked him to head the new fifth army corps, Porter was sent to Hanover Junction to clear McDowell's path of Confederate troops. His orders were to protect McClellan's right flank by driving Confederate soldiers away from Hanover Court House *(which was north of Richmond)* because McClellan was about to attack the Southern capitol. In this, as in most of his endeavors for McClellan, Porter was successful.

❧ 50 ❧

Kangaroo Court

If once a man indulges himself in murder,
Very soon he comes to think little of robbing;
From robbing he next comes to drinking and Sabbath breaking,
And from that to incivility and procrastination.
"Murder considered one of the Fine Arts"

Thomas De Quincy, 1827

Secretary of War Edwin Stanton's role in the trial and conviction of General Fitz John Porter was not trivial. The trial was the most important military trial of the century to that time. Porter's conviction was a supreme tragedy. What Stanton did in packing the kangaroo court, in accepting false testimony, and in closing his eyes conveniently to John Pope's and Irvin McDowell's guilt, was a crime.

Secretary Stanton added insult to injury by fighting tooth and nail to stop any possibility of a rehearing for Porter that might have shown the light of truth on the allegations, all despicable acts by a man in one of the most important jobs in America in 1863.

Tragedy and comedy are close cousins. I placed De Quincy's satiric quotation at the head of the chapter to reflect a need for my readers (*and I most of all*) to see the comedy in this twenty-year drama. Perhaps, as well, to illustrate a saying I recall from years ago on the mastiff of the Detroit Times newspaper that I delivered as a boy to my fifty-odd country customers in 1938; *'What Fools We Mortals Be....'*

The first prosecution witness for the trial who would decide General Fitz John Porter's guilt or innocence was, as you might have guessed, John Pope. Pope was summoned and his time as a witness stretched over a period of four days in December, from the second to the fifth. As Pope testified, his answers were devious. He had to have been nervous, aware that *he* might *also* face charges for his ineptitude at Manassas. He tried, with his testimony, to save his skin at the trial and pass the blame to the chosen easy mark: Porter.

John Pope succeeded in avoiding Porter's fate, but in the long run justice was served on Pope. After all, the administration had hand-picked John Pope for the job of leading the Army of Virginia. For Stanton to blame the true villains for the loss of Second Manassas was not an option for the Republican administration. To admit their bad choice at a time when the government might fall for the string of lost battles to the rebels, facing the hundreds of coffins lining the docks in the port of New York, was not an option. Pope's leadership had been an utter failure. Such an admission would have shaken the people's confidence mightily in the government.

Pope's failures as a general and as a man were no secret. Most persons high in government knew Pope was a poor leader and a bad general. Soon after the trial John Pope was banished to the hinterlands and sent to the West to fight Indians.

McDowell, who deserved a share of the blame for Manassas, received his just due as well. Never again was he given a leadership position. Pope and McDowell may have received some small share of what they deserved for their failures on the Plain of Manassas, but the destruction and the damage they left in their wake was the ruination of a good man's life.

TRIAL AND TESTIMONY

The trial began in the winter of the second year of the war, 1862. Major General Hunter, the president of the court, read the first charge.

"Major General Fitz John Porter received a lawful order from Major General John Pope, his superior and commanding officer, on August 27 while at Warrenton Junction. Major General Porter did then and there disobey the said order, being at the time in the face of the enemy. This occurred at or near Warrenton, in the State of Virginia, on or about the 28th of August, 1862. The order read as follows:"

'The Major General commanding directs you start at 1 o'clock tonight, and come forward with your whole corps, or such part of it as with you, so as to be at Bristoe Station by daylight tomorrow morning. Hooker has had very severe action with the enemy, with a loss of about 300 killed and wounded. The enemy has been driven back, but is retiring above a railroad. We must drive him from Manassas, and clear the country between that place and Gainesville where McDowell is. If Morell has not joined you, send word to him, to push forward immediately, and send word to Banks to hurry forward with all speed, and take your place at Warrenton Junction. It is necessary, by all accounts that you should be here by daylight. I send an officer with this dispatch, who will conduct you to this place. Be sure to send word to Banks, who is on the road to Fayetteville, probably in the direction of Bealeton. Say to Banks, also, that he had best run back the railroad trains to this side of Cedar Run. If he is not with you, write him to that effect.'

'P.S. If Banks is not at Warrenton Junction, leave a regiment of infantry and two pieces of artillery as a guard until he comes up, with instructions to follow you immediately. If Banks is not at the Junction, instruct Colonel Clary to run the train back to this side of Cedar Run, and post a regiment and section of artillery with it.'

This order from General Pope typifies Pope's liking for wordiness and a lack of clarity and precise instructions. Later, the famous *Joint Order* was a prime example of Pope's lack of clarity. Further, that order created problems for Pope that helped Pope lose the battle.

Note: Hereafter, when a witness offered testimony during Porter's general court martial, the source of that testimony is directly from the Official Records of the Proceedings, from Series I, Volume XII, Part One Supplement, as shown by page(s) number, followed by total number of pages of the text. Example: *(P. 100:379)*.

The Prosecution called General Pope as its first witness.

Court: "Explain the reasons for the urgency of the *(1 AM)* order, as indicated, to arrive at Bristoe Station *by daylight.*"

Pope offered a lengthy explanation of his reasons for the urgent need to comply with his 1 AM order *(P. 13:379)*. For the sake of brevity Pope's order for Porter to arrive by morning, he argued four points:

Hooker's division faced Ewell's forces four miles west of Bristoe Station and he needed help.

Hooker was almost out of ammunition with five rounds left per man. His situation was perilous and Porter's presence was essential.

If A.P. Hill learned how weakened Hooker's forces were, without help, Hooker would be overrun. If that happened, A.P. Hill would probably attack at first light. This point was to stress the need for Porter to arrive at Bristoe Station with his division as soon as possible.

The facts were these:

Despite the unusual difficulty in marching on a moonless night on an unfamiliar road filled with all manner of obstacles, Porter brought his 9,000 men the three miles to Bristoe Station by 9 AM with his troops ready for action by 10 AM.

By the time Porter arrived, the Confederate general, Richard Ewell, was long gone to join Jackson on Stony Ridge above the Warrenton Turnpike.

Pope never told Porter about Hooker's lack of ammunition and Hooker's insufficient forces against Ewell's Confederates. As it turned out, Porter sat on his hands all that day at Bristoe Station waiting for orders and receiving none, until the next morning.

When Porter arrived at Bristoe Station, he wrote a note to Pope to detail for the record why he was unable to bring his 9,000 infantrymen to Bristoe Station until nine o'clock instead of early morning; a delay of three hours. That all-important note and its contents were an important part of Porter's defense. It would have shown Porter's reason for the delay and, by Pope's acceptance of the note's contents, Pope's acknowledgment of those reasons. Pope was asked about the note. He shrugged his shoulders and admitted he could not find it; which was contrary to army regulations, especially during battle.

Court: "Did Porter explain the reason why he did not obey your order?

Pope: "He wrote me a note. I have mislaid the note." *(P. 14:379)*

As the reporter of Porter's affair I trust my readers will remember and be impressed with Pope's claim that he *'mislaid'* the note, which note, if present before the court would have *entirely invalidated the First Charge.*

Porter stopped the interrogation about the missing note. He interrupted the testimony. That missing note was a crucial piece of defense evidence. He wanted the note in evidence.

He asked Pope, "Have you looked for the note?"

Pope replied, "I have looked for it but I have not been able to find it." (*P. 14:379*)

Pope never *denied* having such a note. He was asked repeatedly about the note and each time the subject came up, Pope claimed it had been *'misplaced'* and that he would search his papers.

Knowing Pope's determination to place all the blame for the loss at Manassas on Porter, anyone at the trial who knew that a government conspiracy was taking place. They would know it was most unlikely Pope would ever find the all-important note. In wartime the first rule of military communications is that any writing relating to a battle; a scrap of paper, a note, a dispatch, a letter or a telegram *must* be filed and carefully preserved.

That crucial note gave clear reasons why Porter *could not* obey the 1 AM order exactly. Far more to the point and proof of what the note contained was the testimony. Much of trial testimony, which supported the truth of Porter's claims, was kept from President Lincoln. Further, much of the evidence supporting Porter's innocence *was never made a part of the judge advocate's final report*.

The testimony from the four generals and several officers of high rank who were there at Manassas during those three days in August 1862, verified the truth of Porter's testimony. Hundreds of supply wagons clogged the narrow road with no wagon master in command, troops marched with no sleep after a long march the day before, in darkness so great regiments got lost. Men fell into deep ditches and ravines. Streams had to be crossed in darkness. Flimsy, broken plank bridges stretched precariously over streams where more than one horse fell to the waters below in the dark night crossing. The railroad track, next to the narrow road, was broken with upturned ties and a path no column of men could follow in the utterly black night.

These difficulties weighed against strict compliance to the 1 AM Order. These obstacles were what made General Porter (*fully supported by his division heads*) arrive at a viable decision as to the best way to obey the spirit of the order and still be ready to fight in the morning. To delay the march two hours, until it was light enough to see the way without falling over one another and getting lost, was the only way to carry out the spirit of the order. Military law, based on Napoleonic battle strategy, states unequivocally that a general in the field, when his superior is absent, has the right and the duty to make necessary changes in an order that will yet comply with the spirit of the order.

That is what Porter did.

Every man, who was there that dark rainy night of August 27, confirmed the hard conditions of Porter's march with sworn testimony. Porter's decision to march at 3 AM instead of 1 AM was the right thing to do. It was what military principles demanded.

Why did the court choose to ignore testimony which established the truth? This is not hard to understand. This court had an *absolute imperative* from powerful Secretary of War Edwin Stanton, and from aging but still powerful General in Chief Henry Wager Halleck, that Porter must be found guilty.

An interesting aside is a comment Lincoln made. He described Halleck as *'little more than a first rate clerk.'*

General Pope, when he gave his testimony, cast aside all of Porter's reasons for the delay in marching. Pope claimed to the court that the obstacles Porter cited *did not exist*. Yet, a dozen credible witnesses testified that Porter was right and Pope was wrong. General Heintzelman, Dr. Abbott, General Morell, Captain Fitfield, Lieutenant Weld, Lieutenant Colonel Locke, General Griffin, General Reynolds, Major Hyland, General Sykes, General Butterfield, and Lieutenant Colonel Brinton confirmed Porter's testimony.

Court: "What was the character of the night? Was there starlight?"

Pope: "It was a clear night. There was no difficulty in marching. There was no obstruction to the movement of infantry. If there were blockages, the railroad tracks were clear." *(P. 14-15: 379)*

And he didn't even stutter when he told those lies.

Dr. Abbott was the next witness. Surgeon Robert O. Abbott was well respected as an honest and direct person. After the battle, Abbott was appointed medical director for the many military hospitals in Washington. He was with General Porter that night and Judge Advocate Holt asked Abbott about the conditions on the road. *(P. 74-81:379)*

Court: "When you were with General Porter in the night, between August 25 and 28, state the condition of the road?"

Dr. Abbott: "The road was a great deal blocked, with wagons and straggling troops."

Court: "At what time did reveille sound that morning?

Dr. Abbott: "We started very early, I recollect, soon after daylight. Some of the troops were in advance of us already."

Court: "What was the character of the night, dark or clear?"

Dr. Porter: "It was a dark night."

There was a curious conversation before the arrest and trial, between General Porter and General Pope at the Fairfax Courthouse in Washington on September 28. This is as near as truth to what occurred, given by the testimony of men who were there.

Porter came to Pope asking why McClellan had sent Pope a copy of a letter urging Porter to support Pope in the coming fight at Manassas. Such a letter would have no earthly reason for being sent by McClellan to Pope *unless* something or someone had stated or written disparaging remarks about Porter's loyalty to Pope, his superior.

The truth is this: McClellan had seen copies of letters Porter wrote to Burnside. General Ambrose Burnside was in command of a division and he was so well respected by the administration that he had twice been asked to lead *all the armies of the Union*. He refused, until later in the Civil War.

In some of Porter's private correspondence to his friend Burnside, Porter was candid about his lack of confidence in Pope's leadership. He was right of course,

Pope was a bad leader, but it was a mistake to make such feelings known and Porter paid dearly for his indiscretion.

The letters reached General in Chief Halleck. Halleck, most likely, instructed McClellan in the strongest terms to set his protégé Porter straight, and back the commanding general in the battle to come at Manassas. Burnside, Porter's friend, had sent the letters to Halleck to help Porter's case. Burnside was trying to show Halleck that the job at Manassas was too much for Pope, and time proved that was certainly the case in spades.

That day on the steps of the Fairfax Courthouse, Porter had his conversation with Pope about the letters. He wished to let John Pope know, regardless of his personal feelings, at all times he had been loyal to Pope as his superior officer, which was true by any measure based on what Porter did during the battle.

"I always did my best to carry out all of your orders," he told General Pope.

Pope's reply to Porter's statement was words to the effect, "I am satisfied with you."

At the time Pope's reply meant to Porter that Pope agreed Porter did nothing that Pope had reason to complain of. Porter left that thirty-minute meeting *(Porter's recollection of the time)* confident that despite rumors Porter had heard, Pope planned to take no action against Porter for the letters. Instead, after that meeting, John Pope testified that the letters had *'opened his eyes'* to Porter's desire to undermine Pope's command. When asked later, Pope denied any memory of his remarks to Porter.

Court: "Did you express yourself satisfied?"

Pope: "I have no remembrance of that."

Pushed, Pope lied.

"I told him I was I was *not* satisfied with his duties, his disobedience at Bristoe Station, and the absence of Griffin and Piatt on the battlefield. The conversation lasted three minutes."

Pushed further, Pope admitted, "Perhaps five minutes."

Pushed again by cross examination, he said. "The conversation might have lasted longer, but not a half hour."

The single important charge against Porter could have been boiled down to less than 30 words. General Porter opened his defense with a statement.

"The only point on which I should have been charged with disobedience was in commencing my march at 3 o'clock in the morning, instead of at 1 o'clock."

Porter was asked a few questions having to do with the state of the troop's fatigue from the earlier long march that day. He was asked whether the ten-mile march did commence at 3 AM. Porter answered in the affirmative and his answers were fully corroborated by the other witnesses. Counsel for Porter, Reverdy Johnson, called General George Sykes to tell about the staff meeting Porter held with his division commanders, prior to making the decision to delay the march. General George Sykes was Porter's second division commander.

Reverdy Johnson: "Describe the staff meeting."

General George Sykes: "At 10 PM, 27 August, General Porter sent for me. In his tent I met General Morell, General Butterfield and Captain DeKay. I was told about the order to march at 1 AM and we talked it over. We agreed nothing could be gained by marching at 1 AM, rather than at dawn. My reasons were that a night march was always injurious to the troops and exceedingly fatiguing. My command had already marched 12 to 14 miles that day and the darkness would cause confusion. A constant stream of wagons had passed ahead of us all afternoon. If we waited two or three hours, daylight would come, perhaps by in three hours. We would march in much better order and more rapidly if we started then at 3 AM instead of at 1 AM." *(P. 217-218: 379)*

Johnson: "And what were the conditions and the state of visibility for marching?"

Sykes: "The night was unusually dark. I sent an aid-de-camp to find the road. He returned and told me the darkness was so great he could not distinguish the road. We marched at 3 AM and two miles from camp, we ran upon a train of wagons encumbering the roads for miles. My mounted escort had to draw sabers to make way for my troops. General Porter made all the wagons to park so the troops could get through. At one point a column was delayed an hour by the wagons. In my military life I have never had so much trouble with wagons as I had that night." *(P. 219-221:379)*

General Morell, commanding Porter's first division, was the next defense witness to offer testimony.

Johnson: "General Morell, when you moved at 3 o'clock did you encounter difficulties in the march?"

Morell: "Yes, sir, until we had the advantage of daylight, there was a great deal of difficulty. Men got lost in the dark, wagons blocked the way and men marched through many small streams, over ruts and ditches in the road that caused the troops to stumble and fall into confusion." *(P. 178-180:379)*

General Morell was asked to testify as to the darkness of the night and the condition of the weather that night.

Morell: "We all expressed in strong terms the difficulty of moving at 1 o'clock rather than 3 o'clock. It was a very dark night and threatening to rain. It did rain before morning. If we had marched at 1 o'clock the men would have been kept up all night. Some of the men did not get into camp until dark." *(P. 180-185:379)*

General Griffin, the next witness, had led the second brigade, and was even more emphatic. When asked by Counsel Johnson if, considering the need for having General Porter's troops at Bristoe Station quickly, starting at 1 o'clock as ordered would have been judicious or expedient. His reply was short.

Griffin: "Decidedly not." *(P. 197:379)*

Asked about the hazards of marching in darkness he replied with equal stress.

Griffin: "If we had started at daylight, we would have arrived at Bristoe Station even sooner that we did by starting at 3 o'clock. We would not have had the stoppages that we had; we had to use candles to get through a piece of woods. Several times we were forced to halt." *(P. 197-201:379)*

Johnson: "Why were you forced to halt?"

Griffin: "Part of my brigade got lost in the darkness." *(P. 203:379)*

Griffin's battle reports told in detail how an entire regiment strayed off the road in the blackness into the dense woods beside the road. Men fell on one another, some strayed farther in to the dark and it took nearly half an hour to find the lost souls and gather the regiment together, with candles to light the way.

General Butterfield was asked the same questions.

Johnson: "How far had your men marched on the previous day?"

Butterfield: "They were very much fatigued. They had marched from Ellis Ford to Bealeton and from there to Warrenton; almost all the way, 14 miles, without water and in the dust. It was very warm." *(P. 227-230:379)*

General Porter questioned Major George Hyland, the officer who was a part of the 13th New York Regiment, who marched to Warrenton on the day and the night of August 27th. This march ended near midnight of the 27th and just as General Porter received the order from Pope to begin a new march at 1 AM to Bristoe Station.

Porter: "What was the condition of your regiment when you arrived August 27?"

Hyland: "They were very much fatigued and worn out. They also needed provisions as they had had no provisions that day to any amount." *(P. 214:379)*

Heintzelman commanded the entire third corps, five thousand troops. Like General Porter, Heintzelman had been part of McClellan's Army of the Potomac before he was transferred to Pope's command. Heintzelman testified next. *(Trial proceedings text, P. 156,157:227)*

Court: "What was the condition of the road between Warrenton Junction and Bristoe Station on the evening of August 27?"

Heintzelman: "It was a narrow road, in tolerable condition. A part of it ran through some woods. It was not a very good road. The troops could only march in line. There were a few little ditches that were bad crossing, and the road crossed a railroad once or twice. These crossings were bad."

Court: "What obstructions on that road would have impeded the movement of a large number of troops?"

Heintzelman: "There was a large train of wagons in front of the command, a considerable obstruction. The road was obstructed by wagons. The five miles of road to Bristoe Station was filled with army trains and wagons bumping into each other." *(P. 97:379)* *(Two or three thousand wagons, led by teams of horses, were on that road, according to other testimony.)*

Court: "What was the character of the night?"

Heintzelman: "The night was very dark. In the course of the night we had a drizzling rain. Our tents were not pitched and we lay down in the rain. We had difficulty getting our wagons up. It was so dark, moving the wagons out of the road for Porter's five-mile march in the pitch darkness, would have been an impossible task." *(P. 98, 99:379)*

Lieutenant Colonel Brinton, of the Second Pennsylvania Cavalry stationed at Catlett's Station nearby, offered his recall of that night.

Colonel Brinton: "The night was very dark and overcast. It was difficult to distinguish the road or any objects on it. The road was blocked with wagons and we ran into them constantly. Near Catlett's Station the road is a narrow one. It leads into a wood and it was difficult for us to get along. We ran into a tree on one hand, or a wagon on the other, without being able to distinguish until we were upon it." *(P. 253-254:379)*

Johnson: "Would orderly movement of masses of troops along that road have been practicable?"

Brinton: "They may have marched in single file, following each other in that way. I think it was almost impossible to move a body of cavalry or infantry over that road at night." *(P. 254-256:379)*

Counsel Reverdy Johnson argued to the court that General Porter's distinguished record ought to put him beyond any possible question of wrongdoing. After his statement, Johnson questioned Porter by asking Porter about his conversation with Pope's emissary, Captain DeKay. DeKay had been responsible for guiding Porter's troops over the road to Bristoe Station.

Johnson: "Did Captain DeKay say anything about having difficulty as a guide in showing the road?"

Porter: "He made some remark to the effect that it would be hard work to find the way."

Porter summarized what he knew of the situation that night.

"The order commanded me to hasten forward as soon as possible from Warrenton Junction to Bristoe Station, in order to be ready there as early as practicable to cooperate with my force against the enemy. I received the order at 10 PM that night."

"It had been written three hours earlier by General Pope who was five miles away. General Pope could not have known the character of the night at 1 AM. He did not know the condition of my troops, who had marched ten miles without delay or rest. General Pope did not know, when his order reached me, the roads were obstructed and impassable for masses of my 10,000 troops in the darkness."

"There was no moon and it was raining. My artillery got stuck fast more than once, yet I had to bring my guns forward. The order called for me to leave two guns with Banks. I could not leave my artillery behind. For my men to go into battle without artillery would be madness. Another time, threading our way through some dense wood, the men had to light candles to find their way."

"Before we marched, I sent two officers to ascertain the condition of the road in the darkness. By marching at 1 AM in the early morning of 28 August, instead of 3 AM as I did, I would have lost time and greatly impaired the strength and efficiency of my troops upon arrival at Bristoe Station. I decided, in concurrence with my other generals, to march at 3 AM, which was done. Even at 3 AM the troops fell into confusion from the darkness and the crowded road. Part of the column was forced to halt and wait for daylight to extricate the artillery from the marshy ground from where it had become stuck fast."

A fact glossed over by the judge advocate and never asked was what happened *after* Porter and his men arrived at Bristoe Station.

"General Pope's 1 AM Order informed me that I must bring my troops to assist Hooker's division quickly. He claimed that I failed to do so when I knew Hooker's ammunition was nearly gone."

This was mentioned by Porter, because if Porter had known Hooker's ammunition was gone, he could and would, almost certainly, sent horses ahead with wagons and ammunition so that Hooker's men could continue their fight.

"General Pope stated that the want of ammunition in General Hooker's division, who was near the vicinity of Bristoe Station, was his (Pope's) immediate and principal cause of the urgent terms in his order directing me to hasten forward. But I was *never informed of this* and *no such cause of urgency* was alluded to in General Pope's order."

"Although the Order makes express reference to the state and position of General Hooker's division, there was *not a single word of proof* tending to show that I knew or suspected, or in any way could have known, that his ammunition was nearly exhausted."

"It should also be born in mind that the very trains upon the railroad, which General Pope directed me to have used to hurry forward to Bristoe Station, were under the supervision of Colonel Clary, *and were themselves laden with ammunition* which, though I did not know the fact, was there and needed for General Hooker."

Porter concluded.

"I rest my defense upon the grounds stated. I executed the order in its full spirit and meaning, to the best of my judgment and ability. The only point of which I am charged with disobedience to is in commencing my march at three o'clock in the morning instead of at one. The right of a general commanding an army corps to exercise judicious discretion in regard to the best method of executing an order from his commanding general at a distance is too well settled in military law and military practice to admit of question."

General Porter followed his statement with a citation of one of Napoleon's maxims on obedience to a military order.

Reading from his notes, he quoted, *'A military order exacts passive obedience only when it is given by a superior, who is present on the spot at the moment when he gives the order. Having knowledge of the state of things, he can listen to objections and give the necessary explanations to him who should execute the order. This is not only military law and authority; it is the only view compatible with the nature of military dictates of common sense.'*

Porter summarized his defense to the charges.

"I am not guilty of this charge or of any of the charges. I performed my duties at all times in keeping with Napoleon's maxim. Good judgment in hindsight leads me to believe I should have waited even longer *(than 3 AM)*, until dawn, before marching. Had I fixed the hour at 1 AM and caused reveille, with my corps already almost broken down from fatigue and long marches, I would have made worse their stumbling about their camps in the thick darkness of the night in order to attempt to move into the road and grope and stagger and struggle about in vain through the night to no use and only to have the day dawn on inextricable confusion and broken strength a mile or two beyond camp. I would have done an act of wanton cruelty to my command and at the same time perpetrated a gross and inexcusable military blunder."

By this time General Porter was weary. The court martial was long and tiring for the defendant. When he finished a summary statement of his defense he returned to his seat. He stood ramrod straight and displayed not the least sign of the grueling examination, and the certain injury of Pope's lying testimony and convenient loss of memory.

❧ 51 ❧

First Charge

The *SECOND SPECIFICATION* to the FIRST CHARGE was for disobeying the *Joint Order*. The specification dealt with an order issued by Pope around 10:30 in the morning of August 29. It was when the battle along the Warrenton Turnpike was about ready to explode. The order was referred to as the *Joint Order* because it had been addressed to Porter and also to Porter's senior officer, Irvin McDowell.

Porter received his copy of the Joint Order about noon of that day, just before his troops encountered the first of Longstreet's troops, which were the right wing of Robert E. Lee's army, near Dawkins Creek on the road to Gainesville.

The court's president, General Hunter, read the *SECOND SPECIFICATION* to the FIRST CHARGE, Porter's violation of the Ninth Article of War.

"Major General Fitz John Porter, on the morning of August 29, 1862, did receive from Major General John Pope, his superior and commanding officer, a lawful order, which order Major General Porter, did then and there disobey, in the following figures and letters, to wit."

Note: So that the reader may better understand Pope's mind and why Pope made the order knowing parts of the order were based on wrong facts, the Joint Order has been separated into parts. Despite the confusing verbiage in the Order, the italicized parts of the sentences below will more clearly illustrate Pope's intentions.

1. You will please move forward with your joint commands toward Gainesville. I sent General Porter written orders to that effect an hour and a half ago. Heintzelman, Siegel, and Reno are now moving on the Warrenton Turnpike and by now must be not far from Gainesville.

2. I desire that, as soon as communication is established between this force and your own, the whole command shall halt.

3. *It may be necessary to fall back behind Bull Run, at Centreville tonight.* I presume it will not be so because of our supplies.

4. I have sent no orders of any kind to Ricketts, and *none to interfere in any way with McDowell's troops,* except what I sent to his aid-de-camp last night, which was to hold his position on the Warrenton Pike until the troops from here should fall on the enemy's flank and rear. I do not even know Ricketts' position, as I was not

able to find out where General McDowell was until a late hour this morning.

5. General McDowell will take immediate steps to communicate with General Ricketts and instruct him to join the other divisions of his corps as soon as practical.

6. If any considerable advantages are to be gained by departing from this order, *it will not be strictly carried out.*

7. One thing must be held in view: that the troops must occupy a position from which they can *reach Bull Run tonight or by morning.* The indications are that the whole force of the enemy *is moving in this direction at a pace that will bring them here by tomorrow night or the next day.* My own headquarters will for the present be at Heintzelman's corps, or at this place."

Pope's long rambling message occupied an entire page of vague, confusing and difficult rhetoric. It included some information that did not really concern Porter, and it left out some information that would have helped Porter. In spite of the smoke and sounds of firing in the west, on the afternoon of August 28th, Pope was still in the dark as to *Jackson's location.* Jackson's odd movements all the previous day and that morning kept Pope on needles and pins. Nevertheless, he was still certain that Jackson was retreating toward an escape through the Thoroughfare Gap.

Longstreet's arrival on the battlefield was another matter entirely. Although Pope continued to act and speak as though he was unaware of Longstreet's arrival, the italicized phrase of the seventh part of the order say plainly otherwise. He must have known. *He had been told* earlier of the approach of a large enemy force, not once, but by several different officers. Pope was told four times that Longstreet had arrived.

Pope received *FOUR SEPARATE REPORTS* that Lee was coming:

1. On the morning of August 29, Porter had ridden in late to the staff meeting. He gave Pope his assessment of the enemy's position, based on his first-hand experience. Porter informed Pope that General Morell's troops were at Dawkins Branch on the afternoon of the day before. He reported that Morell faced Longstreet's skirmishers all that previous afternoon.

Porter said, "I believe the troops Morell fought with were probably the same force General Buford had reported earlier."

Pope's reaction was astonishing.

"You skirmished with Jackson's rescue force. That is all they were."

With that brief statement Pope turned to other matters.

Porter testified at his court martial, "I tried to convince Pope that the force I had been fighting was a very large force. My warning was in vain. He put no confidence in what I said."

2. General Banks, under McDowell's command, had spotted troops on the Turnpike early on the morning of August 27. Banks immediately sent word to Pope: *'It seems apparent the enemy is moving upon the Valley of the Shenandoah.'*

3. On the evening of August 28, General McDowell met with Pope. He showed

General Pope John Buford's dispatch that a heavy Confederate force had passed through Gainesville at 8:30 AM that morning. Pope interpreted Buford's report to mean that Longstreet was coming to support Jackson's retreat. It was only a rear-guard action.

4. General Banks, guarding supplies and the supply trains at Warrenton, said to Pope in a dispatch that 'a *large force of the enemy* had been sighted near the Thoroughfare Gap.'

Pope's own Joint Order assumed this was the case. The Joint Order specified a *'move to Bull Run.'* Why? Obvious to the writer, it was because of a possible need to defend against Longstreet's approach behind ready-made defenses.

Pope's last statement of the Joint Order that *'a force of the enemy is moving in this direction at a pace that will bring them here by tomorrow night or the next day'* belies his certain knowledge they had *already* arrived. Pope gave an order, *ignoring his received information, for Porter to attack Jackson with* Longstreet's army in Porter's way, and Porter could not attempt to reach Jackson without risking his entire force to Longstreet's flank attack.

This part of the Joint Order illustrated Pope's gravest error; that Pope knew of a certainty, by his own testimony, that Longstreet was through the Gap by nine o'clock in the morning of August 28. Pope reasonably knew that Longstreet had deployed his 25,000 troops on the battlefield and was ready to do battle by 1 PM of that same day and not, as the Joint Order indicated Pope's fantasy, *'they will be here by tonight or tomorrow.'*

Pope criminally misjudged the importance of all reports; whether from an inability to comprehend the first-hand reports he had heard, or worse perhaps from an unwillingness to sway from his obsession with capturing Jackson and the myth of Jackson's retreat. Maybe he did not believe Longstreet had arrived in force because he did not want to believe it. Whatever the reason, from that time on and for the next seventy-two hours, all of Pope's decisions were colored by his stubborn fixation on an enemy retreat and that any other enemy sighting was merely a rescue operation for Jackson. Yet, in spite of all that, from the words of the Joint Order, *some part of Pope's mind* had accepted the possibility he was wrong and Longstreet *was* an immediate threat.

Perhaps that strange myopia and an unwillingness to face facts was a part of Pope's mental state under pressure. If true, although he had ample opportunity to take advantage of Porter's valiant all-day defense against Longstreet, Pope did nothing.

As the reader you are in a position to see all the facts, which Porter would have given everything to have had when he was faced with defending himself at the court martial, establishing a valid defense which *was proven* in his favor many years after the court martial, at his rehearing in 1878.

The other parts of the Joint Order reflect Pope's ignorance of the facts. The Order refers to Heintzelman's, Siegel's and Reno's positions. They were *nowhere near Gainesville*. They were three miles from Gainesville and none of them could ever have reached Gainesville against Longstreet's attacking force already on the field and advancing swiftly. This was the same reason that Porter could not reach Reynolds' division *(Heintzelman's corps)* to obey that part of the order.

The Joint Order gave Porter the option of remaining in position if he was forced to do so, asserting that he could fall back to Bull Run. Reverdy Johnson, Porter's counsel, questioned General Roberts, Pope's chief of staff.

Listen to the way the court threw up a smoke screen when Reverdy Johnson got too near any facts that would have shown Porter to have *obeyed* the Joint Order.

Reverdy Johnson: Is it not true that the Joint Order gave Porter discretion whether or not he must move to Gainesville and attack Jackson, depending on the situation?

(This was the part of the Joint Order which said, *'If any considerable advantages are to be gained by departing from this order, it will not be strictly carried out.'*)

Before Roberts could answer the question a member of the court stopped Roberts. He objected to the question and the courtroom was cleared. The judge advocate announced that the question was *not* to be answered. If Roberts had answered "Yes" then Porter could not have been accused of failing to attack the enemy.

The Joint Order gave Porter a command that was impossible to obey. Not then, not ever, was it possible *at any time* for Porter to *'fall on Jackson's flank and rear.'* Pope had ample opportunity and repeated warnings that Longstreet would have prevented that. After the battle all three of the leading Confederate generals: Lee, Longstreet, and Hood *testified to the truth of that fact.*

General Pope's Joint Order was a confusing rambling of vague directions and uncertainties. Mainly, it repeated the 6:30 PM, August 27th order for Porter and McDowell to march to Gainesville. This order was more detailed, specific, with added instructions, however confusing it may have been. The court martial charge, Porter's failure to *'push forward in the face of the enemy,'* was a military euphemism for cowardice. That unfair and insulting accusation must have caused Porter more pain and distress than any other.

When Pope testified at Porter's court martial he explained to his questioner, "When I issued the Joint Order sending Porter to Gainesville, I was not certain at what point, if any, of the Warrenton Turnpike east of Gainesville the enemy could be brought to a stand."

"My reasons," Pope made clear, "for sending Porter and McDowell to Gainesville was so that their two commands could meet the enemy anywhere on the Turnpike if necessary."

Pope was referring to an enemy he considered to be Stonewall Jackson and not Longstreet. Despite numerous warnings that Longstreet was on the battlefield, Pope continued to focus entirely on Jackson alone.

The *FOURTH AND FIFTH SPECIFICATIONS* to the FIRST CHARGE, like the other specifications, were read by the Court.

"In that the said Major General Fitz John Porter, being at or near Manassas Junction, on the night of the 29th August, 1862, did receive from Major General John Pope, his superior and commanding officer, a lawful order, which Major General Porter did permit one other brigade attached to his command to march to Centreville."

The Specifications contended that Porter allowed General Piatt and his brigade to run off to Centreville, instead of staying with Porter's fifth corps and carrying out

Pope's order to attack at Manassas when his brigade was needed at the battlefield. Piatt remained with his brigade in Centreville all day Saturday, August 30, near Manassas Station doing not much else but resting and eating hardtack and boiled pork.

The problem was Pope's. Pope had given Piatt's brigade to Porter... but he had never *told* Porter that Piatt was a part of his command. As a result, leaderless Piatt wandered around on his own without Porter's knowledge of the addition to his force. That was not the first time Pope was careless in his assignments. General Rufus Hatch's whole division of four brigades and 2,000 infantrymen had been given to Porter. Then Pope allowed McDowell to take Hatch away from Porter when Porter needed Hatch's division most: when he faced Longstreet's 29,000 Confederates.

Reverdy Johnson, Porter's lawyer, questioned Pope. He asked him to tell the court how and in what way General Porter disobeyed those two orders to march to Gainesville. Pope's answers as he spoke became a compelling insight into John Pope's thinking process. More than that, it revealed the true reason for Pope's complaint: he *had* to shift blame from himself.

As Pope was asked question after question, he scrambled to give convincing answers, answers that would support his claim of Porter's disobedience. Little by little, gradually, as he replied, a clear picture of Pope's duplicity was revealed.

Counsel Johnson began by asking the court to read Porter's note to Pope, which told Pope what was preventing Porter from executing the Joint Order or the 4:30 Order to attack Jackson. The court read Porter's desperate note.

'I found it impossible to communicate by crossing the road to Groveton. The enemy is in strong force on this road and they appear to have driven our forces back; the firing of the enemy has advanced and ours retired. I have determined to withdraw to Manassas. I have attempted to communicate with McDowell and Siegel but my messengers have run into the enemy. They have gathered artillery and cavalry and infantry. The advancing masses of dust show the enemy coming in force. I am now going to the head of the column to see what is passing and how affairs are going. Had you not better send your trains back?'

Signed F. J. Porter

All of his messengers had been killed or captured. When he wrote this dispatch it was in the hope this one might get through. At that hour, when he wrote this dispatch, these were the facts:

Longstreet with 29,000 men, cavalry and artillery was passing between Porter and the Warrenton Turnpike. Longstreet was on his way to attack Pope's left flank, something which Pope was still unaware.

The sounds of artillery and musket fire from Pope's forces on the Turnpike had died down. Porter believed Pope was retreating to behind Bull Run, as the Joint Order warned might happen.

Soon after he had sent this dispatch, Porter rode close to the front where Morell was holding the enemy. He saw a resumption of the fight at Groveton and on the Turnpike proving Pope *had not retreated*. Therefore, he decided to stay and fight his way toward the battle near Groveton to support the Federal army, which he did within the hour.

Counsel Johnson began his interrogation of John Pope.

Johnson: *"When did you receive this note?"*

Pope: *"The night of August 29."*

Johnson: *"Did you receive another note from the accused, and, if so, have you that other note? (Porter sent a second dispatch informing Pope that he was fighting his way to the aid of Reynolds and Heintzelman on the Turnpike).*

Pope: *(Pope equivocated)* *"The only information I received was Porter's position on the field."*

Johnson: *"Recollect, if you can, whether you received a second note stating Porter was holding his position and, if he could have King's division, he would attack, and that Morell was ready to engage the enemy?"*

Pope: *"I am not sure, perhaps my aid told me, or, perhaps, Porter sent me word. I am not quite sure about that, that if he had King's division he could make a dash, or something of the kind. Whether I was told or whether it was by note, I am not clear."*

Pope was becoming quite proficient in mislaying Porter's notes. The ones he mislaid were the same notes that would have exonerated Porter from wrongdoing and disobedience.

Johnson: *"Where was the accused when you issued your 4:30 order?"*

Pope: *"I do not know. I supposed he was somewhere on the Manassas-Gainesville Road."*

Johnson: *"Without knowing the relative positions of the enemy and accused at 4:30 PM, how could you be certain if it was in the power of the accused to turn Jackson's right flank?"*

Pope: *"I knew Jackson's position. Porter's march would take him directly to Jackson's right flank."*

Johnson: *"Did you know that at 4:30 PM, Longstreet's forces had already joined Jackson's forces and were moving in force on your flank?"*

Pope: *(One might imagine he shifted, sweating and squirming in his seat like a frog on a hot griddle)* *"I had feared the junction of those forces at any moment. I expected Longstreet's movement during the afternoon of August 29." (P. 38:379)*

Pope's statement that he feared "the junction of those forces at any moment" conflicted with his order. His Joint Order stated clearly, *'The indications are that the whole force of the enemy is moving in this direction at a pace that will bring them here by tomorrow night or the next day.' Pope was testifying with a new tune to cover his ineptitude, after not heeding his generals' information and only following his manic delusion that Jackson was retreating.*

Counsel Johnson began a new line of questioning, asking Pope on repeated occasions if he knew Longstreet's line of march, where Longstreet was, and where Porter was at the time Pope issued the 4:30 Order. Answers to *fourteen questions* on these subjects caused Pope to flounder. He gave vague answers that were not to the point.

Finally, Counsel Johnson asked,

Johnson: "Without knowing where Longstreet was or what he was doing, how did you know Porter could certainly obey the 4:30 Order?"

Pope: "I do not believe a considerable number of Longstreet's forces had reached Jackson." *(P. 39:379)*

Again, *(P. 41:379)* Pope says, "By 7 o'clock in the evening I knew from General Buford's report that a portion of Longstreet's force, numbering perhaps one-half the force under General Porter and certainly not more than two-thirds, as General Buford estimated, had passed through Gainesville."

The fact was Longstreet outnumbered Porter *three to one*. Porter had 9,000 men and Longstreet had 29,000 men and they were all in position for battle.

When asked once again in what way Porter disobeyed the order, Pope fell back on the absence of Griffin's and Piatt's force. Since they were out of the action and under Porter's command, he stated that therefore Porter disobeyed the attack order.

Here Pope had made two major mistakes. The facts were these: after Pope gave Porter the order on August 28, to go to Centreville, a part of Morell's division, losing sight of Griffin's division in the lead, got lost. Morell, believing Pope's earlier order to move to Centreville, proceeded to Centreville. When Morell reached Centreville, on the morning of August 29, as soon as he heard the sound of the guns at Groveton, without orders, he marched to the scene and joined the fight.

Piatt's brigade was a different case. Piatt was under Pope's orders. Pope had never ordered Piatt to join Porter's command and so Piatt's brigade vegetated all that day at Centreville out of the action.

The judge advocate's prejudice, which from time to time showed its face, popped up now. Porter and Counsel Johnson put their heads together and Porter suggested an idea to Johnson.

"Try logic on Pope," Porter whispered. "He admitted he knew Longstreet had appeared at Gainesville 8:30 that morning. He admitted he knew the distance to Groveton from Gainesville is no greater than five miles. Any military man knows an army moves at least a mile in an hour. Especially Lee's forces, which have moved as fast as a man can walk, two or three miles in an hour. There can be no doubt they were on the field by 10 AM and Hood reached Jackson's right side by 1 PM"

"How then, at 4:30 PM, eight hours later, when he issued the 4:30 order, and which I didn't receive until sunset, could Pope not have *known* there was no possible way for my men to get to Jackson's flank with Hood's division already there and the rest of Longstreet's 29,000 men in my front? Ask him how I could have joined Reynolds' division on the Turnpike, as his Joint Order stated, and still have reached any part of Jackson's force?"

Counsel Johnson questioned Pope. Before Pope could open his mouth, the court objected to the question.

Court: "The opinion of the witness has no bearing one way or another." *(P. 45:379)*

The court was cleared.

Bear in mind, time after time, Judge Advocate Holt had asked witnesses for their opinions based on their first-hand experience. This was exactly the same case. Reverdy Johnson asked General Pope of the Army of Virginia his opinion. Major General Pope was the *one man* whose opinion should have been based on facts, which he knew, or should have known, better than any of his officers.

When the court reopened, the judge advocate announced, "The witness shall not answer the question propounded by the accused." *(P. 45:379)*

Once more the court's pro forma intention to convict Porter was made obvious. Counsel Johnson's question to Pope was meant to give the lie to the charge of disobedience.

Johnson: "Did, or did not, General Porter engage the enemy on August 29? If he did not, was it not in violation of your orders?"

Reverdy Johnson was trying another tack to corner Pope in yet another lie. If Pope said that he knew Porter was fighting the enemy on August 29, he could not claim Porter disobeyed him. He had to have known Porter was fighting an enemy from the notes he acknowledged Porter sent him that afternoon and from McDowell, who had seen the enemy skirmishers fighting Morell's troops. If Pope said that Porter disobeyed him, how could he have justified his three orders to fight the enemy?

Once more the judge advocate saved Pope's bacon. *He objected to the question.* After clearing the court on his return the judge decided to pose the question this way.

Court: "Did the accused engage the enemy on August 29?"

Pope: "I do not know of my own knowledge that he did so." *(P. 47:379)*

Here the examination of the witness was closed on that specific matter.

At 5:20 AM of the 29th Porter received a dispatch from General Pope. He was directed to *'move upon Centreville at dawn.'* The order had surprised Porter. He said so later, in the following conversations.

"It seemed to me that the directive would carry me away from the likely scene of action at Manassas. I wasn't satisfied and I grilled the staff officer for more information about the reason for the order."

The officer gave him nothing. He had no other information.

Porter said, "I put my column on the road right after breakfast and arrived at Manassas Junction about 8:30 AM. It was there I met Captain Piatt of Pope's staff."

"Captain Piatt had a verbal order for McDowell. The order directed McDowell to turn King's command over to me. He also told me that General Pope wanted me to reverse direction and march to Gainesville."

"Just then General McDowell rode up. We reviewed the events of the previous 16 hours and we spoke for nearly an hour. I knew by his conversation McDowell was not pleased that a part of his corps *(King's Division)* had been assigned to me."

"About then, while McDowell and I were engaged in conversation, General Gibbon rode up. He had a second order from Pope. When the order was read I could see the contents did not make McDowell feel any better. The second order *repeated* Pope's order to place King's division with my fifth corps."

"McDowell asked me to place King's division on his right. This was so his three divisions would be better concentrated, he said."

"When I rode back to my troops, I discussed the enemy situation with General Morell. By noon I had deployed my artillery and all four of my divisions to be ready for the attack I expected. Longstreet had arrived on the other side of Dawkins Creek and in the timber beyond, across from the Manassas-Gainesville Railroad."

"I did not think James Longstreet had any idea what Union forces faced him. From the sounds coming from his forces, like myself, for the next two hours they went about the business of deploying forces for battle."

Porter, afterward, aimed his chief criticism of the court martial and the fallacious charges against another person, besides John Pope.

"The greater villain, in this case, was Irvin McDowell."

"General McDowell's testimony has astonished me beyond measure. It did me more harm than all the rest put together. He told the court that I was a criminal. Why did he say this? He said it because I told him that I thought it would hurt General Pope if Pope left our wounded behind. McDowell accused me of a *'sneering manner'* toward General Pope."

"Another time, he testified I seemed *'indifferent'* about getting more ammunition during the fight at Dawkins Branch. In fact, at that time, I had already sent two of my men to get ammunition. I was determined not to fall back."

During Porter's defense at the court martial, and later during his rehearing, General Porter explained what *really* happened between him and McDowell that day before McDowell elected to leave him and take his corps to the action at Groveton. Porter's statements were supported by Generals Sykes and Morell, who overheard the conversation.

The reader will better understand the specific wrongs that McDowell perpetrated on Porter by a review of the conversation between Porter and McDowell at Dawkins Branch that day. This was while Longstreet's skirmishers were already engaged with Porter's troops. As the two generals talked, the sounds of muskets and artillery were plainly audible.

Porter: "McDowell said to me that day about midday of August 29, *'Porter, this is no place to fight a battle; you are too far out already.'* This remark was heard by General Morell and by General Sykes. McDowell's order to *'stay where I was,'* to which I agreed, *is nowhere hinted at in the charges against me.*"

"McDowell, when he testified, claimed that he told me to *'Put your force here and I will take mine to Sudley Springs Road, on the left of the troops engaged with the enemy.'* In his testimony, he justified this claim by adding, *'I left General Porter with the belief and understanding that he would put his force in at that point.'*"

"McDowell's true order was overheard by my Chief of Staff Colonel Lock, and by Captain Martin, officers in General Morell's Division. *It did not happen* as McDowell testified. McDowell did not tell me nor did he imply that I should attack... An order to attack under the circumstances I faced was the chief of the false charges against me. General McDowell was utterly in error on this point."

During the trial, General Porter offered Colonel Elisha G. Marshall's deposition as an important part of his defense. The Joint Order and the 4:30 Order were both received by General Porter on the same day; the first at about noon and the second after sunset. The circumstances were intertwined with Porter's reasons and inability to carry out both orders at the time Pope expected. Marshall's testimony makes clear the reason for Porter's actions in both cases.

Marshall, commanding the 13th New York Regiment, made a careful and continuous reconnaissance of the enemy which Porter faced that day. In addition, Colonel Marshall studied first hand Jackson's position on the right of Longstreet's forces.

Colonel Marshall's testimony was offered while Marshall was confined to his bed after receiving a grievous and near-fatal wound at the recent Battle of Fredericksburg *(several weeks after the loss at Manassas)*. Colonel Marshall had commanded one of the six regiments led by Colonel Charles Roberts. Roberts in turn reported to General Morell, who was General Fitz John Porter's first division head.

Marshall was a Regular Army man. He had seen action with Porter at Mechanicsville and on Malvern Hill. A West Pointer, the 33-year-old officer had been an Indian fighter and had come through the Civil War unscathed, that is until Fredericksburg.

Now quite ill, his face was pale with loss of blood. His eyes, however, were bright and keen with intelligence and the spirit of a true soldier. What he had to say was spoken with an exactness of detail, confident precision, and conviction of its accuracy. General Porter conducted the interrogation.

General Porter: "Where were you on the afternoon of the 29th of August?"

Colonel Marshall: "I was on the road leading to Gainesville, the road from Manassas Junction."

Porter: "What was your duty?"

Marshall: "I was on duty with General Morell's division, in General Porter's corps, and commanding my regiment."

Porter: "Please specify the character of the duty you performed."

Marshall: "About 1 o'clock I was detailed by General Porter to go with my regiment across all open country, and across ravine and some timber that was facing our line of battle. I deployed my skirmishers to find out the position of the enemy, and anything else that I could find out concerning them."

Porter: "State the position and the force of the enemy in the immediate vicinity of General Porter's command, as far as you know it."

Marshall: "Immediately after going toward the enemy force, my skirmishers were fired upon by a body of dragoons (cavalry). Shortly afterward there was a section of artillery which opened fire upon General Porter's command. Soon after that, perhaps about two o'clock, the head of a large column came to my front. They deployed their skirmishers and met mine. (Colonel) Webb returned their fire until about three o'clock when they drove my skirmishers into the edge of the timber."

"We were all on the left of the Manassas Railroad, going toward Gainesville. Their force continued to come down all day; in fact, until one o'clock at night. It was a very large force and they were drawn up in lines of battle as they came down."

"I reported at different intervals to General Morell, my immediate commander, the position of the enemy. At one time I deemed it so important that I did not dare trust orderlies or others with messages, and I went myself to confer concerning the enemy. This was about dusk. General Morell told me he had just received orders from General Porter to attack the enemy; to commence the attack with four regiments."

"General Morell seemed to be very much troubled and he asked my advice, my opinion. I told him by all means not to attack. It was certain destruction to do so. I told him that I for one did not wish to go into that timber and attack the enemy. Their position was a very strong one. They were certainly in force at that time and twice as strong as our own force; that is, all of General Porter's corps."

"General Morell had expressed to me the tenor of General Porter's order (*the 4:30 Order*). I also felt we had executed that same order with reference to General Pope's army by keeping this large body at our front at bay better than we would have by attacking them. I believed that if we attacked them it was certain destruction. We would have had to move our line across a large ravine and into timber. Perhaps our line of retreat would have been entirely cut off from General Pope's army. I must also say that this army that came down in our front was a separate and distinct army of the enemy from which was fighting General Pope's army."

Much time had passed since Colonel Marshall had begun his lengthy testimony. General Porter wished to stop the proceedings to give Colonel Marshall a rest. He appeared weaker and he had grown paler. At times, Marshall paused for several seconds to regain his strength and go on with his deposition.

There were several other persons in the room while the witness gave his testimony. Beside a doctor and a nurse in attendance, there were several officers and civilians acting as witnesses for the deposition. Porter was concerned for the welfare of his fellow officer, knowing he was in pain and in critical physical condition because of his wound. Porter wished to stop for a time to give Marshall some rest and time to gather his strength.

Colonel Marshall would not hear of it. He was determined to give his listeners and the court all of his recollections of that fateful day. Marshall knew how important his testimony was to prove General Porter's innocence and support Porter's actions as correct.

"Colonel, let us stop for a while. So you may rest and the doctor may minister to you."

"No, no, general, "Marshall replied. "I must continue while I have the strength and my mind is clear."

"Very well," Porter agreed and they continued the examination.

Marshall: "… While I was on reconnaissance, and before I went in to General Morell, I could hear and judge the result of the fighting between the forces of the enemy and general Pope's army. From where my regiment was, I could see Union troops on General Pope's left and I could also see the enemy's right during the greater part of the day. The fighting was about two miles off, perhaps a little diagonally to our right."

"The enemy set up their cheering and appeared to be charging and driving our men. Not a man of my command would have been uncertain; General Pope's army was being driven from the field."

Marshall, of the U.S. Regular Army, had seen much fighting, and knew what he was seeing.

Marshall: "In the different battles I have been in I have learned there is no mistaking the enemy's yell when they are successful. It is different from that of our own men. Our men give three successive cheers, and in concert. There was a cheering without any reference to regularity … a continual yelling."

"Afterward, at dark, I was sent for by General Porter and questioned very stringently with reference to the enemy. My remarks to him were the same as I am now making and as I made to General Morell. I also stated in conversation with General Porter I felt our right was very weak. I felt the pickets should be increased for there was danger of our being cut off entirely from general Pope's army."

"I was given one regiment under my command to go to the right of me, and four companies of another regiment to go to the left of me, as pickets. General Griffin (*Morell's second brigade*) also was ordered to place a strong force on my right and to connect with me."

Porter: "As to the position of the enemy being as it was between 5 o'clock and dusk, and the position of General Porter at that time, was it possible, without the greatest danger for General Porter, to have made that movement on his right, to attempt to reach and destroy Jackson on his right?"

This was as leading a question as one might have heard in any courtroom. It would have had an immediate objection from the plaintiff or the prosecutor. However, as part of a deposition, by one who was not an attorney, the question and Marshall's answer was included in the trial transcript.

Marshall: "No, sir; it was impossible to have done so. In the first place it was impractical to cross the country in that position during the day. We would have been obliged to have whipped this very force in front of us, as large as it was. To have got there (Jackson's right) was very doubtful if we could have done it."

Porter: "Do you know that the order to attack, sent to general Morell (from General Pope) was predicated upon the news, which General Porter had received that the enemy was retiring?" (This news came earlier from General McDowell.)

Marshall: "General Morell told me that the news was that the enemy was retreating. He said, 'We knew the reverse. They were not.'"

It was Judge Advocate Holt's turn to question the witness. The judge began with an inquiry about what Marshall saw or knew of Longstreet's advance through Thoroughfare Gap.

Court: "Did the force of which you speak (*Longstreet*) seem to come from the direction of Thoroughfare Gap?"

Marshall's replies to the grilling lasted for almost an hour. Reading the transcript of Holt's questions and Marshall's answers, it became apparent to the reader that the judge advocate was trying his best to establish a fact that would help convict General Porter. Holt finally asked Marshall the single question he had been leading to.

Court: "Did you withdraw in the presence of the enemy?"

If Marshall had withdrawn, it would only have been on Porter's order. Therefore, any such answer would support Pope's allegation that Porter was a coward, who had fled in the face of an enemy. Marshall's reply was one Holt may not have expected.

Marshall: "Yes, sir. My opinion on the 29th while I was on duty was that after I saw that the enemy desired to remain on the defensive it appeared they wanted us to attack them." *(Longstreet's army was setting a trap.)*

According to a letter written after the war by James Longstreet to Porter, this was true. General Porter was a good enough soldier that he knew this also. He waited as long as he could, holding Longstreet from advancing and crushing Pope's army before Pope could get away. Porter saved the Union army. Porter finally left, after five hours, only when he knew it was time to retire in order, or suffer the loss of his own army before Longstreet's three-to-one advantage.

Judge Advocate Holt turned his questioning in a new direction. For the next thirty minutes he challenged Colonel Marshall's estimate that Longstreet's corps was more than twice that of Porter's force. Marshall's replies give us a good insight into a soldier's experienced eye of guessing with some accuracy the size of a distant and advancing enemy.

Court: "Did you make your estimate of the amount of that force principally from the extent of the line as indicated by the clouds of dust, or had you other means than that of judging?"

Marshall: "No, sir. You cannot tell the difference, except by the quickness of movement of these columns. They seemed to move more quickly, which caused me, before going on this duty, to judge that it was the enemy coming. I judged that the advance of the enemy were dragoons, from the fact there was always dust ahead of and disconnected from the main column, which moved quicker even than the rest of the line; and, therefore, before going on this duty, I judged that the enemy were coming down to our front."

Judge Advocate Holt struck at Colonel Marshall's observations, analysis, and reasons, why Porter did not attack Jackson's left flank as he had been ordered to do. Judge Holt wanted to know whether such a march could have been direct, or would it have had to be circuitous. He wanted to know about the terrain and the character of the country. He wanted to know how far Porter would have had to march to reach Jackson. He wanted to know how long such a march would have taken Porter.

To each of these questions Marshall gave a clear estimate and a cogent, reasonable reply.

Marshall: "The road was heavily obstructed by broken country and heavily timbered. It was not possible to carry artillery and Porter would have been under heavy enemy fire at all times. It would have taken several hours, perhaps half a day."

The judge advocate ended his questioning of Colonel Marshall. The hearing continued the next day in the 10th Avenue Washington Justice building courtroom. General Porter called Major George Hyland to the witness box. Major Hyland led the infantrymen of the 13th New York Second Regiment, commanded by Colonel Marshall on 29 August.

General Porter questioned Major Hyland about that morning, as he had earlier of his superior, Colonel Marshall.

Porter: "What was your duty on 29 August?"

Major Hyland: "I and my skirmishers were employed in duty from 1 o'clock of the afternoon, all night until daylight the next day. The 22nd Massachusetts and Berdan's sharpshooters were placed with us, on the same duty and forming in line. I could hear the commands clearly as if forming in line (for battle), and I also heard the movements of their artillery coming into position."

Porter: "Have you any knowledge of forming for an attack that morning?"

Hyland: "Yes, sir. I could hear the commands plainly as if forming into line; I could hear the artillery coming into position."

Judge Advocate Holt questioned Hyland in his turn.

Court: "What was the character of the country?"

Hyland: "The country in front of us was heavily timbered. After the timber there was an open ground with a deep ravine and a stream running through the ravine. After the open ground there was more heavy timber, and some scrub pine."

Court: "Can you state the force of the enemy that was in front of you?"

Hyland: "It was a very large force, indeed, perhaps 10,000. They were adding to their strength and more troops were coming, perhaps 12,000 to 15,000 men."

Court: Could they have made a successful resistance to General Porter's entire corps?"

Hyland: "I do believe so."

In cross-examination by the judge advocate, General Morell testified that the enemy's position and growing forces were impregnable as he led Porter's forces on the afternoon and the evening of 29 August, as had been confirmed earlier by Hyland, Marshall and others.

Earlier in the trial John Pope's chief of staff, General Benjamin S. Roberts, testified as a witness for the prosecution.

Court: "What do you know of Longstreet's forces facing near Porter's corps?"

Roberts: "I traversed the greater part of the battlefield during 29 August. Furnished with an eye-glass by General Pope, and directed to watch from afar the advance of the reinforcing bodies of the enemy as they appeared to have come from the Gap, I did carefully watch the clouds of dust, which they raised. In my judgment, and I have no doubt, that the masses of the enemy were mostly moving on the Warrenton Turnpike between Gainesville and the battlefields. During my rides over the field, I caught one or two glimpses of some portion of General Porter's force, but I did not pretend to have seen anything of his force after 1 o'clock."
(*P. 60:379*)

Hearing Pope's man say these things, that no enemy faced Porter that day, General Porter's cool and controlled exterior broke for a moment with a flash of anger at the patent lie.

History does not say much of Benjamin Stone Roberts. Perhaps for good reason; Roberts was not a likeable person. While he held a brief command in 1863, General B.S. Roberts is known to have sent people who held Confederate views to a camp prison. What made Roberts' actions against Confederate civilians unusual was that several of those persons he sent to prison were women and children. He was soon replaced in his command and faded from the pages of history.

General Porter replied to Roberts' claim of *'no large enemy in front of Porter.'* Based on Roberts' allegation that he was close enough to know whether or not Porter could have attacked Jackson, Porter revealed the lie in Roberts' testimony by pointing out that Roberts was not in the same area.

"General Roberts testified that he *'thought he was, at one time, within a mile and a half of my forces.'* Roberts could not possibly have seen my fifth corps. A thick wood intervened between him and me. He could see nothing of my force. Roberts said he could not see the ground in my front, in which the enemy was posted. He testified that *'for the entire afternoon, there was in my front no enemy save for some cavalry and some light artillery.'"*

"I respectfully contend that neither General Pope nor the government can offer any testimony or evidence to challenge the testimony of the mass of enemy in my front."

The truth was that Roberts was lying through his teeth to support and protect Pope's malfeasance.

In his own defense of the charges, Porter stated,

"The charge alleges that I disobeyed the order of the 29th of August, addressed jointly and severally to General McDowell and myself. The substance of the order is that General McDowell and I were to proceed to Gainesville and make a junction with other specified corps. Then we were to halt. The order gave me the right to use my judgment as to how I should carry out the order. The order concludes by commanding me not to move so far that I could not fall back to Bull Run by the night of the 29th or the next morning."

It was plain to the watchers that Porter was working hard to keep his anger and his outrage under control.

"General Pope has said that I disobeyed this order. I asked General Pope in what manner I disobeyed his order. His reply was that I *'partially obeyed it and partially disobeyed'* the order. When I asked him in what way I disobeyed, he claimed that I failed to attack the enemy in flank, as he directed me to do."

"The Joint Order directed me to proceed toward Gainesville."

Porter's voice was even but there was no mistaking the indignation that he felt.

"The Joint Order *did not direct me to attack Jackson's flank.* That order was part of the *4:30 Order.* It was *not* a part of this order."

Porter was his usual calm, studied self again as he continued.

"When I received the Joint Order directing me to bring my force toward Gainesville, I was already proceeding toward Gainesville under the previous 8:50 PM order. I made all efforts within my power to affect a junction with the forces of Generals Heintzelman, Reno and Ricketts, as the order specified."

He paused to remind his judges of the importance of McDowell's action in removing King's 3,000 troops from his command, and thereby weakening his forces (*McDowell reclaimed King's division without Pope's knowledge*).

"I had been relying on King's division. In spite of all my efforts I could not make a junction with the other corps. I faced three obstacles. First, the unexpected force of the enemy before me was greater than my own." (*Longstreet's army had arrived on the battlefield.*)

"Second, because we were not anywhere near Gainesville; not the short distance others have claimed, but nearly four miles away."

"Third, my troops had to march that whole distance over deep ditches, through thick woods and heavy brush, and across rocky ravines. All of this time my troops would have been under heavy musket and artillery fire."

Porter returned to another part of the Joint Order.

"When General McDowell and I met that morning to discuss the Joint Order he assumed the role of commanding Officer, as was his right under military law. He directed me to '*remain where I was.*' The verbal order was given to Colonel Locke, my chief of staff."

McDowell denied this. He testified that he '*did not recollect*' giving the message to Colonel Locke. However, Colonel Locke, a man of unquestioned good character and veracity, had affirmed that he received the message from General McDowell. As Porter's senior officer, General McDowell had modified the Joint Order.

Porter: "I did then continue to hold my position until I was ordered away from it some hours afterward, at sunset, when I received General Pope's 4:30 PM Order. I obeyed these orders, or a legal interpretation of them, in every regard."

Historical Note: It was confirmed during Porter's rehearing in 1878 that McDowell's convenient memory was to protect his friend, Pope. A few months after the battle, Irvin McDowell faced a military Board of Inquiry and escaped censure by the skin of his teeth. In 1879, when a Board of Review commissioned by President Rutherford B. Hayes issued its final report recommending a pardon for Porter, they also attributed much of the loss of the battle to McDowell. In their report McDowell was depicted as indecisive, uncommunicative, and inept. Repeatedly, he failed to answer Porter's frequent requests for information, he failed to forward information of Longstreet's position to Pope, and he neglected to take command of the Union Army Left Wing, as was his duty under the Articles of War.

McDowell escaped worse penalties by testifying against Pope. Despite his escape from censure, he spent the next two years in exile from any kind of leadership position.

⤙ 52 ⤚

Second Charge

The Court labeled Porter's disobedience to the *4:30 Order* as the *THIRD SPECIFICATION* to the original FIRST CHARGE. Here, once more, as polite as the words of the court martial record appear, they minced no words. The court read the third specification.

"Major General Fitz John Porter, having been in front of the enemy during the battle of Manassas, on Friday, August 29, 1862, did on that day receive from Major General John Pope, his superior and commanding officer, a lawful order, which said order Major General Porter did then and there disobey, and did fail to push forward with his forces into action either on the enemy's right flank or rear, and in all other respects did fail to obey said order."

In hindsight and knowing everything that transpired that day, one cannot help but laugh (*or cry*) over Pope's myopia and his stubborn refusal to face facts. Longstreet's 29,000 troops slammed into Porter on Porter's flank. Getting through Longstreet's maelstrom of bullets and artillery was risking almost certain destruction. Besides the barrage of enemy musket fire, the ground was a mass of gullies and rocks, thick brush, and heavy dense woods.

Pope's 4:30 Order commanded General Porter: *'Your line of march brings you in on the enemy's (Stonewall Jackson) right flank, and if possible, on his rear, keeping your right in communication with General Reynolds. The enemy is massed in the woods in front of us, but can be shelled out as soon as you engage their flank. Keep heavy reserves, and use your batteries, keeping well closed to your right and rear, so as to keep you in close communication with the right wing.'*

After the witnesses were heard, Porter offered his defense to the charge that he disobeyed the 4:30 Order to attack Jackson's left flank. One of his most important witnesses was Colonel Elisha G. Marshall, who not only had been in the thick of the fight that day near Dawkins Branch, but also lost nearly half the men in his platoon. One hundred of the 240 men of Colonel Marshall's 13th New York Infantry were killed or wounded.

At the beginning of the fight, as Longstreet had approached, Porter had given Colonel Marshall the job of a continuous reconnaissance of the enemy that was fast gathering on Porter's immediate front. Marshall saw it all. He saw Longstreet's five divisions coming and he was a witness to the moment when John Bell Hood's division reached Stonewall Jackson.

Aware of Pope's order for Porter to attack Jackson's left flank, Colonel Marshall paid particular attention to where Jackson's right and left flanks were located. At the same time, when he saw the incredible and unexpected sight of Longstreet's huge force of rebels that were fast approaching, he knew the rules of the game had changed.

Colonel Marshall's testimony was taken while he was confined to his bed. He had been grievously wounded at the battle of Fredericksburg on December 13, 1862, and his wound had been nearly fatal. In Porter's defense, Counsel Reverdy Johnson cited from the record Marshall's eye-witness testimony.

Marshall: 'I was detailed by General Porter to go with my regiment across open country and a ravine to some timber that was facing our line of battle. I deployed skirmishers to find the position of the enemy and anything else I could find out concerning them.' *(P. 233:379)*

'Their force continued to come down all day, in fact, until 1 o'clock at night. It was a very large force, and they were drawn up in lines of battle as they came down. The enemy was in force and twice as large as all of General Porter's forces. Had we attacked and moved forward to the timber, our line of retreat would have been cut off as well. *(P. 233-234:379)*

Porter pointed out to his listeners, "The 4:30 Order read, in part, *'Your line of march brings you in on the enemy's (Stonewall Jackson) right flank, and if possible, on his rear, keeping your right in communication with General Reynolds...'* and further states that I must place my forces, *'keeping well closed to your right and rear, so as to keep in close communication with the right wing.'*"

Porter said, "General Pope wrote the 4:30 Order believing that when I received his order my forces would be near Jackson's right flank. I *was* in the presence of the enemy, but they were not Jackson's troops; they were Longstreet's forces. Longstreet's forces were in much greater numbers than my own. They were impregnably posted in my direct front. The order and Pope's belief was that I could attack Jackson's right, while at the same time, according to the order, I was required to keep a connection with General Reynolds, and this was not within the realm of the possible."

Fitz John Porter's indignation at the unreasonableness of Pope's order was reflected in the tenor of his voice and the whitening of his knuckles as he held the copy of the record in his hand. He spat out the next words.

"For my men to have attacked Jackson's right flank, even had it been possible with 29,000 Confederate troops on my front, would have led me in one direction, while for me to keep a connection with General Reynolds' division, I would have been forced to advance in a nearly *opposite* direction."

He finished quietly.

"Both of these movements, when the order was written and when I received the order at sunset, were so *utterly* impracticable and so *surely* disastrous that no commander in his right mind, knowing what I knew, could possibly have attempted to execute both parts of the order at the same time."

He picked up another page of the record.

"I may say that the army that came down on our front was a *separate and distinct part of the army General Pope was fighting.* Colonel Marshall went to the front, where General Morell was directing our defenses. Here is Marshall's testimony on that matter."

Marshall: 'The army in my front, Longstreet's main force, was an entirely different army than that Pope was fighting. At the same time, from my vantage point I could see, hear and judge the result of the fighting between General Pope's army and Jackson. For the greater part of the day I saw the enemy's right about two miles off diagonally to our front and to the right. The enemy set up cheering and appeared to be charging and driving us, but what was certain was that General Pope's army was being driven from the field.'

Porter's Counsel turned to other testimony.

"We might rely on Colonel Marshall's testimony alone, since it is entirely conclusive. However, Major Hyland's testimony further confirms General Porter's claims."

He read from the court records.

Hyland: 'I could hear the commands plainly as if forming in line. I heard their artillery coming into position." *(216: 379)* 'I could not state the numbers or the divisions. I judged from movements and from commands given, there was a very large force. They were larger than ours and more were coming from Thoroughfare Gap.' *(P. 216:379)*

Porter said, "Generals Griffin and Morell confirmed that we could not have gotten our troops to our right and toward the Turnpike. If we had tried our men would have been exposed to a murderous fire all day long. I did not retreat. Since I could not attack or cross to the front to the enemy, I chose to take my forces down the Sudley road to assist General Pope's forces on the Warrenton Turnpike near Groveton, which I did."

"I affirm and have, as I contend, fully proved before the court, first, that complete obedience to the order was impossible. Even if I had received the order at the moment the time purports to have been written, that is at 4:30 PM on the 29th of August, such complete obedience to the order by me was for yet stronger reasons wholly impossible. As a military movement such obedience would have been wholly inexpedient, injudicious, and improper, even if it had been possible at the hour when I did receive the order; that is to say, at or nearly at 6 PM of the 29th, when the sun had set, or was setting."

"Second, I affirm and contend that I have fully proved before this court that I was in compliance, so far as possible, with the manifest spirit, purpose and meaning of the order. I did take measures to carry out the spirit and accomplish that purpose. Those measures taken by me were the only practical measures for me to adopt under the circumstances. They were far more useful than any attempted liberal compliance with the order could have been. Any such attempt, literally, to obey the order, which I might have made at the time I received it, would have been nothing less than delinquency, if not a crime."

"The fundamental averment of the order, upon which the charge against me rests, is entirely untrue. The Joint Order of August 29 claims that my line of march on that day, brought me to my enemy's right flank. The fact is my line of march that day brought me directly upon the front of a separate force of the enemy (*Longstreet's divisions*), ten to fifteen thousand strong. When the order was written, General Pope was entirely ignorant of that force before me. He must plead total ignorance of this truth as his sole possible justification for sending me this order."

"It is proved abundantly that if I had executed, or attempted to execute the order literally, either at the moment it was written or the moment I received the order, by falling upon Jackson's right flank, my column would have suffered one of two separate disasters. If I had tried to move cross-country in a direct line to Jackson's right I would have been exposed to a murderous attack by the enemy posted in my front to my left. My column would have been under fire through a country through which I could only have passed in extreme disorder and without artillery."

"If, on the other hand, I adopted the only other course available to me, falling back to Bethlehem Church, and then following in General McDowell's track to the battlefield, the enemy in my front would have fallen on my rear with such crushing effect as to destroy my whole column."

"The presence of Longstreet's army was 1200 to 1500 yards from directly in my front. It was a great force of artillery, infantry and cavalry, which I could not attack because his right flank extended farther southward than my extreme left. Furthermore, I could not attack the enemy's left flank because the country was impassable (*deep gullies, thick woods, and heavy brush*) and the resulting disorder of my troops because of the character of the country, my column, as it moved along, would have been exposed to an assault by Jackson's right. At the same time, my troops would have to face the entire force, without cover, of the massed artillery and guns of the enemy."

REPEAT OF THE 4:30 PM ORDER

Pope sent another order at 8:50 PM, repeating his 4:30 PM order. That second, more strident directive read as follows:

'Immediately upon receipt of this order, the precise hour of receiving, which you will acknowledge, you will march your command to the field of battle of today, and report to me in person for orders. You are to understand that you are expected to comply strictly with this order, and to be present on the field within three hours after its reception, or after daybreak tomorrow morning.'

As one might suppose, when John Pope sent this second order to Porter, four and a half hours after his first, 4:30 order, with no result that his order had been heeded, he was livid with anger. The wording and the terseness of the order could not have been more deliberate or insulting to a fellow officer. Pope was deeply concerned. He knew by this time he was not likely to win the battle and destroy Thomas Jackson; he was in very real danger of losing his shirt.

The reason Pope was in this pickle and ready to lash out at anyone but himself was because he had, for two days, refused utterly to accept the news, from Reynolds, McDowell, Banks and Porter that Robert E. Lee was in the field with Longstreet's army about to join Stonewall Jackson and smash into the Federals. General Porter

369

had been the lynch-pin of Pope's entire strategy; that is, to catch Jackson in a vice. To Pope's mind, Porter had disobeyed his explicit orders.

Even in that late hour, Pope refused to face reality. That reality was a catastrophe in the making that Pope had made for himself. General Porter could not have advanced to strike Stonewall Jackson's right flank; Longstreet's many thousands of rebels were in his way. Nevertheless, with Longstreet's cannons and infantry blasting away at his flanks, Porter tried that hopeless task, knowing the odds and he lost hundreds of his men.

In spite of the hopeless ordeal Porter faced, he held Longstreet's army in place for five hours. Those five hours of the extra window of time gave Pope's army the opportunity to escape annihilation and retreat over the Bull Run Bridge to the defenses of Centreville and Washington forty miles away.

Porter added, "It is alleged that I disobeyed the order of 8:50 PM of the 29th of August. The order directed me, immediately to march to the field of battle and report in person to General Pope. The same charge alleges that I disobeyed in that I permitted General Griffin's brigade and General Piatt's brigade to march to Centreville, out of the way of battle, and remain there the entire day of Saturday, the 30th of August. Thereby I greatly delayed the arrival of these two brigades on the field of battle, on the 30th of August."

"The facts are these. Upon my receipt of the 8:50 PM, August 29 order, which I did not received *until 3:50 AM on the 30th of August,* nine hours later, I did at once proceed to take my command to the battlefield. General Pope states explicitly in his testimony that he made no complaint at the time. A portion of my command arrived upon the field, four hours before the fighting. I site the testimony of General Morell."

Morell had testified, "A short time before daylight on the 30th, I received a written order from General Porter, which said, *'Lose not a minute in withdrawing and coming down the road to me. The wagons, which went up, send down at once, and have the road cleared; send me word when you have all in motion.'*"

General Porter was finished with his defense. He finished with heat, although he was tired from the six-hour ordeal. He knew the signs; the Stanton-picked court had already ruled against him. Porter had made clear to the court two incidents which were never explained: the 8:50 PM 'immediate' order given to him nine hours late, and General Pope having made no complaint at the time of Porter's arrival on the field. Porter had presented evidence that went a long way toward exposing Pope's mistakes for which Porter was found guilty. Porter was blamed for the loss of the Battle of Second Manassas, instead of Pope and McDowell where all the blame should have rested.

❧ 53 ❧

Summation

When the trial was concluded, Porter summed up his defense. In his last ditch desperate attempt to get through to the stone-faces of the judges he pulled all stops.

"My defense is now concluded. Before I deliver it into your hands I wish to be indulged in some remarks more exclusively personal. To speak of oneself is always unpleasant and is generally against the laws of good taste—but there are occasions when it becomes unavoidable."

"The sensibility, which it then wounds, must bear the inflictions because a higher sensibility demands the sacrifice."

"When a soldier's honor is impeached, when his loyalty is assailed, when cowardice is even insinuated against him and when the safety of his country has been purposefully and causelessly hazarded against him in the indulgence of some low, petty and contemptible motive, it cannot be expected he is to be restrained by the delicacy which belongs to the ordinary intercourse between gentlemen."

"If his past life gives the lie to the charge; if the charges exhibit conduct totally inconsistent with the truth, if it speaks of a nature that would revolt at even the thought of the other; if his past evinces a long and perilous course of duty, a consistent zeal for the honor of his flag and an undying devotion to its service; ... if he has given himself with sleepless vigilance and amidst countless hazards to do what he could to put down this vile rebellion and reinstate the authority of the government. If until the unfortunate Virginia Campaign of last summer his services were approved by the public, by his brothers in arms and signally approved by the president, if these facts are true then I may well be excused for invoking them as an answer to the base and groundless imputations against my duty and my honor as a citizen and as a soldier."

"What has been my history? That I served while a mere youth throughout the Mexican War, throughout the resplendent campaign of Lieutenant General Scott, and was actively engaged in several battles of Vera Cruz, Contreras, Molino Del Rey, Chapultepec and the City of Mexico. I entered into that service as a brevet second lieutenant."

"Second, I was ordered by then secretary of war, Mr. Holt, your judge advocate, to proceed to Texas for the purpose of withdrawing as many of the troops as I could from that state and thereby counteracting, as far as possible, the effects of the base and unexampled treachery of General Twiggs. Amidst great difficulties and much personal peril, I succeeded in rescuing seven companies, in all five hundred men. I posted two at Tortugas, two at Key West and taking three to New York. The whole duty was performed to the perfect satisfaction of the Department."

"Third, in May of 1861, I was commissioned as colonel in the regular army and in August as a brigadier general of volunteers and afterward served in the Peninsula Campaign under Major General McClellan. At the siege of Yorktown, he constituted me as director of the siege."

"In the battle of Hanover Court House I commanded the fifth corps of the Army of the Potomac. In the Battle of Gaines Mill, my command being about 29,000 men, I lost in killed and wounded about 9000 men which tells of the severity of the conflict. In the Battle of Malvern Hill, which site I selected, I succeeded in stopping 30,000 to 40,000 of the enemy, evidently the bravest that ever trod a battlefield."

"I live now amid whatever discouragements war may cause us and the gloom, cheered by the anticipation that all may yet be well. The Union will yet merge from its present danger even stronger than before from the trials through which we pass. It will be once more a strong and united people. We shall glory in the thought that our country shall once more serve to light the world by its example. Our country will become again a monument to past glory and a tribute to the pledge of future glory until time's last echo shall have ceased to sound."

General Porter's final statement to the court that had found him guilty was a ringing cry of an innocent patriot against the injustice that had been heaped upon him by an unjust court.

"Traitor to my country? When did treason so peril and labor to rescue it from destruction? If the charge had not assumed the solemn form that has been given to it, it would be received everywhere where my whole conduct is known, as ludicrous, false, or the creation of a morbid and distempered brain."

❧ 54 ❧

Conviction

The court published its ruling:

FITZ JOHN PORTER IS CASHIERED OR DISMISSED FROM THE ARMY FOR DISCIPLINARY REASONS AND FOREVER DISQUALIFIED FROM HOLDING ANY OFFICE OF TRUST OR PROFIT UNDER THE GOVERNMENT OF THE UNITED STATES.

President Abraham Lincoln relieved Porter by Special Order from the War Department, Adjutant General's office. The Special Order was dated January 21, 1863. The signed President's Order relieved Major General Fitz John Porter of his command and gave Porter's corps to Porter's friend, Major General Ambrose Burnside.

In the hundred-word missive Lincoln included these words: *'Fitz John Porter shall be relieved from the command of the corps he now commands in said army, and that Major General Burnside shall take command of said corps.'*

On January 22, 1863, in the third year of the Civil War, The New York Times carried the latest news from Washington. First, there was news of interest to the Cosmopolitan New Yorkers:

'Mr. Bullet was appointed the Collector of New Orleans, recently of Kentucky. The appointment was regarded as a most excellent one.'

'Utah was admitted to the Union. Judge Cradlebaugh gave a speech which made astounding revelations in regard to one Brigham Young and his Mormon Church appointments.'

'The Senate Military Committee considered repealing the law limiting the number of Generals in the Union Army, but came to no conclusion.'

'The Senate Committee for Indian Affairs decided on a plan for colonizing and concentrating the various Indian tribes in the new Western States.'

'The War Department, under General Order No. 11, dismissed Colonel R.C. Murphy from the service of the United States for allowing his command at Holly Springs, Mississippi, to be surprised by the enemy while his troops were asleep in their beds.'

Newspaper headlines told of more fighting, the battles of South Mountain and Crampton's Gap, and of a 'glorious' Union victory at Antietam. THE BACK OF THE CONFEDERACY HAS BEEN BROKEN the New York Times blared proudly.

It was much too soon to say that. Antietam might have been lost because of McClellan. Although he outnumbered Lee's army by more than two to one, McClellan sent his brigades into battle against Lee in ragged piecemeal. He should have destroyed Lee's army at Antietam. Instead Lee lived to fight again for two more years.

Porter's fifth corps was there, his last command before his trial and conviction in January of 1863. McClellan should have used Burnside but McClellan would not risk his last reserve.

At bloody Antietam, John Reynolds would die, along with thousands of his comrades and gray-shirted Southern boys. On September 22, 1862, Lincoln would issue the Emancipation Proclamation, giving slaves their freedom effective January 1, 1863. In that same year the Dakota war against the Indians would begin and, on the fourth of July, 1863, the Battle of Gettysburg would break the back of the Confederacy to send them on the lonely way to a final surrender in 1865.

The newsboys, peddling their newspapers on the corners of the snowy streets of Washington, shouted the newest headline: 'Extra! Extra! Biggest military trial in century! General Porter convicted of treason. Extra! Extra!' The headline that covered the masthead of the New York Times that day in January displayed the words,

'PORTER CONVICTED'

The two column article and subhead that followed said

IMPORTANT FROM WASHINGTON:

GEN. FITZ JOHN PORTER CASHIERED

AND DISMISSED FROM THE SERVICE

Special Washington Dispatch – Washington, D.C. Wednesday, Jan. 21.

'The verdict of the Court in General Fitz John Porter's case was approved today by the President. Contrary to former reports, the court found him guilty of the charges proffered and he was accordingly cashiered and dismissed from the service. The court met to try General Porter. Present were Generals Hunter, Hitchcock, King, Ricketts, Casey, Slough, and (James A.) Garfield (who would later become president). General N.B. Buford was another member, half-brother to General John Buford. Lastly, General Roberts was the Inspector General. The prosecutor was Colonel J. Holt, the Advocate General.'

After the trial, the editor of the New York Times gave a bizarre opinion of what should serve as justice and for the correctness of Porter's sentence.

'To every reasonable man, the bare knowledge of the court was composed of seven officers of such personal character, such unquestioned integrity and such professional ability as, by itself, ought to be a sufficient guarantee of the correctness of the action and without a perusal of a line of the testimony on which that action was founded. There is not a civil tribunal in the land, whose competence and ought sooner to accredit its decision.'

In plain words, according to the mental giants and moral arbiters of the New York Times editor, when the judges who sit on the court are men of 'unquestioned integrity,' then hang the evidence. By every possible measure, John Pope owed Porter his gratitude. Instead, to fix blame for the loss of the Second Battle of Manassas and remedy his own reputation, Pope placed the blame on Porter—and his false charges stuck.

So it was over.

Porter had been efficiently and neatly done in by a criminal and conspiratorial administration. His career was over; he was stripped of rank and turned out with ignominy.

But that wasn't the end of it. Nothing could ever restore the lost years and the terrible tragedy Porter must have suffered. Nothing could ever give him back the achievements he might have reached as one of the Civil War's greatest generals. Nothing could make right the travesty of justice Porter and his family suffered. It would take time; all of 16 years, to correct the great wrong that had been done to him by the calculating pedagogues who saw only their own self-aggrandizement, but Porter would live to see his name and reputation restored.

Reverdy Johnson
Statesman

❧ 55 ❧

Long Road Back

It took over 20 years before Major General Fitz John Porter's conviction was reversed.

Porter began his mission immediately after the Court pronounced the horrific sentence. Not the least of the purgatory Porter suffered was the Washington newspapers. The Republican press savaged Porter as a traitor who should have been hung. Fitz John Porter must have felt quite alone in 1863. For nearly two decades Porter suffered the tortures of the damned for his conviction. He was exonerated by a special commission ordered by President Rutherford Hayes, and conducted by General John Schofield in 1878. President James A. Garfield succeeded Hayes, and Garfield having voted to convict Porter earlier, would not reverse his sentence. Porter's sentence was not commuted until 1882, by President Chester Arthur. Republicans still harbored resentment at Porter. Porter did not receive an official pardon until 1893 from President Grover Cleveland, (the first Democrat in almost 50 years) when the U.S. Congress restored his commission as infantry colonel and backdated the decision to 1861. Can you imagine how Porter must have felt; from being one of the brightest stars of the Union Army, a man among men, brave and courageous with a brilliant record, to suddenly being dashed to earth among the lowest of the low without honor or a proud name?

The years after court martial passed like bleak signposts for Fitz John Porter, once a major general of the Union Army. Each day was a constant reminder of the condemnation of all that he once was. For years he had been banished from the army and forbidden to hold any public office. He was alone with no one to share the anger and bitterness of what the conspiracy had wrought on his life, except for his wife of thirty years. Harriet Pierson Cook Porter continued to support her husband and was the one person with whom Porter could unburden his troubled mind.

The strength of character of this man is nowhere more in evidence than the fact that he held on to his pursuit of righteousness for all those long years, fighting tooth and nail for justice. For any man to be found legally a coward, who refused to obey a lawful order in the face of the enemy, what greater cross of shame and humiliation can a good man carry to his grave?

Porter worked tirelessly to prove his innocence. Right after the trial he began his long, lonely way back to find his stolen dishonor and set the matter straight. Carefully surveying the Manassas battlefield, Porter made wonderfully detailed maps of every foot of the ground. He was painstaking in his attention to detail: every bush, tree, hill and gully were included, along with broken railroads, country roads and streams. His maps covered everywhere his troops went during those three trying days of Second Manassas.

Porter's conviction did not end the controversy. Friends used their influence to persuade state and local lawmakers to pass resolutions condemning the government for dismissing him from the army. He drew attention to the make-up of the court, a court that was composed of hand-picked military men who owed their allegiance to Secretary of War Edwin Stanton. Stanton had the power to make or break these men, depending upon how they testified. In spite of the clear evidence of Fitz John Porter's innocence it became clear that Secretary Stanton and his servants had conspired to rule against Porter from the start.

Major General George McClellan became, once more, a powerful political voice in the Democratic Party. McClellan asked his friends to write letters in Porter's defense and request a new trial. After the Union losses at Fredericksburg, the near mutiny of Burnside's officers during the 'mud march,' and the resurgence of the Democratic Party, raised voices became sufficient to commence a special commission to exonerate Porter, and eventually overturn Porter's conviction.

After the war Porter wrote to Robert E. Lee and James Longstreet. He asked for their help. He needed their cooperation so that he could gain access to the captured papers of the Confederacy. Other men supported Porter including Ulysses S. Grant, William Tecumseh Sherman and George Thomas; all-important high-level members of the *Republican Party*. These were brave men and their support of Porter's innocence caused their decline in popularity with members of their own political party. With peace and the United States once more a united country, Robert E. Lee, James Longstreet, as well as Union heroes William Tecumseh Sherman and Ulysses S. Grant; were some of those that wrote letters in Fitz John Porter's defense.

State and local resolutions were passed condemning the trial and the government for dismissing Porter.

With the slanted make-up of the kangaroo court, the disingenuous speed and conduct of the hearing, the evidence ignored, and the fallacies taken as fact, the court arrived at their findings. Judge Advocate Holt's court was roundly criticized as a body designed to rule in favor of the war administration's interests regardless of the truth.

Time and the truth revealed the shortcomings of Irvin McDowell and John Pope, and that least of all was Porter responsible for the loss of the Battle of Second Manassas. McDowell was brought up on charges. Miraculously, McDowell was exonerated of any wrongdoing but never again served in a leadership role commanding troops.

Secretary Stanton had some apparent investment in finding Porter guilty, whether to save face for his poor choices in appointing generals whose acts helped to lose the Battle of Second Manassas, or to appear less culpable to the president through the use of Porter as a scapegoat. Stanton's influence and power soon became apparent. Several of the officers who perjured themselves during the court martial hearing received promotions shortly after the trial. Secretary Stanton repeatedly blocked any attempt by the government to re-investigate the matter. He saw to it that any officer who spoke out *in support* of Porter was punished.

MCDOWELL SPEAKS OUT

Soon after Porter's conviction in 1863, Irvin McDowell was brought to answer for his part in the Battle of Second Manassas in his own Court of Inquiry. Irvin McDowell, by all the evidence, had more character than Pope, his partner in the crime. A twinge of conscience may have driven McDowell to speak out. At that court McDowell exonerated Porter of all wrongdoing. He recommended that Porter should be returned to command. Nevertheless, so powerful was Stanton's influence that this clear vindication had no effect.

JOHN MCALLISTER SCHOFIELD

It was only sixteen years after Porter's conviction in the Kangaroo court of 1862 that President Rutherford B. Hayes commissioned a board of inquiry to re-open the conviction. The new Secretary of War, the man who replaced Stanton, was assigned to be in charge of Porter's retrial. That man was Major General John Schofield, and he headed the special commission.

John McAllister Schofield was hardly a person one might have expected to establish a board of inquiry that would set Fitz John Porter free. Schofield graduated from West Point ten years before the Battle of Second Manassas and, in his last year at the Point, Schofield's career nearly ended with an ignominious dismissal.

Schofield's near dismissal was reminiscent of Porter's ending. While he was a teaching assistant at West Point, John Schofield was charged with allowing his fellow cadet candidates to tell off-color jokes to the class and, for the more artistically gifted West Pointers, he permitted racy sketches of scantily clad ladies penned in chalk on the blackboard instead of math formulas. Schofield's prissy superior officer considered the chalk drawings and the jokes offensive.

Schofield's dismissal was appealed to the Secretary of War. The matter went to a board of inquiry. The majority of the appeals board saw the matter for what it was; nothing more serious than student horseplay and they overturned Schofield's expulsion. However, two of the officers on the board of inquiry voted to sustain the expulsion. One of them, General George H. Thomas, arguably a mediocre Civil War commander, would later be Schofield's commander during the war. Needless to say, there was no love lost between the two men.

John Schofield was a good soldier during the Civil War. At the battle of Wilson's Creek, in August of 1861, he acted with 'conspicuous gallantry' and was awarded the Medal of Honor for bravery. Following the war, he rose in rank and favor. Given a secret task to investigate the strategic potential of a United States presence in the Hawaiian Islands, it was Schofield that recommended the United States should establish a naval port at Pearl Harbor.

By 1876 Schofield had risen to be the superintendent of the United States Military

Academy and President Rutherford B. Hayes asked him to reopen the case of Major General Fitz John Porter. After Schofield had studied a mass of new evidence that came, not from the North, but from Confederate generals, who had no axe to grind for or against Porter, Schofield found *to his certainty* that Porter had been *wrongly convicted*. He further opined that Porter's action *might have saved the entire Union army from complete defeat caused by the ineptitude of John Pope and his second in command, Irvin McDowell.*

Attorney John Christian Bullitt was counsel for the petitioner at Porter's board of inquiry, special commission hearing. Porter's first meeting with Bullitt in 1878 was dramatic. When Porter was ushered into John Bullitt's office, Bullitt rose from his chair and came to meet Porter when he entered.

"I am so happy to meet you, General Porter," Bullitt said. "Your counsel during your trial has spoken of you in the most glowing terms."

Porter knew Bullitt was referring to Reverdy Johnson, the attorney who had defended him during his court martial in 1862.

REVERDY JOHNSON

Reverdy Johnson was a controversial character in political circles. Johnson was a Whig Democrat, and in 1858 he represented a slave owner in a Federal hearing. The slave owner wished to retain ownership of Dred Scott. Scott was a freed man and later once again made a slave when he returned to a slave state. After being black-listed by the Republican Lincoln administration for several years, Reverdy Johnson was better accepted in the more tolerant years of the Democratic Andrew Johnson administration.

In 1868 Reverdy Johnson was appointed as foreign minister representing the United States in Great Britain. John Bullitt was a close friend of Johnson's and it was Reverdy Johnson that had suggested to Porter to ask for Bullitt's help. Attorney John Bullitt had read all of the 1862 court martial proceedings. He had also carefully studied Porter's evidence, which supported Porter's innocence. When he had finished the hundreds of pages of testimony and evidence, Bullitt was determined to defend this innocent man, a great soldier that had spent nearly two decades to right one of the great injustices of American history.

"Please come in. Sit down," Bullitt said, "General Porter, I am honored that you should have asked me to represent you at the rehearing and I do so most willingly. I know you are not only innocent of the spurious charges, but I completely agree with President Grant. I also agree with many others who know you and were present at the Second Battle of Manassas, that it was your actions that saved the Union Army from destruction."

With that auspicious beginning between the two men, Bullitt called for coffee from his secretary and moved his chair to the side of his desk to be closer to his guest.

"We have two months before your rehearing. Let us begin."

❧ 56 ❧

The Rehearing

On January 6, 1878 the rehearing of the 1863 court martial conviction of General Fitz John Porter opened at West Point. It was a quiet Monday morning. Except for the sound of rustling papers and nervous coughs among the witnesses and the muted sounds from the training grounds outside the windows where commands were being given to the cadets, the room was silent. The board had convened in the matter of Fitz John Porter, recently a major general of the Civil War for the United States.

Inside the main building, the dark paneled hearing room was quiet. General Schofield, the presiding judge advocate, tapped his gavel lightly twice on the broad oak table before him. The two dozen witnesses, the several reporters, and the concerned friends of the accused sat up a little straighter. Every person present knew this hearing was the culmination of almost two decades of waiting to remove a painful dishonor for the man sitting at the petitioner's table.

This rehearing was the last bit of history to a bitter war that had taken half a million lives and caused untold damage to millions of others. The Porter court martial and the cashiering of a brave officer was perhaps one more poignant reminder of the dreadful collateral damage caused by the War Between the States two decades earlier.

The large wall clock at the side of the conference room stood exactly at 10 AM. The three officers, who sat around the large oak table, were all distinguished men of the regular army. Chairman John Schofield had held major commands during the Civil War. Like Porter, Schofield was a Democrat but since the emancipation of the Black man, attitudes had begun to change dramatically, especially in the North among Democrats.

President Andrew Johnson had selected Schofield as secretary of war in 1868. Schofield replaced the bitterly prejudiced Edwin Stanton, who had worked so hard to end Porter's career and had been the architect of Porter's wrongful and unjust conviction.

Note: Hereafter, when Porter's counsel refers to the testimony and the evidence during the rehearing, the source of Bullitt's facts and figures comes from the full text of *'Argument of John C. Bullitt, Counsel for the Petitioner, Fitz John Porter, Before the*

Advisory Board of Officers at West Point, January 6, 1879, U.S. Archives.' The sources of Bullitt's statements are shown, following his statement, as a page number, followed by total number of pages of the complete text. *Example: (P. 100:260).*

After Schofield, the other two board members were attorneys of high standing for the army and graduates of West Point: General A.H. Gerry and Colonel George Getty. The court recorder, a diminutive gentleman of advanced age, had the appearance of a chipmunk busy counting nuts as he wrote the words of the rehearing for posterity. Porter's counsels, three prominent lawyers, were John Bullitt, Joseph Choate, and Anson Maltby, and they sat at the petitioner's table with Porter.

Porter's Chief Counsel, John Bullitt, began his opening statement.

"May it please the Board; the accusations against General Porter may be stated as follows:

"First, General Porter did not march, as he was ordered, at 1 AM of August 28, 1862, from Warrenton Junction to Bristoe Station and delayed moving his troops until 3 AM. "

"Second, he did not obey the Joint Order of the morning of August 29, 1862, to move toward Gainesville."

"Third, on the night of August 29, 1862, being with his corps between Manassas Station, and within sound of the guns and in the presence of the enemy, and knowing that a severe action was being fought, and that his corps was badly needed, he did fail all day to bring his force to the field and did shamefully fall back retreat."

"Fourth, while a severe action was being fought on August 29, 1862, and believing General Pope was sustaining defeat and retiring from the field, he did fail to go to the aid of General Pope and retreated from the presumed defeat and failed to make any attempt to avert the disaster and aid in averting misfortune and endangering the Capitol of this country."

"Fifth, he disobeyed an order of 4:30 PM to attack an enemy on his flank or rear."

"Sixth, He disobeyed the 4:30 Order to attack the enemy and retreated from the advancing forces of the enemy, with no attempt to engage them, or to aid the troops, who were already fighting greatly superior numbers, and were relying on Porter's flank attack, to secure victory, which would have followed in compliance with said order."

"These six propositions are the substance of all the accusations upon which General Porter was found guilty by the court martial, which tried him and rendered its decision on January 10, 1863."

The attorney waited, allowing seconds to pass before completing his thought.

Looking up quickly, and searching the faces of the several board members, he said, "It appears to me, that the first inquiry should be the precise object of this rehearing and the nature of your duties in connection with it. The president has directed you to examine the court martial records, hear new evidence, and advise the president of what, in your judgment may be his duty regarding this matter. In a sense, you are acting as an appellate court. You are to examine the findings and the opinion submitted by Judge Advocate General Holt to the president. You are to determine whether the evidence submitted to the court martial was sufficient to warrant the findings of guilt. However, you are not to stop at that point. After you have examined all that is before you, you are to determine whether the findings of the court martial should be allowed to stand."

"The burden of proof is on the petitioner. The laboring oar is upon us. The onus is upon us to show the error of the court martial for want of new facts before this board. Therefore, if we can show that President Lincoln approved the findings of the court martial *because of misinformation,* you have the right to disregard his approval altogether."

Next he turned to the stack of interrogatories and official records before him.

"Let us examine the proceedings of the court martial. Let us see how far the evidence submitted to them sustains the charges that were made."

(Here followed ten pages of Counselor Bullitt's argument. This writer has endeavored to condense the points of his argument fairly and accurately)

THE 1:00 AM ORDER

Bullitt repeated the testimony of Generals Butterfield, Sykes and Warren, in regard to the charge that Porter failed to obey the 1:00 AM Order *(P. 18-22:254)*. These three generals restated three different points in harmony; the night was shrouded in a moonless darkness, the road was filled with nearly 3,000 supply wagon teams, and the troops had already marched all that day and were in no condition to fight without sleep.

Bullitt held the written record up before the board.

"Their testimony was ignored by Judge Advocate Holt *(P. 8-15:254)*. All the weight was given to Captain Duryee's statement that he *'did not experience any difficulties going out that night.'* Furthermore, the fact that Duryee started his march in daylight and halted at midnight was ignored. Also, the remainder of Duryee's testimony was not counted."

Here, Bullitt held up other papers.

"These are a portion of testimonies, which the judge advocate chose *not* to include with other evidence supporting General Porter's claims; those of Duryee, Myers, and Barstowe.

"Judge Advocate Holt asked Duryee, 'Was the road obstructed by wagons or otherwise?'"

"Captain Duryee's answer: *'The march was very slow. We halted every ten or fifteen minutes. It was a very tedious march.'*" *(P. 9:254)*

"Judge Advocate Holt then relied on Major Barstow's statement. Barstow had said, *'I have no vivid recollection of that night as we moved over that road. It seemed to be like other nights we moved.'* *(P. 10-12:254)* However, Major Barstow marched in *daylight* and camped at 9 o'clock."

"Lieutenant Colonel Myers, chief quartermaster for McDowell, answered Holt's question, *'I know of nothing that would have hindered troops marching along the railroad which runs parallel to the road, although I may be mistaken in that opinion.'* *(P. 11-12:254)*

"John Reynolds was questioned. *(P. 12-14:254)* The judge advocate asked Reynolds, *'You say the night was dark. Would it have been practicable to march over that road with a guide?'* Reynolds replied, *'I suppose it would.'*"

"Please note that Holt had *neglected* to include in his posed question to Reynolds the added obstruction of three thousand wagon teams."

"Reynolds was also asked, *'Was the night too dark to march troops in masses over an unfamiliar country?'* And General Reynolds' reply was to say, *'I should think so. I do not think it possible to march troops on such a night. I should have considered it a very precipitous undertaking.'*"

"When Porter's counsel asked General Reynolds these questions, for reasons I will not venture to explain, and I confess *I do not understand,* Judge Advocate Holt *omitted* those questions and Reynolds' answers from the record."

Boring in on the point, Bullitt said, "It is clear that the judge advocate also relied heavily on General Pope's testimony. *(P. 14:254)* Pope had declared when asked, *'In my opinion the night was good for marching and the road was clear. Even if there had been obstructions, the railroad track was clear.'*"

Bullitt's censure of John Pope was plain.

"It might be inferred from General Pope's statement, that the march would have been a pleasant summer evening's excursion. He seems to think there should have been not the slightest difficulty in marching ten thousand men with artillery over railroad tracks whose ties were torn up and whose rails were broken in several places."

"I do not believe anybody but such a man as Pope, who had everything to lose with any other testimony, would claim that a railroad track was a reasonable road for a private citizen to go over, much less an army, marching in the darkness."

Bullitt continued. "General Heintzelman said, *'It is very difficult to march over railroad tracks at night. Some of the tracks were torn up, ties were piled on the tracks, culverts were destroyed, and bridges burned.'* *(P. 18:254)*"

"If the judge advocate had given a fair or full summary or statement to the whole of the evidence, the exact reverse of the inferences drawn by him would have been conclusively established."

Speaking without notes, Counselor Bullitt summed up his argument against the judge advocate.

"The judge advocate said, *'The manner in which Porter marched was an indication that General Porter was not trying to execute the order in good faith.'*"

Bullitt paused, and fixing his eyes on the men at the table, said, "Porter ordered Colonel Brinton, at midnight, to clear the road. Porter sent requests to Pope asking for help to clear the road of the wagons, which were under Pope's order. Porter exerted himself, with the help of his officers to get the wagons out of the way so his men could get through."

Bullitt allowed himself a slight smile of derision for Pope's statement.

"Pope's own admission was that he knew *'Porter was coming along the road slowly and pushing the wagons out of the way.'*"

"Testimonies of Generals Sykes, Butterfield, and Warren *(P. 8:254)* confirm the extreme difficulty of marching under these conditions. Porter's general officers, without exception, asked General Porter to delay the march until daylight, and that is on the record. Butterfield stated that his troops were in no condition to march without some sleep. Porter insisted that the order *must* be obeyed. It was only after Porter saw for himself his general officers' contentions that darkness was *'so apparent,'* it was *'impossible to move,'* and that *'nothing could be gained by marching early, best at a later hour, three or four in the morning,'* did he defer to his general officers."

"All this evidence had no weight with the judge advocate. He brushed them away as though they were feathers, while the slightest expressions of an adverse character, no matter the source, were magnified to the last degree."

"This trial was the most important in the history of this nation. The sentence of the court martial was the severest that could be imposed, short of death. To an honorable man, sensitive and high-toned, that sentence was worse than death. General Porter enjoyed the highest degree of confidence from the president. He had won signal honor and distinction on more than one battlefield. With his devotion to country, his soldierly attainments, and his power to command, he was regarded as the peer of the truest and best of his comrades in arms."

"I shall try to show next, how erroneous was the opinion the judge advocate submitted to the president on January 19, 1863. Lieutenant Colonel Myers was a wagon master. He had never marched troops. He admitted he had two to three thousand wagons on that road that night that filled the road and parked where they chose."

Bullitt added, "Myers was not a military man. He had never tried to march troops over a railroad. This was a railroad with broken ties and breaks in the line. To march 10,000 men in darkness over a broken railroad filled with obstructions; can any sane man say that a road filled with wagon teams, marching on such a dark night, is not facing a serious obstruction to marching along that road?"

Bullitt concluded with a damning statement.

"I submit that the evidence cited by the judge advocate shows the entire mistake into which he had fallen on this whole subject. His mind was so filled with prejudice, so poisoned against General Porter, that he was unable to review this evidence as it ought to have been examined at the time. Of the four pages of testimony only 36 lines were disclosed to the president, while all of the rest supporting Porter's innocence of the charge *were not given to President Lincoln.*"

Bullitt's voice rose to emphasize he words.

"There *is no military rule which imposed upon General Porter the necessity of trying to move at 1:00 AM that night.* Therefore, the opinion and the finding of the court martial on this point was manifestly an error."

THE JOINT ORDER

Counselor Bullitt's presentation had taken nearly an hour. Water was brought to the table and a moment of recess gave the board members time to review their notes. Counselor Bullitt picked up his papers and looked up to address the listening members of the board with the next charge.

"We now come to the next proposition, which is the charge that General Porter disobeyed the *Joint Order* of the morning of August 28, 1862, given to Generals McDowell and Porter to move toward Gainesville. The Order reads,

'*To Generals McDowell and Porter: You will please move forward with your joint commands toward Gainesville. I sent General Porter written orders to that effect an hour and a half ago. Heintzelman, Siegel, and Reno are now moving on the Warrenton Turnpike and by now must be not far from Gainesville. I desire that, as soon as communication is established between this force and your own, the whole command shall halt. It may be necessary to fall back behind Bull Run, at Centreville tonight. I presume it will not be so because of our supplies. I have sent no orders of any kind to Ricketts, and none to interfere in any way with McDowell's troops, except what I sent to his aid-de-camp last night, which were to hold his position on the Warrenton Pike until the troops from here should fall on the enemy's flank and rear. I do not even know Ricketts' position, as I have not been able to find out where General McDowell was until a late hour this morning. General McDowell will take immediate steps to communicate with General Ricketts and instruct him to join the other divisions of his corps as soon as practical. If any considerable advantages are to be gained by departing from this order, it will not be strictly carried out. One thing must be held in view: that the troops must occupy a position from which they can reach Bull Run tonight or by morning. The indications are that the whole force of the enemy is moving in this direction at a pace that will bring them here by tomorrow night or the next day. My own headquarters will for the present be at Heintzelman's corps, or at this place.*'"

"I wished to make clear, gentlemen, that no order or information was received by General Porter from General Pope *after* Porter received this Joint Order, until,"

Here Bullitt paused *to* look at his notes,

"Until Porter received delivery of what is known as the 4:30 Order late in the afternoon, at about sunset."

Bullitt stopped to emphasize another point.

"Pope had set up new headquarters. Now he had moved to from Centreville to near the intersection of Sudley Road. He was to the immediate rear of Siegel, Reno, and Heintzelman on the Warrenton Turnpike. General Porter did not know this. Porter also was unaware at that time, when the Joint Order was given to him, that there was fighting on the Turnpike. Therefore, we must consider General Porter's conduct in light of the Joint Order, the changing circumstances, as they existed that morning, and as they developed until he received the 4:30 Order that night."

Bullitt made wry half-grin as he held up a copy of Pope's Joint Order.

"I must admit I had trouble understanding this vague and confusing order. My difficulty might be my lack of a military education." (*It was a kind way for Bullitt to say the order was confusing as hell.*) However, you and I must try to *analyze* the Joint Order for its meaning. We must know what Pope intended."

Bullitt began by saying, "Its directions are these."

He moved a step to a wooden tripod stand behind him. On the stand was a 30-inch by 40-inch illustration board. It had been covered with a cloth. He removed the cloth and on the board several points had been listed:

"Porter and McDowell were to move to Gainesville. They were to contact Heintzelman, Reno, and Siegel. They were moving that way. Then they were to halt. They were told, '*When you have halted, be at a place where you can fall back to Centreville that night or by morning.*' The order stated, '*If any other advantage comes up, this order does not need to be obeyed.*' Finally, both men were instructed to tell General Ricketts to '*join General McDowell as soon as he can.*'"

"The five parts seem clear enough. But let's look deeper. Let us try to know what Pope really wanted of Porter and McDowell. First, consider the part of the order that said, '*If any considerable advantages are to be gained by departing from this order, it will not be strictly carried out.*' Pope then added the warning, '*It may be necessary to fall back behind Bull Run, at Centreville tonight.*' Finally, Pope stated, '*The indications are that the whole force of the enemy is moving in this direction at a pace that will bring them here by tomorrow night or the next day.*'"

Bullitt waited for the impact of these instructions from Pope to be clear to his audience. After five seconds he volunteered an opinion that was reasonable.

"It appears from the wording of the order that Pope aimed to avoid a general engagement until *all* his forces were behind Bull Run. With this in mind, and having impressed his generals to avoid a general battle, they *still* had discretion to attack Jackson, but to *avoid* a general battle, in case Lee's main Confederate force should form on their front which did in fact occur. Apparently that probable eventuality was unforeseen by Pope, or at least, Pope denied he thought it probable."

(Here Bullitt paused to allow time for that information to sink into the minds of his listeners).

"Here is the question. Did Porter act according to his best judgment that afternoon?"

Without waiting for an answer Bullitt changed the topic.

Picking up another set of papers he said, "Let us go back for a moment, to the day before, August 27. What did Pope know and when did he know it?'

"He knew Hooker had met and had fought Richard Ewell's Confederates at Bristoe Station. He knew Jackson had gone on to Manassas Junction. He knew Jackson's troops had burned the Union supplies there and was moving toward Centreville. He knew that Longstreet was coming through Thoroughfare Gap."

This time Bullitt waited a full minute before proceeding. He wanted to point out an important fact.

"Pope had at least *four* several early warnings of Longstreet's approach: from Porter, from Reynolds, from Banks and from McDowell, yet he acted, by all we know, as though Longstreet was unimportant, a cipher in his plans to capture Jackson."

Counselor John Bullitt was laying out the facts of the case as though he was building a house, step by step, so that the evidence and the facts would be completely understood by every member of the board.

"Porter had been told to move toward Gainesville. This was intended by Pope so that Porter's forces might catch Jackson before he could escape through Gainesville into Thoroughfare Gap and join Longstreet's forces. McDowell's force, Pope assumed, would hold off Longstreet at the Gap should he appear."

"Then Pope changed his orders. At 9 PM, August 27, McDowell was ordered to go to Manassas, instead of Gainesville, where Pope thought Jackson might be. To be more certain that Longstreet would remain bottled up in the Gap, McDowell left Ricketts' division in Gainesville."

Bullitt continued with a review of the situation to that moment.

"Beginning in the morning of August 28, until just after midnight, this was the situation; all day Ricketts held Longstreet at the Gap until he was forced to fall back at nightfall. King's division, on the Warrenton Turnpike, at evening of that day had a sharp engagement with Jackson, who had set his defenses on Stony Ridge above the Pike."

"Just after midnight of August 28, at 3 AM of August 29, Pope was yet *unaware* that Jackson was on Stony Ridge. In fact, Pope did not know that Jackson had attacked King on the previous late afternoon. Not knowing any of these things, and *thinking Jackson was at Centreville,*"

His voice gained emphasis.

"Pope, issued new orders to Porter, Hooker, and Kearney. They were sent to Centreville to attack Jackson."

"Matters were becoming confused because of Pope's ignorance. As Porter moved toward Centreville, McDowell intercepted Porter at Manassas Junction. He told Porter about King's hard fight on the Turnpike and that King had been forced to retreat to Manassas. He also told Porter that Ricketts' men at the Gap had retreated before Longstreet's advance. McDowell told Porter to follow that part of the Joint Order, which said to form his troops behind Bull Run and wait for reinforcements from McClellan, and that Franklin's corps was expected any moment. And finally, Porter was ordered *not to bring on a general engagement* until reinforcements had arrived."

"Porter obeyed his senior officer, General McDowell. He began his move to Centreville, but, before he had gone two and a half miles from Manassas toward Centreville, *new orders* came from Pope. Now General Porter was directed to move in the opposite direction; toward Gainesville for the second time. He was told to take King's division with him." (P. 31:254)

"The messenger, Captain Piatt, gave McDowell the same message. Whereupon, McDowell, who was embarrassed to give up an entire division to a junior officer, sent a request to Pope. He asked Pope to allow him to keep King's division and *not to give King to Porter*. In spite of the startling fact that this new order would be to *remove and weaken Porter's strength* by several thousand fighting men, should he meet Longstreet, *Pope agreed.*"

Counsel Bullitt stopped, with an expression of incredulity at Pope's act. Then, after a slight pause, he continued his careful narration of the events of those three days.

"I wish to emphasize this point: Porter remonstrated against losing King. He knew from McDowell that Ricketts had been forced back at the Gap. Porter knew Longstreet was coming and there was no one to stop him. He badly needed King's division. Yet, it was his duty to stop Longstreet, so, following orders, he turned about and headed back to Gainesville."

"At the same time Porter had received several other *verbal orders* from Pope that were contradictory. Seeing the possibility of a dangerous confusion, he asked General Pope that his orders be in writing in the future. Porter's request was a very wise and reasonable request. It was also necessary in light of Pope's lack of specificity and carelessness in issuing orders."

"What Porter expected might happen, did happen; when Porter reached Dawkins Branch at about 11:30 AM, he met Longstreet's forces coming from Gainesville. The distance to Thoroughfare Gap was nine miles. Since he had captured Longstreet's scouts and he could see the dust rising above the trees, he had every reason to believe it was Longstreet who confronted him."

"What did he do? The first thing he did was to throw out skirmishers to find out what he faced. Then he sent Butterfield's men to move forward, seize a commanding position and cover the deployment of his troops. Divisions under Morell, Sykes and King were set in line of battle."

"While these movements were in progress, from the content of Pope's several orders, it seemed Pope's purpose was to place Porter and McDowell between Jackson and Longstreet to prevent their linking up, and also to capture Jackson. The terms of the Joint Order were difficult. It was obscure. It was complex. Any officer, given such an order should be expected to be given liberality in its execution."

John Bullitt paused. He leaned toward the assembled board to further emphasize the seriousness of the problem Pope had caused.

"Now, Gentlemen, I call your attention to this point. It is a point I consider most extraordinary. The Joint Order says plainly by Pope that the *'indications were that the whole force of the enemy was moving at a pace that would bring them here by tomorrow night or the next day.'*"

He lowered the timber of his voice until the dozen spectators at the rear of the room could hardly hear him. Several leaned forward to catch his words.

"Yet, Pope was well aware from Buford's note of *'17 divisions, artillery and 500 cavalry'* that Longstreet was already through the Gap. We know that the main purpose of the Joint Order was to prevent Longstreet from joining Jackson. Pope knew Ricketts had been forced to retreat. That is the reason why Pope reassigned Ricketts to Porter along with reassigning King's division, to give Porter enough men so *he could stop Longstreet.*"

Bullitt, who almost always spoke in a calm and quiet manner, now changed. His voice grew stronger.

"John Pope *knew* when he issued the Joint Order, in which he stated that Longstreet *might* arrive by night or the next day, Longstreet was actually *nine miles away*. He would arrive on the battlefield, by the most generous of estimates, that same day."

As if counting the points, he raised a forefinger.

"Pope *admitted* he knew the truth. At the court martial Pope testified, *'I knew Longstreet could be expected certainly that afternoon of the 29th.'*"

A second finger was raised.

"Pope knew Longstreet was no more than a day's march from the Gap on the 27th. Pope knew that Longstreet was *in the Gap on the 28th*. Pope knew at 10 o'clock in the morning, when he sent the Joint Order that the Confederate army was within an easy half-day's march from the field of battle."

Bullitt waited a full minute before continuing. Then he made his most damning statement of the day.

"Now, I say to you, what General Pope did is the most extraordinary part of this whole affair. Here is a commanding officer, who has given General Porter, his subordinate, an important command. He sends him on a mission of the first magnitude. He places twenty thousand men under that subordinate's command for the purpose of discharging a duty, a duty so vital that upon the result of that duty rests the fate of the commanding officer's *own army*, and *the fate of his government*."

The Counselor stopped, as though the words he spoke were too terrible and implausible to be believed.

Continuing in a voice of condemnation, he said, "Yet, although that same commanding officer *knew* that the main force of the enemy was within an easy half-day's march of his men, he told his subordinates that this force *would not appear upon the battlefield until the night of the next day*."

Counselor Bullitt lifted his hands and raised his brows in astonishment at his own words, staring at the officers sitting before him. Dropping his arms, he became immediately more formal. When he asked the next question it seemed he was chastising someone not in the room for the injustice which the court martial had lain upon Fitz John Porter.

"Consider, Officers, is it fair to hold that subordinate officer responsible for the non-performance of duty under an order so inconsistent with the known facts?"

Note: Eleven pages (P. 24-36:254) of the complete text of Attorney John C. Bullitt's argument on Porter's behalf to the Schofield Advisory Board has been condensed for brevity. Every essential part has been retained for a clear and accurate representation of the crucial points made in the text and Bullitt's appeal.

Counselor Bullitt offered his explanation of the *meaning* of the Joint Order.

"Porter's and McDowell's common purpose of doing duty together was to move toward Gainesville and regain the ground lost by Ricketts' fifteen thousand troops. Pope's intent was that Ricketts' and King's divisions, when united with Porter's corps, would be large enough to stop Longstreet's forces at Gainesville. At the same time an attack could be made on Jackson's right flank."

Bullitt paused here to hit hard on a point that needed to be made clear.

"Further, there was *nothing in the Joint Order* that allowed Porter and McDowell's corps to be divided. Yet McDowell left Porter and divided their forces contrary to the Joint Order's imperative."

He summed up.

"Considering the accusations against Porter for not obeying the Joint Order we must consider all that happened that day."

"First, by noon Porter had encountered the enemy at Dawkins Creek."

"Second, Porter received his copy of the Joint Order."

"Third, while Porter was deploying his troops and studying the confusing Joint Order, McDowell arrived. *His appearance automatically, as senior officer, gave him command of Porter's corps.*"

"Fourth, McDowell, seeing Porter was in the midst of deploying his troops against the enemy, exclaimed, *'Porter, you are too far out.'*" (P. 40:254)

"Porter understood what McDowell meant for him to do. Since McDowell's direction was based on the Joint Order, and the Joint Order required both men to fall back to Bull Run to meet the enemy with the entire army, McDowell meant that Porter was being ordered to stop deployment and move his troops toward Bull Run. And moving through Manassas was the quickest way to Bull Run."

"At McDowell's command, Porter stopped all deployment preparations. To further convince Porter of the need to fall back to prepare to meet the enemy as a unit, McDowell told him of Buford's report of that morning of, *'17 divisions, artillery, and 500 cavalry sighted moving through Gainesville at 9 AM.'*"

"Fifth, from the words of the Joint Order, both Porter and McDowell were informed by Pope that Longstreet was expected."

Here, Bullitt stopped. Holding his audience while they were temporarily frozen in rapt attention, he finished.

"...but not *'until tomorrow night or the next day.'*"

He followed that quote with an excerpt of Pope's testimony from the court martial record.

"Let me call your attention to Pope's own testimony. He says, on page 33 of the record, *'I had feared the junction of these corps at any moment, as I knew from information that Longstreet was pushing forward to join Jackson. I therefore expected that movement of Longstreet's army certainly during the afternoon of the 29th.'*" (P. 37:254)

Counselor Bullitt put all of the complex parts of the Joint Order together to illustrate McDowell's last crippling response to Porter.

"Pope had given King's division to Porter. However, in a ride through the woods it became obvious because of the enemy's presence, that *there was no way McDowell could send King's division to Porter.* Thereupon, McDowell rode off without any further word of explanation."

"When Porter called after him for orders, asking, *'What shall I do?'* McDowell's only response was a wave of his hand. Porter, on his own, had to decide his course of action."

"What did Porter do? Well, gentlemen, he decided to attack Longstreet, or hold him in position, with or without King's added forces, until he knew what was going on with the rest of Pope's army."

Bullitt's description of Porter's quandary at that moment, after McDowell had ridden off, was so clear to his listeners that they could almost see themselves in General Porter's place. Bullitt supplied the answers by giving them the reasonable access into Porter's reasoning as another soldier.

"Since Porter had decided to fight, he still needed King. When he sent word to McDowell asking for King to be returned to his forces, McDowell replied with a negative. McDowell, for his reasons whatever they were, had decided to keep King's division."

Bullitt interjected his narrative with a point of importance.

"In his reply, McDowell *also ordered* Porter to *'Stay where you are. Fall back, if necessary, to Bull Run.'*"

Once more paused, Bullitt raised his tone of voice to a higher level of emphasis, and said clearly, lest anyone miss his meaning.

"That was a *most important order* from McDowell. If that order had seen the light of day at the Porter court martial, it would have *cleared Fitz John Porter of the charges.*"

Bullitt framed a clear indictment of Irvin McDowell.

"But McDowell claimed *he never sent the order.*"

"Now, I say, this is the most extraordinary part of this whole affair. Testimony at the retrial has revealed that the charge of Porter's delay in the march to Gainesville was *without foundation*. The Joint Order was written about 10 AM. Porter did not receive the order until noon. Furthermore, all the evidence shows that General Porter not only anticipated the order, but he fully executed the order *ahead of time.*"

"He moved forward with his command toward Gainesville as far as he could go. He fully complied with the part of the order which said, *'I desire that as soon as communication is established between this force (Heintzelman, Siegel and Reno) and your force, the whole command shall halt.'* He established communication with this force and he formed a line to engage Longstreet on his immediate front."

"Even General McDowell testified Porter had *complied* with the directions of the order *before it reached him*. All the facts show that General Porter gave an intelligent and prompt compliance with this order and the two preceding orders, which he received that day."

"The proof also shows that General McDowell, who was senior to Porter, was present when Porter received the order. McDowell assumed command and thereby *became responsible for the movements of General Porter's corps.* McDowell's *own words* in his testimony during the Porter court martial were, *'At that time I conceived General Porter was under me. When the Joint Order reached us we were doing what the Joint Order directed us to do. That Joint Order found the troops in the position in which it directed them to be.'*"

Counselor Bullitt continued.

"Soon after, Morell reported to Porter, *'An attack will bring on a disastrous repulse. It will be followed by a strong pursuit.'*"

"Porter agreed. After hearing reports from his other divisions, Porter also saw the extreme danger in *pushing an attack.*"

"It was nearing sunset. The day was nearly spent. Thereupon General Porter gave orders for his troops to retire for the night but remain in position to hold the enemy on the following morning. His order read, *'Put your men in position to remain during the night, and have out your pickets. Put them so that they will be in a position to resist anything.'" (P. 52:254)*

"What could be clearer than that to show Porter was *willing and ready* to attack?"

THE 4:30 PM ORDER

Bullitt held up a sheet of paper. It was a copy of the now infamous *4:30 Order.*

"As the day was ending and it was growing dark, the 4:30 Order arrived. Here occurred another error by the judge advocate during the Porter court martial. Judge Holt believed the 4:30 Order arrived to Porter's hand *before* Porter told his troops to hold positions for the night. The facts now show that the 4:30 Order arrived *after* he had ordered Morell to hold position for the night." *(P. 53:254)*

John Bullitt read the order from General Pope:

'Your line of march brings you in on the enemy's (Stonewall Jackson's) right flank, and if possible, on his rear, keeping your right in communication with General Reynolds. The enemy is massed in the woods in front of us, but can be shelled out as soon as you engage their flank. Keep heavy reserves, and use your batteries, keeping well closed to your right and rear, so as to keep you in close communication with the right wing.'

"Here is a new conundrum," Bullitt said. "Please follow this reading closely."

"That evening, *before* he received the 4:30 Order, Porter sent duplicate messages to McDowell, hoping one of them would get through. The messages said, *'I have no communication from you. I may have to retire for food and water. The enemy is going to our left and our rear. I have no more messengers or cavalry. Let me know your designs, whether you retire or not. Have lost a few men.'"*

Bullitt was a lawyer. Good lawyers use drama to their advantage. Good lawyers have also learned that over-emphasis or too much drama soon becomes a detriment to clear argument. Bullitt was not only an excellent lawyer; he was an experienced proposer of argument. During the rehearing he had used emphasis to advantage. Most of the time his words were stated with measured objectivity of a statement of the facts. Now, once more the subject was worthy of special emphasis.

"These messages to McDowell were NEVER PRODUCED at the trial."

"They *were* finally produced, after twenty years, for the first time at this meeting, during the taking of testimony from General McDowell. Because the judge advocate did not see these orders, an erroneous impression was created. McDowell, in his original testimony at the trial, indicated that the 4:30 Order arrived *before* General Porter had ordered Morell to *'post his men for the night.'"* *(P. 53:254)*

"This would, indeed have been cowardice and a refusal to face the enemy—had that been true. But it was *not* true."

"The undisputed truth is that the 4:30 Order came long *after* Porter's directive to General Morell to *'post his men for the night.'"*

"These dispatches contain intrinsic evidence that they were written *before* General Porter had received the 4:30 order. The language found in them could not have been used by Porter if he had already received the order to attack, as contained in the 4:30 Order." *(P. 54:254)*

"Immediately, within minutes, after General Porter had the 4:30 Order in his hand he sent Colonel Locke to General Morell with an order to *'Move forward with your division and attack with your whole force.'* Thereafter, Porter rode to Morell. Porter realized when he arrived at Morell's headquarters that it was so late it was impossible to follow the 4:30 Order to attack that day so he told Morell to put his men in position for the night."

Bullitt took a deep breath and placed the papers he had been holding in his hand on the table before him. He looked at each of the board members.

Nodding his head in an apparent expression of wonder and utter bafflement, he said, "It is difficult for me to comprehend how, with these facts before us, General Porter could have been found guilty of disobedience to the Joint Order. What Porter did after receiving the order is the best refutation of the charges. McDowell took away two-thirds of the force with which he was to execute the Joint Order. From that moment successful execution became impossible. He was left by McDowell in such a position that he was compelled to exercise his best discretion in the use of his force. He acted with honesty, zeal, and fidelity, all of which are demonstrated by the dispatches he wrote during that afternoon."

Counselor Bullitt had concluded his reading of the defense. He turned the hearing board members' attention to the several important errors, which had been committed by the court martial board and the judge advocate, which had added to and exacerbated indications of General Porter's perceived guilt of the charges.

"Indeed, the answer to this problem is solved when the serious errors and mistakes made by the court martial are perceived. It was an error for the court to assert that McDowell took command of Porter's force *before* the Joint Order was received. This happened *long after* Colonel Piatt and General Reynolds had passed Pope's order to Porter to change his movement from Centreville to Gainesville."

"Yet recall, from the time Porter first saw McDowell and McDowell was told King's division had been assigned to Porter, what did McDowell do? He loitered and hung around Porter's skirts hoping to get King back until he got an answer from Pope returning King. That happened only when he received his copy of the Joint Order and he took charge of Porter's force."

"What did McDowell claim during the court martial? On page 91 of the record he says very distinctly, *'General Porter and I started out from Manassas with the understanding that under the Articles of War applicable in such cases, I had command of the whole force; his own and my own.'*" (P. 58-59:254)

"I repeat to this board the all-important fact that McDowell claimed, incorrectly, he took command over Porter *before* he, McDowell, received the Joint Order. Yet, please remember, *McDowell was not in command* of Porter's forces *until* the Joint Order gave him that legal right."

"This egregious error does not stand in isolation. Allow me to list the errors, which were made by the court martial and its advocate general."

❧ 57 ❧

Condemnation

John Bullitt bent over backwards to avoid casting any hint or slightest of aspersions on the members of the Porter court martial or that any hint of a conspiracy existed between the court or any of the witnesses. Now, however, a note of deeper criticism stole its way into his remarks.

"The Porter court martial *chose* to believe differently. They believed that Porter had been under McDowell's command *before* the Joint Order was given to the two men. That belief was *wholly an error* on the part of the judge advocate. There is *not a fact to sustain it*. General Gibbon's testimony is to the contrary. In addition, the court martial record itself clearly shows if and when McDowell took command of Porter's corps."

Counselor Bullitt found a page of the trial testimony, touched his glasses to place them more securely on his nose, and read Gibbon's testimony. *(P. 61-63:254)*

"Gibbon states: *'General Porter placed the order in McDowell's hands. McDowell read it and he expressed dissatisfaction that part of his command was assigned to General Porter. I recollect McDowell requested General Porter to place King's division on Porter's right so he could keep his command together.'*"

He continued reading Gibbon's testimony.

"The judge advocate questioned Gibbon: *'Was there any other conversation, other than McDowell's request of Porter?'*"

Before reading Gibbon's answer to the question, Bullitt gave his listeners a wry smile and said, "Gentlemen, I think you know that generals in charge do not make requests, *they give orders.*"

"Gibbon's answer was, *'I think not. I don't recall any.'*"

Bullitt continued.

"The question: *'Did you understand that at that time McDowell asserted any right to take command of Porter's forces?'*"

"Answer: *'Not at all. On the contrary, I assumed that McDowell's request was proof positive that he had not assumed command.'*"

With a subtle change in the tenor of his words, Bullitt underscored Gibbon's testimony from the record as a matter of great importance.

"Consider General McDowell's conduct after he received the Joint Order, and his testimony at the trial. It is an illustration of how much McDowell tried to make the evidence *conform* to what he deemed proper for his own vindication... without regard for the facts as they really occurred. McDowell had the legal right to assume command. It was his duty. It was then, after he came up to Porter with the Joint Order in his hands, which gave him what he wanted so badly, King's division, that he took command. As the superior in charge he could then take back King from Porter. *Then, and only then* did he assume command."

Bullitt continued. "Now let us turn to another error that was made by Judge Advocate Holt," Bullitt said. "This error made by the court martial was the substratum, the beginning upon which all other errors were founded."

"McDowell testified that when they met to discuss the Joint Order, '*Porter's forces were three miles beyond Bethlehem Church.*' This was close to Jackson's line and, if it had been true, Porter had no obstacle before him for an attack as ordered."

"It was *not* true."

"General Porter never got beyond Dawkins Creek, two miles from Bethlehem Church. He faced Longstreet's 25,000 Confederates at Dawkins Creek three miles from Jackson's line."

"How then did the court come to this error?"

Bullitt answered his own question.

"They came to this egregious error by McDowell's testimony alone. At the trial, McDowell was questioned on this matter. He was asked, '*Was there a considerable force of the enemy in front of Porter?*' McDowell replied to the Court, '*I have no positive knowledge on that point. I have not supposed there was, but I cannot say.*'"

"McDowell was asked, '*Was General Porter close enough to attack Jackson?*'"

"McDowell replied, '*The distance from General Porter's head of column to the road was not so great as to have enabled a large force of the enemy to be between them.*'" (P. 64-65:254)

"It is no wonder the court assumed it to be true; McDowell was the *only person that* authored the allegation that Porter was close to Jackson, and yet Porter retreated. The facts are these. If Porter had been where McDowell claimed that he was, Porter would have been within enemy lines." (P. 66:254)

Bullitt allowed himself the liberty of a poorly repressed chuckle of derision.

"McDowell committed an error of the most material character to mislead the court from arriving at the truth with reference to the charges made against him. It is a pity. By his deception McDowell lost a great opportunity for his own self-aggrandizement. If he had taken command and ordered Porter to halt, as Porter did on his own, McDowell would now have the credit of having deferred the disaster that fell upon Pope by one full day. Thereby McDowell, *and not Porter,* would have saved Pope's army."

John Bullitt was in most cases before a jury, a self-contained, unflappable officer of the law. Now, however, Bullitt's disdain and scorn for McDowell became plain.

"Instead, what did Irvin McDowell do? McDowell used his right as senior commander to take 17,000 men from Porter and retire while leaving Porter to meet Longstreet's 29,000 troops with one-third the men."

"Now I come to still one *more* of the errors into which the court martial must have fallen. McDowell was determined to justify his decision that *'there were considerable advantages to be gained by departing from the Joint Order.'* That is to say, McDowell claimed that by moving his forces along the Sudley Springs Road toward the field of battle then being fought by General Pope and the main army, his purpose was to throw himself on the enemy's center. At the same time, he wished General Porter to attack the enemy's right flank."

"McDowell testified this was the case. First, he conveyed the impression there was serious fighting on his right. From McDowell's testimony the judge advocate concluded that McDowell had been listening for between five and six hours to the battle raging on his right: *'I heard the sound of battle, which seemed to be at its height on our right, toward Groveton.'* (P. 85 of the court martial record)

"McDowell calculated to produce the impression upon the mind of the court martial that this battle was raging within their hearing. Yet we know from all other testimony there was a lull upon the field. There was some artillery firing at long range but no infantry fighting. However, McDowell implied infantry fighting and not merely long-range artillery."

"He knew his statement was wholly untrue."

Bullitt continued. "This was said by McDowell to prove that Porter shrank coward-like away from the performance of his duty to his comrades, who were struggling in an unequal battle of forces at Groveton. He was planting poison in the minds of the court martial and the judge advocate. He was himself in danger, and not following the manly course and remaining with Porter to meet Longstreet."

"Unfortunately for Porter, unfortunately for the cause of justice, unfortunately for the cause of truth, aye, unfortunately for the sake of General McDowell himself, I fear his heart had never had a manly beat to meet such an issue and stand where only an honest man should stand. Instead, he threw the responsibility upon the shoulders of another fellow officer."

Now Bullitt fell silent. He straightened, took a deep breath, and resumed his argument, more quietly but with measured force.

"Now the time has come to rectify these mistakes. After sixteen years this investigation can be conducted free of bias or prejudice. The circumstances that took place and the influences that were then operating at that time in 1862, that made the minds of men inflamed, had made them ready to receive extravagant statements."

"Then there was a great national disaster. There had been a series of defeats. Popular feeling was to find someone upon whom the consequences of the disaster could be turned. No matter how calm and deliberate the judges may have been during that terrible time, it was almost impossible for the human mind to resist those influences and look at the question candidly, unbiased, and unprejudiced."

Now that John Bullitt was certain he had established Porter's absolute innocence, his speech turned to an opportunity to mend fences, to lighten his harsh criticism, which he had leveled at the members of the Porter court martial, and at the judge advocate.

"With all due respect for the court martial and its judge advocate, this record, from beginning to end shows the influences of which I speak. General McDowell and General Pope produced stories that were inconsistent and contradictory. But men did not weigh these stories with coolness and deliberation so soon after the disaster of that battle on the Plain of Manassas."

Bullitt took time to praise one man on the court martial board; the recorder, Major Gardner. No doubt, Fitz John Porter was very grateful and had directed Bullitt to recognize Gardner's contributions to Porter's final judgment of innocence.

"Major Gardner, the official recorder, performed his duty to supply General Porter with every part of evidence available. He made available every reasonable facility, papers and information with the greatest of zeal and good will. Thus, with his willing assistance, General Porter was able to present his case during this rehearing in completeness and with clarity."

THE JACKSON REPORT

Counselor Bullitt presented his case.

"There was one other curious document that I wish to present for your inspection. It was a booklet, a kind of journal written by Irvin McDowell. It purported to quote Thomas Jackson's battle reports written after the battle and before Stonewall Jackson's death," Bullitt said.

"In preparation for this rehearing, General Porter's counsel and my fellow counsel, Joseph Choate, deposed General McDowell to testify as to McDowell's confusion to his Abstract of the published report of Jackson's Battle Report of August 29 and 30, 1862. That Abstract, and McDowell's wrong interpretation of dates were most damaging to Porter's defense of the charge of cowardice and retreat in the face of the enemy."

"McDowell prepared and circulated this printed abstract from Thomas 'Stonewall' Jackson's report of the events of battle of August 29 and 30, 1862. Stonewall Jackson is now deceased. In order for McDowell to justify his *'misstatements,'* McDowell altered the date of the battle from the 30th to the 29th. Then he paraded the article to show and to justify his *misstatements,* to which he testified. McDowell's Abstract of Jackson's writing was to show that Porter was near the sound of heavy fighting, near Jackson's line, on the Turnpike on August 29. Yet, he testified that Porter retreated in cowardly fashion to Dawkins Branch, two miles from the fighting."

"It is idle to contend that General McDowell fell into these misstatements of dates innocently. It would be too severe an attack on credulity to suppose McDowell did not see that Jackson's battle report related to August 30, and not August 29. If McDowell did not see this he was guilty of such recklessness as to preclude the possibility of putting reliance to truth on *any statement he made.*"

"If McDowell was innocent of intentional perversion, then he was so reckless as not to be entitled to have any reliance put upon his statements. If McDowell was guilty of willful misstatement, then it would prove a want of truthfulness that would sweep out of the case the whole effect of the evidence."

Then Porter's alternate attorney, Counselor Joseph Choate, stood and took Bullitt's place at the head of the table. Choate picked up the Abstract and held up a thin booklet for the board's inspection.

"This treatise, an Abstract written by McDowell after the Porter trial, was the further proof McDowell needed to justify his actions on August 29 and his testimony to the court martial. McDowell had authored this booklet to support a further defense of his actions during the Battle of Second Manassas. The booklet was called *'The Jackson Report.'* It was a treatise written by McDowell, containing, supposedly, Jackson's report of August 29 and 30."

"When McDowell was questioned for disposition prior to this rehearing on the obvious errors of the dates in his writings, he protested any wrongdoing. He claimed the extract contained in his writing is from General Thomas Jackson's report of the battle of August 30, 1862. McDowell claimed it was a true report of the battle as it occurred on August 29, at the time he was with Porter at Dawkins Branch. He claimed it was the reason he withdrew his forces from Porter and went toward Groveton."

Counselor Choate continued.

"His purpose was plain. It was to magnify Porter's failure to attack Jackson's right on August 29. It was to show a terrific battle had actually occurred that day. He altered the dates and then paraded the alteration to show the facts were as he testified. This was no innocent blunder."

"He was questioned numerous times for the rehearing about the discrepancy of dates in his writing. I asked him, *'Do you know what you printed and circulated as an extract from General Jackson's report of the battle of the 29th, was in fact an extract from Jackson's report of the 30th?'*

"McDowell's reply was vague. He said further, *'I thought it was the 29th. I made it in the spring after these events. Jackson mixed up the 29th and the 30th and some parts belong to one and some parts belong to the other.'*

Choate stated further regarding his conversation with McDowell, "When I said, *'I speak of this part, which you published as the report of the 29th. Do you now know that this report was of what took place on the 30th?'* He replied, *'I supposed the report referred to the 29th. I heard afterward that it referred to the 30th. I mixed the 29th and the 30th together.'*"

Counselor Choate continued, "I tried once more to elicit a reasonable response from General McDowell, saying, *'Do you suppose so now?'*"

"McDowell fell back on an excuse stating his report was *'human error, which may have been caused by the passage of time.'* That was his excuse for the error, without admitting anything. McDowell said, *'I made that report six months after the battle. After time passes a person can be mixed up.'* I asked if he was an active participant in the events of both the 29th and the 30th of August. His reply was *'Yes, sir.'*"

Counselor Choate continued to read from the record of McDowell's disposition conducted earlier.

Choate: 'Does not your personal knowledge of the events of those two days enable you to form a judgment as to whether your Abstract contained a truthful account of the 29th or of the 30th and which?' (*In other words, did Jackson have his dates right when he wrote the report?*).

McDowell: *'I think Jackson mixed the two days together. Jackson was confused.'*

Killed a few months after the Porter trial, at Chancellorsville, Stonewall Jackson, the master strategist and one of the most careful and clear-minded of soldiers, was exacting in his orders and his reports. Jackson must have turned over in his grave at McDowell's answer.

Counselor Choate turned to the board.

"As you know, I complained to General Schofield that General McDowell had not answered the question. Thereupon, General Schofield questioned McDowell."

Again Choate read from the testimony record.

Schofield: *'The question now is whether the witness now believes his abstract is about the events of both days, or only the 30th, or only the 29th?'*

McDowell: *'I think the two days were mixed up in Jackson's mind.'*

Counselor Choate went on. "McDowell continued to blame Jackson. He carefully sidestepped the question, since he, McDowell, was *on the scene both days,* and couldn't discern the difference between what occurred on each of those two days."

"Finally, after being harshly and repeatedly cross examined, McDowell blew up. He placed blame for the wrong dates on the dead General Jackson as being a confused person. He said to his questioner, thoroughly exasperated and boxed into a corner for his lies, *'THIS IS THE EIGHTH TIME I HAVE TOLD YOU THAT IT WAS A MISTAKE BASED UPON JACKSON'S CONFUSION.'"*

Counselor Choate finished with his review of the Jackson Report and McDowell's erratic answers. Choate concluded his part of the defense argument. His final remark was to call Irvin McDowell a liar in the most flowery of legal terms.

Joseph Choate stated, "It might take some use of a mental chisel to scrape away the veneer of fine words, and to dig down and reveal Irvin McDowell's character. It requires a broader mantle of charity than is usually thrown over the testimony of witnesses, to condone such an offense against fair dealing and truth telling as this was. It requires charity to admit its author to the fold of those upon whose words the fate of a fellow man can be made to depend."

Counselor John Bullitt resumed his argument for the defense.

"Probably the most fatal blow General Porter suffered in his defense was General McDowell's allegation that he, McDowell, had assumed command of Porter's corps, when he had not. McDowell had ordered Porter to attack Jackson and when Porter did not, on that word from McDowell, the judge advocate found Porter was guilty of violation of duty."

"Now the question comes: Was it true that McDowell gave any such order to Porter to attack Jackson? Bear in mind the Joint Order. That order from the commanding general stated Pope's wish for the *combined* forces under Porter's *and* McDowell's commands to replace the retreating Ricketts, to interpose themselves between Longstreet and Jackson and also, if possible, destroy Jackson's army. It did not allow McDowell to withdraw, take two-thirds of Porter's troops and leave Porter alone to hold off Longstreet. Was it not McDowell's duty to carry out the Joint Order?"

"No sooner did McDowell receive his copy of the Joint Order than he took back King's division and marched away, thus breaking up the force, which general Pope had united to carry out his order. McDowell made it impossible to carry out the dictates of the Joint Order when he marched away from Gainesville and went to Groveton."

"Let me ask you, if McDowell believed it was his duty to tell Porter to make the attack, why didn't he make it himself as well, when he had all those troops there, instead of cutting the Federal force by two-thirds and leaving Porter's one-third to carry out the order?"

"In answer to the question as to his motives that day, McDowell's answer was, *'I was not looking at the close of the day. I was going on the plan that 'sufficient unto the day is the evil thereof.'*"

"For McDowell to take his troops away is inconsistent with his pretense that he gave Porter an order to attack in force while he was at Dawkins Creek talking to Porter. It is true that a man who relates facts from his imagination does not always remember what he says. Tell the truth and you cannot be tripped up by any question."

"For example, McDowell forgot what he said earlier; *'Porter could not go farther toward Gainesville. General Patrick, a part of King's Division, had gone as far as he could go.'* McDowell imputed to Porter, in his testimony, that *'Porter's disposition was to shrink from a fight.'* McDowell laid the groundwork for the judge advocate to believe that Porter was cowardly and treacherous."

Counselor Bullitt continued. "The saddest and worst of the allegations against General Porter was the charge that he refused to offer battle and that he retreated in the face of the enemy. That accusation was dastardly. Listen to the language of Porter's court martial testimony from page 287 of the court record."

'On the morning of August 29, as I pushed toward Gainesville as ordered, I held an all-important position that day and through an anxious afternoon. My forces held the massing forces of the enemy. We were able to divide and distract, holding the massing forces in check.'

'When I received the 8:50 Order commanding me to advance to Gainesville, I left my strong position and thus I opened the road for the enemy. I feared he would make his furious onset upon our left flank. Personally, I was glad to be with my corps when the fight raged on the 30th. But I state my deliberate judgment as a military man, that except for that peremptory order from General Pope commanding me to withdraw—I say, it was a false military movement.'

'Had we been permitted to hold the enemy there, the terrible attack on the army's left flank would never have been made. I would have stopped Longstreet's attack then and there, as I stopped it the day before. I asked General Pope to produce the note I sent to Pope at dusk in reply to the 4:30 Order. That note would prove and support what I have said.'

Counselor Bullitt asserted, "That note and seven others, which Porter had sent to Pope and to McDowell on those two days, were never produced until much later, after the trial and after General Porter's conviction."

"This is astonishing. It is the duty of any superior officer in command of an army to preserve the correspondence between him and his subordinates. The missing notes would have and did explain and confirm Porter's innocence and claims. Could Pope and McDowell have laid hands on the missing notes during the court martial, and not waited until three months after the finish of the trial proceedings?"

"A reasonable person might suppose the notes were not produced because they would not only have proven Porter's innocence of the charges, but they would also, perhaps, have lain the true cause for the debacle on August 30, 1862, on the two men who truly *were* responsible."

"McDowell's testimony was accepted by the judge advocate as true. The charges against General Porter, when you look at them, were prepared by somebody who intended to throw a drag net around General Porter and cover all his actions on August 29. How is it possible that McDowell said any of these things to Porter? If he had said it, it would have been his duty to report it and it would have appeared in the charges and specifications. But it is not there. It would appear that from the beginning of the trial before the court martial, the mind of the judge advocate had been imbued with deep and bitter prejudices against General Porter."

"There was bias in McDowell's favor, especially by General Pope and also by the judge advocate. When you examine Pope's testimony, all of the judge advocate's questions were addressed to the witnesses as though there was *no doubt* that Porter violated the 4:30 Order."

Counselor Bullitt continued. "I wish to read from pages 15, 16, and 17 of the trial record. It shows there was strong prejudice against Porter. McDowell's examination followed Pope's. It is not difficult to understand how well inclined McDowell must have been to respond to expectations as to his evidence, which were foreshadowed by Pope's examination. His testimony to the judge advocate illustrates, I think, the errors and mistakes that were made."

Judge Advocate Holt: 'Was there any engagement then pending?'

Pope: 'Fighting was then going on along the turnpike; that is, from Centreville to Warrenton. Fighting was going on quite sharply.'

Judge Advocate Holt: 'Did the march of General Porter's command, as indicated in the order, lead him towards the battle?'

Pope: 'Yes, sir. It led him towards the flank of the enemy.'

Counselor Bullitt: "I call to the board's attention facts already known. First, Pope was east of Groveton, on the Warrenton Turnpike and about two miles from Gainesville. Second, Pope's 4:30 Order to Porter was to '*march toward Gainesville;*' *not* toward the Groveton battle."

"Pope's answer to the question implied that Porter's march would lead him directly to the battle. It would not. It led, if Longstreet's 25,000 troops had not stopped him, to the battle on the *flank of the enemy* near Gainesville. That objective was two miles from the '*battle*' at Groveton to which Pope referred in his answer."

"The question was then asked of Pope, 'What is the distance between Manassas Junction and the scene of the engagement of which you speak?'"

"**To this, Pope answered,** 'Between five and six miles. I have not been over that road.'"

Counselor Bullitt continued. "General Pope had already described the engagement, which was near Groveton on the Turnpike. Yet, now he states that the road between Manassas and the *'scene of the battle'* is one with which he is unfamiliar. Now Pope speaks, without doubt of the target of Porter's 4:30 Order, which was Gainesville and near Jackson's right flank, not east of Groveton. He could not have it both ways. Did Pope mean Gainesville was to be Porter's objective? Or did he intend that Porter should change his line of march and veer off to the east to go to the battle on the Turnpike near Groveton?"

"Apparently Pope was confused. Unfortunately for General Porter, Judge Advocate Holt chose to believe the two places were one and the same, and therefore, Porter disobeyed the 4:30 Order by not marching to the *'scene of the action.'* After all, McDowell was able to march to the scene of the action near Groveton."

"Never mind that the Groveton fight was *not* where McDowell had been ordered to go. Never mind that he *should* have remained with Porter. The combined forces of Porter's and McDowell's armies would have moved between Longstreet and Jackson's left flank and changed the course of the battle. Never mind that Porter, by remaining alone against a force three times his size, held the Confederate army at bay all day and saved Pope's army from disaster."

Counselor Bullitt continued. "Pope jumped in again to save his friend, McDowell."

"The record states that Judge Advocate Holt asked Pope, *'You have stated that McDowell obeyed the Joint Order, so far as to appear on the battlefield with his command?'"*

"Pope answered, *'Yes, sir.'"*

"Now, let me ask the board to consider for a moment *how* had General McDowell obeyed the Joint Order? What single act did McDowell perform in fulfillment of or compliance with the Joint Order?"

"The only thing he did was to take command of the force long enough to destroy the effect of the spirit and purpose of that order. He took King's and Ricketts' divisions away from Porter. Taking them to Sudley Springs Road near the scene of the Groveton battle site was certainly not the fulfillment of that order in any possible sense. It is doubtful whether the discretion allowed by the order covered any such an action, no matter how far you stretch it. It would be like saying that McDowell obeyed an order to go from Albany to New York by way of the Hudson River, had obeyed the order, when he instead took the train and went to Chicago."

John Bullitt had been reeling off fact after fact supported by incontrovertible new evidence. Now he stopped.

Almost as if he was speaking to himself, he said, "I do not believe that the trait of courage is one that needs to be spoken much or often in a soldier. It is expected of him. In this army at Second Manassas the want of courage was not common to the men or the officers. They behaved with a degree of stubborn courage, which is not excelled since by soldiers or troops anywhere."

"I do not say McDowell was a coward. He had his reasons, whatever they were, to leave Porter and march toward Groveton. For that reason, more than any other he would never have ordered Porter to attack alone. Perhaps his memory was faulty.

As he dwelt upon the events of that day, his conviction grew that he may have thought he told Porter to attack. But one is utterly inconsistent with the other. Either he left Porter knowing Longstreet's forces were too strong and the army must unite at Bull Run, leaving Porter to act on his own discretion, or he gave Porter the order to attack, then left him with one-third of the force Pope intended he should have to attack, according to the Joint Order."

"Possibly McDowell did not recollect having said, with a wave of his hand, *'Porter, you should put your forces into the woods near Dawkins Branch and remain there to hold the enemy in check while I go off up the Sudley Road.'* His memory probably took one of those sudden twists as it did before, when he *'took the view'* that Porter should move against the enemy. Then later he said he *'directed Porter to attack the enemy in flank.'*"

"The judge advocate relied on McDowell's testimony and in particular, McDowell's statement that *'Porter's forces were near enough to Jackson that he could have easily attacked Jackson. Porter's corps had passed a point three miles in advance of Bethlehem Church and they were very near the Turnpike.* McDowell lied and the judge advocate believed him."

"The truth and the evidence proved that Porter was never closer to the Turnpike than Dawkins Creek, five miles from Jackson with the entire Confederate army in his way. There Porter held Longstreet's main force for the entire afternoon."

John Bullitt's face was drawn and pale with subdued anger and emotion, as he spoke of McDowell's acts of calumny and deceit.

"Irvin McDowell was a man that had, at one time, been selected as the commander of the armies of his government. This was the man who was the trusted and chosen adviser of General Pope. This was the man who knew the circumstances of that day. This was the man who knew what the Joint Order meant and knew his duty and upon whom, more than any other man, General Porter relied upon for a true statement of the facts."

"Yet we know now that what McDowell said was wholly untrue. Feeling himself in danger, General McDowell brought down General Porter to save himself. Instead, he threw it upon the shoulders of Fitz John Porter, another officer who happened to be in a position where it *could* be thrown upon him. General McDowell intentionally gave a false impression to the court martial when he made that statement: He knew it was a lie when he made it."

❧ 58 ❧

Lee

One defense argument on behalf of General Porter stands out among the others. The argument was written by the man who ended the Civil War for the North and later became President of the United States, Ulysses S. Grant, who stated:

"And now it is known by others, as it was known to Porter at the time, that Longstreet, with some 25,000 men, was in position confronting Porter by 12 o'clock on the 29th of August, four and a half hours before the 4:30 Order was written."

Another enlightening fact came from Robert E. Lee, the general who opposed John Pope that day in 1862. Lee said of his right wing, led by General James Longstreet, *"Longstreet's command arrived within supporting distance of Jackson on the 29th of August, 1862, between 9 and 10 AM, and his lines were formed by noon. My command arrived at 9 AM, the 29th of August, near Groveton. Longstreet's command was deployed in a double line for an attack between 10 AM and 12 PM on the 29th, extending from Jackson's right across the Turnpike and Manassas Gap Railroad. Longstreet was ready to receive any attack after 11 AM and we were particularly anxious to bring on the battle after 12 PM; myself more so than any other."*

Pope's own chief of division for artillery, Captain Martin, admitted he received a report of the battle between Longstreet and Porter on August 29, from Lieutenant Charles Hazlett, General Porter's Fifth U.S. Artillery Regiment. Hazlett had set up a 6-pound Parrott gun and his crew was firing toward the woods where the enemy had been spotted earlier. Lieutenant Hazlett stated, *"The enemy opened up on us with a 10-pounder Parrott and another rifled gun. At the time clouds of dust were seen rising in the woods near the enemy's battery. Shortly afterward a large column of infantry appeared."*

After the rehearing was finished, General Schofield made a revealing assessment of General Porter's true value in the Battle of Second Manassas.

He asserted, "The fact is that Longstreet and his four divisions of 29,000 men were on the field. Porter, with his two divisions saved the Army of Virginia that day from disaster."

President Lincoln was purposely misled about the trial. Lincoln, then president, approved the sentence of the court. He approved the sentence on the argument by Judge Advocate Holt, who purposely misrepresented the evidence. However, the proceedings were never examined by him.

One accusation of which Porter was found guilty was the claim that Porter retreated. This was based on the moment when Porter was convinced his orders required him to take his troops to Bull Run, as the Joint Order stated he must do should there be reason for that movement. Porter believed that Pope's forces were being overrun on the afternoon of August 29, 1862. There was no way he could break through Longstreet's forces to reach the Warrenton Turnpike on that afternoon or evening. When, moments later, Porter determined the firing on the Turnpike had died away, Porter was sure that the army was not retreating. Immediately he changed the orders to his men to stay where they were and hold the line against Longstreet.

The court martial chose to believe Porter retreated. They took this unformed idea as fact. When President Lincoln was presented with the evidence of Porter's guilt, his son, Robert Lincoln (P. 902 of the record) testified that President Lincoln made *'harsh expressions.'* Lincoln was under the conviction that Porter had retreated or fallen back as indicated by a note from McDowell to King. As indicated by that erroneous note Lincoln was *'strong in his condemnation.'*

That note was a lie.

The truth was that Lincoln was presented with a bald naked lie that this untruthful dispatch had been sent, which claimed General Porter had retreated. Not a fact to controvert this lie was ever laid before the President. Therefore, it was no surprise that President Lincoln did so express himself. The truth and dispatches supporting Porter's innocence were never presented to the President.

Schofield remarked during retrial, *"Lincoln, great-hearted and great-minded executive that he was, was grossly betrayed by the servants in whom he trusted."* Lincoln had later learned that he was misled. But before he could act on that new knowledge he was assassinated.

When the hearing was finished on March 19, 1879, Schofield concluded with a personal judgment.

"This was the most important military trial in the history of this nation. The sentence of the court martial was the severest that could have been imposed short of death, and to an honorable, high-toned, and sensitive nature, it was perhaps worse than death. The accused had enjoyed the highest degree of confidence on the part of the president, of the army, and of the nation. He had won signal honor and distinction on more than one hard-fought battlefield. In soldierly attainments and qualities, in devotion to his country and to the cause in which he enlisted, in energy, zeal, and perseverance, and in the power of command, he was regarded as the peer of the truest and best of his comrades in all areas. We may well imagine the effect on the mind of President Lincoln when he found that a general of such character, and one in whom he had put such trust and confidence had been convicted by a court of his fellow officers, of such crimes."

The Schofield Board concluded these facts with a statement: *"We believe not one of the gallant soldiers on that bloody field was less deserving of such condemnation by the court martial than General Fitz John Porter."*

The Schofield Board of Officers had gathered the most complete and best available material and evidence and studied all of it. The board was composed of men of character, higher learning, and integrity, and they acquitted Porter. But they also gave that soldier the highest possible eulogy for his gallant conduct. They stated:

"In accordance with the President's order, justice requires such action as necessary to set aside the findings and sentence of the court martial in the case of Major General Fitz John Porter, and restore him to the position which that sentence deprived him. Such restoration to take place from the date of his dismissal from service."

In 1879, Ulysses S. Grant was no longer president. John Schofield asked President Rutherford Hayes to set aside the court martial of Fitz John Porter, and attributed the loss of the Battle of Second Manassas to Pope and McDowell. But Porter was a Democrat and President Hayes a Republican, and Hayes could not get Republican Party support for the pardon. Many Republicans still incorrectly believed that Porter was a traitor. It was not until 1882 that President Chester Arthur commuted Porter's sentence. And it was not until 1893 that President Cleveland, a Democrat, officially pardoned Porter.

Union General
Ulysses S. Grant

☙ 59 ❧

Grant

No other similar case in human history ever took so many twists and turns as the Porter court martial and the resolution of the case years afterward.

Prior to the Schofield Commission hearing which completed in 1879, Porter tried for many years to appeal his sentence which included an ongoing dialogue with Ulysses S. Grant. This chapter shows what led up to the Schofield Board retrial, and the assistance Grant provided after the rehearing and after Grant was no longer president.

Porter's case was one of the most unbelievable convictions known, and has been revealed as an alarming misuse and corruption of government power. That infamy was made starkly visible in 1866, three years after Porter had been cashiered from the army. The old maxim that *'Power corrupts and absolute power corrupts absolutely,'* was at work by the men who should have served the country and its president. From 1864 to 1877, Ulysses S. Grant held successive positions as general-in-chief, secretary of war, and then was served two terms as president. Fitz John Porter made application to Grant during this period for a rehearing of his case. Porter's request was based on testimony which had not been available at his trial or before the court martial in 1863. It was after the war was over that information, evidence, and testimony became available from high-ranking generals in the Confederate army.

Porter had friends. Many men believed in his innocence: ex-presidents, a Justice of the Supreme Court *(who had been present at Porter's trial)*, and many other able men. A rehearing of Porter's case was urged by senators, representatives in Congress, governors, generals and other army officers. The reason for their strong support was that the new evidence Porter offered was sustained by high-ranking Confederate army officers, who had fought at Second Manassas. They knew the truth, first hand, of the events that were brought forward at the Porter trial.

President Grant favored Porter's appeal.

He told Porter, "In four days you shall receive an order for a Board to meet at West Point to rehear the evidence."

Grant was so convinced that Porter was innocent that he said, *"Not only ought he to have the rehearing, but every member of the court which sentenced him should be glad to have the opportunity to join in the appeal."*

He added, *"If injustice has been done by the finding of the court, resulting in a severe sentence, damaging him professionally and otherwise, every opportunity which the law allows should be given to exculpate himself."*

Then suddenly, the freedom train for Porter screeched to a halt.

The prosecutor and chief witness against Porter, John Pope, was Grant's former schoolmate. Grant trusted Pope. He had faith in Pope's integrity. John Pope and certain officials, upon whom Grant thought he could rely, came to him like a plague with a flood of annoying begging protests *against* a rehearing. President Grant yielded to their demands and requests. Grant withheld the order.

Correspondence between President Grant and Fitz John Porter ceased. What follows are Porter's letters, showing a gradual evolution and change in Grant's ideas. Grant's initial belief in Porter's innocence had been taken away from Grant by the continuing lies and deceit from Pope, McDowell and other officers, who had served on the kangaroo court in 1862.

When Grant had time to examine for himself the merits of Porter's case, he shook off the bias and false statements of other men. Grant saw the harm that he had, unwittingly, done Porter. He saw the error into which he had fallen. He labored to correct his former mistake and remove the burden that baser men had placed upon an innocent man. The letters that follow are examples of the writings of two men of the highest integrity and nobility, and what led up to the Schofield Board of Inquiry.

Porter's first two letters to Grant in September of 1866, right after the Civil War, were finally answered and declined. Colonel Adam Badeau, Grant's secretary, wrote an answer for Grant. The reply, October 1, 1866, was short. One telling phrase in the curt letter spoke volumes: *'General Grant instructs me to say, that since Secretary Stanton is still Secretary of War and he sees no change in your status of guilt, I must decline your request for a rehearing.'* Edwin Stanton was not about to let Porter off the hook after going to such trouble to pack the court and arrange Porter's conviction.

By 1867, Grant was no longer general in chief of armies; he had taken Stanton's job and he was the secretary of war. Porter's next attempt brought heavy guns to Porter's request. His appeal had been supported by ex-presidents Fillmore and Pierce, Judge Curtis, Senators Wilson, Foster and Harris, Governor Curtin, Governor Winthrop, Horace Greely, General Banks, Edward Everett, and others. Grant was careful. He qualified any possible rehearing by stating the obvious: that Porter must justify the need for a rehearing with new evidence. Until there was new evidence there would be no rehearing.

Grant's reply on September 18, 1867, threw one more roadblock before Porter's request; Porter must first convince the attorney general. If the A-G agreed an appeal was worthwhile, Grant could reconsider. Meanwhile, to make sure he was acting within the law, Grant wrote to the A-G.

To the War Department,

September 19, 1867:

'Is there authority, after so many years, to try a second time by a military court a person whose case has been disposed of according to law? If so, how do we make the proceedings legal? What method should be used to find and show all evidence, new and old, to prove innocence?'

Respectfully, U.S. Grant

Porter submitted to the attorney general, upon his request, the documents and the evidence in support of his appeal. What happened next was no surprise. Knowing the history of the forces that had worked from the beginning to make Porter the scapegoat for Pope's and McDowell's mistakes, and the important people in the Lincoln administration that had worked so hard and so carefully to pack the court and arrange the evidence to convict, it was not a surprise what happened next. In some mysterious way by persons unknown, the evidence, and all traces of that evidence, vanished like snow in a hot summer's sun. It disappeared from the War Department's files as though they never existed. The only sign that Fitz John Porter had ever sent *anything* to the attorney general was an empty file with a label on it that read *'Porter's Appeal.'*

The only explanation for the disappearance was a letter dated February 27, 1868.

'General Fitz John Porter,

Your application and accompanying paper for a re-examining of your case seem to have been mislaid. When we find them they will be returned or processed as you desire, Your Obedient Servant,'

It was signed by an underling ten grades below the A-G.

President Grant was rather conservative during his presidential years, but mellowed with time and became more amenable to hearing all sides of the story. Later, Porter tried again. This time he asked for a personal meeting so he could answer Grant's views about his conduct *(as the court martial found from the perjured testimony in 1862)* during the Battle of Second Manassas. Porter leaned heavily on Grant's well-known sense of fairness and open-mindedness.

Grant replied.

In his answer to Porter he said, *'As soon as I can find a day I will take great pleasure in seeing you. I shall listen without prejudice. If you convince me I was wrong in my former opinions, I will correct them.'*

Very truly yours,

U.S. Grant'

In a letter dated October 31, 1876, Grant offered Porter a time and a place for an appointment.

'Call any day at my office about 11 o'clock. I will give you the interview and I will keep persons from coming to my office while we talk.'

Very truly yours,

U.S. Grant'

November 19, Grant wrote again. He had received a copy of a letter from Major General Alfred Terry. The contents of Terry's letter are unknown. However, Terry's words had a strong effect on Grant. He wrote to Porter, '*General Terry's letter is manly, to say the least. I exonerate you so far as the judgment of one very intelligent member of the court goes…*'

Very truly yours,

U.S. Grant'

Congress was about to meet. Porter was anxious to have Grant's decision and whether his appeal should go through the President or through Congress. December 1, he asked for another meeting.

Grant replied, saying, '*I will be glad to see you anytime. I have taken all of your evidence to my house to go over carefully… but every evening I have had company. With what I have seen thus far, you will meet with no opposition from me in obtaining relief. I shall finish examining your papers in the next few days. If my judgment convinces you have been wronged, I will say so.*

U.S. Grant'

Porter, wisely, did not ask for a meeting. He waited until Grant had finished his examination of the evidence.

December 9, Grant wrote to General Porter. He asked him to call '*Next Monday, about eleven o'clock.*' Grant was effusive in his apologies. He said, '*I can say now, from what I have read, I believe I have done you an injustice, both in thought and speech…*'

December 19, 1876, Grant wrote Porter a second letter.

'*I am through reading. I am ready to meet you any morning after tomorrow.*'

Fitz John Porter's conviction was investigated by the Schofield Commission in 1878. Rutherford Hayes, who succeeded Grant as president in 1877, had commissioned this board, and Schofield asked to set aside the court marital.

Porter received the letter he had waited 18 years to read. It was from Grant. Inside Grant's cover letter there was his letter to President Hayes. The long, two-page letter was a ringing salutation to the guilt and suffering of an innocent brave soldier.

President Rutherford Hayes

Washington, D.C.:

Dear Sir,

'*I have recently reviewed the trial and testimony furnished before the Schofield Court of Inquiry, held in 1879, giving the subject three full days of careful reading and consideration, and much thought I am convinced that for these nineteen years I have been doing a gallant and efficient soldier a great injustice. When I was President I had the power to have ordered a hearing, which he only got at a later day. In justification for my injustice to General Porter, I can only state that after the war closed I based my decision on wrong information. It is incumbent upon me to remove the stain upon his good name from him and his family and repair my own unintentional injustice to General Porter. I ask you give the subject some thought and the same study I have given to it and ask that the matter be placed before the Attorney General for his opinion.*'

'Hoping you will do this for an officer who has suffered for nineteen years a punishment that should never have been inflicted upon any but the most guilty.'

I am very truly yours.

U.S. Grant'

Grant had called in all his chips. When Grant spoke people listened. The General, who had helped save the Union and who had brought the Confederacy to its knees in defeat was welcome everywhere. Grant sent similar letters to every senator and representative in Congress, every judge and man in high office that had supported Porter. In each of them Grant admitted his own injustice to Porter and asked for their help to make Porter's complete exoneration a legal and national fact.

U.S. Grant created a dialogue to advocate for Porter's rehearing, and helped to gain acceptance of Porter's innocence among his peers. When Grant was no longer president, he had no power to hold a new trial despite his support. However, he wrote extensively as to his opinion that Porter's name should be cleared.

By 1882, President Chester Arthur was in office. Ulysses S. Grant, suffering from illness which would eventually take his life, wrote an extensive and detailed article which was published in the North American Review, Volume CXXXV. The 8-page treatise covered the entire Battle of Second Manassas and Porter's part in the three-day conflict. The writing reviewed troop movements, Pope and McDowell's orders and activities. As a measure of the man that Grant was, he apologized for his part during the calumny wrought upon Porter in his court martial.

Grant wrote:

'If a solemn and sincere expression of my thorough understanding and belief in the entire innocence of General Porter will tend to draw the public mind to the same conviction, I shall feel abundantly rewarded for my efforts. It will always be a pleasure to me, as well as a duty, to be the instrument, even in the smallest degree, of setting right any man who has been grossly wronged, especially if he has risked his life and reputation in defense of his country.'

'I feel, as stated on a previous occasion, a double interest in this particular case, because, directly after the war, as General of the Army, when I might have been instrumental in having justice done to General Porter, and later as President of the United States, when I certainly could have done so, I labored under the firm conviction that he was guilty; that the facts of the receipt of the 4:30 Order were as found by the court, and that the position of the troops and numbers were as given.'

'I have become better informed. I at once voluntarily gave, as I have continued to give, my earnest efforts to impress the minds of my countrymen with the justice of this case, and to secure from our government, as far as it could grant it, the restitution due to General Fitz John Porter.'

ULYSSES S. GRANT

John McAllister Schofield
Lieutenant General Union Army

❦ 60 ❦

Schofield Report

On March 19, 1879, the Schofield Commission issued its report to President Hayes. The Board recommended that *"Justice requires such action as may be necessary to annul and set aside the findings and sentence of the court martial in the case of Major General Fitz John Porter, and to restore him to the positions of which that sentences deprived him… such restoration to take effect from the date of his dismissal from the service."*

Furthermore, the court found General Porter innocent of any wrongdoing during the course of action on August 29, 1862, and, in fact credited General Porter with saving the Union army from an even greater defeat.

The detailed report of the Board of Army Officers in the Case of Fitz John Porter was dated in New York City, on March 19, 1879. It was directed specifically to President Rutherford Hayes, the man whose responsibility it was to use the report and recommendations, either for the conviction or exoneration of the charges against Porter, and take direct action. Porter had now been found innocent, but Rutherford Hayes could not get Republican congressional support to exonerate Porter. Following the Schofield Commission decision, the Board of Army Officers wrote in 1879:

'SIR: WE, THE BOARD OF OFFICERS, appointed by order of the President to examine the evidence in the case of Fitz John Porter, late Major General of Volunteers, and to report, with reasons for our conclusions, what action (if any), in our opinion, justice requires should be taken by the President on the application for relief in this case, have the honor to make the following report.'

The single-spaced, 20-page Report made several claims as the basis of their findings, and is outlined in this chapter, indicating a more correct view of events of 1862. Although this chapter repeats some of the correspondence during the Battle of Second Manassas, it is repeated here to show the correct logic the Schofield Board employed in proving Porter was not guilty.

The Court was thorough and diligent in looking at every side of the story. They examined every available fact, studied detailed maps of the battleground and heard testimony from officers of the late Confederate army as well as Union officers who were on the field of battle. The result was to establish, beyond reasonable doubt, all of the facts essential to effect a correct judgment based on the merits of

Porter's case.

The evidence, which this court was presented were several kinds.

1. Inaccurate and wrongful statements of certain witnesses and inaccurate maps and incorrect positions of the Federal and Confederate forces, presented to the original 1863 court.

2. Opinions of prominent officers based upon imperfect knowledge.

3. Far more complete and accurate statement by large numbers of eye witnesses at the battle and from both of the contending forces.

4. Accurate maps of the battlefield and accurate positions of the contending forces.

5. Conflicting testimony, interpretation of orders, motives of commanding officers and responsibilities of the different commanders during the battle.

What followed next in the Schofield Report was a narration of the events which gave rise to the charges against General Porter, giving a synopsis of how Pope was able to blame Porter, while Schofield attributed the loss of battle to Pope and McDowell.

In August of 1862, McClellan's army was withdrawing from its position near Richmond, *(which McClellan had failed to capture)* on the James River. Halleck ordered Pope to hold the line on the Rappahannock River, and to stand on the defensive until all the Federal forces could be united. When that was done, General Halleck intended to take command of McClellan and Pope's combined forces. McClellan was told he would take direct command under Halleck.

That was not to be. Five days later, Lincoln took the command away from McClellan and gave it to John Pope. General Porter, who joined General Pope at that time, had the impression the army would continue to operate with a defensive character as it had under McClellan.

Two things changed everything. Lincoln was tired of McClellan's 'slows.' He wanted action. At that same time Stonewall Jackson marched 28,000 men around Pope's rear and threatened Washington D.C. General Pope turned his forces around at the Rappahannock and ordered they rendezvous in several train stops and crossroads towns as a staging area before going after Jackson on the Manassas Plain.

Pope, at his headquarters at Warrenton, ordered his six corps (60,000 troops) forward toward Gainesville and the Manassas Plain, where he thought he would find Jackson. Porter, Siegel, Heintzelman, Reno, Banks, and McDowell were to rendezvous near Gainesville.

Porter came to headquarters and was sent to Gainesville with Heintzelman and Reno. Banks guarded the trains that moved supplies and troops to Manassas; then Banks also was ordered to Warrenton Junction.

When Pope learned that Hooker's division, (Heintzelman had sent him ahead) was engaged with Jackson at Bristoe Station, Pope ordered Porter to move his troops forward to support Hooker in his fight. Pope sent Porter the following order:

'The Major General commanding directs you start at 1 o'clock tonight, and come forward with

your whole corps, or such part of it as with you, so as to be here (Bristoe Station) (Parenthesis are those of the author) by daylight tomorrow morning. Hooker has had very severe action with the enemy, with a loss of about 300 killed and wounded. The enemy has been driven back, but is retiring above a railroad. We must drive him from Manassas, and clear the country between that place and Gainesville where McDowell is. If Morell has not joined you, send word to him, to push forward immediately, and send word to Banks to hurry forward with all speed, and take your place at Warrenton Junction. It is necessary, by all accounts that you should be here by daylight. I send an officer with this dispatch, who will conduct you to this place. Be sure to send word to Banks, who is on the road to Fayetteville, probably in the direction of Bealeton. Say to Banks, also, that he had best run back the railroad trains to this side of Cedar Run. If he is not with you, write him to that effect.'

'P.S. If Banks is not at Warrenton Junction, leave a regiment of infantry and two pieces of artillery as a guard until he comes up, with instructions to follow you immediately. If Banks is not at the Junction, instruct Colonel Clary to run the train back to this side of Cedar Run, and post a regiment and section of artillery with it.'

Pope intended *(from the order)* that Porter was to arrive early on August 28, prepared and ready to attack, drive Jackson away from Bristoe Station, and clear the country. Hence Porter had to arrive at Bristoe in condition to fight.

The evidence shows that Porter showed an earnest desire to comply with the order. However, the court found that if he had marched his men (who had no sleep) at 1 o'clock, when they arrived they would be would be in poor condition to perform adequately. A vigorous pursuit, with hard marching after an enemy who had left Bristoe and was some distance beyond, would have greatly fatigued the troops and thrown them into disorder. General Porter exercised the very ordinary discretion of a corps commander, which was his plain duty, in delaying the march until 3 o'clock. General Porter remained at Bristoe, under orders from Pope, until the morning of August 29, 1862.

McDowell sent Ricketts' division to Thoroughfare Gap to meet and resist the advancement of reinforcements for Jackson from the main body of Lee's army. Banks was at Warrenton Junction and Porter was at Bristoe. The rest of the army moved to find and attack Jackson at Manassas Junction.

Jackson withdrew during the night of the 27th and the morning of the 28th and went toward Groveton on the Warrenton Turnpike. Heintzelman and Reno followed Jackson, by way of Centreville. McDowell and Siegel, after they started for Manassas Junction, changed direction to follow Jackson with the others.

King's division *(part of McDowell's corps)*, while they marched along the Warrenton Turnpike, was struck by part of Jackson's forces from the ridge above the Turnpike. The contest lasted until dark.

The other troops came up to join in the fight. Reynolds came to the right of King and Siegel positioned his force on Reynold's right, near the Stone House. Heintzelman and Reno were still at Centreville. Ricketts was fighting Longstreet at the Gap. Pope hoped to strike Jackson a decisive blow before re-enforcements could. Under these conditions, Pope sent Porter an order;

'GENERAL: McDowell has intercepted the retreat of Jackson. Siegel is immediately on the right of McDowell. Kearney and Hooker march to attack the enemy's rear at dawn. Major-

General Pope directs you to move upon Centreville at dawn of day with your whole command, leaving your trains to follow. It is very important that you should be here at a very early hour in the morning. A severe engagement is likely to take place, and your presence is necessary.'

Signed by Colonel George Ruggles, Chief of Staff

Porter promptly marched toward Centreville. As he passed Manassas Junction at the head of his column, he was halted and given new orders because of changes in the battle the night before on the Turnpike.

King had withdrawn from his position on the Turnpike and fallen back to Manassas Junction. Ricketts had fallen back from the Gap, first to Gainesville and then to Bristoe Station.

The way was open for Jackson to retreat to Thoroughfare Gap or for the advance of Longstreet. They had plenty of time to affect a junction of their two armies either at the Gap or at Groveton and before a larger force could stop them. There was no longer any chance of attacking Jackson's divisions alone.

When Pope learned of King's withdrawal from the Turnpike, he sent a verbal message to Porter to retrace his steps and move toward Gainesville. He followed this verbal order with a third order, which was received by Porter at 9:30 AM of August 29.

To Major General Porter:

'Push forward with your corps and King's division, which you will take with you, upon Gainesville. I am following the enemy down the Warrenton Turnpike. Be expeditious or we will lose much.'

Major General John Pope, Commanding

Knowing the military situation, Porter advanced promptly. He was followed by King's division and they took the direct road from Manassas Junction toward Gainesville. While near Manassas Junction, General McDowell met with Porter and they talked about Pope's order, which had placed King (*McDowell's First Division*) under Porter's command. Under the Sixty-Second Article of War, Porter and McDowell conceded McDowell had the right as the senior officer, to command Porter and King in a united command. However, he waited and wrote Pope for confirmation and did not take command of Porter or King.

At 11:30 AM, the head of Porter's column reached Dawkins Creek, about three miles from Gainesville and 9 miles from Thoroughfare Gap. There he met the enemy's cavalry and captured some of Longstreet's scouts. The clouds of dust in his front and on his right and going all the way back to Thoroughfare Gap, showed Porter that the enemy was coming in force. In fact, the Confederate army had already arrived on the battlefield.

Porter deployed his first division, Morell. Sykes' division closed up more closely for support. King's division followed. Morell sent a regiment forward across the creek as skirmishers and Butterfield's brigade (part of King's division) started across the creek in front and somewhat to the right, ready to advance in support of Butterfield's brigade.

Sometime between 11:30 and noon McDowell returned. He arrested Porter's movement Porter had been making, saying to him, *"Porter, you are too far out. This is no place to fight a battle,"* or words to that effect.

Minutes before this time, McDowell had received a dispatch from Buford. Buford had informed McDowell that seventeen regiments of infantry, a battery, and some cavalry had passed through Gainesville at 8:45 AM that same morning, and moved down the Warrenton Turnpike *(Centreville Road)* toward Groveton. Therefore, McDowell reasoned, that force must have been in front of Siegel and Reynolds for two hours.

Information the Schofield court received showed that the entire Confederate army was already on the field by noon of August 29. The enemy army covered an area from Gainesville toward Groveton on the Turnpike. McDowell's troops (Ricketts' division) had delayed Longstreet from passing through the Gap from noon until dark of the day before, August 28. Hence, Lee had had 18 hours by the morning of the 29th to close up in mass near the Gap and seven hours on the morning of the 29th to march 8 miles and form a line of battle. Jackson had not retreated but had held his position. Siegel, who had been pursuing Jackson, had been stopped and remained in position ear Groveton.

All of this maneuvering boiled down to this: Lee's army was in line and ready to start his offensive. Porter's arrival at Dawkins Creek forced Lee and Longstreet to delay the Confederate advance. Furthermore, the evidence and the facts support Porter's contention that he knew the enemy was in his immediate front. This belief, Porter conveyed to McDowell by word and gesture that convinced McDowell of the truth of Porter's belief.

In contrast, only Porter's 9000 men were ready for action against the 29,000 men of Longstreet's left wing. Banks' troops were still at Bristoe without orders to move from that point. Ricketts' men were so worn out by constant marching that they were of little use. King's division, just in front of Porter, were fatigued and worn out with Pope's orders of constant marching.

Maps, supplied by the confederacy, show that there was a gap of two miles in the Union lines between Porter and Reynolds, who was at Groveton fighting Jackson. This was the military situation when McDowell took charge of Porter's fifth corps and King's division. The effort to destroy Jackson before he could be reinforced had failed. The Confederate army was on the battlefield and the Federal army was not ready. The time to assume a defensive posture against Lee was due and long past due.

On his way to the fighting on the Turnpike, McDowell had received a copy of an order from Pope. It was the same order Porter received the moment before McDowell had arrived at the head of Porter's column at 11:30 or Noon.

GENERAL ORDERS NO. 5

Generals McDowell and Porter:

'You will please move forward with your joint commands toward Gainesville. I sent General Porter written orders to that effect an hour and a half ago. Heintzelman, Siegel, and Reno are now moving on the Warrenton Turnpike and by now must be not far from Gainesville. I desire that, as soon as communication is established between this force and your own, the whole command shall halt. It may be necessary to fall back behind Bull Run, at Centreville tonight. I

presume it will not be so because of our supplies. I have sent no orders of any kind to Ricketts, and none to interfere in any way with McDowell's troops, except what I sent to his aid-de-camp last night, which were to hold his position on the Warrenton Pike until the troops from here should fall on the enemy's flank and rear. I do not even know Ricketts' position, as I have not been able to find out where General McDowell was until a late hour this morning. General McDowell will take immediate steps to communicate with General Ricketts and instruct him to join the other divisions of his corps as soon as practical. If any considerable advantages are to be gained by departing from this order, it will not be strictly carried out. One thing must be held in view: that the troops must occupy a position from which they can reach Bull Run tonight or by morning. The indications are that the whole force of the enemy is moving in this direction at a pace that will bring them here by tomorrow night or the next day. My own headquarters will for the present be at Heintzelman's corps, or at this place.'

John Pope,
Major General, Commanding

Since under the Sixty-Second Article of War, McDowell was in command of the combined forces, and Pope was absent from the field, Porter and McDowell acted upon this interpretation of the law. The two-mile wide gap between Porter and Reynolds at Groveton had to be filled.

The situation was critical. If Longstreet attacked, as he seemed ready to do, Porter's 9,000 men were all that stood between Longstreet and the rest of Pope's disorganized army. The two men reconnoitered the woods ahead, and McDowell decided to take King and go and set up next to Reynolds. McDowell very hurriedly announced his decision to Porter and rode off. As he left Porter called after him, *"What shall I do?'*…or words to that effect. McDowell gave no audible answer.

After McDowell rode off Porter continued his planned move with Morell. Morell's men had not gone more than a half mile when Confederate artillery opened up on them and they were forced to take cover. Several times Porter sent scouts through the thick woods to let McDowell know he had run into heavy opposition. Each time Porter's scouts were either driven back, killed, or captured. They were unable to reach McDowell.

King did not reach the place McDowell had sent him to cover. McDowell, failing to place King with him, left the two-mile gap in the Union defense line open. Porter tried four times to send written dispatches to McDowell to let him know the situation; the Gap was open and he was under heavy attack.

General Pope was still fixated on destroying Jackson before he could retreat or be reinforced. He ordered his troops to begin a coordinated all-out offensive against Jackson's right and left flank. Kearney was ordered to attack Jackson's right starting at 5 PM. Porter received an order at 4:30 to attack the enemy's right or his rear. The order was not delivered in time and Porter did not receive the order until sunset. When Porter heard the sound of guns diminishing by Siegel, it suggested to Porter that Siegel was being driven back. If that was true, Porter saw that the situation was extremely perilous. He must instantly decide what he must do to avert disaster. Porter's order to his first division head, General Morell, shows his intention.

General Morell:

'Push over to the aid of Siegel and strike at his rear. If you reach a road up which King is moving and he has got ahead of you, let him pass, but see if you cannot give help to Siegel. If you find him retiring, move back toward Manassas, and should necessity require it, and you do not hear from me, push to Centreville (as the Joint Order allowed). If you find the direct road filled, take the one via Union Mills, which is to the right as you return.

Look to the points of the compass for Manassas.'
F. J. Porter.

This would have left Porter with Sykes alone to hold the Manassas Road and cover the retreat of Ricketts' worn-out troops, which were stretched out along for 4 or 5 miles from Sudley and back toward Manassas. Before Morell had time to start, a report came to Porter the enemy was moving down to attack his front and flank. They were coming in force. Porter might have to meet an attack of 20,000 men. Porter sent a second dispatch to Morell.

General Morell:
'Hold on to your present place. Who is passing?'
F. J. Porter

He sent a third message.

General Morell:
'Tell me what is passing quickly. If the enemy is coming, hold on to him and I will come up. Post your men to repulse him.'
F. J. Porter

And again, with Morell's advice that they had better retire, Porter replies,

General Morell:
'We cannot retire while McDowell holds on.'
F. J. Porter

The 1862 court martial which had found Porter guilty, had used testimony from the prosecution that contradicted these facts. The original court martial claimed, in its fifth specification of the First Charge, that Major General Porter disobeyed General Pope's order in that Porter did *'permit Brigadier General A.S. Piatt's brigade to march to Centreville and thereby greatly delayed the arrival of Piatt's brigade on the field of battle.'* However, the Schofield Board was able to show that Porter ordered Piatt's brigade, 800 men, to move back to Manassas Junction and take up a defensive position to cover the expected retreat of the Federal army.

General Porter tried several times to report what he knew to General McDowell.

Generals McDowell and King:
'I found it impossible to communicate by crossing the woods to Groveton. The enemy is in great force on this road, and as they appear to have driven our forces back, the fire of the enemy having advanced and ours retired, I have determined to withdraw to Manassas. I have endeavored to communicate with McDowell and Siegel, but my messengers have run into the enemy. They have gathered artillery and cavalry and infantry, and the advancing masses of dust show the enemy coming in force. I am now going to the head of the column to see what is passing and shown affairs are going, and I will communicate with you. Had you not better send your trains back?'

F. J. Porter
Major General

Again Porter tried to reach McDowell...

Generals McDowell and King:
'I have been wandering over the woods and failed to get a communication to you. Tell how matters go with you. The enemy is in strong force in front of me, and I wish to know your designs for tonight. If left to me, I shall have to retire for food and water, which I cannot get here. How goes the battle? It seems to go to our rear. The enemy is going to our left.'
F. J. Porter
Major General

Again...

General McDowell:
'The firing on my left has so far retired that, as I cannot advance and have failed to get over to you except by the route taken by King, I shall withdraw to Manassas. If you have anything to communicate, please do so. I have sent many messengers to you and General Siegel and get nothing.'
F. J. Porter
Major General

Porter's short message seems like the wail of the lost and abandoned, but still fighting on against hopeless odds:

'An artillery duel is going on now; been skirmishing for a long time.'
F. J. P.

Porter sent one more message before 6 PM.

General McDowell:
'Failed in getting Morell over to you. After wandering about the woods for a time I withdrew Morell and while doing so artillery opened upon us. My scouts could not get through. Each one found the enemy between us, and I believe some have been captured. Infantry are also in front. I am trying to get a battery, but have not succeeded as yet. From the masses of dust on our left and from reports of scouts I think the enemy is moving largely in that way. Please communicate the way this messenger came. I have no cavalry or messengers now. Please let me know your designs, whether you retire or not. I cannot get water an am out of provisions. Have lost a few men from infantry firing.'
F. J. Porter
Major General Volunteers
August 29, 6 PM

Now, suddenly, the situation changed. Porter discovered that the sounds of artillery had deceived him; Pope's troops were still fighting. Porter recalled Piatt and ceased all further preparations for a retreat.

At 5:30 PM Porter received a report from scouts at his right that the enemy was in full retreat. Heavy sounds of musketry showed Porter that serious work was going on near Groveton. Porter was not certain so he ordered Morell to make a reconnaissance to learn the truth. Morell, from his recent fighting, knew the report was false. Morell prepared to support the reconnaissance with his whole division. It was at that time that the 4:30 Order came to '*attack the enemy in flank or rear.*'

The 4:30 Order read:

Major General PORTER: 'Your line of march brings you in on the enemy's (Stonewall Jackson) right flank, and if possible, on his rear, keeping your right in communication with General Reynolds. The enemy is massed in the woods in front of us, but can be shelled out as soon as you engage their flank. Keep heavy reserves, and use your batteries, keeping well closed to your right and rear, so as to keep you in close communication with the right wing.'
John Pope
Major General Commanding

The Court found that Porter did not receive the 4:30 Order until 6:30 PM. The evidence introduced at General Porter's court martial in 1862 was that Porter had received the order at 4:30 PM. This was testimony given by the officer who carried that order and one of the orderlies that accompanied him.

Neither of these two witnesses carried a watch. Their estimates were based on the time they took to ride from General Pope to General Porter. In fact, 4:30 PM is when General Pope *started to write the order* and not the time then messenger left Pope to deliver the order. Moreover, these two messengers *did not and could not have ridden over the route they claimed to have taken*. These witnesses deliberately made false statements in regard to the route taken. In addition to all of these facts, one of the witnesses was found to have made other admissions and statements which were not true.

General Sykes' testimony was that the order was received at sundown. Lieutenant Colonel Locke, Captain Montieth, Lieutenant Ingham and Lieutenant Weld testified that the 4:30 Order was delivered about sundown. Now, a new and independent witness, Captain Randel, confirmed their testimony.

The moment Porter received the order, he instructed General Morell to make the attack at once. He sent a dispatch to Pope stating this, then rode to the front. When he found Morell, Morell had completed preparations for the attack, but darkness had set in. It was not possible to attack in the dark. The contest at Groveton had spent its force and the Federals there would not have received any aid from Morell. The order was based on such erroneous conditions that *it was not possible for Porter to carry out Pope's 4:30 Order.*

Porter placed his troops in position, so they would be ready to attack in the morning. He had a further disability; the enemy had 2500 cavalry near his flank, while Porter had only a few mounted men.

At that time McDowell's weary men had been passing the rear of Porter's forces and several miles from where they were supposed to be to help in the Union defense; the Union army was not ready for battle. The court found facts that clearly showed evidence of General Porter's true character. *Nothing Porter did or failed to do indicated that any part of Porter's conduct was deserving of criticism, and much less so of censure or condemnation.*

Porter's duty that day was plain and simple. His duty was to hold his position and cover the deployment of McDowell's troops. It is perfectly clear that Porter had no thought whatever of retreating from the enemy. When the enemy advanced as if to attack, Porter's orders were, *'If the enemy is coming, hold on to him.' 'Post your troops to repulse him.' 'We cannot retire while McDowell holds on.'*

The trial court assumed that Porter had orders to attack an enemy, or any aggressive action, *before* he received the 4:30 Order. All this was the exact *reverse* of the truth. An attack by Porter would have been a violation of the spirit of his orders. It would have been a criminal blunder leading to an inevitable disaster. In short, Porter had no choice, as a faithful soldier, but to do what he did.

Testimony from Confederate officers confirms that Longstreet had 29,000 men on the field and Porter had 9,000. Testimony from Confederate officers confirms that Robert E. Lee was on the field two or three hours before Pope arrived on the field.

Porter's conduct was obedient, subordinate, faithful, and judicious. Porter and his two divisions saved the Army of Virginia from disaster. The Schofield Board of Officers also found that General Pope was wholly in the dark about the presence of the enemy in force. Porter repeatedly reported to Pope the presence of the enemy in force in his front. Porter's 4 PM dispatch and a 6 PM dispatch to Pope reported the situation clearly. However, contrary to military policy, Pope did not preserve those dispatches.

This is the end of the Board's statement of the facts. Incorrect facts were the basis of the charges for which Porter was pronounced guilty by the 1862 court martial trial. What follows has no bearing on the Board's findings of fact and recommendation of Porter's full reinstatement. However, a narration of the events, which followed on August 30, gives a full understanding of the Union's defeat that day.

Pope ordered Porter to withdraw from his position and march to the battlefield. This is demonstrated in the 8:50 PM order of August 29 and the two, 12 Noon Orders of August 30. These orders, to attack Jackson's left wing, allowed Lee to press forward unopposed by Porter. It was the cause of the Union defeat.

Nevertheless, as Longstreet pressed forward to strike Pope's exposed left wing and flank, Porter's troops, General Warren's brigade, sprang into the gap and breasted the storm until but a handful of his brave men were still alive. Then General Sykes, with his disciplined brigades, and General Reynolds, with his gallant Pennsylvania Reserves, seized the commanding ground in the rear. Like a rock Reynolds' men withstood the Confederate advance. Porter saved the Union army.

Schofield, Terry and Getty concluded with this.

'These events were excluded from evidence before the 1862 court martial that tried General Porter. Justice requires that they should be said here, especially on the question of animus, the deep-seated resentment and hostility, which so strongly was a part of Porter's case. Therefore, having given the reasons for our conclusions, we have the honor to report that in our opinion justice requires at the President's hands such action as may be necessary to annul and set aside the findings and the sentence of the court martial in the case of Major General Fitz John Porter, and to restore him to the positions of which that sentence deprived him, that restoration to take effect from the date of his dismissal from the service.'

J.M. SCHOFIELD, *Major General U.S. Army*

ALFRED H. TERRY, *Brigadier General U.S. Army*

GEORGE W. GETTY, *Brevet Major General, U.S. Army, Colonel 3rd Infantry*

Former Secretary of State John Hay made an observation, which summed up the reasons for Porter's trial and conviction: "Porter was ruined for his devotion to McClellan."

❦ **61** ❦

Rules of War

When Porter discovered Longstreet's army was at his front, should General Porter have attacked Longstreet? McDowell had left him. The Joint Order had ceased to be mandatory, although Porter was still mandated to fall back to Bull Run if it became necessary. He could no longer think of going to Gainesville with the force on his right. Yet he was bound to fall back to Bull Run that night. Whether to attack or not was the question.

The rule that applies in such cases is well stated in certain extracts. A French work, recently published in Paris, is entitled, *'The Method of War.'* It refers to Napoleon Bonaparte, General Arthur Wellesley Duke of Wellington, and Archduke Charles of Teschen of Austria, men whose reputations entitle them to consideration.

Napoleon stated: *"A military order requires passive obedience only when it is given by a superior who, being present at the moment when he gives it, has knowledge of the state of things, can listen to objections, and can give explanations to the one who is to execute the order."*

This from The Method of War, describing General Wellesley, the Duke of Wellington:

'It was a general order from the camp of Jensen, dated November 11, 1803. In making known to the army the decision given by the court martial in the affair of Captain (not named), Major General Wellesley thinks proper to explain to the troops that it is necessary to well distinguish the cases in which it is allowable or not for an officer to act at his own will.'

'It may frequently happen that an officer receives an order which is impossible to execute, through circumstances unknown at the moment of giving it by him who gave it. Or at the execution of which would be so difficult or so dangerous that there would be a moral impossibility to conform to it. In a case of this nature, Major General Wellesley would be very far from wishing to prevent detached officers from acting freely. But Captain (not named) was not in this situation, which the officer who had given him his orders did not also have. It was his duty to obey.'

Jourdan's French army was in the Rhine Campaign of 1796. He forced his troops' passage of the Lahn River into Germany. The first intention of General Wartensleben, who commanded the Austrian corps under the command of Archduke Charles of Teschen, had been to fall back behind the Weida River. This was because the French, having found the garrison of Hamburg to fall back upon in the town of Usingen, were already threatening Wartensleben's line of retreat. On July 9, having received a dispatch in which the Archduke Charles wrote to him to 'withdraw from the environs of Friedberg, only after having tried the fortune of arms.' Wartensleben changed his design. He resolved to attack Jourdan that same day. General Wellesley gave his interpretation:

'However, Wartensleben, in his position at the time, should not have attempted an attack. He should have directed the attack against the center of the French army. Since moving his left, he had Jourdan at Hamburg on his rear. In advancing on his right, he abandoned his line of retreat upon Frankfort.'

'In spite of these dangers, he had the temerity to attack… and in what a situation! With forces inferior in number, in a position in which his wings, deprived of support and threatened with being constantly outflanked, he had no reserve.'

'In vain will it be said that the order, which the Archduke Charles had sent him, was the grounds of this resolution. Wartensleben had the right not to execute the order. The Archduke Charles, then near Pforzheim, did not know his situation when he gave him the order.'

'A General-in-Chief, who indicates to subordinates, detached afar, their lines of operation and strategic points of their defensive positions, has performed his duties. One cannot expect from him precise and detailed orders when their execution depends not only on the circumstances of the moment, but also on the actual position of the troops.'

Counselor Bullitt, during the rehearing, added his opinion of these historical military precedents accepted in modern military procedures and law.

"I should suppose there was great good sense in that. The rule is one which accords with natural reason. In this case General Porter was acting practically under the rule laid down by Archduke Charles. Ought Porter to have attacked Longstreet? He thought he should not do so, as he knew was the case."

That Porter knew Longstreet was before him, there can be no doubt. The learned Recorder of the Porter court martial said, "Porter was being tried according to his *not* knowing Longstreet's force was present. Yet, *everyone* knew Longstreet had arrived on the battlefield. Porter would have been wild and insane to have attacked 29,000 Confederate troops with barely 9000 men. Pope knew it. McDowell knew it, yet McDowell and Pope framed their answers in such a way as to show Porter did not know and still refused to attack Jackson."

Counselor Bullitt: "Under the rules laid down by Napoleon, by the Duke of Wellington, and by the Archduke Charles of Austria, General Porter could only be held responsible for the honest and faithful exercise of the discretion given to him by the situation. Any movement by him, except for the one he made, to hold Lee in check, would have most certainly resulted in the destruction of the Army of Virginia."

Bullitt concluded this precedent in his summation.

"I have presented the facts of the case to induce you, by your findings, to restore General Porter's name to that page of history, which thus far has been a blank. Restore his name with the purity and integrity and the honor for which he exerted himself as a soldier and which he has always endeavored to maintain as a man."

Union General
Fitz John Porter

❧ 62 ❧

Quietus

In 1878, a special commission under General John M. Schofield exonerated Porter by finding that his reluctance to attack Longstreet probably saved Pope's Army of Virginia from an even greater defeat. It was not until 1882 that President Chester A. Arthur reversed Porter's 1863 court martial sentence. A special act of the U.S. Congress restored Porter's commission as an infantry colonel in the U.S. Army, backdated, but without any back pay due. Porter, vindicated, retired from the army at his own request. An official pardon did not come until 1893, from President Grover Cleveland.

Porter was later involved in mining, construction and commerce. He served as the New York City Commissioner of Public Works, the New York City Police Commissioner, and the New York City Fire Commissioner. Porter died in Morristown, New Jersey. His body is buried in Greenwood Cemetery, Brooklyn, New York, and his grave can be found in Section 54, Lot 5685/89. There is a statue of Porter in Haven Park, in Portsmouth, New Hampshire, and the World War II Liberty Ship, *SS Fitz John Porter* was named in his honor.

Today all cadets at West Point and the United States Air Force Academy are required to memorize a quotation from one of Schofield's graduation addresses. It is a statement of a man's character that might well have been said of Fitz John Porter's ways of commanding his men.

'The discipline which makes the soldiers of a free country reliable in battle is not to be gained with harsh treatment. On the contrary, such treatment is far more likely to destroy than to make an army. It is possible to impart instruction and give commands in such a manner and such a tone of voice as to inspire in the soldier no feeling but an intense desire to obey, while the opposite manner and tone of voice cannot fail to excite strong resentment and a desire to disobey.'

'The one mode or the other of dealing with subordinates springs from a corresponding spirit in the breast of the commander. He who feels the respect which is due to others cannot fail to inspire respect for himself. While he who feels, and hence manifests, disrespect toward others, especially his subordinates, cannot fail to inspire hatred of himself.'

A hundred and fifty years have passed since those three days in August. I like to think Porter is among the greats, as the parade of the fallen from battle pass before us through history, leading the silent blue and gray columns are the generals and officers who fought and died with their men; Thomas Jackson, John Bell Hood, Philip Kearney, John Reynolds and so many thousands of others. Fitz John Porter's shade, after so many years of waiting to be given back his honor, marches with them.

In Greenwood Cemetery, Brooklyn, New York there is a large gray granite tombstone. On its face there are the names of the two people whose bodies lie there beneath the green grass of the park-like grounds. On the left side of the stone Fitz John Porter's name is written. Below his name are inscribed the titles he earned, including General of the Army.

Porter's birth and death are recorded; 1822 to 1901. On the right side of the granite face, opposite Porter's name there is the outline of a cross. Below the cross is written the name of the one person who knew Porter best; Harriet Pierson Cook, his wife of forty-three years. Harriett was buried next to her husband after she had been Porter's widow for another twenty years. I believe her memories were both terribly painful and wonderfully beautiful. The six simple words on their gravestone is a fitting statement for both their lives.

'I have fought the good fight.'

A BEGINNING

BIBLIOGRAPHY

Second Manassas; Time-Life Books, Alexandria, Virginia.

Second Battle of Manassas- Historical Report; Troop movements, John Hennessy, August 1862. U.S. Dept. of the Interior, Forestry Service.

This Hallowed Ground; Bruce Catton, Doubleday and Co., New York, NY 1956.

A Glorious Army; Jeffrey Wert, Simon and Shuster, New York 1946.

Glory Road; Bruce Catton, Doubleday and Co. 1952.

Twenty Years of Congress, Lincoln to Garfield; Henry Hill Pub. 1884.

Encyclopedia Americanna; Vol. vii Americanna Corp.

Significance of Railroads in the Civil War; Lee Meridith 330 Muster of the Round Table.

Supreme Court Argument, Amistad Case; Feb 22-March 2, 1841.

Amistad Rebellion; June 27, 1839; Internet.

The Way We Weren't; David Von Drehle, Yahoo News, Time.

The Porter Court Martial; New York Times January 10. 1862.

An Undeserved Stigma; North American Review, Vol cxxxv.

Civil War Medicine; Charles Sweeny, M.B.A

Rifled Musket-Fish or Fowl? Charles Sweeney. M.B.A.

Court-Martial of Fitz John Porter; Wikipedia.

The Fiery Trial, Speeches and Writings of Abraham Lincoln; Oxford U. Press. 2002.

The Lincoln Papers; Vol. 1 and 2, David C. Mearns, 1948 Garden City Press.

Lincoln's Speeches and Writings; 1832-1865, Viking Press.

A People's History; Howard Zinn, Harper Perennial 1995.

Webster's Encyclopedia of Dictionaries, History of the United States: Civil War; 1978 Edition.

Second Manassas, 1862; Robert E. Lee's greatest victory, John Langellier, Praeger Publishers. 2004.

Second Manassas, Longstreet's Attack and the Struggle for Chinn Ridge; Scott C. Patchan, Potomac Books, Washington, D. C. 1966.

Return to Bull Run, the Campaign and Battle of Second Manassas, John J. Hennessy; Simon and Shuster. 1992.

To the Gates of Richmond, the Peninsula Campaign; Stephen W. Sears, Tichnor and Fields. 1992.

Lee Takes Command from Seven Days to Second Bull Run; Time-Life Books.

The Civil War, A Picture History; Bruce Catton; Bonanza Books.

Unholy Sabbath; Brian M. Jordan, Savas Beattie, New York and California.

Civil-War-Trust/ Second Bull Run. Wikipedia. Org./ Wikipedia

Hard Tack and Coffee; John D. Billings, George M. Smith & Co. 1887

Detailed Minutiae of Soldier Life; Carlton McCarthy; Carlton McCarthy & Co.; 1882.

Philadelphia Weekly Times, Sparks from the Camp Fire; Joseph W. Morton, Keystone Publishing Co. 1890; Southern Historical Society Papers, June, 1882.

The Heart of Abraham Lincoln, Man of Kindness and Mercy; Historical Bulletin No. 6 Madison: Lincoln Fellowship of Wisconsin, 1948 pp.11, 12.

Rochester Express Newspaper (New York); Quotation by F. B. Carpenter, Signing of the Emancipation Proclamation. 1863.

The Irish Brigade and its Campaigns; Capt. D. P. Conynham; Wm. McSorley and Co. New York.

Battlefields of the South, Bull Run to Fredericksburg; By an English Combatant. John Blackburn, N.Y. 1864.

Life in the Confederate Army; William Watson; New York Scribner and Welford, 1886.

Personal Recollections of a Cavalryman; J. H. Kidd; Sentinel Printing Co., Ionia, Michigan 1908.

The Blue and the Gray, Story of the Civil War as Told by Combatants; Edited by Henry Steele Commager, Fairfax Press, New York, 1902.

One of Jackson's Foot Cavalry; John H. Worsham; the Neale Publishing Co., 1902. Reprinted 1981 Time-Life Books.

A Summary of the Case of Fitz John Porter; Theodore A. Lord, 1883, San Francisco.

Fighting the Confederacy; General Edward Porter Alexander, University of North Carolina Press, 1989.

Extraordinary Circumstances: The Seven Days Battles; Brian K. Burton, Bloomington, Indiana University Press, 2001.

Wikipedia Free Encyclopedia; 2012, 2013

Lincoln and Douglas, The Debates that Defined America; Allen C. Guelzo, Simon & Shuster, 2008.

One Man's War; David Hamer.

New York Herald; Sept. 8, 1862.

The Underground Railroad; Kvie, Africans in America, 1780-1862, Internet, 3/6/2013.